ABOUT THE AUTHORS

Suzanne Peregoy is Professor Emerita of Education, San Francisco State University, where she coordinated the M.A. and Reading/Language Arts Specialist Credential programs while also teaching courses in language and literacy development. She earned an M.A. in Spanish literature and linguistics from the University of California, Santa Barbara. Her Ph.D. in language and literacy from the University of California, Berkeley, focused on bilingual reading, second language acquisition, and language issues in American Indian education. Previously, she taught ESL to adults and elementary grades in a bilingual education program, and she directed a multicultural preschool program. She was active in writing California's guidelines for preparing in-service teachers to work with English language learners. She has published articles on bilingual and second language literacy in the *Journal of the National Association for Bilingual Education, The Reading Teacher, Canadian Modern Language Review, Educational Issues of Language Minority Students, Hispanic Journal of Behavioral Sciences*, and *Theory into Practice*.

Owen Boyle is Professor Emeritus of Education, San Jose State University, where he coordinated the Bilingual and ESL Program, chaired the Language and Literacy Department, and headed the Reading Specialist Credential and M.A. programs in literacy. At San Jose State he taught courses in second language literacy, language acquisition and reading, multicultural literature, and reading assessment. He received his doctorate at the University of California, where he was Coordinator of the Learning from Text Program and researched and taught students. As Assistant Director of the Bay Area Writing Project, he worked with teachers from all over the world including those from Germany, Panama, Alaska, and California. He served on the California State Superintendent's panel that developed guidelines for preparing teachers of reading and was instrumental in developing a reading instruction test required for a California multiple subject teaching credential. He has published articles and research in *Journal of Educational Issues of Language Minority Students, Hispanic Journal of Behavioral Sciences, Bilingual Research Journal, Journal of the Association of Mexican-American Educators, Journal of College Reading and Learning, The Reading Teacher*, and *Reading Research and Instruction*. He taught elementary and secondary school where he worked with second language learners for 12 years.

Karen Cadiero-Kaplan is an Associate Professor at San Diego State University in the Department of Policy Studies in Language and Cross Cultural Education. She serves as coordinator and advisor for the department's Master of Arts Program in Curriculum Development for Social Justice. Dr. Cadiero-Kaplan's publications cover literacy ideologies and practice, English language development, and bilingual education policy and practice. She also has several publications on critical uses of technology for language and literacy development. Her recent books include *Bilingual Education and the Literacy Curriculum* (Peter Lang, 2004) and a co-edited book, *The Living Work of Teachers: Ideology and Practice* (California Association for Bilingual Education, 2006).

In addition to her research, Dr. Cadiero-Kaplan provides state and national leadership in the area of English teaching and language policy. In 2006–2007 she served as President of the California Association of Teachers of English to Speakers of Other Languages (CATESOL); and as a member of the Bilingual Design Team for the California Commission on Teaching Credentialing, advising the commission on standards development for bilingual teacher education. Dr. Cadiero-Kaplan also works with lobbyists from various English learner advocacy groups to inform the State Board of Education and the State Assembly on issues related to English learners. She presently serves as Vice President of Californians Together, a statewide coalition of parent, teacher, and civil rights groups concerned with ensuring the best possible education for English learners in California.

FIFTH
EDITION

Reading, Writing, and Learning in ESL

A RESOURCE BOOK FOR TEACHING K–12 ENGLISH LEARNERS

SUZANNE F. PEREGOY
San Francisco State University

OWEN F. BOYLE
San Jose State University

with contributions by

KAREN CADIERO-KAPLAN
San Diego State University

BOSTON   NEW YORK   SAN FRANCISCO
MEXICO CITY   MONTREAL   TORONTO   LONDON   MADRID   MUNICH   PARIS
HONG KONG   SINGAPORE   TOKYO   CAPE TOWN   SYDNEY

Executive Editor: *Aurora Martínez Ramos*
Series Editorial Assistant: *Kara Kikel*
Executive Marketing Manager: *Krista Clark*
Production Editor: *Annette Joseph*
Editorial Production Service: *Black Dot Group/NK Graphics*
Composition Buyer: *Linda Cox*
Manufacturing Buyer: *Linda Morris*
Electronic Composition: *Black Dot Group/NK Graphics*
Interior Design: *Black Dot Group/NK Graphics*
Cover Administrator: *Linda Knowles*

For related titles and support materials, visit our online catalog at www.pearsonhighered.com.

Between the time Website information is gathered and then published, it is not unusual for some sites to have closed. Also, the transcription of URLs can result in typographical errors. The publisher would appreciate notification where these errors occur.

ISBN-10: 0-205-59324-0
ISBN-13: 978-0-205-59324-8

Library of Congress Cataloging-in-Publication Data

Peregoy, Suzanne F.
  Reading, writing and learning in ESL : a resource book for teaching K-12 english learners / Suzanne F. Peregoy, Owen F. Boyle.—5th ed.
    p. cm.
  Rev. ed. of: Reading, writing and learning in ESL. 4th ed. 2005.
  ISBN 978-0-205-59324-8 (alk. paper)
  1. English language—Study and teaching—Foreign speakers.   I. Boyle, Owen.   II. Title.
  PE1128.A2P393   2008
  428.0071—dc22   2007051130

Printed in the United States of America

10   9   8   7   6   5   4   3   2   1   HAM   12   11   10   09   08

Credits appear on page 460, which constitutes an extension of the copyright page.

Allyn and Bacon
is an imprint of

www.pearsonhighered.com

CONTENTS

vii

6 Words and Meaning: English Learners' Vocabulary Development 200

ix

xiii

CONTENTS

xiv

PREFACE

Reading, Writing, and Learning in ESL: A Resource Book for Teaching K–12 English Learners, Fifth Edition, is a comprehensive, reader-friendly text that provides a wealth of teaching ideas for promoting oral language, vocabulary, reading, writing, and content area development in English for K–12 English learners. The book provides up-to-date language acquisition theory, classroom organization, teaching strategies, and differentiated instruction and assessment procedures for effective English learner instruction. Our goal has always been to offer a **single, comprehensive professional resource** for teachers working with English learners. As such, it is an ideal text for preservice and in-service ESL and bilingual methods classes. It also makes an excellent staff development tool for teachers to use during in-service workshops and throughout the school year as a reference.

Our purpose in the fifth edition remains the same as in the earlier editions: We wish to open a window on classrooms in which English learners are actively involved in learning about themselves, their classmates, and the world around them. In these classrooms, students often pursue topics of their own choosing, using oral and written English to discuss and confer with their classmates, read, write, report, and share in the ongoing process of learning. Gradually, they advance their knowledge of English, expanding their discourse repertoires and refining their control of grammar, pronunciation, spelling, and mechanics. Ideally, they will use their growing academic, linguistic, and sociocultural competence to create better worlds for themselves and those around them.

New in This Edition

We have put a great deal of thought and effort into making the fifth edition as thorough and up to date as possible, while maintaining a user-friendly style with numerous new visuals, including cartoons to give you a little comic relief. Of primary importance, we have added a brand new chapter on English learners' **vocabulary development** (Chapter 6). The new chapter presents current research on this important topic, including which words students need to know, how to differentiate assessment and instruction, features of an excellent vocabulary program, and strategies for beginning and intermediate English learners.

Our second major effort is a completely updated and revised Chapter 3, **Effective English Learner Instruction and Assessment.** The new Chapter 3 highlights the current *TESOL PreK–12 English Language Proficiency Standards* (TESOL, 2006) and illustrates how they inform our rationale for **Content-Based and Differentiated Instruction.** These two instructional features are incorporated into a new model of effective English learner instruction, which is presented in Chapter 3 and applied in subsequent chapters of the book.

Finally, each chapter offers new and updated Internet sites and new and updated suggested readings. In addition, we have added new material to each chapter.

PEARSON
myeducationlab Your Class. Your Career. Everyone's Future.
Where the Classroom Comes to Life MyEducationLab is a research-based learning tool that brings teaching to life. Through authentic in-class video footage, interactive simulations, rich case studies, examples of authentic teacher and student work, and more, MyEducationLab prepares you for your teaching career by showing what quality instruction looks like.

MyEducationLab is easy to use! At the end of every chapter in the textbook, you will find the MyEducationLab logo adjacent to activities and exercises that correlate material you've just read in the chapter to your reading/viewing of multimedia assets on the MyEducationLab site. These assets include:

Video: The authentic classroom videos in MyEducationLab show how real teachers handle actual classroom situations.

Case Studies: A diverse set of robust cases illustrate the realities of teaching and offer valuable perspectives on common issues and challenges in education.

Simulations: Created by the IRIS Center at Vanderbilt University, these interactive simulations give you hands-on practice at adapting instruction for a full spectrum of learners.

Readings: Specially selected, topically relevant articles from renowned education journals expand and enrich your perspectives on key issues and topics.

Student & Teacher Artifacts: Authentic preK-12 student and teacher classroom artifacts are tied to course topics and offer you practice in working with the actual types of materials you will encounter daily as teachers.

Other Resources:

Lesson & Portfolio Builders: With this effective and easy-to-use tool, you can create, update, and share standards-based lesson plans and portfolios.

News Articles: Looking for current issues in education? Our collection offers quick access to hundreds of relevant articles from the New York Times Educational News Feed.

New Material in Each Chapter

Chapter 1:

- Revised sections on "How Cultural Differences Affect Teaching and Learning," "Becoming an Effective Participant–Observer in Your Classroom," and "Who Am I in the Lives of My Students?"
- Expanded discussion on standards and assessment

Chapter 2:

- New activity box, "Language in the Attic: Constructing Your Language Family Tree"

- New activity box, "Sharing Your Experiences Learning a New Language"
- Revised and expanded section on "Age and the Interplay of Sociocultural, Personality, and Cognitive Factors"
- New discussion of world Englishes

Chapter 3:

- Completely revised and updated chapter
- New discussion of 2006 TESOL standards
- New discussion of content-based instruction
- New discussion of differentiated instruction
- New discussion of the sheltered instruction observation protocol (SIOP) model for observing sheltered instruction
- Revised model of effective English learner instruction
- Revised material on scaffolding and English learner assessment

Chapter 4:

- New discussion of differentiated instruction for oral language development

Chapter 5:

- New discussion on emergent literacy and explicit, direct instruction
- New discussion of differentiated instruction in emergent literacy

Chapter 6 (*ALL NEW!*):

- Research on English learners' vocabulary development
- Words students need to know
- How students learn new words
- Differentiating vocabulary assessment and instruction
- First and second language proficiency considerations for vocabulary development
- Different kinds of dictionaries to address diverse English learner needs
- Vocabulary strategies for beginning and intermediate English learners
- Assessing English learners' vocabulary progress
- Planning differentiated, content-based vocabulary instruction

Chapter 7:

- New discussion on key ideas for working with errors of beginning and intermediate second language writers

- New chart (Figure 7.15) for students to use to self-correct papers based on teacher response
- New discussion of differentiated instruction for writing development

Chapter 8:

- New discussion of strategies and materials for promoting independent reading
- New discussion of guidelines for selecting appropriate reading materials
- New suggestions for selecting quality multicultural literature
- New discussion of differentiated instruction for reading and literature

Chapter 9:

- New discussion of differentiated instruction for academic, content-based instruction

Chapter 10:

- New discussion of differentiated instruction for academic literacy and content-based instruction

Chapter 11:

- Revised model of assessment in the classroom

Features of the Book

We have included several features to make this book easy for readers to use:

- Each chapter begins with a short **introduction** and **guiding questions** so readers know at a glance the focus and general content of the chapter.
- Each chapter includes numerous **classroom examples** and **vignettes** of teachers and students, giving life to the text and illustrating important ideas as they apply to classroom life.
- Each chapter offers an **Internet Resources** box indicating Websites and suggested activities to extend readers' learning opportunities relevant to the chapter content.
- **MyEducationLab activities** are provided throughout the book to extend student learning.
- Each chapter concludes with a **summary of teaching strategies** that were presented in the chapter and grade levels at which each strategy may be used.
- Each chapter ends with **suggested readings, discussion questions,** and **activities** for readers to carry out.

- To facilitate use as a **handy reference and resource,** the book includes **a detailed table of contents** to enable readers to quickly peruse, identify and locate topics and teaching strategies in each chapter. Similarly, **author** and **subject indexes** and **references** at the end of the book offer quick reference guides.

Organization of the Text

The book consists of eleven chapters, sequenced as follows:

- Chapter 1 summarizes background information on English learners, including the impact of culture on learning, language support program types, and education policy affecting English learners.
- Chapter 2 presents an overview of first and second language acquisition theories as these relate to students, classrooms, and teaching practices.
- Chapter 3 develops a coherent model of effective English learner instruction and assessment, including differentiated and content-based instruction.
- Chapters 4–10 present teaching and assessment strategies, addressing oral language development for beginning and intermediate English learners (Chapter 4); early literacy development (Chapter 5); vocabulary development (Chapter 6); writing (Chapter 7); reading and literature study (Chapter 8); and academic content area literacy (Chapters 9 and 10).
- Chapter 11 offers an in-depth view of reading assessment and its application to instructional decision making.

Using the Instructor's Manual and Test Bank

Upon adopting the text for your classroom, you will be given instructors' access to the website (www.pearsonhighered.com/irc) which contains chapter summaries and goals, key vocabulary, classroom activities for students' involvement and pages that can be used for overheads, and a test bank that includes multiple choice questions and essay questions for each chapter.

Acknowledgments

As we complete the fifth edition of this book, it is with great pleasure that we introduce you to Dr. Karen Cadiero-Kaplan, who has worked with us to prepare this new edition. Dr. Cadiero-Kaplan is an Associate Professor of Policy Studies in Language and Cross Cultural Education at San Diego State University. Her contributions to our work have been invaluable, particularly in the areas of critical literacy and differentiated instruction. Her expertise, professionalism, and enthusiasm added life and encouragement to what is ultimately a rather difficult task. Thank you, Karen!

Because this book culls from our own learning experiences, past and present, we also wish to acknowledge the following individuals who played a significant role in our professional development: Drs. Marilyn Hanf Buckley, Lily Wong Fillmore, Martha Haggard, Robert Ruddell, and Sid Tiedt.

Next, we would like to acknowledge our university students, most of whom are prospective teachers or practicing teachers. They have helped us learn along the way and provided invaluable information for this edition. We also deeply appreciate the teachers who have welcomed us into their classrooms and shared materials with us, including Linda Chittenden, Debbie Dee Clark, Audrey Fong, Jennifer Jones, Jay Kuhlman, Anne Phillips, Reina Salgado, Juana Zamora, Cathryn Bruno, Don Mar, Angela Campbell, Juana Feisel-Engle, Peggy Koorhan, Gloria Lopez-Guiterrez, Rosemarie Michaels, Elda Parise, Debi Quan, and Pam Thomas.

We would also like to thank our reviewers: John Douglas Battenburg, California Polytechnic State University; Gypsye Bryan, Southern Louisiana University; Dorothy Valcarcel Craig, Middle Tennessee State University; Emily Catherine Day, Eastern Michigan University; Zohreh R. Eslami, Texas A&M University; Deanna Nisbet, Regent University; Jon Reyhner, Northern Arizona University; and Hollis G. Stein, University of Maryland.

1

English Learners in School

In this chapter, we address the concerns of teachers when they first encounter students who are new to English in their classrooms, discussing such questions as the following:

1. Who are English learners?
2. How can I get to know my English learners when their language and culture are new to me?
3. How do cultural differences affect the way my students respond to me and to my efforts to teach them?
4. How can I ease newcomers into the routines of my class when they understand little or no English?
5. How do current policy trends affect English learners?
6. What kinds of programs exist to meet the needs of English learners?

First, come with us into Buzz Bertolucci's classroom. It is the first day of school in Mr. Bertolucci's first-grade class. All the children are seated on the rug and have just finished the opening routines with the calendar. After introducing the children to each other through a song, Buzz places a Big Book of *The Gingerbread Man* in front of the class. With its large print and colorful illustrations, the 30-inch-tall Big Book not only captures the children's attention but also helps them understand the story's events. Mr. Bertolucci reads the book to the entire class, points to the pictures, puts on a gingerbread man mask, and acts out words such as "Run, run as fast as you can. You can't catch me. I'm the Gingerbread Man!" The entire book is "read" and acted out by members of the class on this, their first day of school. When the story is finished, one of the school cooks enters the room and hands a note to Mr. Bertolucci. He reads it to the class: "I jumped out of your book and ran to the cafeteria. Come and meet me! The Gingerbread Man." Teacher and children leave for the cafeteria but cannot find the Gingerbread Man there. They ask the cooks if they've seen the Gingerbread Man, but they haven't. Finally, one cook suggests that they look in the oven, and there they find another note from the Gingerbread Man: "I've gone to the janitor's storeroom by the bathrooms. See you there!" The class finds the janitor and asks if he's seen the Gingerbread Man, but he replies that the Gingerbread Man has gone to the nurse's office. When they meet the nurse, the children learn that the Gingerbread Man has gone to the counselor's office and then to the principal's office. Finally, the principal reports that the Gingerbread Man has returned to their classroom. When the children return to the classroom, each one finds a Gingerbread Man cookie at his or her desk.

As the children eat their cookies, Mr. Bertolucci reads *The Gingerbread Man* again. He has introduced his children to literature in an involving way. In addition, he has introduced the new children to their school and to the many people and places in the school they will need to know. He has also presented the literature and its simple theme in a concrete and interesting manner. The children in his class will look forward to the next book he reads, and they will look forward to reading and writing themselves.

It may surprise you to learn that more than half the children in Mr. Bertolucci's class are new to the English language, coming from homes in which languages such as Spanish, Cantonese, or Japanese are spoken. Such linguistic variety was not always the case, but changes in the neighborhood over the past 10 years have been dramatic. Mr. Bertolucci has responded to these changes by keeping many of his favorite teaching routines, such as *The Gingerbread Man*, but modifying them to meet the needs of his English learners. Given today's immigration patterns, you may be facing similar changes in your school. In this book, we will show you how to develop and modify oral language, reading, and writing instruction to meet the needs of your students who are new to English. But first we want to introduce you to the great diversity among the children who are called English learners, to help you better understand and integrate them into your classroom and school. We use the term *English learners* to refer to non-native English speakers who are learning English in school. Typically, English learners speak a primary language other than English at home, such as Spanish, Cantonese, Russian, Hmong, or French. English learners vary in their proficiency in their primary languages. Of course, they vary in English language proficiency as well. Those who are beginners to intermediates in English have often been referred to as **limited English proficient (LEP)**, a term that is used in federal legislation and other official documents. However as a result of the pejorative connotation of "limited English proficient," most educators prefer the terms **English learners**, **English language learners**, **non-native English speakers**, and **second language learners** to refer to students who are in the process of learning English as a new language. The terms **English as a Second Language (ESL)** and **English for Speakers of Other Languages (ESOL)** are often used to refer to the acquisition of English as a non-native language. We continue to use the former term because it is widely used and descriptive, even though what we refer to as a "second language" might actually be a student's third or fourth language. A synonym for ESL that you will find in this book is **English Language Development (ELD)**.

Who Are English Language Learners?

Students who speak English as a non-native language live in all areas of the United States. The number of English learners has steadily increased in recent decades, nearly doubling between 1994 and 2004 when survey results estimated that 5,119,561 English learners were enrolled in U.S. public schools in grades preK-12. During that time, English learner enrollment increased at almost seven times the rate of total student enrollment (National Clearinghouse for English Language Acquisition, 2006). States with the highest numbers of English learners are California, Texas, Florida, New York, and Illinois. In recent years, however, EL populations have surged in the Midwest and South and in Nevada and Oregon. Spanish is by far the most prevalent primary language, spoken by 80% of ELs. Many English learners are sons and daughters of immigrants who have left their home countries to seek a better life. Some recent immigrants have left countries brutally torn apart by war or political strife in regions such as Southeast Asia, Central America, the Middle East, and Eastern Europe. Others have immigrated for economic reasons. Still others come to be reunited with families who are already here or to seek educational opportunities they may find in the United States. Finally, many English learners were born in the United States, and some of them, such as American Indians of numerous tribal heritages, have roots in U.S. soil that go back for countless generations.

Whether immigrant or native born, each group brings its own history and culture to the enterprise of schooling (Heath, 1986). Furthermore, each group contributes to the rich tapestry of languages and cultures that form the basic fabric of the United States. Our first task as teachers, then, is to become aware of our students' personal histories and cultures, so as to understand their feelings, frustrations, hopes, and aspirations. At the same time, as teachers we need to look closely at ourselves to discover how our own culturally ingrained attitudes, beliefs, assumptions, and communication styles play out in our teaching and affect our students' learning. By developing such understanding, we create the essential foundation for meaningful instruction, including reading and writing instruction. As understanding grows, teacher and students alike can come to an awareness of both diversity and universals in human experience, as shared in this poem by a high school student who emigrated with her parents from Cambodia (Mullen & Olsen, 1990).

3

"You and I Are the Same"

You and I are the same
but we don't let our hearts see.
Black, White and Asian
Africa, China, United States and all other
countries around the world
Peel off their skin
Like you peel an orange
See their flesh
like you see in my heart
Peel off their meat
And peel my wickedness with it too
Until there's nothing left
but bones.
Then you will see that you and I
are the same.

(Kien Po, "You and I Are the Same." 1990. San Francisco:
California Tomorrow. Reprinted with permission of the author.)

How Can I Get to Know My English Learners?

Given the variety and mobility among second language groups, it is likely that most teachers, including specialists in bilingual education or ESL, will at some time encounter students whose language and culture they know little about. Perhaps you are already accustomed to working with students of diverse cultures, but if you are not, how can you develop an understanding of students from unfamiliar linguistic and cultural backgrounds? Far from a simple task, the process requires not only fact finding but also continual observation and interpretation of children's behavior, combined with trial and error in communication. Thus the process is one that must take place gradually.

Getting Basic Information When a New Student Arrives

When a new student arrives, we suggest three initial steps. First of all, begin to find out basic facts about the child: What country is the child from? How long has he or she lived in the United States? Where and with whom is the child living? What language or languages are spoken in the home? If the child is an immigrant, what were the circumstances of immigration? Some children have experienced traumatic events before and during immigration, and the process of adjustment to a new country may represent yet another link in a chain of stressful life events (Olsen, 1998).

Second, obtain as much information about the student's prior school experiences as possible. School records may be available if the child has already been enrolled in a U.S. school. However as you are not likely to receive a cumulative folder forwarded from another country, you may need to piece the information together yourself, a task that requires resourcefulness, imagination, and time.

Some school districts collect background information on students when they register and administer English language proficiency tests. Thus, your own district office is one possible source of information. In addition, you may need the assistance of someone who is familiar with the home language and culture, such as another teacher, a paraprofessional, or a community liaison, who can ask questions of parents, students, or siblings. Keep in mind that some children may have had no previous schooling, despite their age, or perhaps their schooling has been interrupted. Other students may have attended school in their home countries. Students with prior educational experience bring various kinds of knowledge to school subjects and may be quite advanced. Be prepared to validate your students for their special knowledge. We saw how important this was for fourth-grader Li Fen, a recent immigrant from mainland China who found herself in a regular English language classroom, not knowing a word of English. Li Fen was a bright child but naturally somewhat reticent to involve herself in classroom activities during her first month in the class. She made a real turnaround, however, the day the class was studying long division. Li Fen accurately solved three problems at the chalkboard in no time at all, though her procedure differed slightly from the one in the math book. Her classmates were duly impressed with her mathematical competence and did not hide their admiration. Her teacher, of course, gave her a smile with words of congratulations. From that day forward, Li Fen participated more readily, having earned a place in the class.

When you are gathering information on your students' prior schooling, it's important to find out whether they are literate in their home language. If they are, you might encourage them to keep a journal using their native language, and if possible, you should acquire native language books, magazines, or newspapers to have on hand for the new student. In this way, you validate the student's language, culture, and academic competence, while providing a natural bridge to English reading. *Make these choices with sensitivity, though, building on positive responses from your students.* Bear in mind, for example, that some newcomers may not wish to be identified as different from their classmates. We make this caveat because of our experience with a 7-year-old boy, recently arrived from Mexico, who attended a school where everyone spoke English only. When we spoke to him in Spanish, he did not respond, giving the impression that he did not know the language. When we visited his home and spoke Spanish with his parents, he was not pleased. At that point in his life, he may have wanted nothing more than to blend into the dominant social environment, in this case an affluent, European American neighborhood saturated with English.

The discomfort felt by this young boy is an important reminder of the internal conflict experienced by many youngsters as they come to terms with life in a new culture. As they learn English and begin to fit into school routines, they embark on a personal journey toward a new cultural identity. If they come to reject their home language and culture, moving toward maximum assimilation into the dominant culture, they may experience alienation from their parents and family. A moving personal account of such a journey is provided by journalist Richard Rodriquez in his book *Hunger of Memory* (1982). Another revealing account is the lively, humorous, and at times, brutally painful memoir, *Burro Genius*, by novelist Victor Villseñor (2004). Villaseñor creates a vivid portrayal of a young boy seeking to form a positive identity as he struggles in school with dyslexia and negative stereotyping of his Mexican language and culture. Even if English learners strive to adopt the ways of the new culture without replacing those of the home, they will have departed significantly from many traditions their parents hold dear. Thus for many students the generation gap necessarily widens to the extent that the values, beliefs, roles, responsibilities, and general expectations differ between the home culture and the dominant one. Keeping this in mind may help you empathize with students' personal conflicts of identity and personal life choices.

The third suggestion, then, is to become aware of basic features of the home culture, such as religious beliefs and customs, food preferences and restrictions, and roles and responsibilities of children and adults (Ovando, Collier, & Combs, 2003; Saville-Troike, 1978). These basic bits of information, though sketchy, will guide your initial interactions with your new students and may help you avoid asking them to say or do things that may be prohibited or frowned on in the home culture, including such common activities as celebrating birthdays, pledging allegiance to the flag, and eating hot dogs. Finding out basic information also provides a starting point from which to interpret your newcomer's responses to you, to your other students, and to the ways you organize classroom activities. Just as you make adjustments, your students will also begin to make adjustments as they grow in the awareness and acceptance that ways of acting, dressing, eating, talking, and behaving in school are different to a greater or lesser degree from what they may have experienced before.

Classroom Activities that Let You Get to Know Your Students

Several fine learning activities may also provide some of the personal information you need to help you know your students better. One way is to have all your students write an illustrated autobiography, "All About Me" or "The Story of My Life." Each book may be bound individually, or all the life stories may be bound together and published in a class book, complete with illustrations or photographs. Alternatively, student stories may be posted on the bulletin board for all to read. This assignment lets you in on the lives of all your students and permits them to get to know, appreciate, and understand each other as well. Of particular importance, this activity does not single out your newcomers because all your students will be involved.

Personal writing assignments like the one mentioned lend themselves to many grade levels because personal topics remain pertinent across age groups even into adulthood. Students who speak little or no English may begin by illustrating a series of important events in their lives, perhaps to be captioned with your assistance or that of another student. In addition, there are many ways to accommodate students' varying English writing abilities. For example, if students write more easily in their native tongue than in English, allow them to do so. If needed, ask a bilingual student or paraprofessional to translate the meaning for you. Be sure to publish the student's story as written in the native language because you will thereby both validate the home language and expose the rest of the class to a different language and its writing system. If a student knows some

English but is not yet able to write, allow her or him to dictate the story to you or to another student in the class.

Another way to begin to know your students is to start a dialogue journal with them. Provide each student with a blank journal and allow the student to draw or write in the language of the student's choice. You may then respond to the students' journal entries on a periodic basis. Interactive dialogue journals, described in detail in Chapter 5, have proven useful for English learners of all ages (Kreeft, 1984). Dialogue journals make an excellent introduction to literacy and facilitate the development of an ongoing personal relationship between the student and you, the teacher. As with personal writing, this activity is appropriate for all students, and if you institute it with the entire class you provide a way for newcomers to participate in a "regular" class activity. Being able to do what others do can be a source of great pride and self-satisfaction to students who are new to the language and culture of the school.

Finally, many teachers start the school year with a unit on themes such as "Where We Were Born" or "Family Origins." Again, this activity is relevant to all students, whether immigrant or native born, and it gives teacher and students alike a chance to know more about themselves and each other. A typical activity with this theme is the creation of a world map with a string connecting each child's name and birthplace to your city and school. Don't forget to put your name on the list along with your birthplace. From there, you and your students may go on to study more about the various regions and countries of origin. Clearly, this type of theme leads in many directions, including the discovery of people in the community who may be able to share information about their home countries with your class. Your guests may begin by sharing food, holiday customs, art, or music with students. Through such contact, theme studies, life stories, and reading about cultures in books such as those listed in Example 1.1 you may begin to become aware of some of the more subtle aspects of the culture, such as how the culture communicates politeness and respect or how the culture views the role of children, adults, and the school. If you are lucky enough to find such community resources, you will not only enliven

---

EXAMPLE 1.1 • A Few Important Books on Multicultural Teaching

---

Banks, J. A. (2003). *Teaching strategies for ethnic studies* (7th ed.). Boston: Allyn and Bacon.

Darder, A. (1991). *Culture and power in the classroom: A critical foundation for bicultural education.* Westport, CT: Bergin & Garvey.

Garcia, E. (2001). *Understanding and meeting the challenge of student cultural diversity.* (3rd ed.). Boston: Houghton Mifflin.

Igoa, C. (1995). *The inner world of the immigrant child.* New York: St. Martin's Press.

Nieto, S. & Bode, P. (2007). *Affirming diversity: The sociopolitical context of multicultural education* (5th ed.). Boston: Allyn and Bacon.

Tiedt, P. L., & Tiedt, I. M. (2006). *Multicultural teaching: A handbook of activities, information, and resources.* (7th ed.). Boston: Allyn and Bacon.

your teaching but also broaden your cross-cultural understanding (Ada & Zubizarreta, 2001).

Not all necessary background information will emerge from these classroom activities. You will no doubt want to look into cultural, historical, and geographical resources available at your school or community library. In addition, you may find resource personnel at your school, including paraprofessionals and resource teachers, who can help with specific questions or concerns. In the final analysis, though, your primary source of information is the students themselves as you interrelate on a day-to-day basis.

How Do Cultural Differences Affect Teaching and Learning?

The enterprise of teaching and learning is deeply influenced by culture in a variety of ways. To begin with, schools themselves reflect the values, beliefs, attitudes, and practices of the larger society. In fact schools represent a major socializing force for all students. For English learners, moreover, school is often the *primary* source of adaptation to the language and culture of the larger society. It is here that students may begin to integrate aspects of the new culture as their own, while retaining, rejecting, or modifying traditions from home.

Teachers and students bring to the classroom particular cultural orientations that affect how they perceive and interact with each other in the classroom. As teachers of English learners, most of us will encounter students whose languages and cultures differ from our own. Thus we need to learn about our students and their cultures while at the same time reflecting on *our own* culturally rooted behaviors that may facilitate or interfere with teaching and learning (Trumbull, Rothstein-Fisch, & Greenfield, 2000). In this section we define basic aspects of culture in the classroom as a starting point for looking at ourselves and our students in this light.

Definitions of Culture

Culture may be defined as the shared beliefs, values, and rule-governed patterns of behavior, including language, that define a group and are required for group membership (Goodenough, 1981; Saville-Troike, 1978). Thus defined, culture comprises three essential aspects: what people know and believe, what people do, and what people make and use. Culture thus serves to ensure group cohesion and survival. Every child is born into the culture of a particular group of people, and through the culture's child-rearing practices every child is socialized, to a greater or lesser extent, toward becoming first a "good boy" or "good girl" and ultimately a "good man" or "good woman" in the eyes of the culture. Thus, culture may be thought of as the acquired knowledge people use both to interpret experience and generate behavior (Spradley, 1980).

It is important to note that cultures are neither monolithic nor static. Rather they include many layers and variations related to age, gender, social status, occupation, wealth, and power. Cultural changes occur as people encounter or develop new ideas and ways of being. Technology offers a handy example of cultural change if you consider the impact of cell phones on how people stay in contact. Contrast how people today keep up with each other in the United States, for example, compared to the days of the Pony Express just 150 years ago! Bearing in mind the complexity of culture, we offer some ways to consider its effects on classroom interactions, including developing your skill as an effective participant–observer.

Becoming an Effective Participant–Observer in Your Own Classroom

When you make observations in your classroom, you are actually using some of the tools used by anthropologists when they study another culture through *ethnography* (e.g., introspection, interviewing, observation, and participant observation). As the teacher, you are automatically both **participant** and **observer** in the classroom culture. To learn about yourself and your students through personal interactions, you may need to hone your skills in observing and interpreting behaviors, including your own behavior. Observation skills are especially important when you first meet your students, whether at the beginning of the school year or when they first enroll in your class. One procedure to help focus your observations is to keep a journal in which you jot notes at the end of each day concerning your interactions with students and their responses to you. Does she seem comfortable seeking help from you? Is he starting to form friendships? In which activities does your new student appear most comfortable: small-group activities, individual seatwork, listening to stories, drawing pictures? In which activities is the student reluctant? By noticing activities that are most comfortable for students, you can make sure that your newcomer has frequent opportunities to participate in them. In this way, you build a positive attitude toward what may as yet be an alien environment: school. From there, you may gradually draw the student into other school routines.

To make the most of your introspective reflections and observations, you may need some concepts to guide interpretations. In other words, it's one thing to notice that Nazrene "tunes out" during whole-class lessons but quite another to figure out why, so that you can alter your instruction to reach her. To provide you with some interpretive touchstones, we suggest you consider for a moment some aspects that constitute culture because these represent potential sources of overt conflict or silent suffering if your classroom rules and structures conflict with those already culturally ingrained in your students.

For a start at describing aspects of culture, we summarize in Table 1.1 "cultural content" with questions outlined by Saville-Troike (1978) categorized into various components, including (1) family structure; (2) definitions of stages, periods, or transitions during a person's life; (3) roles of children and adults and corresponding behavior in terms of power and politeness; (4) discipline; (5) time and space; (6) religion; (7) food; (8) health and hygiene; and (9) history, traditions, holidays, and celebrations. Table 1.1 provides a number of questions that you might ask yourself about these aspects of culture. As you read the questions, try to answer them for your own culture and for a different cultural group to get a sense of similarities and differences across cultures. Do you find potential points of conflict in the classroom context? How might you deal with them?

9

TABLE 1.1 • CULTURAL CONTENT AND QUESTIONS

CULTURAL CONTENT	QUESTIONS
Family structures	What constitutes a family? Who among these or others live in one house? What are the rights and responsibilities of each family member? What is the hierarchy of authority? What is the relative importance of the individual family member in contrast to the family as a whole?
Life cycles	What are the criteria for defining stages, periods, or transitions in life? What rites of passage are there? What behaviors are considered appropriate for children of different ages? How might these conflict with behaviors taught or encouraged in school? How is the age of the children computed? What commemoration, if any, is made of the child's birth and when?
Roles and interpersonal relationships	What roles are available to whom, and how are they acquired? Is education relevant to learning these roles? How do the roles of girls and women differ from those of boys and men? How do people greet each other? What forms of address are used between people of differing roles? Do girls work and interact with boys? Is it proper? How is deference shown and to whom and by whom?
Discipline	What is discipline? What counts as discipline and what doesn't? Which behaviors are considered socially acceptable for boys versus girls at different ages? Who or what is considered responsible if a child misbehaves? The child? Parents? Older siblings? The environment? Is blame even ascribed? Who has authority over whom? To what extent can one person impose his or her will on another? How is behavior traditionally controlled? To what extent and in what domains?
Time and space	How important is punctuality? How important is speed in completing a task? Are there restrictions associated with certain seasons? What is the spatial organization of the home? How much space are people accustomed to? What significance is associated with different locations or directions, including north, south, east, and west?
Religion	What restrictions are there concerning topics discussed in school? Are dietary restrictions to be observed, including fasting on particular occasions? When are these occasions? What restrictions are associated with death and the dead?
Food	What is eaten? In what order and how often is food eaten? Which foods are restricted? Which foods are typical? What social obligations are there with regard to food giving, reciprocity, and honoring people? What restrictions or proscriptions are associated with handling, offering, or discarding food?
Health and hygiene	How are illnesses treated and by whom? What is considered to be the cause? If a student were involved in an accident at school, would any of the common first aid practices be considered unacceptable?
History, traditions, and holidays	Which events and people are sources of pride for the group? To what extent does the group in the United States identify with the history and traditions of the country of origin? What holidays and celebrations are considered appropriate for observing in school? Which ones are appropriate only for private observance?

When students in our university classes discuss the questions in Table 1.1 according to their own family traditions, interesting patterns emerge. Although many students identify with middle-class, European American cultural values, such as punctuality, some also add special traditions passed down from immigrant grandparents or great grandparents, including special foods and holiday traditions. Other students come from families who have been in this country for centuries, yet maintain particular regional traditions such as herbal healing practices. In addition, some students have maintained strong religious traditions, such as Buddhist, Catholic, Greek Orthodox, Hindu, Judaic, Muslim, and traditional American Indian beliefs. From these discussions, we find that each individual actually embodies a variety of cultures and subcultures.

One student found the cultural questions an interesting way to look at her own family. Her parents had met and married in Germany, her father an Egyptian and Coptic Christian, her mother a German Catholic. From there they moved with their three young children to the United States. Najia reflected, with some amusement, on how different her German relatives were from her Egyptian relatives. For example, her German relatives visited once or twice a year, making plans well in advance and staying a short, predetermined amount of time. Her Egyptian relatives, in contrast, "couldn't seem to get enough of each other." They loved long visits, with as many of the family together as possible. Najia's German mother emphasized orderliness and punctuality in the home, with carefully scheduled and planned meals. The family ate at the specified hour, and all were expected to be there on time. With such differences concerning time and space, Najia wondered that her parents were able to make a highly successful marriage. She attributed their success in part to their individual personalities: her mother, an artist, is by nature easygoing and flexible; her father, an electronic engineer, is an organized thinker and planner. As individuals, they seemed compatible with many of each other's cultural ways. Najia's reflections are a reminder that people's behavior combines both cultural and individual differences.

Sociolinguistic Interactions in the Classroom

One particularly important aspect of culture that can affect teaching and learning has to do with the ways you use language during instruction. Because teaching and learning depend on clear communication between teacher and students, the communicative success of teacher–student interactions is crucial. Early on, difficulties may arise from lack of a common language. However, communication difficulties may persist even after students have acquired the basics of English if the student and teacher are following different sociocultural rules for speaking (Cazden, 1986). For example, if the home culture values strict authority of adults over children and if children are only supposed to speak when spoken to, then these same children may be reluctant to volunteer an answer in class. You might quite logically interpret this reluctance as disinterest or lack of knowledge, when in fact the student may simply be waiting for you to invite him or her to respond. On the other hand, some students may not want to answer your questions because displaying knowledge in class amounts to showing off, causing them to stand out, uncomfortably spotlighted at center stage (Philips, 1983). Some students consider enthusiastic knowledge display impolite because it might make their friends appear ignorant. These examples illustrate how cultural values affecting language use may impede teacher–student communication in either English or the home language.

Language use differences can be especially confusing in the realm of teacher questioning. Research has shown that teachers often do not allow much *wait time* after asking a question in class (Rowe, 1974). It turns out that what is considered enough wait time in everyday conversations varies across cultures, as do rules concerning how and when to interrupt and the number of people who may speak at once (Bauman & Scherzer, 1974; Ochs & Schieffelin, 1984; Schieffelin & Eisenberg, 1984; Shultz, Erickson, & Florio, 1982). In addition, students must learn classroom rules regarding who can speak with whom and when (Mehan, 1979). These rules may vary with the activity structure (e.g., teacher-led lesson versus small-group projects) and from one teacher to the next. Thus, it is important to make *your* rules explicit for speaking in class and to allow sufficient wait time for students to respond. Helping students find their comfort zone for expressing themselves appropriately in class will pay off in learning, self-esteem, and social relationships.

Another potential problem area is the known-answer question (i.e., questions used to assess student knowledge for which the teacher already knows the answer). For some students, these known-answer questions might be considered odd or of dubious purpose (Heath, 1983; Mehan, 1979), resulting in student reluctance to participate in such interrogations. You might want to reflect on your own questioning practices in terms of wait time, question types, and the actual phrasing you use. If your questions are greeted with blank stares, try altering your questioning style, or perhaps reserve discussion questions for small-group activities. Another possibility is to introduce question and answer sessions with a brief explanation of what you are trying to accomplish and why. That way, if students are unaccustomed to your question types, you will at least help them understand your purpose for asking them.

Culturally Related Responses to Classroom Organization

There are other cultural differences that may interfere with student participation in learning activities in the classroom. One of these is the social organization of lessons (Mehan, 1979). Within the constraints of time and adult assistance,

 INTERNET RESOURCES

The California Teachers of English to Speakers of Other Languages (CATESOL) site is a good place to begin your exploration of issues relating to English language learners (**www.catesol.org/index.html**). For example, the CATESOL news link contains articles and reports on recent events (e.g., James Cummins' views on No Child Left Behind and ELL students). Another link contains official position papers on important topics such as the Role of English as a Second Language in Public Schools Grades K-12, Language Policy, and Literacy Instruction for English Language Learners. You might also want to visit the National Clearinghouse for English Language Acquisition (NCELA) Website at **www.ncela.gwu.edu** to explore the extensive resources, online library, databases, frequently asked questions, classroom ideas, and more, all aimed at improving teaching and learning for ELLs. The site will also link you to current K-12 education policy briefs. You might want to choose one of the frequently asked questions to answer and discuss with your classmates.

teachers typically use whole-class, small-group, and individualized formats for instruction. It is important to recognize that these formats represent distinctly different types of **participation structures** (Philips, 1983), each with its own rules about when to speak and how. Students may experience various degrees of comfort or discomfort with these various formats based on both cultural and individual differences (Au & Jordan, 1981). For example, the use of small groups for cooperative learning is intended to increase learning for all students but especially for ethnic minority students (Kagan, 1986). The rationale is that many ethnic minority cultures instill strong values of group cooperation and that such instruction will therefore build on familiar cultural experiences. In addition, cooperative groups provide students with practice in getting along with people different from themselves to the extent that groups consist of students with different backgrounds. We are convinced that cooperative group learning is a valuable tool for teachers for the reasons described. However, it is important to keep in mind that some students may feel that the teacher, as the academic authority, is the only proper person to learn from in the classroom. One way to accommodate such students is to balance your use of group work with necessary teacher-directed instruction. When you do ask students to work in cooperative groups, you need to explain your reasons for doing so, thereby showing that group learning is valid academically. In fact, parents may need to hear your reasons as well. We knew one child who was functioning beautifully in cooperative groups, yet during parent conferences, his father politely asked when we were going to start teaching! Cultural differences in teaching practices thus present challenges to teachers, students, and parents alike.

In summary, we know that different students may be more comfortable with some instructional formats than with others and that their feelings stem from both cultural and individual preferences. We suggest you *use a variety of formats to meet the multiple needs of your diverse students*. Your best route is to be aware of how you create the participation structures of learning (i.e., grouping formats) to observe and interpret student responses with thoughtful sensitivity, making modifications as needed. In so doing, you **differentiate instruction** (Tomlinson, 1999) according to particular student needs, a topic we discuss in Chapter 3 and apply in subsequent chapters.

Literacy Traditions from Home and Community

As you approach the teaching of reading and writing to English learners, you will want to be aware of the literacy knowledge your students bring with them. Literacy knowledge stems not only from prior schooling but also from experiences with the ways reading and writing are used in the home and community (Au & Jordan, 1981; Boggs, 1972; Heath, 1983). It is helpful to become aware of how reading and writing are traditionally used in the community because these traditional literacy uses will influence your students' ideas, beliefs, and assumptions about reading and writing. You will want to build on these ideas and make sure to expand them to include the functions of literacy required by U.S. schools and society. Let us make this concept more clear through some examples.

Gustavo, age 7, entered the first grade of an urban elementary school in February, halfway through the academic year. He had come from rural Mexico, and this was his first time in school. He didn't even know how to hold a pencil.

13

At first, he was so intimidated that he would refuse to come into the classroom at the beginning of the school day. With persistent coaxing from the teacher and her assistant, he reluctantly complied. Once in, Gustavo was anxious to fit into the normal class routines. He loved to wave his hand in the air when the teacher asked a question, although at first he didn't know what to do when called on. That part of the routine took a little time to master.

One day, as we were chatting with Gustavo, he began to tell us all about his little town in Michoacán, about the travails of the trip *pa' 'l norte* (to the north), and then about an incident when his 2-year-old sister became critically ill. His mother, he recounted, knew what medicine the baby needed, but it was only available in Mexico. So they had to find someone who could write to send to Mexico for the medicine. They did, and Gustavo's baby sister recovered.

What does this story tell us about the concept of literacy that Gustavo offers for the teacher to build on? First, we can surmise that Gustavo has not had extensive opportunities to explore reading and writing at home. He probably has not been read to much nor has he been provided with paper and pencils for dabbling in drawing and writing—the very activities so highly recommended today as the foundation of literacy development. On the other hand, he is well aware of how important it is to be able to write—it was a matter of life and death for his sister! Furthermore, he is aware of the inconveniences, not to say dangers, of illiteracy. Thus, Gustavo, at the tender age of 7, brings a deeper understanding of the importance of literacy than many children whose rich early literacy experiences allow them to take such things for granted. Gustavo's motivation and understanding provide the foundation for the teacher to build on. Gustavo needs daily exposure to the pleasures and practical functions of print through stories, poems, rhymes, labels, letters, notes, recipes, board games, instructions, and more. With practice and hard work, his proudest moment will come when he himself writes the next letter to Mexico.

In contrast to Gustavo, students who are older when they immigrate often bring substantial experience and skill in reading and writing in their home language. These experiences and skills provide a good foundation for learning to read and write in English. Students who read in their home language already know that print bears a systematic relationship to spoken language, that print carries meaning, and that reading and writing can be used for many purposes. Moreover, literate students know that they are capable of making sense of written language. Such experience and knowledge will transfer directly to learning to read and write in English, given English language development and appropriate literacy instruction (Cummins, 1981; Dressler & Kamil, 2006; Hudelson, 1987; Odlin, 1989). Thus, when students arrive with home language literacy skills, teachers do not have to start all over again to teach reading and writing (Goodman, Goodman, & Flores, 1979; Peregoy, 1989; Peregoy & Boyle, 1991, 2000). Rather, they can build on an existing base of literacy knowledge, adding the specifics for English as needed, a topic developed fully in subsequent chapters.

In addition to literacy knowledge, newcomers with substantial prior education often bring academic knowledge in areas such as mathematics, science, history, and geography. It is important to find out about such expertise to recognize it, honor it, and build on it. You might also seek ways for your students to share their particular knowledge with the rest of the class. To conclude our discussion of culture, we suggest you take another look at your own cultural ways again to focus on how your attitudes, beliefs, and assumptions might play out in your classroom.

Who Am I in the Lives of My Students?

Working effectively with students from diverse cultures presents challenges and opportunities. As the teacher, you are in a position to inspire your students and open their eyes to the future in ways that no one else can. As you think back on your own schooling, you probably recall teachers who made a difference in your life. Because teachers have such great impact on their students, it's important to acquire the habit of self-reflection with regard to our own teaching practices and interpersonal relationships with students. For example, one deeply committed high school teacher we know undertook an action research project in which she tape-recorded her writing conferences with individual students. Upon transcribing her data, she discovered that she ended her conferences with White students by saying she looked forward to the next conference, but with her Black students she merely bid them good-bye. She was shocked by this distinct difference in treatment and upset to the point of tears, especially so because one of her stated curriculum goals was to empower *all* her students through writing. Through the process, however, this teacher was able to change her conference style to treat all students equitably with the same encouragement. At the same time, she gained a powerful insight into how easily a teacher can unintentionally disempower, rather than empower, students, perpetuating inequalities inherent in the dominant society rather than transcending and transforming them for the better. Through her critical self-examination process, this fine teacher had attained a new level of **ideological clarity** (Bartolomé, 2000; Cadiero-Kaplan, 2007). Teaching, like parenting, allows significant opportunities for a deeper understanding of ourselves and our influence on the lives of others.

How Can I Ease Newcomers into the Routines of My Classroom When They Know Little or No English?

As you begin to know more about your students, you will be better able to offer them social and emotional support. Only when new students become comfortably integrated into your classroom's social and academic routines will optimal second language acquisition and academic learning occur. Thus you'll need to give special effort and attention to those who are newcomers to the country. Adapting from Maslow's hierarchy of human needs (Maslow, 1968), we discuss basic strategies for integrating new children into your classroom. Two basic needs you will want to consider are (1) safety and security and (2) a sense of belonging. By paying close attention to these basic needs, you lay the foundation for meeting your students' self-esteem needs and for their growth in language and academic abilities.

First Things First: Safety and Security

When English language learners first arrive in school, a "first things first" approach is helpful, following Maslow's views. Thus the first concern must be with creating a feeling of safety and security. To address this need, there are several things you can do. First, it is helpful to assign a personal buddy to each newcomer, and if possible, one who speaks the newcomer's home language. The buddy must be a classmate who already knows the school and is comfortable there. The buddy's job is to accompany the newcomer throughout the day's routines to make sure he or she knows where to find such essentials as the bathroom, the cafeteria, and the bus stop. The newcomer needs to learn not only where things are but also the various rules for using them. For example, each school has its own rules about how to line up and collect lunch at the cafeteria, where to sit, how to behave, and when to leave. Furthermore, there are culturally specific rules about how to eat particular kinds of food; rules that we take for granted but that may be totally foreign to a new arrival. Perhaps you yourself recall feeling tentative and intimidated the first time you ate in the school cafeteria. If so, you will have some idea of the anxiety that can accompany the first days of school for a youngster who is new not only to the school, but also to the entire culture it represents. The personal buddy helps the new student through these initial days, helping alleviate anxieties and embarrassments that are bound to occur.

Another way to address the safety and security needs of newcomers is to follow predictable routines in your daily classroom schedule. Most teachers follow a fairly stable schedule within which instructional content varies. Predictability in routine creates a sense of security for all students, but it is especially important for students who are new to the language and culture of the school. In fact, your predictable routines may be the first stable feature some students have experienced in a long time, especially if they have recently immigrated under adverse circumstances.

Creating a Sense of Belonging

An additional way to promote security and create a sense of belonging is to assign your student to a home group that remains unchanged for a long time. In classrooms in which student seating is arranged at tables, the home group may be defined by table. The purpose of the home group is to develop minicommunities of interdependence, support, and identity. If such groups are an ongoing aspect of classroom social organization, with rules of caring, respect, and concern already in place, then the home group provides an ideal social unit to receive a newcomer.

Regardless of how you organize your classroom, it is always important to seat new students toward the middle or front of the classroom, in a place where you can observe them closely and where they can observe the classroom interactions of other, more experienced students. We don't recommend placing new students at the back or other far reaches of the room. In our experience, students who speak little or no English tend to be placed at the periphery of the classroom where they sometimes blend into the woodwork and are forgotten. Even if you feel a child can't understand a word you are saying, you can integrate the child into the class by simply looking his or her way while speaking. We encourage conscious integration of newcomers into the social fabric of the classroom so as to avoid unconscious marginalization.

By paying close attention to the social and emotional needs of your new students, you will be laying the foundation for the early stages of language

When students share information about their home countries, they grow in self-esteem while broadening the horizons of their peers.

17

acquisition. For example, the one-on-one attention of the personal buddy offers numerous opportunities for your newcomer to learn many basic English words and phrases at the survival level. In addition, repetition of classroom routines provides non-English speakers with ideal language learning opportunities because the words and phrases that accompany such routines are constantly repeated within a meaningful, concrete context. If you count up the number of times a child hears such functional phrases as "It's lunch time now" and "The quiet table may line up first," you will get an idea of how valuable such **context-embedded** (Cummins, 1980) language can be for rapid learning of basic English expressions. Finally, integrating newcomers into cooperative groups provides further social and academic language learning opportunities, as discussed in detail in Chapter 3. Thus by attending to the security needs of your limited English proficient students, you also lay a firm foundation for English language acquisition.

   As English language acquisition progresses and students begin to become a part of the social fabric of your class, they are well positioned to grow in self-esteem through successful participation in both the social and academic aspects of classroom life. Thus Maslow's theory provides a useful way to look at the initial needs of newcomers. As the social-emotional foundation is laid, all the other aspects of personal growth may begin to interweave and support each other, with social and academic competence creating self-esteem and reinforcing feelings of security and belonging. In the process, English language development will be further enhanced.

Current Policy Trends Affecting the Education of English Learners

Whether you are new or experienced in the field of education, media reports have no doubt introduced you to various reform efforts in education; many of which have been promoted by federal and state education policy. Because disparate needs and interests are served by education policy and because there are always divergent points of view as to how any problem may be solved, the arena of educational policy is filled with controversy and debate. In this section, we briefly discuss education policies affecting English learners across the nation and offer additional resources on this complex topic.

Academic Standards and Assessment

The implementation of academic standards and assessment permeates all levels of education today. If you are in a teaching credential program, for example, chances are your coursework is organized to teach and assess what you should know and be able to do to be an effective teacher. Similarly, standards have been delineated for K–12 students that specifically define the knowledge and skills that students must attain for promotion and graduation in subjects such as reading, math, science, social science, and English language arts. In addition, standards have been developed that specifically address English language development for students new to English (e.g., Teachers of English to Speakers of Other Languages [TESOL], 2006; California State Department of Education, 2002). Teachers generally need to become familiar with the standards of the content areas they teach and with standards specific to English learners. In this section, we introduce you to basic issues in standards-based reforms. In Chapter 3, we discuss how teachers implement standards-based instruction in their classrooms.

The standards and assessment movement traces its origins to *A Nation at Risk* (National Commission on Excellence in Education, 1983), a national report funded by the U.S. Congress that called for improvement in education across the country. Among the outcomes of the report was the development of the National Assessment of Education Progress (NAEP), a large-scale, national assessment program that permits comparisons among states on student achievement in reading, writing, and mathematics. By conducting periodic assessments of students in grades 4, 8, and 12, NAEP is able to provide the public with a report card on how well students are doing across the nation. NAEP findings have been used to spur education reforms, such as the reading instruction reforms of the 1990s, aimed at increasing student achievement. The current focus on rigorous academic standards, assessment, and accountability can all be traced back to the reforms called for in *A Nation at Risk*.

In line with today's emphasis on standards and assessment, a large-scale effort to serve English language learners has been undertaken by the World-Class Instructional Design and Assessment (WIDA) Consortium (www.wida.us/) involving 15 states serving more than 420,000 English learners in grades preK-12. Among their many accomplishments, WIDA developed English language proficiency standards that served as the basis for TESOL's *PreK-12 English Language Proficiency Standards* (TESOL, 2006), which address social language and academic language development in the content areas, including performance expectations for listening, speaking, reading, and writing. (See Chapter 3 for more information on the TESOL standards.) The WIDA Consortium has also developed an English language proficiency test aligned with their standards and a variety of other standards and assessment tools to help teachers and administrators better serve English learners. Furthermore, WIDA has developed primary language resources, including Spanish language proficiency standards and test report forms to parents or guardians in 19 languages. The WIDA Consortium merits a visit to their website because new resources are continually added.

In recent years the push for high academic standards and achievement has gained momentum. For students to achieve high academic standards, Congress encouraged national education organizations and state departments of education to develop rather detailed descriptions of curriculum content to be taught across the grades in subjects such as reading, mathematics, social science, science, and English language arts. Standards documents are generally structured to include (1) content standards that delineate what students should know and be able to do, (2) benchmarks that specify expected knowledge and skills for each content standard at different grade levels, and (3) progress indicators that describe how well students need to do to meet a given content standard (Laturnau, 2003). Criteria for achievement are thus built in to the standards.

High-Stakes Testing

Hand in glove with the use of curriculum standards is the implementation of high-stakes, standardized testing to measure how well standards are being met. Serious consequences may be applied when standards are not met, supposedly to motivate achievement and increase accountability (Ananda & Rabinowitz, 2000). For example, performance on a high school exit exam may determine whether a student will receive a high school diploma, regardless of passing grades in all required high school coursework. Similarly, standardized test performance may play a part in deciding grade retention or promotion of students in elementary, middle, and high school. School funding may depend on raising test scores. Furthermore, teachers and principals may be held directly accountable for student achievement (Afflerbach, 2002). Low-achieving schools, for example, may be subject to restaffing measures, in which teachers and principal are moved elsewhere and a totally new staff brought in.

The teeth in the jaws of high-stakes testing have been sharpened by the No Child Left Behind Act (NCLB), federal legislation reauthorizing the Elementary and Secondary Education Act (ESEA) originally passed in 1965 to improve academic performance among lower-achieving, "economically disadvantaged" students. Although standardized tests have long been used to identify students who qualify for educational assistance, the new law raises standardized testing to a higher pitch, requiring states to implement "accountability systems" covering all public schools and students. All students in grades 3 through 8 are to be tested by rigorous standards in reading and math. In addition, states are to establish and meet "progress objectives" ensuring that *all* groups of students reach academic proficiency within 12 years. To monitor the progress of "all groups," "test results are to be broken out by poverty, race, ethnicity, disability, and limited English proficiency" (U.S. Office of Elementary and Secondary Education, 2002, p. 1).

Schools that meet or exceed their progress objectives will be eligible for an "achievement award," whereas those who fall below must improve or be subject to "corrective action," such as restaffing. The NCLB act thus places tremendous pressures on schools serving groups who tend to score lower on standardized tests than their middle- and upper-class, White counterparts.

Over the decades *socioeconomic status* has proven to be one of the strongest predictors of standardized test performance. Children from low-income families consistently score lower than those in more affluent circumstances, and racial, ethnic, and language minority students are overrepresented in the lower income brackets. Unfortunately, it is not clear that mandating achievement will improve learning or even raise test scores, especially with the high pressure atmosphere it creates. For example, we have heard young children anxiously voice concern that their test performance might cause their favorite teacher to be moved to another school.

Equally problematic is the danger that test scores may be used inappropriately either to retain students or to sort them into less challenging instructional programs. Even worse, high-stakes testing may actually increase the already high dropout rate among racial, ethnic, and language minority students. Because of the lifelong consequences of educational decisions based on high-stakes testing, it is essential that these tests be proven both fair and valid for all students, especially those living in poverty. Therefore, constant scrutiny is needed to monitor the effects of high-stakes testing to ensure that all students are provided meaningful and equitable access to a high quality education, one that welcomes them in rather than pushing them out and one that broadens their life choices rather than narrowing them (Escamilla, Mahon, Riley-Bernal, & Ruteledge, 2003; Valdez Pierce, 2003).

In addition to issues related to socioeconomic status, testing and progress mandates such as those in NCLB pose special problems for many students new to English. First of all, *English proficiency* affects student performance and may render test results inaccurate if not totally invalid (Abedi, 2001; Abedi, Leon, & Mirocha, 2001). If performance is low, it may not be clear whether the cause is limited English knowledge, insufficient content knowledge, or a combination of both. In addition to English language proficiency, other factors may affect English learners' preparedness for successful performance, including the amount, quality, content, and continuity of prior schooling relative to the content and format of the test (TESOL, 2003).

Furthermore, the NCLB actually requires an *accelerated learning pace* for English learners to close the achievement gap between them and the general student population. With research showing that it takes 5 to 10 years to development academic language proficiency (Thomas & Collier, 1997, 2002), this progress mandate is ill informed and highly unrealistic for many English learners. Finally, it is important to remember that English proficiency is necessary but not sufficient for academic achievement in an English language curriculum. It takes more than knowledge of the language to make progress in school. Quality instruction, a safe and supportive school environment, student motivation, and parental support are also factors that come into play.

In summary, in recent decades we have witnessed a tidal wave of movement calling for high educational standards and assessment. In the past, curriculum content has been generally similar in schools across the country, but states and local communities have always retained control over the specifics. However the national standards and assessment movement is leading toward a standardized, uniform national curriculum. Whether these reforms will finally help or hinder learning among *all* students remains to be seen. More problematic is the implementation of high-stakes testing, the effects of which have the potential to create larger divisions between rich and poor and between those with power and those without.

Education Policy Specific to English Learners

Although English learners are affected by general education policy, they are also subject to policies specific to their English proficiency status. Federal law requires schools to identify and serve students in need of educational support based on English language proficiency. The purpose of such educational support is twofold: (1) to promote English language development and (2) to provide meaningful instruction so that students may learn academic content appropriate to their grade level. Schools are free to choose the kind of program that will best meet the needs of their students, including whether students' primary language will be used for instruction or not. Since 1968 when the ESEA Title VII Bilingual Education Act was passed, bilingual education programs have been developed throughout the country, using languages such as Spanish, Vietnamese, Chinese, Japanese, French, and Portuguese. In addition, bilingual programs have served numerous American Indian languages such as Navajo, Cherokee, and Crow. However with the passage of NCLB, the bilingual education provisions of ESEA Title VII have *not* been reauthorized for the first time in history. The current re-authorization of the ESEA thus effectively eliminates federal support for (but does not prohibit) bilingual instructional programs.

Instead of supporting bilingual instruction, the comprehensive NCLB Act places heavy emphasis on English language proficiency, not only for students but also for teachers, who must be certified as proficient in written and oral English. Although leaving schools choice of program type, the act requires them to use instructional methods that research has proven effective. To increase accountability, the act requires states to establish standards and benchmarks for English language proficiency and academic content. Academic content standards are to be aligned with those established for the general K-12 student population.

The elimination of federal support for bilingual education represents the culmination of several decades of heated debate, not just among lawmakers and educators, but among the general public as well. Arguments against bilingual education have often centered on the effectiveness of bilingual instruction in teaching English, with no attention given to potential benefits of bilingualism or primary language use and maintenance. Proponents and opponents both cite research and statistics to support their cases regarding the effectiveness of bilingual instruction (cf. Crawford, 1999; Faltis & Hudelson, 1998; Lessow-Hurley, 2000; Ovando, 2003; Ovando, et al., 2003). However research seldom provides absolute, unequivocal findings. Instead, results have to be interpreted based on the research method, including background information on students and teachers in the study, the type of program implemented, the extent to which teachers follow the program model, and many other variables. Because it is difficult to control for these variables, research results are usually open to criticism on either side of the debate. In the final analysis, research findings tend to play a smaller role than attitudes, values, beliefs, and ideology in the effectiveness debate. We offer additional resources on bilingual education in Example 1.2.

EXAMPLE 1.2 • USEFUL RESOURCES ON BILINGUAL EDUCATION

Brisk, M. E. (2005). *Bilingual education: From compensatory to quality schooling* (2nd ed.). Mahwah, NJ: Lawrence Erlbaum Associates.

Crawford, J. (1999). *Bilingual education: History, politics, theory and practice* (4th ed.). Los Angeles: Bilingual Educational Services.

Cummins, J. (2001). *Negotiating identities: Education for empowerment in a diverse society* (2nd ed.). Los Angeles: California Association for Bilingual Education.

Faltis, C. J., & Hudelson, S. J. (1998). *Bilingual education in elementary and secondary school communities: Toward understanding and caring.* Boston: Allyn and Bacon.

Lessow-Hurley, J. (2005). *The foundations of dual language instruction* (4th ed.). New York: Addison-Wesley Longman.

Ovando, C. (2003, Spring). Bilingual education in the United States: Historical development and current issues. *Bilingual Research Journal, 27*(1), 1–24.

In addition to the effectiveness issue, anti–bilingual-education sentiment is fueled by the belief that to unify diverse groups, English should be used exclusively in public settings. The use of languages other than English in hospitals, social service agencies, schools, voting booths, and other public venues is considered anathema by members of the "English-only" movement, promoted by groups such as U.S. English and English First. Resentment against immigrants and resources allocated to serve them adds fuel to the English-only movement. These sentiments have found their way into a variety of ballot initiatives in states, such as California and Arizona, aimed at (1) eliminating bilingual education, (2) restricting public services to immigrants, and (3) requiring English as the "official language" to the exclusion of all others. Whether such initiatives are upheld in the courts or not, they send a chilly message that finds its way into our classrooms as we attempt to create positive learning environments for English learners (Gutierrez, et al., 2002).

In summary, English learners are subject to both *general* education policy and to policy *specific* to their English learner status. Educational reform in the United States has become extremely politicized in recent decades. Now more than ever, state and federal legislators are mandating not only the content of the curriculum, but at times also the method of instruction. Greater and greater emphasis is being placed on English as the exclusive language of instruction. These trends are leading to greater uniformity and standardization in curriculum and instruction. The current emphasis on detailed and specific curriculum standards and concomitant high-stakes testing has placed tremendous pressure on students, teachers, and principals to get students to test well. These trends existed before the passage of NCLB and are likely to continue when the ESEA comes up again for reauthorization. Now as never before educators need to form a strong voice in the political processes that create education policy.

LA CUCARACHA   **BY LALO ALCARAZ**

La Cucuracha © 2002 Lalo Alcaraz. Dist. by UNIVERSAL PRESS SYNDICATE. Reprinted with permission. All rights reserved.

What Kinds of Programs Exist to Meet the Needs of English Learners?

If you are fairly new to the enterprise of educating English learners, you might be interested in the kinds of programs in place throughout the country to serve them. We offer such information in the following sections so that you will have an idea of what some school districts are doing. If your school has just begun to experience growth in English learner populations, these general descriptions may provide a starting point for considering a more formalized English language learner support program. It is important to reiterate that *federal law* requires that all English learners be provided with an educational program that provides them (1) *access to the core curriculum* and (2) *opportunities for English language development*. Districts are given substantial latitude in selecting program types and choosing whether to use the students' home language for instruction. *State laws govern program requirements at a more specific level*. Thus as you consider program development for your English learners, you will want to seek information from your state and local offices of education.

Bilingual Education Programs

English language learners find themselves in a wide variety of school programs, from those carefully tailored to meet their specific linguistic and cultural needs to programs in which little is done differently to accommodate them. Perhaps the simplest distinction among programs is whether two languages or one is used for instruction. Bilingual education programs are defined as educational programs that use two languages, one of which must be English, for teaching purposes. Bilingual education programs have taken many forms, but two goals are common to all: (1) to teach English and (2) to provide access to the core curriculum through the home language while students are gaining English language proficiency (Lessow-Hurley, 2005).

The following are brief sketches of some of the most prevalent bilingual program models. As you read these descriptions, think of them as skeletons that may vary considerably in the flesh as differences in communities, students, teachers, and administrators affect program implementation. In addition, bear in mind that some program models may overlap and that a single model may be called by a different name from the one given here.

In the program model descriptions we indicate whether the program serves language minority students, language majority students, or both. In the United States and other English-speaking countries, **language minority students** are those who speak a language other than English at home. In other words, their home language is a minority group language such as Cantonese, Crow, or Spanish. **Language majority students** are those whose primary language is English, the predominant national language or majority language. In this book, we are concerned with language minority students who are learning English in school, thus the term *English learners*. However a discussion of bilingual program models would be incomplete without some mention of the immersion model developed in Canada, in which language majority students learn a minority group language in school. The extensively researched Canadian immersion model, discussed subsequently, has been highly successful and has influenced instructional development in second language teaching throughout the world (Lessow-Hurley, 2005).

TRANSITIONAL BILINGUAL EDUCATION. Transitional bilingual education programs are designed to serve language minority students who are limited English proficient. Primary language instruction is provided for one to three years. The purpose of primary language instruction is to build a foundation in literacy and academic content that will facilitate English language and academic development as students acquire the new language. After the transition to English instruction, no further instruction in the home language is offered. The goal is to develop English language proficiency for limited English proficient students as soon as possible.

MAINTENANCE BILINGUAL EDUCATION. Maintenance bilingual education is designed to serve language minority students who are limited English proficient. It differs from transitional bilingual education in that primary language instruction is provided *throughout* the elementary grades and in some cases continues in middle and high school. English language instruction is also provided throughout the grades. The purpose of the maintenance model is to help language minority students develop and maintain their primary language and become fully proficient in oral and written English. Thus the program goals include full bilingualism and biliteracy for English learners.

IMMERSION EDUCATION. Originally developed in Canada, immersion programs are designed to teach a minority language to language majority students. For example, in Canada, native English-speaking students often learn French as a second language. In the United States, native English-speaking students learn languages such as Spanish or Cantonese. In immersion programs, students receive subject matter instruction through their second language to develop second language proficiency while learning academic content. Special techniques are used to help them understand, participate, and learn in the new language. Language, content, and literacy instruction take place in the students' new language in the early grades, with the gradual introduction of English language arts as students progress up the grades. The ultimate goal is full bilingualism and biliteracy in English and the minority language for native English-speaking students. Immersion programs are therefore *bilingual* programs designed to serve language majority students. Canadian immersion programs have been extensively studied and evaluated by the Ontario Institute for Studies in Education (Genesee, 1984, 1987; Swain & Lapkin, 1989). The success of the Canadian immersion model has influenced program development in two-way immersion described in the next section and structured English immersion and sheltered instruction (cf. Krashen, 1984) discussed in a subsequent section.

TWO-WAY IMMERSION PROGRAMS. Two-way immersion programs, also called developmental bilingual education (Christian, 1994), combine elements of Canadian immersion and maintenance bilingual education to serve *both* language majority and language minority students. Two-way immersion programs group more or less equal numbers of native English-speaking students and native speakers of a minority language together for instruction. In the early grades the non-English language (e.g., Spanish) is used for instruction in an immersion approach, that is, second language acquisition through content instruction in the second language. This procedure provides second language development for English speakers and intensive primary language development for the native speakers of the minority language early on. Instruction through English, including reading and writing, begins with about 20 minutes a day in kindergarten and is gradually increased as students move up the grades until approximately equal time is given for each language (Reynolds, Dale, & Moore, 1989). As English language instruction increases, native English speakers develop their primary language (English) skills, and native Spanish speakers develop their second language (English) skills. At the same time, both groups develop skills in the minority language. Alternatively, some two-way programs use both languages from kindergarten on up the grades in approximately equal proportions. In any case, the goal is full bilingualism and biliteracy for *both* language minority and language majority students. For example, the English speakers acquire Spanish or Cantonese and the Spanish or Cantonese speakers acquire English. Both groups develop and maintain their home languages. Emphasis on primary language maintenance for language minority students is a goal shared by the maintenance bilingual education model. The two-way program model has been carefully developed, researched, and evaluated in school districts throughout the United States with positive results (cf. Christian, 1994; Lindholm, 1990; Lindholm & Gavlek, 1994; Lindholm-Leary, 2001; Peregoy, 1991; Peregoy & Boyle, 1990a).

NEWCOMER PROGRAMS. Newcomer programs are designed to support the initial adjustment of immigrant students to the language, culture, and schooling of their new country. All students in newcomer programs are recent arrivals from other countries. Newcomer programs emphasize the integration of academic and personal–social support to help students adjust (Chang, 1990). Newcomer programs may make use of students' home languages for instruction, but they also emphasize systematic English language instruction. Newcomer programs are short term, often only one year, and are intended to prepare students to succeed in regular schooling situations, where they may continue to receive bilingual instruction, English language development, and sheltered English content instruction, also referred to as Specially Designed Academic Instruction in English (SDAIE). (Full discussion of SDAIE is provided in Chapter 3.)

English Language Instructional Programs

Bilingual education programs serve only a small percentage of eligible students. Much more common are instructional programs that make use of only one language, English, for teaching. In many urban and suburban areas today, classrooms include students from several language groups, making bilingual instruction difficult to implement. Program types that use only English for instruction include the following:

SHELTERED ENGLISH OR SPECIALLY DESIGNED ACADEMIC INSTRUCTION IN ENGLISH (SDAIE). In these programs, students are taught subject matter entirely in English. Subject matter instruction is organized to promote second language acquisition while teaching cognitively demanding, grade level appropriate material. Special teaching techniques are used to help students understand English instruction even though they are still limited in English language proficiency. Sheltered instruction, or SDAIE, is most effective for students who have already achieved intermediate English language proficiency. Primary language support may be provided separately according to district resources and student needs.

ESL PULLOUT. In these programs, English learners receive the majority of their instruction in regular classrooms alongside their monolingual English-speaking peers. However, they are pulled out of the classroom on a regular basis to receive additional help from an ESL teacher or aide. The help they receive consists of English language development activities and reinforcement of subject matter being taught in the regular classroom. The goal is to help students get by while becoming proficient in oral and written English.

ENGLISH LANGUAGE DEVELOPMENT. In these programs, English learners are taught all subject matter using English as the language of instruction in a class taught by a teacher with special knowledge of second language development. The majority of students in such classes are usually non-native English speakers with various levels of English language proficiency. At the elementary school level, English language development teachers are responsible for teaching students English language and literacy skills and the full elementary school core curriculum, including mathematics, science, and social studies. The goal is full English language, literacy, and academic development. At the secondary level, English language development teachers are primarily responsible for English language and literacy development; content is taught by subject matter specialists using sheltering or SDAIE techniques. The term *English Language Development* is sometimes used synonymously with ESL and ESOL.

STRUCTURED ENGLISH IMMERSION. In these programs English learners are taught all content through English using sheltering techniques to make instruction understandable. It is important to distinguish structured English immersion from the Canadian immersion model described previously. Specifically, structured English immersion does not promote primary language literacy, whereas the Canadian model docs. Therefore, the goal of structured English immersion is language, literacy, and content learning in English only, whereas the Canadian model aims for full bilingualism and biliteracy. Some states have passed laws through ballot initiatives limiting language assistance through structured English immersion to one year only. This time limit flies in the face of research showing that ELs need *at least* five to seven years to acquire sufficient English for academic participation in general education classes (Cummins, 1979; Thomas & Collier, 2002).

English Learners in the "General Education" Classroom

Although various bilingual and monolingual English support programs have been designed specifically for English learners, many students find themselves in classrooms where little, if any, special assistance is provided. These students face a sink-or-swim situation. Increasingly, however, sound practices in second language teaching are reaching the general education or "regular" classroom teacher. In this book, we offer information and ideas for developing language and literacy skills in English as a non-native language. We believe that these ideas can be applied by teachers, regardless of the type of program: bilingual, ELD, or English only. Just as our students bring diverse backgrounds, so also will programs exhibit diversity as we all join forces to move our students toward educational success and integration into the larger society.

Quality Indicators to Look for in Programs Serving English Learners

We have seen that English learner programs vary widely. However there are certain basic elements recognized by professionals in English learner education that any quality program should include. These elements are summarized in the following statement on the education of K-12 language minority students in the United States issued by TESOL, the international, professional organization for educators working with English learners (TESOL, 1992).

> TESOL supports programs which promote students' growth in English language proficiency, enhance cognitive growth, facilitate academic achievement, and encourage cultural and social adjustment. Such programs include:
>
> - comprehensive English as a Second Language instruction for linguistically diverse students which prepares them to handle content area material in English.
> - instruction in the content areas which is academically challenging but also is tailored to the linguistic proficiency, educational background, and academic needs of students.
> - opportunities for students to further develop and/or use their first language in order to promote academic and social development.
> - professional development opportunities for both ESOL and other classroom teachers which prepare them to facilitate the language and academic growth of linguistically and culturally different children.*

27

---

*Copyright 1992 by Teachers of English to Speakers of Other Languages (TESOL), Alexandria, VA. Reprinted with permission of TESOL.

Using Research and Expert Views to Inform Practice

Over the past decade or so, education policy makers have called for systematic reviews of research and expert opinion to identify best practices in the field of English learner education. One such effort funded by the U.S. Office of Education addresses "effective literacy and English language instruction for English learners in the elementary grades" (Gersten et al., 2007). The complete report is available from http://ies.ed.gov/ncee. We summarize the report's five major recommendations for you here. *First*, **formative assessments** of English learners' reading should be carried out to identify students who may need extra help learning to read. *Second*, **small group interventions** are then recommended to provide focused instruction in areas of assessed need. *Third*, **vocabulary instruction** is highlighted. Essential content words should be taught in depth along with instruction on common words, phrases, and expressions not yet learned. *Fourth*, **academic English** instruction should be provided to develop students' ability to use English for academic discourse, reading and writing text, and formal argument. *Fifth*, **peer-assisted learning** opportunities should be provided frequently. In particular, students should work in pairs to complete structured, academic tasks. Paired students should represent different levels of ability or English language development. As you read through the book you now hold in your hands, you will discover *our* effort to connect theory, research, and best practices in English learner education. In this process, we include discussions of the topics highlighted in the report previously mentioned.

Summary

In this chapter, we have highlighted the rich diversity among students who are learning English as a second language in school. In our descriptions, we focus on children's different experiential backgrounds and strengths, while pointing out particular challenges they face in school. Because we believe strongly in building on each student's prior knowledge and experience, we suggest a variety of ways you can get to know your English learners, even though you may not yet share a common language. These activities include personal writing topics, interactive journal writing, and writing by students in their home language. Knowing that cultural differences can create an initial source of miscommunication, we have pointed out various components of culture defined by anthropologists, while suggesting ways to recognize and honor cultural differences among students in the classroom. We have also discussed how classroom organization and language use may be more or less comfortable for students as a result of both cultural and individual differences. We suggest cooperative group learning as one strategy for integrating students into the classroom fabric and promoting English language acquisition. Because we are convinced that social and emotional security form an essential base for learning, we have also provided a variety of ways to promote newcomers' sense of belonging from day one, using Maslow's hierarchy to give attention to their social–emotional needs. Finally, we offered an overview of the kinds of classrooms and programs in which English language learners find themselves. In the next chapter, we will present the details of second language acquisition, maintaining our emphasis on students' experiences and reactions to the processes and motivating factors that lead to learning their new language, English.

As we come to the conclusion of this chapter, an experience comes to mind that happened 30 years ago during the summer after my (Suzanne's) first year teaching second grade in a Spanish/English bilingual maintenance program in Guadalupe, California. I had gone to my mother's home reservation, the Flathead Indian Nation in northwestern Montana, to visit relatives and enjoy the summer celebrations. From there we proceeded to the Crow Fair in southeastern Montana, where people gathered from all over the United States and Canada for singing, dancing, stick games, fry bread, beadwork and turquoise jewelry, and festivities at what is billed as the "biggest tipi encampment in the world." You meet a lot of new people at Crow Fair. One afternoon while relaxing in the shade with my relatives near the Little Bighorn River, we met a family from Canada: mom, dad, and three teenagers. The father, a lanky, long-haired man in his late 40s, asked me what my work was. I replied that I was a bilingual teacher in California and that my second-graders were mostly immigrants from Mexico. I was proud of my work. He paused reflectively and then asked, "Why aren't you helping your own people?" These words stunned me. My words stuck in my throat and would not form themselves into a meaningful reply. Into the silence, my grandmother intervened, "They are *all* her children."

In today's world, these words take on even greater meaning, as the diversity among our students increases daily. Few teachers will go through their careers without encountering students different from themselves in language, culture, race, religion, social class, or land of birth. For teachers of English learners, such differences are a given, representing the challenge and reward inherent in our professional lives. Facilitating English learners to speak, read, write, and learn in a new language has become the task of an increasing number of teachers each day. Without a doubt, it is a task that calls for new learning, not only about theories of language and learning, but also about other people, other cultures, and about ourselves.

The essence of our message throughout this book calls for creating a welcoming classroom climate, one that provides each student with a variety of ways to be an active participant and successful contributor. We do not downplay the challenge of creating classroom unity out of student diversity, but we believe strongly that it can be done. Teaching linguistically and culturally diverse students presents an exciting learning opportunity for all of us. Is it easy? Certainly not! The opportunity for any learning and growth, our own and that of our students, is accompanied by great challenge and risk. Successful teaching with culturally diverse students calls for a willingness to go the extra mile, to observe ourselves critically, to question our assumptions, and perhaps to try doing things a little differently: teachers continually learning with open eyes, open minds, and open hearts!

In recalling his younger years, novelist John Steinbeck spoke of just such a teacher:

> In her classroom our speculations ranged the world. She breathed curiosity into us so that each day we came with new questions, new ideas, cupped and shielded in our hands like captured fireflies. When she left us, we were sad; but the light did not go out. She had written her indelible signature on our minds. I have had lots of teachers who taught me soon forgotten things; but only a few who created in me a new energy, a new direction. I suppose I am the unwritten manuscript of such a person. What deathless power lies in the hands of such a teacher.

May you be such a teacher!! (*CTA Journal*, November, 1955)

29

Suggestions for Further Reading

Becker, H. (2001). *Teaching ESL K–12: Views from the classroom with commentary from Else Hamayan*. Boston: Heinle & Heinle.

This is a good introductory book for teachers and administrators alike. It discusses topics including ESL curriculum, program models for secondary and elementary schools, assessment issues, special education, and parent involvement. The discussion with commentary offers a unique look at ESL programs. From the back cover of the text: "Teaching ESL K–12 shows the kind of meaningful professional conversation that teachers can have as they relate their 'wisdom of practice' to the social discourse of research and policy-making."

Cadiero-Kaplan, K. (2004). *The literacy curriculum & bilingual education*. New York: Peter Lang. Cadiero-Kaplan's excellent book discusses issues of policy, ideology, and politics in terms of how they influence literacy instruction. Chapters include: Schooled Literacy Ideologies, Public Policy: Literacy & Bilingual Education, Engaging Factors of Hegemony & Historicity of Knowledge, Engaging Literacy Ideology & Pedagogy, and Institutional Practices & Effects of Literacy Ideologies, and Creating Knowledge through Praxis. The book is an excellent guide for teachers who want to make a difference in our educational system.

Christensen, L. (2000). *Reading, writing, and rising up: Teaching about social justice and the power of the written word*. Milwaukee: Rethinking Schools. The author sees the teaching of reading and writing as ultimately political acts. The book looks at teaching for social justice and contains lots of samples of student writing. Chapters topics include: Building Community Out of Chaos, Unlearning the Myths that Bind Us, Writing the Word and the World, The Politics of Language, Poetry, Immigration, Portfolios, and Untracking English. Ultimately the book aims at "creating quality education for all students."

Díaz-Rico, L. T., & Weed, K. Z. (2006). *The cross-cultural, language and academic development handbook: A complete K–12 reference guide* (3rd ed.). Boston: Allyn and Bacon.

This 334-page book outlines all the basic information considered essential for the California English learner credential. Chapters cover information on second language acquisition and teaching; assessment; culture and cultures in contact; program models; and language program policies and issues. This resource is both comprehensive and up to date in its presentation of theory, research, and practice.

Garcia, G. (Ed.). (2003). *English learners: Reaching the highest level of English Literacy*. Newark, DE: International Reading Association.

This edited text contains articles from top teachers and researchers in second language literacy. There are three sections: Teaching English Learners to Read: Current Policy and Best Instructional Practice; Teaching English Language Development: Rethinking and Redesigning Curriculum; and Optimizing Culture as a Bridge to Literacy Learning. This is an excellent, informative collection of articles.

Hall, J. K. & Eggington, W. G. (Ed.). (2000). *The sociopolitics of English language learning*. New York: Multilingual Matters Ltd. This edited book focuses on the political, cultural, and social dimensions of English language teaching. It has three major sections: Language Politics, Language Practices, and English Teaching; The Social, Cultural, and Political Dimensions of Language Education; and Possiblities for Action. Some sample articles by top people in the field are: "Linguistic Human Rights and Teachers of English" by Tove Skutnabb-Kangas; "The Social Politics and Cultural Politics of Language Classrooms" by Alastair Pennycook; and "Disciplinary Knowledge as a Foundation for Teachers Preparation" by William Grabe, Fredricka Stoller, and Christine Tardy. This is an excellent place to start if your interested in going beyond the basic areas of language teaching and methodology.

Hinkel, E. (Ed.). (2005). *Handbook of research in second language teaching and learning*. Mahwah, New Jersey: Lawrence Erlbaum Associates. This excellent, informative book contains 57 different articles on second language literacy and learning under eight different major headings: Important Social Contexts in Research on Second Language

Teaching and Learning, Methods in Second Language Research, Applied Linguistics and Second Language Research, Second Language Processes and Development, Methods and Curricula in Second Language Teaching, Second Language Testing and Assessment, Identity, Culture, and Critical Pedagogy in Second Language Teaching and Learning, and Language Planning and Policy and Language Rights. We recommend this book to every teacher.

Meyer, L. (Ed.). (2000a). *Theory into practice, 39* (4). Columbus, Ohio State University.

This themed volume brings together an exciting array of articles that portray issues and insights related to the diversity of children and languages in U.S. schools. Articles address immigrants learning English and "learning America," loss of family languages, American Indian languages and tribal sovereignty, barriers to meaningful instruction for English learners, and English learners learning to read English. In addition there is an eye-opening

dialogue among four bilingual, African-ancestry teachers, and finally an article on two-way immersion in the United States. Lily Wong Fillmore's article on the loss of family languages has won a national award.

Tomlinson, C. A. (1999). *The differentiated classroom: Responding to the needs of all learners.* Alexandria, VA: Association for Supervision and Curriculum Development. This short book (132 pages) presents differentiated instruction (DI) in theory and practice. Chapters include: What is DA, elements of differentiation, ethinking how we do school—and for whom, learning environments that support DA, good instruction as a basis for differentiated teaching, teachers at work building differentiated classrooms, instructional strategies that support differentiation, and how do teachers make it all work. This book, with classroom examples, is all you need to get started with a truly differentiated approach to instruction.

31

Activities

1. As you look at Table 1.1, try to answer as many of the questions as you can regarding your own family traditions. For example, when you think of family, are you thinking about your mother and father and perhaps a sister or brother or are you thinking of hundreds of cousins, uncles, and aunts who get together every year for the holidays? Compare your answers with those of another adult. What are the similarities and differences?

2. Take the opportunity to visit a school near you that enrolls newly arrived students from other countries. Obtain permission from the principal to visit one of the classrooms. As you observe, try to find out where the students are from and what kinds of special help they are receiving. Use a checklist containing questions such as: What language(s) do the students speak? What assistance are they receiving? Is there a paraprofessional who speaks the students' language(s) or does the teacher use the language? Are there special materials available in the

students' home language? What kind of program would you design for these students to promote language development and content-area learning if you were the teacher?

3. Meet with a teacher who specializes in teaching English as a second language. Ask his or her views about the effects of students' cultural and prior educational backgrounds on their school performance. What accommodations does the teacher make to help students adjust? What kinds of programs does the teacher consider best for English learners and why? What kinds of materials or activities has the teacher used with success with English learners?

4. Talk with a child who is learning English as a non-native language. Ask what it is like to learn English in school; what the hardest part is; what has been fun, if anything; and how long it has taken so far. Ask the student to tell you what program, materials, and activities seem to work best for her or him.

5. Begin an informal study of an ethnic group that you would like to know more about. Begin charting information about the group by listing and noting specific information from Table 1.1, such as the family structures, life cycles, roles of men and women in the culture, discipline structures, religion, values, and the like. In addition, after you've gathered descriptive information, look for literature to read by members of that group to get a sense of the culture from an inside view.

PEARSON
myeducationlab
Where the Classroom Comes to Life

Video Homework Exercise
The Importance of Culture

In the video teachers and other English learner education experts discuss the role of culture in the process of second language acquisition, especially as it plays out in classroom interactions among students and teachers. Various aspects of culture are highlighted, including what people do, think, and believe about what constitutes appropriate ways to interact in the classroom; cultural norms concerning the meaning of eye contact, gestures, and facial expressions; and how much distance to maintain from others during conversations. The importance of learning about and validating students' home cultures is emphasized.

Go to MyEducationLab, select the topic "Diversity," and watch the video entitled "The Importance of Culture."

1. Compare the aspects of culture presented in the video with the information in the Chapter 1 section, "How Do Cultural Differences Affect Teaching and Learning?" Develop your own definition of culture, providing three examples of how it applies to classroom interactions and student learning.

2. The video emphasizes learning about and validating students' home cultures. Describe several ways you can learn about students' home cultures. You may wish to refer to the Chapter 1 section "Classroom Activities That Let You Get to Know Your Students."

3. In the video, mention is made of the friction and emotional stress that may occur when cultural norms are violated. Examine Table 1.1, and identify one specific cultural aspect that might be a source of friction or stress as a result of differences between home and school norms. How might you resolve the issue, while at the same time respecting the home culture?

Second Language Acquisition

> " Words were medicine: they were magic and invisible. They came from nothing into sound and meaning. They were beyond price; they could neither be bought nor sold. "
>
> —N. Scott Momaday (Kiowa), *House Made of Dawn*, 1968

> " Language is acquired, whining is learned. "
>
> —Woody Allen

In this chapter, we describe theories about how people acquire a second language, focusing on children and young people learning English in school. The following questions are discussed:

1. What do we know when we know a language? What are some ways experts have defined language proficiency and communicative competence?

2. How does language function as a symbol and instrument of power, social standing, and personal identity?

3. What theories have been proposed to explain first and second language acquisition?

4. What factors have researchers identified as important in acquiring a second language?

5. What are some important social, emotional, cultural, and educational factors that influence English learners' language acquisition experience in school?

We know a young Nicaraguan girl, Judith, who came to California at the age of 7. Her parents struggled to make a living for their seven children, and Judith was quite protective of them, always looking to lighten their load. Once we asked about her younger brothers and sisters, but Judith admonished us never to mention the topic to her mother, who was still grieving the loss of an infant. Judith was virtually non-English speaking in the third grade; her English grew very slowly in her fourth and fifth grades, though her native language remained fluent: She could make up extensive and complex Spanish stories on the spot, given a patient audience. For a long while we didn't see Judith, but then we happened to visit her school one day. We entered the main office to check in, and there answering the telephone in fluent English was Judith, now a sixth grader, who had earned the prestigious job of student assistant. What a transformation! We greeted her at once and complimented her on her efficient office management skills. And then we just had to comment: "Your English is so good! How did you do it?" With hardly a moment's reflection, she replied: "I waited." And wait she had, a good four years, though much more went into the process than her answer implied.

Judith's story gives a glimpse of second language acquisition from the inside view. In this chapter, we look at how researchers and theorists have described the process. As you read on, you will find that Judith's brief answer carried the weight of truth. There is, of course, more to be said to understand what it is like to learn the language of the school and the larger society as a non-native language. In the following few sections, we first discuss what you know when you know a language, to highlight the complex territory English language learners must cover to become proficient. We next present an overview of first and second language acquisition theories. Finally, we discuss various factors that impinge on the process, including the nature of the language learning situation, the effects of age, the importance of social interaction and "comprehensible input," and the treatment of learner errors.

What Do You Know When You Know a Language? Defining Language Proficiency as Communicative Competence

In general, language proficiency may be defined as the ability to use a language effectively and appropriately throughout the range of social, personal, school, and work situations required for daily living in a given society. In literate societies, language proficiency includes both oral and written language. For our purposes as educators, we want our students to become competent in four language processes: listening, speaking, reading, and writing.

Our definition of language proficiency emphasizes not only the grammatical rules governing sounds, word forms, and word orders to convey meaning (phonology, morphology, syntax, and semantics) but also knowledge of social conventions of language use (e.g., how to start and end a conversation smoothly; how to enter a conversation without interrupting other individuals; how and when to use informal expressions such as slang as opposed to more formal ways of speaking; how, whether, and when to establish a first-name basis in a formal relationship). Thus as you can see, judgments concerning language proficiency are deeply rooted in social and cultural norms. For this reason, the term *com-*

municative competence is often used instead of *language proficiency* to empha-size the idea that proficient language use extends beyond grammatical forms to include language functions and the social conventions of language to achieve communication (Canale & Swain, 1980; Wallat, 1984).

Classroom Example of Language Use in Social Context

It is important to note that when people use language, they must coordinate all language subsystems (i.e., phonology, morphology, syntax, semantics, pragmatics) simultaneously in a way that is appropriate to the social situation to communicate effectively. Let's look at a brief conversation as an example. In Ms. Baldwin's second-grade class, the children have planted a vegetable garden, and a group of eight students is now getting ready to go outside to care for their plants.

TEACHER: Let's get ready to go out to the garden. Who remembers what our vegetables need?

CLASS: Water.

TEACHER: That's right. So I will turn on the hose and each of you will get a turn to water one row. What else do we have to do?

CLASS: Pull the weeds.

TEACHER: OK, anything else?

With this brief example, we can look at how various language subsystems operate simultaneously for communication to be achieved. First of all, the social context, as noted previously, is a second-grade classroom situation, with the teacher in charge of a group of students. The social situation constrains how talk will occur. For example, the conversational structure in this exchange is particu-lar to classroom settings, with the teacher initiating the dialogue and the students responding, often as a group. The children know from experience that in this sit-uation they are free to call out their answers. They are not required to raise their hands to be called on, as they are at other times. The teacher initiates the conver-sation with two utterances that serve to organize and regulate the behavior of the children as they get ready to go out into the garden. When the teacher asks, "Who remembers what our vegetables need?" her question serves two pragmatic functions. First, the question focuses children's thoughts to regulate their behav-ior when they go out to the garden. At the same time, the question serves an aca-demic teaching function, which is to review plant knowledge learned recently. We have thus defined the **social context** and examined the **pragmatics** of the utter-ances in the conversation. All of the teacher's utterances are aimed at essentially the same functions: organizing the children's behavior and reviewing plant care concepts. The children's responses serve to display that they know what to do when they go outside. This sequence, teacher initiation-student reply-teacher evaluation, is typical of classroom conversations (Mehan, 1979).

Now let us look at how these utterances are formed to convey meaning. Lan-guages convey meaning by the systematic and coordinated use of rules governing sounds, including intonation, pitch, and juncture **(phonology)**, word formation **(morphology)**, and word order **(syntax)**. Each language in the world uses a finite set of sounds that make a difference for meaning: **phonemes**. Phonologists demonstrate phoneme differences by examining word pairs with minimal sound differences, such as pin/bin. Because a pin is different from a bin, that is, they have

Internet Resources

Vivian Cook's site on Second Language Acquisition (SLA) Topics **(homepage.ntlworld.com/vivian. c/SLA/)** is broken into several major categories which contain several links. Some categories are: Main SLA Approaches, Multicompetence: L2 user theory, Methodology, Learning and using, Bilingualism, Individual differences, Controversial questions, and Language Teaching. This is a valuable site for both students and teachers. You might also explore the ERIC Clearinghouse on Language and Linguistics site: **www.cal.org/siteMap.html.**

The site contains, among others, short articles on important topics by key writers and researchers. A few categories explored are: assessment, English as a second language, language diversity, technology and language learning, bilingual education, two-way immersion, and second language learning. You might explore one of these topics in preparation for a paper or a presentation in class.

different meanings, we can conclude that the two sounds, /p/ and /b/, are phonemes of English because the sound differences make a difference in meaning. In the previous classroom conversation, the children responded to the teacher that they were going to "pull the weeds." If they had said "pull the seeds," varying the response by only one phoneme, it would still make sense but would change the meaning completely, in a way that would be disastrous for the garden! If the children had said "pull the tzekl," they would have used a combination of sounds that is not English at all. Each language allows certain sound sequences but not others. If the children had said "weeds the pull," they would not have made any sense because they would have violated English word order rules, or syntax. At the level of morphology, if the children had said "pull the weed" instead of "pull the weeds," it would not have been quite right because they needed the plural form with the *-s* suffix rather than the singular to convey meaning accurately. Prefixes, suffixes, and root words are the building blocks, or **morphemes**, from which words are formed. All three rule-governed systems, phonology, morphology and syntax, work together simultaneously to help create meaningful sentences.

So far we have discussed language forms as they combine to convey meanings. The study of linguistic meaning, per se, is yet another area of study called semantics. When linguists study meaning in different languages, they often analyze the lexicon, or vocabulary of the language, examining, for example, synonyms, antonyms, kinship terms, and other aspects of the meanings of words in different contexts. Words and their meanings reflect the physical and cultural realities of the people who use the language. The ways in which languages serve to put meaning at the service of human communication are remarkably complex and interesting though not yet fully understood. Beyond lexical analysis, another way to study meaning is to analyze how languages convey information about actions indicated by the verb, including who or what instigates the action, who or what is affected by the action, where the action takes place, and a number of other cases that describe the meaning relationships among the elements in a sentence (Fillmore, 1968). For example, consider these two sentences:

Diego Rivera painted that mural.

That mural was painted by Diego Rivera.

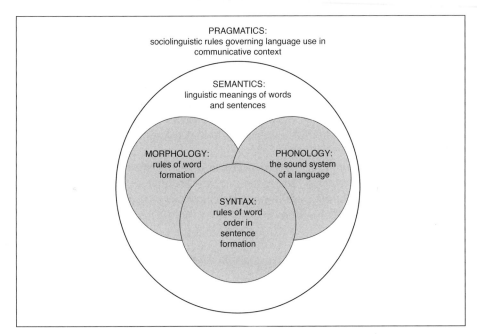

FIGURE 2.1

LANGUAGE SUBSYSTEMS

The action in both sentences is conveyed by the verb *painted*. The agent is *Diego Rivera*, and the object is *that mural*. Both sentences yield the same semantic analysis, even though they differ grammatically. Our examples provide a simple illustration of a complex and interesting linguistic theory, just to give you a taste of one way linguists have attempted to characterize how languages operate to convey meaning. The exciting part is that thousands of person hours have been spent trying to understand how language works, but even though it is not yet well understood, children the world over have no trouble acquiring their native tongues, and many become bilingual or multilingual!

This discussion of linguistic subsystems is intended to give you an idea of the complex nature of language proficiency. Figure 2.1 summarizes the subsystems of language, with pragmatics as the overarching aspect. This depiction illustrates our view that all language subsystems serve the purpose of communication, for the prime impulse to use language is the need to communicate.

Literal and Figurative Language

Beyond literal meanings conveyed by words and their sequence in utterances, most of us use figurative language, such as metaphors and idiomatic expressions, every day. I remember my father sometimes saying, "That guy's a real bird." I knew that the person described was a bit wacky, but I did not expect him to have wings. Similarly, when someone says, "That car of mine is a real lemon," we understand that the car breaks down a lot. We do not expect it to produce lemonade. In these examples, *bird* and *lemon* are used metaphorically. Young children and second language learners have to grapple with these nonliteral uses of words as they become proficient speakers of their new language.

We are reminded of our experience teaching English as a second language (ESL) to a group of men from Mexico and Central America who were working in the agricultural fields of California's central coast. We decided to bring in

37

some practical material on cars and car buying, so we brought in a book on cars we had at home. We started with a chapter called "How Not to Pick A Lemon." We hadn't really given any thought to the title, but the minute we held up the book to introduce the chapter, we had to start by explaining the title. As it happened, all of our students were lemon pickers! They certainly understood the literal meaning of the phrase, and we had a great laugh as we explained its figurative sense. This topic turned out to be one that engaged the most interest that semester. In fact, we ended up giving the book away to one of the students.

Idioms, like metaphors, are fixed expressions whose meaning does not correspond literally to the words that comprise it. Like metaphors, idioms present challenges to young children and second language learners, a topic we address in Chapter 6. As you read the following idioms, visualize both the literal meaning and the figurative one.

- He's got himself in a real pickle now!
- Everything's coming up roses.
- No sweat!

THE FAR SIDE® BY GARY LARSON

© 1983 FarWorks, Inc. All Rights Reserved/Dist. by Creators Syndicate

"Hang him, you idiots! Hang him! ... 'String him up' is a figure of speech!"

Related to idioms are pat phrases or sayings such as the following:

- The coast is clear.
- There's a pot for every lid.
- Butter wouldn't melt in her mouth.
- If wishes were horses, beggars would ride.

In addition to using figurative language, it is possible to say something but mean its opposite, as in irony or sarcasm. For example, if you have just received notice that your insurance rate has gone up, you might say, "Oh great!" But you really mean "Oh no!" or "Oh how awful!" or perhaps something much more colorful. These examples of nonliteral language illustrate how complex linguistic communication really is.

In summary, language proficiency represents a large and complex array of knowledge. As we have seen, appropriate language use involves both social and grammatical knowledge. People adjust their linguistic style from formal to informal, oral to written, according to their needs and purposes. Fully developed language proficiency, or communicative competence, thus includes the development of a repertoire of oral and written language skills from which to choose to achieve communication across a range of social situations, including academic situations.

Students learning English as a new language face a complex task that must take place gradually over time. Simultaneously, many will also develop and maintain proficiency in their home language, including literacy skills, thereby becoming bilingual and biliterate. For children living in bilingual communities, maintenance of the home language represents a vitally important aspect of communicative competence: bilingual communicative competence (Grosjean, 1982; Romaine, 1989). Consider, for example, the fact that the home language may be a child's only means of communicating with parents or grandparents. As a result, the home language becomes the primary vehicle for the transmission of cultural values, family history, and ethnic identity—the underpinnings of self-esteem (Wong Fillmore, 1991a, 1991b). In addition to the important social and emotional advantages of home language maintenance, research suggests that primary language development supports second language development (Cummins, 1980, 1981) and that bilingualism itself may lead to cognitive flexibility (Hakuta, 1986). Although we focus on second language literacy in this book, we want to underscore the importance of the first language as an integral part of our students' lives, socially, emotionally, cognitively, and educationally.

Language, Power, Social Standing, and Identity

The fact that words may be listed and defined in a dictionary or that pronunciation and grammar rules may be catalogued can draw attention away from the dynamic nature of language. Russian theorist Mikhail Bakhtin suggests that when people communicate via language, they engage in more than an exchange of words: They engage in an exchange of consciousness as meaning is negotiated and understanding achieved or not achieved (Bakhtin, 1981; Moraes, 1996). Words take on different meanings based on the social and power relationships between speakers. And that meaning is intrinsically related to the social, cultural, political, and historical contexts in which a conversation takes place.

In this section, we briefly discuss how language acts as an instrument of social, cultural, and political power. In this context we bring up the volatile topic of dialect. Finally, we discuss how the mother tongue is deeply connected to personal identity and self-esteem, and how adding a new language involves the forging of new identities (cf. Norton, 1997). Understanding these ideas helps us recognize and honor students' home languages and ways of speaking, while facilitating development of English as an additional language or dialect. Dialect issues are especially relevant because English language development (ELD) classes may include native English speakers who are learning Standard English as a second dialect.

ACTIVITY 2.1

Languages in the Attic: Constructing Your Language Family Tree

One way to recognize and honor students' home languages is through an activity we use in class called Language in the Attic (Murray, 1992), which can be adapted for use with secondary and elementary age students. You start by drawing a family tree on a plain piece of paper, with your name in the center. On one side you list your father's name and then the names of his parents. On the other side you list your mother's name and the names of her parents. Beside each family member, list the language or languages that each one speaks or spoke. Try going back as many generations as you can. What you end up with is your linguistic family tree. Looking at your language family tree, try to answer the following:

1. What circumstances led to maintenance or loss of your "languages in the attic"?

2. What family feelings have you discovered about your ancestral languages?

3. How have education, literacy, and employment in your family contributed to language maintenance or loss?

As you and several classmates share your linguistic family trees, try to identify interesting patterns in language maintenance, shift, and change.

1. How do these patterns reflect social, cultural, economic, and political realities in the lives of your parents and forebears?

2. How do men's and women's or boys' and girls' experiences differ?

Other activities include: (1) making a graph of all attic languages in your class to see how numbers compare; (2) identifying the number of languages that came from each continent in the world; and (3) researching and identifying the world language families represented in the class (cf. Crystal, 1997, or search the Internet with key words "language families"). Finally, don't miss the opportunity to highlight and share feelings of wonder and pride in the linguistic diversity of your particular group of students.

Language as an Instrument and Symbol of Power

Languages don't live in a vacuum. They live, breathe, proliferate, change, and die according to the vicissitudes of the lives of their speakers. For example, the Latin of ancient Rome is no longer spoken, even though it can be studied in its written form. As the Roman Empire spread to parts of Europe, northern Africa, and central Asia, Latin gradually became the dominant language in commercial, legal, and administrative affairs. After Rome fell, Latin had gained such a strong hold in parts of Europe that it remained the primary language spoken even after the Romans lost power. In those areas, Latin gradually evolved into what we know today as the Romance languages: Italian, Spanish, Portuguese, Rumanian, and French. The spread of spoken Latin and also the Roman alphabet to the outlying provinces of the Roman Empire was one of many sociocultural effects of Rome's political domination on the diverse groups of people it conquered.

It is estimated that 4,000 to 8,000 different languages are spoken in the world today (Fromkin, Rodman, & Hyams, 2003). Mandarin, English, Hindi, and Spanish have the largest number of speakers. Some languages have few speakers, and are therefore at risk of extinction. The languages of the world have been classified into 100 or so overarching language families based on linguistic similarities. Most European languages, including English, belong to the Indo-European language family, which also includes several Germanic and Gaelic languages and all modern languages that have descended from Classical Latin, Greek, and Sanskrit. Other language families include Afro-Asiatic, Amerindian, Austroasiatic, Malayo-Polynesian, and Niger-Congo. Some languages, called isolates, do not seem to fit into any known language family, such as Euskara, the language of the Basque people of the Pyrenees Mountains in France and Spain (Crystal, 1997). Another isolate is Kutenai, the American Indian language of some of my (Suzanne's) ancestors, which is still spoken by a small number of people in Montana, Idaho, and British Columbia. The world's linguistic diversity is truly immense, and it reflects the tremendous diversity of cultures throughout the world.

Language or Dialect?

One reason that numerical estimates of the world's languages vary so widely is disagreement over whether to classify a particular linguistic system as a language or a dialect. Generally, we say that when there are systematic differences in the way different groups of people speak the same language, they are using different dialects or varieties of that language. Systematic differences in phonology, morphology, syntax, semantics, and pragmatics have been found, for example, in the English spoken by certain groups of African Americans, American Indians, European Americans, and Latino Americans in the United States (Fromkin et al., 2003). Mutual intelligibility is often cited as a criterion to test whether two language varieties are dialects of the same language. However this test does not always work. For example, the so-called dialects of Chinese are not all mutually intelligible, yet they are generally called dialects, except for Mandarin, which is the official language of mainland China. By the same token, languages such as Spanish and Portuguese are mutually intelligible. Yet they are classified as separate languages. In these cases, political status rather than mutual intelligibility plays the deciding role in distinguishing language from dialect, thus the assertion that a language is "a dialect with an army and a navy."

To illustrate how a dialect with an army and a navy assumes power, let's consider Spanish as an example. In this case we will look at a particular dialect of Spanish, Castilian, which became Spain's standard language beginning with several events in 1492. In that year, not only did Columbus claim the New World for Spain, but the Moors were also driven out of Granada, culminating the 700-year struggle to regain the Peninsula from its Muslim conquerors; all Jews were expelled from Spain, except those who were willing to convert to Christianity; and Antonio de Nebrija compiled a Castilian grammar, one of the first modern language grammars ever published. Language, religion, nationhood, and empire coalesced all at once under Ferdinand of Aragon and Isabella of Castille. Isabella's dialect (not Ferdinand's) became the standard, rather than Galician or Catalonian or some other Hispanic dialect. As Spain spread its empire to other parts of the world, Spanish supplanted numerous indigenous languages while continuing to evolve. What Rome had done to Spain, Spain was now doing to people in the Americas.

Today the Spanish Empire no longer exists. However as its linguistic legacy, Spanish is spoken by some 310 million people mostly in South America, Central America, North America, and Spain (Katsiavriades, 2000). A correlate of that legacy, however, is the loss and extinction of many indigenous languages, a process that continues today. Because Spanish continued to evolve in the Americas, the standard varieties of Spanish of countries like Argentina, Mexico, and Puerto Rico are different from each other and different from the Castilian spoken in Spain.

In a similar fashion, English spread worldwide with the imperial expansion of Great Britain and the national growth and expanded influence of the United States. Today English is considered a prestigious international language, knowledge of which is said to hold the key to economic opportunity and success as a result of its widespread use in education, government, the mass media, and business throughout the world. Although perhaps true for some, these beliefs suggest that English is one monolithic standard that spreads its influence equally among all. On closer examination, however, we find that this is not so, rather an underlying paradox emerges. Even as knowledge of English opens doors, it can also contribute to significant social, political, and economic inequalities based on the relative prestige of the *variety* of English used, along with a complex array of other factors that affect power relations among individuals, groups, and nations.

To illustrate how language variety relates to power and prestige, a model depicting three concentric circles has been suggested (B. Kachru, 1983). The **inner circle** portrays countries in which English is the primary national language, such as Australia, Canada, the United Kingdom, and the United States. Having originated in England, English migrated with its speakers in centuries past to areas that became inner circle countries. The **outer circle** depicts countries in which English, often coexisting with indigenous languages, is used in major institutions such as education, civil service, and government. In outer circle countries, English was usually imposed during colonial rule and remains in use as a major or official language. The outer circle consists of many countries in Asia, Africa, the Middle East, and the Caribbean and Pacific islands. Outer circle countries include, for example, Ghana, India, Nigeria, Philippines, and Singapore to name just a few. The **expanding circle** includes countries in which English is taught as a second language for international communication purposes but has no role in domestic institutions, as in Japan, China, Russia, and many European and Latin American countries. The varieties of English used in all three circles have come to be known as World Englishes and have been studied extensively during the past three decades (Y. Kachru, 2005).

Some experts suggest that the spread of English is overall a positive phenomenon because it offers access to a wider world of communication with corresponding personal, social, and economic benefits (B. Kachru, 1983). Others argue that the global expansion of English, together with the emergence of its regional varieties, is largely negative because it contributes to political, social, and economic inequality; primarily to the benefit of inner circle individuals and institutions (Phillipson, 1992). In this view, language is used to maintain the political power, prestige, and hegemony of the inner circle. The sociocultural and political effects of World Englishes are enormously complex, and this discussion barely scratches the surface. To put a face on the topic, we offer the case of Edna Velasco described by Tollefson (2000).

Edna is from the Philippines, an outer circle country, where English is an official language used widely in government, education, business, and mass media. A graduate of a prestigious, private college in the Philippines, Edna was educated *through English* from elementary school through college. Edna is bilingual in Filipino and English, using a variety of English common to highly educated individuals living in and around Manila, the country's capital. When Edna decided to pursue a doctoral degree in applied linguistics in the United States, she was required to pass an English language proficiency test to qualify for admission, which she did. Subsequently, to qualify as a teaching assistant in ESL at the university, she was required to take a test of spoken English, including accent and speaking style. Even though she saw herself as a native English speaker, Edna felt nervous and worried about how the examiners would judge her Filipino English. The fact that she was required to submit to testing illustrates the lower status of her variety of English in this situation. Yet in Philippine society, Edna's English was indicative of high status, opening doors of opportunity economically and professionally.

Edna's case not only illustrates differential language status, but it also points to broader issues in the teaching of English. Which variety of English will we teach and why? Whose English is worthy as a model for English learners and why? How should we address language differences in the classroom that reflect language variety norms as opposed to mistakes of grammar and usage? How and when should students be made aware of different varieties of English? These issues take on greater significance as mobility, immigration, and communication increase around the world, and as speakers of World Englishes come into greater contact with each other, face-to-face and via telephone, television, and the Internet.

In summary, this brief discussion has illustrated several points: (1) how languages migrate, evolve, and change over time; (2) how languages connect with power and may be used to consolidate political hegemony of nations and empires; (3) how political status plays a major role in determining dialect or language status; and (4) how language variety can contribute to the maintenance of social, political, and economic inequalities among users. Thus far in our discussion, we have examined the impact of language varieties across nations. But language varieties occur *within* nations as well, with similar effects on status and power relations, a topic we take up next.

THE ROLE OF A STANDARD LANGUAGE. When a dialect comes into power as a standard, its status is usually reinforced by its widespread use in three major arenas: (1) in written media, such as newspapers, magazines, books, and articles; (2) in oral broadcast media, such as radio and television; and (3) in academic settings in both oral and written forms. Connoting higher social and educational status, the standard language becomes an instrument of power for those who use it. At the same time, facility in the standard language may offer access to broader social, economic, and political opportunities. For these reasons, fluency in the standard language is an important educational goal. Optimally, students will maintain fluency in the home language as well, keeping communication lines open with family, friends, and community (Wong Fillmore, 1991a, 1991b), while forging a personal identity that accommodates both languages and cultures.

MISUSE OF THE TERM DIALECT. When language scholars use the term *dialect*, they use it as a descriptive term to refer to regional and social variations within a particular language. However, in everyday usage, it often carries a negative, pejorative connotation. Judgments are made about people based on how they speak. To some people the term *dialect* may imply inferiority. Even worse are judgments that the speaker is using bad grammar or lazy pronunciation, when in fact the language they are using is a rule-governed, fully developed linguistic communication system. The fact is that each of us speaks a particular variety or dialect of the language we are born into, and all language varieties are legitimate and equal as communication systems. The social and political reality, however, is that certain dialects carry more prestige and power than others. For example, the ability to use Standard English may offer access to economic, social, and political opportunities, which are otherwise denied. For these reasons, we want all students to develop fluency in Standard English, adding to the home language rather than replacing it.

Making judgments about students' grammar and usage tends to be second nature for many of us. However, it is crucial not to slip into negative, stereotypical judgments based on students' language. This is where ongoing self-reflection and self-awareness are essential. Finally, we must recognize the validity and importance of diverse community languages and language varieties. When students sense that you as the teacher truly recognize and value their home language and culture, they are more likely to feel positive about school and learning. At the same time, you build students' senses of identity and self-worth while creating the effective foundation for students' academic success. Because you as the teacher may represent the new language and culture, your positive attitude may also help students identify more positively with their new language and culture as well.

Personal Identity and Ways of Speaking: The Case of Ebonics

James Baldwin (1924–1987), the brilliant African American novelist and essayist, was eloquent in his use of language. Baldwin grew up in New York City and lived much of his adult life in Paris. He drew on his experiences at home and abroad to develop his essays on racism, language, and power. In 1979, he published an article in the *New Yorker* on the topic of "Black English," now sometimes referred to as Ebonics (Baldwin, 1979/1998). In the article, he talks about how one's language is intricately connected to one's identity:

> It [language] is the most vivid and crucial key to identity: It reveals the private identity, and connects with, or divorces one from the larger public, or communal identity . . . To open your mouth . . . is (if I may use Black English) to "put your business on the street": You have confessed your parents, your youth, your school, your salary, your self-esteem and, alas, your future. (p. 68)

In so few words, Baldwin crystallizes what we have taken several paragraphs to try to explain! But why does he say "and, alas, your future"? We interpret this statement as a reference to the way language functions as a gatekeeper, keeping some people down and preventing their access to social mobility and power. This is where access to standard language forms comes in, as noted previously.

So what is Ebonics? Ebonics, or African American language, is a variety of English spoken at least some of the time by many African Americans in the United States. Ebonics has been widely studied, and its particular rules of grammar, pronunciation, and discourse have been described by linguists (e.g., Baugh, 1999; Dillard, 1972; Labov, 1972; Perry & Delpit, 1998; Smitherman, 1986, 1998a,b). Like all other languages, Ebonics has a history that mirrors that of the people who speak it, in this case the descendants of African men and women who were captured to work as slaves on American soil. Because its features draw on and reflect aspects of the Niger-Congo languages spoken in West Africa, some call Ebonics Africanized English (Smitherman, 1998b). Baldwin (1979/1998) suggests that when the slaves were given the Bible by their White masters, the formation of the Black church began, and "it was within this unprecedented tabernacle that Black English began to be formed." Baldwin tells us, "This was not, merely . . . the adoption of a foreign tongue, but an alchemy that transformed ancient elements into a new language" (Baldwin, p. 69). Clearly, Ebonics is a rich and expressive communicative resource, a fully formed language, and hopefully, a source of solidarity and pride for its speakers.

In summary, as human beings each of us is born into a family and community where we acquire basic ways of acting, believing, and making sense of the world around us. The language or languages we use and particular ways of speaking are part and parcel of this sociocultural learning. As children we are all socialized through language, and in the process we acquire it. Because the language we speak is so intricately interwoven with our early socialization to family and community, it forms an important element of our personal identity, our social identity, our racial identity, our ethnic identity, and even our national identity.

Significantly, our first language is often referred to as the mother tongue. We identify deeply with our mother tongue and with our family's ways of speaking: If you denigrate my language, you attack my mother, my father, my family, my neighborhood. As children growing up we become aware, sometimes painfully, of the social status of our ways of speaking. Yet the home language remains an integral part of our identity and may be the only way to communicate with parents and grandparents. As a result, the home language is essential for communicating cultural values, family history, and ethnic pride. Teachers can assist students by recognizing and honoring their home languages and ways of speaking. Finally, it is essential to realize that adding Standard English as a new language or dialect involves much more than learning grammar, vocabulary, and syntax. It also requires the expansion of one's personal, social, racial, and ethnic identity to make room for the new language and all that it symbolizes and implies. Developing a bilingual, bicultural identity is a dynamic, challenging, and sometimes painful process that continues well into adulthood.

Language Acquisition Theories

As we proceed with our discussion of how youngsters acquire a second language in school, we must take a moment to summarize basic language acquisition theories related to first and second language development. Our purpose is to acquaint you with those aspects of theory and research that are helpful to teachers in understanding both first and second language learners. It is important to note that neither first nor second language acquisition is yet fully understood. As a result, many controversies and disagreements prevail among experts. For this reason, continued interdisciplinary research in psycholinguistics, sociolinguistics, and education is needed to help us better understand processes of language acquisition and use. The issues are complex enough to keep many researchers busy for decades, if not centuries, to come. With that, let us summarize some basic theories.

First Language Acquisition Theories

Our favorite first language learner is our young granddaughter, Hope. When Hope visits us, we enjoy playing hide-and-seek, reading books to her, and just listening to her talk. Recently, while playing a board game with Hope, Grandpa pronounced the *r* in rabbit as a *w*, saying, "It's a wabbit!" Hope was tickled by this. She immediately grinned with knowing amusement and giggled, "Him don't say it right!" At 3 Hope was confident enough about her own knowledge of phonology to point out the phonemic impropriety of an adult's pronunciation. At the same time, she remained oblivious to her own grammatical infelicities. We didn't correct Hope's grammar because we assumed that with time she would outgrow that phase to become mature in her language use, and eventually she did. Many parents and grandparents have similar stories to tell.

How do language acquisition theories explain observations such as these? Three basic theories of first language acquisition have been put forward over the years: behaviorist, innatist, and interactionist (Lightbown & Spada, 1993). We now discuss each briefly.

BEHAVIORIST THEORY. You are probably familiar with behaviorism as a major learning theory emphasizing stimulus, response, and reinforcement as the basic elements of learning. For language acquisition, behaviorists hypothesized that children learned their first language through stimulus, response, and reinforcement as well, postulating imitation and association as essential processes. For example, to learn the word *ball*, the child would first associate the word *ball* with the familiar spherical object, the stimulus. Next the child would produce the word by imitation, at which time an adult would praise the child for saying *ball*, thereby reinforcing the child's correct verbal response. Behaviorists assumed that the child's mind was a *tabula rasa*, a blank mental slate awaiting the scripture of experience.

Behaviorist concepts of imitation and reinforcement could not account for typical child utterances like "Him don't say it right," which were clearly not imitations of adult speech. Moreover, behaviorists could not explain how any novel utterance was produced, even those that were grammatically correct. Yet most utterances we produce in conversation or writing are in fact original. That is, they are not pat phrases we have learned by hearing and repeating. In addition, child language researchers noticed that parents typically reinforce their children for the meaning of their utterances, not for grammatical correctness. These and other concerns were boldly pointed out as Noam Chomsky (1957) engaged in a heated debate with behaviorist B. F. Skinner (1957), attacking behaviorist theory as inadequate to explain observations of child language development.

INNATIST THEORY. Chomsky was able to garner some strong arguments against the behaviorist explanation of language acquisition, using examples from children's developing grammars, such as our example from Hope. Skinner and his behaviorist colleagues were experts in psychology, applying their theories to verbal behavior. Chomsky, on the other hand, was a linguist with a genius for analyzing syntax. In fact, his early work on syntax and transformational grammar revolutionized the field of linguistics (Chomsky, 1957, 1959). Chomsky's explanations of grammatical rules and transformations became the subject of psychological research on language use in the interdisciplinary field of psycholinguistics.

As Chomsky pondered the complex intricacies of children's development of grammar, he concluded that language acquisition could only be accounted for by an innate, biological language acquisition device (LAD) or system. Infants must come into the world "prewired for linguistic analysis." Specifically, Chomsky claims that infants universally possess an innate "grammar template," or universal grammar, which will allow them to select out the many grammatical rules of the language they hear spoken around them, as they gradually construct the grammar of their mother tongue.

From the innatist perspective, children construct grammar through a process of hypothesis testing. For example, a child may hypothesize the rule that *all* plural nouns end with an -*s*. Thus when they come to a word such as *child*, they form the plural as *childs*, or when they come to the word *man*, they say *mans* for the plural. Gradually, they will revise their hypothesis to accommodate exceptions to the plural rule. Thus children create sentences by using rules rather than by merely repeating messages they have heard, as assumed by behaviorists. This application of rules accounts for the generative nature of language. With a finite set of rules, people can generate an infinite number of novel utterances. Children acquire the rules, according to Chomsky, with little help from their parents or caregivers. But as Harvard psychologist Howard Gardner stated (Gardner, 1995, p. 27), the Chomskyan view is "too dismissive of the ways that mothers and others who bring up children help infants to acquire language." Gardner argues that, "while the principles of grammar may indeed be acquired with little help from parents or other caretakers, adults are needed to help children build a rich vocabulary, master the rules of discourse, and distinguish between culturally acceptable and unacceptable forms of expression." This interest in the role of people in the social environment provides the focus of the next theoretical perspective on language acquisition that we discuss, the interactionist perspective. In response to Chomsky's emphasis on innate grammar mechanisms centered in the infant, interactionists have brought back an interest in the role of the social environment and the influence of parents and caregivers on children's language acquisition.

47

Copyright 2003 Paul Gruwell. Used with permission.

48

INTERACTIONIST THEORY. According to the interactionist position, caregivers play a critical role in adjusting language to facilitate the use of innate capacities for language acquisition. This is in sharp contrast to the innatist view that adapting language has little effect on a child's acquisition process. The interactionist view thus takes into consideration the importance of both nature and nurture in the language acquisition process.

Interactionists study the language mothers and other caregivers use when caring for infants and young children, with special attention to modifications they make during these social interactions to assist children in communication. One strategy often observed between English-speaking, middle-class mothers and their toddlers is conversational scaffolding (Ninio & Bruner, 1978), as illustrated in the following conversation:

CHILD: Birthday cake Megan house.
MOTHER: We had birthday cake at Megan's house. What else did we do at Megan's house?
CHILD: Megan dolly.
MOTHER: Megan got a doll for her birthday, didn't she?

In this conversation, the mother repeats the child's meaning using an expanded form, thereby verifying her understanding of the child's words while modeling adult usage. In addition, the mother assists or scaffolds the toddler's participation in the conversation through prompting questions at the end of each of her turns. In this way, scaffolding provides conversational assistance and focused linguistic input tuned to the child's own interests and language use at that moment. By preschool age, this kind of scaffolded conversation is no longer necessary. Whether scaffolding is actually necessary for language acquisition has not been verified. In fact, ways in which infants and young children are spoken to varies across cultures (Ochs & Schieffelen, 1984; Schieffelin & Eisenberg, 1984). Nonetheless, caregivers generally facilitate children's vocabulary development, their ability to use language appropriately in social situations, and their ability to get things done through language.

Children's language develops over time, not within a single interaction. As children develop language, they must construct the meanings of thousands of words. Adult assistance in this process is illustrated in the following dialogues, as British linguist M. A. K. Halliday and his wife (1984, 1994) interact with their son, Nigel. This transcript captures Nigel's "ongoing construction" of the concept of cats as it transpired over a period of eight months. In these dialogues, we witness Nigel's semantic development as he both contributes and receives information to help him construct the concept cat.

Nigel at 2; 10; 22 (2 years; 10 months; 22 days)

NIGEL: And you [that is, "I"] saw a cat in Chania Falls.
MOTHER: Yes, you saw a cat in Chania Falls.
NIGEL: And you picked the cat up. Mummy, do cats like meat?
MOTHER: Yes, they do.
NIGEL: Do cats like bones? Do cats like marrow?

Nigel at 3; 0; 26

NIGEL: How do the cat's claws come out?
FATHER: They come out from inside its paws. Look, I'll show you.
NIGEL: Does it go with its claws?
FATHER: Not if it's going along the ground.
NIGEL: And not if it's climbing up a tree?
FATHER: Yes, if it's climbing up a tree it does go with its claws.

Nigel at 3; 5; 12

NIGEL: Cats have no one else to stop you from trossing them . . . cats have no other way to stop children from hitting them . . . so they bite. Cat, don't go away! When I come back I'll tell you a story. [He does so.]

Nigel at 3; 6; 12

NIGEL: Can I give the cat some artichoke?
MOTHER: Well, she won't like it.
NIGEL: Cats like things that go; they don't like things that grow.

Nigel at 3; 6; 14

NIGEL: I wish I was a puppet so that I could go out into the snow in the night. Do puppets like going out in the snow?
FATHER: I don't know. I don't think they mind.
NIGEL: Do cats like going out in the snow?
FATHER: Cats don't like snow.
NIGEL: Do they die? [He knows that some plants do.]

FATHER: No, they don't die; they just don't like it.

NIGEL: Why don't puppets mind snow?

FATHER: Well [hesitating] . . . puppets aren't people.

NIGEL: Yes, but . . . cats also aren't people.

FATHER: No, but cats are alive; they go. Puppets don't go.

NIGEL: Puppets do go.

FATHER: Yes, but you have to make them go, like trains.

NIGEL: Trains have wheels. Puppets have legs.

FATHER: Yes, they have legs; but the legs don't go all by themselves. You have to make them go.[*]

Halliday (1994) says: "Interpersonally, it (the dialogue) evolves into a dynamic modeling of question, answer, challenge, contradiction, and the like that is the essential component of the resources out of which all conversation is constructed" (p. 79). Most important, this is not talk for talk's sake but a serious effort over time to build a concept through interaction between parent and child.

As we saw with Nigel, interactions do not necessarily lead to immediate understanding. Rudimentary understandings must be developed and refined over time, often through misunderstandings. For example, during salary negotiations between hockey players and club owners, there was a lot of talk about salary caps. When a sportswriter's young son heard that the strike had been settled, he asked his father, "Will the players have to wear their salary caps now?" An explanation followed. Children are constantly constructing meaning as they interact with people and the world around them, and through these interactions, they gradually sort out the nuances and construct the multiple meanings of words and phrases. The interactionist perspective acknowledges the important roles of both the child and the social environment in the language acquisition process.

SUMMARY OF FIRST LANGUAGE ACQUISITION THEORIES. Table 2.1 summarizes the behaviorist, innatist, and interactionist perspectives on language acquisition by comparing (1) the focus of linguistic analysis, (2) how each theory accounts for the process of acquisition, (3) the role of the child, and (4) the role of the people in the social environment. Of the three approaches, the behaviorist approach, which places primary weight on children imitating what they have heard, has proven least adequate for explaining observed facts in child language development. The innatist view, in contrast, places primary weight on the child, and particularly on innate, biological mechanisms to account for language acquisition. The interactionist perspective, acknowledging both the child's role and that of caregivers in the social environment, emphasizes the importance of social interactions aimed at communication as the essential ingredient in language acquisition. To the extent that more research is needed on both the biological and social mechanisms in language acquisition and use, innatists and interactionists are likely to add important information to the overall understanding of language acquisition now and in the future.

---

[*]"Listening to Nigel: Conversations of a very small child," by M. A. K. Halliday, 1984, Sydney, Australia: University of Sydney, Linguistics Department. Reprinted with permission of author.

TABLE 2.1 • COMPARISON OF BEHAVIORIST, INNATIST, AND INTERACTIONIST THEORIES OF LANGUAGE ACQUISITION

ACQUISITION ASPECTS	BEHAVIORIST PERSPECTIVE	INNATIST PERSPECTIVE	INTERACTIONIST PERSPECTIVE
Linguistic focus	Verbal behaviors (not analyzed per se): words, utterances of child and people in social environment	Child's syntax	Conversations between child and caregiver; focus on caregiver speech
Process of acquisition	Modeling, imitation, practice, and selective reinforcement of correct form	Hypothesis testing and creative construction of syntactic rules using LAD	Acquisition emerges from communication; acts scaffolded by caregivers
Role of child	Secondary role: imitator and responder to environmental shaping	Primary role: equipped with biological LAD, child plays major role in acquisition	Important role in interaction, taking more control as language acquisition advances
Role of social environment	Primary role: parental modeling and reinforcement are major factors promoting language acquisition	Minor role: language used by others merely triggers LAD	Important role in interaction, especially in early years when caregivers modify input and carry much of conversational load

Second Language Acquisition Theories

Theories about how people learn to speak a second (or third or fourth) language are directly related to the first language acquisition theories described previously. There are two reasons why. First of all, because first language acquisition is a universal achievement of children the world over, researchers and educators interested in second language acquisition and teaching have often used first language acquisition as an ideal model, one that may inform us about how a second language might be taught. Until Chomsky, however, ideas about how a first language was acquired were not fully developed and researched. Behaviorists, for example, did not analyze closely the speech development of young children, but rather extended general learning theory principles to language development.

With the advent of Chomskyan linguistics, however, a whole generation of psycholinguists was inspired to go out and tape record the speech of infants and young children to analyze and describe the process of acquiring their mother tongue. The focus of the research was to describe the grammatical development of young children. Chomsky's contribution to the study of child language was his new way of looking at syntax. Researchers applied his methods of describing syntax to the problem of describing children's interim grammars at different ages and stages of language development. As a result, a remarkable amount of information was generated about first language acquisition in languages as diverse as Turkish,

Mohawk, Spanish, and Japanese. This information provided a natural resource for second language acquisition researchers, not only in terms of theory, data collection, and data analysis, but also in terms of framing the research questions themselves. One of the first questions was simply: Is a second language acquired in the same way as the first? If so, what are the implications for classroom instruction? Because first language acquisition is so successfully accomplished, should teachers replicate its conditions to promote second language acquisition? If so, how? These questions are not fully answered yet but remain pertinent today.

Even as information began to accumulate from the study of child language, however, behaviorist views predominated in educational practice, heavily influencing methods of second language teaching in schools, emphasizing drill and practice of grammatical forms and sentence structures. Meanwhile, as researchers began to go into people's homes to tape record children's speech, the impact of the social environment in various cultural milieus emerged as an interesting variable in language acquisition and use. In fact, some early language acquisition researchers were thwarted in their data-collecting efforts when they discovered that their tape-recording procedures conflicted with cultural norms about how to talk to children! Sociologists and anthropologists were ready to combine their interests and insights about culture and language to inform what became the interactionist viewpoint on language acquisition.

The study of first language acquisition has now emerged as a necessarily interdisciplinary field involving anthropology, psychology, education, and linguistics. As you can imagine, careful attention to social and cultural conventions is essential in investigating how a second language is learned, given the intimate connections between language and culture. In the following section, we will introduce you to how second language acquisition is described and explained from the three perspectives examined for first language acquisition: behaviorist, innatist, and interactionist. We will also discuss their implications for teaching, and then offer a picture of our own understandings of second language acquisition in classrooms. See whether you can identify the theories that we have taken to heart in our viewpoint.

BEHAVIORIST PERSPECTIVE IN SECOND LANGUAGE ACQUISITION. Behaviorist theories of language acquisition have influenced second language teaching in a number of ways that persist today in many classrooms. If you have taken a foreign language in high school or college, you are probably familiar with the methods informed by behaviorist learning theories. One behaviorist language teaching method popular in the 1960s is the audiolingual method, in which dialogues are presented on tape for students to memorize, followed by pattern drills for practicing verb forms and sentence structures. Students are first taught to listen and speak and then to read and write based on the assumption that this is the natural sequence in first language acquisition. (This sequence has been disputed, as you will see in Chapter 4.) For behaviorists, the processes involved in second or foreign language learning consisted of imitation, repetition, and reinforcement of grammatical structures. Errors were to be corrected immediately to avoid forming bad habits that would be difficult to overcome later. If you were taught with this method, you may remember the drill-and-skill practice, often carried out via audiotapes in a language laboratory. How well did this instruction work for you? When we ask our students this question in classes of 40 or so, only 1 or 2 report successful foreign language competence acquired through the audiolingual approach.

INNATIST PERSPECTIVE IN SECOND LANGUAGE ACQUISITION. Just as Chomsky's theories inspired psycholinguists to record and describe the developing grammars of young first language learners, they also influenced research on second language learning. One such theory put forth to account for second language development was the **creative construction theory** (Dulay, Burt, & Krashen, 1982). In a large-scale study of Spanish-speaking and Chinese-speaking children learning English in school (Dulay & Burt, 1974), English language samples were collected using a structured interview based on colorful cartoon pictures. Children were asked questions about the pictures in ways that elicited the use of certain grammatical structures. Children's grammatical errors were then examined to determine whether they could be attributed to influence from the first language or whether they were similar to the types of errors young, native English-speaking children make. Data analysis showed that the majority of errors were similar to those made by native English-speaking youngsters as they acquire their mother tongue. Based on these results, the authors proposed that English language learners creatively construct the rules of the second language in a manner similar to that observed in first language acquisition. Dulay and Burt therefore concluded that second language acquisition is similar to first language acquisition.

Dulay and Burt (1974) also used their findings to refute the hypothesis that learner errors will generally be predictable from a contrastive analysis of the learner's mother tongue and the developing second language. Contrastive analysis is a procedure for comparing phonological, morphological, and syntactic rules of two languages (the learner's mother tongue and his or her second language) to predict areas of difficulty in second language development. For example, Spanish creates the plural by adding an *-s* or *-es* ending to a noun (e.g., *casa, casas; lápiz, lápices*). This rule is similar to English pluralization. Thus by contrastive analysis, it would be predicted that plurals in English will not be difficult for native Spanish speakers to learn. When the rules of two languages are quite different, contrastive analysis predicts learner difficulty. For example, Cantonese has no plural marker. The idea of plural is conveyed by context. Thus it would be predicted that Cantonese speakers would have difficulty forming plurals in English. Although predictions based on contrastive analysis sometimes held true in their data analysis, Dulay and Burt found that most English language learner errors among their subjects were best described as similar to errors made by children acquiring English as a first language.

KRASHEN'S FIVE HYPOTHESES. Continuing in the innatist tradition, Stephen Krashen (1982) developed a series of hypotheses about second language acquisition that have taken root in the field of second language teaching due in part to Krashen's desire to address classroom second language learning. Krashen's five hypotheses are: (1) the acquisition-learning hypothesis, (2) the monitor hypothesis, (3) the natural order hypothesis, (4) the input hypothesis, and (5) the affective filter hypothesis. Each of these is discussed here.

The Acquisition-Learning Hypothesis. One of Krashen's first assertions was that there is a distinct difference between acquiring and learning a second language. Acquisition, Krashen asserts, is a natural language development process that occurs when the target language is used in meaningful interactions with native speakers, in a manner similar to first language acquisition—with no particular attention to form. Language learning, in contrast, refers to the formal and conscious study of language forms and functions as explicitly taught in foreign language classrooms.

Krashen goes on to make two claims about the acquisition-learning distinction that have generated considerable controversy in the academic community: (1) that learning cannot turn into acquisition, and (2) that it is only acquired language that is available for natural, fluent communication. Krashen's critics have pointed out that it would be extremely difficult, if not impossible, to detect which system, acquisition or learning, is at work in any instance of language use (McLaughlin, 1987). Furthermore, the two terms require much finer definition to be subjected to experimental study. These criticisms notwithstanding, Krashen's emphasis on second language acquisition by using the new language for relevant communicative purposes has had substantial, positive influence on classroom practice, especially in regard to the move away from the drill-and-practice pattern aimed at language learning.

The Monitor Hypothesis. Krashen has suggested that the formal study of language leads to the development of an internal grammar editor or monitor. As the student produces sentences, the monitor "watches" the output to ensure correct usage. For a student to use the monitor three conditions are necessary: sufficient time, focus on grammatical form, and explicit knowledge of the rules. Thus it is easier to use the monitor for writing than for speaking. Krashen maintains that knowing the rules only helps learners polish their language. The true base of their language knowledge is only that which has been acquired. From this assumption, he recommends that the focus of language teaching should be communication, not rote rule learning, placing him in agreement with many second language acquisition and foreign language teaching experts (cf. Celce-Murcia, 1991; Oller, 1993).

The Natural Order Hypothesis. According to the natural order hypothesis, language learners acquire (rather than learn) the rules of a language in a predictable sequence. That is, certain grammatical features, or morphemes, tend to be acquired early, whereas others tend to be acquired late. Figure 2.2 illustrates this view.

A considerable number of morpheme studies support the general existence of a natural order of acquisition of English grammatical features by child and adult non-native English learners. However, individual variations exist, as do variations that may result from primary language influence (Lightbown & Spada, 1993; Pica, 1994).

The Input Hypothesis. Central to Krashen's view of second language acquisition is the input hypothesis. According to the input hypothesis, the acquisition of a second language is the direct result of learners' understanding the target language in natural communication situations. A key element of the input hypothesis is that the input language must not only be understandable, thus the term **comprehensible input**, but should contain grammatical structures that are just a bit beyond the acquirer's current level of second language development (abbreviated as $i + 1$, with i standing for input and $+1$ indicating the challenging level that is a bit beyond the learner's current level of proficiency). Krashen suggests that acquirers are able to understand this challenging level of language input by using context, extralinguistic information such as gestures and pictures, and general background knowledge. In other words, input can be made comprehensible as a result of these extra cues. Moreover, acquisition is facilitated by a focus on communication and not grammatical form.

FIGURE 2.2 • ACQUISITION OF ENGLISH MORPHEMES

English morphemes acquired early:	
-ing: Verb ending	John is going to work.
-/s/: Plural	Two cats are fighting.
English morphemes acquired late:	
-/s/: Possessive	We saw Jane's house.
-/s/: Third person singular	Roy rides Trigger.

In summary, according to Krashen, language is acquired (not learned) by understanding input that contains linguistic structures that are just beyond the acquirer's current level of competence ($i + 1$). Speech is not taught directly but emerges on its own. Early speech is typically not grammatically accurate. If input is understood and there is enough of it, $i + 1$ is automatically provided. According to Krashen, we do not have to deliberately program grammatical structures into the input. Although Krashen's theory is particularly concerned with the grammatical structures contained in the input, vocabulary is also an important element in $i + 1$. Krashen emphasizes free-choice reading on topics of interest to students as an excellent way to acquire both vocabulary and other aspects of language.

The Affective Filter Hypothesis. Krashen's fifth hypothesis addresses affective or social–emotional variables related to second language acquisition. Citing a variety of studies, Krashen concludes that the most important affective variables favoring second language acquisition are a low-anxiety learning environment, student motivation to learn the language, self-confidence, and self-esteem. Krashen summarizes the five hypotheses in a single claim: "People acquire second languages when they obtain comprehensible input and when their affective filters are low enough to allow the input in [to the language acquisition device]" (Krashen, 1981a, p. 62). For Krashen, then, comprehensible input is the causative variable in second language acquisition. In other words, listening to and understanding spoken language is the essential ingredient in second language acquisition. For this reason, Krashen urges teachers not to force production, but rather to allow students a **silent period** during which they can acquire some language knowledge by listening and understanding, as opposed to learning it through meaningless rote drills.

In summary, Krashen's second language acquisition theories have been influential in promoting language teaching practices that (1) focus on communication, not grammatical form; (2) allow students a silent period, rather than forcing immediate speech production; and (3) create a low-anxiety environment. His notion of comprehensible input provides a theoretical cornerstone for sheltered instruction, or specially designed academic instruction in English (SDAIE), described in Chapter 3. These practices have benefited students in many ways. More questionable theoretically, however, are his acquisition/learning distinction and the notion that comprehensible input alone accounts for language acquisition. The importance of output, that is, speaking and writing, cannot be ignored in a balanced view of language acquisition (Swain, 1985). Finally, evidence indicates that some grammatical forms may not develop without explicit instruction (Harley, Allen, Cummins, & Swain, 1990).

INTERACTIONIST PERSPECTIVE IN SECOND LANGUAGE ACQUISITION. The idea that comprehensible input is necessary for second language acquisition also forms a basic tenet of the interactionist position. However, interactionists view the communicative give and take of natural conversations between native and non-native speakers as the crucial element of the language acquisition process (Long & Porter, 1985). Their focus is on the ways in which native speakers modify their speech to try to make themselves understood by English-learning conversational partners. Interactionists are also interested in how non-native speakers use their budding knowledge of the new language to get their ideas across and to achieve their communicative goals. This trial-and-error process of give-and-take in communication as people try to understand and be understood is referred to as the **negotiation of meaning**. As meaning is negotiated, non-native speakers are actually able to exert some control over the communication process during conversations, thereby causing their partners to provide input that is more comprehensible. They do this by asking for repetitions, indicating they don't understand, or responding in a way that shows they did not understand. The listener's natural response is then to paraphrase or perhaps use some other cue to convey meaning, such as gesturing, drawing, or modified speech (sometimes referred to as "foreigner talk," which is somewhat analogous to caregiver speech in first language acquisition).

In addition to the importance placed on social interaction, some researchers have looked more closely at output, or the speech produced by English language learners, as an important variable in the overall language acquisition process (Swain, 1985). We have seen that the language learner's output can serve to elicit modification of input from conversational partners to make it more comprehensible.

The three theoretical perspectives bear certain implications for instruction, as outlined in Table 2.2. As you read the chart, you will see how the three theoretical perspectives compare in terms of the source and nature of linguistic input to

TABLE 2.2 • INSTRUCTIONAL IMPLICATIONS OF SECOND LANGUAGE ACQUISITION THEORIES

INSTRUCTIONAL COMPONENTS	BEHAVIORIST	INNATIST	INTERACTIONIST
Source of linguistic input	language dialogues and drills from teacher or audiotape	natural language from the teacher, friends, or books	natural language from the teacher, friends, or books
Nature of input	structured by grammatical complexity	unstructured, but made comprehensible by teacher	unstructured, but focused on communication between learner and others
Ideal classroom composition	all target language learners of similar second language proficiency	target language learners of similar second language proficiency so $i + 1$ can be achieved	native speakers together with target language learners for social interaction aimed at communication
Student output	structured repetitions and grammar pattern drill responses	output is not a concern; it will occur naturally	speaking occurs naturally in communication with others
Pressure to speak	students repeat immediately	"silent period" expected	no pressure to speak except natural impulse to communicate
Treatment of errors	errors are corrected immediately	errors are not corrected; students will correct themselves with time	errors that impede communication will be corrected naturally as meaning is negotiated; some errors may require explicit corrective instruction

learners, ideal classroom composition vis-à-vis native speakers and second language learners, student output, pressure to speak or produce output, and treatment of learner errors.

Beyond Social Interaction in Second Language Acquisition Theory

Social interaction with native speakers represents an important theoretical corner-stone in explaining second language acquisition. However, placing second language learners and native speakers in a room together does not in itself guarantee social interaction or language acquisition. We also need to look closely at the larger social and political contexts in which our students live and learn because they can affect relationships between native speakers and English learners. Who are the native speakers? Who are the English learners? Are the two groups from the same social class or not? Are they from the same ethnic group or not? Will the two groups want to interact with each other? To what extent will particular English learners choose to interact with particular native English speakers and adopt their ways of speaking? How will English learners cross the linguistic, social and cultural boundaries needed to participate socially among native speakers?

Stereotypes, prejudices, and status and power differences may make interaction difficult. Furthermore, natural tendencies to affiliate with one's own linguistic, social, and ethnic group (Sheets & Hollins, 1999) may also work against the kind of social interaction that facilitates language acquisition. Two-way immersion programs described in Chapter 1 represent one of the few educational alternatives that explicitly promote equal status between language minority and language major-ity students, with both groups learning the native language of the other while devel-oping full bilingualism and biliteracy. Even in multilingual classrooms, however, you are in a position to promote positive social participation through heterogeneous grouping discussed in Chapter 3. To the extent that linguistically, culturally, and academically diverse students are able to work together to accomplish learning tasks, thinking through procedures and problems as a group, they create the moment-to-moment sharing of linguistic and cognitive resources that can lead to not only academic learning, but also respect and rapport among each other (Gutierrez, Baquedano-Lopez, & Alvarez, 2001). As you begin to address intergroup relations in your classroom, you might want to select one or two multicultural education resources from Example 1.1 (Chapter 1) for closer study and discussion with your colleagues at your school or in your university classes.

Learning a Second Language in School: Processes and Factors

We have just reviewed the complex nature of language proficiency and some the-oretical perspectives on the process of language acquisition. What does this mean for students learning English as a second language in school? In this section, we discuss essential processes and factors influencing English learners in school, par-ticularly the social context of second language acquisition, age and the interplay of social and cognitive factors in the second language acquisition process, social

ACTIVITY 2.2

Sharing Your Experiences Learning a New Language

If you have studied or acquired another language, share your language learning story with the group. Using the stories, discuss the effects on second language acquisition of differences, such as age, culture, and language learning situation, and opporutnies to use the new language with native speakers.

Reflecting further, what do you recall as the hardest part? Why was it hard? What was easy? Why was it easy? How proficient did you become? What affected your degree of proficiency? Can you identify a theory underlying the teaching approach (e.g., behaviorist, innatist, interactionist)?

versus academic language use, comprehensible input and social interaction, and the treatment of language learning errors in the classroom. As we discuss these factors, you will see how theory has affected our views.

Second Language Acquisition Contexts: Formal Study Versus Immersion in a Country Where the Language Is Spoken

One factor that affects second language acquisition is the social context in which the second language was learned. Have you ever studied another language, or do you know someone who has? How did you learn it? And how well did you learn it? When we ask our students this question, we hear a wonderful variety of second language learning stories. Most of our students have had the experience of studying a foreign language in high school or college. They often recall specific foreign language teaching techniques for learning the grammar, pronunciation, and vocabulary, usually of a European language such as French, German, or Spanish. Many also remember activities such as choral repetition of sentence patterns, memorization of vocabulary items, and perhaps in-class opportunities to put these together in writing or simulated conversations.

Under these learning conditions, some basic knowledge of the language may have developed. However, few people report reaching a substantial level of communicative competence unless they spent time in a country where the language was spoken. The opportunity for foreign travel or residency often bears fruit for second language development based on the seed of classroom instruction. In contrast, students who have come to the United States as immigrants have a different language learning story to tell. Many hold vivid memories of entering elementary or high school knowing not a word of English and feeling frightened and baffled at the world around them. They struggled for months, perhaps years, to become acclimated to the new language and culture. All too often, immigrant students are overcome by these demands and drop out of school. Yet others learn English well enough to be successful in university classes, though perhaps retaining a foreign accent. Reflecting on your own language learning experiences and talking with other people about how they learned a second language can provide insights into the process of second language acquisition. What can we learn from different language learning stories?

Perhaps the first thing we can see is a distinction between studying a foreign language for one period a day in school and learning a language through immersion in a social environment, including the school, where the target language is used regularly for day-to-day communication. Differences between these two language acquisition contexts directly affect the language learning process. Students immersed in an environment in which the new language is spoken have the advantage of being surrounded with opportunities to hear and use it. The larger social environment features the new language, not only in the classroom but also everywhere else—in shopping malls, at the theater, on television, in newspapers, and more. As a result, classroom learning can be solidified and expanded to the extent that learners interact within the larger community (Dulay et al., 1982). In addition, students learning the language of their new country are likely to be motivated, because success in acquiring strong English skills is important for day-to-day functioning and full participation in society.

In a social immersion situation in which learners live in a country where the target language is spoken, second language acquisition is facilitated by the rich language exposure available and by the inherent **need to communicate**. At the same time, students are challenged to the highest levels of oral and written acquisition because they will need native-like skills to qualify for future education and employment opportunities. In contrast, foreign language study tends to be limited in opportunities and necessity to use the language for functional communication. Similarly, the expectations for accomplishment are correspondingly lower. When students enter your class knowing little English, they have the benefits of an immersion situation because the new language is used both in school and in the larger environment. At the same time, some may feel pressured by their need to learn the new language as quickly as possible.

Age and the Interplay of Sociocultural, Personality, and Cognitive Factors

Another factor affecting second language development is the learner's age when second language acquisition begins. Among native-born children who speak another language at home, such as Spanish, Cantonese, or Crow, English language acquisition usually begins prior to or upon entry to elementary school. For immigrants, on the other hand, the process may begin at any age, depending on how old they are when they arrive in their new country. Age on arrival bears heavily on second language acquisition processes and eventual levels of attainment. Why is this so? The influence of age on second language acquisition stems from the complex interplay of sociocultural, cognitive, and personality factors (cf. Brown [2007] for a thorough discussion of these factors).

As we begin our discussion, let's bear in mind that learning a new language in school is a demanding task, no matter what the age when acquisition begins. The magnitude of the task is revealed by research showing that it takes *at least* five to seven years to reach a level of English language development sufficient for academic success in English (Cummins, 1979; Collier, 1987, 1987/1988; Thomas & Collier, 2002). In addition, the idea that learning a new language is easy for young children has not been borne out in research. In fact, there is evidence to suggest that adults may be *superior* to young learners in terms of literacy, vocabulary, pragmatics, and schematic knowledge (Scovel, 1999). To illustrate how age interacts with sociocultural, personality and cognitive factors, let's look at the case of Montha, a university student who came to the United States from Cambodia at age 12.

SOCIAL AND CULTURAL FACTORS. Montha was the eldest of six children. She had been educated in Cambodia and was literate in Khmer when she arrived, but her education took place entirely in English after she moved to the United States. The family spoke Khmer at home but nowhere else did she use or hear her home language. Montha remembers how difficult it was to fit in at school, where she knew neither the language nor the customs of her schoolmates. She felt frightened and isolated, because there were no other Cambodians in her school. To exacerbate the situation, at age 12 she was self-conscious and concerned about being different. Nonetheless, she gradually found her way into school social groups and began to acquire English.

Reflecting back, Montha feels that her younger siblings had more chances to interact with fluent English speakers than she did. For one thing, as the eldest daughter, Montha was expected to help her mother daily with household chores, whereas her sisters were permitted to play with other children in the neighborhood. In addition, as an adolescent, she was not permitted to date or to go out with friends in cars, an accepted pastime of many U.S. teenagers. For these activities, she had to wait until she had graduated from high school and no longer lived with her parents. In these ways, we see how the age differences between Montha and her younger siblings affected social participation with English-speaking friends based on her family's cultural expectations.

From this brief example, we can see how age interacted with social and cultural factors to constrain Montha's social language learning opportunities. First of all, she entered the U.S. social scene at an age when cultural expectations of teenagers differed considerably between her home culture and that of the larger society. Remaining at home to help her mother, she was restricted from certain aspects of social participation that might have helped her learn English. In contrast, her siblings were young enough to be permitted to play with English-speaking neighborhood children, and this type of play was acceptable to Montha's parents. In other words, Montha's siblings, by virtue of their age, were permitted a broader range of age-appropriate social activity acceptable to both Cambodian and U.S. parents, and this, very likely, facilitated language acquisition.

PERSONALITY FACTORS. Despite these external social and cultural restraints, Montha did become proficient in English, no doubt due in part to certain personal attributes, including unflagging determination and persistence in achieving her goals. At this point in her life, she was dedicated to becoming a teacher of English learners, and was working on passing the basic skills test required to enter the teaching credential program. Another personal attribute was her particularly sensitive and empathetic attitude toward others, which certainly played a role in her desire to teach and may also have motivated her English language acquisition. Given that there were no other Cambodian families in her school or neighborhood, her social contacts required English, and Montha was a person who thrived on social relationships.

COGNITIVE FACTORS. Montha was a successful English learner who went on to earn a baccalaureate degree at a state university. By age 12 when she came to the United States, she had developed substantial cognitive, literacy, and academic abilities in her first language. These abilities no doubt contributed to her success in high school and college, given the fact that well-developed academic skills and strategies transfer between a bilingual's two languages (Cummins, 1981). Montha's journey was nonetheless a difficult one. Academic development in her primary language ceased on her arrival, and she had a great deal of academic English to acquire before she could qualify for the university. Once there, she struggled to earn the grades that would allow her to go on for a teaching credential. In addition, she had difficulty passing the timed reading, writing, and math examinations required for the teaching credential. Without her persistent nature and her commitment to helping children reminiscent of her former self, she would most likely not have been able to push through and become a teacher. But she did!

Montha's English developed fully, though she retained some pronunciation features that set her apart from native English speakers. She also maintained fluency in Khmer and a strong ethnic identity. As a postscript, Montha tells us that her mother never did learn English. Being an adult, her mother was not required to attend school daily as her children were. Nor did she seek work outside the home as her husband did. Thus, she did not find herself in social contexts that might have provided the exposure and motivation needed for English language acquisition. These days, Montha's mother takes a great deal of pride in Montha's accomplishments as a bilingual teacher and serves as a valuable resource when Montha needs a forgotten phrase in Khmer or some detail of a cultural tradition to include in her curriculum at school. Montha's case highlights how her age on arrival interacted with sociocultural, cognitive, and personality factors in her language acquisition process and in her journey to becoming a bilingual teacher.

DIFFERENCES IN SCHOOL EXPECTATIONS OF YOUNGER AND OLDER LEARNERS. Another age-related factor affecting second language acquisition is the level of cognitive-academic functioning normally expected across the grades from elementary through high school. A general task for all English language learners is to gain enough English proficiency to carry out school tasks about as well as their English fluent peers. For kindergarten and first-grade children, the linguistic performance gap between English language learners and their English-speaking age mates is relatively small. After all, monolingual children are still developing both language and concepts during the primary grades. Furthermore, learning for all young children is best derived from direct experience, manipulation of concrete objects, and social interaction with adults and peers. As kindergarten teachers know, younger children learn more by talking while doing than by listening to a long verbal explanation from the teacher. The same holds true for young English language learners. Thus, learning environments that are age appropriate for younger monolingual children tend to be optimal for young English language learners as well. Nevertheless, special accommodations are needed to help young English learners adjust to a school, understand instruction, learn English, and succeed socially and academically.

For older immigrant students, academic learning presents greater demands on second language proficiency than for younger newcomers (Ovando et al.,

Students who begin learning English in secondary school face substantial linguistic and academic challenges.

62

2003). They have further to go and less time to catch up than their younger brothers and sisters, as we saw in Montha's case. From middle school on, and sometimes earlier, we expect students to be able to learn from lecture-style verbal instruction at least some of the time. Furthermore, subject matter grows increasingly complex and abstract. Thus, students who are older on arrival have a larger language gap to fill before they will be able to function academically in English at a level commensurate with their English fluent peers. On the other hand, precisely because they are older, they bring the advantages of a well-developed cognitive and conceptual system. Moreover, they may have had sufficient schooling in their home country to be facile in literacy and numeracy skills. If so, they stand a good chance of academic success, provided that their new school offers systematic support for both second language development, social-cultural adjustment, and continued content area learning. Other students may have had little schooling, or their educational opportunities may have been interrupted by war, political turmoil, or the struggles involved in leaving their home country. In such cases, students will need extra support as they grapple with academic literacy, content area learning, and social-cultural adjustment in their new country.

Teacher Expectations for English Learner Achievement

Neither we as teachers nor our students have any control over their age on arrival. Yet when students enter school with little or no knowledge of English, they are faced with the dual challenge of learning a new language and trying to fit into school routines both socially and academically—no small task! What do we know about second language acquisition processes that can facilitate these adjustments? First, we have seen that the process of acquiring a second language is facilitated when learners and speakers of the target language have the opportunity and desire to communicate with each other. Thus students need opportunities to interact with fellow students and negotiate meaning by sharing experiences through activities, such as group work, drama, readers' theater, art, and writing. Making use of natural cognitive and linguistic processes similar to those involved in acquiring their first language, English language learners take the language they hear spoken around them and use it gradually to acquire the new language—its vocabulary, sound system, grammatical structure, and social conventions of use.

In the earliest stages of second language acquisition, students grapple with understanding their teacher and peers and with somehow making themselves understood. As they begin to talk, learners grow in the ability to use their new language with fluency and ease, though as yet imperfectly. Eventually, as opportunities for higher-level thinking and problem solving are provided, students acquire the formal language competence necessary for more advanced instruction in mathematics, science, social studies, literature, and other subjects. Thus students must learn to engage in complex social and cognitive transactions through their second language, both orally and in reading and writing.

When we say that students must become capable of complex social and cognitive transactions through their second language, we are putting forward the goal of full English language and literacy development. That is, we are expecting them to attain the same level of English language proficiency as their native English-speaking counterparts. For English language learners, this means acquiring the essentials of English phonology, morphology, syntax, semantics, and pragmatics and being able to integrate them for use in a wide variety of social contexts. Ultimately, we want our students to be at ease in English with their peers, potential employers, insurance agents, bank representatives, university recruiters, and the full range of social contacts that occur in daily life. Moreover, we want them to be capable of using both oral and written language in formal ways for academic purposes. This latter goal is one of the main charges of schooling for all students and represents access to the employment and social mobility available in U.S. society. If, in addition to English language skills, students have been able to develop their primary language, they will enjoy further options afforded by their bilingualism. In other words, teachers' expectations of English learners must be high, and social and academic support must be provided for these goals to be achieved.

63

Language Used for Social Interaction Versus Language Used for Academic Learning

Some experts make a distinction between language used for basic social interaction and language used for academic purposes (Cummins, 1980). **Basic Interpersonal Communication Skills (BICS)** are language skills needed for social conversation purposes, whereas **Cognitive Academic Language Proficiency (CALP)** refers to formal language skills, including listening, speaking, reading, and writing, used for academic learning. Research shows that students may demonstrate basic social competence in a second language within six months to two years after arrival in a new country. In other words, they can speak English well enough to interact with their peers, talk on the telephone, and negotiate meanings with adults. However, the ability to demonstrate academic competence in the new language orally and in writing at a level commensurate with that of their native-speaking peers may take five years or more (Cummins, 1979; Thomas & Collier, 2002). Current preliminary research findings suggest that students with no prior schooling and no primary language support may take much longer, as much as seven to ten years, to acquire academic skills in their new language (Thomas & Collier, 2002). In other words, newcomers may need substantial time and educational support to develop English skills such as those needed to understand academic lectures, to make and defend logical arguments orally or in writing, to read school texts efficiently, and to write effectively for academic purposes.

Let's take a moment to consider some aspects of academic language use that students must control with increasing sophistication as they progress from elementary through middle school and high school. Reading and writing are two obvious aspects of academic language use, particularly reading and writing essays that compare and contrast, persuade, describe, and summarize content area material. However, academic learning involves a variety of cognitively demanding oral language uses as well. For example, students need to be able to follow their teachers' or peers' oral explanations of complex concepts and procedures in science, mathematics, and the social sciences. They need to understand such explanations well enough to apply them in carrying out their own experiments, in solving mathematical problems, and in debating issues and explaining their views of topics in social science and history. Academic language use, whether oral or written, requires a growing reservoir of background knowledge pertinent to any given discipline, along with knowledge of the conventions of how to organize information orally and in writing. If we assume that the basis for these academic skills is ideally established among monolingual students by fifth or sixth grade, it is not surprising that acquiring such skills takes English learners five to seven years, or longer. We provide strategies to promote oral and written academic language development in Chapters 3 through 10.

Information on how long it takes for students to acquire English sufficient for academic purposes is important to us for two reasons. First, it reminds us that, even though students may appear fairly proficient in English during basic social interactions, they are still likely to need special support to be able to learn and display their knowledge of complex academic material through their second language. Second, it gives us a direct index of the long-term nature of the language acquisition process. We usually have students in class for just one year, and it is helpful to know that we are unlikely to witness full-blown language development in our students during that short time.

Although we may not control the timetable of language development, there are numerous strategies we, as teachers, can use to promote that development. Thus, throughout this book, we will point out ways to assist English learners to develop the kind of linguistic competence that will facilitate their academic success.

Learning to Use English in Socially and Culturally Appropriate Ways

Academic language use is a major goal for all students. Equally important for students new to English is explicit instruction in socially and culturally appropriate ways of using English, oral and written. Early childhood teachers are quite accustomed to this type of socialization because it is a natural part of the curriculum. Reminding children to say "please" and "thank you," asking for a toy instead of grabbing it, waiting a turn instead of interrupting: All of these are second nature for teachers of young children. And all of them reflect social and cultural conventions of English in this society. Similarly, teachers help students learn the special classroom rules for taking turns, talking, listening, and responding to other points of view. Writing party invitations and "grace notes" to show gratitude or sympathy are other examples of language bound by social and cultural guidelines that are taught in school. The elementary curriculum provides many opportunities to help students learn socially and culturally appropriate language use.

If you teach English learners who arrived in this country in middle or high school, the social and cultural conventions of both oral and written language use continue to be of utmost importance. Older students typically have extensive social and cultural repertoires for primary language use. They may also know various conventions for English, but they need to add new ones as they become increasingly proficient. Explicit instruction with role-playing is often helpful as students learn both the phraseology and social protocol appropriate to everyday situations, such as using the telephone, eating at a restaurant, applying for a job, meeting new friends at a party, going to the doctor or dentist, and asking the teacher for help after school (cf. Jones, 2003). Making small talk is another aspect of communicative competence that can be quite difficult and thus merits explicit instruction. Appropriate phrases and ways of expressing emotions such as gratitude, impatience, empathy, enthusiasm, and even anger are all needed as students develop full communicative competence in English. We recommend that you use the teachers of English to speakers of other language (TESOL) standards (TESOL, 2006) to help you build social and cultural language competence into your preK-12 curriculum.

Comprehensible Input and Social Interaction

As noted earlier, comprehensible input refers to language used in ways that make it understandable to the learner even though second language proficiency is limited (Krashen, 1982). Paraphrasing, repetition of key points, reference to concrete materials, and acting out meanings are some of the ways speakers can help convey meaning and thus make language more understandable. When we pair two communication channels, the verbal and the nonverbal, words and meanings become discernible to the learner, as for example, when a picture of the digestive system is displayed and pointed to during an explanation of the digestive process. In this way, language is not only understood but also forms the raw material from which learners may gradually construct the new language system for themselves. During the earliest stages of language learning, face-to-face social interactions between learners and speakers of the target language provide optimal language learning opportunities.

Language learning opportunities are richly present during social interactions because participants are likely to be focused on communicating with each other, and they will naturally make use of all their resources to do so—facial expression, dramatization, repetition, and so forth (Wong Fillmore, 1982, 1985). Furthermore, the non-English speaker can communicate at a rudimentary level through actions, nods, and facial expressions. As communication is worked out or negotiated, a great deal of understandable language is generated, thereby providing comprehensible input from which language may be acquired. Take for example an interaction we observed between two boys, Marcelino, new to English, and Joshua, a native English speaker. They were coloring a drawing they had created of a helicopter. When finished, it was to be posted on the bulletin board with drawings of other transportation vehicles.

JOSHUA: Here, Marcelino. Here's the green *[hands Marcelino the green crayon].*

MARCELINO: *[Marcelino takes the green crayon and colors the helicopter.]*

JOSHUA: Hey, wait a minute! You gotta put some red stars right here. OK?

MARCELINO: Huh?

JOSHUA: Red stars. I'm gonna make some red stars . . . right here. *[Joshua draws four red stars, while Marcelino continues coloring with the green crayon.]*

MARCELINO: OK.

In this interaction, the hands-on, context-embedded activity conveyed much of the meaning. Marcelino understood the purpose of the task and was able to interact with Joshua with minimal English to negotiate division of labor. With much of the meaning conveyed by the situation and the concrete materials, Joshua's language provided comprehensible input. Thus, Marcelino is apt to retain for future use words such as *green* and *red,* and phrases such as "Wait a minute." Working one-on-one with a partner also permitted Marcelino to convey his need for Joshua to clarify his concern over the red stars. While focused on the task of coloring the helicopter, Marcelino participated in the conversation with his minimal but functional vocabulary. At the same time, he was afforded quality English input from Joshua through conversation pertaining to the hands-on activity. Interactions such as this provide important elements for language acquisition—a functional communication situation, comprehensible input, and social interaction around a purposeful task.

As the teacher, the language you use can be a valuable source of comprehensible input, whether you are working with the whole class, small groups, or individuals. In Chapter 3, we show how you can tailor your talk and your lessons to make them optimally understandable to students, thereby enhancing content learning and second language acquisition. This kind of instruction is often referred to as sheltered instruction or Specially Designed Academic Instruction in English (SDAIE). Finally, it is important to note that written language also affords comprehensible input when students read, provided the material is relatively easy to understand (Krashen, 1993), a topic addressed in Chapter 8.

What about Language Learning Errors?

As we have seen, the question of learner errors in language acquisition is a topic of great interest and controversy. How should we treat second language errors in the classroom? Should we correct students' errors or not? If we do correct, when and how do we do so? We will give you our ideas on this complex issue, but you will need to decide for yourself how you will proceed on a case-by-case basis.

There are several considerations to think about in deciding whether to correct learner errors. Your first consideration is the English language development stage of the learner. Many errors are developmental and will eventually be replaced by conventional forms without your intervention. You will recall that certain morphemes develop early, such as the *-ing* form of the verb and the plural -/s/. Other morphemes develop late, such as the -/s/ for the third-person plural. The latter error continues to appear in some English learners' speech many years

Working in groups while using English promotes academic learning, social development, and second language acquisition.

after they begin to learn English. For students in the early stages of second language acquisition, errors that impede communication may be corrected in a sensitive and natural way, especially those involving vocabulary. Consider the following example from a third-grade English language development classroom in which five English learners are playing a board game with the teacher standing nearby. Natalia, a native Russian speaker, has been in this country four months and is a beginner in English.

NATALIA: I putting the marker on the points.
TEACHER: Those are called dots. You're putting the marker on the dots.
NATALIA: The dots.

The teacher focused on the vocabulary item *dots,* and her gentle yet explicit correction was well received. However, the teacher did not correct Natalia's use of *I* instead of *I am* or *I'm*. Why? First, lack of the verb or its contraction does not make a difference in meaning. Second, this is a common beginner error, and appropriate verb use is likely to develop with time. Third, it is doubtful that correction of this grammatical form would result in Natalia's being able to produce it in another context. Corrections that focus on meaning tend to be easier to learn than those that focus on grammar alone. As a rule of thumb, you may provide words and word forms to beginning English learners to help them make themselves understood, thereby maintaining a communication focus.

As second language acquisition proceeds, there may be some grammatical errors that persist and become permanent or *fossilized* (Selinker, 1972). We have seen, for example, that the third person singular, present tense verb marker *-s* develops late, and sometimes not at all. A possible explanation for its tardy appearance may be that the "person" and "tense" information conveyed by the -*s* can be understood through context. Because English requires that the subject be explicitly stated, subject–verb agreement is redundant, and the tense can be inferred from context, as illustrated by the following sentence pairs. Notice that the grammatical errors do not impede communication.

Renae bakes cookies for me.	Renae bake cookies for me.
The cat sits in the sun.	The cat sit in the sun.

What should you do if such grammatical errors persist among intermediate and advanced students? Our view is that grammatical errors are best dealt with in the context of student writing. For one thing, writing can be looked at and analyzed in a leisurely way, whereas speech goes by quickly and unconsciously and then disappears. A student may not be able to perceive that a spoken error occurred unless it was tape recorded. Even then, the student may not hear the error. On the other hand, a written error is visible and preserved. It can be pointed to and discussed. When patterns of error recur in a student's writing, specific mini-lessons can be tailored for the student so that he or she may self-edit. Details of this process are discussed in Chapter 6 on editing during process writing.

In summary, the way you treat English learner errors will depend on your own judgment, taking into consideration the student's English language developmental level, the prevalence of the error type, the importance of the error type for communication, and your specific goals for the student in terms of English language development. There is not sufficient research on the specifics of English language development to give you error correction recipes. Even if there were, individual differences would obviate their usefulness. Finally, you should keep in mind that error correction is not the major source of English language development; meaningful experiences, using the language for a variety of oral and written purposes, play a much larger role. Nonetheless, grammatical refinements in speech and writing may require explicit instruction. Thus the error correction guidelines and examples we provide are suggestive, not prescriptive. Your own trial and error will provide you with further information, as you work with English learners to promote their school success.

Summary

In this chapter, we discussed second language acquisition as children experience it in school. First, we defined language proficiency, pointing out grammatical and social aspects of both communicative competence and communicative performance. Next we summarized behaviorist, innatist, and social interactionist theories of first and second language acquisition. We then examined a variety of factors that researchers and theorists have noted as important in second language acquisition: the language learning environment (immersion versus foreign language), age, cognitive development, the cultures of the home and school, and ways in which all of these interact to motivate and give purpose to second language acquisition. Finally, we discussed comprehensible input, social interaction, learner errors, and differences between social and academic language development.

●●●●●●●●

Suggestions for Further Reading

Brown, H. D. (2000). *Principles of language learning and teaching* (4th Ed.). White Plains, NY: Addison Wesley Longman. This is a classic text that should be in every second language teacher's library. Chapters include: Language, Learning, and Teaching; First Language Acquisition; Age and Acquisition; Human Learning; Styles and Strategies; Sociocultural Factors; Communicative Competence; and Theories of Second Language Acquisition.

Ellis, R. (1997). *Second language acquisition.* Oxford: Oxford University Press.

This book, one in the Oxford Introductions to Language Study series, is 147 pages long. Short chapters include topics such as describing and explaining L2 acquisition, the nature of the language learner, interlanguage, social aspects of interlanguage, individual differences in L2 acquisition, and instruction in L2 acquisition. This excellent, short book also contains a glossary and annotated bibliography.

Fromkin, V., Rodman, R., & Hyams, N. (2007). *An introduction to language* (8th ed.). Boston: Thomson Heinle.

This classic text, in its eighth edition, is an excellent introduction to language study. Clearly written chapters include topics such as: brain and language, morphology, sentence patterns, language in society, language change, and writing.

Hall, J. K. & Eggington, W. E. (Eds.). (2000). *The sociopolitics of English language teaching.* Clevedon, England: Multilingual Matters.

This edited volume brings together under one cover an array of important topics, offering research-based perspectives on the political, social, and cultural dimensions of English language teaching. Topics include policy and ideology in the spread of English, linguistic human rights, official English and bilingual education, and non-native varieties of English. Contributors also offer ideas for transforming language education practices and for becoming sociopolitically active.

Hinkel, E. (Ed.). (2005). *Handbook of research in second language teaching and learning.* Mahwah, NJ: Lawrence Erlbaum Associates.

This comprehensive handbook offers 57 chapters by experts in the many, various topic areas within the field of second language teaching and learning. The chapters are divided into 8 sections, all of which refer to the main topic of second language teaching and learning: (1) social contexts in research; (2) research methods; (3) applied linguistics and second language research; (4) second language processes and development; (5) methods and curricula in second language teaching; (6) second language testing and assessment; (7) identity, culture and critical pedagogy; (8) language planning and policy and language rights. This handbook provides an important, up-to-date resource for teachers, university students, and researchers.

Lightbown, P., & Spada, N. (2006). *How languages are learned* (3rd ed.) Oxford: Oxford University Press.

This excellent, friendly text, completely revised and updated, relates complex issues in a clear and concise manner. Chapter topics include learning a first language, theories of second language learning, factors affecting second language learning, learner language, second language learning in the classroom, and popular ideas about language learning. Using a scale from "strongly agree" to "strongly disagree," the text begins with 12 provocative questions regarding language learning; the questions provide an excellent advance organizer for a course and for this book. A chapter reviewing classroom research is particularly excellent because it analyzes research based on language acquisition theories such as behaviorism and interactionism. This is a short book, 135 pages, that presents valuable information in an accessible manner.

Mitchell, R. & Myles, F. (2002). *Second language learning theories*. New York, NY: Oxford University Press.

This short book, just over 200 pages, is an excellent introduction to second language learning theories. Chapters include second language learning, key concepts and issues, recent history of second language learning research, cognitive approaches to second language learning, functional/pragmatic perspectives on second language learning, and sociocultural perspectives on second language learning.

Parker, F. & Riley, K. (2000). *Linguistics for non-linguists: A primer with exercises* (3rd ed.). Boston: Allyn & Bacon.

This is the perfect book for teachers who are new the field of linguistics but would like to build their understanding of language. Chapter topics include pragmatics, semantics, morphology, language variation, first-language acquisition, second-language acquisition, writing, and language processing. Each chapter contains supplementary exercises which help readers use and consolidate their linguistics knowledge.

Activities

1. After reading this chapter, which language acquisition theory do you favor? Or do you favor a combination of the different views? Do you think any one theory seems to account for all the variables in language acquisition? Discuss these issues with someone else who has read the chapter.

2. Taking each of the language acquisition theories in turn—that is, behaviorist, innatist, and interactionist—think of how each view might help you organize your classroom for maximum language learning. Compare and contrast each of the views in terms of a classroom context. For example, look at Table 2.2, which delineates the different theories, and determine what a classroom that strictly followed one theory might be like: Would desks be in rows or circles? Would the teacher always be in the front of the class or moving around the class most of the time? Would students have many choices of classroom activities or would the teacher determine almost all lessons? Finally, describe what theory or combination of theories accounts for the kind of classroom you think is ideal for second language learners with varying degrees of English language proficiency.

3. Think of your own experiences learning or using a language. What were the contexts in which you felt you were most successful in learning a language? Did you learn best in a classroom context, or, if you have visited a country where you had to learn at least some basics of a second language, how did you go about doing it? What helped? What didn't help? If you were to need to learn a language for something important like getting a job, how would you go about it?

4. If you are currently learning a language, you might try keeping a journal of your language learning and language acquisition experiences. For example, how do you feel as a language learner under different kinds of circumstances? How do you react, positively or negatively, to circumstances in which you aren't fully proficient in the language? What humorous situations have you experienced as a result of learning a new language?

Where the Classroom Comes to Life

....

Video Homework Exercise

Culture and Self-Esteem

Go to MyEducationLab, select the topic "Diversity," and watch the video entitled "Culture and Self-Esteem."

The teachers in this video discuss the connection between cultural diversity and self-esteem, including: the importance of supporting the culture and strengths that students bring to the classroom; how teaching is not just the delivery of information to students by a teacher, but rather the establishment of a connection among students and teachers in that each shares what they know and each learns; and the importance of fostering success in tasks every day because self-efficacy is a major contributor to self-esteem and development.

Complete the homework questions that accompany it. You may print your work or have it transmitted to your professor as necessary.

71

Classroom Practices for English Learner Instruction

> *Any subject can be taught effectively in some intellectually honest form to any child at any stage of development.*
>
> —JEROME BRUNER, *The Process of Education*

In this chapter, we describe effective classroom practices for English learners, addressing the following questions:

1. How are curriculum standards used in classrooms serving English learners?
2. What is differentiated instruction, and why is it important for English learners?
3. What is content-based instruction (CBI), and how is it related to sheltered instruction or specially designed academic instruction in English (SDAIE)?
4. What goes into planning sheltered instruction or SDAIE?
5. How can group work, theme study, and scaffolding facilitate language and literacy development?
6. How are English learners assessed?

R ecently we walked into Jamie Green's ninth-grade sheltered history class where a unit on ancient Egypt was underway. Her classroom was like the inside of an ancient pyramid: Brick walls and ceilings had been created from butcher paper, hieroglyphics were posted on the paper walls, and Egyptian scenes adorned the bulletin boards. We were literally transported to a different time and place!

Earlier that week Jamie had asked her students, mostly intermediate English learners, to share what they already knew about Egypt. As students brainstormed words such as *pyramids*, *tombs*, and *desert*, Jamie created a cluster (see Figure 3.1), drawing a picture next to each word. She then gave students ten minutes to share in small groups all they knew about Egypt. When they reported their ideas back to the class, she added the new information to the cluster. Next she shared a short film on ancient Egypt, after which she invited students to add any new ideas to the cluster.

Jamie then handed out a K-W-L worksheet (see Figure 3.2) and asked the groups to list in the "K" column everything they now knew about Egypt and in the "W" column what they wanted to learn. She explained that they would be creating a study question from the "want to know" column, so it was important to decide on something they really wanted to explore. The "L" column would be used later for summarizing what they had learned about their topics. In subsequent weeks, students worked in their groups researching and reporting their findings to the class. As they made their reports, students helped one another by suggesting additional resources. For example, when one group reported on mummies, another student told them about a cool book she had seen about mummies in the library.

73

FIGURE 3.1

STUDENT-GENERATED
CLUSTER ON EGYPT

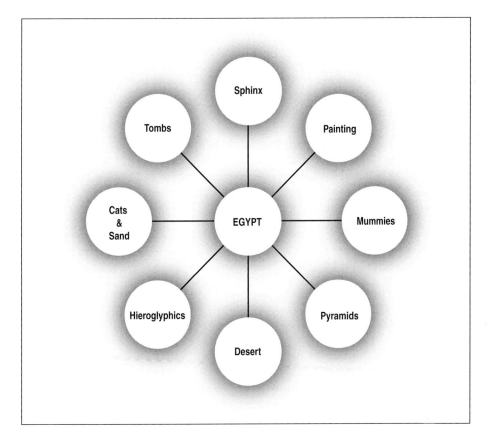

FIGURE 3.2

ONE GROUP'S K-W-L
EGYPT WORKSHEET

K (KNOW)	W (WANT TO KNOW)	L (LEARNED)
Pyramids were tombs where pharoahs were buried.	How did the pharoahs live and how did they rule the people so they would build pyramids?	
Mummies were the way they preserved the pharoahs.	How did they make mummies and why did they do it?	
Hieroglyphics were the way they wrote.	Can we learn how to write in hieroglyphics?	

Thus students served as resources for one another. Later, groups prepared exhibits for an upcoming family night, when students would act as docents, explaining their projects and displays to their visitors.

In this complex unit, Jamie implemented a number of practices that are recommended for effective English learner instruction. First, she assessed what students knew about the topic *before* instruction by creating a cluster of ideas and by having them work in groups to fill out the K-W-L sheet. Next, she involved students in collaborative groups in which they chose and carried out their own research projects. At every step, she supported student comprehension and learning by accompanying verbal explanations with pictures, graphs, gestures, and careful use of language. Finally, by asking them to serve as docents on family night, she motivated them to higher levels of content learning and communicative performance.

In this chapter, we provide an overview of components of effective English learner instruction that experienced teachers like Jamie use with their English learners to promote English language and academic literacy development, content area learning, and positive social cultural development. We begin with a discussion of curriculum standards because these will guide you in choosing content and assessing student learning. Thereafter we address: (1) differentiated instruction; (2) content-based language instruction, including sheltered English instruction; (3) group work; (4) and scaffolding. We conclude the chapter with a discussion of English learner assessment. Figure 3.3 provides an overview of the components of effective English learner instruction.

Standards-Based Instruction and Assessment

In Chapter 1 we introduced you to standards-based reform efforts of the last decade or so. These reforms have resulted in the development and widespread use of standards in every curriculum area including English language development (ELD). In this section, we discuss how teachers use curriculum standards to help them plan instruction and assess learning. As noted previously, standards consist of three components: (1) content standards that delineate what students should know and be able to do; (2) benchmarks that specify expected knowledge and skills for each content standard at different grade levels; and (3) performance standards or

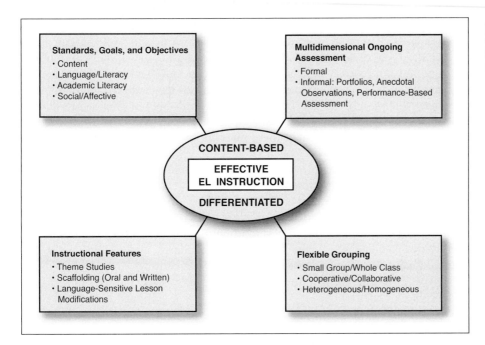

FIGURE 3.3

EFFECTIVE EL
INSTRUCTION

progress indicators that describe how students will show they have met the standard (Laturnau, 2003). Assessment criteria are thus built in to teach each standard.

Ideally, standards-based instruction will help you focus on high expectations for all students, while motivating you to tailor instruction to meet individual student needs. It also encourages multiple modes of assessing learning, including careful observation as students carry out particular tasks, such as writing an essay or conducting an experiment. Finally, standards-based instruction and assessment potentially will permit students to attain and demonstrate their knowledge and skill in a variety of ways. These are all worthy goals for effective English learner instruction.

If you are new to curriculum standards, you might find them a bit daunting at first, especially if you have to contend with various sets of standards in several curriculum areas. If you are an experienced teacher at your grade level or subject, the content is likely to be familiar but perhaps stated in more detail or from a different point of view than what you are used to. Also, don't be surprised to find a variety of formats and wording across different sets of standards: Standards documents are not yet standardized!

Your first task, then, is to study the standards you are expected to use for your grade level and subject, and align them with your state's English language development standards. It is helpful to meet with other teachers to deepen your understanding and to share ways to teach and assess your English learners according to the standards. Some schools provide staff development days for this purpose. As you gain experience in using the standards, you may discover new ways to meet them or perhaps the need to modify them. If so, you will want to discuss your ideas with your teaching colleagues and principal.

For promoting your students' English language acquisition, many states use the *PreK-12 English Language Proficiency Standards* (Teachers of English to Speakers of Other Languages [TESOL], 2006), a revision of the 1997 TESOL standards. Building on work by the World-Class Instructional Design and Assessment

(WIDA) consortium discussed in Chapter 1, TESOL's new version presents **five standards** elaborated by grade level for English learners in preK through grade 12. Standard 1 addresses the kind of English needed for social, intercultural and instructional purposes, whereas Standards 2 through 5 address the academic language needed for success in four core content areas: language arts, math, science, and social studies, respectively. The TESOL standards are not intended to replace your district's content area standards. Rather, they show you how to address the needs of English learners to help them meet those standards, as required of all students.

The TESOL standards' focus on academic language development through content area instruction represents a long-standing emphasis in English learner education (e.g., Brinton, Snow & Wesche, 1993). Moreover, the integrated language and content area focus responds to federal legislation (*No Child Left Behind*, 2001) requiring states to develop English language proficiency standards that (1) are grounded in state academic content standards, and (2) address the language domains of listening, speaking, reading, and writing. The new standards also provide **sample performance indicators**, that is, examples of "observable, measurable language behaviors" expected for each standard across different grades and English language proficiency levels. The concrete wording of the performance indicators illustrates what to look for to assess whether a student has met the standard. Figure 3.4 provides an example for you of a TESOL standard matrix.

For ease of use, the **sample performance indicators** for each of the five standards are grouped together by **grade level cluster**, that is, PreK–K, 1–3, 4–5, 6–8, and 9–12. Thus, for example, all performance indicators for all five standards pertaining to grades 1–3 are presented in one section. The sample performance indicators for each standard are presented in matrix charts broken down by (1) **language domain**, that is, listening, speaking, reading, and writing; (2) **content topic**, based on state and national standards for English language

FIGURE 3.4

EXAMPLE OF TESOL STANDARD AND PERFORMANCE EXPECTATIONS

Source: PreK-12 English language proficiency standards by TESOL, 2006. Reprinted with permission of Teachers of English to Speakers of Other Languages (TESOL).

GRADE LEVEL 6–8		STANDARD 4				
English language learners communicate information, ideas, and concepts necessary for academic success in the area of SCIENCE						
DOMAIN	TOPIC	LEVEL 1	LEVEL 2	LEVEL 3	LEVEL 4	LEVEL 5
S P E A K I N G	Atoms Cells Molecules	Identify elements within models or diagrams according to oral directions	Match oral descriptions of functions of various elements with models or diagrams	Arrange models or diagrams based on sequential oral directions (e.g., stages of mitosis or fission)	Reproduce models or diagrams based on visually supported tapes, CDs, videos, or lectures	Design or construct models or diagrams from decontextualized oral discourse
L I S T E N I N G	Solar System	Repeat definitions of key objects in the solar system (e.g., planets, asteroids) with a partner	Describe appearance and composition of objects in the solar system with a partner	Compare appearance and composition of objects in the galaxy with a partner	Present or discuss illustrated processes involving planetary objects (e.g., measuring distance or time spans)	Explain, using technical terms, the structure of the universe using examples of planetary components (e.g., stars and galaxies)
NATIVE LANGUAGES & CULTURES						

development, language arts, science, math, and social studies; and (3) **language proficiency level**, using a 1–5 scale, representing a continuum with the descriptors *starting, emerging, developing, expanding,* and *bridging* for levels 1–5 respectively. To present all the information in an easily readable format, the performance indicators for *listening* and *speaking* are presented on one page, with those for *reading* and *writing* on the next.

As you read the performance indicators across the page, you will get an idea of how student performance expectations require greater English language proficiency as you move from level 1 to level 5. Notice that the performance behaviors for *listening* require students to *do something* based on *oral directions* of gradually greater complexity, thereby demonstrating their comprehension of English. On the other hand, the *speaking* performance indicators require students to *say something*, with complexity increasing gradually across the five language proficiency levels, from merely *repeating* at level 1 to *explaining in technical terms* at level 5. At the bottom of the matrix chart, you will see the phrase, *native languages and cultures*, which serves as a reminder that English learners bring their own linguistic and cultural resources to the task of English language acquisition. For example, newcomers educated in their home country bring substantial knowledge and experience that can be applied to academic learning in English. Thus it is helpful, whenever possible, to use the primary language to tap into that knowledge base.

In summary, the new TESOL standards help teachers (1) facilitate English language acquisition for social, intercultural, and instructional purposes; and (2) conceptualize grade-appropriate curriculum and assessment in the major content areas in ways that address varying English language proficiency levels. Content-based instruction is thus implicit in the standards. Performance indicators across English proficiency levels illustrate how to tailor instruction and assess learning according to students' various English proficiency levels, including ideas for building in supports such as pair work, the use of visuals, and opportunities to use the primary language when appropriate. It is important to reiterate that the TESOL standards do not replace your state's curriculum standards. Rather, they are to be used alongside your other standards documents as examples of how to build in "differentiated" support for English learners in various content areas across the language proficiency continuum. In the next two sections, we elaborate on two important instructional cornerstones inherent in the TESOL standards: **differentiated instruction** and **content-based instruction**.

Differentiated Instruction (DI)

We have just seen how the TESOL standards can help you tailor your instruction and assessment to meet the varying levels of English language proficiency among your students. Sensitivity to language variation represents one important facet of **differentiated instruction**, an approach in which teachers acknowledge, respect, accommodate, and build upon a wide array of student differences to facilitate optimal growth for all (Tomlinson, 1999). In addition to English

FIGURE 3.5

ONGOING ASSESSMENT
FOR DIFFERENTIATED
INSTRUCTION

WHEN	WHY
Before instruction	To determine prior knowledge of lesson content To determine particular student strengths/needs
During instruction	To check for student understanding To modify lesson to meet student needs To identify students who need additional help
After instruction	To assess student achievement of standards/objectives To inform next steps for teaching/learning

78

language proficiency, teachers consider each student's prior knowledge and experience relevant to the topic or procedure to be taught, using the primary language as a resource when possible. They also look for each student's strengths and preferences for taking in, processing, and showing their understanding of ideas and information, whether through linguistic means, such as talk and print; non-linguistic means, such as pictures, diagrams, charts, and figures; or physical and kinesthetic means, such as demonstration, drama, and pantomime. Teachers also consider student preferences for social or solitary learning experiences and strive to provide a balance of both cooperative and independent learning opportunities. To capitalize on student differences, teachers first need to learn what those differences are. Differentiating instruction thus calls for **ongoing assessment** relative to the curriculum and constant and careful observation of students as they engage in a variety of learning activities. Through such assessment and observation, teachers can begin to determine the best starting points for each student and plan optimal learning experiences for all.

As you can see, differentiated instruction (DI) highlights the importance of ongoing assessment during all phases of instruction, including a renewed emphasis on various ways to assess students *before* instruction, as well as during and after. In addition, differentiated instruction calls for a classroom climate that actively promotes mutual **respect and caring** among students and teacher, a climate in which each student is valued for his or her particular talents, a climate that provides each one the support needed to learn, grow, and thrive. Finally, differentiated instruction calls for **variety and flexibility** in classroom organization, learning materials, and grouping. Every one of these statements applies equally to effective English learner instruction. Because DI addresses individual differences, and because English learners bring a multiplicity of such differences, DI is both natural and necessary for effective English learner instruction. DI emphasizes accommodating a wide array of student traits, talents, and special needs. Effective English learner education must do the same but with added depth in addressing English language proficiency levels; primary language knowledge; cultural differences; and varied prior knowledge students bring from their diverse cultures and life experiences. One approach that addresses linguistic and cultural differences among ELs is sheltered instruction, also referred to as Specially Designed Academic Instruction in English (SDAIE). Sheltered instruction represents one type of content-based instruction, which we define next, followed by a detailed discussion of sheltered instruction.

Content-Based Instruction (CBI)

Content instruction, whether it relates to a piece of literature, a science experiment, or the study of ancient civilizations, can promote oral and written academic learning and second language acquisition. Using the target language as a medium of instruction to teach language and content simultaneously is known as **content-based instruction (CBI)** (Brinton, Snow, & Wesche, 1993; Snow, 2005; Snow & Brinton, 1997; Stoller, 2002). CBI is used to teach a second or foreign language in a variety of programs from kindergarten to college. Programs vary considerably in staffing formats, students served, and the extent to which teachers are responsible for content learning, language learning, or both. For example, CBI may be found in university foreign language classes, such as Japanese, in which all students are at the same level, and language development is the main goal with content serving as the vehicle. The French immersion programs in Canada serving native English speakers in elementary school provide another example of CBI. In these programs, French language acquisition and content learning are major goals, with French/English bilingualism and biliteracy the eventual, desired outcome. A third example can be seen in sheltered English programs K-12, in which both academic content and English language development are goals for ELs. Essential to all CBI programs is the modification of teacher language and instruction in ways that permit students to understand, participate, and learn in a new language. In other words, instructional language is made usable as "comprehensible input" by pairing it with visuals, concrete objects, and other cues to convey meaning. In addition, opportunities may be created for students to use the new language through small group activities involving content-oriented tasks. (You may wish to look back at our discussion of comprehensible input and social interaction in Chapter 2.)

Research has shown that the rich linguistic exposure provided by content instruction is excellent for second language learning, but not sufficient for attaining native-like proficiency (Swain, 1985; Harley, et al., 1990). Therefore, in addition to addressing language outcomes through content teaching, CBI makes room for **explicit instruction** on particular skills and strategies that will help students attain greater proficiency in the new language across a wide spectrum of activity. For example, such instruction might focus on vocabulary, grammar, or discourse strategies appropriate to particular social situations. Similarly, such instruction might highlight strategies for learning from academic texts or for writing in formats and discourse styles used in a particular academic discipline (Met, n.d.; 1998). The purpose of explicit instruction, then, is to address specific aspects of oral and written language use that do not emerge on their own during the natural course of content instruction. Teachers gauge specific language learning needs through ongoing classroom assessments, providing instruction to those who need it, often in small groups that meet on a short-term basis. In this way, teachers differentiate instruction according to student needs.

Reflecting back, you can see that CBI supports ELs' achievement of the TESOL standards (1) by integrating language and content learning; (2) by addressing the language domains of listening, speaking, reading, and writing; and (3) by providing support for various English language proficiency levels. Our approach to effective English learner instruction is content based. Therefore, throughout this book, we show you how to promote oral language and literacy development through content area instruction. The particular approach to CBI that we recommend and discuss next is sheltered instruction, sometimes referred to as specially designed academic instruction in English (SDAIE).

Sheltered Instruction or Specially Designed Academic Instruction in English (SDAIE)

Sheltered instruction or specially designed academic instruction in English (SDAIE) has evolved over the last several decades as an effective means of helping English learners succeed in school (Echevarria, Vogt & Short, 2008; Northcutt & Watson, 1986; Schifini, 1985). As a content-based approach, sheltered instruction or SDAIE uses the target language for instruction, with special modifications to ensure student comprehension and learning. Sheltered instruction addresses three main goals: (1) grade-appropriate content area learning, (2) English language and literacy development, and (3) positive social and affective adjustment.

Sheltered instruction is implemented with various staffing patterns depending on school organization and student needs. For example, in self-contained classrooms typical at the elementary school level, one teacher may be responsible for meeting all three goals. In high school, where classes are usually departmentalized, the English as a Second Language (ESL) teacher may be responsible for English language and literacy goals, with the content teacher responsible for subject matter attainment. Yet both ESL and content teachers use sheltering strategies, integrating language, and content instruction, preferably with ongoing coplanning and coordination. In addition to language and content learning, social and affective adjustment is another important piece of effective English learner instruction. To the extent that you establish positive relationships to form a community of learners, you also promote social development and self-esteem among your students (Gibbs, 1994). The social-emotional climate you establish also provides ELs opportunities to see themselves as worthy, capable, and contributing members of the classroom community, both socially and academically (Cummins, 2001; Cummins, Brown & Sayers, 2007).

Now let's look at some snapshots of sheltered instruction in action. We suggest that you first examine the Sheltered Instruction (SDAIE) checklist in Figure 3.6. Then, as you read the following examples, tick off the strategies teachers use.

A Science Example with Fourth Graders

Ms. Bloom's fourth grade consists of a mixture of ELs and native English speakers. They have been studying raptors and have recently visited the local natural history museum.

Ms. Bloom greeted her fourth-graders, who stood lined up at the door after mid-morning recess. She put her finger to her lips and quietly announced that today was the special day they had been waiting for. Then she asked them to tiptoe to their seats at their cooperative group tables. They took their seats, but not too quietly, because their curiosity was piqued by what they found at the

FIGURE 3.6

EFFECTIVE ENGLISH
LEARNER INSTRUCTION
CHECKLIST

Source: Adapted from
Schifini, 1985.

1. **The teacher organizes instruction around grade-appropriate content, often theme based (e.g., literature, math, science, integrated themes, social studies)**
   a. Instruction provides ìaccess to the core curriculumî
   b. Content is academically demanding
   c. Language objectives are established according to studentsí English language proficiency in relation to language demands of lesson
   d. Language and content learning are integrated
   e. Content is presented from multicultural perspectives
2. **The teacher designs appropriate learning sequences.**
   a. Assesses and builds upon studentsí interests and prior knowledge, including cultural knowledge
   b. Explains purpose of activity
   c. Helps students develop learning strategies for reading, writing, thinking, problem solving
   d. Provides multiple opportunities for students to process information verbally and nonverbally (draw, dramatize, discuss, review, question, rehearse, read, write about)
3. **The teacher modifies language used during instruction.**
   a. May use slightly slower speech rate
   b. Speaks clearly, repeating if needed
   c. Defines new words in meaningful context
   d. Paraphrases in simple terms when using more sophisticated forms of expression
   e. Limits use of idiomatic speech
4. **The teacher supports verbal explanations with nonverbal cues.**
   a. Gestures, facial expressions, action to dramatize meaning
   b. Props, concrete materials
   c. Graphs, pictures, visuals, maps
   d. Films, videotapes, overhead projector, bulletin board displays
5. **The teacher plans ways to ensure participation of all students, keeping in mind English proficiency of each.student**
   a. Monitors lesson comprehension and clarifies concepts as needed
   b. Reviews main ideas and key vocabulary
   c. Plans for students to actively participate in learning activities verbally and nonverbally according to functional English abilities
   d. Provides opportunities for students to contribute based on their modalities of strength: visual, auditory, kinesthetic, oral, written, pictorial
6. **The teacher provides a variety of flexible grouping formats to provide opportunities for social, linguistic, and academic development**
   a. Heterogeneous groups
   b. Pair work
   c. Short-term skill groups
   d. Teacher-student conferencing
7. **The teacher provides a variety of assessment methods that permit students to display learning through their modalities of strength (e.g., oral, written, visual, kinesthetic, auditory, pictorial).**
   a. Performance-based assessment
   b. Portfolio assessment
   c. Learner self-assessment
   d. If used, standardized tests are modified to accommodate English learners (e.g., extra time to complete)

center of each table: a small oval object wrapped in aluminum foil, a slender, five-inch probing instrument, and a graphing sheet depicting what turned out to be different kinds of rodent bones. Ms. Bloom waited for all to be seated and quiet. Then she proceeded to give her instructions:

"Yesterday we visited the Natural History Museum, and we saw a diorama of the life cycle of owls. Who remembers what Table Three wanted to know more about after visiting the museum? (Students at Table Three answer: 'We wanted to know more about what owls eat.') OK, so I promised you I would give you a chance to investigate, or find out for yourselves. At your table, you have something wrapped in foil. (Ms. Bloom holds up an example.) This is called an owl pellet. After an owl finishes eating, it *regurgitates* the pellet, or throws it up out of its mouth. (Teacher dramatizes with a hand gesture.) After everyone understands what to do, I want you to take the pellet apart, examine it carefully, and together decide what information you can figure out about what owls eat. I want you to look, to talk together, and to write down your ideas. Then each group will share back with the whole class. Take a look at the instruction card at your table and raise your hand when you are sure you know what to do."

Students went ahead, and with some assistance from the teacher, they got started. Because the groups included more advanced and less advanced English speakers, they were able to help each other understand what to do. After sharing their findings with the rest of the class, each group graphed the kinds of bones they found and then discussed the original question further in light of their findings.

Even in this short example, you probably noticed how Ms. Bloom made use of many techniques to facilitate English learner comprehension, participation, and learning, including the following: (1) organization of instruction around cognitively demanding content, in this case, science; (2) explanation of the lesson's purpose, with attention to understanding what was to be done; (3) building background for lesson content by visiting a museum; (4) careful use of instructional language, including definition and repetition of key words like *owl pellet* in context, developing meaning through direct experience with the actual object; (5) acting out or paraphrasing the meaning of words like *regurgitated*; (6) use of direct experience when examining the owl pellets; and (7) opportunities for students to help each other through cooperative group work. Perhaps you have found that you already include many of these sheltering techniques in your teaching. If so, keep up the good work. Now let's look at a sheltered lesson with kindergarteners.

A Literature Example with Kindergarteners

Last week we were in Roberto Heredia's kindergarten classroom of beginning and intermediate English language learners. Roberto was reading the predictable book *The Very Hungry Caterpillar* (Carle, 1986), part of a literature study on the author, Eric Carle. You may remember this simple pattern story about the little caterpillar who eats through page after page of luscious fruits and fattening foods until he turns into a chrysalis and then emerges as a beautiful butterfly. As you read about Roberto's presentation of the book, you may wish to refer to Figure 3.6 to tick off the sheltering strategies he uses.

Roberto features the story by posting a picture of a caterpillar next to the large class calendar. Next to the caterpillar, you see labeled pictures of the caterpillar's food as depicted in the story: one apple, two pears, three plums, four strawberries, five oranges, and the many rich foods that the caterpillar surfeited himself with that Saturday. Roberto also had paper cutouts on popsicle sticks of the caterpillar and all of the different foods he ate.

After the calendar routine focusing on the days of the week, Roberto read the story from the book. When the children asked to hear it again, he reread the story using the popsicle stick props of the caterpillar and foods. As Roberto read the first sentence, "On Monday the very hungry caterpillar ate one apple," the children chimed in eagerly: "But he was still hungry." As he read "Monday," he pointed to the word Monday on the calendar; when he read "hungry caterpillar,"

Internet Resources

Jim Cummins has been a researcher/writer/ teacher on bilingual education and second language policies and literacies for years. His website on second language acquisition and literacy development is an excellent one: **www.iteachilearn. com/cummins/**. The site contains lesson plans, articles, discussions of important ideas such as BICS and CALP, and many other links that will help you explore policies and ideas related to second language acquisition and literacy. The site of the TESOL organization (Teachers of English to Speakers of Other Languages) is invaluable to educators: **www.tesol.org/**. We suggest you find the Pre-K–12 Standards in the site and develop a mini-lesson based on a standard that interests you. With the lesson you develop, discuss specific objectives based on the standard and discuss how you will assess and determine the lesson's success.

he waved the caterpillar cutout; and when he read what the caterpillar ate, he mimicked the caterpillar eating the paper cutout of the apple. The children begged for another reading, so Roberto read it one more time, holding up the caterpillar and food cutouts while the children chimed in.

The next day Roberto read the story using sentence strips in a pocket chart, pointing to each word as he did so. By this time, the children were completely familiar with the story and its predictable pattern. Roberto now prepared the children to write their own story using a caterpillar or one of the other animals in the wall dictionary and following the pattern in the original story. Children worked in groups to write their first story together, which they published in a booklet made by folding a piece of paper in a special way previously demonstrated. When the groups finished their books, they read them aloud to the class. A part of one group's story, "The Very Hungry Dinosaur," begins as follows:

On Monday, the very hungry dinosaur ate a green horse.
On Tuesday, the very hungry dinosaur ate two red cars.
On Wednesday, the very hungry dinosaur ate three brown houses.
On Thursday, the very hungry dinosaur ate four purple elephants.

Finally, because the children enjoyed the stories so much, Roberto had the children make the books into big books to be kept in the classroom library. On the next day, children made small individual stories, which they took home to read to their parents. Roberto's goal was to allow each of the beginning students to participate in English at his or her own level in an enjoyable manner with no pressures to perform. However, he found that almost all of the students, both beginners and intermediates, already saw themselves as successful English speakers, readers, and writers through the lesson.

A Social Science Example with High School Students

Ed Broach, a social studies teacher in an inner-city high school, has long been highly effective in teaching first and second language learners. An excellent teacher, he always made sure his students were, in his words, "getting it." How

83

did he do this, and how did the concept of sheltered instruction improve his teaching?

One social science curriculum standard requires students to understand and explain how a bill in Congress becomes a law. To begin the unit on this topic, Ed asks his students to consider the word *law*, giving them a few minutes to share with a partner any experiences they've had with laws in this country or elsewhere. He then creates a cluster on the chalkboard that categorizes aspects of the laws that students have experienced. In the process, Ed engages students in a discussion of the need for good, fair laws. Ed explains that they should keep this discussion in mind because they are going to have a chance in class to create a new law or change an old one, following procedures used by the U.S. Congress. In this way, Ed provides a practical purpose up front for motivating student interest in the topic.

Next, Ed provides each student with a list of important vocabulary words for the unit, such as l*egislature, Congress, House of Representatives, Senate*, and *bill*. Then, using an overhead projector, he shows students pictures of Congress and explains a flowchart that illustrates how an idea becomes a bill and how a bill becomes law. As he does so, he emphasizes terms on the vocabulary list. Next, he has students work in groups to check their levels of knowledge and understanding of these terms. For each term, students discuss whether they recognize the word, whether they can use it in a sentence, and whether they can explain its meaning to others. Ed uses this information to determine additional concept and vocabulary development that might be needed. At this point, students read a selection from the textbook on the legislative process using a study guide Ed devised for them.

With this preparation, students are ready for a short film on the topic, which furthers student learning. Ed continues to check for student comprehension during and after the film. Next, he sets up a mini-congress. Students work as congressional committee members to write up a bill and take it through all the steps required to enact it as a law. For example, one group decided to pass a law to change school disciplinary procedures. During group work, Ed circulates through the classroom, making notes as he checks for student involvement and understanding. Afterward, Ed reviews and clarifies essential concepts by summarizing the legislative processes his students have just experienced.

Let's look at how Ed has modified his teaching to make it more effective for English learners. Originally he assigned the reading first and did the simulation game last, followed by the multiple-choice test with essay questions. Now he does several things differently. First, he spends more time before students read the text to set the purpose for the unit, key into their prior experiences and knowledge of the topic, and provide an overview of concepts and vocabulary using visual aids. Second, he has become more conscious of modifying instruction according to student needs, including the pace and complexity of his own instructional talk. Third, he checks carefully for student understanding at every step. Fourth, he watches to be sure that groups are functioning smoothly and that everyone has a chance to participate. Fifth, he assesses student learning in a variety of ways: through checklists while students are in groups and through individual portfolio conferences and by more traditional means. These modifications have worked well. In fact, Ed recently told us that he has to make his tests a little tougher these days because students were all passing his old ones so easily. Through sheltered instruction, Ed has taken excellence to yet a higher level, improving learning opportunities for all his students.

We have just seen three teachers using sheltered instruction. Next let's look at what goes into their planning.

Planning for Differentiated, Sheltered English Instruction or SDAIE

As you sit down to plan instruction, you need to keep two things in mind at once: (1) your students in all their diversity and (2) the curriculum you are required to teach. Your job is to bring the two together, meeting each student at his or her level to facilitate learning. When you tailor your instruction to your ELs' language proficiency levels and prior knowledge, you are **sheltering instruction**. When you further modify instruction based on your students' varied talents, strengths, and learning needs, you are **differentiating instruction**. Your planning requires you to address four questions: what, who, how, and how well?

What: Content you will teach based on curriculum standards

Who: Your students; their English language proficiency levels; primary language and cultural backgrounds/experiences; learning strengths and needs

How: Instructional strategies and materials tailored to student strengths and needs; individual, small group, or whole-class activities; modifications for language proficiency levels and other special needs

How well: Performance expectations and assessment procedures

As noted previously, sheltered instruction or SDAIE integrates content, language, and social/affective development. We therefore suggest that you establish objectives for each category. Figure 3.7 shows one planning format that addresses the topics of the foregoing discussion.

You establish **content objectives** based on your district's curriculum standards. Bear in mind that you may need to adjust the amount of material you cover for some students, particularly those in the earlier stages of English language development. To do so, you carefully review and evaluate your curriculum to identify those concepts most essential for continued academic development and success. By honing curriculum concepts in this way, you adjust the cognitive load for those who need it but not the grade level of the material (Meyer, 2000b; Tomlinson, 1999). Similarly, you may need to think of ways for more advanced students to extend their learning beyond your lesson objectives. In this way you provide everyone access to the same curriculum while differentiating instruction based on your students' particular strengths and needs.

Next you establish **language objectives**, varying them according to your students' language proficiency levels, using the TESOL standards or your state's ESL/ELD standards as a guide. One way to identify language objectives is to review the learning tasks you are planning and analyze the **language demands** and **language learning opportunities** they offer for students at different levels. For students new to English, for example, your objectives may focus on comprehension rather than production. If the lesson requires specific vocabulary or grammatical structures, such as the past tense, these may become the basis of your lesson's English language objectives. You need only a few language objectives, aspects that

FIGURE 3.7

LESSON PLAN FORMAT

Planning Guide for Sheltered Instruction/SDAIE

Theme/Topic _____ Grade _____

Student Traits: English language proficiency levels, cultural backgrounds, special needs

Standards:
      Content
      Language

Objectives:
      Content
      Language
      Social/Affective

Pre-assessment (what do students know before instruction? used to inform instructional procedures, grouping and selection of varied materials to support learning)

Grouping

Materials

Instructional sequence with strategies to support your talk and student involvement
      1. Introduction: tie in to students' interests and prior knowledge; stimulate curiosity
      2. What you say and do/what students say and do
      3. Closure: Review accomplishments; tell what's coming next

Post-assessment (what do students know after instruction? differentiated to permit students to display learning through modality of strength; used to document learning and inform next steps in instruction)

---

you will focus on and assess, drawing from the domains of listening, speaking, reading, and writing.

In addition to language objectives, you need to plan **language-related lesson modifications**, particularly how you will modify your instructional delivery to support English learners' comprehension. First, you will want to plan ways to accompany your instructional talk with visuals, concrete objects, direct experience, and other nonverbal means to convey lesson content. Second, you need to plan what to say to get your point across, including particular phrasing and vocabulary. Third, you will want think of ways to rephrase information and define new words in context if needed. This detailed attention to your own language use may be difficult at first. With practice, however, it will become a natural part of your instructional planning process. During lesson delivery, you need to check to be sure all students understand and follow your ideas and explanations. If some do not, you might take them aside for further help. This process is part of ongoing assessment of student learning and differentiation of instruction.

Finally, you need to examine your individual, whole-class, and small-group activities to identify social interaction opportunities that serve as the basis for your **social/affective objectives**. Social/affective objectives concern social-cultural adjustment, interpersonal relationships, empathy, self-esteem, and respect for others. For example, social/affective objectives might refer to students cooperating on a task, responding sensitively to each other's ideas, accepting opinions divergent from their own, and respecting the home languages and traditions of others. Social/affective objectives will reflect what you value in student behavior. Your values will, of course, reflect your particular cultural point of view, and that is fine. In reality, you create your own classroom culture, which will be somewhat different from anyone's home culture, including your own. It is important to be conscious of what you value so that you can explicitly state the social/affective behaviors you wish students to display.

Because social interaction is conducive to both language acquisition and subject matter learning, **classroom organization** for English learners includes frequent opportunities for students to work together in pairs or groups. When you organize groups, it is important to vary group membership according to your particular academic, language, and social/affective objectives. Heterogeneous groups are usually preferable for language, social, and academic development. At times, however, you may call together a small group of students who need **explicit instruction** on a particular skill or topic, usually on a short-term basis. However, be careful to avoid inflexible, long-term ability grouping, which has been shown to have negative effects on student learning and self-esteem (Eder, 1982).

The last step in the instructional sequence is **assessment of student learning**. Basing your assessment on the standards, goals, and objectives you outlined previously, you need to provide students a variety of opportunities to display their learning. Assessment outcomes permit you to document student progress and decide on your next steps in instruction. In this way, you differentiate assessment and instruction to facilitate optimal student performance and continued growth.

This short section has described basic planning procedures for sheltered instruction. In the next three sections, we elaborate on three important instructional strategies to incorporate into your teaching: group work, theme studies, and scaffolding. Lastly, we discuss English learner assessment.

87

Group Work

Group work is an important element of sheltered instruction or SDAIE. When you provide opportunities for English learners to interact with their English-speaking peers, receptive and productive language learning opportunities abound (Wong Fillmore, 1982). Imagine, for example, a group of three or four students working together to create a mural. Language will be used naturally to accomplish the task at hand. In addition, the language that is used will be context embedded (Cummins, 1981), that is, directly related to concrete objects at hand. The mural, the paints, the children themselves, and their actions support comprehension of task-based talk. Moreover, if words are used that are not understood, collaborative group work permits learners to ask for repetition and clarification if needed. Thus, learners themselves have some control over fine-tuning the input generated in carrying out the collaborative project. English learners are also challenged to speak during group work, thereby providing excellent practice in articulating their ideas in English. Collaborative group work therefore provides opportunities for both social and academic language development, with proficient English-speaking peers providing good models for English learners. For these reasons, collaborative projects generate particularly rich language learning

TABLE 3.1 • A FEW TYPES OF COLLABORATIVE GROUPS

TYPE	PROCEDURE	PURPOSE
Buddy system	Pair students; one more capable is paired with a student less proficient in English. The buddy helps the student in and out of the class until the second language learner becomes proficient and knowledgeable about class and school routines.	Helps the new second language learner become a member of the classroom society. Helps the student become comfortable in the school.
Writing response groups	Students share their writing with one another, concentrate on what is good in the papers, and help one another improve their writing. The teacher begins by modeling good response partners and giving students specific strategies for improving their papers.	Writing response groups have several purposes: making students independent; helping students improve their writing; and giving students an audience and immediate response to their writing.
Literature response groups	Teacher first models response to literature, emphasizing the variety of acceptable responses. Students learn to value individual responses and support responses with what they have read. Students focus on individual feelings first and later on structure and form of literature.	To help students use their own background knowledge to respond to literature, to value students' individual responses and to help them become independent readers of literature.
Cooperative groups	Students are given specific roles and responsibilities for group work. Students become responsible for the success of one another and they teach and learn from one another, creating success for all members of the group.	Build individual and group responsibility for learning. Build success for all members of the group. Develop creative, active learners.

contexts, especially when groups include advanced or native English speakers. Because group work provides opportunities for individuals to display their talents and to procure assistance from peers, it is an important component of differentiated instruction. Of course, the teacher continues to be an important language model and source of input as well. Table 3.1 depicts several different kinds of collaborative groups. Writing and literature response groups will be described in subsequent chapters; cooperative groups are discussed next.

Organizing Group Work

There are many ways to organize group work to suit the purpose at hand; some are informal and student centered, whereas others are more structured and require students to learn the cooperative processes before academic work can actually begin. For the purposes of second language acquisition and differentiated learning opportunities, the specific structure of collaborative groups is less important than the quality of the opportunities they provide for interaction. To organize informal group work, for example, you might provide activity centers as a free choice in the afternoon, with three to six students permitted at each center. By offering games, manipulatives, and problem-solving activities aimed at different levels of language and content knowledge, you differentiate instruction while encouraging informal collaboration among students. Another possibility for collaboration is to create specific tasks for small groups to work on together. For example, to introduce a unit on animals, you might divide the class into groups of three or four students and provide each group with a set of photographs of different animals. One task would be to categorize the photos and then to explain and justify the criteria for their groupings. The task is rich in natural opportunities for the use of academic language related to higher-level thinking, such as comparing, contrasting, categorizing, explaining, and justifying. Furthermore, because students carry out the task in small groups, everyone gets a chance to contribute in a low-risk, low-anxiety atmosphere. The relaxed atmosphere, or low-anxiety environment, is considered conducive to content learning and language acquisition (Dulay et al., 1982; Krashen, 1981a).

To the extent that the target language, English, is used during group work, students practice their new language and gain context-embedded input for further acquisition. In some situations, you may explicitly encourage the use of English for group activities. For example, if most students in the class speak the same native language and varying levels of English, students may tend to use the home language instead of English. If so, you may choose to encourage English explicitly as the designated language for activity centers. In multilingual classrooms, English becomes the one language common to all students, the *lingua franca*, and students consequently choose it as a matter of course. The ideal learning situation occurs when the class includes advanced and native English

89

This group of girls worked together cooperatively to prepare their oral presentation to the class.

speakers with whom English learners may interact during group work. However, research suggests that students who are quite new to English have difficulty understanding and learning during group work conducted in English only (Saunders & O'Brien, 2006). For these students, access to lesson content through their first language (L1) may help, either from the teacher or from a peer. In summary, informal collaboration can promote English learners' language, content and social development when implemented with careful attention to students' language abilities, and other individual strengths and needs. Next we discuss more structured approaches to cooperative learning.

Cooperative Learning Methods

In addition to informal group collaboration, a great deal of work has been carried out on more structured cooperative learning methods (Cohen, 1986; Dishon & O'Leary, 1984; Johnson, Johnson, & Holubec, 1986; Kagan, 1986). Cooperative learning may be defined as an instructional organization strategy in which students work collaboratively in small groups to achieve academic and social learning goals. In cooperative learning, you establish heterogeneous groups. That is, members are either randomly assigned, or else you set up membership to ensure that each group includes a variety of students in terms of gender, ethnicity, language proficiency, and academic achievement (Cohen, 1986). You may also balance groups in terms of personality characteristics: shy/outgoing, quiet/talkative, and so forth. In addition to heterogeneous grouping, procedural roles are assigned to students in each group, such as recorder, observer, encourager, or reporter. These roles are rotated so that all group members have a chance to experience them. In this way, leadership and other roles are distributed among all students, rather than falling on certain ones all the time.

In addition to heterogeneous grouping and role distribution, cooperative learning procedures are set up to build positive interdependence among group members. That is, students come to share and support each other's learning in socially appropriate ways. This occurs because members of a cooperative group succeed only if every member succeeds. Thus, to be successful, all students must care about the work of all the other group members. To build positive interdependence,

Calvin and Hobbes © Watterson. Reprinted with permission of UNIVERSAL PRESS SYNDICATE. All rights reserved.

assignments are established that require group members to cooperate smoothly. For example, you may assign a group project with each group member responsible for one part. In this way, the final goal cannot be achieved without each member contributing. Furthermore, the quality of the final project depends on the quality of each member's contribution. Thus, individuals are accountable for their own learning and that of the group, and they develop autonomy in their group learning.

Phases of Cooperative Group Development

You may find that many of your students have had little or no experience in group interactions. In addition, some students may not consider group work academically appropriate based on the values and assumptions of their home cultures. Therefore, we recommend that you gradually implement group work in your classroom. A first step is to place students in partnerships in which they can work together on specific tasks, such as buddy reading or cleanup duties. Next, you may place students in groups of three as they become comfortable working in groups. Finally, you may create cooperative/collaborative groups of four or five students.

Even this gradual and careful grouping will not guarantee effective group work. You still need to provide feedback to help students listen, take turns, stay on task, and work together effectively as a group (Cohen, 1986, 1994). Some teachers have groups evaluate *themselves* on the mechanics of cooperation addressing questions such as (1) Did we stay on task? (2) Were we courteous and respectful to one another even when we didn't agree? (3) How can we be more successful next time? Such checklists help students develop an awareness of their group dynamics, increasing their chances for success.

Whether homogeneous or heterogeneous in membership, groups will go through phases on their way to working autonomously. In the first phase, let's call it the get-along phase, you may find students need a lot of help. They may not know how to get along or how to resolve conflicts. They need to know that they are responsible for the behavior of others in the group and themselves (Cohen, 1986). You will need to work closely with them to help them move to the next phase, developing relationships, in which students determine one another's strengths and decide who is best suited for various aspects of group work. During this phase, you may need to help groups that are dominated by one or two individuals, especially if the groups include native and non-native English speakers. To meet individual needs and thus differentiate instruction, we recommend that you have a multiplicity of ways students can display their knowledge, such as drawing a picture, creating a graph, demonstrating a procedure, or completing a scientific experiment. When groups are asked to perform a variety of tasks, it's more likely that all students in a group will be involved.

Once students have developed a successful pattern of relationships, they can move to the phase of production, in which they begin to become efficient group workers who can bring their task to completion. Sometimes groups will reach a final phase of autonomy, in which they require minimal help from the teacher, develop many of their own topics, and seem to move from one task to another without any help. Whatever phase your students are in, you will need to work with them closely to help them advance to more productive phases of group work, always working toward group autonomy. To do this you may have to resolve conflicts and clarify directions groups are taking in their work. Finally, help students self-monitor by using checklists or by having successful groups role play for others how they work together. Successful group work is accompanied by a teacher who gives clear directions and works with students to help them grow as group members (Cohen, 1986; 1994).

Jigsaw

In one cooperative technique, called jigsaw (Aaronson, 1978), one segment of a learning task is assigned to each group member, who then works to become an "expert" in that area. After researching their special areas, the experts from each group meet to compare notes and extend their learning. Finally, the original groups meet again, and the experts report back to their original groups. For example, Mary Ann Smith created "base groups" consisting of three students each to help her students learn about spiders. She then assigned each member in the base group different pages from a selection on spiders. One student in each base group was responsible for pages 1 to 3, another for pages 4 to 6, and the third student was responsible for the final three pages. When students had read the assigned pages, Mary Ann met with the specialists on each section. These students became experts on the information they read, discussing and sharing their understanding of the reading with their expert peers and planning how they would teach the information to members in their base groups. All experts returned to their base groups and shared their special expertise with their peers. In this way, all group members were availed of the whole spectrum of information on spiders. In jigsaw processes such as this, students may then apply their knowledge to a group task or to an individual task, assuring individual accountability for all information.

A final aspect of the jigsaw process is the development of group autonomy: Groups become responsible for their own learning and smooth functioning. Thus, the teacher needs to step back at times to let students solve their own procedural and conceptual conflicts. In this way, students use their critical thinking abilities and social skills to work things out on their own.

To summarize our discussion thus far, we have seen that ELs, by virtue of their immersion in a new language and culture, have the benefit of natural exposure to the new language both in and out of school. In addition, they have real and immediate life needs that motivate them to learn. They also bring to the learning task a variety of talents, skills, and prior knowledge for the teacher to build upon. At the same time, they must reach high levels of proficiency in order to succeed. In order to learn their new language, they need comprehensible input and opportunities to use the new language in day-to-day social interactions. Teachers can provide high-quality comprehensible input for both social and academic language use in the classroom by using sheltering techniques, by differentiating instruction, and by creating opportunities for collaborative group work in which English will be used with peers. Another excellent strategy to use with English language learners is thematic instruction. The next section explains why and how.

Thematic Instruction

For many years, teachers have used themes or topics as focal points for organizing curriculum content (Enright & McCloskey, 1988; Pappas, Kiefer, & Levstik, 1990). One teacher we know, Reina Saucedo, uses corn as the central topic for a unit that integrates math, social studies, science, and language arts. She begins the unit with a feast of *quesadillas*, which are toasted corn tortillas filled with melted cheese. Next comes a discussion about corn as the basic ingredient for tortillas. From there, the class embarks on a study of corn, a native American plant originally cultivated by indigenous peoples in North, Central, and South America. Reina's students read, illustrate, and dramatize corn legends; sprout corn seeds and record their growth; and create a world map, citing locations where corn is grown and eaten today. Some students choose to research how corn is prepared in different countries, creating an illustrated international corn cookbook. The class learns about the nutritive value of corn, finding out, for example, that it combines with beans to form a complete protein. They also learn how to dye corn kernels and string them into necklaces to wear or to give as gifts. As a culminating activity they create a menu based on corn and prepare a nutritionally balanced meal for the class.

Though more prevalent in the primary grades, thematic instruction lends itself to virtually any content and any grade level. For example, an extensive cooperative theme project, "Building Toothpick Bridges" (Pollard, 1985), would be appropriate for upper-elementary grades through high school. In this integrated science-math-building project, students work in groups of six, forming "construction companies," to design and build a bridge out of toothpicks. The unit begins with readings on the history of bridge development, analysis of bridge designs, and information about how bridges work. Students may visit local bridges to examine their architecture and consider how they are structured to bear weight and constant use. Each construction company member assumes a role, selecting from project director, architect, carpenter, transportation chief, and accountant. The goal is to design and build the strongest bridge possible, staying within the company's projected budget. In the planning stage, companies design their bridges, estimating the quantity and cost of necessary materials. On certain days, the "warehouse" is open for purchase of materials, paid for by check. At the end of the project, the strength of the bridges is tested to the breaking point, and the strongest bridge wins a prize. The bridge breaking is an exciting media event, described by students in an article for the local newspaper. This collaborative project is a highly involving, fun project that integrates the use of oral and written language with a wide variety of science and math concepts. The theme-based collaborative project serves many purposes: to teach science and math concepts and applications, promote the use of library resources, provide students with a chance to work together cooperatively, and help them become better readers and writers as they negotiate meanings for themselves and others. Finally, the purposes in a unit, such as this one are met seamlessly as the students engage in activities that are involving and meaningful.

In summary, we recommend the use of thematic instruction for English language learners for several reasons. First, thematic instruction creates a meaningful conceptual framework within which students are invited to use both oral and written language for learning content. The meaningful context established by the theme supports the comprehensibility of instruction, thereby increasing both content learning and second language acquisition. In addition, theme-based collaborative projects create student interest, motivation, involvement, and purpose. Moreover, as students work together on their projects, they naturally use both oral and written language to question, inform, problem solve, negotiate, and interact with their peers. Through such engagement, both social and academic language and literacy development are challenged and promoted. But keep in mind that most students, whether English learners or native English speakers, need time and assistance to be integrated into project-oriented, collaborative classrooms. Nevertheless, when combined with opportunities for thematic instruction, it creates optimal content, language, and literacy learning opportunities for both native and non-native English speakers.

Organizing Thematic Instruction

We offer six criteria for organizing thematic instruction to promote language development, critical thinking, independence, and interpersonal collaboration for English language learners. Our criteria represent basic learning principles that we have adapted from Enright and McCloskey (1988).

MEANING AND PURPOSE. The content of the theme study is interesting and relevant to the students. One way to ensure interest and relevance is to provide opportunities for students themselves to guide the choice of topics, activities, and projects within the theme study. As students make choices, they invest themselves in their own learning, thereby creating self-direction and purpose.

BUILDING ON PRIOR KNOWLEDGE. The theme study builds on students' prior knowledge, including that gained from life experiences and the home culture. In this way, students' varied cultural experiences can be incorporated into their schoolwork, providing understanding of themselves and others.

INTEGRATED OPPORTUNITIES TO USE ORAL AND WRITTEN LANGUAGE FOR LEARNING PURPOSES. The teacher is conscious of creating opportunities for oral language and literacy to be used for learning purposes established in concert with students. The teacher broadens the students' experiences with different forms and functions of print suited to student interests and goals.

SCAFFOLDING FOR SUPPORT. Thematic instruction is provided in a classroom atmosphere that respects each student, builds on their strengths, supports their efforts, and values their accomplishments. One way to support students is to use sheltering techniques and various kinds of scaffolds, discussed later, to assist students in participating successfully, even if their English language/literacy proficiency is limited. Another way is to give students varied opportunities to display and share their learning.

COLLABORATION. Students are given many opportunities to work together on theme-related projects and activities. Collaboration in pairs and small groups provides students with opportunities to process complex information actively in a low-risk, low-anxiety situation. In this way, language and content learning is productive, and positive social relationships can be promoted. At the same time, language and literacy are used purposefully, promoting acquisition of both.

VARIETY. Variety permeates the learning process—in topics of study, in the ways that learning is shared with others, in the functions of oral and written language used, in roles and responsibilities, and in task difficulty. Variety and flexibility characterize learning groups—pairs, small groups, and the whole class. Thus interest remains high.

The process of developing thematic instruction is dynamic, ideally involving input from the students themselves at all levels of decision making. The first step is to choose the topic or theme that will serve as the focus of interest. There are many sources for themes and topics, including state and local curriculum guidelines and personal interests and curiosities expressed by the students. Not least, your own special interests provide an excellent source of topics and themes, and you are likely to have or know of resources and materials to share with your students. Enthusiasm is contagious, and when you bring your own curiosity and joy for learning into the classroom, you reveal your personal self, thereby deepening your relationship with your students and modeling lifelong learning. Likewise, when you build on your students' interests and curiosities, you can catch their wave of enthusiasm and embark on exciting new learning adventures yourself.

Once a theme is chosen, the next step is to brainstorm ideas related to the theme. One way to conduct the brainstorming is to create a cluster or word web on the chalkboard as you and your students generate ideas around the theme. During brainstorming, it is important to accept and write down every idea contributed by your students. Based on the words generated during brainstorming, related ideas can be grouped together, resulting in a map of the major subtopics to be investigated. Under each subtopic, activities and projects are listed together, as shown in the map in Figure 3.8. It is helpful to post the thematic map in the classroom to keep the organization and planning available at a glance.

Another way to generate and organize learning activities and projects around a theme is to write the chosen theme or topic on a large piece of butcher paper and invite students to list "what we know already" and "what we wonder about," as Jamie Green did with her theme cycle on Egypt. Students may then form interest groups around the "wonder topic" of their preference, and together with the teacher, establish a plan to find out more. In this approach, groups conduct research with teacher guidance as needed, each group presenting its findings to the class in some form: oral, written, pictorial/graphic, or dramatic. Students are encouraged to combine at least two or three of the presentational modes so as to "shelter" their presentations for their classmates. For example, an oral presentation to the class might explain a mural. Finally, the butcher paper list is reviewed and revised with a new category: "What We Know Now." This theme study (Altwerger & Flores, 1991) may then be repeated by adding "What We Wonder Now," as students pose new questions and choose new areas of investigation. The thematic instruction provide students with opportunities for functional and purposeful language use in the classroom, which we discuss in more detail next.

95

FIGURE 3.8

TREES: AN INTEGRATED THEMATIC UNIT

Source: From Marilyn H. Buckley and Owen Boyle, *Mapping the Writing Journey* (Berkeley: Bay Area Writing Project, 1981), p. 28. Reprinted with permission of the publisher.

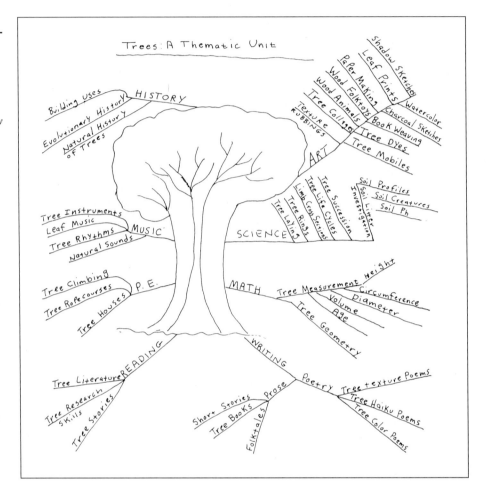

Functional and Academic Literacy Uses in Thematic Instruction

From the standpoint of second language learning, one of the teacher's major responsibilities is to make sure to incorporate a variety of functional and academic literacy uses into the projects and activities undertaken by the students (Heath & Mangiola, 1991). The following list describes different forms and uses of reading and writing to consider as you expand your students' repertoires.

In addition to exposing students to a variety of literacy forms and functions, you will want to make sure that scaffolding supports, described in the next section, are available to facilitate student participation, even if English language proficiency is limited. Therefore, as the final step in developing a theme study, you will want to examine the project and activity plans while considering the special strengths and needs of your students. Using questions such as the following may help you differentiate instruction and guide your students' involvement:

1. Which aspects of the project can be carried out by students with minimal English proficiency (e.g., painting, coloring, short answers, use of the student's native language)?

FIGURE 3.9

Forms and Classroom Examples of Print Functions

FUNCTIONAL LITERACY FORM	PURPOSE
Lists	For organizing and remembering information
Order forms	For purchasing items for classroom activities
Checks	To pay for classroom book orders
Ledgers	To keep account of classroom responsibilities
Labels and captions	To explain pictures on bulletin boards or other displays
Personal journals	To generate ideas on a project, record feelings
Buddy journals	To develop or promote a personal relationship
Record-keeping journal	To keep track of a project or experiment
Interactive journal	To converse in writing; to promote a personal friendship
Notes	To take information down so it will be remembered
Personal letters	To share news with a companion or friend
Business letters	To apply for a job; to complain about a product
Dramatic scripts	To entertain the class by presenting stories dramatically
ACADEMIC LITERACY FORM (ESSAY)	**PURPOSE**
Narrative	To relate stories; to share tales about people and places
Enumeration	To list information either by numbering or chronologically
Comparison/contrast	To show how two or more things are different and alike
Problem/solution	To discuss a problem and suggest solutions
Cause/effect	To show cause/effect relationships
Thesis/proof	To present an idea and persuade readers of its validity

97

2. How can I build on special talents or prior knowledge of the theme topics?

3. Which aspects of the project involve literacy uses that may be supported by literacy scaffolds and/or by peer assistance (e.g., writing a story based on the repeated pattern of a predictable book such as *Brown Bear, Brown Bear, What Do You See?* [Martin, 1967] or *Fortunately* [Charlip, 1997]; writing a letter in cooperative pairs; paired reading)?

4. What special resources might be of help to a particular group (e.g., books, encyclopedias, films, community members, school personnel)? What resources can I provide to address special talents and needs of particular students in my class (e.g., simpler texts, more advanced texts, primary language material)?

5. How might this project lead to particular kinds of language and literacy uses (e.g., a letter to a company protesting its use of laboratory animals, the contribution of an article to the school newspaper, oral reading of the poems discovered in researching the theme, the use of a log to record plant growth). For more teaching ideas to use with thematic instruction, check out Chapter 6 on vocabulary and Chapters 9 and 10 on content area reading and writing.

Creating Variety in Language and Literacy Uses

Your role in generating a variety of oral and written language uses is crucial for optimal language and literacy development through thematic instruction. To support students' successful involvement, you will want to consider the students' performance levels and find ways to stretch them. As you consider how to assist your students with their projects, two questions should be kept in mind: (1) How can I assure successful participation by each student? and (2) How can I encourage each student to perform at his or her best?

We believe that both participation and motivation are promoted by encouraging students to make choices. For example, if your curriculum requires the study of your state's history, you might start with local history by posing the questions: Has our town always been here? What do you suppose it was like here 100 years ago? Your discussion may lead students to other questions, such as: What and who was here? How did people live, work, and learn? How did they dress? What did they use for transportation? What did they do for fun? Students may form interest groups by choosing which questions they want to work on. Further choices may be made as to the books and materials they will use to answer their questions. Perhaps some students will choose to interview long time local residents. Finally, students may choose the format they wish to use for presenting their findings—publishing a factual book on local history, creating a mural to depict the town as it was 100 years ago, creating a diary that might have been written by a local child 100 years ago, or creating a series of letters that might have been written to a cousin in another state. Your job is to be on hand to listen to students and make suggestions as needed. By offering students choices, you broaden their horizons, while allowing them to invest more fully in their own learning, thus sparking interest and involvement as well.

Active participation is also enhanced when students work in groups to accomplish self-selected tasks. Groups provide support and motivation to get things done. Furthermore, your English learners may prove more capable than anticipated when allowed to work in a small group. In any case, you will want to move from group to group to observe students' progress and interaction. If necessary, you may suggest ways to involve new English language learners. For example, if a student speaks virtually no English, you might pair him or her with another student to illustrate the group's book or to copy captions for the illustrations. You need to be observant, intuitive, and imaginative when making such suggestions for newcomers and others with limited English proficiency. Therein lies the art of teaching: knowing when to encourage and when to stand back!

Finally, as students reflect on their new knowledge, they are in a position to evaluate their own learning. Through the process of posing their own questions, researching to find possible answers, and presenting their findings to their classmates, they can see for themselves how much they have learned. At the same time, they may wish to note those areas still open to question, thereby generating questions for their next theme study. The theme study thus replicates the knowledge generation process used in formal research. In our approach to theme studies, we emphasize the use of scaffolding, a concept we now discuss in detail.

Scaffolding

Russian psychologist Lev Vygotsky (1896–1934) introduced a useful concept about learning and development when he pointed out that what the learner can do with assistance today, he or she can do alone tomorrow. Teaching, he urged, must aim not at today's but at tomorrow's development, or, as he called it, the

zone of proximal development (ZPD) (Vygotsky, 1962). Learners need to be challenged, but with support and assistance that permit them to perform at the next level. The support and assistance that permits this performance is called **scaffolding**. The idea of the ZPD is similar to Krashen's notion of *i* + 1, discussed in Chapter 2, which suggests that input in second language acquisition should be just a little beyond the learner's current language proficiency. Vygotsky's idea refers to learning in general, whereas Krashen is concerned specifically with second language acquisition. The sheltering techniques discussed previously that make language comprehensible are a form of scaffolding.

Scaffolding refers to temporary structures used to facilitate construction of a building. In learning and development, students are constructing the ability to carry out complex processes, such as talking, reading, writing, thinking, and understanding the social and physical worlds around them. We define **scaffolds as temporary supports, provided by more capable people, that permit learners to perform a complex process before they are able to do so unassisted**. Assisted participation offers practice and development of a skill as an integrated whole, rather than drill on smaller aspects of the skill one at a time. Once proficiency is achieved, the scaffold is no longer needed and may be dropped.

For a concrete example, consider a 12-month-old child who is just beginning to walk but still has a tendency to fall flat on her well-padded bottom. Her father offers his hand to help her make it across the room. She succeeds with pride and delight. For a while, she needs the hand-holding support from more capable others to scaffold this complex process of coordinated psychomotor activity. Before long, though, she is able to walk by herself, and the scaffold is no longer needed. If some day she chooses to do more "advanced walking," such as walking on a balance beam, the same hand-holding scaffold may assist her. Thus, a similar scaffold may be applied later as more sophisticated versions of the complex process are attempted. In the sections that follow, we examine scaffolding as it applies to school learning.

SCAFFOLDING LANGUAGE ACQUISITION. Research in first and second language acquisition has shown how adults and more proficient language users may take a simple cue from a novice language learner, and restate the meaning in a more elaborated form. For example, a toddler might say, "Mommy, birdie" to which the mother might reply, "Yes, there's a pretty blue bird on the fence, isn't there?" The reply serves to acknowledge and elaborate the child's topic. At the same time, the mother's response provides linguistic input that is directly geared to the child's interest and language development level, thereby providing a scaffold for language acquisition. Similar kinds of scaffolding have been observed in classrooms serving second language learners, as teachers and more proficient peers repeat and elaborate on English learners' communicative efforts (Peregoy & Boyle, 1990a).

ROUTINES AS SCAFFOLDS. As a teacher, you no doubt spend considerable time at the beginning of the year getting your students used to your daily routines, including roll call, group work schedules, transitions, behavior expectations, and the like. That time pays off later in creating a smoothly functioning classroom. You may not have thought of it, but those routines also serve to scaffold language and literacy acquisition. For example, as the routine repeats, so does the language used. That repeated language is readily learned by novice English learners. At a more sophisticated level, process writing and guided reading also represent scaffolding routines.

FIGURE 3.10

DEPICTING SCAFFOLDING

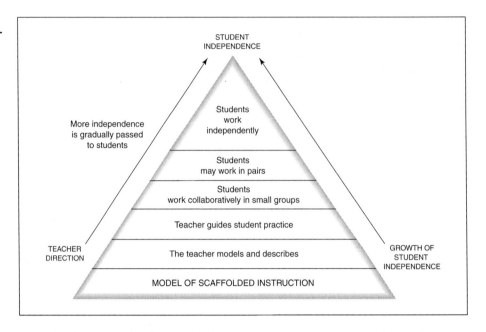

Consider for a moment the words of Catherine Snow (1977), "We think of routines as simple and unsophisticated...but their simplicity allows for the introduction, into slots created by the routine, of fillers considerably more complex in structure and/or content than could possibly be dealt with elsewhere" (p. 49). In process writing, for example, students get used to working a piece over until it is deemed publishable. Through the built-in routines of response and feedback, with corresponding revision and editing, students are scaffolded to a much higher level of performance than they could have achieved otherwise. Process writing, in fact, is an overarching scaffolding routine that incorporates **multiple, embedded scaffolds** (Peregoy, 1991; Peregoy & Boyle, 1990a, 1999a, 1999b) in each of the phases of the writing process: topic generation, writing, revising, editing and publishing. Figure 3.10 illustrates how teachers gradually relinquish responsibility to students through scaffolding.

A KEEP Example

One educational program that incorporates Vygotsky's ideas about scaffolding is the Kamehameha Elementary Education Program (KEEP) in Honolulu, Hawaii. KEEP was established in the late 1970's as a research and development center to meet the educational needs of native Hawaiian children descended from the original Polynesian inhabitants of the island chain (Tharp & Gallimore, 1988). These children, ethnic minority group speakers of Hawaiian Creole English, were not achieving well in school, particularly in reading (Au & Jordan, 1981). Through the concerted efforts of a team of psychologists, anthropologists, linguists, and educators, an innovative educational program was established, which became a laboratory and demonstration school.

Two especially interesting innovations were made. First, a communication feature of the children's home culture was incorporated into reading lessons. That is, discussion of stories was carried out through co-narration, or the joint narration of a story by two people. Co-narration, or "talk story," the researchers had found, was a feature of the native Hawaiian storytelling tradition to which the children were accustomed. In their home culture, co-narration of a story not only conveyed information, but it also served to reaffirm the relationship between the co-narrators. With this familiar communication style incorporated into reading lessons, children were more inclined to participate in lessons. In time, reading achievement scores increased and remained at national-norm levels for over a decade (Tharp & Gallimore, 1988, p. 116).

The second KEEP innovation over the decades has been the implementation of a teaching model based on the Vygotskian notion of assisted performance in the child's zone of proximal development. The teaching model emphasizes the teacher's ability to respond to the child's developmental level and to stretch the child's performance accordingly through modeling, feeding back, instructing, questioning, and other processes (Tharp & Gallimore, 1988). The teacher thereby "scaffolds" the child's development to the next level.

To illustrate the complex nature of scaffolding, as carried out in a KEEP kindergarten, Tharp and Gallimore (1988, pp. 138–146) provide a detailed description of an activity in which the teacher leads a group of six children in making peanut butter and jelly sandwiches. The experience later serves as the basis of a dictated story, or in this case a dictated recipe, using the traditional language experience approach (Allen, 1976; Stauffer, 1970). The "instructional conversation" between the teacher and children during the sandwich-making creates natural opportunities for the teacher to model, question, and instruct, thereby scaffolding children's linguistic and cognitive performance.

Gathering the children at a small table, the teacher begins with an improvised chant about making peanut butter and jelly sandwiches. Placing the peanut butter and jelly jars on the table with a loaf of sliced bread, she introduces the activity with a statement and a question (Tharp & Gallimore, 1988):

TEACHER: We're gonna make our peanut butter sandwich. What is the first
thing I'm going to need? [Produces a jar of peanut butter, a jar
of jelly, and a loaf of sliced bread in a bag.]

J: Get the bread!
[Child points to bread; reaches across the table and pats the bag
of bread.]

TEACHER: I need to get a piece of bread. What am I going to do with it?
[Reaches into the bag and retrieves a slice. J. nods approval.]

J: Put this first . . . and put this second.
[Touches peanut butter jar; touches jelly jar.]

TEACHER: Put it . . . [Hesitates]

J: Oh, no. Put this first . . . and this second.
[Touches jelly jar; touches peanut butter jar.]

R: Get the knife first, no get the knife in and spread it.

JK: Put the jelly on the sandwich, then that on the sandwich.
[Points to peanut butter.]

TEACHER: I put the jelly on top of the sandwich?
[Places jelly jar on top of sandwich.]

CHILDREN: (chorus) No! No! No!
[Two stand up; another points; they laugh and smile
with surprise and amusement.]

R: You open it.
[Takes jelly jar from teacher and removes lid.]

JK: Then you put it in.

TEACHER: Oh I need to twist the lid off the jar?

CHILDREN: Yes, yes and then you make like that.

R: First you have to do peanut butter . . .

J: No. That!
[Gestures toward jelly, disagreeing about which ingredient is applied first.]

R: [Shakes head in disagreement.]

TEACHER: I have to spread the peanut butter first? Are you sure?

R: Yeah, cause I tried it, that's [the truth] everybody's [looking at it].

TEACHER: How do I spread it? Do I take my finger, stick it in, and rub it all over the bread?

J: No this! You stick that in . . .
[Picks up knife; makes spreading motion with knife over bread.]*

At this point, the children get the idea that they are going to have to tell their teacher methodically, sequentially, and step-by-step exactly how to make this sandwich. The instructional conversation continues, with questioning, modeling, and feedback from the teacher. By requiring the children to organize the procedure logically and to provide explicit directions through language, not gesture, she is inviting them to perform in their zone of proximal development both cognitively and linguistically. Making language clear enough to stand on its own without gestures or reference to objects in the environment is a cognitive-academic skill required for school literacy. In fact, in the next phase of this activity children will produce a written recipe by dictating the procedure to the teacher. This language experience activity guided children's thinking and language toward forms acceptable for schoolwork and academic literacy, an important transition for all students, and especially for those whose ways of using language differ from those of the school (Heath, 1983; Michaels, 1979).

Scaffolds for First and Second Language Reading and Writing

Building upon scaffolding research, we have applied the metaphor to reading and writing, creating what we call **literacy scaffolds** (Boyle & Peregoy, 1990; Peregoy & Boyle, 1990b). Literacy scaffolds are reading and writing activities that provide built-in teacher or peer assistance, permitting students to participate fully at a level that would not be possible without the assistance. In other words, literacy scaffolds make it possible for students to work in their zones of proximal development in reading and writing, thereby challenging them to reach their next level in literacy development. Criteria defining literacy scaffolds are as follows:

1. Literacy scaffolds are applied to reading and writing activities aimed at functional, meaningful communication found in whole texts, such as stories, poems, reports, or recipes.

---

*Reprinted with permission from Roland J. Tharp and Ronald Gallimore, *Rousing minds to life: Teaching, learning, and schooling in social context* (New York: Cambridge University Press, 1988), pp. 138–139.

2. Literacy scaffolds make use of language and discourse patterns that repeat themselves and are, therefore, predictable.

3. Literacy scaffolds provide a model, offered by the teacher or by peers, for comprehending and producing particular written language patterns.

4. Literacy scaffolds support students in comprehending and producing written language at a level slightly beyond their competence in the absence of the scaffold.

5. Literacy scaffolds are temporary and may be dispensed with when the student is ready to work without them.

Perhaps the clearest example of a literacy scaffold is the interactive dialogue journal, in which student and teacher carry on a written conversation. Dialogue journals have proven useful for English language learners of all ages, from kindergartners to adults (Kreeft, 1984; Peregoy & Boyle, 1990a). Typically, the student makes a written entry in his or her journal, perhaps accompanied by an illustration, and the teacher then responds in writing with a comment or question that furthers the conversation. The dialogue journal thus duplicates, in written form, the scaffolding opportunities we saw earlier in the informal instructional conversations between adults and young children at home and at school. In their responses, teachers may model written language patterns by incorporating and expanding upon the students' entry, just as adults sometimes do in conversations with young children. Thus, the dialogue journal affords the teacher regular opportunities for scaffolding through questioning, modeling, and feedback. However, the scaffolding is always embedded in the natural flow of the written conversation between the student and teacher, with the focus on the personal interchange between them. Other examples of literacy scaffolds are described in

Reading her own published story, this little girl celebrates an achievement that was scaffolded by the process approach to writing.

the subsequent chapters, including shared reading, patterned writing, mapping, directed reading-thinking activity, and readers theater.

In summary, scaffolding helps students perform at a level somewhat beyond their unassisted capability. As teachers, we are constantly aiming to help students reach their next developmental level in all areas of learning and development. Few classroom teachers have the luxury of a research team to inform them of the nuances of their students' home cultures. However, classroom teachers have something that research teams generally do not have—the benefit of a deep, ongoing reciprocal relationship with students over time. Through the special teacher-child relationship and through thoughtful and sensitive trial and error, you will be in a position to judge which scaffolding routines work with your students and which do not. In fact, as you systematically observe your students, as you reflect on what you know about their families, and as you interpret their responses to you and your teaching, you will be expanding your role from teacher to teacher-researcher. Another area that requires research skills is assessment of student learning, a topic we turn to next.

Assessment of English Learners

Assessing students has always been a challenge no matter who your students are. Today's emphasis on standards-based instruction and accountability has increased dramatically the time, effort, and dollars devoted to assessment. In this section we discuss assessment as used for the purposes of: (1) English learner identification and program placement, (2) program evaluation, and (3) documentation of student progress. First, we provide background on basic concepts that underly current assessment procedures, both formal and informal, including discussion of standardized tests and performance-based assessment. We end the chapter with principles for classroom-based assessments. Specific assessment procedures are integrated into all subsequent chapters for oral language, vocabulary, early literacy, reading, writing, and content area literacy.

English Learner Assessment: Definition and Purposes

When we talk about **assessment**, we are referring to systematic procedures used to gather, analyze, and interpret information on student learning, achievement, or development. Assessment data deliver information, which may be stated, for example, in terms of a percentile, a raw score, or a verbal description. Careful **evaluation** of assessment data provides the basis for appropriate programmatic and instructional decisions. As teachers of English learners, we are primarily interested in assessing subject matter learning and English oral language, reading, and writing development. Bilingual teachers must also assess primary language and literacy development. Assessment serves three important purposes:

- Identification and program placement of students in need of special language support services
- Program evaluation for reporting to local, state, and federal education agencies

- Documentation of student learning and progress to
  - **a.** inform instructional decisions
  - **b.** communicate progress to parents

Student placement and program evaluation are generally initiated at the district level, whereas documentation of student learning and progress are the teacher's responsibility. Assessment procedures will depend on the purpose, as we shall discuss.

Basic Concepts and Terms Used in Assessment

Whenever we assess students, we have to observe their performance on a particular task in order to infer or estimate their knowledge, skill, or competence in that area. Assessment data may come from a variety of sources, including formal and informal measures. **Formal assessment** measures include standardized tests, such as group-administered standardized achievement tests in reading, language arts, and mathematics. Formal measures also include individually administered tests, such as those used to identify special learning needs. **Informal assessment** measures include such items as teacher-made tests, miscue analysis of oral reading, checklists, anecdotal observations, and student work samples. As a teacher of English learners, you will probably use all of these at different times with each of your students.

Formal assessment measures are designed according to rigorous testing theory and principles, including field testing to establish **validity** and **reliability**. A test is considered to have **content validity** if its items closely reflect the knowledge or skill it purports to measure. Suppose, for example, that you want to measure the essay-writing ability of all sophomore students. A test that collects an essay sample will be more valid than one that simply consists of multiple-choice items on punctuation, because the essay sample more closely reflects the skill being evaluated. A test is **reliable** if it yields similar results when retaken, usually with the use of two equivalent forms to lessen the possibility of a learning effect between testing and retesting.

Formal and informal assessment measures have different purposes, strengths, and limitations. In general, formal measures are designed to compare individuals or groups with a previously established **norm** or **criterion**. For **norm-referenced tests**, the test publisher determines the norm, that is, the average or mean score achieved by a large group of students broadly representative of those for whom the test is intended. A problem with norm-referenced tests stems from the fact that the norming population usually consists primarily of fluent English speakers, making comparisons with English language learners at best difficult to interpret, if not unfair and misleading. To interpret your English learner's performance on such a test, you need to bear in mind that you are comparing him or her with a primarily English proficient group. **Criterion-referenced tests** set up cut-off scores to determine the competence level achieved. If you have taken the California Basic Education Skills Test (CBEST), you have taken a criterion-referenced test for which the cut-off score is meant to indicate the basic level of skill in reading, writing, and mathematics needed to be a teacher. Standards-based assessments are criterion-referenced in that they establish a specific level of performance for determining whether a student has met the standard. When evaluating English learner performance on such tests, you have to consider whether the criterion is reasonable for your students.

In contrast to formal measures, **informal measures** compare individuals with themselves and with small groups, such as other students in your class. Informal measures are generally based on student work samples and student interactions during naturally occurring classroom situations, that is, direct measures of student ability. Formal measures are relatively easy for the teacher to administer and score but tend to be anxiety-producing for many students. On the other hand, informal measures are not as anxiety-producing for students, given that data are usually drawn from student performance during day-to-day classroom activities. However, considerable thought must go into collecting, organizing, and storing the information. In addition, analyzing the collection of student products requires time, effort, and thought from both the teacher and the student.

Efforts have been made to combine some of the best features of both formal and informal assessment in what is called **performance assessment** (cf. Fradd & McGee, 1994). The inclusion of performance indicators or benchmarks in curriculum standards illustrates the impact of this development. Performance assessment involves the direct observation and measurement of the desired behavior. For example, if problem solving using graphing is a curriculum goal, then assessment will consist of observing and evaluating students in the process of problem solving using graphs. Similarly, if the curriculum goal is for students to know how to write an autobiographical narrative, then assessment will elicit an autobiographical narrative to be evaluated. In this regard, performance assessment incorporates an element of informal assessment, that is, direct measure of the desired behavior. When performance assessment is used to compare student performance in different districts in a state, as with writing assessment, it incorporates an element of formal assessment, that is, cross-group comparison. In other words, data are collected in a systematic, standardized fashion so that valid group performance comparisons may be made. Assessment experts continue to struggle to find ways to meet the varying assessment demands for program evaluation and classroom use. This brief discussion has provided an overview of basic issues. Let us now consider how English learners are assessed, formally and informally, for the three purposes: student identification and program placement, program evaluation, and documentation of student learning and progress.

Identification and Placement of Students Needing Language Education Support Services

English learners are entitled by law to educational assistance that provides access to the core curriculum and English language development. The first order of business, therefore, is to identify students who need the support of a bilingual, ELD, or other language education support program. An established procedure for such identification involves two steps. First, a **home language survey** is sent to parents to find out whether a language other than English is spoken in the home. School districts usually have these surveys available in the various home languages of students in their communities. At times, a follow-up phone call may be necessary from an intepreter. If a language other than English is used in the home, the student must be tested for English language proficiency. Commercial, standardized English language proficiency tests are available for this purpose, with subtests for oral language, reading, and writing. Examples include the *Language Assessment Scales* published by CTB-McGraw Hill and the *IDEA Language Proficiency Tests* (IPT) published by Ballard and Tighe. For general information about language proficiency tests, you may visit the National Clearinghouse for English Language Acquisition website (AskNCELA, at http://www.ncela.gwu.edu/) or type in the test names as key words in an Internet search.

In the last decade or so, states have begun to develop their own language proficiency tests. For example, the WIDA Consortium has developed the WIDA-ACCESS Placement Test (W-APT) now used in 15 states to determine initial program placement. WIDA has also developed a test to measure annual gains in English language proficiency, ACCESS for ELLS®. For more information on the WIDA Consortium standards and assessments, visit www.wida.us. California uses it own California English Language Development Test (CELDT) for both program placement and for measuring annual progress in English language proficiency. If you are interested in the CELDT, we recommend the CELDT Communications Assistance Packet for Districts/Schools (California State Department of Education, 2003) available on the Internet.

Tests vary considerably in the kind of language elicited and in the methods used to analyze them. However, for a full picture of English language proficiency, and to meet current federal requirements, tests must address listening, speaking, reading, and writing. Oral language samples may be elicited by asking questions or by asking the student to tell a story about a picture or sequence of pictures. Reading tests usually include passages with multiple-choice comprehension questions to answer, whereas writing tests often elicit a writing sample for analysis. Scoring and analysis are usually conducted by the school district or by the test publisher. Test results are finally interpreted to yield a level of second language proficiency. For example, the WIDA framework identifies five language proficiency levels each, for listening, speaking, reading, and writing; the CELDT discriminates five levels as well. Regardless of the number of language proficiency levels, three categories emerge as important for program placement (1) non-English proficient (NEP), (2) limited English proficient (LEP), and (3) fully English proficient (FEP). School districts must provide support services for NEP and LEP students, with redesignation to FEP as the overall goal.

Limitations of Standardized Language Proficiency Tests

Standardized language proficiency tests have certain limitations that can lead to inappropriate program placement. For example, the fact that a student's score is based on a single performance sample elicited out of the context of routine classroom activity may lead to inaccurate appraisal of language proficiency. In addition, test performance is easily affected by nonlinguistic variables, such as lack of familiarity with the testing procedure, disinterest, and fatigue. Furthermore, to the extent that a student feels the pressure of a testing situation, performance may be affected by anxiety. Finally, different standardized language proficiency tests sometimes yield different levels for the same student. Use of a single test within a given state is helpful in this regard, but the problem persists if students move from one state to another. Because of these limitations, it is important for you to be aware of the possibility that a student has been inappropriately placed in your classroom based on language proficiency test performance. If you suspect a student has been misassigned to your classroom based on English language proficiency, you should check with your principal concerning procedures for retesting and reconsideration of the placement. Your judgment is extremely important and likely to be more accurate than the student's test performance.

Redesignation to FEP

Just as English learners have a legal right to alternative language support programs, they also have a legal right to exit these programs once they have gained sufficient English proficiency to succeed in the general education program. Redesignation to FEP is thus a critical matter requiring careful assessment of a student's ability to succeed educationally without special language support (Linquanti, 2001). Such assessment must be multidimensional, that is, based on multiple measures, including formal and informal measures of oral and written English, achievement test scores, and perhaps measures of academic performance in the primary language. In addition, it is important to include the judgment of teachers, parents, and any other resource personnel who have worked with the student.

Program Evaluation

School districts must comply with federal and state assessment requirements, which usually include annual standardized achievement testing in reading, language arts, and mathematics. Sensitive and thoughtful teachers have seriously questioned the validity of standardized tests for English learners, and rightfully so. Students must be able to read English if a test written in English is to measure performance accurately. Beginning and intermediate English learners are at a distinct disadvantage in this regard by virtue of English language proficiency alone. Another disadvantage stems from the timed format of standardized testing. Research shows that reading in a second language is slower than native-language reading, even at advanced stages of second language development (Fitzgerald, 1995). Thus second language test takers may score low, not because of a lack of knowledge, but because of the need for more time to finish the test. A final difficulty with standardized achievement tests is interpreting individual English learner performance. For English learners, the test publisher's norms are not appropriate unless the test was normed on English learners, which is seldom if ever the case. Furthermore, large-scale standardized achievement tests are technically not designed to reflect any individual's performance accurately, only group performance. Yet individual scores are reported to teachers and parents and are sometimes used to make decisions about a student's instructional program. In recognition of these problems, some school districts are limiting or modifying the use of standardized testing with English learners. At the least, it is important to consider a student's English language proficiency when interpreting his or her score.

As a teacher of English learners, you need to be informed about language proficiency and standardized testing instruments and procedures used in your district. In addition, you need to understand the strengths and limitations of these tests. Moreover, it is important that you know how to interpret and evaluate test results so that you can explain them to parents and consider them in your instructional planning. However, your greatest assessment responsibility will be the documentation of each student's learning and progress to make future instructional decisions and to communicate student performance and progress to parents.

Classroom-Based Assessment of Student Learning and Progress

Classroom-based assessment requires a systematic approach to inform instruction and document student learning. Previously we pointed out how effective teachers make a point of assessing students prior to instruction on a particular topic, skill, or procedure so as to modify or fine-tune their lesson planning to meet the needs of each individual. This type of assessment may include a short question-answer session, brainstorming as part of a K-W-L activity, or an anticipation guide. Another important source of information is student performance on previous assessments related to the current topic, skill, or procedure. Last but not least, you should also consider your own personal knowledge of each student's special interests, talents, and aspirations as you get ready to teach something new.

As you strive to obtain a clear picture of your students' progress on curriculum standards, keep your eyes open to allow for students to display breadth and depth of learning beyond the stated performance expectations. Your students might surprise you with what they are able to do during classroom projects and group work when these are relevant and important to their lives and interests. To catch your students at their best, you need to become a careful observer and data collector. The following principles, based on Ruddell and Ruddell (1995), provide guidelines for your classroom-based assessment, often referred to as **authentic assessment:**

1. Assessment should be based on observations of students as they engage in authentic learning tasks.
2. Assessment should be tied directly to your curriculum standards, instructional goals and teaching.
3. Assessment should be continuous, based on observations over a substantial period of time.
4. Assessment should take into consideration the diversity of students' cultural, linguistic, and special needs.
5. Assessment should be collaborative, providing opportunities for students to evaluate their own work.
6. Assessment should be multidimensional, that is, based on a variety of observations, in a variety of situations, using a variety of instruments.
7. Assessment should be based on current research and theory concerning language, literacy, and knowledge construction.

KEEPING CULTURAL CONSIDERATIONS IN MIND. We have already mentioned that a student's English language proficiency can affect test performance if the test is in English. Similarly, a student's cultural and experiential background

109

might also interact with your assessment procedures to cloud or clarify the results. Because schooling practices tend to conform more or less to middle-class European American experiences and values, students from other cultural backgrounds may be misassessed by virtue of cultural and other experiential differences. For example, middle-class European American students are often accustomed to telling about events as a routine activity at home. You have probably heard someone say to a child, "Tell Aunt Rosie about your trip to the zoo," or "Tell me what you did at school today." In this way, adults prompt what researchers call event casts (Heath, 1983; Schieffelin & Eisenberg, 1984). Narratives of this type are thus familiar discourse routines for many children. However, in some cultures event casts are seldom, if ever, asked of children. Children with event cast experience may be more able to participate when similarly prompted at school, as might occur in retelling an experience orally or in writing, or in retelling a story as part of a reading comprehension assessment. This is but one example of the subtle ways in which students' prior cultural experiences may prepare them differently for school tasks.

There are many ways in which cultural differences might affect student performance in your class, as discussed in Chapter 1. As the teacher, you can optimize your students' chances for success by offering a variety of formats in which to display knowledge, including individual, small-group, and whole-class instructional formats. In addition, you will want to provide students a variety of opportunities to display knowledge through their modalities of strength: for example, visual, auditory, kinesthetic, oral, written, or pictorial. Finally, it is important to offer private knowledge display opportunities, such as journal entries or individual conferencing, given that some students may be uncomfortable with public knowledge displays. As we mentioned previously when discussing scaffolding, you will not always know which of your classroom routines are best suited to the cultural and personal experiences of each student. However, by providing a variety of routines, by observing how individual students respond, and by modifying your procedures accordingly, you become a culturally responsive teacher, increasing student comfort and success in your classroom. In so doing, you become a better evaluator of student learning as well.

PLANNING SYSTEMATIC, CLASSROOM-BASED ASSESSMENT. Most of your classroom-based assessment will make use of informal assessment methods. These methods include direct observation, teacher–student conferences, student journals or learning logs, writing samples, running records of oral reading, and teacher-made tests. To be systematic, it is important that you decide which of these methods you will use and when. In addition, you will need to decide how to record, interpret, and store the assessment results for each student.

One way to compile assessment results is the **portfolio**. A portfolio is a folder that contains a variety of samples of student work related to a particular curriculum area. Students and teachers together decide which pieces of work to include in the portfolio, to display the student's best work. In writing, for example, students may keep a **working folder** of drafts and rewrites. Periodically, perhaps every four to six weeks, they select their best piece or pieces from their working folder to be placed in the portfolio. By the end of the semester, students have a set of writing samples that will show their progress over time. If students include all drafts for one of their portfolio entries, a picture of the work involved in arriving at publication is illustrated. Other items that may be included in a portfolio include interest inventories, lists of topics written or read about, running records of oral reading, unit tests, titles of books read, and any other classroom-based measurements that you believe will provide a rich and representative picture of your students' academic performance. Be sure to involve your students, not only in choosing items for inclusion in the portfolio, but also in devising ways to organize the contents that will make them easy for parents and others to read. For example, you may wish to include a table of contents and tabs to separate categories.

We have discussed many ways you can assess student learning. As you do so, you may also want to find ways to assess your own teaching. One useful resource is the *Sheltered Instruction Observation Protocol* or the SIOP model (Echevarria, et al., 2008), a 30-item list of observable teacher behaviors that comprise effective planning, delivery, and assessment of sheltered instruction or SDAIE. The protocol includes a 0- to 4-point rubric to mark each item, covering a range from highly evident to not evident. Figure 3.11 outlines components of SIOP content with corresponding examples. Over the last decade, the SIOP model has been carefully researched and refined. Large-scale evaluation studies have shown it to be a valid and reliable way to assess effective implementation of sheltered instruction. It can be used informally for self and peer evaluation or more formally as part of program evaluation.

In summary, English learner assessment is vitally important for student placement, program evaluation, and documentation of student learning and progress. In Chapter 11, we provide indepth discussion of individual literacy assessment. In addition, details on portfolios and other classroom-based assessments are provided in subsequent chapters as we discuss oral language, early literacy, writing, reading and literature, and content instruction. As always, it is important to consider the effects of English language proficiency and cultural differences in assessing English learners and interpreting their performance in classroom activities.

COMPONENT	EXAMPLE FEATURES
Preparation	Language and content objectives; Supplementary materials; Adaptation of content
Building Background	Explicit links to prior experience and past learning; Instruction on key vocabulary
Comprehensible Input	Speech modified to learner needs; Clear explanation of tasks; Variety of cues to support meaning
Strategies	Scaffolding; Variety of question types with sufficient wait time; Grouping; Social interaction opportunities; Clarify concepts in L1
Practice Application	Opportunities to apply language and content learning; Integration of 4 language skills
Fffectiveness of Lesson Delivery	Language and content objectives clearly supported; High student engagement; effective pacing
Lesson Review/Evaluation	Review of concepts and vocabulary; Feedback; Ongoing assessment of comprehension and learning

FIGURE 3.11

SIOP MODEL COMPONENTS AND EXAMPLE FEATURES

Summary

In this chapter, we have described and illustrated three interrelated instructional approaches: sheltered instruction, SDAIE; collaborative group work; and theme studies. We provided a detailed checklist of sheltering, or SDAIE, strategies and discussed how collaborative group work provides rich language and content learning opportunities as students discuss, debate, review, and otherwise negotiate meaning in their groups. Finally, we showed how thematic instruction gradually builds learners' background knowledge each day, providing children with maximum opportunities for becoming proficient communicators, readers, writers, and learners in their non-native language. We also discussed the concept of scaffolding as an important metaphor to help us identify teaching strategies that promote language and literacy development. Finally, we discussed important issues in English learner assessment. The following chapters build on this instructional framework and provide over one hundred specific strategies for language, literacy, and content learning.

Suggestions for Further Reading

Celce-Murcia, M. (Ed.). (2001). *Teaching English as a second or foreign language* (3rd ed.). Boston: Heinle & Heinle.

This edited text, in its third edition, is thoroughly comprehensive, with sections on teaching methodology, language skills (listening, speaking, reading, and writing), integrated approaches, "focus on the learner," and skills for teachers. We've relied on this excellent text for many years, and this edition adds nine new articles. Every teacher should have this one.

Cummins, J., Brown, K., & Sayers, D. (2007). *Literacy, technology, and diversity*: *Teaching for success in changing times*. Boston: Pearson/Allyn and Bacon.

This highly readable volume addresses literacy, pedagogy, assessment, and technology for promoting achievement and empowering minority and low-income students. Taking a critical approach, the authors analyze education policy and its impact on students and offer various specific program efforts to promote access and use of technology and promote student engagement in literacy, social studies, and mathematics.

Echevarria, J., Vogt, M., and Short, D. J. (2008). *Making content comprehensible for English learners: The SIOP Model* (3rd ed.). Boston: Pearson/Allyn & Bacon.

This book presents a systematic, research-based checklist for observing and evaluating how well sheltered instruction is implemented in any given lesson. The book provides theoretical background and classroom examples to help readers understand sheltered instruction and the model for evaluating its implementation. The complete observation protocol and an abbreviated version are provided in the appendix. The book also comes with a CD-ROM. Every teacher should have this book.

Gianelli, M. C. (1990). Thematic units: Creating an environment for learning. *TESOL Journal, 1,* (2), pp. 13–15.

Don't let the date of this excellent article on thematic units deter you. The author describes in some detail how she set up a thematic unit and its effect on her English learners. The results of using a thematic unit were that her students both improved their language abilities in addition to gaining knowledge in all areas of the school curriculum.

Herrell, A. & Jordan, M. L. (2007). *Fifty strategies for teaching English language learners* (3rd ed.). Upper Saddle River, NJ: Merrill/Prentice Hall.

This practical book contains fifty strategies you can integrate into your classroom. At the beginning of the text each strategy is categorized according to its function: supports comprehensible input, encourages verbal interaction, supports contextualizing language, reduces anxiety, encourages active involvement, and provides assessment information.

Rhodes, R. L., Ochoa, S. H., & Ortiz, S. O. (2005). *Assessing culturally and linguistically diverse students: A practical guide*. New York/London: The Guilford Press.

This volume offers a comprehensive, highly readable, hands-on guide to assessing culturally and linguistically diverse students. Step-by-step procedures and guidelines and a number of reproducible checklists and worksheets for immediate use by teachers and other educational personnel are offered. Topics include a detailed description of linguistically diverse populations in the United States, legal and ethical requirements in assessing diverse students, types of educational programs serving them, guidelines for using interpreters, cultural issues in assessment, language proficiency assessment in English and the native language, and guidelines for cognitive and academic assessment of diverse students. Highly recommended reading.

Richard-Amato, P. (2003). *Making it happen: Interaction in the second language classroom* (3rd ed.). White Plains, NY: Longman.

This textbook introduces a variety of approaches and classroom strategies for teaching English as a second language to students of any age. Examples of classrooms in different types of programs are provided.

Teachers of English to Speakers of Other Languages (2006). *PreK-12 English language proficency standards*. Alexandria, VA: Author.

This valuable resource provides English language proficiency standards with sample performance indicators for social and instructional language and for academic language use in language arts, social studies, science, and math.

Wink, J. (2004). *Critical pedagogy: Notes from the real world* (3rd ed.). New York: Addison-Wesley Longman.

If you have read about critical pedagogy but wondered how to turn its theoretical ideals into day-by-day practice in your classroom, this book is for you. Joan Wink invites us on a lively and engaging journey as she defines critical pedagogy succinctly and clearly, explains its origins, and then offers numerous examples of how theory can come alive through such classroom activities as problem posing, dialogue journals, and a useful problem-solving activity she calls "the mess." Finally, she wraps up with a discussion of why such pedagogy matters in the twenty-first century. This is a book that speaks to the heart and the mind with a vision for a better future for all.

113

Activities

1. Reread the vignette on *The Very Hungry Caterpillar*. Using the information in this chapter, discuss all of the things Roberto did to help his young, beginning English learners comprehend the story and write their own book. Do you find any strategies that have not been discussed in this chapter? Can you think of some strategies that Roberto should have used but didn't? How would you improve the lesson?

2. With a partner discuss the following ways of learning and rank each one from most to least helpful: learning from direct experience (including movies, pictures, and simulation games), learning from writing, learning from reading, learning in a large class lecture (in which there is little opportunity for questions and interaction), and learning in a small collaborative group (in which students can share their knowledge and help one another define terms). After you've ranked yours, share with your partner and discuss how each approach might be better depending on the situation. See how others in your class ranked the activities.

3. Think back to a memorable learning experience you had in elementary school. Jot down the experience as you remember it, making note of what you were learning about and what you were doing in the process of learning. Now

analyze the lesson to see how many, if any, sheltering techniques were used. Were any techniques used that we now define as sheltering techniques? If sheltering techniques were not used, to what do you attribute the strength of your memory? What made the situation memorable to you? What implications can you draw for your own teaching?

4. Take a lesson plan from a published source or one you have written yourself. Critically review the plan to analyze its comprehensibility for English learners. What modifications or additions could you make to ensure comprehension and participation by English learners? Is the lesson thematically oriented? Does the lesson involve collaborative group work? Does the lesson shelter information for students in a variety of ways? How would you change the lesson based on the information you now have

concerning some of the ways teachers provide instruction of English learners?

5. Try a theme study with a small group of children. Begin by brainstorming the question, "What are some things we would like to know more about?" Next, as a group, choose one topic to focus on. Write the topic on a piece of butcher paper and create two columns for listing "what we know" and "what we want to know." With the children, decide which question to investigate and how. With student input, create a list of books, people, and places to obtain the needed information. Students may choose to work alone or in pairs to present the final product of their learning to the rest of the group. When finished, make a new butcher paper list of "what we know now" and "new questions we have now." Discuss the pros and cons of working with children within a theme study.

PEARSON
myeducationlab
Where the Classroom Comes to Life

Video Homework Exercise
Teaching to Diverse Learning Styles

In the video we learn about strategies teachers may use to address the varied learning strengths and needs among students in their class, such as scaffolding; opportunities for social interaction; and offering a variety of ways to comprehend ideas and demonstrate learning through varied modalities (e.g., kinesthetic, auditory, visual). We then see a reading lesson which illustrates these strategies. Working with the whole group, the teacher reads a flip book about the character's feelings when preparing to make a speech to the class. During the reading, the teacher asks one student, Amber, to role play the character's actions and feelings. After reading, the teacher asks students to use Amber's actions and their personal experience to describe how the character felt.

Go to MyEducationLab, select the topic "Differentiating Instruction," and watch the video entitled "Teaching to Diverse Learning Styles."

1. Compare the strategies suggested in the video with the components of effective English learner instruction depicted in Chapter 3, Figure 3.3. Why is "teaching to diverse learning styles" an essential aspect of English learner instruction?

2. Looking closely at the flip book lesson, what does the teacher do that would be especially effective with English language learners? What additional modifications would be needed to accommodate students who are beginners in English language acquisition?

3. Consider Amber's performance as she role-plays the story while the teacher reads. What language skills does Amber need to role play successfully? How easy or difficult would the task be for a beginning English language learner? Why?

4

Oral Language Development in Second Language Acquisition

> **❝** Conversation is the laboratory and workshop of the student. **❞**
>
> —EMERSON

In this chapter, we discuss oral language development and its relationship to literacy and academic development. We also provide suggestions for promoting and assessing oral language development in second language acquisition. The following questions are addressed in the chapter:

1. What are the relationships among listening, reading, speaking, and writing? How do these relationships inform classroom teachers?

2. How do language form, communicative function, and social context combine to affect students' oral language performance in the classroom?

3. What are some characteristics of beginning and intermediate levels of second language oral proficiency in English?

4. What strategies will assist beginning and intermediate students in developing oral language proficiency?

5. How can structured observation tools, checklists, and anecdotal observations be used to describe and document oral language performance and development?

We look forward to visiting Lisa Garcia's third-grade classroom because her students are always so actively involved and because Lisa sees oral language as foundational to everything she does. When we enter her room we see children dancing and singing; we see them pantomiming snowflakes; we see them talking about books they have read or heard; we see them discussing the growth of the class bunny; and we see them preparing puppet shows. In addition, we know that when we enter the class, the children will expect us to be a part of the daily events. They often want to share their recent writing with us, or they will read or recite a pocket poem to us. In Lisa's class children get recognition for reading a favorite poem to anyone who enters the class or for reading the poem to someone in the schoolyard at recess time. The children carry favorite poems in their pockets, and when they recite a poem to someone, that person signs the poem.

Another reason we look forward to visiting Lisa's class is that something exciting and unpredictable happens every day. One day the children gave Lisa a surprise birthday party and presented a skit about their class. They laughed hilariously as one child played Lisa while others played themselves in the little drama. Because Lisa and her children value the social, dramatic, poetic, academic, and other functional uses of oral language in her classroom, they enjoy daily opportunities to forge understandings, create new meanings, and promote interpersonal relationships through talk.

Oral Language in Perspective

Walter Loban, a favorite professor of ours and a pioneer in researching oral language development of students from kindergarten through 12th grade, used to say:

> We listen a book a day,
> talk a book a week,
> read a book a month,
> and write a book a year.
>
> (cited in Buckley, 1992)

With this saying, Loban highlighted the pervasiveness of oral language in our lives; it is so pervasive, in fact, that we easily take it for granted—until plagued with a case of laryngitis. Reading and writing also play vitally important roles in our lives, but oral language interactions account for the bulk of our day-to-day communications, remaining the primary mode of discourse throughout the world.

For students learning English as a second language in school, oral language development plays a key role as well. When students are working or playing together, their conversations are based on concrete, here-and-now topics of current interest. As a result, opportunity abounds for them to negotiate meaning through requests for clarification, reference to objects at hand, and other face-to-face communication strategies. At the same time, the language used becomes comprehensible and usable as input for second language acquisition. To optimize classroom oral language learning opportunities, we need to make time each day for students to talk to each other while working in a variety of situations, including paired reading, group research projects, group work at learning centers, brainstorming a writing topic, sharing news with the entire class, and just visiting quietly while carrying out tasks. Although classroom oral language opportunities such as these may seem obvious to you, research indicates that teachers do from 65 percent to 95 percent of the talking in most classrooms (Lowery, 1980). Language development should be vocal and visible in classrooms where talk is valued as a learning tool.

Task-directed talk, including teacher talk during instruction, is useful in and of itself for second language acquisition if sheltering techniques are used, as discussed in Chapter 3. Talk is also important for helping students clarify concepts and arrive at their own understandings. As academic content increases in complexity, the use of small- and large-group discussion plays a vital role in promoting students' conceptual understanding and learning. Consistent with the value we place on oral language interactions, we incorporate opportunities throughout this book for students to develop their own thinking through talking and responding as they read, write, and learn in English, because it is the integrated use of oral and written language for functional and meaningful purposes that best promotes the full development of second language proficiency.

Integration of Listening, Speaking, Reading, and Writing

What does it mean to integrate listening, speaking, reading, and writing? In natural, day-to-day experience, oral and written language uses are not kept separate and isolated from one another. Instead, they often occur together, integrated in specific communication events. For example, when you are reading the Sunday newspaper, you may comment on an article to your roommate or spouse, engendering a discussion about it. Such discussion may lead you to reread parts of the article to clarify questions that emerged in the discussion. Similarly, when the phone bill arrives, you might have an extended discussion of its written contents to decide who owes what, or whether one or more members of the household needs to stop making so many long-distance calls. If your parents were immigrants and spoke little English when you were a child, you may have had the experience of translating for them and helping them fill out forms at the doctor's office. In each of these real-life situations, oral and written language uses intermingle as people go about the business and pleasures of life, and the intermingling of oral and written language occurs in literate societies across ethnic and social class boundaries (Heath, 1983; Vásquez, 1991).

Listening, speaking, reading, and writing also occur naturally together in learning events in school at all grade levels, even though traditionally they were taught separately. (See Chapter 3 for more discussion.) In primary grades, for example, the teacher may read a picture book aloud, taking time along the way to let children orally predict what will happen next or to discuss the characters or plot. Older students may perform a play from a written script, engaging in lengthy discussion over the fine points of interpretation, with the final result being a dramatic oral performance of the play. When students write stories, they read what they write, ask others to read and comment on their writing, and perhaps read their writing aloud to celebrate its completion. In all these situations, a written text has been the subject of oral discussion and interpretation, demonstrating how oral and written language become naturally interwoven during a particular communication event. In school, you enrich each school day when you give children opportunities to interweave oral and written language for functional, meaningful learning purposes.

117

"My boy, Grand-père is not the one to ask about such things. I have lived eighty-seven peaceful and happy years in Montoire-Sur-le-Loir without the past anterior verb form."

Source: © The New Yorker Collection 1973 Everett Opie from cartoonbank.com. All Rights Reserved.

Relationships Among Listening, Speaking, Reading, and Writing

Another way to look at the integration of the four language processes is to consider how they interrelate during language development. In first language acquisition, we know that all children, barring severe abnormalities, become grammatically competent speakers of the mother tongue by about age 5. Subsequent language development relates primarily to vocabulary acquisition and expansion of the functions for which language is used. Competence in reading and writing, on the other hand, is a much later development and one not universally achieved. Thus, oral language development occurs earlier and more fully than written language development in first language acquisition.

Various patterns emerge among students who are learning English as a second language in school. For young English learners with little literacy in the home language, basic oral language competence is likely to emerge earlier than competence in reading and writing (Fradd & McGee, 1994). For older students who know how to read in their first language, however, the pattern may be different. Some of these students may develop competence in written English earlier than oral English. In either case, a good deal of time is spent simultaneously developing both oral and written language abilities. We also know that English language learners do not need to be fully proficient in oral English before they start to read

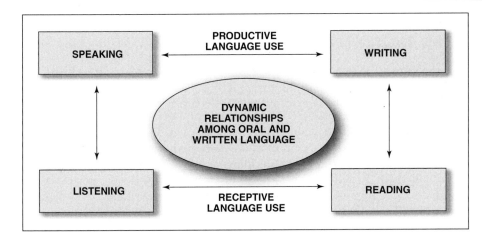

FIGURE 4.1

RELATIONSHIPS AMONG
WRITTEN AND ORAL
LANGUAGE

119

and write (Hudelson, 1984). Furthermore, second language knowledge can be developed from written and oral input, provided that the text is comprehensible to the language learner (Elley & Mangubhai, 1983). The relationships among listening, speaking, reading, and writing during development, then, are complex relationships of mutual support. Practice in any one process contributes to the overall reservoir of second language knowledge, which is then available for other acts of listening, speaking, reading, or writing. For this reason, it is important to provide abundant exposure to functional, meaningful uses of both oral and written language for all learners.

Figure 4.1 illustrates the interrelationships among listening, reading, speaking, and writing. More specifically, listening and reading are receptive uses of language: Messages are received by ear or by eye, and meaning is reconstructed based partly on prior knowledge. Listening and reading are not passive processes, however. Listeners and readers must actively take the speaker's words and recreate the message to comprehend it. Thus, when you assist students with listening comprehension, you are assisting them with reading comprehension. Conversely, speaking and writing are productive uses of language: The speaker or writer must *create* the message for an audience. When you assist students with spoken composition, therefore, you are assisting them with written composition. Moreover, reading can be one of the most important ways we develop oral vocabulary, and writing helps us learn how to compose in oral language. Thus, in our day-to-day lives oral and written language are interwoven like threads in a tapestry, each supporting the other to create the whole picture (Boyle, 1979).

We have spent some time discussing the integration of listening, speaking, reading, and writing to emphasize the importance of creating learning opportunities that involve using all four interrelated language processes. We have described two general reasons for this recommendation. First, in the course of day-to-day living, people move back and forth from oral to written modes during communication because both serve essential functions. The same holds true for the kinds of communication that promote learning in the classroom. Thus, the integration of listening, speaking, reading, and writing is functionally appropriate. Second, practical use of each language process provides both specific development of that process and overall language development in English. As teachers, we want to develop each student's abilities to the fullest as listeners and speakers, readers, and writers.

Form, Function, and Social Context in Oral Language Use

As you begin to focus on your students' oral language use, you need to take into account language forms, functions, and social contexts. As you begin to facilitate students' oral language competence, you will want to consider how social context affects choice of language form for a given language function or purpose. The social context consists of the social setting, the speakers, and the social and power relations among them. Language forms include choice of words, grammar, and pronunciation. Language functions are the communicative intentions or purposes of speakers' utterances (see Table 4.1). For example, consider a social setting consisting of parents, grandparents, and three teenage boys having dinner at home. One of the teenagers wants the salt, which is near his younger brother. He says, "Hey, gimme the salt, woudja?" If the salt were near his grandmother, he might say instead, "Grandma, can you pass me the salt?" He might even say "please." If this same family were having dinner at a formal banquet, the teenager might be a little more formal in his request of his brother, saying perhaps, "Could ya pass the salt over here please?" The teenager's choice of language form has varied according to formality of the social setting and his relationship with the person to whom he addressed his request. The social context in which language is used plays an important role in communication, setting parameters, of formality or politeness, for example, that guide linguistic choices.

The social context of language use places different cognitive and social demands on speakers that may affect the quality of their oral language performance. The same thing can happen, though perhaps less obviously, in one's native language. Consider, for example, the difference between a casual chat with a friend about a movie you have just seen and a formal job interview in which six interviewers are seated around a boardroom table facing you. The two situations differ considerably in the extent to which you "watch your language" and attempt to be clear, precise, and grammatically correct. For English language learners, the more formal and cognitively demanding situation can trigger noticeably more errors in pronunciation, grammar, and vocabulary than would generally occur in a less formal situation. This being the case, you can see why it is important to observe students in various social contexts or communication situations, formal and informal, to accurately assess their oral proficiency.

As we discuss students' oral language proficiency, we will refer not only to language forms but also to language functions. Table 4.1 illustrates **Halliday's functional categories** (1985) for oral language use along with corresponding classroom examples. You can develop specific activities in your classroom to expand students' ability to use language to carry out a variety of communicative functions. For example, Halliday's interactional function deals with getting along with others and can be translated into cooperative group work in your classroom. Group work enhances students' growth in language, building on conversational skills they already possess and easing adaptation to school routines. As teachers, we are charged with the task of developing students' abilities to use language effectively for heuristic (scientific discovery and problem solving) and informational functions. Thus K-12

TABLE 4.1 • LANGUAGE FUNCTIONS AND ANALOGOUS CLASSROOM EXPERIENCES

FUNCTIONS	CLASSROOM EXPERIENCES
Instrumental: I want; language as a means of getting things, of satisfying needs	Child clarifying instructions from morning routines; asking for supplies in play store or kitchen; asking for book in class library
Regulatory: Do as I say; controlling the behavior, feelings, or attitudes of others	Developing pantomimes and role-playing routines with partners or in groups; determining steps for completing projects
Interactional: Me and you; social interaction, getting along with others	Working in cooperative and collaborative groups on projects, art activities, and play
Personal: Here I come; pride and awareness of self, expressions of individuality	Sharing and telling about oneself; dictating language experience stories to others; sharing personal experiences
Heuristic: Tell me why; seeking and testing knowledge	Asking the teachers and students how something works; explaining the ideas in a story or retelling a story
Imaginative: Let's pretend; making up stories and poems; creating new worlds	Using wordless books to create new stories; using pictures to create stories; using creative dramatics to act out original ideas
Informative: I've got something to tell you; communicating information, description, ideas	Sharing ideas about what should be studied in a project or theme cycle; explaining what happened during a school event or describing a favorite television show
Divertive: Enjoy this; jokes, puns, riddles, language play	Telling riddles and jokes during special time devoted to this purpose

schooling serves to expand children's and young adults' repertoires in a variety of oral language functions.

While keeping in mind our philosophy concerning the integration of the four language processes serving a variety of communicative functions, we will spend the remainder of this chapter discussing English learners' oral language development. We begin with a discussion of oral language proficiency characteristics of beginning and intermediate English learners. Next, we provide descriptions of classroom activities that promote oral language development, followed by procedures for documenting oral language performance and development during classroom activities.

Describing Oral Language Performance of Beginning and Intermediate English Learners

We have undertaken to provide instructional strategies for English learners who are not yet fully proficient in English. We assume that fully proficient English learners will be able to benefit from the same instructional program, provided you validate them personally and culturally in the educational process. Most of the reading, writing, and learning ideas in this book are appropriate or can be adapted for all students, not just beginning and intermediate English learners. Thus, you may use the strategies with fully proficient English learners and native English speakers as well, according to your judgment.

In keeping with our concern for English learners described as limited in English proficiency and to facilitate your use of this book, we have taken the larger category of limited English proficiency (LEP) and divided it into two subcategories of English learners: (1) beginning and (2) intermediate. We use these categories in this chapter in reference to oral proficiency and in subsequent chapters to describe second language reading and writing proficiency. We include non-English speakers in our beginner category because the strategies we suggest work as well for them as for children who have already begun to speak the new language. As you read on, bear in mind that these are broad, general guidelines, not levels set in stone. We designate activities as appropriate for beginning and intermediate English learners for your convenience. However, please keep in mind that no activity should be withheld from any particular student solely on the basis of perceived English language proficiency. It is all too easy to misjudge a child's language competence because language performance varies across situations and from week to week as a result of the dynamic and context-specific nature of language proficiency. Moreover, motivation tends to stretch children's performance. Therefore, we recommend that you allow students the choice to take part in more difficult activities according to their interests and desires. You may be in for some pleasant surprises!

Second Language Oral Proficiency of Beginning English Learners

The beginner phase of second language development starts immediately on exposure to the new language. Early on, the child may neither understand nor speak a word of English. Soon, however, language comprehension develops as a result of opportunities for social interaction with speakers of the new language and the comprehensible input that is generated. Although it is important not to force beginners to speak, the fact is that shortly, within perhaps a week to a few months, most students will naturally begin to speak on their own (Terrell, 1981). At this point, their speech is likely to be limited to simple phrases and expressions that have highly functional communicative payoffs, such as "OK," "No," "Wanna play," "I wanna she go, too," and "I donno" (Wong Fillmore, 1983). As beginners develop, they are able to generate utterances according to simple grammatical rules, enabling them to carry out various tasks according to their own needs and purposes. The conversation in Example 4.1, described by Lily Wong Fillmore (1980), shows a young beginner's attempt to get an eraser back from her friend Cathy.

EXAMPLE 4.1 • BEGINNING-LEVEL SECOND LANGUAGE DEVELOPMENT

CATHY: Gimme 'raser! [*Takes Kim-girl's eraser.*]
KIM-GIRL: [*Looks up crankily. Turns to Lily Wong Fillmore and complains:*]
Can I eraser? Se took my 'raser. Se want 'raser.
This Edlyn gip me.
                [*She grabs microphone that has been placed right in front of her and says into it:*]
Gip me 'raser, yah!
Gip me pencil, yah!
Gip me chopstick, no!
Gip me crayon, yah!
Can I hab color? No way!
That's all! Bye-bye!

Source: Lily Wong Fillmore, "Learning a Second Language: Chinese Children in the American Classroom," J. E. Alatis, ed., *Current Issues in Bilingual Education: Georgetown University Roundtable on Languages and Linguistics* (Washington, D.C.: Georgetown University Press, 1980), p. 323.

Kim-girl is at the table doing seatwork. Cathy, Sin Man, Suh Wah, and Chui-Wing are at the same table; they have been arguing over the possession of a pink eraser all morning. As you can see in the example, Kim-girl makes use of various formulaic expressions, such as "That's all," "Bye-bye," and "No way." In addition, in this conversation, she demonstrates her ability to use simple present tense grammar for statements and questions when she says: "Can I eraser? Can I hab color? Se want 'raser. This Edlyn gip me." Her pronunciation shows some influence from her native language, Korean, in the use of se for she and gip for give. As a beginner in English, Kim-girl is resourceful in using her rudimentary English knowledge to try to get her eraser back. She also takes the opportunity for pattern practice with her litany of "Gip me" sentences. With limited formal language knowledge in terms of grammar, vocabulary, and pronunciation, Kim-girl is effective in achieving her communicative goal: the return of the eraser.

Your initial concern for beginners when they first arrive is to provide social-emotional support by assigning new students to a home group and a buddy, preferably one who speaks the child's home language. The buddy accompanies the newcomer everywhere throughout the school day, including to the bathroom, cafeteria, and bus stop. Meanwhile the home group assumes responsibility for the new child during routine classroom activities. Some teachers set up home groups of four to five students each at the beginning of the school year. These groups remain fairly stable throughout the year to create interpersonal support and cohesion. With such groups in place, much responsibility for caring for a new student may be transferred from the teacher to the home group. These assignments help meet the safety, security, and belonging needs of a new student and create the social interaction matrix from which language acquisition begins to grow.

At the beginner level, support for participation in lessons comes from three sources: the teacher, the other students, and the newcomers themselves. Early on, you may provide some tasks that do not require speech but rather invite a non-verbal participatory response. For example, if a group is working on a thematic

When English learners work and play with native English speakers, language learning opportunities occur naturally and often.

124

project, the newcomer may be involved in drawing, painting, or coloring a mural with the assistance of the other group members. In this way, the child contributes actively to the group project, while interacting through concrete and context-embedded language. Drawing or painting a mural is actually a high-level cognitive activity. Information gleaned from the theme study must be synthesized and portrayed accurately and meaningfully. Thus art becomes a valid academic learning tool for English language learners, just as it can be for native English speakers. Working on the mural project can also promote language development because active involvement in a low-risk, small-group activity means that a good deal of talk will go on, providing excellent input for language acquisition.

Similarly, you and the other students can make use of sheltering techniques, such as gestures, paraphrasing, and checking for understanding, to help make lessons and routine activities more understandable to the newcomer. Finally, you can make sure that small-group activities take place frequently, to create numerous opportunities for social interaction. With this kind of support, beginners will gradually advance toward the intermediate phase described next.

Second Language Oral Proficiency of Intermediate English Learners

Intermediate English learners are able to understand and speak English in face-to-face interactions, and they are able to speak with minimal hesitation and relatively few misunderstandings. Nevertheless, because their grammatical abilities (syntax, semantics, phonology) are still developing, you may notice features in their speech that are not typical of standard English. For example, students may at times confuse *he* and *she*. They may not conjugate verbs conventionally, saying things like, "My friend, she like to read a lotta books," using *like* instead of *likes*.

Even though these speech differences may nag at you for correction, we recommend that you control the natural tendency to constantly correct students' grammar in the middle of a conversation. Instead, make a point of noticing how much the child can now do with the new language. Show interest by asking questions that focus on the activity at hand, encouraging the student to tell you more. Build in and model appropriate grammar and vocabulary as you respond, thereby providing input that is tailored to the student's immediate linguistic needs and interests. You may be surprised to find that with patient listening your student is able to understand and discuss ideas at a fairly complex level. For example, intermediate students may be able to recall the details of a story, identify main ideas, predict what will come next, and, perhaps, summarize a plot. However, at this phase of development, students are likely to struggle to formulate their ideas in their new language, both orally and in writing. To get an idea of an intermediate English learner's oral language, take a look at how Teresa

---

EXAMPLE 4.2 • INTERMEDIATE-LEVEL SECOND LANGUAGE SPEAKER

SUZANNE: Was it scary?

TERESA: No, it wasn't escary. But, well . . . First it was scary but then the other one no. Because there was . . . First a little girl . . . There was a television and the father was sleeping in the . . . in a . . . *sillón*? in like a chair. And then the little girl pass the television and she said, "Right here!" Then . . . then a hand get out of the television and she said, "Ouch!" And then a little boy was sleeping and the little girl sleep here and the boy here and then he see all the time a tree and then . . . then . . . there was outside a tree . . . a tree. But it look ugly in the night. It look like a face . . . And then he was escary. Then he tell his father and his father said OK. Just count 1, 2, 3 to not escare. Then . . . then . . . the . . . he . . . the little girl and the little . . . the two brothers go in with the mother and her father because they're still escare.

---

described the movie *Poltergeist* to us (Example 4.2). Teresa, a fifth-grader whose first language is Spanish, has been learning English since the third grade.

As you can see, Teresa is quite expressive in English and is able to provide a rather detailed account of the movie. She employs her developing vocabulary with a variety of grammatical rules, using both past and present tense forms. Furthermore, she is able to coordinate her linguistic knowledge without hesitation much of the time. The aspects of Teresa's speech that indicate her intermediate level of English language development consist primarily of (1) her unconventional verb use (e.g., "hand get out," "little girl sleep," "it look ugly"), (2) nonidiomatic expressions (e.g., "he see all the time a tree," "the little girl pass the television"), and (3) occasional groping for appropriate vocabulary items (e.g., "*sillón*, in like a chair" and variations of the word *scare*: scare, scared, scary).

During the intermediate phase of second language development, you can support students' participation in learning activities by continuing with the sheltering techniques and small-group collaboration discussed previously. In addition, now is the time to involve students in more linguistically demanding tasks. For one thing, intermediate English language learners know sufficient English to be able to serve as the buddy of a newly arrived non-English speaker. In terms of classroom learning activities, the intermediate student will be able to hold a speaking part in a story dramatization or readers' theater, or any other more formal language activity that permits rehearsal. In addition, during this phase, students may enjoy participating in small-group discussions of stories, science experiments, and other activities.

As intermediate-level English language learners progress, they may appear able to use English with nearly as much facility as their native English-speaking counterparts. Their speech may be fluent, and you might find them responding with enthusiasm during whole-class and small-group discussion. Their reading and writing may be relatively fluent as well. At this point, it is important to continue both sheltering techniques and group collaboration. More advanced intermediate students are capable of understanding steady streams of verbal instruction, but you still need to accompany your words with charts, graphic organizers, concrete objects, and pictures to convey meaning. These efforts will enhance learning for all students. In addition, intermediate students can benefit

125

from hearing the teacher use technical vocabulary, provided that it is introduced with concrete experiences and visual support, such as graphs and pictures, that parallel your verbal explanations.

Promoting Oral Language Development in the Classroom

The classroom is a natural environment for a large variety of oral language learning opportunities, and you will find that the following chapters build on and integrate this oral language foundation with writing and reading. As the teacher, you can organize your classroom in ways that encourage the two most important elements of oral language development: **comprehensible input** and **social interaction**. Keep in mind that a predictable schedule helps students adjust to the classroom and provides easily acquired basic vocabulary with the repeated routines.

In addition to the basic routines of roll call, recess, snack, lunch, and dismissal, the use of routine instructional events also provides oral language learning opportunities. Some typical routine instructional events include circle time, journal time, literature study circles, process writing, projects, theme studies, and other lesson sequences in content areas, such as math, science, and social studies. To the extent that these instructional events maintain the same structure while the content changes, they provide a familiar routine with repetition of familiar language that scaffolds student participation and learning (Boyle & Peregoy, 1991; Peregoy, 1991, 1999.) For example, a literature study circle has a small-group discussion format centered on one book. The format remains stable throughout the year, but the content, that is, the book being discussed, changes. Another stable feature of the literature study circle is the discussion of literary elements and the informal turn-taking procedures. Thus students become familiar and comfortable with the literature study circle as an interactional format that supports their oral language use and development.

Whether you are engaging your students in literature study, process writing, or theme studies, it is always important to review your own instructional delivery to incorporate additional cues to convey meaning, especially nonverbal cues, such as dramatization, gesture, pictures, graphic organizers, and concrete objects. As a teacher–researcher you can analyze and evaluate ways in which classroom activities and verbal/visual adaptations work with your English learners by keeping a daily log or by videotaping lessons for later analysis. Verbal strategies that help students understand your talk include paraphrasing, repeating key vocabulary in context, and summarizing main points. Social interaction can be promoted in the classroom by encouraging students to work in pairs and groups. These strategies for sheltering, scaffolding, and group work were described in detail in Chapter 3.

In addition to the oral language development opportunities available during managerial and instructional routines, there are a number of wonderful learning activities that showcase oral language use in ways that promote acquisition. Interestingly, many of these activities are based on the arts. This makes sense if you stop to consider that the arts employ nonverbal media of communication. When these media are combined with language use, a natural scaffolding is provided for comprehension and production of oral language. The activities described in the following pages can be integrated into literature study, theme studies, and process writing, or they can take on a life of their own. Because they provide opportunities for negotiation of meaning through social interaction, they facilitate oral language development. Each activity can be easily adapted for beginning- or intermediate-level students. In most cases we give examples of possible adaptations that make student participation easier or more difficult so that you may adjust the level to challenge your students appropriately.

Using Games in Second Language Classrooms

In our teaching at the elementary, secondary, and college level, we have used games, such as simulation games, drama games, pronunciation games (Tatsuki, 1996), grammar games, story games, and writing games, to improve student learning and to create an atmosphere of ease, creativity, and fun. We especially enjoy and recommend drama warm-up activities like those in Spolin (1963/1983) and described at the end of this chapter. We believe that any lesson that allows us to use a game improves student learning and attitude. Games create experiences with language and ideas, and "experience is the glue that makes learning stick." Throughout this book we give examples and recommend games for motivating, engaging, and getting feedback from students (Wisniewska, 1998). At the end of this chapter we recommend a classic book full of games for beginning, intermediate, and advanced English language learners (Wright, Betteridge, & Buckby, 2002). You can start with this classic book and easily adapt ideas for your own classes. For example, older students can make board games based on content they are studying. Younger students might create games based on the stories they are reading. Finally, with your guidance, students can make and play their own games based on a game, such as Monopoly (Yang, 1992). You won't be disappointed if you try games.

Songs

Sing a song a day at least! Songs bring levity, laughter, and beauty into your classroom. Songs also promote a feeling of unity in the class, particularly important when differences among students prevail. In addition, all students can participate at some level, regardless of English language proficiency. Some songs may be related to a theme or topic of study, whereas others may be favorite tunes suggested by your students. Bear in mind that songs are language based, so you will need to provide cues to meaning, such as pictures, pantomime, or gestures. We recommend that you post song lyrics accompanied by pictures or rebus symbols to convey meaning. In addition, you may wish to copy lyrics for each student to illustrate and keep in a song book. Because songs are popular with all ages, this activity can be successful throughout the grades. Just make sure your students have some say in which songs they get to sing.

One final note: Although we suggest songs for English language development, you might also want to invite any and all willing students to share a song with the class in their home language by bringing a recording or by singing it. It can be a fine cross-cultural experience for everyone. We remember the day an East Indian girl, Barjinder, sang a beautiful song in her native language. When she finished, the class sat in awed silence and then broke out in spontaneous clapping. Barjinder looked down with a smile, beaming with pride at her classmates' enthusiastic response.

INTERNET RESOURCES

Randall's Cyber Listening Lab (**www.esl-lab.com**) contains hundreds of listening activities at easy, medium, and hard levels. It also contains information on speaking and pronunciation. Activities are listed under categories such as general, academic, and vocabulary. If you want to explore further the site has much more than just oral language information and activities. The Region 10 Education Service Center **www.region10.org/** contains specific lesson plans in various content areas and downloads in areas such as sheltered instruction for secondary math and science, literacy stations in the bilingual classroom, language transfer issues and the EL, improving writing instruction for adolescent linguistically and culturally diverse students, word bag activity, and scaffolding language and learning: literacy strategies for ELs. The site also contains links to many other valuable sites

Drama

Acting out stories and events in math, science, history, literature, or theme studies can be a highly motivating way for students to process and present information they have studied. Dramatic enactments in the classroom range from informal to formal. For drama at its least formal, you can provide props in a dramatic play center of your classroom. During free time, students create their own dramas within the context of the props. Changing the props from time to time is important to stimulate new interest and new topics for dramatic play. Another dramatization technique has been developed by early childhood educator Vivian Paley (Weinborg, 1989). In this self-expression process, children first dictate a story for you to write down. Later, a child dramatizes the story with help from friends as you read the story during group time. A third way to encourage informal dramatization is to make props available for enacting stories that are currently being read in the classroom.

A favorite book of ours, *Improvisations for the Theater* (Spolin, 1963/1983), outlines numerous drama techniques, beginning with simple pantomimes, progressing to brief, context-embedded dialogues, and moving on to one-act plays. For example, early in the year students might develop warm-up routines in which they mirror a partner's every move; later, they mime catching a ball that changes from a basketball to a soccer ball to a tennis ball. The nonverbal warm-up activities involve all students and create confidence and concentration, preparing them for later activities that require oral language use.

The next level of activities involves students in brief improvisations based on a situation for which they create a dialogue. For example, the teacher might say that the children are stuck in an elevator for 10 seconds, and then for five minutes, and, finally, for two hours. The students then create appropriate dialogue for each of the situations. Gradually, the activities lead students to where they can improvise little plays of their own. Drama activities provide students with a variety of contextualized and scaffolded activities that gradually involve more participation and more oral language proficiency; they are also nonthreatening and a lot of fun. The Spolin book and other books containing hundreds of developmentally appropriate activities are annotated at the end of this chapter.

Dramatizing Poetry

Poetry also provides an excellent springboard for dramatization (Gasparro & Falletta, 1994) and is effective with English learners of all ages. Selecting the right poem is essential. Poems that present minidramas or that express strong emotions, attitudes, feelings, or opinions work best (Tomlinson, 1986). One such poem that appeals to all ages is "The Crocodile's Toothache" (Silverstein, 1974), a hilarious dialogue between a crocodile and his dentist. For poem enactment, you begin by reading the poem aloud, modeling not only pronunciation but also dramatic intonation and stress. You may wish to have the poem copied on chart paper with some pictures to help convey meaning. During the first readings, you need to clarify difficult or unusual words, making sure that your students generally understand the poem. If you like, you may next invite all your students to read the poem chorally. Finally, in pairs or groups, your students prepare a dramatic rendition of the poem to be presented to the entire class. If you find that you and your students enjoy dramatizing poetry, you will want to start a collection of poems that fit in with content areas and themes you teach. In this way, poem dramatizations will become integrated into your curriculum.

Recently, we had the opportunity to observe fourth-grade English learners performing a skit on the California Gold Rush, a topic designated by the state curriculum framework. In this integrated curriculum project, students incorporated songs, poems, and dramatizations in ways that promoted oral and written language development. The teacher began by providing a variety of experiences to give the students a feel for the Gold Rush era. The class visited historical museums where they learned about people arriving from all over the world by horse, by foot, by wagon train, and by ship to try their luck in the California foothills. Students sang songs of the era, such as "Sweet Betsy from Pike," and read poems and newspaper articles from the period. They saw films depicting gold panning, sluice boxes, and tent towns. They learned that miners wore denim jeans, giving the Levi Strauss Company its start as a factory outlet in San Francisco. They also made sourdough bread and sourdough pancakes. They even had the chance to pan for gold at a nearby park. The "gold" (painted rocks) had been planted beforehand by their industrious teacher. After these experiences, the children decided they wanted to write a play about a family moving to California to join the Gold Rush. The teacher divided the class into four groups, and each group put together a script for a short drama. Next the groups gathered props for their skits. The teacher set aside an hour a day for one week for rehearsal. Finally, each group performed its 10-minute skit for the rest of the class as a culminating event. As it happened, the student teacher had arranged to videotape the skits, adding to students' excitement and pride.

In developing their skits, these fourth graders used oral language for a variety of functions. In addition, they used written language to scaffold their oral performance of songs, poems, and the skit itself. First, they synthesized large amounts of information and selected aspects they wished to portray in their skit. They did this through informal discussion in small groups, proposing and evaluating ideas and then making decisions by consensus. Next, they created a basic story to tell in their skit, selected characters to play different roles, and wrote out dialogue. Some groups incorporated songs and poems learned during the theme study. One group read aloud a letter written to a relative back home to convey the character's inner feelings. During rehearsal, students used a great deal of directive language to organize, practice, and perfect the skit. Finally, each group gave a formal performance of their skit. As a follow up, the students critiqued the performances, including oral performance aspects, such as diction, volume, and pace. Because the skits had been videotaped, the children were able to see and hear themselves over again. As you can see, the oral language development opportunities in this theme study were rich and varied, while optimal oral performance was scaffolded by group support, the chance to work from written scripts, and multiple rehearsals.

As you develop instructional sequences with and for your students, you can begin to make note of the oral language opportunities inherent in them. From there, you can look for ways to incorporate more such opportunities, increasing the variety of functions and interactional formats available, such as pairs, small groups, and whole-class performances. It is important to point out that performances should take place only after students have had plenty of practice before the spotlight. Be sure to allow student choice in such events.

Show and Tell

Show and tell, a strategy teachers have used for years, involves children bringing a favorite object, such as a teddy bear, to the class and telling the class about it. The situation is context embedded because all the children can see the prized possession, making it easier for the audience to understand the child's words. This is a beginning activity for young language learners that can be expanded to more advanced, context-reduced oral language use by simply asking children to place the favorite object in a paper bag so that it is not visible to classmates. Then the owner of the object begins describing the object to the class. Because the object is not visible, the speaker must be more specific about the object to assist classmates in guessing what it is. Later in the year, students can work with more difficult objects that are not in a bag but in their imagination, or they can have pictures in front of them that they describe to others. The variations of show and tell can scaffold children's early speaking with objects on hand and can induce more accurate descriptions when their comfort and language levels are more advanced.

One Looks, One Doesn't

In an activity called "One Looks, One Doesn't," you place a transparency of a picture on an overhead projector after telling students that one of them may look at the transparency while the other one looks away. The student who looks at the transparency describes it to his or her partner, who attempts to draw a picture of it. Because the describers can see their partner drawing the picture, they can adjust their language to assist the drawer; thus, the task is both easy and fun for the students. After five minutes or so the picture is revealed to all of the students and they get to see how accurate their communication was. This activity can also be developed for different levels of language use and proficiency. For example, the first transparencies used might be quite concrete, such as a picture of a red car with a number of people in it; later transparencies can be more abstract or complex, such as a picture of a fantasy scene with wizards and goblins.

Another way you can change the complexity of the task as students become more proficient in their oral language is to ask the describer and drawer to place a book or some other object between them so that the describer cannot see what the artist is doing. This then tests the accuracy of the describer and the listening accuracy of the artist. The first activity, in which the two could see one another, is similar to an oral language conversation and is context embedded because the individuals conversing can check to see if the person they are talking to is understanding them; the second approach is closer to a written message, context reduced, and causes the communicator to be more specific and accurate to make sure that the response to the communication is effective.

Tape-Recording Children's Recreations of Wordless Book Stories

Working with partners, students can use a wordless picture book to create and tape-record a story based on the pictures. Then they can play the story as they show the pictures to the rest of the class. You might have all the students share the same book at first, later on preparing different books to present to one another. Because listeners can see the pictures as each original rendition of the wordless book is being presented, story comprehension is scaffolded. Following is a list of some of our favorite wordless books for older and younger students. In Chapter 7 we present more information on wordless books for students of all ages.

Briggs, R. (1978). *The Snowman*. New York: Random House.

Carle, E. (1971). *Do You Want to Be My Friend?* New York: Harper.

Day, A. (1989). *Carl Goes Shopping*. New York: Farrar.

Goodall, J. (1985). *Naughty Nancy Goes to School*. New York: Atheneum.

McCully, E. (1984). *Picnic*. New York: Harper.

Tafuri, N. (1988). *Junglewalk*. New York: Greenwillow.

Turkle, B. (1976). *Deep in the Forest*. New York: Dutton.

*Wiesner, D. (1988). *Free Fall*. New York: Lothrop.

*Wiesner, D. (1991). *Tuesday*. New York: Clarion.

Taping and Dubbing a Television Show

One activity students enjoy is taping and dubbing their favorite television show, such as a cartoon, a sports event, or a situation comedy. We have found that older students enjoy using soap operas and action/adventure stories to share with one another. You begin by taping the show and showing it to the students without the sound. Alternatively, the original program may be played all the way through with sound first if you think it will help your students understand the original

---

*Books for older students.

story. Then your students create their own script for the show and dub it either on the original videotape or onto an audiotape to play along with the video. Students work with partners or in small groups to recreate their own television show, which is then played back for their classmates. It's especially fun to see the different ways each group has treated the same visual story. It can also be interesting at this point to play the original show to compare it with the meanings students have imputed in their scripts. If you have questions about your particular use of a television show, check copyright laws.

This taping and dubbing activity allows students to choose some of their favorite television programs, negotiate the meaning of the pictures, and create their own drama to present to the class. Because they are familiar with the show, they are able to use its story structure to create their own play. Moreover, in small groups children assist one another in understanding and recreating their own stories. Because the scene is visual, it provides an additional channel of communication for English learners. Perhaps most important, script development of this sort is highly motivating, thus promoting functional and fun involvement in a multimedia language and literacy event. When this dramatic activity is used in classrooms, students and teacher often laugh heartily at the outcomes of each group's drama, motivating them to create more scripts!

Choral Reading

Have you ever been to a large gathering where there is community singing and found that you couldn't remember all the words to the song? You may have been able to succeed in the group singing because you could fake it: When you weren't sure about the next word you could often sing the word a split second after others around you. In a sense you were experiencing the way a group singing scaffolds an unsure singer. Choral reading, a strategy involving students reading together, scaffolds English learners reading in a classroom in the same way. By involving students in selecting the readings, you can ensure that students of all ages are afforded the benefits of choral reading.

When you use choral reading with English learners and other students, you need to select materials that are age appropriate and a little beyond what your students can read on their own, that is, in their zone of proximal development (McCauley & McCauley, 1992). Next, you read the materials to students several times while showing the words to a poem or story. Then students can practice through repeated reading before they perform. During this practice phase, the students may brainstorm different ways to act out or pantomime the actions in the reading. Finally, students read the story together and act out the actions.

One of the powers of choral reading is that you can select books and have children select books for varying degrees of language and reading ability. Books and poems that lend themselves to more concrete actions and that have repeatable patterns, such as *The Very Busy Spider* (Carle, 1984), will be easier for students to understand. As students develop ability, they can still be challenged with more difficult books. We recently observed one first-grade class performing a choral reading of *Madeline* (Bemelmans, 1939). When they read each part of the story, they acted out the actions. For example, when the children in the story brushed their teeth, the choral readers brushed with much vigor; when the children ate, the performers pretended to eat as well. Dramatization, when combined with choral reading, allowed these English learners to be actively involved and reinforced the meaning of the story phrase by phrase.

Research indicates that choral reading helps children learn the intonation of English stories and improves their diction and fluency (Bradley & Thalgott, 1987). In addition, choral reading raises the enthusiasm and confidence of early readers (Stewig, 1981) and helps them expand their vocabulary (Sampson, Allen, & Sampson, 1990). Finally, children find great joy in choral reading and are eager to try it over and over with some of their favorite books. Choral reading need not be limited to young children. Poems, song lyrics, and picture books that appeal to older learners can serve as the basis for this enjoyable, low-anxiety oral language activity. You may select passages from literature such as *The House on Mango Street* (Cisneros, 1994) or poetry selections suggested in the district curriculum. Finally, consider asking your students to suggest song lyrics.

These first-graders put in a lot of effort preparing to present a choral reading to the fifth-graders of a favorite book. Their rehearsals had a real purpose, motivating them to perfect their reading through repetition and practice.

133

Riddles and Jokes

Riddles and jokes can be a lot of fun for students at the intermediate English proficiency level. You will need to consider the extent to which the age and cultural backgrounds of your students will affect their understanding of the humor, though. You might read some riddles and jokes that you think are appropriate for the age, language level, and cultural backgrounds of your students, modeling for them what they will do when they have practiced their own riddles and jokes in small groups. Then you can set aside a day for your students to share the jokes. As an alternative, you might make riddles and jokes a part of your regular classroom routine, inviting student participation on a volunteer basis. The activity allows students to have fun with something they enjoy doing, helps them become more comfortable speaking in front of the class, and gives them a chance to rehearse before making their presentation.

In summary, there is a variety of oral language development opportunities available through drama, songs, poetry, riddles, and jokes. The activities described in this section facilitate oral language development in at least three ways: (1) They encourage students to work in groups on motivating projects; (2) they provide various scaffolds for oral language performance, including informal rehearsal, written scripts, and choral readings prior to spotlighted performances; and (3) they focus on fun uses of oral language, reducing the anxiety sometimes associated with using a non-native language. Finally, although these activities may be implemented solely for the sake of language development and community enjoyment, some can and should be integrated into academic projects in content-area learning, at least some of the time.

Oral Language Development Through Content-Area Instruction

In addition to integrating drama, music, and poetry into your academic curriculum, each of the content areas presents specific oral language demands and learning opportunities. In this section, we discuss mathematics, science, and social studies to illustrate how content-area instruction provides both content learning and academic language development if comprehension and learning is supported with sheltering strategies. Our discussion concerning second language development and content instruction applies to learners of all ages but is especially pertinent for upper elementary, middle, and high school.

Oral English Development and Use in Mathematics

To tailor your mathematics instruction to the language and learning needs of your English learners, consider the particular cognitive-linguistic demands that mathematics instruction places on your students. Mathematics is a formal and systematic approach to using numbers and number concepts for solving problems in daily life and other areas, including research in the physical, social, and biological sciences. Most elementary math concepts (e.g., addition, subtraction, multiplication, and division; fractions and mixed numbers; inverse operations; and patterning and probability) can be illustrated through demonstration and manipulation of concrete objects, such as unifix cubes, beans, buttons, and pattern blocks. Using concrete objects is one way to make math concepts meaningful and more accessible. In fact, current mathematics pedagogy emphasizes extensive use of manipulatives to promote discovery of basic mathematics concepts, in a sequence that goes from concrete to pictorial to abstract (National Council of Teachers of Mathematics, 1989; Reys, Suydam, & Lindquist, 1991). Another way to make math concepts more meaningful and understandable is to embed them in real-life situations that your students have experienced.

All students, regardless of age or home language, must develop both the concepts and the academic language that mathematics uses to convey these concepts. Mathematical language, whether conveyed in English, Spanish, Chinese, or any other language, is specific, precise, and logical. As with all content instruction, English learners are best prepared to benefit from math instruction if they have attained at least an intermediate level of English language proficiency. However, English learners' prior math background, the difficulty of the material, and the extent to which the concepts can be conveyed nonverbally also affect the ease with which English learners learn math. Where feasible, primary language support for conceptual understanding may be helpful for many. Let us take a look at some aspects of English as used in mathematics that English learners and others need to control for successful learning.

Mathematical language includes unique vocabulary, sentence structures, semantic properties, and text structures, both oral and written, as discussed in full by Dale and Cuevas (1987) and summarized here. You generally teach these aspects of mathematical language through oral instruction or oral instruction supported by writing words, formulas, and equations on the chalkboard. Math vocabulary includes words that are specific to the discipline, such as *numerator, denominator, addend,* and *sum.* In addition, math vocabulary includes words students may already know but must now learn with a new meaning, such as *column, table, rational,* and *irrational.* As you consider the cognitive–linguistic load present in mathematics instruction, you need to keep in mind that certain difficult vocabulary may require review, preferably in the context of solving problems related to your students' daily experiences. For example, students need to learn that addition can be signaled by any of these words: *add, plus, combine, and, sum,* and *increased by.* Similarly, subtraction may be signaled by such words as *subtract from, decreased by, less, minus, differ,* or *less than.* These addition and subtraction examples come from Crandall, Dale, Rhodes, and Spanos (1985), cited in Dale and Cuevas (1987).

One of the best ways to promote cognitive processing of math concepts is through pair work and small-group problem solving. Here we have an ideal situation for development of cognitively demanding oral language use. As students discuss how to approach a problem, they become conscious of problem-solving strategies. If you teach such strategies, you will help students develop both metacognitive skills and the kind of language we employ to guide our own thinking efforts—the heuristic function of language, in Halliday's terms (1985). Word problems provided in written format can be analyzed and discussed orally and converted to appropriate mathematical formats to be solved. As you can see, mathematics requires substantial linguistic processing for students to understand and apply mathematical concepts and operations to problem solving.

Oral English Development and Use in Science

Science abounds with cognitively demanding oral language uses, provided that it is taught using a process-oriented inquiry approach (Kessler & Quinn, 1987). Within such an approach students work in pairs or groups to define a problem, state a hypothesis, gather data, record observations, draw conclusions relating data to the hypothesis, and explain and summarize findings. Scientific inquiry requires students to use academic language to convey the thinking involved in observing, classifying, comparing, measuring, inferring, predicting, concluding, synthesizing, and summarizing. In fact, researchers concerned with quality education for English learners have found that process-oriented science classes provide excellent language and content learning for students learning English (De Avila & Duncan, 1984; Kessler & Quinn, 1984; Mohan, 1986; Thomas & Collier, 2002).

The success of inquiry-based science projects for English learners is attributable to three major factors: (1) Students investigate real science problems that engage their natural curiosity about the world, such as plant growth, the solar system, electricity, and magnetism; (2) students are actively engaged in investigations involving hands-on activities, actual observations, and lab work rather than solely reading facts and theories in a textbook; and (3) students carry out investigations in groups that promote talking out their thinking and planning. What we see, then, is that inquiry-based science provides many opportunities for higher-level thinking through use of context-embedded oral language aimed at solving scientific problems, creating ideal opportunities for both language and content learning.

You will increase motivation and facilitate comprehension of science concepts if you connect these concepts to students' prior knowledge. For English learners, prior knowledge is apt to reflect different cultural assumptions from your own. You will want to bear in mind that every culture has its own theories and beliefs about many domains of science, such as classification of plants and animals and explanations for the movements of celestial bodies. Kessler and Quinn (1987) point out that miscommunications may arise with English learners when your students start with different assumptions from yours about the world. For these reasons, you will need to find ways to identify your students' prior knowledge, beliefs, and assumptions about phenomena you are studying. Students' observations and thinking may conflict with previous notions about the physical world, and these conflicts are most likely to come to light during group discussions. Such "sociocognitive conflict" is a natural part of scientific learning that we all go through, however, and should be considered as positive (Kessler & Quinn, 1987). We recall writer Eudora Welty (1983) telling about a short story she had written in which she described the moon rising in the west. Her editor promptly advised her to be more accurate in her settings, creating both sociocognitive conflict and an immediately relevant learning opportunity for Welty!

There are certain kinds of academic language use associated with science that all students, including English learners, need to learn. Vocabulary related to a particular scientific domain is necessary for precision in identifying and describing concepts (e.g., *periodic table, element, ion*) and naming materials and tools (e.g., *microscope*). In addition, students need to develop the ability to put together logical descriptions of experimental procedures and findings. Logical descriptions require careful sequencing of information held together by cohesive ties such as *however, therefore, because*, and *in conclusion*. Research shows that using cohesive ties in both oral and written language is especially difficult for English learners, a topic addressed in detail in Chapter 9 (Goldman & Murray, 1989, 1992). Oral discussions in pairs or groups will assist students in conceptually organizing their results for a clear presentation, oral or written.

As you can see, full participation in inquiry-based science requires at least an intermediate level of English proficiency, although beginners may benefit as well, particularly if sheltering strategies are used and if primary language support is provided by the teacher or paraprofessional. In addition to rich oral English learning opportunities, science projects offer natural and necessary math applications. We describe strategies for integrating oral language, literacy, and content areas, including strategies for reading and writing research reports, in Chapters 9 and 10.

Oral English Development and Use in Social Studies

In some ways, the concepts, generalizations, and understandings required for social studies depend heavily on oral and written verbal descriptions and explanations. This is especially true for a discipline such as history, which concerns people and places no longer available for direct viewing. Nonetheless, social studies topics may be made more concrete for students through films, pictures, videotapes, and museum visits. In addition, students may study their own communities and family histories as a personally relevant social science project through which they can learn social science inquiry methods, such as survey, interview, and observation. Finally, students will benefit from group discussions to help them understand and communicate what they have learned. In addition to research efforts carried out through oral language interactions, students need access to information that may be available only in written form. Literacy skills are thus essential. We provide many strategies for content-area reading and writing in Chapters 9 and 10. Here we will briefly review some of the oral language development opportunities inherent in the study of the social sciences.

The social sciences present oral language opportunities in a variety of ways. Chances are you will be presenting information orally to students some of the time through a lecture format. If you use pictures, graphs, flowcharts, gestures, and other visual supports to convey meaning, you will increase students' concept development while providing oral language development opportunities. All of the sheltering strategies presented in Chapter 3 are appropriate not only for social studies instruction but for other content areas as well.

Social studies also provides opportunities for students to present simulations or reenactments of historical or political events. We saw previously how fourth graders wrote and presented a play depicting the Gold Rush, incorporating songs and poems. Playing the part of legislators, students may debate a proposed bill or dramatize the process of enacting legislation. In addition, groups of students may select particular topics to study in depth, as in the jigsaw cooperative group procedure described in Chapter 3. As experts, they then present their findings to the class. When students make presentations to the class, they should always support their talk with visuals they have prepared to convey meaning. Through presentations such as these, presenters organize information and rehearse it for effective oral delivery. Listeners benefit in content and language development from the sheltered delivery provided by their peers. As you gain practice in analyzing the social studies content you teach, you need to find (1) ways to present the content through visuals, dramatizations, and other multimedia; and (2) ways to increase students' use of oral language to discuss, analyze, synthesize, and summarize information—that is, their academic language use.

In summary, we have briefly described oral language development demands and learning opportunities inherent in mathematics, science, and social studies. Our discussion is intended to illustrate ways of looking at the content you teach in terms of the oral language required for learning. If you are a content-area teacher, you know your subject area in depth. As you review your lesson plans, you will want to think about the kinds of oral and written language required for your English learners to understand the concepts and to demonstrate their learning. In all content areas, sheltering strategies should be used along with hands-on, direct experiences for inquiry and discovery. In addition, students should be given time and opportunity to process information orally in pairs and groups. They also need time and opportunity to rehearse for oral presentations. Given such time and opportunity, your students will advance in English language development while learning subject matter with greater understanding and retention than would otherwise be possible.

Classroom Assessment of English Learners' Oral Language Development

In Chapter 3 we described formal, standardized language proficiency tests, which serve the purpose of program assignment. In this section, we describe ways to document and assess students' oral language progress through classroom observation using checklists, anecdotal observations, and a structured oral language observation instrument called the Student Oral Language Observation Matrix (SOLOM). The SOLOM focuses your attention on five oral language traits: comprehension, fluency, vocabulary, grammar, and pronunciation. Checklists can be constructed to include any of a variety of oral language behaviors that you wish to document, including particular grammatical structures, vocabulary, conversational interactions, and presentational skills. Anecdotal observations consist of on-the-spot narrative accounts of student oral language use during particular classroom activities. Each of these observation techniques allows you to evaluate your students' use of oral language forms as they are used to serve communicative functions in particular social contexts in the classroom. We discuss the SOLOM oral language performance checklists and anecdotal observations here.

The Student Oral Language Observation Matrix (SOLOM)

Teacher judgment is one of the most important and accurate measures of English learners' oral language development. One observational instrument that teachers can use to assess their students' oral proficiency is SOLOM, shown in Figure 4.2. With this tool, your observations of student oral language use during day-to-day classroom activities stand in place of formally elicited language samples used by the commercial tests, such as the language assessment scales and others described in Chapter 3. As the teacher, you will be able to observe your students periodically over the year in a variety of naturally occurring classroom situations. As a result, your cumulative observations of student oral language use will be much richer, more natural, and more educationally relevant than a standardized test (Goodman, Goodman, & Hood, 1989). In addition, your students will be focused on the classroom task, alleviating the anxiety factor typical of testing situations. By combining your focused observations over time with the descriptive evaluations in the SOLOM, you will be able to document student progress in English oral language development.

While you observe students during day-to-day classroom activities, the SOLOM is organized to focus your attention on general oral language traits, that is, comprehension, fluency, vocabulary, grammar, and pronunciation. Thus, you are, in fact, evaluating student language on several analytic dimensions. Your ratings are ultimately subjective and require substantial linguistic sensitivity to be accurate and meaningful. However, we believe that you can develop such sensitivity through guided experience in language observation and analysis. Research, in fact, supports teacher efficacy in rating students' second language oral proficiency, using procedures similar to the SOLOM (Jackson, 1980; Mace-Matluck, 1980, 1981).

To use the SOLOM, you observe a student during a classroom activity that promotes oral language use, such as group work. You may spend five minutes or so listening to the speech interactions among the members of the group, paying particular attention to the student or students you wish to evaluate. During the observation itself, or shortly afterward, you fill out one observation form per student according to the descriptive traits outlined for you on the form. If you are using the SOLOM to document student progress over the course of the year, you need to make sure that the social context of your observations is similar each time to ensure comparability of performance. For example, you may wish to make cooperative group work your primary observation time. To get a richer picture of your student's oral proficiency, you should observe several different contexts, such as formal presentations in front of the class, cooperative group work, and individual conferences with you when

	1	2	3	4	5
A Comprehension	Cannot be said to understand even a simple conversation.	Has great difficulty following what is said. Can comprehend only "social conversation" spoken slowly and with frequent repetitions.	Understands most of what is said at slower-than-normal speed with repetitions.	Understands nearly everything at normal speed, although occasional repetition may be necessary.	Understands everyday conversation and normal classroom discussions without difficulty.
B Fluency	Speech is so halting and fragmentary as to make conversation virtually impossible.	Usually hesitant; often forced into silence by language limitations.	Speech in everyday conversation and classroom discussion frequently disrupted by the student's search for the correct manner of expression.	Speech in everyday conversation and class-room discussions generally fluent, with occasional lapses while the student searches for the correct manner of expression.	Speech in everyday conversation and classroom discussions fluent and effortless, approximating that of a native speaker.
C Vocabulary	Vocabulary limitations so extreme as to make conversation virtually impossible.	Misuse of words and limited vocabulary; comprehension quite difficult.	Student frequently uses the wrong words; conversation somewhat limited because of inadequate vocabulary.	Student occasionally uses inappropriate terms and/or must rephrase ideas because of lexical inadequacies.	Use of vocabulary and idioms approximates that of a native speaker.
D Pronunciation	Pronunciation problems so severe as to make speech virtually unintelligible.	Hard to understand because of pronunciation problems. Must frequently repeat to make himself or herself understood.	Pronunciation problems necessitate concentration on the part of the listener and occasionally lead to misunderstanding.	Always intelligible though one is conscious of a definite accent and occasional inappropriate intonation patterns.	Pronunciation and intonation approximate that of a native speaker.
E Grammar	Errors in grammar and word order so severe as to make speech virtually unintelligible.	Grammar and word-order errors make comprehension difficult. Must often rephrase and/or restrict himself or herself to basic patterns.	Makes frequent errors of grammar and word order that occasionally obscure meaning.	Occasionally makes grammatical and/or word-order errors that do not obscure meaning.	Grammatical usage and word order approximate that of a native speaker.

139

FIGURE 4.2 • SOLOM: STUDENT ORAL LANGUAGE OBSERVATION MATRIX

SOLOM PHASES: Phase I: Score 5–11 = non-English proficient; Phase II: Score 12–18 = limited English proficient; Phase III: Score 19–24 = limited English proficient; Phase IV: Score 25 = fully English proficient.
Based on your observation of the student, indicate with an "X" across the block in each category that best describes the student's abilities. The SOLOM should be administered only by people who themselves score at level "4" or above in all categories in the language being assessed. Students scoring at level "1" in all categories can be said to have no proficiency in the language.

Source: Courtesy of California State Department of Education, 1981.

discussing schoolwork. These contexts are not test contexts, but rather involve students as they carry out routine classroom activities. As a result you are evaluating authentic oral language used for real, day-to-day classroom purposes.

Figure 4.2 explains how to score the SOLOM. As you can see, each trait (i.e., comprehension, fluency, vocabulary, pronunciation, grammar) receives a rating from 1 to 5, according to the descriptors. After writing an X on the appropriate descriptors, you tally the ratings for all five traits. The SOLOM yields four phases of English language proficiency: Phase I, 5–11, non-English proficient; Phase II, 12–18, limited English proficient; Phase III, 19–24, limited English proficient; and Phase IV, 25, fully English proficient. You will notice that both Phases II and III are described as limited English proficient.

For an example of a SOLOM evaluation, let us return to Teresa, the fifth-grader whose *Poltergeist* narrative we offered as an example of an intermediate English speaker previously in this chapter (Example 4.2). Teresa, a fluent Spanish speaker who came to California in the third grade, is fluent in oral and written Spanish. She has been enrolled in a bilingual program since her arrival, and she has been learning English for two years. We have reproduced Teresa's narrative below for you to read again, this time with some additional conversational interchanges lasting a total of 85 seconds. As you read through the transcript, consider how you might evaluate Teresa's oral language performance based on the SOLOM descriptors for comprehension, fluency, vocabulary, grammar, and pronunciation.

SUZANNE: But at least you got to see *Poltergeist*.

TERESA: Yeah.

SUZANNE: Was it scary?

TERESA: No, it wasn't escary. But well . . . at first it was scary but then the other one no. Because there was . . . First a little girl . . . There was a television and the father was sleeping in the . . . in a . . . *sillón?* in like a chair. And then the little girl pass the television and she said, "Right here!" Then . . . then a hand get out of the television and she said, "Ouch!" And then a little boy was sleeping and the little girl sleep here and the little boy here and then he see all the time a tree and then . . . then . . . there was outside a tree . . . a tree. But it look ugly in the night. It look like a face . . . And then he was escary. Then he tell his father and his father said OK. Just count 1, 2, 3 to not escare. Then . . . then . . . the . . . he . . . the little girl and the little . . . the two brothers go in with the mother and her father because they're still escare. Then the other night . . . the little boy was . . . everyday he was counting and counting and he get up to . . . up to 2,000. He say 2,000, 2,001 and the hand of the tree get up like that . . . and the hand of the tree get up like that . . . And the . . . then the other escare that . . . because he broke the window. The tree. And the hand. And he get the boy and he said, "Mommy, mommy help me!" And then . . . But the tree was . . . I think the house was . . . it was haunting because there was a lot of the . . . of the . . . in the movie there came out many . . . um . . . many men but they are bad. They was ugly.

SUZANNE: Ooh, were they skeletons?

TERESA: Yeah.

SUZANNE: Or were they ghosts?

TERESA: They look like a ghost. They were a ghost and . . .

At this point another student interrupted. Discussion of the movie ended.

Now let's evaluate Teresa's oral language based on this sample. First, take a look at the descriptors for comprehension. Because Teresa does most of the talking, we do not have a great deal to go on to evaluate her comprehension. Based on her responses to questions and her comprehension of the movie itself, we give her a 4: "Understands nearly everything at normal speed, although occasional repetition may be necessary." For fluency, we have some trouble deciding between a 3 and a 4. Reviewing the transcript, we try to decide *how frequently* Teresa's speech is disrupted because of lack of fluency. Many of Teresa's repetitions and restarts are similar to those of native English speakers. In and of themselves they do not disrupt communication. However there are three instances in which Teresa seems to be searching, somewhat unsuccessfully, for a way to express herself. The first time is at the beginning when she says, "No, it wasn't escary. But well . . . at first it was scary but then the other one no. Because there was . . . First a little girl." It takes her five tries to get into the narrative. After that, however, she is off and running until she says, "Then . . . then . . . the . . . he . . . the little girl and the little . . . the two brothers go in with the mother and her father . . . ." Here again she is disfluent. She seems to have been searching for a word meaning "brother and sister." The closest word in English, though not commonly used in conversation, is *siblings*. Teresa apparently uses a direct translation of *los hermanos*, the brothers.

In Spanish *los hermanos* can mean "the brothers," but it can also mean "the brothers and sisters," or "the brother and sister." Therefore it has a broader range of meaning than "the brothers" in English. As a result, when Teresa uses the direct translation, her meaning becomes confused. The third example of disfluency occurs at the end when she says, "And the . . . then the other escare that . . . because he broke the window. The tree. And the hand. And he get the boy and he said, 'Mommy, mommy help me!'" These three instances of disfluency go beyond repetitions and restarts found in natural, spontaneous speech of native and nonnative speakers alike. We decide that these disruptions are infrequent enough to rate this oral language sample as a 4: "Speech in everyday conversation and classroom discussions generally fluent, with occasional lapses while the student searches for the correct manner of expression."

For vocabulary, we are again torn between 3 and 4 to describe Teresa's oral performance. As with the fluency trait, it is the word *frequently* that we have to consider carefully. We decide on 4: "Student occasionally uses inappropriate terms and/or must rephrase ideas because of lexical inadequacies." For example, she uses the word *sillón*, rephrasing it as *chair*. Although her vocabulary is not rich, we think that it is usually adequate for her purposes, thus the 4.

For evaluating pronunciation we rely on the audiotape because our written transcript conveys only a few aspects of her pronunciation. We rate the sample as a 3: "Pronunciation problems necessitate concentration on the part of the listener and occasionally lead to misunderstanding." Teresa is not "very hard to understand" as in the descriptor for a 2, nor "always intelligible" as in the descriptor for a 4. Therefore, the 3 rating fits well. For grammar, we find ourselves trying to decide whether Teresa's grammatical errors are frequent—3—or occasional—4. We decide on a 4, primarily because her grammar and word-order errors do not obscure meaning for us. She demonstrates one error consistently: the omission of the -*s* on third-person singular verbs, such as *he see* and *it look like*. In a similar vein, she says, "a hand get out." Teresa uses the present tense form for indicating both present and past tense, a fairly typical strategy that often persists rather late in second language acquisition, but which does not seriously impede communication. She also uses non-native English word order at times, such as "he see all the time a tree" and "there was outside a tree." For us, these errors do not impede communication, so we are comfortable with the 4 rating.

Now that we have rated Teresa's oral language performance on the SOLOM traits, we add the scores for a final rating.

Comprehension:	4
Fluency:	4
Vocabulary:	4
Pronunciation:	3
Grammar:	4
Total:	19, or Phase III: limited English proficient

Let's talk for a moment about the rating process for the SOLOM. You must have noticed that we had difficulty choosing between ratings on some dimensions. You might have rated Teresa's sample differently yourself. In fact, when we ask our students to fill out the SOLOM for Teresa's narrative, there are always some variations in trait scores and the resulting total score. For one thing, the taped narrative, though useful as an introduction to the SOLOM, lacks the major strength inherent in the tool: *in-person observation of natural language use in your own classroom*. If you were getting ready to make instructional or programmatic decisions for Teresa, you would need several in-person observations on which to base your SOLOM ratings. Another factor influencing ratings is the extent to which raters are accustomed to the non-native speech patterns of English learners. The important thing in using the SOLOM is to apply the descriptive criteria as consistently as possible. It is also important to notice that a broad range of scores, from 14 to 24, yields a "limited English proficient" label, though divided into Phase II and Phase III. Thus the SOLOM offers additional descriptive detail and analysis within the category "LEP," highlighting the fact that "LEP" actually covers a rather broad range of second language development. In summary, the SOLOM provides a general index of oral language proficiency that is based on actual oral language use during day-to-day classroom activities, such as group work, teacher–student conferences, and classroom presentations. By building a set of observations over time, you will obtain a developmental picture of oral language progress.

What instructional implications can be drawn for Teresa? First, Teresa has sufficient English oral language proficiency to benefit from academic instruction delivered in English, provided that sheltering or specially designed academic instruction in English (SDAIE) techniques are used to ensure lesson comprehension. Moreover, substantial exposure to academically demanding material in English is precisely what she needs to challenge her to higher levels of second language development. However, Teresa still needs the educational support of a bilingual or English language development program. She will benefit from reading, writing, and making oral presentations in English with scaffolding provided by the teacher and other students who are more advanced in English language development. At the moment, she struggles when reading in English, though she is fluent, successful, and enthusiastic when reading in her home language, Spanish. We would encourage her continued Spanish literacy use and development, while providing structured opportunities for her to read and use a wide variety of English language materials supported by opportunities for buddy reading, story mapping, literature discussion, and other strategies for intermediate-level students described in Chapters 7 through 10.

In summary, oral language assessments based on the SOLOM may be used as one source of information, among several, to inform decisions to reclassify students to the category of fully English proficient, as discussed in Chapter 3. In addition, SOLOM data may be collected periodically and placed in a student's language development portfolio. For this purpose, the descriptive statements and total score are more useful for documenting student progress than the designations of non-English proficient (NEP), limited English proficient (LEP), and fully English proficient (FEP). By including periodic SOLOM observations in the student's portfolio, you form a developmental picture of oral language progress over time that will provide a solid basis for instructional decisions.

Checklists and Anecdotal Observations

The SOLOM provides a general index of oral language proficiency. Two other assessment tools—checklists and anecdotal observations—may also be used to provide additional information about your students' ability to use oral English for a variety of purposes. Checklists can be useful because you can tailor them to your specific evaluation needs. In addition, checklists are convenient to use because they list the behaviors to look for and merely require a checkoff. However, when you devise a checklist, you need to try to include any and all potential behaviors, and leaving a place for "other" so that you can list unexpected behaviors. Another benefit of checklists is that evaluations are based on holistic observations of students in the course of day-to-day classroom language use, as is the case with the SOLOM and anecdotal records.

An anecdotal record is a running account of an observed oral language event, written on the spot, describing the event and quoting the participants as closely as possible to convey how the interaction unfolds in real time. Anecdotal observations require considerable effort and focused attention because you must observe and interpret the flow of a social interaction while simultaneously recording it. The benefit of anecdotal observations is that you record interactions as they occur, rather than filling in a checklist. They are thus much more open-ended and provide much richer detail of student behavior. As you make your written account, you provide some on-the-spot analysis, but you also have a narrative record to review later, at which time you might see and understand something that was not evident to you during the observation. A drawback to anecdotal observations is that they start with a blank page. It takes some practice and training to know what to look for and how to "see" when observing, because what you see depends a great deal on how well you understand what you are observing. In addition, the quick pace and complexity of student interactions can be difficult to capture on a page. Some teachers, particularly those interested in conducting their own classroom research, have chosen to use videotapes to back up their on-the-spot observations.

We offer two oral language observation forms in Figures 4.3 and 4.4. These two forms combine the use of checklists and anecdotal observations. If your

FIGURE 4.3 • INFORMAL CHART TO FOLLOW THE ORAL LANGUAGE DEVELOPMENT OF YOUR STUDENTS

CLASSROOM INVOLVEMENT	BEGINNING LEVEL	INTERMEDIATE LEVEL	ADVANCED LEVEL
Functions: Informal talk Reporting Discussing Describing Explaining Questioning Debating Evaluating Persuading			
Interaction patterns: Partners Small groups Large groups			
Linguistic elements: Vocabulary Syntax Organization Ideas Audience sensitivity			
Other Comments:	Student Name_____		Date_____

Source: Based on M. H. Buckley, *Oral Language Guidelines*, unpublished workshop handout, 1981.

instructional program requires that you document your student's oral language development with greater specificity than standardized tests or the SOLOM provide, we recommend that you consider these two forms and modify them according to the goals and objectives of your program. Both forms focus your attention on participation structures or interaction patterns. These are the grouping structures within which students interact during your observation. Your form will need to reflect the actual grouping structures that you use in your classroom. Each form also lists a number of language functions often served during classroom interactions. As we observe English learners, we want to see how well they are able to achieve communicative goals and purposes through their developing English skills. Each of the two forms offers examples of classroom language functions that you might look for as your students interact. The language functions in Figure 4.3 are based on Buckley (1981), whereas those in Figure 4.4 are based on Halliday (1975), described previously in this chapter. You may want to add, elaborate, or modify classroom language functions to suit your curriculum. Finally, each form includes linguistic elements or language forms to call your attention to grammar, pronunciation, vocabulary, and your students' ability to coordinate these as they produce different oral discourse structures, such as conversations, debates, and formal presentations to the class.

144

Student Name_____   Subject _____   Date _____

ACTIVITY	ANECDOTAL OBSERVATIONS
Participation structure: Formal presentation — individual — group Structured cooperative group work Informal group work Pair work	
Language functions: 　Heuristic 　　Hypothesizes 　　Predicts 　　Infers 　　Considers 　　Asks 　　Reports 　Informative 　　Describes 　　Explains 　　Synthesizes 　　Summarizes 　　Clarifies 　　Responds 　　Retells 　Instrumental 　　Requests 　　Asks for 　Regulatory 　　Directs 　　Commands 　　Convinces 　　Persuades 　Personal and interactional 　Divertive and imaginative	
Language forms: Vocabulary: particular to domain and general vocabulary Sentence structures: 　　declarative 　　question 　　command 　　exclamation 　　grammatical correctness Morphology: Phonology: Discourse:	Overall evaluation:

FIGURE 4.4

ORAL LANGUAGE OBSERVATION CHART

Source: Based on M. A. K. Halliday, *Learning How to Mean: Exploration in the Development of Language* (London: Arnold, 1975).

145

Although both forms address (1) participation structure, (2) language functions, and (3) language forms, the two forms are designed to be used differently. The chart in Figure 4.3 is a modified checklist in which you determine on the spot whether the student is performing at a beginning, intermediate, or advanced level. For each category, there is room for you to jot notes that describe aspects of student performance that support your judgment. The chart in Figure 4.4 is set up for you to keep a running record of the entire interaction. To use this chart, you first fill out the name, subject, and date, and then circle the participation structure you are observing. Next, you write a narrative that describes what is happening, who is saying what to whom, and what is accomplished during the interaction. The descriptors listed under language functions and language forms serve as reminders of forms and functions that your student might use during the interaction. After the observation, you review the narrative and make an overall evaluation of the student's performance in terms of language forms and functions within this particular type of grouping format or participation structure.

In summary, the detail with which you document oral performance among the English learners in your classroom will depend on the goals and objectives of your instructional program. General observations such as those prompted by the SOLOM may suffice. If greater specificity is needed, language observations structured along the lines of the charts just discussed may be implemented. In that case, you will probably need to develop documentation forms that are tailored to your program, your students, and your classroom organization patterns. Systematic observations carried out periodically are appropriately placed in a student's portfolio and will provide a record of oral language development over time.

Differentiating Instruction for Oral Language Development

Differentiating instruction for oral language development requires us to consider each student's oral English proficiency *in relation to* lesson standards, objectives, and performance expectations. Your daily interactions with students should give you a good sense of their various oral abilities. In addition, you may wish to focus your observations using assessment procedures described in this chapter (Figure 4.2), language use for classroom interactions and involvement (Figure 4.3), and the types of oral language engagement for participation (Figure 4.4). These tools will help you match instruction and performance expectations with students' oral language abilities. In addition, knowing your students' oral English levels will help you decide how to group students for optimal participation, such as pairs and triads. For example, you may want *small groups* of students with *varied oral English proficiency* levels for some activities to encourage oral language use. It is also helpful to know your students' primary language abilities. You may, for example, want to pair a newcomer with a bilingual student to help the newcomer understand directions and get started. Next, you determine the strategies and materials you will use to facilitate content learning among students of varied oral English proficiency levels. Finally, you decide how to determine and document learning.

In this chapter, and throughout the book, we have set up several features to help you differentiate instruction. To begin with, the teaching activities we described are grouped, broadly speaking, for beginning and intermediate English learners. In addition, Figure 4.5 indicates different grade levels for which each strategy is appropriate. These features, together with your assessment of a student's oral English using strategies we describe, should give you a good start for planning differentiated instruction. In addition, you may recall our framework from Chapter 3 addressing the questions: **who**, **what**, **how**, and **how well**. We use that framework now to illustrate differentiated planning for a lesson that forms part of a larger study on travel. This particular theme study integrates mathematics (calculating distances), social studies (history of transportation), and English language development.

Who: Students in grades 2 to 4 identified as **beginning** to **early advanced** in oral English proficiency. The students are from a variety of primary language backgrounds and cultures; most have had experiences using public transportation and personal vehicles both in their home cultures and in the United States.

What: Students use oral language to plan and present a poem that incorporates familiar and new vocabulary in the construction of simple prepositional phrases. The poem follows the scaffolding structure seen here, taken from *Let's Write and Sing a Song* (Pertchik, Vineis, & Jones, 1992). Students work in small groups to write three verses, each identifying a different vehicle (airplane), the place it travels (sky), and the title of the operator (pilot).

We go from here to there, from there to here, but if it's too far to walk what will we do?

We can ride in/on _____, in/on _____ with _____
  (vehicle)   (place it travels)   (person who operates it)

Students are given the following three examples. Using Total Physical Response (see Chapter 6), they perform the poem/song along with the teacher.

Vehicle	Place it travels	Person who operates it
in a boat	on the water	with the captain
in a plane	in the sky	with the pilot
on a skateboard	on the sidewalk	our friends

How: Students will work in triads to compose three verses of the poem based on the model, working in homogeneous groups that mirror their instructional levels and abilities. Students may use their primary language to clarify directions and identify forms of transportation; thereafter they may refer to dictionaries or peers for English terms they don't know. Those who are **beginning** will be given picture dictionaries to determine vocabulary. Students who are **intermediate** and **advanced** will draw on their knowledge of English, with monolingual English and bilingual dictionaries available as well. As a culminating activity, each group will write and perform the poem in a group for the class.

How Well: The SOLOM will be used to assess oral language use in small groups. A rubric checklist that includes correct use of prepositional phrases, appropriate syntax, and pronunciation will be used to assess oral performance of the poem during the culminating activity.

Summary

In this chapter we focused on oral language development in second language acquisition. We began by describing how listening, speaking, reading, and writing are intertwined in daily use. We also noted that each of these language processes supports the others during language development. We showed how natural oral language functions can be connected to your classroom routines, and we discussed the importance of integrating oral language with reading and writing activities. Strategies for oral language development, oral language demands, and opportunities inherent in academic subjects, such as mathematics, science, and social studies, were discussed. Next we described developmental oral language characteristics of English learners by presenting an oral language observation instrument, the SOLOM, followed by examples of speech from beginning and intermediate English speakers. Finally, we offered ideas for structuring your observation and evaluation of students' oral performance by using modified checklists and anecdotal observation records.

We believe that by integrating drama, poetry, and songs into your curriculum, by creating a secure climate where all students want to share, and by providing opportunities for students to process and present academic material in small groups and in front of the class, you will assist English learners with oral language development.

In Figure 4.5 we summarize the strategies discussed in the chapter. The chart provides a general grade-level guideline for using strategies in the chapter, but

FIGURE 4.5

GRADE LEVELS AT WHICH STRATEGIES MAY BE USED

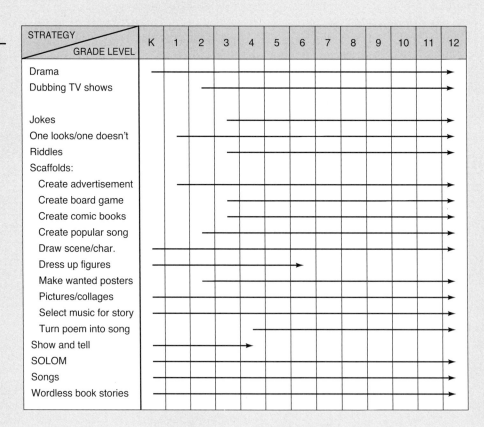

only you can make the best decision concerning whether children are prepared to work with various strategies in your classroom.

•••••••••

Suggestions for Further Reading

Ernst-Slavit, G., & Wenger, K. J. (1998). Using creative drama in the elementary classroom. *TESOL Journal, 7*(4), 30–33.

The authors discuss using drama with elementary students, and secondary teachers could easily use the guidelines here to use drama in their classrooms and to help students act out familiar stories. The authors list several benefits students derive from drama: a defined context for language use, extended oral communication repertoires, improved reading and writing, expanded listening skills, emboldened risk taking, and advanced problem-solving skills. Moreover, they give specific examples of how to set up a story-telling classroom.

Genesee, F., Lindholm-Leary, K., Saunders, W. M. & Christian, D. (Eds.). (2006). *Educating English language learners: A synthesis of research evidence.* Cambridge University Press.

This excellent synthesis of research includes chapters on oral language; literacy: crosslinguistic and crossmodal issues; literacy; instructional issues; and academic achievement. Each chapter contains a discussion of research and issues and a chart several pages long of the pertinent research. An excellent, readable synthesis of research on English language learners.

McCauley, J., & McCauley, D. (1992). Using choral reading to promote language learning for ESL students. *The Reading Teacher, 45*(7), 526–533.

An excellent article on choral reading that gives a rationale, procedures for using poetry in particular, and several examples of second language children adapting poetry and drama together. To adapt choral reading to English language learners, the article shows how to add gestures and acting out to make the material more comprehensible for novice and more advanced English learners.

Nunan, D. (Ed.). (2003). *Practical English teaching.* New York: McGraw-Hill. Experts on topics such as methodology, listening, speaking, reading, learning styles and strategies, content-based instruction (CBI), classroom-based assessment, and writing each present a chapter in their area of expertise. After a discussion of the topic, the chapter suggests further readings and helpful websites. This is an excellent book for introducing ideas to students new to the area of English learner instruction.

Richards, J., & Renandya, W. (Eds.). (2002). *Methodology in language teaching: An anthology of current practice.* Cambridge: Cambridge University Press.

This is one of the best books of its type. It contains 41 short articles on topics ranging from speaking and listening to reading and writing, grammar and pronunciation, and assessment and technology. Articles are written by known experts in specific aspects of second language learning. If you could buy only one book, this might be the best choice.

Silverstein, S. (1974). *Where the sidewalk ends.* New York: Harper & Row.

A book full of poems children love to hear, act out, and read over and over again. The poems range from nonsense poems to fantasy to more serious. Our own classes have loved, among others, "Ickle Me, Pickle Me, Tickle Me Too," "Captain Hook," "Listen to the Mustn'ts," "I'm Making a List," and "Boa Constrictor."

Spolin, V. (1963/1983). *Improvisations for the theater.* Evanston, IL: Northwestern University Press.

This is a classic drama text for actors that we have used from the first year we began to teach. It starts with silent improvisations such as asking pairs to act out being mirrors of one another. It moves to small talking parts in which, for example, strangers are stuck in an elevator for 10 seconds, then five minutes, and finally for two hours. It ends with students acting out plays. The book contains over a hundred meaningful activities for the classroom. This book is our favorite, but the author Viola Spolin also has several other useful books available through the same publisher.

Wright, W., Betteridge, D., & Buckby, M. (2002). *Games for language learning: New edition.* Cambridge: Cambridge University Press.

Games for Language Learning is in its 24th printing since 1983 and there's a reason why: It is an excellent resource for teachers who want to add to their repertoire in language learning and have fun at the same time. The authors provide activities ranging from controlled to guided to free, thus giving appropriate amounts of direction for students at beginning, intermediate, and advanced levels of language. There is a brief but useful introduction to using games in classrooms.

Activities

1. Discuss with a partner or in a group the various oral language activities you have been involved in throughout your schooling. Were your teachers anxious to have you involved in group work or were you required to sit still and be quiet most of the time? Did you put on plays, puppet shows, or readers' theater after reading books, or were you in a class in which the book was read and the teacher asked questions about the book? Were you involved in panel discussions? Did you give formal speeches in class? What effect did your involvement or noninvolvement in oral language activities have on your overall interest in school and your capacity to learn?

2. It has been said that young children learn through their talking, that through talking they are able to think (Buckley, 1981). You will hear young children talking even when they are playing by themselves. Children will talk aloud while they play with dolls or Legos or other toys. What would be the effect on children's language growth of organizing a class to be silent most of the time? What kind of classroom organization provides children with the greatest opportunities for language growth? In terms of language acquisition, are input and output equally important? Whose input and output?

3. If possible, observe a classroom in which students are involved in literature circles or literature response groups. How involved are the English language learners in this activity that relies mainly on language? Does the silence of some students mean that they are not involved? Would they be more involved if the same group of students were preparing a puppet show about a story they had read or if they were creating a poster advertising the story? Observe a class that uses various scaffolds for students and determine whether beginning English learners are more involved when scaffolds such as murals, drawings, or collages are used. What seems to involve intermediate and advanced English learners the most?

4. Help intermediate and advanced English learners set up a debate about a topic that particularly concerns them and have them present the debate in front of the class. Help students learn formal rules of debate and assist them with practicing before they present it. Provide students with a chart of specific guidelines for debating, preferably making the debate more like a discussion than a competition with winners or losers. Debates may be carried out in teams. Let students evaluate themselves based on the guidelines you provided at the beginning.

5. Demonstrate for students literature study circle responses and discussions. Read a story to the students first and then model a possible discussion concerning the literature. If possible, make or get a videotape of a successful literature circle discussion and show it to your students. Create guidelines for a literature study circle with your students and discuss with them what might work best. Next, read a story and ask students to discuss the story using the guidelines you have created. For more advanced students, let them read a story they've selected and discuss it in their groups. After the first group discussions, ask students to discuss how the group worked together and how they could make their group discussions even better.

6. Observe an elementary school and a high school serving English learners. Arrange to observe a sheltered science lesson (or other content area) in each. When you observe, make a note of how the teachers use language and nonverbal cues to convey lesson content. In addition, make a note of how students interact during whole-class instruction and small-group work. After your observations, compare the elementary and high school lessons in terms of (1) the teachers' talk and sheltered instructional delivery, (2) the cognitive demands of the lesson content, and (3) the opportunities for oral language development made available through the lesson. What conclusions do you draw concerning the challenges teachers and students face? What are the similarities and differences between the elementary and secondary school lessons?

7. Make a focused observation of one English learner during small-group work when free talk is appropriate. Based on your observation, fill out the SOLOM observation chart. Discuss your evaluation with the teacher to see how your evaluation compares with the teacher's judgment. If there are discrepancies between your evaluation and that of the teacher, what might be some sources of these differences? Based on your experience, what are some of the advantages and disadvantages of the SOLOM?

Where the Classroom Comes to Life

....

Video Homework Exercise
Making Presentations

In the video, the teacher introduces an assignment in which each student is to read a biography of an explorer and make an oral presentation to the class about the life of the explorer while dressed up as the explorer. The teacher points out that students need to organize their ideas in advance of the oral presentation and that they may use note cards to help them remember what they want to say.

Go to MyEducationLab, select the topic "Speaking," and watch the video entitled "Making Presentations."

1. How does this assignment integrate the use of listening, speaking, reading, and writing as discussed in the Chapter 4 section "Oral Language in Perspective"?

2. What sheltering techniques would you suggest students use to make their presentations more understandable to their English learner classmates?

3. What special strategies would you use to help beginning English learners prepare for their oral presentation? What about intermediate English learners?

Other Videos: Memory EPV5 and Motivating Through Problem-Based Learning EPV6.

5

Emergent Literacy: English Learners Beginning to Write and Read

> ❝I won't know what my story is about until I finish my picture!❞
>
> —OSVALDO, age 5

> "Tis a lesson you should heed, Try, try again.
> If at first you don't succeed, Try, try again."
>
> —THOMAS PALMER (*Teacher's Manual*, 1840)

In this chapter, we discuss English learners' early literacy development, home–school relationships, classroom strategies to involve your students in reading and writing, and assessment procedures to document their progress in the early stages of reading and writing development. The following questions will guide your reading for the chapter:

1. What does research tell us about the early literacy development of English learners?
2. What are the "emergent literacy" and "reading readiness" perspectives, and how do they influence early literacy instruction?
3. How can teachers and parents work together to enhance home–school relationships and promote early literacy development?
4. How can you organize your classroom to maximize early literacy development for all students?
5. What classroom strategies can you use to provide a firm foundation for English learners' early literacy development?
6. How can you assess early literacy development?

A few years ago, we spent some time in a two-way Spanish immersion kindergarten observing and helping the teacher. Children were immersed in a print-rich environment where they drew and wrote daily in journals, listened to predictable stories and poems, rewrote stories, and played in literacy-enriched dramatic play centers that included a post office, restaurant, office, grocery store, blocks, arts, and writing areas. We were interested in how these kindergartners would approach the task of writing in a classroom such as this, where children were invited to draw and write to their hearts' content but were not given much explicit instruction on writing.

During English language arts one day, I (Suzanne) asked a group of six children (native Spanish speakers, native English speakers, and bilinguals) to write a story in English to take home to my husband. I passed out the paper, which was lined on the bottom half and plain on the top, and the children began writing without hesitation. As they wrote, I made note of how each child approached the task, and as they finished, I knelt down to ask each one to tell about their story. Lisa had written the words "I love my mom" in legible script and had illustrated her story with hearts and a picture of herself next to her mother. Rosa had drawn a picture of her seven family members and had filled several lines with block letters evenly spaced. Osvaldo was the last child to finish his work. He had filled the lined half of the page with indecipherable letters and punctuation and was now busy drawing. Three times I asked him to tell me about his story and three times he simply replied, "I don't know yet." The fourth time I interrupted his drawing, he explained in desperation, "I won't know what my story is about until I finish my picture!" His story (see Figure 5.1) was about a boy kicking a soccer ball, a shiny black and white triangular sphere that nearly flew off the page to hit me in the face of my ineptitude!

These kindergarten children had never been told how to write or what to say. Yet somehow they were quite comfortable with this request to write a story someone else would read. The forms of their writing varied from wavy lines to apparently random arrays of block letters to conventional print. The topics of their stories came from their own interests and experiences. They knew their stories had a purpose of a sort: My husband would enjoy reading them. Yet the children seemed more focused on their own purpose: personal expression of a message from within. It was clear that all six children knew at least something about both the forms and functions of print. Furthermore, they were all confident that they could write a story, one that would at least have meaning for themselves. They differed, however, in the extent to which they were able to approximate conventional

FIGURE 5.1 • OSVALDO'S SOCCER STORY

153

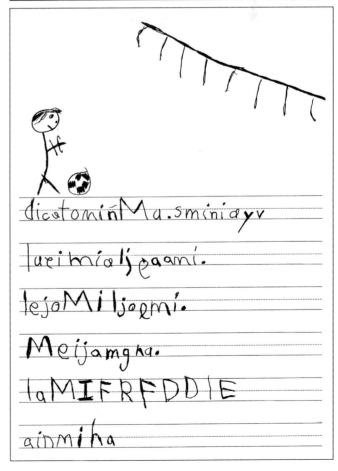

writing forms to convey their meaning. Indeed, they differed in their understanding of whether print has anything to do with meaning at all! For Osvaldo, the writing had no meaning until the picture was complete.

When I returned to the classroom after spring break, Osvaldo asked, "How'd your daddy like the story?" In typical kindergarten fashion, he had created an equivalence between husband and dad. But his question revealed something more than his developing understanding of human relationships. It illuminated his sense of audience! Osvaldo provides us with a rich example of the many aspects of writing children must eventually coordinate: forms, functions, and illustrations and the need to shape these in a way that will please one's audience. In the early stages of literacy development, young children typically understand and control some aspects of the task better than others. And they must grapple with these complexities while still constructing their understanding of the social and physical world around them: Virtual reality is complex.

The kindergarten children just described were demonstrating early literacy development in an emergent literacy environment. In this chapter, we examine early literacy development as it has been researched over the past two decades. In doing so, we will briefly contrast two viewpoints on children's literacy development: the emergent literacy viewpoint and the reading readiness viewpoint. We will spend some time discussing the main tenets of the emergent literacy perspective, illustrating our points with samples of children's writing and reading, and describing how teachers implement such a perspective in early childhood classrooms. Finally, we describe ways to assess English learners' early reading and writing development. In our discussion we also address a pressing concern of many teachers: How do I help older English learners who have not yet learned to read or write in any language?

What Does Research Tell Us About the Early Literacy Development of English Learners?

A large body of research investigates early literacy development in a first language. As a result, we now have a substantial amount of exciting and interesting information about young children's early literacy development in English, Spanish, and other languages (e.g., Chi, 1988; Clay, 1975; Ferreiro & Teberosky, 1982; Harste, Woodward, & Burke, 1984; Teale, 1984; Teale & Sulzby, 1986). However, relatively little research documents early literacy development in English as a second language, particularly among students who have not had literacy instruction in their first language. Nevertheless, the research we do have shows that English reading and writing development processes are essentially similar for both English learners and native English speakers (Edelsky, 1981a, 1981b; Goodman & Goodman, 1978; Hudelson, 1984; Urzúa, 1987). That is, in reading, all learners gradually come to use their developing English language knowledge, their world knowledge, and their understanding of print conventions to make sense of written text. Similarly, in writing, they use their developing English language knowledge, world knowledge, and understanding of print conventions to put their ideas on paper. For all learners, literacy development is a complex process that takes place over a lengthy period during which they demonstrate gradual approximations to mature versions of reading and writing. In both reading and writing, all learners must learn the forms of print in English, including the letters of the alphabet and how these are sequenced into words, sentences, and paragraphs to create letters, stories, recipes, and other forms of written communication. At the same time, all learners must learn to select from this rich array of written discourse forms to achieve the communicative functions at hand, whether to direct, inform, persuade, entertain, complain, or console. Finally, written language use takes place in a social context and serves personal and social purposes. Furthermore, literacy learning is achieved through interpersonal relationships in the varying social contexts in which literacy instruction takes place. Literacy development thus evolves through social interactions involving written language from which children develop ideas about the forms and functions of print. They also become aware of the ways print is used in different social contexts for a wide variety of purposes.

Although many aspects of reading and writing development are essentially similar for English learners and native English speakers, there are important differences as well. Two important differences are a student's English language proficiency and ability to read and write in the primary language (Hudelson, 1987). Students at the beginning stages of English language development are still acquiring basic knowledge of English while learning to read and write English in school. Research shows that English learners can benefit from English literacy instruction well before they have developed full control of the language orally. In other words, oral and written English can develop more or less simultaneously (Goodman, Goodman, & Flores, 1979; Hudelson, 1984, 1986; Urzúa, 1987), provided that instruction is carefully organized to be meaningful and relevant, a topic we discuss throughout this chapter.

If your English learners are literate in their primary language, they may bring knowledge, skills, and attitudes about reading and writing that transfer to the task of English reading. In fact, research and theory consistently support the benefits of teaching children to read and write in their primary language first, not

 INTERNET RESOURCES

The English as a foreign language (EFL) specific sites **(http://members.tripod.com/~ESL4kids/links. html)** contain links to many other sites for hundreds of resources. Boggle's World contains collections of materials for elementary and middle school students. Dave Sperling's ESL Café is one of the most extensive ESL sites on the Web. The CanTeach site offers lesson plans for beginning reading and writing and resources for grades K-4.

The Center for Adult English Language Acquisition (CAEL) site offers information on adult learners: **www.cal.org/caela/ esl_resources/digests/ Familit2.html**. If you teach older students, you'll want to go to this site. You might try to evaluate some of the sites to see which ones would be most appropriate for different grade levels and different abilities or you might actually try some of the specific activities or strategies available in the sites.

only because it is easier to read and write a language you already know, but also because literacy skills transfer from the primary language to English, as English language proficiency develops (Cummins, 1981; Peregoy, 1989; Tragar & Wong, 1984). In summary, research shows that English language proficiency and primary language literacy contribute to the ease with which English learners develop English reading and writing skills. Other factors may contribute as well, including cultural factors that affect classroom communication, teacher perceptions of student abilities, student motivation, and teacher–student relationships as discussed in previous chapters.

In our discussion of early literacy in this chapter, we focus on beginning and intermediate English learners who are new to reading and writing in English as a second language. Most of our discussion applies to beginning readers and writers under age 7. However, we also discuss early literacy instruction for a special group of English language learners: older children and adolescents who have never learned to read or write in any language. Our teaching recommendations for non-native English speakers draw heavily on first language research, applied with caution and sometimes modified to accommodate linguistic and cultural differences. If you are a bilingual teacher, you should note that many of the teaching strategies we describe for beginning literacy in English can be used to teach beginning reading and writing in the primary language, with occasional modifications based on the writing system of the primary language you are teaching.

156

Contrasting the Emergent Literacy and Reading Readiness Perspectives

Ideas about when and how young children should be taught to read and write have always been subject to a variety of influences. This is not surprising if you stop to consider that two different sources of advice, a culture's traditional child-rearing practices and scientific thought of the day, have played a part in forming views of how young children should be educated. In this section we will discuss two theoretical perspectives that have influenced literacy instruction: reading readiness and emergent literacy. We then elaborate on the emergent literacy perspective, the perspective we believe offers the most effective teaching practices for native English speakers and English learners alike.

Reading Readiness Perspective

The **reading readiness** perspective held sway in many parts of the world during much of the twentieth century. Based on maturationist theories of development (see Gesell, 1925) and the standardized testing movement of the 1930s and 1940s, reading readiness proponents adhere to the belief that children are not developmentally ready to read until they reach a mental age of 6.6 years (Morphet & Washburn, 1931). In practical terms, this translated into the postponement of reading until first grade. Writing instruction was also postponed until first grade and aimed at proper letter formation rather than composing or communicating. Kindergarten was to serve the purpose of socialization and oral language development, not literacy.

Reading readiness practices in kindergarten were further influenced by the testing movement of the 1920s and 1930s. Test developers created tests of specific subskills that correlated with reading achievement, including auditory discrimination, visual discrimination, left-to-right eye progression, and visual motor skills. Some educators fell into the trap of assuming a causal relationship in the correlations, believing that early reading success resulted from subskill acquisition, rather than just being somehow linked with it. As a result, it became common practice to teach these "readiness skills" in kindergarten to "get children ready to read" in first grade. Reading readiness subskill activities were translated into corresponding kindergarten objectives as shown in the following list. When basal reader publishers incorporated readiness subskills into workbooks as part of their reading series, reading readiness theories became effectively established in classroom practice nationwide.

The list here provides examples of reading readiness subskills and corresponding learning objectives for kindergartners (Morrow, 1983, 1993).

Reading Readiness Subskills	Sample Objectives
auditory discrimination	• identify and differentiate familiar sounds (car horn, dog barking, siren)
	• identify rhyming words
	• identify sounds of letters
visual discrimination	• recognize colors
	• recognize shapes
	• identify letters by name
visual motor skills	• cut on a straight line with scissors
	• color inside the lines of a picture
	• hop on one foot
large motor skills	• skip
	• walk on a straight line

Several years ago we had a personal experience that called our attention to reading readiness practices in school. When our neighbor's child, Aretha, entered kindergarten, she could already read and write stories. She used to sit at a little table in the living room and churn out pages of imaginative stories that often began with "Onc upn atym." Occasionally, she would ask her mother or father how to spell a word, but she usually used her own spelling. Perhaps because her parents were teachers, she loved to play school and "teach" her little brother how to read using her mother's kindergarten materials. By first grade, Aretha was already a writer and could read books from the second- and third-grade classes.

But when Aretha's mother and father met with her kindergarten teacher during parent conferences, they were astounded to hear that Aretha was not ready for first-grade reading instruction. The teacher explained that Aretha was still having trouble with some basic kindergarten tasks: cutting with scissors and hopping on one foot. Aretha's parents could not see the connection between these motor skills and learning to read. Moreover, they knew Aretha could already read and write. To remedy the situation, Aretha's father asked the teacher to listen to Aretha read a book. After Aretha successfully and fluently read out of two textbooks, her teacher concluded that Aretha was indeed ready for reading instruction. Though well meaning and conscientious, Aretha's teacher held some false assumptions about reading that blocked her ability to recognize Aretha's capabilities and potential, a reminder that we must always examine and reexamine our assumptions about learning and teaching.

In summary, reading readiness is a traditional view of literacy instruction that assumes that children must be able to perform certain auditory, visual, psychomotor, and linguistic tasks in order to show the maturity needed for reading instruction. Children like Aretha would be tested to see if they could tie their shoes, skip properly (one of the things Aretha had trouble with and still does at age 19), trace pictures, hear the difference between similar words such as *pin* and *tin*, and so on, all as prerequisites for reading instruction. Problems with the reading readiness perspective came to light when children like Aretha proved they could read without having developed some of the so-called prerequisite readiness skills. For English learners, the language-related prerequisites for reading were often especially inappropriate, such as hearing the difference between initial consonants in two otherwise identical words (e.g., *pin–bin, chair–share*), or the expectation that oral language should be fully developed before reading instruction could begin. For native English speakers and English learners alike, many reading readiness subskill prerequisites turned out to be unnecessary hindrances to literacy development.

Emergent Literacy Perspective

The basic tenets of the reading readiness perspective were called into question as a result of research in the 1960s on children who learned to read before receiving reading instruction in school (Durkin, 1966). These early readers had not been drilled on auditory and visual discrimination tasks, nor did they wait until they could hop proficiently on one foot before they engaged in reading. On the other hand, they didn't learn to read by age 2 while hiding alone in a closet either, as philosopher Jean-Paul Sartre (1967) claimed to have done. Rather, these early readers set their sights on doing what they saw other people doing, and they engaged the adults at home in answering their questions about print and reading. Gradually, they figured the rest out for themselves. The percentage of children who learn to read without formal instruction is quite small. However, by investigating these children's literacy development processes, researchers documented the need for a theory of early literacy development that could accommodate their findings. The stage was set for a new perspective: the emergent literacy perspective.

According to the **emergent literacy** perspective, pioneered by Marie Clay (1975) in New Zealand and Emilia Ferreiro and Ana Teberosky (1982) in Latin America, children begin to develop written language knowledge from the moment they are first exposed to reading and writing at home during their preschool years, possibly from the time of birth (Clay, 1982). Literacy development is viewed as somewhat parallel to oral language development in process (Peregoy & Boyle, 1993). That is, as children are immersed in social environments where people are reading and writing for a variety of purposes, they take note of how the written word is used around them in lists, notes, letters, storybooks, road signs, product labels, magazines, and other environmental print. From this highly functional written input, children gradually construct knowledge of the functions and forms of print. Of course, little ones want to get into the act as well and will take to pencil, paper, and books readily. You may have seen preschoolers pick up a storybook and "read" it to their stuffed animals, turning the pages and pointing out the pictures as they go along. Given the opportunity, children will also try out writing on paper with drawing, scribbling, and various other forms of writing that gradually begin to approximate conventional writing. Thus, comprehensible input, social interaction, and children's gradual approximations to mature reading and writing are important factors in early literacy development, just as they are in oral language development.

Although early research on emergent literacy highlighted children's natural tendencies to develop literacy concepts through immersion, another line of inquiry took hold in the 1990s (Neuman & Dickinson, 2002, Snow, Burns & Griffin, 1998) that focused on how explicit, direct instruction might help "emergent literate" children learn to decode written words. In particular, researchers examined aspects of the alphabetic principle that children eventually need to know in order to move along in literacy development (Adams, 1990a, 1990b). Inherent in the alphabetic principle are three basic concepts: (1) the speech stream can be broken down into sounds or phonemes; (2) letters of the alphabet can represent these speech sounds; and (3) knowing letter-sound correspondences permits a reader to "recode" words from written form to oral. The outcome of the research effort has been an emphasis on explicit instruction on **phonemic awareness** (the ability to discriminate speech sounds in words) and **phonics**, specific letter-sound correspondences. These research efforts have led to education policies calling for a **balanced approach** that includes explicit instruction on phonemic awareness, phonics, reading fluency, vocabulary, and comprehension (for more information go to www.nationalreadingpanel.org). These goals are best accomplished within a rich literacy environment that highlights the meaningful, functional uses of print. We discuss these ideas in greater detail later in this chapter.

An important aspect of the emergent literacy perspective is that literacy development begins at a young age at home amid day-to-day family and community activities. As a result, with literacy learning no longer considered the sole province of the school, family involvement in early literacy is highlighted. Whereas advocates of reading readiness discouraged parents from teaching their children to read, emergent literacy educators encourage parents to involve their children in naturally occurring literacy events at home, such as reading stories and making grocery lists, emphasizing the importance of home–school relationships in early schooling.

To summarize, we have examined two viewpoints on beginning reading and writing development: reading readiness and emergent literacy. The reading readiness perspective was based on the best scientific knowledge available in the first half of the century. However, literacy research in recent decades refutes the major assumptions of the reading readiness perspective and calls into question many of its practices, especially practices that withheld from children opportunities to engage in authentic, purposeful reading and writing, however rudimentary their efforts might be. Emergent literacy research has led to the following teaching recommendations, which we consider applicable to native English speakers and English learners alike.

1. Acknowledge that all children bring literacy knowledge to school, although recognizing that children vary in their sophistication in literacy concepts and skills.

2. Immerse children in a variety of functional reading and writing experiences that display the purposes of literacy while demonstrating and modeling the processes of reading and writing.

3. Enrich dramatic play centers with functional print, including lists, tablets, prescription forms, phone books, and other props, to encourage children to experiment with reading and writing during play.

4. Accept and celebrate children's progress in their gradual approximations to conventional literacy.

5. Encourage children to read and write at home and to talk to their parents about their reading and writing.

6. Offer explicit instruction on phonemic awareness and phonics based on assessed need.

Specific strategies to implement these recommendations for English learners are described in the remainder of this chapter.

Differences Between Oral and Written Language Development

The emergent literacy perspective emphasizes similarities between oral and written language acquisition. Although there are many similarities between oral and written language acquisition, there are also some significant differences, summarized in Figure 5.2. First, oral language is universally achieved, whereas literacy acquisition is not. No one has posed an innate "literacy acquisition device" comparable to Chomsky's (1959) "language acquisition device." Thus, there are some cultures that never developed literacy, and there are some individuals in literate cultures who do not learn to read and write.

Another difference between oral and written language development is that oral language is learned with relatively little explicit instruction, whereas written language development requires substantial explicit instruction and practice. For example, young children self-correct as they move from saying, "Him don't say it right" to "He doesn't say it right." No one needs to teach them. In contrast, almost all students need explicit instruction on particular reading and writing

FIGURE 5.2 • SOME SIGNIFICANT DIFFERENCES BETWEEN ORAL AND WRITTEN LANGUAGE ACQUISITION

ORAL LANGUAGE DEVELOPMENT	WRITTEN LANGUAGE DEVELOPMENT
Every culture develops oral language.	Not every culture develops written language.
Every child learns the language of his or her community with rare exception.	Not every child learns the written language of his or her community.
Oral language is learned with little explicit instruction.	For most children written language must be learned with a lot of explicit instruction.
Oral language is the primary vehicle for meeting our basic needs.	Written language is not the primary vehicle for meeting our basic needs.

conventions. One reason explicit instruction is needed is simply that it saves time to tell a third grader to spell -*tion* at the end of words instead of the more logical -*shun* that the child has been using or to break long words into parts or to use letter/sound cues to promote early independence in reading. Speaking of explicit instruction, we are reminded that emergent literacy pioneer Marie Clay is also the developer of Reading Recovery (1975), an early intervention program that provides explicit phonics instruction integrated with meaningful reading and writing for first graders experiencing difficulty learning to read.

Differences between oral and written language acquisition tend to be differences in degree rather than kind (Snow, 1983). For example, the fact that literacy acquisition is not universally achieved in literate societies may be partially attributable to the difference in degree of functionality between oral and written language. You can't get by in life very well without talking because oral language is used so often to meet basic needs. Written language is certainly functional, but it does not have the immediacy of oral language. No child is required to read the word *Cheerios*® in order to get breakfast. As teachers, we need to increase and highlight the functions of literacy in our classrooms. As literacy uses proliferate, your students will be motivated to read and write. In addition, the more you read and write in the classroom, the more your students will be able to see how it is done and why. You are a powerful model. As students work with the medium of written language, they will develop many conventions on their own. When necessary, though, you should feel free to use explicit instruction, especially when children ask you for it. And they will!

Highlighting Literacy Functions in Your Classroom

It takes some thought and imagination to create and highlight literacy functions in your classroom. When you create a variety of literacy purposes for your students, you broaden their understanding of literacy functions and motivate them to learn how to read and write. If your students have little prior experience with reading and writing, it is all the more important that you explicitly talk about how these can be used for different purposes, such as a card to send birthday wishes to a friend far away, a list to help you remember what to buy at the store, a journal to keep a record of the events of a trip to visit relatives, and a personal phone book to keep your friends' numbers handy. Table 5.1 cites additional examples of literacy functions that children use at home and at school.

Exploring the Visual Form of Written Language

One fascinating aspect of early literacy development is young children's explorations of the visual form of the writing system they see used around them, whether alphabetic as in English, logographic as in Chinese, or syllabic as in the Cherokee writing system developed by Chief Sequoyah in the nineteenth century (see Crystal, 1997). Just as children acquire the oral language forms spoken around them, they also experiment with the written forms that they see others using. Figure 5.3 illustrates 4-year-old children's attempts at writing in English, Arabic, and Hebrew, each of which uses a different alphabetic writing system, in which letters represent language sounds (Harste, et al., 1984). Although not yet conventional, each child's writing is

TABLE 5.1 • Written Language Functions and Classroom Experiences

FUNCTIONS	CLASSROOM EXPERIENCES
Instrumental I want	Order forms in play store
Interactional Me and you	Message board for notes from teacher to children; class post office; dialogue journals
Personal Here I come	Books about self and family with captioned pictures; individual language-experience stories
Heuristic Tell me why	Question box; single-concept books; science experiments; learning logs; response journals
Imaginative Let's pretend	Story reading; readers' theater read-along books and records; comic strips
Informative I've got to tell you	Message boards and bulletin boards; notes to pupils paralleling school messages to parents; class newspaper; content textbooks; resource books
Regulatory You should	Daily schedule posted; directions for feeding the class pet posted; behavioral rules posted

recognizable as a precursor of the conventional form of the corresponding alphabet. These examples of young children's early attempts at writing show us their efforts to represent the visual aspects of the alphabetic writing system they have seen used around them. Their writing approximates the mature writing systems, but not well enough yet to be clearly decipherable.

Research suggests that children learning logographic writing systems, in which written characters represent words, may also go through similar stages, from scribbling to inventive character forms to standard character formation (Chi, 1988). Figures 5.4 and 5.5 show young Taiwanese writers' approximations in constructing characters of the Chinese writing system. Figure 5.4 shows early iconic pictographic writing in which the child's writing looks like the actual item. That is, for the word *bed* the child draws a picture of a bed. Below each item is the Chinese character for the word. Figure 5.5 gives an example of more advanced, invented pictographic writing that closely approximates conventional Chinese characters (Chi, 1988).

Development of Alphabetic Writing: Connecting Symbols and Sounds

The examples of children's emergent writing in Figures 5.3, 5.4, and 5.5 illustrate youngsters' attention to the visual aspects of writing systems. In this section, we take a look at two studies that show how children working with alphabetic writing systems gradually connect the visual symbols with the sounds they represent to make their written messages decipherable to others. Elizabeth Sulzby, an emergent

FIGURE 5.3

EMERGENT WRITING IN ENGLISH, ARABIC, AND HEBREW

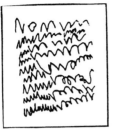

Dawn, a 4-year-old from the United States, writes in unconventional script using a series of wavy lines. Each line is written from left to right. Dawn creates a page of such lines starting at the top of her page and finishing at the bottom of her page.

Source: Reprinted by permission of Jerome C. Harste, Virginia A. Woodward, and Carolyn L. Burke, *Language Stories and Literacy Lessons*, (Portsmouth, NH: Heinemann, a division of Reed Elsevier Inc., 1984).

Najeeba, a 4-year-old from Saudi Arabia, writes in unconventional script using a series of very intricate curlicue formations with lots of "dots" over the script. When she completes her story she says, "Here, but you can't read it, cause I wrote it in Arabic and in Arabic we use a lot more dots than you do in English!"

Ofer, a 4-year-old from Israel, prints, first right-to-left then left-to-right, using a series of rectangular and triangular shapes to create his story, which his grandmother says ". . . looks like Hebrew, but it's not." Her concern because he sometimes writes "backwards" sounds like the concerns of many parents and teachers in the United States, with the difference being that left-to-right is "backwards" in Hebrew, and right-to-left "backwards" in English.

literacy researcher, examined the writing of 24 English-speaking kindergarten children (1985). She identified six categories of writing strategies that the children used, but cautioned that these categories did not necessarily represent developmental sequences. The categories were:

1. Writing via drawing
2. Writing via scribbling
3. Writing via letterlike forms
4. Writing via reproducing well-learned units or letter strings
5. Writing via invented spelling
6. Writing via conventional spelling

As shown in Sulzby's research (1985), when children first begin to use letters, they may not use them to represent sounds. Eventually, however, children represent sounds with letters. At this stage, they create their own invented spellings, which are logical and readable but not yet fully conventional. When children create invented spellings, they are demonstrating advanced emergent literacy. It is

FIGURE 5.4

CHINESE ICONIC PICTO-
GRAPHIC WRITING.
These pictographs were
written by a 5-year-old
Chinese boy. Beneath his
pictographic writing is
the conventional Chinese
character and the meaning
in English.

Source: Original data,
reprinted with permission,
courtesy of Dr. Marilyn Chi.

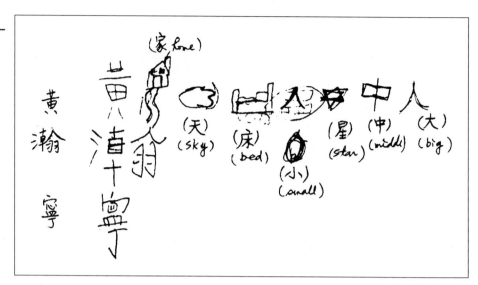

164 **FIGURE 5.5**

PICTOGRAPHIC INVENTED
WRITING.
This 5-year-old Chinese
boy is using symbols that
look like the conventional
Chinese character, as
shown in parentheses.

Source: Original data,
reprinted with permission,
courtesy of Dr. Marilyn Chi.

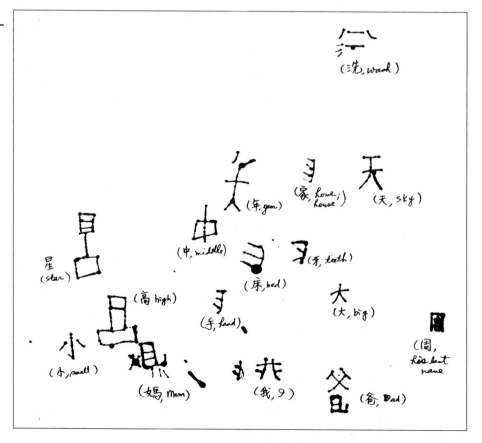

through children's invented spellings that we see them really working through the sound/symbol puzzle inherent in writing English (Gentry, 1980).

In our own research in the two-way Spanish immersion kindergarten described at the beginning of this chapter, we analyzed journal entries made by eight Hispanic American children who were native Spanish speakers writing in Spanish (Peregoy & Boyle, 1990a). We identified seven developmental scripting strategies in Spanish that correspond closely with those found by Sulzby in English. Our categories, shown in Figure 5.6, are distributed along a continuum from least advanced to most advanced: scribble writing, pseudo letters, letters, pseudo words, copied words and phrases, self-generated words, and self-generated sentences. Like Sulzby, we found that these were not discrete developmental sequences. In fact, some children used two or more scripting strategies in the same journal entry. You may want to adapt Figure 5.6 as a teacher–researcher and chart the developmental progress of your own emergent writers.

In our emergent writing research in the Spanish immersion kindergarten, we were able to document ways in which native Spanish-speaking Mexican American children took control of their own Spanish literacy development in a constructive manner

FIGURE 5.6 • A CONTINUUM OF DEVELOPMENTAL SCRIPTING STRATEGIES

WRITING TYPE	DEFINITION	EXAMPLE
scribble writing	wavy lines or forms that don't look like letters, but look a little like writing	
pseudo letters	forms that look like letters but aren't	
letters	recognizable letters from the alphabet; often seen in long rows	
pseudo words	letter or pseudo letters that are spaced so they appear to be words	
copied words	words that have been copied from displays in the classroom	
self-generated words	words that students created that are close enough to conventional spelling to be recognized	
self-generated sentences	conventional or nearly conventional sentences that communicate ideas	

Source: Suzanne F. Peregoy and Owen F. Boyle, "Kindergartners Write! Emergent Literacy of Mexican American Children in a Two-Way Spanish Immersion Program," *The Journal of the Association of Mexican American Educators* (1989–90), p. 12. Reprinted with permission of the publisher.

165

similar to that reported in other studies (Ferreiro & Teberosky, 1982; Sulzby, 1985). They used drawing to assist them with the task of developing ideas for writing, and they wrote about topics related to home and school, including topics initiated during circle time. In addition, these kindergartners used the print that surrounded them in and out of the classroom as a form of input for scripting. They took note of words in the wall dictionary, labels from around the room, alphabet charts, and their own names, and incorporated these into their journal writing. Several of the children made significant progress in constructing literacy in the emergent literacy kindergarten. However, some children made relatively little progress, the result, in part, of the teacher's extended absence because of illness that year. More research is needed on children who struggle in emergent literacy development.

Finally, it is important to note that the children in our study varied in prior literacy experiences gained at home. In some cases the children's parents had attained less than a sixth-grade education, whereas other parents were high school graduates. One child, whose mother we met at school, was already being encouraged to write at home. Therefore, it is not surprising that he was the most sophisticated writer in our study. We regretted that we were unable to visit each child's home to find out what kinds of literacy materials were available and how the family incorporated literacy events into day-to-day activities.

In summary, in this section we examined ways in which young children explore the visual forms of written language. As they experiment with written language, they may gradually reconstruct the spelling system well enough to convey written messages without having to explain their meaning. To achieve accuracy in conventional spelling and other aspects of written language generally requires formal instruction. In the next section, we take a closer look at some of the concepts about print that students need to develop to use the alphabet for reading and writing.

Print Concepts That Emerge in Emergent Literacy

We have suggested that children begin to develop their own literacy knowledge through exposure to meaningful, functional literacy events in a process similar to oral language development. What are some basic literacy concepts and insights that develop during the emergent literacy phase? In addition to an ever-broadening understanding of the many communicative functions and personal purposes served by written language, emergent readers and writers must grasp the following ideas about print:

1. Print carries meaning. It conveys a message.
2. Spoken words can be written down and preserved.
3. Written words can be spoken, that is, read out loud.
4. In English, words are read from left to right, top to bottom.
5. In English and other languages that use alphabets, the speech stream can be divided into sounds, and these sounds are represented by letters or groups of letters. This is the alphabetic principle.
6. The speech stream has a linear sequence in time that corresponds to written language's linear sequence on the page.
7. Sound/symbol correspondences are consistent, but in English there are many exceptions.

As you read this list, you probably noticed how abstract all this sounds. It is abstract! You could never teach children these things by trying to have them memorize these statements! It is through immersion in a literacy-rich environment with lots of stories read aloud and lots of opportunities for children to write on their own that they begin to understand the marvelous truths about print, its relationships to spoken language, and its power to communicate across time and space.

The first four of the preceding list of print concepts probably seem extremely obvious to you. For young children, however, there is still a great mystery to the printed word, and children have to come to understand gradually that print can convey meaning and that it does so by representing language. You will recall our friend Osvaldo, the kindergartner whose writing had no meaning until his picture was complete. Osvaldo did not yet grasp the specific relationship of print to meaning and language. On the other hand, he did understand that writing should convey a message, and he was interested in knowing how his story was received!

The last three print concepts, which sound technical to many who hear them for the first time, all relate to the alphabetic principle, that is, the idea that language sounds are represented by letters and letter sequences. The first alphabet was created over 3,000 years ago by the great Semitic trading people of the Mediterranean, the Phoenicians. Theirs was a brilliant discovery, one that is reconstructed daily by children learning to read and write. What does it take to reconstruct the alphabetic system that children see in use around them? Let's consider the idea that the speech stream can be divided into sounds. If this idea seems obvious to you, it is probably because you read and write and have therefore had many opportunities to work with the **graphophonemic units**, or letter–sound correspondences, of your language. A phoneme, you may recall, is the smallest unit of sound that makes a difference in meaning in a language, and a **grapheme** is the letter or letter combination, such as *d* or *th*, that represents that sound (Stahl, 1992). The streamlike nature of speech is more evident when you listen to someone speaking a foreign language. Then it's hard to discern individual words, much less individual sounds: It's all a flow of sound. Young children are confronted with the speech stream in a similar manner, except that they are further distracted from listening for sounds by their attention to the meaning of the speech stream. Young children do, however, know how to play with language sounds, an ability that develops around age 4 or 5. Evidence that children can divide the speech stream comes from word play, such as spontaneous rhyming. For example, you may have heard children who take a word like *cake* and generate a litany of rhymes: *take, lake, Jake, rake.* They do this for fun, but it shows that they understand the concept of a speech sound because they have replaced the initial consonant, a single speech sound, in each word to create a new rhyming word. In so doing, they are demonstrating **phonemic awareness**, or awareness of individual sounds that constitute spoken words. In fact, one way to assess a child's level of phonemic awareness informally is to ask him or her to tell you words that rhyme.

Research suggests that phonemic awareness is an important aspect of early reading development in English and one of the best predictors of native English-speaking children's future success as readers (Adams, 1990a, 1990b). This makes sense when you consider that the alphabet is a graphic system that relates letters to speech sounds. As students learn the relationships between speech sounds and the letters in written words, they gain access to one of the main cueing systems in reading (along with syntax and semantics): phonics or graphophonics (Goodman, 1967; Stahl, 1992). Key research suggests that once children grasp (1) the idea that words consist of different phonemes and (2) that letters represent these phonemes, they can benefit from phonics instruction (Ehri & Wilce, 1985; Frith, 1985; Juel, Griffith, & Gough, 1986; Perfetti, Beck, Bell, & Hughes, 1987). However, phonics instruction should address sound/symbol correspondences that students have not acquired already through meaningful experiences with print and through their own personal efforts at reading and writing.

You can no doubt see how important the concept of speech sounds is to the development of the alphabetic principle. Phonemic awareness should not be considered a prerequisite for literacy instruction, however. Indeed, we believe that exposure to written language promotes phonemic awareness by showing children how oral language sounds are divided, sequenced, and represented by letters and letter sequences. Reading poems, stories, and song lyrics aloud while students read along is one way. Giving them opportunities to write is another. Your students' emergent writings demonstrate the extent of their understanding of the alphabetic principle and other concepts about the forms and functions of print. In fact, one of the best ways for learners to work on phonics is through their own writing using invented

FIGURE 5.7 • SAM'S WRITING

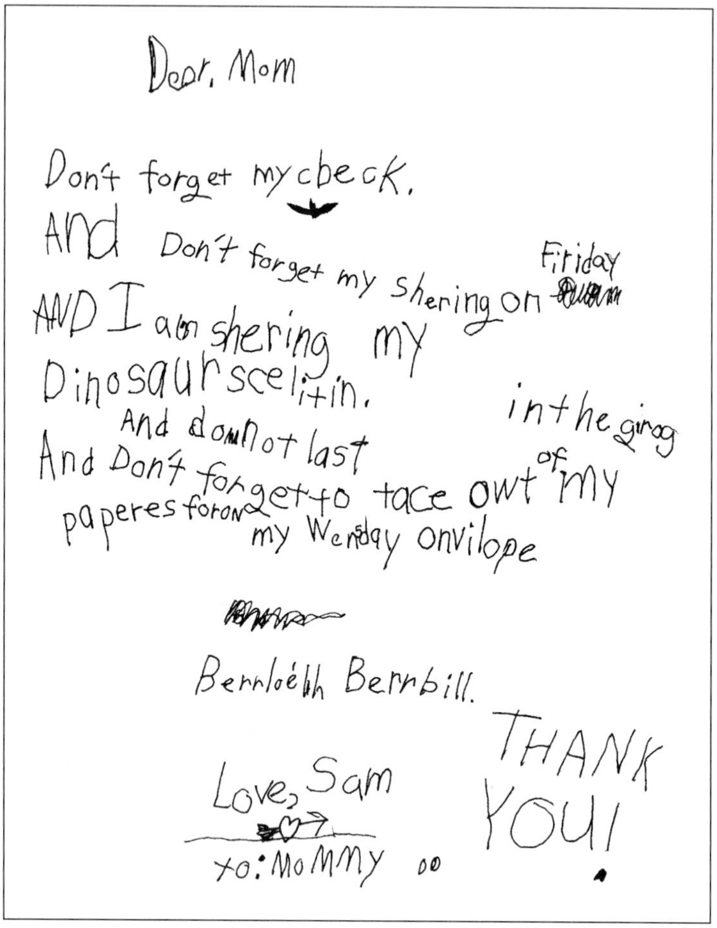
Dear, Mom

Don't forget my cbeck.
And Don't forget my Shering on Firiday
AND I am shering my Dinosaur scelitin. in the girag
And don not last
And Don't forget to tace owt of my paperes foron my Wendsday onvilope

Berrloéth Berrbill.

THANK YOU!

Love, Sam

to: Mommy

or temporary spelling. Just as children's oral language "errors" (e.g., "he goed" for "he went") represent logical, developmental hypotheses about grammar, so also children's and older students' invented spellings (e.g., *bar* for *bear*) represent their logical, developmental hypotheses about how to spell. You need to be well prepared to explain invented or temporary spelling to parents as a high-level cognitive process in which students "think through" how sounds and letters relate to one another. Invented spelling represents an important step on the way to conventional spelling while providing individualized phonics practice that will assist both reading and writing development.

Invented or Temporary Spelling: Children Working Out Sound/Symbol Correspondences

We have talked about invented spelling at some length. Now let's look at two children's writing samples to examine the logic inherent in their invented spellings. Sam is a 7-year-old Farsi/English bilingual who is proficient in English, whereas Martha is a 6-year-old native English speaker. In Figure 5.7, we see a note Sam wrote to his mother, a university student. Because she is not always home when Sam gets out of school, the two of them post notes, messages, and letters on the refrigerator door to keep one another apprised of events of the day or coming events.

Sam uses some interesting spelling strategies. For example, he spells *Friday* "Firiday," because that's how he hears it. Notice that each of the words he invents or constructs is decipherable by sounding out the word phonetically with a little help from the context. So we get "shering" for *sharing*, "scelitin" for *skeleton*, "girag" for *garage*, "owt" for *out*, and so on. We know how he pronounces the word *envelope* because of his spelling, "onvilope." We also get Sam's original spelling for *take*, which we might not expect: "tace." Most important, we see in Sam's writing a consistency as he constructs the sounds he hears in English into his own individual, sophisticated, and logical spelling system. Incidentally, we thought that the words at the end of the letter, *Berrloe'lh Berrbill*, were made up or Farsi words, but his mother told us they were from a favorite book of his—another indication of the effects of a highly literate environment.

In Figure 5.8 we see evidence of 6-year-old Martha's approach to the task of representing her words through invented spellings. For the most part, the consonants she uses are consistent with the sounds she wishes to represent. She has learned the conventional sound/letter correspondences and uses them effectively. In contrast, spelling vowel sounds presents a challenge to Martha. English has numerous vowel sounds, but few vowel letters to represent these sounds, just *a, e, i, o, u*, and sometimes *y* and *w*. Even conventional spelling does not offer a one-to-one correspondence between English letters and sounds. Let's see how Martha is handling this challenge. In her story in Figure 5.8, she consistently uses *"ee"* to represent the long *e* sound as in "hee" for *he* and "finlee" for *finally*. Her double vowel strategy is used inconsistently, however. For example, she uses double *o* in "koodint" for *couldn't*, even though it doesn't have a long *o* sound. In addition, Martha uses a different approach to long vowel sounds, writing "finde" for *find*, "hom" for *home*, and "onr" for *owner*. In these words, she lets the vowel "say its name." Finally, Martha hears the diphthong, two vowel sounds combined, in the word *found*, which she spells "fawnd." Even though Martha's

FIGURE 5.8 • MARTHA'S WRITING

Foow

thar wus a lost dog and hee koodint finde a hom but hee finlee fawnd a onr

vowel spellings are inconsistent, they portray the sounds well enough for the words to be decipherable. Invented spellings as sophisticated as Martha's and Sam's show us how children are working out orthographic representations of language sounds. If you can decipher the message, the child has done an effective spelling job even if it is not completely conventional.

Although Sam and Martha provide interesting examples of invented spelling for us to analyze, their efforts also demonstrate a clear understanding that writing has meaning and purpose. Their messages make sense and serve particular functions: Sam is communicating with his mother; Martha is writing a piece of fiction. Martha is an avid storywriter, in fact, and she uses a number of literary devices in her stories, including openings such as "Wuns upon a time." In addition, her characters tend to have a problem that they solve, evidence of a rudimentary plot. We mention these aspects of the children's writing to highlight that spelling is but one aspect of written language that learners must begin to control as they develop literacy. They will need time, practice, and instructional support to proceed to conventional reading and writing, important topics we develop in Chapters 7 through 10. In addition, we discuss spelling development and instruction later in this chapter.

Emergent Literacy in English as a Non-Native Language

Little research addresses the emergent English literacy development of English learners who have not received literacy instruction in their primary language. Although more research is needed, we believe that English learners will develop emergent literacy concepts following patterns similar to those documented for native English speakers (Hudelson, 1984, 1986). Therefore, the teaching strategies we offer in subsequent sections of this book emphasize immersing students in meaningful, functional uses of reading and writing combined with explicit instruction to assist them in becoming independent readers and writers. National panels reviewing research on the teaching of beginning reading recommend phonemic awareness, phonics, reading fluency, and comprehension as the cornerstones of the curriculum. Students should receive beginning reading instruction in the primary language, if possible (Snow et al., 1998). Complex topics like phonemic awareness have yet to be investigated among students learning English as a second language. However, there will be differences early on in English learners' ability to perceive and produce English speech sounds, depending on the extent of their English language proficiency. For this reason, English learners should not be involved in phonics instruction that isolates sounds and letters from meaningful use of text. That is to say that any phonics instruction should take place in the context of whole texts such as poems, songs, and predictable stories for which understanding and enjoyment have been developed, before focusing on individual words and sound/symbol patterns. In so doing, both language and literacy acquisition are served first, and children receive explicit phonics instruction subsequently.

As with young English learners who are new to literacy, there is little research on older English learners who have minimal prior literacy experience in either the primary language or English. However, Else Hamayan (1994) has given us an interesting report on her experiences teaching ESL to Southeast Asian refugee adolescents in the Philippines in a program designed to prepare families to relocate to North America. For various reasons, the adolescents in her class had never received literacy instruction, and their families were nonliterate as well. Thus, the students had very little experience with functional print. In dialogue journal entries to share with her, Hamayan's students tended to copy print materials they found at home, such as their parents' ESL exercises. They seemed to focus on form, without any idea that print served to communicate a message. Hamayan concluded that their lack of experience with print left them in the dark about its functions and purposes.* Based on her experiences with these students, Hamayan suggests that older nonliterate students need to be introduced gradually to the numerous ways reading and writing are used for communication, that is, written language functions. In addition to constant exposure to literacy functions, Hamayan suggests explicit teaching of reading and writing strategies to help them learn as quickly and efficiently as possible. As Hamayan says, "Although an exclusive use of structural approaches falls short of the needs of children from low-literacy backgrounds, explicit attention to the rules and the structure of writ-

---

*Alternative explanations for these students' approach to writing in dialogue journals might be their unfamiliarity with the genre or their belief that the most important thing was to produce correct forms for the teacher.

ten language can help learners become literate and develop higher-order thinking skills and learning strategies" (1994, p. 290). Hamayan's recommendations echo the ones we make here for younger learners. Because of their age and more advanced cognitive development, older learners may be able to learn some aspects of literacy more quickly than younger children. However, as yet we have insufficient data to draw detailed conclusions about the differences between younger and older learners whose first exposure to literacy is in their second language. If you have such students, you might consider documenting your teaching strategies and corresponding student progress over time. Sharing your experiences in class or at conferences can increase your own understanding while making a worthwhile contribution to the field!

In summary, we have contrasted the reading readiness and emergent literacy perspectives of early literacy development. We elaborated on the emergent literacy perspective, discussing research findings and implications for instruction, including the importance of immersing students in a variety of functional literacy events and providing opportunities for them to construct reading and writing in their own way, gradually approximating conventional written language. We went on to discuss in some detail several early insights learners must achieve in the emergent literacy phase of reading and writing development, most of which related to the alphabetic principle. In our discussion, we emphasized that emergent readers and writers are also expanding their understanding of how print can serve a vast array of communicative functions and purposes. Thus a crucial role for teachers is to illustrate the usefulness of reading and writing for many purposes in classroom and community. Finally, we discussed implications for English learners, noting that more research is needed on the emergent literacy paths taken by English learners, including those who are older when introduced to literacy for the first time.

171

Home and School Environments That Nurture Emergent Literacy

In literate societies, young children's literacy development begins well before kindergarten, and this holds true across ethnic and socioeconomic lines. In many countries, children are exposed to environmental print in the form of road signs, billboards, announcements in store windows, and magazines in doctor's offices, to name just a few. In addition, you will find literacy materials of various kinds in most homes: magazines, newspapers, CD or tape labels, TV guides, books, and paper and writing tools. Many teachers have been led to believe that immigrant families, poor families, and other minority group families neither use literacy at home nor value education in general. A growing body of research now refutes this belief. Although it is true that families vary in the ways children are involved in literacy at home, literacy nonetheless serves numerous functions in most homes, including homes of families living below the poverty level (Chall & Snow, 1982; Taylor & Dorsey-Gaines, 1988), families in which English is not the primary language (Delgado-Gaitán, 1987; Díaz, Moll, & Mehan, 1986; Vásquez, 1991), and families with low educational levels (Heath, 1983; Purcell-Gates, 1995). Perceptive teachers will find ways to recognize and build on children's home language and literacy experiences, thereby transforming deficit myths about English language learners and other language minority students (Díaz, et al., 1986; Flores, Cousin, & Díaz, 1991).

How Do Home Environments Promote Early Literacy?

Parents and other family members provide a powerful model for children every time they pick up a newspaper or magazine; every time they put pen to paper, whether to post messages on the refrigerator, make grocery lists, write letters, or note appointments on their calendar; and every time they cut out grocery coupons or discuss the call-waiting feature announced in the recent phone bill. In so doing, family members model the forms and functions of print for children. These natural, functional, daily uses of written language provide a good foundation for literacy because children see that written language is a wonderful tool. They want to own the mystery of such powerful magic.

Another way families promote literacy development is by answering children's questions about print. Children often initiate literacy events when they ask, "What does that sign say?" The question triggers a response, "That's a stop sign. It means we have to stop at the corner to let other cars go by." I (Suzanne) can remember at age 7 sitting in the front seat as my father was driving home from the store. I saw a big, yellow YIELD RIGHT OF WAY sign, and I asked my dad what it meant. He explained it, but I remember being confused by the concept. Luckily, I didn't need to understand that sign for another 10 years, when I finally got my driver's license! Sometimes children ask parents how to spell a word as they write at home. At other times, children will beg to have a story read. In each case, children *invite* modeling, scaffolding, and explicit instruction from parents and siblings, thereby providing a natural means of language and literacy development at home.

Children also show interest in writing from an early age. As soon as a toddler can grasp a pen or crayon, the impulse to write will appear. This impulse often takes on grand proportions if children gain surreptitious access to a "blank" wall in the house. Perhaps you are one of those early writers/artists who wrote on walls as a child, or less joyful, perhaps you were the parent who had to repaint the wall! Providing children with writing materials early on may not only encourage literacy development but may also save your walls!

What do we know about the literacy concepts children bring to school if a language other than English is spoken in the home? First, we know that for early literacy concepts to develop, exposure to literacy events is what matters most, not the language of the written materials or the language in which the discussion around written materials takes place. Many non-English-speaking parents have feared that using their native language at home might be harmful to their children's acquisition of English. This turns out to be untrue (see Cummins, 1981; Wong Fillmore, 1991a, 1991b). In the case of early literacy in particular, when children are involved in functional literacy activities at home—in, say, Spanish or Cantonese—they begin to form important concepts about how print works in form and function. In the process, they begin to have expectations about print and they want to read and write. These understandings will transfer to English literacy when they go to school. Similarly, with oral language use, it is important that parents talk to children in extended and elaborated ways in the language they know best because doing so helps young children build knowledge of the world that will serve them in school and transfer to English once the second language is developed.

A small percentage of English learners may come to school with extremely limited literacy experience. However, even parents who are not highly educated often expose their children to the functions of print. You may recall the story of Gustavo in Chapter 1. Gustavo at age 6 understood deeply the importance of the written word because his mother had to find someone who could write a letter to Mexico to obtain medicine essential for his baby sister's health. His mother could not write, but the importance of writing was certainly understood. Parents of English learners, whether immigrants or native born, vary in their own literacy development; some are highly educated, others are not. However, nearly all value literacy and education (cf. Delgado-Gaitán, 1987). In fact, many have risked their lives to come to this country for the specific purpose of obtaining a better education for their children.

Some children who are learning English in school come from cultures with strong oral storytelling traditions in the home language, be it Navajo, Spanish, Hmong, or African American English. It is important to note that oral traditions also offer excellent foundations for literacy development. We know, for example, that fables and folktales have predictable story structures, as do television soap operas, which you can watch in Spanish, Chinese, English, and other languages in some areas of the country. Children become familiar with the narrative structures of these genres and with the characters themselves, potentially creating a familiar foundation when they encounter similar stories in print at school. It can be a challenge to find out about the oral traditions of the children in your class, but these stories can provide a rich multicultural resource for early literacy development.

In summary, families promote early literacy in many ways: by modeling a variety of day-to-day literacy uses; by answering children's questions about print and its meanings; by providing children with literacy materials, including paper, pencils, books, and magazines that allow them to play with reading and writing; and by telling stories and reading aloud to children.

173

Family Literacy Programs

Numerous research studies have shown that children who are read to at home tend to achieve better when they go to school (Wells, 1986). Furthermore, the active involvement of parents in children's schooling has a positive impact on their school adjustment and performance (Epstein, 1986; Topping & Wolfingdale, 1985). These research findings have led many educators to become involved in family literacy projects aimed at promoting story reading and other kinds of literacy activities among families, particularly low-income, minority, and immigrant families. Some family literacy projects offer classes for parents in English language and literacy with a focus on promoting parent involvement in their children's schooling. The best family literacy programs assess and acknowledge the language and literacy used at home and build from there.

We have seen family literacy projects of various kinds. A number of projects emphasize teaching parents to read storybooks to their preschool and kindergarten children. Some projects teach specific read-aloud techniques such as asking children to predict what the story will be about or to predict what will happen on the next page or asking children at the end why they liked or disliked the book (Edwards, 1989). Story reading seems to be beneficial in a variety of ways. Perhaps most powerful is the cozy, loving laptime moments that story reading creates. It also provides parents with a chance to exercise their own reading skills, while boosting parental self-esteem in knowing that they are strengthening their child's chances for success in school. Finally, by modeling story reading for children, parents provide a rich source of numerous emergent literacy concepts.

A special kind of family literacy project was instituted in the late 1980s as a result of federal funding: Family English Literacy. These programs serve the parents of children who are learning English in school. The parents themselves are English learners, and the Family English Literacy programs assist parents in learning to speak, read, and write in English. The functional focus of English language use involves parents in reading with their children and listening to their children read; talking about homework and school concerns with their children; and engaging children in literacy-related home activities, such as cooking, writing notes, and marking the calendar for special events.

Among the most promising Family English Literacy projects are those that make a particular effort to learn about, acknowledge, and build on the literacy activities already present in the home (Auerbach, 1991). In such projects, parents use the English literacy class to identify their own needs and concerns in a safe forum for dialogue about family and community issues. At the same time, they learn how to advocate for their children in school. Most important, family literacy projects help forge comfortable connections with the school among parents who previously may have felt alienated from educational institutions, while helping immigrant and other parents take control of their own lives and those of their children.

One particularly interesting family literacy project was undertaken in the Pajaro School District in California (Ada, 1988). In this project, educator Alma Flor Ada invited Spanish-speaking parents to come to the library to study children's literature as a focus for developing their own literacy skills. Many of the parents had never advanced beyond the second or third grade in Mexico and were therefore unsure of themselves in school settings. Children's literature provided a natural, nonthreatening, and inviting means to literacy. As parents attended the sessions, they began to see that there were many ways in which they could become involved in literacy activities at home with their children. They felt validated to know that using Spanish and talking about Spanish language children's literature would have a positive effect on their children's school experiences, including literacy development in English. As a culminating project, parents and children wrote stories about significant events in their lives. Through this project parents had the opportunity to reflect on their relationships with their children, with the school, and with their as yet unwritten futures. In so doing, they took a more active and aware stance in creating and recreating their own life stories.

Promoting Parent Involvement in English Learners' Schooling

Promoting involvement among your English learners' parents can be quite a challenge, especially if you don't share a common language. Cultural differences may also impede the school relationships you wish to achieve, if parents' prior experiences with schools were minimal or if their school experiences emphasized separate, autonomous roles for home and school. We offer some suggestions here that we have gathered over the years.

Make Parent Involvement a Schoolwide Goal

If parent involvement is a school priority, then resources can be provided for increasing home–school communication. For example, school notices can be translated into your students' home languages. Because schools often have numerous different primary languages within the student population, it is essential to have the support of the administration in providing translators. If possible, a community liaison worker can be hired to make phone calls or visit the homes, if needed, to make sure parents receive important information.

Teachers sometimes report difficulties in getting parents to come to school, whether for open house, parent conferences, or other school functions. If children are bussed some distance to school in cities or rural areas, it is often quite difficult for parents to get to the school. In addition, some parents work long hours and are unable to attend school functions because of work schedules. Nonetheless, you can make a special effort to help parents feel comfortable at school by providing notices in the home language that explain the purpose of the school function and what will be happening. We have often been told that the best way to get parents to come to school is to provide a social event that includes food and the opportunity to see their children performing songs, dances, or plays. Because each community is different, you may wish to brainstorm parent involvement ideas with paraprofessionals, community liaisons, teachers, and the principal at your school, especially those who are members of the particular cultural groups you serve.

Taking School Activities Home

In addition to translating notices sent home and making efforts to bring parents to school, you can forge home–school connections and promote language and literacy development through carefully structured take-home activities. We know of one teacher who lets children take home a teddy bear for one day. The next day at school, the child reports to the class what the teddy bear did at home. Similarly, you can implement the use of a "literacy backpack." You will have to buy one or more small backpacks, depending on how many you want to have in use at one time. You place literacy materials in them to be taken home for a specified number of days. One week, you might insert colored markers and several sheets of paper; another week, you might put in a copy of the storybook you have been reading to the class. You need to make sure that the rules on caring for the items and the due date for return are clear. To promote parent involvement, children can be asked to show their parents what they wrote or drew, to read a story to their parents, or to otherwise talk about activities. Children who have taken the backpack home may also report to the class what they did with the materials at home.

Another item to put in the literacy backpack is storybooks with audiotapes that your children have been reading in class, a routine that has been researched and found effective with young English learners (Koskinen, et al., 1995). In this home–school literacy project, the teachers sent home a tape recorder and the storybook and audiotape. They found that 12-inch tape recorders with color-coded buttons, which they marked with colored dots for "play," "stop," and "rewind," worked best. They sent home letters explaining the project translated into the home languages of the parents. Whenever possible, teachers explained the use of books and audiotapes during parent conferences. In this project, five backpacks at a time were available to take home to keep for three to five days. Thus, it took several weeks for each child to have a first turn. Children were given instructions on how to select a book, how to check it out and return it, and how to use the tape recorder to read along with the story. The children were responsible for teaching their parents how to use the tape recorder with the storybooks.

Projects such as these take considerable time, money, and organization, but the rewards in literacy development and home–school relations make them worthwhile. Financial support is sometimes available from parent–teacher groups, professional organizations, local merchants, or fast-food chains.

In summary, as children become involved in using literacy in their homes and communities, they will begin to form ideas about the forms and functions of print—the beginnings of emergent literacy. You can build on these early concepts by offering all children a wide variety of functional literacy experiences, including shared reading, journal writing, shared writing, and immersion in literacy-enriched play centers, as described subsequently.

Classroom Strategies to Promote Early Literacy

In the previous section, we discussed early literacy development and ways to link children's home and school experiences in natural, fun ways to support their developing concepts of the forms and functions of print. Our discussion focused primarily on early childhood classrooms. In this section, we describe classroom strategies that will continue to support early reading and writing development for young English learners. In addition, we make suggestions for adapting these strategies for older English learners whose first exposure to literacy begins later, whether in upper-elementary, middle, or high school.

Early Literacy Goals

Any student, regardless of age, who is just beginning to read and write in English needs to develop (1) awareness and appreciation of the variety of purposes reading and writing serve in everyday life; (2) understanding of relationships between print and oral language, including the alphabetic principle; (3) knowledge of print conventions, such as left-to-right, top-to-bottom sequencing; (4) knowledge of specific sound/symbol correspondences, or phonics; and (5) ability to recognize a growing number of words on sight. During early literacy development, learners need to begin to coordinate all these understandings to read and make sense of simple texts.

All five goals are served by holistic teaching strategies, whereas explicit skill instruction further reinforces phonics and sight word development. We define **holistic strategies** as literacy events involving reading and writing whole texts such as stories, poems, songs, and recipes, that serve real, day-to-day purposes. Holistic strategies, or what we defined as literacy scaffolds in Chapter 3, are especially important for English learners because they provide rich and meaningful print experiences, with comprehension scaffolded by the teacher or other students. Holistic strategies should be used extensively every day. These strategies may then be supplemented by explicit phonics and sight word instruction. Phonics and sight word instruction should be based on words that students have already seen and heard many times in stories, poems, songs, letters, recipes, and other texts used previously. When you offer numerous meaningful, functional print experiences, your students increase their awareness of why we read and write; that is, the functions of print. When you offer explicit phonics instruction, you increase students' knowledge of how print works, or, its form. Both are important aspects of early literacy development.

Creating a Literacy-Rich Classroom Environment

In the early grades, especially kindergarten, you can promote literacy development in many ways. First, you can enrich activity centers with literacy props that encourage children to learn about literacy through play. Some centers reflect familiar aspects of the child's home and community, such as the kitchen and grocery store; others introduce new themes, such as science centers, that are precursors of later academic subjects. For literacy development purposes, each center should be enriched with literacy props. For example, the kitchen can be supplied with calendars, note paper for grocery lists, cookbooks, and recipe cards for boys and girls to enjoy. The other centers can be similarly enriched. With an eye toward literacy opportunities, you can create a plethora of functional literacy opportunities for children to explore and enjoy.

The following list illustrates some ways to enrich your classroom with functional literacy opportunities in several different centers. Figure 5.9 on page 178 gives a sample floor plan showing how you might organize your classroom for children's optimal use of functional literacy opportunities.

Books, Books, Books

Books—not just those that the teacher reads aloud daily, but also books children make themselves—take on new life in early literacy classrooms. Here is a list of the many different kinds of books found in exemplary emergent literacy classrooms (Tease, 1995):

- individually written, child-made books
- published trade books
- children's journals
- poetry books
- books related to theme studies
- holiday books
- Big Books
- dictionaries and encyclopedias
- alphabet books
- phone books
- recipe books
- teacher-made books
- photo album books with pictures labeled
- sign language books
- author of the month books
- collections of songs or poems children have learned at school

With so many books in the classroom, you'll need to find a way to organize them so that children can find them easily and put them away after use. Bookshelves are often organized with labels by subject, author, title, or size (tall, wide, and small). In each case, alphabetical order may provide the sequence. Some teachers put books in color-coded bins according to topics, authors, or level of

FIGURE 5.9

CLASSROOM FLOOR PLAN
OPTIMIZING FUNCTIONAL
LITERACY OPPORTUNITIES

Kitchen Center	Recipe cards
	Notepads and pencils
	Cookbooks
	Cupboard items labeled for putting away
Science Center	Information about class pets posted: name, when and what to feed the pet, whose turn to feed the pet
	Books about science display (e.g., hamsters, rocks)
	Labels on display items
Block Center	Turn-taking chart to limit block use to two or three children
	Books about architecture or about props in the block center (e.g., transportation, farm animals)
Grocery Store Center	Products on labeled shelves
	Receipt books
	Tablets to make grocery lists
	Cash register
Writing Center	Paper of various sizes and colors
	Pens, pencils, markers
	Stationery, envelopes
	Postcards

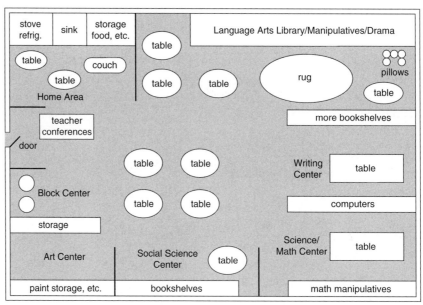

Dramatic Play	Science/Math	Block	Language Literacy
*telephone	*class pet	*shelves labeled	*feltboard and
*telephone book	*list of care and	with diagrams	story pieces
*shelf containing items	feeding instructions	*books related	*library with variety of
with authentic labels:	*names of daily	to building	genres organized
Cheerios, etc.	helpers posted	*order forms	and labeled
*shopping list	*books about	for lumber	*table with paper and
*clothes for drama	hamsters displayed		writing tools
			*typewriter and computer

reading difficulty. Single-book display racks showcase a special theme book, the author of the month, or a current story or poem. All good literacy programs build on children's fascination with books.

Using Daily Routines to Highlight the Forms and Functions of Print

Daily classroom routines can enhance children's awareness of the forms and functions of print. Give some thought to the routines of your classroom so that you may highlight for your students how literacy serves everyday purposes. At the same time, call attention to the actual processes of reading and writing as you go about daily activities.

Morning Message

One classroom routine is the "morning message," in which you preview the day's activities for your students. By writing the day's activities down on the board as you say the words, you model the organizational/ mnemonic function of writing and the form (i.e., the left-to-right, letter-by-letter sequence corresponding to your spoken words).

Classroom Rules and Procedures

Another routine that lends itself to a functional literacy learning opportunity stems from classroom rules and procedures that you and your students establish together at the beginning of the year. As decisions are made, you write down on a large chart the rules and procedures for such duties as table cleaning, floor sweeping, pet care, and any other routine chores. In this way, your students will see the spoken words written on the board. Each duty can be simply illustrated with a broom, an animal, a table, or other appropriate picture to support student understanding of the chart. By highlighting print uses during day-to-day routines, you make literacy so natural and unintimidating that children begin to read without even knowing it.

Wall Dictionary

Another way to incorporate a literacy learning opportunity into your daily routines is to post the alphabet at children's eye level, creating a wall dictionary (Figure 5.10). The first entries in the dictionary are the children's names on tagboard posted below the appropriate letter of the alphabet. If possible, post a photo of each child next to his or her name. During roll call children can place their name tags on the wall dictionary under the appropriate letter: María would place her tag under the letter *M*, for example. For each of us, there is a magic in our names and those of our friends. To be

FIGURE 5.10 • PARTIAL WALL DICTIONARY USING CHILDREN'S NAMES AND FAMILIAR WORDS

A a	B b	C c	D d
Anna	Barbara	Cathy	Don
an	be	cat	Dan
and	bear	can	dad
are	but	car	did
animal	bat	colt	

able to write their own name early in school creates a power over print for children. Later on, favorite words from songs, poems, stories, and theme studies may be added to the wall dictionary. As words accumulate, you may invite children to read, chorally or individually, all the words that begin with *M*, or one word that begins with *M*. Or you might ask children to find all the animal names posted. You can no doubt think of other games to play using the wall dictionary. The wall dictionary provides many opportunities for children to become aware of both the alphabet and its sound/symbol correspondences. In addition, the wall dictionary helps students develop a sight vocabulary that they will use in reading and writing. Finally, the wall dictionary familiarizes students with the concept of alphabetical order.

Reading Aloud to Students

Reading aloud is beneficial for students of all ages. When you read aloud to your students, you involve them in the pleasure function of print, you model the reading process, and you develop general knowledge and literary notions about story plots and characters. Keep in mind, however, that following a story line places heavy cognitive–linguistic demands on listeners in terms of attention, comprehension, and memory. You can help your students listen and comprehend by stopping at certain places in the book to discuss a picture as it relates to the story or to review the plot. You may also focus comprehension by asking prediction questions as you go along. If the book is short and simple, repeated readings will assist comprehension. As you try these techniques, you will find out which ones work best with your particular group of students. Their purpose is to facilitate comprehension for your beginning and intermediate English language learners so that they may enjoy the read alouds.

In reading aloud to students you will want to select age-appropriate books that they will be able to understand. At the same time you will want to gradually move to books that are more demanding for your students, books that increase in length, language level, and plot complexity. If you are new to the act of reading aloud to an audience, we recommend that you practice story reading at first. You can get ideas for oral reading from professionally recorded audio or videotapes. For example, if you listen to Danny Glover reading *How the Leopard Got His Spots* or James Earl Jones reading *Bringing the Rain to Kapiti Plain* (Aardema, 1981), you will get an idea of how professional actors use intonation and other techniques to convey the enthusiasm and wonder that oral readings can bring to a story. Such oral readings greatly enhance anyone's ability to listen.

You will also find reading aloud more fun if you choose some of your own favorite books. Your natural enthusiasm will be contagious. Big Books or oversized books are an excellent choice, because you can point to the words as you read aloud. In this way you model the reading process, promoting development of print concepts, the alphabetic principle, phonics knowledge, and sight vocabulary. Most important, the reading-aloud moments should be a special time when students feel comfortable to simply sit and enjoy listening to stories. Finally, encourage children to bring books they enjoy for you to read to the class; this will give them a sense of ownership during reading-aloud time. Here is a list of some of our favorite books to read aloud for readers of different ages.

Ahlberg, J., & Ahlberg, A. (1981). *Peek-A-Boo*. London: Puffin.
Ahlberg, J., & Ahlberg, A. (1986). *The Jolly Postman*. Boston: Little, Brown.

Anno, M. (1983). *Anno's USA*. New York: Philomel Books.

Brown, M. W. (1947). *Goodnight Moon*, illustrated by C. Hurd. New York: Harper & Row.

Bruchac, J. (1989). *Iroquois Stories*. Cassette tape. Greenfield Center, NY: Good Mind Records.

Bryan, A. (1991). *All Night, All Day: A Child's First Book of African-American Spirituals*. New York: Atheneum.

Carle, E. (1986). *The Very Hungry Caterpillar*. New York: Philomel Books.

Connolly, J. (Ed.). (1985). *Why the Possum's Tail Is Bare and Other North American Indian Nature Tales*. Seattle: Stemmer House.

Delacre, L. (1989). *Arroz con Leche: Popular Songs and Rhymes from Latin America*. New York: Scholastic.

de Paola, T. (1985). *Tomie de Paola's Mother Goose*. New York: Putnam.

Galdone, P. (1979). *The Three Bears*. New York: Clarion.

Garcia, M. (1978). *The Adventures of Connie and Diego/Las Aventuras de Connie y Diego*. Chicago: Children's Book Press.

Griego, M., Bucks, B., Gilbert, S., & Kimball, L. (1981). *Tortillitas para Mamá and Other Nursery Rhymes, English and Spanish*. New York: Holt, Rinehart & Winston.

Kitchen, B. (1984). *Animal Alphabet*. New York: Dial.

Lobel, A. (1970). *Frog and Toad Are Friends*. New York: Harper.

McKissack, P. (1986). *Flossie and the Fox*. Chicago: Children's Book Press.

Myers, W. (1990). *The Mouse Rap*. New York: HarperCollins.

Prelutsky, J. (Ed.). (1983). *The Random House Book of Poetry for Children*, illustrated by A. Lobel. New York: Random House.

Say, A. (1995). *Grandfather's Journey*. Boston: Houghton Mifflin.

Sendak, M. (1963). *Where the Wild Things Are*. New York: Harper.

Steptoe, J. (1987). *Mufaro's Beautiful Daughter: An African Tale*. New York: Lothrop.

Yep, L. (1989). *The Rainbow People*. New York: Harper & Row.

Shared Writing and Reading Through the Language Experience Approach

The language experience approach to writing and reading, discussed fully in Chapter 8, is a literacy approach based on student's dictations that can be used with learners of any age, preschool through adult. A good way to start is to invite your students to dictate stories or ideas as a whole class. As they dictate the words, you write them down on chart paper, inviting students to read the words back as you point them out. This simple use of language experience models functional writing and reading, illustrates the relationship of print to speech, helps develop sight vocabulary, and illustrates sound/symbol correspondences. Finally, the fact that students themselves generate the content ensures a text that is appropriate to their age, experiences, and interests. You can later use these texts as the basis of phonics and sight word instruction. By writing down things students say each day you will be helping them learn to read and write.

Dialogue Journals

Dialogue journals provide an excellent introduction to literacy for English learners of all ages (Kreeft, 1984). As you may recall, in dialogue journals students write regularly on the topic of their choice, and you respond to the content of their entries, not the form. By doing so, you show interest in the students' ideas, ask questions that encourage elaboration, model form and function in writing, and deepen your personal relationship with students. For emergent readers and writers, dialogue journals offer students the chance to work out sound/symbol relationships in the context of an authentic communicative interaction with their teacher. English learners also work on overall English language development through journals, as evident in the following examples from a first-grader working on the phrase "What I like to do is _____." We offer some clarifications of the child's words in italics.

Dec. 1: I like to do is sing for egg de I like to do is it a pizza? *(I like to do is sing for egg day. I like to do, "Is it a pizza.")* Teacher responded: You should teach us an egg song.

Dec. 8: I like to do is sing de He like to do is paly happy sing paly? *(I like to do is sing day. He like to do is play happy sing play.)* (Teacher did not respond that day.)

Dec. 15: I like to play whaat butterfly de vey like to do is play a round bks Butterfly is like to it flsr *(I like to play with butterfly day they like to do is play around bikes. Butterfly is like to eat flowers.)* Teacher responded: I have never played with a butterfly before. It sounds like fun.

Students of all ages enjoy dialogue journals, in part because of the personal attention they receive from the teacher. Journals also provide ongoing writing samples from which to assess students' literacy development over time.

Alphabet Books

We have already mentioned using print in functional and meaningful ways to develop children's appreciation of the purposes and pleasures of print. All of these activities, such as wall dictionaries, language experience stories, rhyming games, the alphabet song, and shared reading, help children develop the alphabetic principle. With the **alphabetic principle**, children come to know that there is a relationship between letters and sounds in the English language. Alphabet books provide yet another avenue for teaching both the alphabetic principle and the alphabet itself. Alphabet books display capital and lowercase letters in interesting ways and can help students become aware of the alphabetic principle while learning the names of the letters. Many of the books teach not only the letters, but concepts as well. Interestingly, alphabet books are available for all ages, from Bruna's *B Is for Bear* for the young to Musgrove's *Ashanti to Zulu: African Traditions* for older students. The best books use enjoyable illustrations that convey meaning and can also help learners begin to make the connection between specific letters and the sounds they make in words the children already know. We've listed some of our favorites here.

Alphabet Books

*Anno, M. (1975). *Anno's Alphabet*. New York: Crowell.

*Base, G. (1986). *Animalia*. New York: Abrams.

Brown, M. (1974). *All Butterflies*. New York: Scribner's.

Bruna, D. (1967). *B is for Bear*. Sydney, Australia: Methuen.

Dr. Seuss. (1963). *Dr. Seuss's ABC*. New York: Random House.

*Dragonwagon, C. (1987). *Alligator Arrived with Apples*. New York: Macmillan.

Duke, K. (1983). *The Guinea Pig ABC*. New York: Dutton.

Eisele, B., Eisele, C. Y., Hanlon, S. M., Hanlon, R. Y., & Hojel, B. (2002). *My ABC Storybook*. White Plains, NY: Pearson Education.

Gag, W. (1933). *The ABC Bunny*. New York: Coward-McCann.

Garten, J. (1964). *The Alphabet Tale*. New York: Random House.

Kitchen, B. (1984). *Animal Alphabet*. New York: Dial.

McNaught, H. (1988). *The Sesame Street ABC Book of Words*. New York: Random House.

*Musgrove, M. (1976). *Ashanti to Zulu: African Traditions*. New York: Dial.

Oxenbury, H. (1972). *Helen Oxenbury's ABC of Things*. New York: Watts.

Rankin, L. (1991). *The Handmade Alphabet*. New York: Dial.

Red Hawk, R. (1988). *ABC's: The American Indian Way*. Albany, CA: Sierra Oaks.

*Van Allsburg, C. (1987). *The Z Was Zapped: A Play in 26 Acts*. Boston: Houghton Mifflin.

Helping Students Recognize and Spell Words Independently

As students progress in their emerging understanding of the functions and forms of print, they have already begun to develop some rudimentary word recognition abilities. You can help them become more effective and efficient in recognizing words by increasing their sight word vocabularies and providing explicit phonics instruction. In this section, we briefly review some of the most useful teaching strategies for these purposes. For a much more comprehensive discussion of word recognition instruction, we recommend Bear, Helman, Templeton, Invernizzi and Johnston (2007), described in the resource list at the end of this chapter. This book was written with native English-speaking students in mind, so you will have to consider the language and cultural needs of your students as you select from the teaching strategies provided.

---

*Books older students enjoy.

Using Big Books to Teach Sight Words and Phonics

Although we discuss the use of Big Books more fully in Chapter 8, we want to point out a few ways you can use them, poems, and song lyrics written in large format on chart paper, to develop word recognition and phonics knowledge early in children's reading and writing development. First, these large-format texts allow children to follow the words that you point to as you read. Second, you can create a window or frame that allows children to focus on only one word at a time in the book. By framing only one word, you provide practice in actually recognizing the word on sight. You can also use predictable books with repetitive patterns and phrases to teach or reinforce sound/symbol correspondences, including consonants, vowels, and letter sequences found in rhyming words. In addition, you may invite children to write their own stories following the pattern in predictable books that they have heard several times. In writing their own stories, your students will have a chance to put their phonics and sight word knowledge into meaningful practice.

The sight word and phonics strategies just described are also applicable to older students who are new to literacy. The key is to find short texts with age-appropriate content. There are a number of predictable books that are appropriate for older students, such as *Fortunately,* by Remy Charlip (1987). In addition, poems and song lyrics are good sources of predictable texts. Songs lyrics, poems, and predictable books can be written in large letters on tagboard or chart paper and used in the same way that Big Books are used with younger children.

Increasing Students' Sight Word Vocabulary

Students begin to develop a sight word vocabulary as a result of immersion in meaningful, functional encounters with print, including writing in dialogue journals, seeing the morning message printed and explained, using wall dictionaries, repeated reading of rhyming poems and predictable books, and shared writing through language experience dictations. All beginning readers and writers need daily opportunities such as these to develop literacy. In addition, you'll need to provide them with explicit instruction on strategies they can use to recognize words they have not encountered before or do not recognize easily when reading.

Certain words occur frequently in any English text, such as *a, and, the, I, we.* If your students have not learned these words through holistic strategies, you may wish to provide practice with these and other words from stories and themes you are studying by using flash cards in a game. Students can do this in pairs or small groups. It is important that your students know the meanings of the words on the flash cards, however, and it may be helpful for the words to be illustrated on the back of the cards. To demonstrate the meaning of articles, prepositions, conjunctions, and other function words, you need to use them in full sentences. If readers do not learn how to recognize sight words automatically, they will plod their way through print and lose the meaning along the way. Next, we give a brief list of high-frequency words adapted from Mason and Au (1990). Students may keep their own word banks or dictionaries with these words along with other words they choose to include.

1. the	11. at	21. was	31. but	41. which
2. of	12. he	22. this	32. what	42. their
3. and	13. for	23. from	33. all	43. said
4. a	14. on	24. I	34. were	44. if
5. to	15. are	25. have	35. when	45. do
6. in	16. as	26. or	36. we	46. will
7. you	17. with	27. by	37. there	47. each
8. is	18. his	28. one	38. can	48. about
9. that	19. they	29. had	39. an	49. how
10. it	20. be	30. not	40. your	50. up

Phonics

The purpose of phonics instruction is to help students recognize words independently, *not* to have them state rules or generalizations. A substantial amount of research on native English readers supports the importance of phonics instruction (Adams, 1990a, 1990b; Anderson, Hiebert, Scott, & Wilkinson, 1985; Bond & Dykstra, 1967; Chall, 1983; Ehri, 1991). Although there is little research, if any, on phonics instruction for English learners, we believe that English learners will also benefit from phonics instruction, judiciously applied. The following principles, developed for native English speakers, apply well to phonics for English learners:

1. Provide ample time for students to read and write for meaningful purposes, allowing students to develop their own understanding of sound/symbol correspondences.
2. Informally assess phonics and word recognition skills your students already use in writing and reading, then focus your teaching on new skills that will promote independence.
3. Always teach phonics and other word recognition skills within a meaningful context; enjoy the story or poem for meaning first, then teach the skill.
4. Generally, teach spelling patterns rather than rules.
5. Remember that phonics and other word recognition strategies are a means to an end: comprehension.

Through thoughtful phonics instruction students can begin to read words that they would otherwise be unable to recognize. Bear in mind, however, that phonics strategies work best during reading when combined with meaning cues provided by the context of the passage. If a student comes across a new word while reading, phonics strategies will provide a tentative pronunciation, while the sentence context will provide the meaning or gist, thereby facilitating comprehension. In fact, mature readers use several cueing systems simultaneously during reading: graphophonic, syntactic, and semantic, for example. We discuss these more fully in Chapter 8.

Word Families

In addition to helping students with phonemic awareness through your daily use of print, it is important to teach students **word families**, sometimes referred to as

185

onsets and rimes. The onset is the initial consonant in a word or syllable, followed by a vowel-consonant sequence, the rime (Stahl, 1992). Thus, in the word *gain* the letter *g* is the onset and the letters *-ain* represent the rime. Adams and others (Adams, 1990a, 1990b; Cunningham, 2005; Ruddell & Ruddell, 1995; Stahl, 1992; Trieman, 1985) have found that "letter sound correspondences are more stable when one looks at rimes than when letters are looked at in isolation" (Stahl, 1992). Thus, you can help students learn words associated with the *-at* rime by simply placing letters in front of the *-at* to make words such as cat, rat, bat, sat, mat, fat, hat, and pat. Or you can make a word wheel containing the rime *(-at)* in the center and the onset *(c, r, b)* on the outside; as children turn the wheel, they create the different words. Likewise, other rimes, such as those found in Stahl's list, which follows, generate nearly 500 words (1992). Knowledge of rimes, along with the consonants that provide the onsets, give students a powerful word recognition strategy that they can use in combination with meaning and grammatical cues to make sense of text.

-ack	-ain	-ake	-ale	-all	-ame
-an	-ank	-ap	-ash	-at	-ate
-aw	-ay	-eat	-ell	-est	-ice
-ick	-ide	-ight	-ill	-in	-ine
-ing	-ink	-ip	-ir	-ock	-ok
-op	-or	-ore	-uck	-ug	-ump
-unk					

One mistake teachers sometimes make is to identify a student's inability to pronounce a word with a lack of phonics knowledge or to consider non-native pronunciation of a word as a reading error. If we give you a word such as *icosahedron*, you might not be able to pronounce it, not because you don't know phonics or can't read, but because you may never have encountered the word before, orally or in writing. Too many students are sent to reading labs for phonics instruction because they can't pronounce a word and have been misdiagnosed as needing phonics instruction. For the purposes of reading and writing, vocabulary instruction highlighting word meaning is a close ally to sight word and phonics instruction because we want students to be able to access the meaning of the word, regardless of pronunciation.

A general sequence of phonics instruction often recommended for native English speakers is the following:

1. single consonants at the beginning of words
2. short and long vowels
3. letter patterns and word families (onsets and rimes)
4. digraphs (two consonants together that make one sound such as *th, ch, ph*) and blends (two consonants together that blend their sounds, such as *cl-, bl-, tr-, cr-, pr-*)
5. syllabication

This sequence is probably useful for English learners whose first exposure to literacy is in English. When you focus on any of these elements, we recommend that you base your instruction on words taken from poems, stories, song lyrics, and other texts you have used in class many times. For example, if you have read *Brown Bear, Brown Bear* (Martin, 1967), you would hold up the book, point to the words *brown* and *bear,* and proceed to talk about the letter *b* and the sound it represents. Next, you might ask your students to tell you other words that begin with the letter *b*, perhaps permitting them to peek at the wall dictionary. In this way you ensure that students understand the words themselves and that they are aware of how letters are related to words in meaningful, whole texts.

An important consideration for English learners is the extent of literacy skill in their first language. In general, students who are literate in their primary language will already possess knowledge of the functions of print. However, they will need to learn the forms of English print and some of its functions, to the extent that they differ from the students' prior print experiences. Bear in mind that students who read a language with an alphabet similar to that of English (e.g., Spanish, French, German) are apt to need less phonics instruction because of transfer of alphabetic knowledge, especially with consonants. The English vowels and their spellings present difficulties for most readers, however, native and non-native English speakers alike.

Besides the many ways students can learn phonics through literacy events, such as reading aloud and journal writing, we recommend using games to help reinforce the learning of individual sound/symbol correspondences when more practice is warranted. We also recommend that you spend a brief time each day going over sound/symbol correspondences you feel students should already know, both to evaluate their phonics knowledge and to determine whether more explicit instruction is needed on word analysis and recognition.

Finally, your students can learn phonics through their own explorations using computers. New software programs are coming out daily that can assist children with learning to read independently, programs that sound out any word children point to as they are reading an animated text. Other programs will read texts in different languages to help English language learners. One other kind of program that is a favorite of ours is "Kids Write," which allows students to write down any word or story and will pronounce the word they have written.

Invented or Temporary Spelling and Word Recognition

We advocate that students write from the first day of class, and we suggest that you accept their temporary or invented spellings. Awareness of word structure and phonics is often best developed through students' own attempts at writing. One study of invented spelling among native English speakers (Clarke, 1989) compared groups of children who used invented spelling with groups of children who were in traditional spelling programs. Results showed that the children who were in the invented spelling groups were better in decoding and comprehension. In addition, "low readiness" students performed significantly higher on spelling and word recognition tests. Many teachers who have used invented spelling techniques testify to the efficacy of encouraging invented spelling and confirm research findings such as these. However, just as with anything else you do in your classroom, you will want to be aware of the progress students are making and adjust your program accordingly.

Developmental Levels in Student Spelling

One way to assess students' progress is to analyze their spelling according to developmental characteristics. We suggest using four developmental levels: prephonetic, phonetic, transitional, and conventional, as defined briefly here and discussed more fully next.

Prephonetic spelling:	Letters or letterlike forms do not represent speech sounds.
Phonetic spelling:	Letters represent sounds; words are decipherable.
Transitional spelling:	Conventional spellings are mixed with phonetic spellings.
Conventional spelling:	Most words are spelled conventionally.

Prephonetic spellers use letters or letterlike forms or even numbers or scribbles that do not as yet represent speech sounds. In other words, prephonetic spellers do not demonstrate understanding of the alphabetic principle, the idea that a letter or letter sequence represents a speech sound. Oswaldo's soccer story at the beginning of this chapter illustrates prephonetic spelling. The examples in Figure 5.11 also illustrate the kind of spelling found at this stage.

Prephonetic spellers need rich exposure to functional uses of written language, the kind provided by reading big books, by writing language experience stories, by discussing word spellings on the word wall, and by generally talking about how print works as you use written language for functional purposes in day-to-day classroom activities. As students develop an understanding of the alphabetic principle, they become able to associate English speech sounds with letters of the English alphabet. When they begin to use this knowledge in spelling, they are on their way to becoming phonetic spellers.

Phonetic spellers use letters and letter sequences to represent speech sounds, thereby demonstrating their grasp of the alphabetic principle (see Figure 5.12). However, they use many spellings that are not conventional. Martha's story on page 169 about the lost dog represents advanced phonetic spelling. Students who are developing the ability to spell phonetically vary a great deal in their approach. Early on, some students may represent a whole word such as *mother* with just one letter, *m*. Gradually they begin to represent each speech sound with one letter. At this point, most phonetic spellings

FIGURE 5.11 • EXAMPLES OF PREPHONETIC SPELLING

Conventional Spelling	Student's Prephonetic Spelling
1. dog	1. mll
2. cat	2. dfg
3. mom	3. trd

students produce are more logical and consistent than many conventional English spellings because English orthography is not based strictly on a one-to-one correspondence between sounds and letters. In other words, some letters consistently represent just one sound, but others do not. Similarly, some speech sounds are represented in several different ways or with several letters, such as long vowel sounds. Figure 5.12 shows examples of phonetic spelling.

FIGURE 5.12 • Examples of Phonetic Spelling

Conventional Spelling	Student's Phonetic Spelling
from	frum
clown	cleeown
cat	kat
city	sity
bake	bac

Phonetic spellers should be recognized and praised for their thoughtful spelling. They should also be encouraged to write more. They will benefit from the kind of exposure to interesting uses of written language recommended for prephonetic spellers. Moreover, phonetic spellers can benefit from basic, formal spelling instruction such as the spelling patterns in the simple word family words provided previously in the discussion of phonics. In this way you can build on what they already know and move them to the next level of spelling development.

Transitional spellers (see Figure 5.13) extend their knowledge beyond the phonetic aspects of spelling and begin to include conventional spellings that are not strictly phonetic. These students are in the transitional phase moving toward conventional spelling. The term *transitional* indicates that they are making the transition from purely phonetic spelling to conventional spelling. Transitional spellers remain adept at phonetic spelling, but they also use a growing number of conventional spelling patterns, such as using the silent *e* for long vowel sounds as in *lake* or two vowels for long vowel sounds as in *beat*. Sam's note to his mother on page 168 provides a good example of transitional spelling.

Students at the transitional level of spelling may be spelling 60 percent to 90 percent of words correctly in their writing. They are on their way to becoming good spellers. They need to continue reading and writing each day for a variety of purposes. In addition, they will benefit from instruction on new spelling patterns as they begin to write longer, more complex words. In this way they will continue developing toward conventional or standard spelling.

Non-native English speaking students may vary somewhat in the developmental patterns just described. Young English learners whose only literacy instruction has been in English are likely to display the developmental patterns noted here. Nonetheless, their phonetic spellings are apt to reflect both their pronunciation and grammar in English, that is, their phonological, morphological, and syntactic development in English. For example, a first-grade English learner recently wrote, "My ma se go st an by de food." ("My mama, she go to the store and buy the food.") The child's pronunciation and grammar are reflected in his spellings. He should be

FIGURE 5.13 • Examples of Transitional Spelling

One day we went to the beech. We played volly ball and we swam arond in the ocean. My friends brought lots of food too. We ate enchaladis and tamalez and we had differen kinds of samiches.

complimented for his ability to convey his idea rather well in English with enough sound/symbol regularity to make it decipherable to his teacher.

Non-native English speakers who begin literacy instruction in English when they are a little older may demonstrate similar English pronunciation and grammar features in their spellings. If they are literate in a primary language that uses an alphabet similar to English, such as Spanish, students may spell using sound/symbol correspondences from their first language. Literacy knowledge in their first language provides them with a starting point for spelling in English. A literate Spanish speaker new to English might write, for example, "I laic to see de circo," for "I like to see the circus." In this case, the word *like* was spelled using Spanish spelling rules. On the other hand, the student is already using the conventional spelling for the words *I, see*, and *to*. The word *circo* is borrowed entirely from Spanish.

The important thing to remember, whether students are native or non-native English speakers, is to recognize the logic of their phonetic spellings and commend for this accomplishment. Phonetic spellers are showing you their ability to hear sounds in words (phonemic awareness) and their knowledge of representing those sounds in a systematic manner, using conventional English sound/symbol correspondences (phonics) at least some of the time. These abilities permit them to spell in ways that make their writing decipherable. Their next challenge is to learn the conventional spellings of words that are not spelled exactly as they sound.

Conventional spellers spell nearly all words conventionally, that is, the way they are spelled in the dictionary. However, even students at the conventional level of spelling development must gradually learn how to spell longer, more complex and more difficult words, a process that takes place over a period of many years. You can expose them to more complex spelling patterns used in English through word study and through vocabulary development in the content areas, including literature study.

We recommend three sources of words that you may use for spelling instruction: (1) misspelled words that recur in the student's own writing, such as journal entries; (2) words related to themes or topics you are currently studying; and (3) words that illustrate particular spelling patterns pertaining to individual speech sounds and to word structure and word formation. At the level of individual sound/symbol correspondences, for example, it is necessary to learn the sounds represented by each consonant letter of the alphabet. Moreover, it is necessary to learn that some consonant letters represent more than one speech sound, such as the letter *c* in *can* and *city*. Likewise, students need to learn that some individual speech sounds are represented by two letters, called *digraphs*, such as *sh, ch, th*. In terms of relating spelling to word formation, it is necessary to learn, for example, that the consonant is doubled at the end of certain words such as *cut, bid*, and *let* when you add *-ing* to make *cutting, bidding, letting*. Thus, you'll want to select words that teach students basic spelling patterns in English, beginning with simple spelling patterns such as those found in the word families presented previously and moving on to more complex spelling patterns related to word structure and formation, including prefixes, suffixes, root words. Of course, students who constantly read will learn new words and new spellings.

Selecting words from students' own writing and from the content of your curriculum is fairly straightforward. However, when it comes to word lists based on spelling patterns, which are rather numerous and complex, we recommend that you avail yourself of published resources on the topic rather than staying up late at night pulling together your own lists. Published lists provide a point of departure for you to modify according to your students' needs and your instructional goals. One resource is provided by published spelling series that your school district may adopt. In addition, we note professional books in the resource list at the end of this chapter that have helped us understand English spelling instruction better.

FIGURE 5.14 • SPELLING LIST DISPLAYING 6-YEAR-OLD STUDENT'S DEVELOPMENT

WORD GIVEN	FALL/NOVEMBER	SPRING/MARCH
monster	mistr	monster
united	vnti	vonited
dress	trste	dress
bottom	botm	boutom
hiked	htiel	hiked
human	hanin	humin
eagle	ell	egole
closed	kuost	klosd
bumped	bode	bumped
type	top	tipe

Using ideas and information from the resources already given, you may wish to construct word lists to inform your instruction that evaluate the kinds of spelling patterns and conventions students know or don't know. Note the spelling list in Figure 5.14, given in November and then in March to a 6-year-old student. With this list the teacher was able to evaluate the student's knowledge and progress and to develop a curriculum for the student.

In summary, spelling is an important skill for writing. It is also influential in early reading development. As students learn the various spelling patterns of English, they can apply this knowledge to word identification during reading and writing. Although developmental spelling details and terminology may vary, the continuum we have offered provides a basic outline for describing students' spelling development in English whether they are first language learners or second language learners. Attention to students' spelling and thoughtful instruction thus yield benefits to students' literacy development.

Summary of Early Literacy Instructional Strategies

In summary, our view is that through authentic, meaningful literacy events students will begin to develop understandings of both the forms and functions of print. Holistic teaching strategies are essential for English learners because they provide many opportunities for students to access the meanings and functions of written language while exposing them to the formal aspects of print. Therefore, we described several holistic strategies and a number of specific word recognition and phonics strategies that we believe promote early independence in reading and writing. As teachers in student-centered classrooms we need to make decisions about how much and what kind of phonics and other skills instruction students may or may not need based on their progress in reading and writing. We strongly advocate continuous use of holistic, meaningful, and functional reading and writing throughout the year in combination with carefully selected skill-based instruction. In Chapters 7 through 10 we provide additional early literacy strategies under the heading of beginning activities for English language learners.

Assessing Emergent Literacy Development

Assessing students' emergent literacy development requires us to focus on what students know, with an eye to moving them to the next developmental level. To document your English learners' emergent literacy development, we recommend keeping a **portfolio** that includes both reading and writing information for each student. For writing, you may select samples from a student's journals and dictated stories. For reading, you may include a list of favorite stories. You may also wish to keep a checklist of your students' knowledge of letters/sounds and sight words and any other word recognition strategies you have taught. In addition, you may wish to use a holistic checklist such as those in Figures 5.15 and 5.16 to document reading and writing development.

Figure 5.15 presents a scale of writing development in which Levels 1 through 6 represent emergent writing behaviors, Level 7 represents transitional writing,

FIGURE 5.15

SCALE OF WRITING DEVELOPMENT

Source: Adapted from L. Lamme and C. Hysmith, "One School's Adventure into Portfolio Assessment," *Language Arts*, 68, 629–640, December 1991. Copyright 1991 by the National Council of Teachers of English. Reprinted with permission.

Level 11:	Child uses a variety of strategies for revision and editing. Child uses a variety of literary techniques to build suspense, create humor, etc.
Level 10:	Child willingly revises and edits. Child writes creatively and imaginatively. Child writes original poetry. Child writes clearly. The message makes sense. Child uses commas, quotation marks, and apostrophes.
Level 9:	Writing includes details, dialogue, a sense of humor, or other emotions. Spelling becomes more conventional. Child willingly revises.
Level 8:	Child writes a story with a beginning, middle, and end. Child uses different forms for several different purposes (narrative, expository, persuasive). Revisions include adding to the story or piece. Child uses basic punctuation purposefully and consistently.
Level 7:	Child writes the start of a story. Child uses both phonics and sight strategies to spell words. Child writes several short sentences. Child rewrites a familiar story or follows the pattern of a known story or poem.
Level 6:	Child invents spellings. Story is a single factual statement. Message is understandable (decipherable).
Level 5:	Child labels or makes statement about drawings. Letters have some connection to sounds. Child writes lists. Child separates words with space or marker.
Level 4:	Letters don't match sounds, but child can explain written message. Child writes strings of letters.
Level 3:	Child copies words he or she sees around the room. Child writes letters and mock letters in a line across the page. Child writes in left-to-right sequence, top to bottom of page.
Level 2:	Child copies words he or she sees around the room. Child writes mock letters, but these may not be in any conventional sequence. Child pretends to write.
Level 1:	Child attempts to write in scribbles or draws patterns.

Level 11: Child reads fluently from a variety of books and other materials.

Level 10: Child seeks out new sources of written information.
Child voluntarily shares information with other children.

Level 9:   Child uses context clues, sentence structure, structural analysis, and phonic analysis to read new passages in a functional, effective, and strategic manner.

Level 8:   Child reads unfamiliar stories haltingly, with little adult assistance.

Level 7:   Child reads familiar stories fluently.

Level 6:   Child reads short texts word by word.

Level 5:   Child memorizes text and can pretend to read a story.

Level 4:   Child participates in reading by supplying rhyming words and some predictable text.

Level 3:   Child talks about each picture (attends to pictures, less so to the story itself).

Level 2:   Child watches pictures as adult reads a story.

Level 1:   Child listens to a story but does not look at pages.

FIGURE 5.16

SCALE OF READING DEVELOPMENT

Source: Adapted from L. Lamme and C. Hysmith, "One School's Adventure into Portfolio Assessment," *Language Arts*, 68, 629–640, December 1991. Copyright 1991 by the National Council of Teachers of English. Reprinted with permission.

and Levels 8 through 11 represent a developmental progression of more mature writing. Figure 5.16 provides developmental descriptors for reading in a manner similar to the writing development scale. Levels 1 through 5 represent emergent reading behaviors, and Levels 6 through 8 represent transitional reading. Levels 9 through 11 represent developmental progressions of more mature reading.

You can use these reading and writing development descriptors to document and evaluate how students are progressing. Although these levels appear to represent steps of a staircase, it is important to note that they should not be considered as lockstep sequences. Students will develop in individual ways, perhaps skipping some levels and intermixing various levels as well. When we use these developmental checklists, we put a check beside each description that pertains to the student's behaviors exhibited during a particular observation period. We are thus able to document what the child can do and set goals for development to the next levels. By making observations over time, we will be able to document their progress, communicate their progress to parents and others, and adjust our instruction.

As students advance beyond emergent literacy, we will introduce them to the idea of editing for publishing, as described in Chapter 7. At that time, we will begin to help them focus on conventional spelling. For now, though, we applaud everything the child produces. Our goal is to allow students the freedom to create as they write—to create the message of their choice while recreating the medium, the spelling system. We also want them to have many choices in reading as they develop into mature readers.

Differentiating Instruction for Emergent Literacy

In order to match instruction to student needs, you start by considering your students' English language proficiency as well as their literacy experiences at home and/or in preschool, both in English and the primary language. Prior literacy experiences in either language are important because they potentially lay a foundation for the early literacy concepts that you will be assessing now to differentiate instruction. In addition, your students' home language literacy knowledge is important because many basic print concepts transfer between languages, as do many higher level literacy skills.

In order to differentiate emergent literacy instruction, you need to assess what your students already know about the forms and functions of print in English. To do so, we recommend that you use the *Scale of Writing Development* (Figure 5.15) and the *Scale of Reading Development* (Figure 5.16). In addition, after reviewing our section on "Print Concepts in Emergent Literacy, you may create a checklist or refer to a **Concepts about Print** checklist based on the work of Marie Clay (1989). Such checklists are available online using the key words "concepts about print" or going directly to http://teams.lacoe.edu/DOCUMENTATION/classrooms/patti/k-1/assessment/print). In addition, you may apply the developmental spelling descriptors to writing your students produce (i.e., prephonetic, phonetic, transitional, conventional). You will want to study the scales and checklists a bit so that you will know what to look for as you observe your students individually and in groups. All of these assessments should be kept portfolios for documenting progress over time.

The checklists suggested above require you to observe students and collect performance samples, such as writing or drawing. Many observations will come from classroom activities. For example, during the first few weeks of school, you will want to offer your students many holistic literacy experiences as described in this chapter, such as journal writing and shared reading with Big Books. A major advantage of these meaningful encounters with print is that they also facilitate oral English development, an important goal for all your students. In addition, holistic strategies are beneficial at all early literacy levels; students take from the activity according to their own level of literacy development. While children are enjoying these activities, *you* will be making informal observations about their literacy knowledge, and recording these afterwards according to the scales and checklists noted above. In addition, you may need to call students individually in order to gather information you were unable to observe during instruction.

After collecting the information, you will be able to group students homogeneously for explicit instruction on areas of assessed need, such as basic print concepts, letter–sound correspondences, and sight word recognition. As you begin instruction, you may need to alter group membership as appropriate based on your on-going assessment of student needs. In addition, these groups should meet on a relatively short-term basis, disbanding when your goals are achieved. You will also continue with holistic reading and writing strategies, in small heterogeneous groups or with the whole class, in order to model fluent reading and writing for enjoyment and learning. By offering both holistic literacy activities and explicit skills instruction based on assessed needs, you will provide **differentiated** instruction in a **balanced** emergent literacy curriculum.

You may recall our planning scaffold for differentiated instruction, addressing the questions: **who**, **what**, **how**, and **how well**. We use that framework now to illustrate a differentiated, emergent literacy lesson, *The Very Hungry Caterpillar* (Carle, 1986). This lesson forms part of a theme study on how living things grow and change. Several children have brought in caterpillars that now live, well-fed, in jars near the window sill.

Who: Kindergarten students from various primary language backgrounds, identified as **beginning** to **intermediate** in English language proficiency. Most of the students know very basic print concepts for English: the front and back of a book; how to turn pages; and reading print from left-to-right. Many are still developing the concept of "word;" all are developing a sight word vocabulary. All are working on letter–sound correspondences while refining phonemic awareness and their understanding of the alphabetic principle.

What: Students follow along visually as you read with a pointer; students chime in on the repeated refrain, "But he was still hungry," during a whole-class, shared reading of a Big Book version of *The Very Hungry Caterpillar*. All students will learn to recognize and understand, orally and in writing, the words: *apple*, *pear*, *plum*, *strawberry*, and *orange*. They will also be able to clap the syllables when pronouncing the words to develop and practice phonemic awareness.

How: Students who are **beginners** in English will be able to match pictures of the fruits to the corresponding written words, thereafter drawing and labeling them in their personal word booklets. Students who are **intermediate** in English and demonstrate basic phonemic awareness will, as a group, dictate three words to the teacher that begin with the same initial sound as *pear* and three that begin with same initial sound as in *strawberry*. They will then copy and illustrate the words in their personal word booklets under two headings: P words and S words.

How well: Student word booklets form the primary means of assessing student learning. While all students are working on their booklets, the teacher visits each one individually to elicit word knowledge and recognition; to determine whether students can hear sounds in words; and to determine how well students can match the beginning sound of a word with its corresponding letter.

195

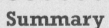

Summary

In this chapter, we described current viewpoints on emergent literacy in contrast to traditional reading readiness views. We described the early insights about the forms and functions of print that learners who are new to the written word must develop, regardless of their age. In addition, we focused on current efforts to forge stronger connections between families and schools, including descriptions of programs to assist the parents of English learners in learning English themselves. We provided a variety of strategies for developing early reading and writing and suggested several ways to assess and document emergent literacy development. Figure 5.17 summarizes the teaching strategies described in this chapter, showing the many age levels to which they may be applied, provided the content is age appropriate.

Most of the strategies in Figure 5.17 will be used in the early grades, of course, but you may find older English learners who have not been to school or did not learn how to read in their primary language. As a result, these older students may be able to profit from some of the strategies teachers normally use with younger learners. Through ongoing evaluation you can make appropriate decisions about which strategies will be most useful to you and your students as you help them become readers and writers. Nevertheless, to bridge a possible gap between home and school you will probably want to start by reading aloud to students of all ages to give them a strong sense of good stories and to start them on the road to becoming competent readers. A good teacher will continually

FIGURE 5.17

GRADE LEVELS IN WHICH STRATEGIES MAY BE USED

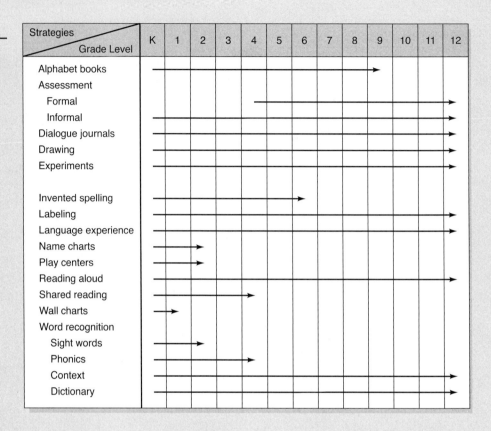

evaluate children's progress and assist them as needed with such skills as sight word recognition and other word analysis skills. But the heart of beginning literacy instruction is reading aloud to children and sharing the wonder and magic in reading and writing for ourselves and others.

Suggestions for Further Reading

Adams, M. (1990a). *Beginning to read: Thinking and learning about print*. Cambridge, MA: MIT Press.

A thorough discussion on beginning reading, this controversial book reviews the literature and research and makes recommendations for integrated approaches to teaching word analysis. We believe that anyone who wishes to advocate for or against phonics instruction should read this excellent, thoughtful book first.

Antunez, B. (2002). Reading and English language learners. WFSU Reading Center. WFSU.org.

Retrieved May 31, 2003, from http://readingrockets.org/wfsu/article/php?ID=409

This excellent seven-page article provides a clear overview of how to teach reading to primary grade English language learners using current research and policy guidelines. It begins with the recommendation to teach beginning reading in children's primary language, if possible. Then it illustrates how to incorporate five components of beginning English reading in a developmentally appropriate manner: (1) phonemic awareness, (2) phonics, (3) vocabulary, (4) reading fluency, including oral reading skills, and (5) reading comprehension strategies. Each section includes special considerations to keep in mind for young English language learners.

August, D., & Shanahan, T. (Eds.). *Developing literacy in second language learners: Report of the national literacy panel on language-minority children and youth.* Mahwah, New Jersey: Lawrence Erlbaum Associates, Publishers. This text comprehensively reviews research on language minority students. If you're interested in research on English learners, this is the place to go.

Bear, D. R., Helman, L., Templeton, S., Invernizzi, M. & Johnston, F. (2007). *Words their way with English learners: Word study for phonics, vocabulary, and spelling instruction.* Upper Saddle River, New Jersey: Pearson: Merrill Prentice Hall. This text is so detailed that you would never be able to use all of the information in it. However, all the theoretical and practical knowledge that you are likely to ever need is here. There are 7 chapters and an extensive index. Chapters range from assessment, to organization, to working with students in the emergent stages, to working with word study, within-word patterns, to affixes and much more. This book is helpful for teachers working at every grade level.

Bolton, F., & Snowball, D. (1993). *Teaching spelling: A practical resource.* Portsmouth, NH: Heinemann.

A companion to their excellent book, *Ideas for Spelling* (1993), this volume offers detailed information on content of the spelling curriculum, including assessment; exploring sound/symbol relationships; the structure of words, creating new words, and shortened words, such as abbreviations and contractions; and the possessive apostrophe. Other topics include alternative spellings and games for playing with words.

Cappellini, M. (2005). *Balancing reading & language learning: A resource for teaching English language learners, K-5.* Portland, Maine: Stenhouse.

This is a practical resource for teachers of young English learners. Chapters include: Knowing English Language Learners, Thematic Planning, Read-Alouds, Guided Reading Groups and Books, Independent Reading and Literature Circles, and Individual Instruction. There are lots of ideas here for elementary teachers.

Carrasquillo, A., Kucer, S.B., & Abrams, R. (2004). *Beyond the beginnings: Literacy interventions for upper elementary English language learners.* New York: Multilingual Matters Ltd. This informative book by authors well-known in second language learning, is both comprehensive and brief (under 200 pages). Chapters include: English Language Learners in United States Schools; English Literacy Development and English Language Learners; Moving Beyond Transition: Struggling English Language Learners in the Regular/Mainstream Classroom; Instructional Writing Strategies for Struggling English Language Learners; Instructional Practices to Promote Reading Development in English Language Learners; and English Literacy Across the Curriculum. A valuable book for every teacher's library.

Hamayan, E. (1994). Language development of low literacy children. In F. Genesee (Ed.), *Educating second language children: The whole child, the whole curriculum, the whole community* (pp. 278–300). Cambridge: Cambridge University Press.

This chapter describes the author's experiences teaching literacy in English to nonliterate, adolescent English learners in a Southeast Asian refugee camp to help prepare them for relocation to North America. The author provides a thorough discussion of teaching strategies, such as dialogue journals, along with the students' responses to her efforts. A combination of holistic and structural (e.g., phonics) instruction is recommended along with a special emphasis on promoting understanding of the purposes and functions of reading and writing.

Peregoy, S. F., & Boyle, O. (2000). English learners reading English: What we know, what we need to know. In L. Meyer (Ed.), *Theory Into Practice,* 39(4), 237–247.

This article looks at some basic elements of reading in a second language. Headings include: "Diversity among English Learners;" "Good Readers Reading in English;" "English Language Proficiency;" "Background Knowledge: Text Content;" "Background Knowledge: Text Structure;" "Phonemic Awareness and Phonics;" "Experience in the Primary Language;" "Types of Writing Systems;" "Writing Systems Similar to English;" "Writing Systems Different from English;"

"Students with Minimal Literacy Experience;" and "Instructional Implications."

Samway, K. D. (2006). *When English language learners write: Connecting research to practice, K-8.* Portsmouth, NH: Heinemann. We recommend any book by Katharine Samway, but this book on writing in the early grades should be invaluable to every teacher of English language learners (ELLs). Following a brief history of writing research, chapters address: Core Research About the Writing of ELLs; Sketches of ELLs Becoming Writers; Gender, Race, Ethnicity, Social Class, and Writing; Reading/Writing Connections; Reflective Writing; and The Influence of the Environment on Children's Writing. This excellent book fills an important gap in ELL education: writing development in a second language.

Snow, C. E., Burns, M. S., & Griffin, P. (Eds.). (1998). *Preventing reading difficulties in young children.* Washington, DC: National Academy Press.

A national panel of experts was given the task of "conducting a study of the effectiveness of interventions for young children who are at risk of having problems learning to read." This book is the report that reviewed research and gave advice on teaching reading. Chapters address the process of learning to read, who has reading difficulties, predictors of success and failure in reading, preventing reading difficulties before kindergarten, instructional strategies for kindergarten and the primary grades and recommendations for practice and research. English language learners are discussed throughout the chapters. Panels that make recommendations about reading always find their critics, and this book is no exception. However, whatever your perspective on reading, this is a book you should read.

Strickland, D. S., & Morrow, L. M. (Eds.). (1989). *Emerging literacy: Young children learn to read and write.* Newark, DE: International Reading Association.

This book contains a collection of articles on emergent literacy by top researchers and practitioners. Articles on topics such as "Oral Language and Literacy Development," "Family Storybook Reading," "Literature for Young Children," "Reading to Kindergarten Children," and "Emergent Writing in the Classroom" give an excellent overall view of many different facets of emergent literacy research and practice. If you could read just one book on emergent literacy, this is the one to read because of its overall perspective.

Activities

1. Identify two or three excellent kindergarten or first-grade teachers serving English learners. To help you in your search, ask a teacher, principal, or supervisor to make recommendations and help you get permission to observe. Spend an hour or so in each class taking note of the physical arrangement of the classroom, the kinds of reading and writing activities children do, and the kinds of things the teacher says and does to engage children in reading and writing. How would you evaluate what you see going on? What do these excellent teachers do similarly? What do they do differently? Can you identify their literacy philosophy based on what you see happening in the classroom (e.g., emergent literacy or reading readiness)?

2. Think about the "ideal" emergent literacy environment for children entering school for the first time. How would you organize your classroom for these children? When and under what circumstances would children be reading and writing? What kind of activities would take place to create a risk-free environment where children can develop completely and confidently?

3. Observe a classroom in which there are many second language learners. Compare and contrast their growth in English writing with young English-speaking children. Do you notice similar kinds of invented spelling or do the English learners seem to be developing along different lines from native English speakers? Do you see areas in which a teacher's knowledge of second language learning would be especially helpful for classroom instruction with these children? What knowledge would that be?

4. What important differences do you see between the emergent literacy and reading

readiness views regarding young developing readers and writers? How would each of these views affect the reading and writing instruction of children in kindergarten or later grades? What information would you give to a teacher who has traditionally taken the reading readiness view of her new kindergarten children?

5. How would you evaluate the writing and reading of English learners in kindergarten and first grade? What is the importance of knowing their prior literacy experiences in their first language and second languages? What differences might you find among children who have been read to a lot before entering kindergarten and those who have not been read to much? If English learners have prior literacy experiences in their first language before entering your class, how will those children be different from English learners who have had little or no literacy experience? What will these differences mean for classroom teachers at different grade levels?

6. What insights does the emergent literacy perspective offer concerning older second language emergent readers and writers? What expectations would you have of these students based on your knowledge of their reading and writing in their first language? How would you teach these students based on this knowledge of their prior literacy experiences?

7. Make yourself available as a literacy tutor for an older, preliterate English learner. With some advice and guidance from the teacher, try a combination of holistic and skill-based literacy strategies with your student. For example, you might keep a dialogue journal, read aloud, or invite the student to dictate stories to you that may be published. Based on these texts, help your student come to understand how print in English reads from left to right, top to bottom. In addition, help your student associate letters and sounds, including word family patterns. Keep a daily log of your experiences and your student's responses and progress. What worked? What didn't work? What did you learn from this experience?

199

PEARSON
myeducationlab
Where the Classroom Comes to Life

Video Homework Exercise
An Interactive Writing Activity

In the video, the teacher has students select a topic to write about and the students begin suggesting what word will go first, next, and so on. The teacher sounds out the first word, *we*, and asks students to write the word on their chalkboards. Next, she writes the word on a chart on the wall so the children can see and check their own spelling. She also has children come up to the chart and write a word they know.

Go to MyEducationLab, select the topic "Writing," and watch the video entitled "An Interactive Writing Activity."

1. These students appear to have English as their first language. Describe those aspects of the lesson that would be effective for English learners. What adaptations would you make to accommodate beginning English learners? What about for intermediate English learners?

2. How many skills in the teacher's lesson can you identify? What are they?

3. Identify and describe several ways in which the teacher encouraged student participation?

6

Words and Meanings: English Learners' Vocabulary Development

> "How beautiful that first slow word
> To those who found it,
> To those who heard,
> Back in the shadowy dawn of Time."
>
> —AUTHOR UNKNOWN

In this chapter, we discuss research on vocabulary learning and teaching, and provide suggestions for promoting vocabulary instruction for English learners. The following questions are discussed:

1. What does research have to say about learning and developing vocabulary in a second language?

2. What does it mean to "know a word"? What words do students need to know?

3. What are some considerations for differentiating vocabulary instruction for English learners? How may such differentiation be accomplished?

4. Which classroom contexts and teaching strategies can best promote vocabulary growth for English learners?

5. How may second language vocabulary be assessed?

Recently, an elderly friend of ours, Mimi, whose eyesight was failing, asked us if we would read to her. We chose favorite books this retired librarian loved such as Jane Austen's *Pride and Prejudice*. One day when we were reading, she told us that she was having trouble sleeping because a word was crowding her out of her bed. "What was the word?" we asked. **"Nomenclature!"** she exclaimed loudly.

We don't all have words crowding us out of our beds, but through words we weave the tapestry of our lives. On school entry and throughout our education, our vocabulary represents one of the most important determinants of our success in reading, writing, and conversing in and out of school. Similarly second language learners' English vocabulary, upon entering school and throughout, will have a large influence on their ability to navigate their coursework in English and communicate broadly in the English-speaking world.

What Does Research Tell Us About Vocabulary Development in a Second Language?

It has been estimated that native English speakers growing up acquire about 1,000 words per year. Thus a kindergartener starts school with about 5,000 words; enters fifth grade with about 10,000; and graduates high school with about 18,000 (Goulden, Nation & Read, 1990; Nation, 2001; Nation & Waring, 2002). There are, of course, differences among English native speakers. For example, research suggests that higher socioeconomic status (SES) first graders know about twice as many words as lower SES children (Graves, Brunetti, & Slater, 1982; Graves & Slater, 1987). Clearly students new to English have their work cut out for them if they are to approximate the vocabulary level of their native English-speaking peers. We also know the critical role of vocabulary for academic literacy, and research has shown that unknown words place a particular burden on English learners' (ELs') English reading comprehension when com-

---

 INTERNET RESOURCES

One excellent site on vocabulary is the Second Language Vocabulary Resources page: **www1. harenet.ne.jp/~waring/vocab/index.html**.

The site contains lists of some of the more common words in English as well as other lists. In addition, it contains a bibliography of second language acquisition and learning as well as many references to vocabulary. You might go to the various lists such as a list of the 2000 most frequent words from a variety of sources, or Paul Nation's list for the Range program, or lists for academic

study. After considering the various lists discuss with fellow students which list or lists would be most appropriate for your students and discuss how you would test your students for word knowledge and have them learn the words on the list. The Ohio University site on Vocabulary for English Language Learners (**www.ohiou.edu/esl/ English/vocabulary.html**) contains links ranging from K-University level vocabulary lessons, activities, and games. You could run a class on vocabulary alone using this site.

pared to their monolingual English counterparts (Jiménez, Garcia & Pearson 1996; Cheung & Slavin, 2005; Dressler & Kamil, 2006). What do we, as teachers, need to know and do to help our students narrow the vocabulary gap as they work toward English language proficiency?

First, let's take a closer look at what you know when you "know a word." Consider a rather common word like *catch*. If *catch* is in your **receptive oral vocabulary**, you will recognize and understand it when you hear it; if it's in your **productive oral vocabulary**, you will be able to use it when speaking. Similarly, if *catch* is in your **receptive written vocabulary**, you will recognize and understand it if you come across it while reading; if it's in your **productive written vocabulary**, you will be able to use it when you write. Thus, we have word knowledge in the four language domains: listening, speaking, reading, and writing. It is worth noting here that we know more words receptively than productively.

To use the word *catch* effectively, you need to know its **form**. What does it sound like; how is it pronounced? What does it look like; how is it spelled? What word parts are there to help you recognize or convey meaning? What is the **meaning** of the word? Now here's the catch. As you know, most words have multiple meanings, and the specific meaning of any word depends upon its **use in context**, including its grammatical function in the sentence or utterance. Consider the following:

Let's play *catch*.

That fellow's a great *catch*.

Alexandra didn't *catch* a single fish today.

I don't want to *catch* your cold.

In the first two examples, *catch* functions grammatically as a noun; in the third and fourth, it's used as a verb. Knowing the word *catch* as a noun also entails knowing how to make it plural (add *–es*) and whether and when it takes an article (*a, an, the*). Similarly, knowing *catch* as a verb entails knowing how it changes form in the various verb tenses. In this case, you have to know that the past tense takes an irregular form, *caught*. Word knowledge therefore includes knowing its grammatical functions and how it "morphs" or changes form to modify meaning.

We offered only four different uses of *catch* in our examples above. In our *Encarta World English Dictionary* (1999), *catch* and its derivatives (e.g., catch-as-catch-can; catch phrase) take up all three columns of an entire page with 30 different meanings as a verb, 10 different meanings as a noun, and 24 different derivative words, phrases, and idiomatic expressions. And we are talking about just one word! Learning the variety of meanings and uses of a word like *catch* requires a great deal of exposure to the word as used in various contexts. Furthermore, breadth and depth of word knowledge are acquired incrementally over time as varied meanings are encountered in different contexts, with wide reading representing a major source of word learning. That said, it remains important to focus on vocabulary as part of daily instruction. How can we do so? We start by narrowing our focus to those words students most need to know, followed by a discussion of how words are learned.

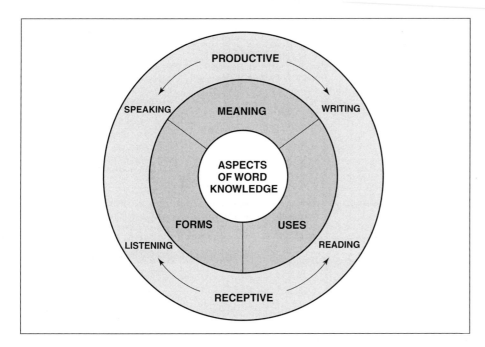

FIGURE 6.1

ASPECTS OF WORD
KNOWLEDGE

What Words Do Students Need to Know?

English learners need to develop a vocabulary that includes general **high-frequency words** along with specific **academic content words** that may occur less frequently but are crucial for learning science, math, history, literature, and so forth. Word frequency estimates point us to those words that occur most often and are therefore important for students to know. For example, the first 1,000 highest frequency words account for about 84 percent of the words used in conversation, and about 73 percent of the words that occur in academic texts (Nation, 2001). When you add the next 1,000 highest frequency words, you now account for about 90 percent of words used in conversation and about 78 percent of words in academic texts. To comprehend a text without help, a student needs to understand about 95 percent of the words. Thus, while a 2,000-word vocabulary works fairly well for *social purposes*, it leaves a student groping in the dark when trying to read or write for *academic purposes*. Interestingly, these figures corroborate Cummins' (1980) distinction between BICS and CALP discussed in Chapter 2. These statistics on word frequencies in conversation vs. academic texts underscore the importance of instruction on both low-frequency **academic content vocabulary** and **high-frequency words**.

High-frequency word lists are readily available on the Internet. Figure 6.2 provides websites for the Dolch list and the first 2000 words list. By looking at the examples provided, you should be able to get a feel for the difficulty level of the lists. Based on words in children's books, the 220-word Dolch list was compiled in the 1930s and 1940s for the purpose of teaching beginning reading to native English speakers. When you look at the Dolch list, you will find that many of the most frequent words are **function words**, for example, *the, to, and, he, a, I, of, in*. Function words (articles, pronouns, conjunctions, prepositions) serve to

FIGURE 6.2

SAMPLE HIGH-FREQUENCY
WORDS

LIST TYPE	USEFULNESS	SAMPLE WORDS
DOLCH list available at: http://literacyconnections.com/Dolch1.html	**Most common 220 words in reading material: Represents 50-60% of words students will see**	the, to, and, he, you, was, said, his, that, she, on, they, him, with, look, is, her, there, some, out, have, about, after, again, all, always, and, any, because, been, before, best, better, big, black, bring, but, buy, came, carry, then, little, could, when, what, were, get, would, come, now, long, very, ask, over, yours, into, just, good, around
First 2000 words available at: http://www.harenet.ne.jp/~waring/vocab/index.html	**First one or two thousand words students will need to know**	action, award, background, beautiful, bridge, candidate, central, change, complete, daughter, decision, definition, democratic, ear, easy, education, entire, father, feeling, girl, government, happy, heart, heavy, important, include, introduce, job, journey, know, lady, language, lunch, manage, meal, national, necessary, objective, office, package, partner, rain, read
Content area words Although there is an academic word list, recent research indicates it has limited use for students (Hyland & Tse, 2007). We recommend concentrating on specific words needed to understand content areas.	**Words used in specific content area** If you use Google and type in your area you can get a content area dictionary for example, science dictionary, social science dictionary, mathematics dictionary, and so forth:	metaphor, angle, ecology, ratio, simile, integers, false positives, experiment, theorem, capitalism, magical realism, anaphoric reference, biology, division, infrastructure, subtraction, identification, taxonomy, acculturation, heredity, anatomy,

show relationships among other words within a sentence. Sometimes, their meaning will depend on a previous sentence or phrase, as is the case with pronouns. In addition, function words such as *nevertheless, moreover,* and *however* show relationships across phrases and sentences. Therefore, function words are best learned through exposure to natural language use, and must be assessed and taught in the context of a sentence or paragraph. Other words on the Dolch list convey relatively concrete meanings, such as *see, ask, good, blue, red, yellow, brown.* These words are referred to as **content words** (different from *content area words*), and consist of nouns, adjectives, verbs, and adverbs. High-frequency content words are good candidates for explicit instruction because they pack so much meaning, even when presented in isolation. Bearing in mind its focus on the simpler language of children's books in an earlier era, the Dolch list remains useful as a guide to words needed in English.

The first 2,000 words website is especially helpful because it also lists the first 500, the first 1,000, and the first 1,500 most frequent words. Unlike the Dolch list, which was based on children's books, these lists are based on materials for older learners and adults. Thus, even the first 500 list includes perhaps 10 words you would not teach in the primary grades, such as *policy, economic,* and *management.* Word frequency lists may help you choose more basic words to use for paraphrasing and defining technical vocabulary for your students.

The lists also provide one source for selecting words to teach, along with your curriculum content, including text materials, literature, and any other material you are using, oral and written.

How Do Students Learn New Words?

Learning a new word is a gradual process that depends on multiple exposures to the word over time. In the process, students move from not knowing the word at all, to recognizing it on hearing or seeing it, to knowing it in limited contexts, to knowing it more fully in a variety of contexts (Allen cited in Tompkins, 2003). Full word knowledge includes both **breadth**, knowing its varied uses and meanings in different contexts; and **depth**, fully understanding the concept represented. When you teach academic content, you are usually introducing new concepts along with corresponding technical vocabulary. These concepts are often fairly complex and abstract, such as *acculturation, fission, integer, magical realism, photosynthesis, simile,* and *quadrilateral.* If a student has studied the topic before and knows the word in the primary language, a foundation for the concept already exists. If not, you may need to spend more time helping students develop and understand the concept. The following guidelines for teaching new words apply in either case:

1. **Relate the "new" to the "known"** by tapping into students' prior knowledge, including primary language equivalents of the new word and its meaning.

2. **Offer repetitions of the new word in meaningful contexts**, highlighting it with verbal emphasis, underlining it, or pointing to it on a word wall.

3. **Provide opportunities for deeper processing of word meaning** through demonstrations, direct experience, concrete examples, and applications to real life.

4. **Engage students in using newly learned words** as they explain concepts and ideas in writing and speaking.

5. **Provide explicit instruction on strategies** for students to use independently for understanding and using new words.

It's important to remember that your students will learn many new words incidentally through conversations as they interact socially with English speakers in school and out. In addition, they will build and consolidate their vocabularies through your carefully designed curriculum that provides (1) exposure to new words during academic instruction supported

Source: Paul Gruwell.

by cues to meaning and opportunities for concept development; (2) experiences reading a variety of material independently and under your guidance; (3) opportunities to write frequently for an audience; (4) explicit instruction on words and word parts; and (5) instruction on vocabulary strategies, including dictionary use, to help students read and write new words independently. Instruction described in items 1–3 above is based on naturally flowing language used in lesson delivery, instructional conversations, books, essays, journal entries, and the like. In other words, in items 1–3 new words are learned in communicative contexts, oral and written. In contrast, instruction described in items 4 and 5 uses words pulled out of context for in-depth study and strategy development aimed at helping students independently deal with new words later on. All of these activities and strategies will help students develop **word consciousness** that will help them recognize, understand, and use new words. Figure 6.3 illustrates the dynamic interactions among the key elements of vocabulary instruction. We'll take a closer look at these interactions next.

When we talk about academic instruction, we are referring to everything you do to teach content, including the texts you assign, your own teacher talk, and the talk among students during group work. The rich, natural language that is part and parcel of academic instruction facilitates vocabulary development provided you use sheltering strategies to develop concepts and make meaning accessible (see Chapter 3). You will also want to follow up with explicit instruction on selected words you judge most important for learning the material under study, using strategies we offer subsequently in this chapter. When you help students develop and apply new concepts and generalizations in any area of study, you simultaneously help them retain the corresponding vocabulary.

FIGURE 6.3

SOURCES OF WORD LEARNING

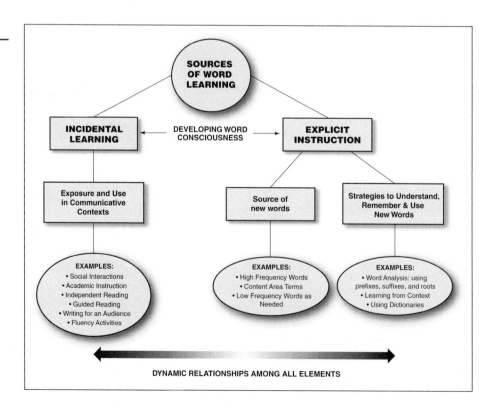

When reading independently or under your guidance, students are dealing with the more or less natural language found in trade books, textbooks, and other materials. During **independent reading**, it is important for English learners to read material geared to their English proficiency and reading ability. As noted previously, if students can't understand most of what they read, about 95 percent of the words in a given text, they will have difficulty inferring the meaning of new words they encounter. If you are on hand to *guide* their reading, students can deal with slightly more difficult texts, and trouble spots offer you the chance to help them apply strategies for dealing with unknown words. Chapters 8 and 11 discuss ways to choose material for independent reading and guided reading at appropriate levels of difficulty. Finally, as students write with opportunities for others to respond, they produce text for communication purposes and get feedback on how well their word choices convey the desired message. To summarize, academic instruction, independent and guided reading, and writing for an audience represent three important avenues to vocabulary development within natural, communicative contexts. We offer numerous ideas for developing and refining vocabulary knowledge in context in our chapters on oral language, emergent literacy, writing, and reading (Chapters 4, 5, and 7 through 11).

In addition to exposure to new words in context, students benefit from **explicit instruction** that focuses their attention on individual words and word parts, such as prefixes, suffixes, and roots (Folse, 2004; Graves, 2004; Nation, 1990, 2005, Schmitt & McCarthy, 2005). Here we are pulling words out of the ongoing flow of oral or written discourse to highlight how they look, how they sound, and what they mean. Analysis of word parts shows students how words are built in English. This knowledge can help them figure out the meaning of new

These girls are using new vocabulary as they explain cloud formation and weather.

FIGURE 6.4

MODEL FOR
INSTRUCTING STUDENTS
ON STRATEGIES

Source: N. K. Duke and P. D.
Pearson, "Effective Practices
for Developing Reading
Comprehension," in S. J.
Samuels and A. E. Farstrup,
eds., *What Research Has
to Say About Reading
Instruction*, 3rd ed.
(Newark, DE: International
Reading Association, 2002),
pp. 203–242.

1) Begin with an explicit description of the strategy	1) Tell students what the strategy is and why it is important for them to learn the strategy
2) Model the strategy in action	2) Teacher and/or students may model the strategy
3) Collaborative use of the strategy	3) Ask students to use the strategy with you as you speak aloud and give them your thoughts
4) Continue with guided practice of the strategy	4) Guide students through the use of the strategy while gradually releasing responsibility to them
5) Finish by having students use the strategy independently	5) Ask students to use the strategy with a specific reading or writing assignment

words they encounter, particularly in reading. Through repeated exposure and review of new words, students gain instant recognition of their form and meaning, or **fluency**, and the ability to use them in communication.

In addition to word study, explicit instruction on **vocabulary strategies** will help your students (1) unlock the meaning of new words they come upon in reading and conversation and (2) choose appropriate and precise words to convey messages when writing and speaking. For teaching particular strategies, you may want to use the scaffolding procedure (Duke & Pearson, 2002) shown in Figure 6.4.

By addressing vocabulary both in and out of natural communication contexts, you provide a **balanced approach** to vocabulary instruction (Decarrico, 2001). The ultimate aim, of course, is for students to be able to use words effectively to achieve their communicative goals across a wide range of communication events; for example, listening to a speech, writing a letter, explaining an idea, reading a story, and so forth. Figure 6.5 illustrates the key elements of an excellent vocabulary program. In later chapters we also present strategies that help students elaborate and deepen their knowledge of words; for example, mapping, clustering, and semantic feature analysis. These elements together will assure you that your students are gaining the vocabulary knowledge they need.

FIGURE 6.5

KEY ELEMENTS OF
SUCCESSFUL VOCABULARY
PROGRAMS

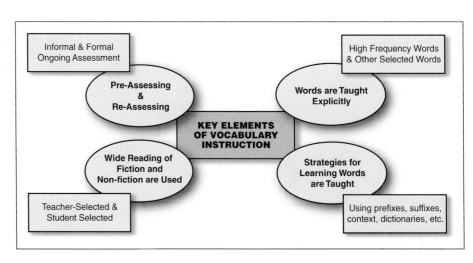

How Do We Differentiate Vocabulary Assessment and Instruction?

To differentiate vocabulary assessment and instruction, you first need to consider each student's: (1) age and grade, (2) English language proficiency (oral and written), (3) primary language proficiency (oral and written), and (4) educational experiences. You already know the age and grade of your students, and that's important for selecting words that are age appropriate and essential for learning grade level curriculum content. Hopefully, you will also have some idea of how much education your student has had both in the primary language and in English as a second or foreign language, as that information gives you a clearer picture of your student's linguistic and conceptual resources, which we talk about next.

English Language Proficiency Considerations

To assess vocabulary and choose words for study, you need to consider each student's English language proficiency. For example, a student new to English might concentrate on words you select from the Dolch list or the first-500 list. On the other hand, an intermediate English learner may benefit more from words on the first-2,000 list. You also need to know whether your student can decode in English. If not, it would be fruitless to assess using a list of written words. Instead, you would need to use pictures or actions to elicit knowledge of a particular word. For instruction, though, it's useful to present both the oral and written forms of a word together for simultaneous acquisition.

Some English learners have studied English formally in their home country. If so, they might display their English proficiency, including vocabulary knowledge, more effectively through writing than through speaking. For these students, you may present a list of words for which the student gives a synonym or a short definition. Students with previous English language study might have developed effective strategies for learning new words, such as memorization and word association. If so, they can use those strategies and share them with their classmates as well. By considering your students' prior knowledge and experiences, you will be able to tailor assessment and instruction accordingly.

Primary Language Proficiency Considerations

Learning about a student's home language use can be helpful, even if you are not teaching bilingually, because aspects of first language knowledge transfer to the second language (Odlin, 1989; Swan, 1997). The extent to which transfer occurs, and whether it helps or hinders, depends on the particular language. In Chapter 5, for example, we saw that decoding ability in Spanish transfers fairly well to decoding in English, with the notable exception of the vowels. That is because both Spanish and English use the Roman alphabet, with consonants (but not vowels) representing similar sounds in the two languages. On the other hand, literacy in a logographic language such as Chinese offers minimal transfer for decoding purposes, positive or negative, because the Chinese writing system is so different from the English alphabet.

For vocabulary, transfer potentially occurs with cognates, words that look and sound similar in two languages, such as *telephone* in English and *teléfono* in Spanish. Because the two words share the same meaning, they are called "friendly cognates." Knowing the word in one language makes learning fairly easy in the other. On the other hand, there are also "false cognates," that is, words with different meanings in two languages even though they look and sound similar. A good example is *embarrassed* in English and *embarazada* in Spanish, which means "pregnant." You can just imagine the potential for confusion there! Cognates, false or friendly, often occur when two languages share the same source language. For example, the Romance languages share many cognates with English due to the influence of Latin and Greek as a source language in their respective histories. As a Germanic type language, English also shares cognates with other Germanic languages, for example, in English and German: house—*Haus*; water—*Wasser*; brother—*Bruder*; sister—*Schwester*. You probably are aware that cognates with non-European languages are much less prevalent. Where they do exist, they tend be loan words to or from English. The point here is that it is helpful for you to learn about your students' primary language proficiency in order to build upon areas of positive transfer, and understand areas of negative transfer when they occur. In so doing, you will be able to further differentiate vocabulary instruction.

We know that in some classes serving English learners, there may be numerous primary languages represented. Learning about all of them can be an onerous task. One way to make use of your students' home languages and promote linguistic awareness is to create a multilingual wall dictionary. For each word you post in English, your students offer the corresponding word in their primary language. From time to time, you and your students may examine the dictionary to identify cognates and other similarities and differences among words in the various languages. In so doing, you demonstrate recognition and respect for students' home languages while motivating interest in cross-linguistic study.

Vocabulary Assessment For Planning Instruction

Broadly speaking, there are two types of words to be concerned with for English learners' vocabulary development: content area words and high-frequency words. Assessing students' word knowledge ahead of time helps you choose study words, based on what they already know and what they need to learn. For important content area vocabulary, you can engage students in brainstorming a topic before teaching about it to assess both prior knowledge and vocabulary. In addition, or alternatively, you might ask students to work in pairs or triads to write anything they know or can guess about a list of words you provide. They write or draw their responses. You may share ideas from these responses with the whole class as a way to generate interest and pave the way for learning about the topic.

Another way you can assess vocabulary is to give students a short list of words you judge to be at about their instructional level. You may select the words from a word frequency list, a teacher's guide, your curriculum standards, or other resource. Next, ask your students to indicate whether they know the word, and if so how well they know it, using the categories in Figure 6.6: (1) I recognize the word, (2) I can define the word, (3) I can use the word in a sentence, and (4) I can use the word in several different contexts. After briefly describing and giving examples of each of the four categories, you might ask them to place

I Recognize the Word	I Can Give a Definition of the Word	I Can Use the Word in a Sentence	I Can Use the Word in Several Contexts

FIGURE 6.6

INFORMAL ASSESSMENT OF VOCABULARY USING WORD LISTS

words under each category of knowledge. For students just starting to learn English, simple pictures are helpful for eliciting word knowledge. For slightly more advanced beginners, you may use more complex, detailed pictures for students to describe. Wordless books, discussed in Chapter 4, may also be used to elicit narratives to informally assess students' vocabulary knowledge. From quick, informal assessments such as these, you can begin to identify different student's word knowledge, and differentiate instruction accordingly.

A Word About Dictionaries

There are many vocabulary resources available, including Internet sites and published materials. One important resource, of course, is dictionaries, and there are many to choose from. To meet your students' varied needs, you will want to consider different types of dictionaries and choose the ones that best suit your students, your grade level, and teaching assignment. In addition to standard English dictionaries you use with native English speakers, publishers offer three types of dictionaries that are especially useful for English learners: (1) picture dictionaries; (2) monolingual, learner dictionaries; and (3) bilingual dictionaries.

Picture Dictionaries

There are a number of picture dictionaries designed for elementary school students such as the *Longman Children's Picture Dictionary* (Longman, 2003) and the *Harcourt Brace Picture Dictionary* (Kelly, 2004). Harcourt Brace also offers a Spanish-English bilingual picture dictionary (Crane & Vasquez, 1994). All of these dictionaries provide colorful illustrations of high interest, high-frequency words. Although designed for younger students, they can be useful for older beginning English learners.

Sophisticated picture dictionaries appropriate for older, intermediate to advanced and fluent English speakers are also available, such as the *Ultimate Visual Dictionary* (Evans, 2006). This dictionary contains high quality, color illustrations and diagrams in 14 topic areas, such as the universe, prehistoric earth, physics and chemistry, the visual arts, music, and sports.

Bilingual Dictionaries

For students who are literate in their primary language, bilingual dictionaries can be helpful. As the name implies, these dictionaries are two-way resources in which you can look up the word in English and find its equivalent in the other language and vice versa. One example is *Simon & Schuster's International Spanish Dictionary* (Gamez & Steiner, 2004).

Monolingual, Language Learner Dictionaries

These dictionaries present all definitions in English, therefore offering no recourse to a student's primary language. Geared specifically to non-native speakers, definitions use restricted vocabulary, some relying on only 2,000 common words in their definitions. They also may include information on grammar and usage. Two examples are the Collins *Cobuild Learner's Concise English Dictionary* (HarperCollins, 2006) and the *Longman Dictionary of Contemporary English* (Longman, 2006), which is also available online www.ldoce.com. Although these two dictionaries are designed for older English learners, you can also find monolingual learner dictionaries for children and teens.

In summary, English vocabulary development looms large in the lives of English language learners. The joint dedication of teachers and students is needed to make word learning effective, efficient, and fun. Students will acquire a large number of words through natural communication, oral and written. In addition, they will learn new words through explicit word study. Next, we offer word learning activities and strategies for beginning and intermediate English learners.

Beginning Level Vocabulary Learners: Characteristics and Strategies

Beginning level English learners possess a rudimentary English vocabulary and are likely to benefit from instruction using words you select from the first 500 to 1,000 high-frequency list. Your content area instruction is also a major source of new English words, as these tend to be highlighted and repeated in meaningful contexts over a period of weeks, thus providing for depth of word learning. At this stage, students will also learn many words during the course of day-to-day classroom activities, provided that sheltering strategies are used to support comprehension. In addition, words associated with daily routines are essential and readily learned. The activities that follow are especially helpful to beginning readers because they give them opportunities to learn new words in a variety of ways.

Total Physical Response (TPR)

Total Physical Response is an approach to language teaching which pairs actions with words to convey meaning (Asher, 2000). Typically, you begin with action words, such as "stand up," "sit down," and "wave good-bye." After saying the word and demonstrating its meaning with gestures and dramatization, the teacher uses it in a command. For example, you say, "Stand up!" and your students respond by standing up. This routine is repeated with other actions words. Through active participation, students learn new action words by watching, imitating and responding to the teacher's commands (Schunk cited in Facella, Rampino, and Shea, 2005). As students progress, the teacher uses more elaborated commands, such as "Put your book on the table." In this way, students learn additional words, including nouns, verbs, adjectives, adverbs, and function words. Not least important, the words are learned in meaningful, grammatical contexts.

A variation on TPR is the game Simon Says. To get ready to play, all students stand up. Then the teacher gives a command while gesturing, such as "Simon Says wave your hands in the air." Students are only supposed to carry out the action if the command is preceded by the words, "Simon Says." Otherwise they have to sit down. The teacher tries to "trick" the students by occasionally giving commands and gesturing, but without first uttering "Simon Says." Both TPR and Simon Says are useful for beginners because (1) actions demonstrate word meaning, (2) students show comprehension by responding, and (3) speaking is not required. However, students eventually may take on the role of the teacher, thereby gaining speaking practice as they give the familiar commands.

We experienced TPR ourselves when James Asher, the originator of the technique, generously agreed to come into our classroom to demonstrate. He gave us commands in Arabic such as "sit, stand, walk over here, walk over there, hold your hands up in the air." Amazingly all of us were able to perform the actions almost right away. One student was even able to take the role of leader, giving commands in Arabic. A week later, an Arabic speaker in our class gave some of the same commands and, remarkably we still remembered the words! We saw for ourselves that TPR offers a fun, effective, low-pressure way to learn new words. Experience is the glue that makes learning stick, and TPR illustrates this concept very well!

Read Alouds

We can't emphasize enough how important it is to read aloud to students at all grade levels, K-12. Through listening to selections read aloud to them, English learners gain exposure to various genres: stories, poems, essays, articles, and more. They also gain familiarity with the sounds and cadences of the English language. Moreover, listening to read alouds introduces students to the organization and flow of written English.

For beginners, short selections usually work best, including poems, song lyrics, and brief stories. Choose selections on familiar topics. Before reading, tap into and build students' prior knowledge by briefly discussing the title or main ideas in the piece as a whole; because building background before reading has been shown to promote vocabulary acquisition (Ulanoff & Pucci, 1999). In addition, consider how you will support comprehension through pictures, actions, and other sheltering assistance as you read. Finally, depending on your students' enthusiasm for the pieces you choose, read them again from time to time. Subsequent readings will be easier for students to understand, and vocabulary knowledge can be consolidated.

It's always important to remember, of course, that listening to any extended stretch of oral language is a demanding task, especially for those new to the language. I (Owen) recently became the godparent of a Oaxacan Mexican baby boy.

To prepare for my new role as *padrino*, I was required to attend a two-hour class of religious instruction in Spanish, a language in which I am perhaps an advanced beginner at best. Even though I was already familiar with the content of the class, I found that I could not concentrate for more than about 10 minutes at a time, making me painfully aware of my beginning status.

Word Cards

Word cards are used to help students consolidate and remember words for which they already know the meaning. To create word cards, students write the English word on one side with a picture, short definition, or translation on the other side. By creating their own cards, your students develop a personal collection geared to their own particular needs and interests. In addition, you can supply important content vocabulary for them to add. Because they keep the cards with them, your students can review their words individually or with a peer when they have a spare minute or two. Once they know the basic meaning of their words, they can consolidate their learning through various games and activities. For example, your students can do **word sorts**, such as grouping their words by meaning, by grammatical category, or alphabetically (for more ideas, see also Cunningham (2005); and Bear, Helman, Templeton, Invernizzi & Johnston, 2007). As your students gain fluency with words and their meanings, they can set them aside as learned, making room in their collections for new words. Word cards can be used with students at any level to help them learn and remember general high-frequency words and specific content area vocabulary.

Word Wall Dictionary

One strategy you can use with beginning students is a word wall dictionary on which you post words for students to learn and review. These words may come from your current theme study, a story you are reading, or any topic you are teaching. You may also use your own judgment and knowledge of your students to select words from an appropriate word frequency list. Next to each word, you may post a short definition or a picture to convey meaning. Lisa Fiorentino uses the wall dictionary throughout the year to help her fourth graders learn new words and review them over time. Each morning after roll call, she takes a few minutes to go over the newest words with students and invites them to evaluate which words they know well enough to take down. Expanding on word walls as presented in Chapter 5 for emergent literacy, word wall dictionaries can also be used to demonstrate the use of ABC order in finding words in published dictionaries, including picture dictionaries (described previously) that are helpful to beginners.

Working with Idioms

Idiomatic expressions are difficult for English learners because their meanings are not literal, but figurative, as you can see in the Peanuts cartoon about "reading between the lines." The best approach is to discuss idioms as they come up in reading material, instruction, or conversation. For a more focused study of idioms, a good starting point can be the Amelia Bedelia books by Peggy Parish and Herman

Source: Peanuts: © United Syndicate, Inc.

Parish. These fun books illustrate humorous situations in which Amelia interprets various words and idioms literally, instead of figuratively, as they are meant to be. For example, to "dust the curtains," she throws dust on the curtains; to make a sponge cake, she uses kitchen sponges. Students have fun in class reading and listening to the books, especially when they already know what the idioms mean before reading. By exposing students to a few idioms, you can alert them to figurative uses of language and help them recognize idiomatic expressions when they come upon them in their reading. Your class may want to compile an idiom book for which each student takes an idiom, illustrates the literal meaning, and describes the figurative one. One handy and comprehensive internet site is www.idiomconnection.com, which lists idioms alphabetically and by topic, such as animals, sports, clothes, colors, food, and money. It also lists the 80 most frequent idioms.

Using strategies such as TPR, read alouds, word cards, word wall dictionaries, and picture dictionaries you can help your students move to up to the intermediate levels.

Intermediate Level Vocabulary Learners: Characteristics and Strategies

Intermediate English learners may know many of the first 2,000 high-frequency words. In addition, many will be competent readers of graded texts and natural authentic texts, depending on their prior educational experiences using English. As with beginning-level learners, you will want to spend the bulk of focused teaching time on the high-frequency words and specific content area words that they need to comprehend their texts. The activities here should be most useful to your intermediate English learners.

Word Wheels

Word wheels can be used to visually portray words that are related in some way, such as synonyms. For example, to help students use more precise terms instead of *said*, a word wheel can be created to show synonyms such as *says, exclaimed, stated, affirmed, related, shouted,* or *yelled* as shown in Figure 6.7. After making sure students know the central word, discuss the different meanings of the

FIGURE 6.7 • WORD WHEEL

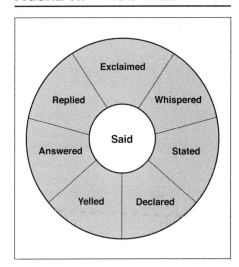

FIGURE 6.8

LANGUAGE WHEEL FOR IRREGULAR VERBS

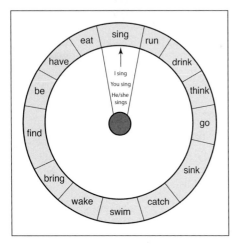

words around the wheel. Your students will enjoy using vivid synonyms for greater precision in their writing and speaking, and they will come to know them receptively as well.

Language Wheels for Verb Conjugations, Adjectives, Adverbs, and Cognates

Language wheels, which are commercially available, can come in handy for English Learners in middle and high school, particularly when writing and preparing for oral presentations. Originally language wheels focused on verb conjugations. Later they were adapted to help students with adjective and adverb forms. In addition, language wheels are available to alert students to false cognates. Made of lightweight tag board, language wheels consist of a bottom circle, about 6 inches in diameter, with a slightly smaller tag board circle attached on top, which you can turn like a dial. Figure 6.8 illustrates how they work with irregular verbs. You simply turn the top wheel to the word you want—*sing*—and the window exposes various conjugated forms: *sing, sang, has sung*.

The same dial-a-word format is used for adjective and adverb forms and false cognates. These tools take us back to our own high-school days learning German and Spanish, and that's a long time ago! For online information about how to find language wheels, type in keywords *language wheel* or *verb wheel*.

Vocabulary Self-Collection Strategy

In the **Vocabulary Self-Collection Strategy** (Haggard, 1986), students select one word they consider important in an assigned reading, pooling their words with those of their classmates to form a study list. The teacher also adds words to the list. Once words are selected from a reading, you and your students work together to define and discuss the words in some detail. Next, you and the class narrow the vocabulary list by eliminating words they already know and selecting words they feel are most important and interesting. Now that you have a study list, you help your students decide on various ways to learn the words, such as testing each other in pairs. In addition, you may wish to post words and definitions on a wall dictionary for reference. Finally, you may wish to test students periodically on words they have studied. The strategy is beneficial in that: (1) students actively participate in selecting in the words for study; (2) it develops a strong sense of word consciousness or awareness; and (3) students learn to take charge of their own vocabulary development.

Word Wizard

Word Wizard (McKeown & Beck, 2004), a research-based strategy, encourages students to actively tune in to new words used in various contexts. After learning new words in class, students take note of their use outside class in different contexts such as conversations, television, radio, magazines, or newspapers. Students then report on their findings when they next meet in class. In sharing their reports, students are encouraged to explain the different ways in which the word was used. One follow-up might be to create a chart summarizing the various ways the word was used along with a tally of how many times a particular use was reported. In the research study by McKeown and Beck on Word Wizard, students were rewarded with points for each new word along with certificates at the end of the week.

Word Wizard focuses your students' attention on new words and opens their eyes to nuanced meanings in different contexts outside class. Perhaps you have noticed how a word you have just learned seems to pop up everywhere thereafter. Word Wizard builds upon this phenomenon and creates enthusiasm among students as they collect words to share in class. Finally, Word Wizard makes a nice complement to the vocabulary self-collection strategy discussed previously.

Contextual Redefinition

Research shows that it is difficult to learn new words from context, even for intermediate and advanced learners (Folse, 2004; McKeown & Beck, 2004; Nagy, Anderson, & Herman, 1987; Nation, 2007). **Contextual redefinition** (Readance, Bean, & Baldwin, 1998; Tierney & Readance, 2000) is a strategy students can apply to figure out the meaning of an unknown word they come upon while reading. For students to be able to determine word meanings from context, they need to have some background knowledge on the topic. In addition, the text should be rich enough in meaning clues to enable reasonable guesses, and those clues are most useful when they stand in close proximity to the unknown word (Schmitt, 2007). Given texts that meet those criteria, contextual redefinition provides a strategy that enables students to figure out unknown words from context by making informed rather than haphazard guesses.

To teach contextual redefinition you use sentences containing words that are important to understanding a passage, and that your students are not likely to know. Your first step is to select such words from an assigned reading, maintaining the entire sentence as context. If the original sentence lacks sufficient context clues, you may need to rewrite the sentence to enrich it. The sentences here illustrate recreated sentences using the words *adamant* and *cachinnation*.

(a) The professor was *adamant* about how students should complete the assignment; he told them he would not accept any other approach.

(b) After she told her joke, there was a great deal of *cachinnation*; everybody laughed a lot.

Without showing the sentences to your students, you present the words *adamant* and *cachinnation* in isolation, pronouncing the words as you do so. Next ask your students to guess the word's meaning and explain their rationale for their ideas. Some guesses may be far from correct, but that's okay because the purpose of this phase of the strategy is to illustrate that it's difficult to guess a word out of context.

Next, you show students the words in context as shown in sentences (a) and (b). Students again guess the meanings of the words, noticing how helpful it is to have the context. At this point, you may want to present another sentence, for which you model your process by "thinking out loud" as you generate possible meanings based on context. In the final step of the strategy, students check the dictionary meaning of words both in isolation and in context to experience the power of context.

Contextual redefinition teaches students how to generate plausible word meanings from context when they are reading on their own. It is rather time consuming, but if your students learn to use context with caution and sophistication, your time will have been well spent.

Vocabulary Journals

You can think of vocabulary journals as an extension of word cards. As students are assigned or come upon new words, they note them in their vocabulary journals along with a definition, a sentence using the word, and any other helpful hint for remembering the meaning. They can also use the journal for reviewing words and becoming fluent with the words. Moreover students can add new sentences when they come across the words again. Thus, the vocabulary journals become a personal dictionary, stimulating interest and building awareness for new words and their meanings.

Dictionary Use

Most of us have used dictionaries often enough to make looking up a word fairly automatic. However, finding the information you need in the dictionary is actually a complex process. To help students out, a seven-step procedure has been developed (Scholfield, 1982) shown in Figure 6.9. As you examine the procedure, consider whether to shorten or simplify it based on your students' age, maturity, and English language development levels. To introduce the procedure, we recommend giving your students a handout of the chart or displaying it on an overhead projec-

FIGURE 6.9

USING A DICTIONARY FOR COMPREHENSION

Source: P. Schofield, "Using the English Dictionary for Comprehension," *TESOL Quarterly* 16(2), pp. 185–194.

STEPS IN DICTIONARY USE	EXAMPLE
Locate word(s) or phrases not understood.	Joe didn't **catch** the drift of the conversation. Student may not recognize he or she didn't understand a word.
If unknown word is inflected, remove inflections to find word to look up.	Example: jump(ed), jump (ing), jump (s); remove the inflections such as *-ed*, *-ing*, *-s*, to get the basic word you want to look up.
Search for unknown word in alphabetic list.	Some students may have to learn the alphabet to do this, especially those with a different writing system.
If you can't find at least one entry for the unknown word, try procedures in the example.	If word seems to be an idiom or set phrase try looking up each main element. If unknown word has a suffix, try the entry for the stem.
If there are multiple senses or homographic entries, reduce them by elimination.	Scan all senses of the word until you find the one that makes the most sense.
Understand the definition and integrate it into the context where the unknown word was found.	Students may also have to look up unknown words that were used in explaining the original definition.
If senses of word don't seem to fit, look for further contextual clues.	Student may have to infer meaning in order to understand.

tor or PowerPoint® screen. Next, model how you would personally use each step, and then have students use the steps to look up words, working in pairs or triads. Learning the strategy takes time and effort, but if students learn to use dictionaries efficiently, they will comprehend more in their reading and will build their vocabulary.

Teaching Prefixes and Suffixes

Prefixes and suffixes (i.e., affixes) are worth teaching if you start out with a small number of the most useful ones. Research has shown that a small number of prefixes can be found in a great number of words students will be reading, and the most common ones may be taught in the early grades with beginners (White, Sowell, and Yanagihara, 1989). For English learners, suffixes for regular verbs are important, such as the *-ed* and *-ing* endings. Your English language development standards, language arts standards, and grade-level curriculum materials will help you choose specific prefixes and suffixes to teach.

Just as you'll want to teach high-frequency words, you'll also want to focus on high-frequency prefixes. For example, the prefixes *un-* and *re-* are used most frequently and begin to occur at about the fourth grade level of reading. Some of the other most common prefixes are *in-*, *im-*, meaning "not". The other most common prefixes on the list are *dis-*, *en-*, *in-*, *im-*.

Once you have selected the affixes most useful to your students, you can begin to think about how you will teach them. Using the model presented by Duke and Pearson (2002) we suggest several steps for teaching prefixes. The same procedure may be used for teaching suffixes.

1. Start by telling students what a prefix is and how they contribute to a word's meaning. Show students several examples of words with prefixes.

2. Provide examples of prefixes such as *un-*, *dis-*, or *en-* and show how the prefix affects word meaning with several words. For example, explain that *un-* means not, and when it is in front of a word, it changes the meaning: for example, *uninterested* means not interested, *unhappy* means not happy, and so forth. You might also show students that when you take a prefix away you still have a base word (Graves, 2006).

3. Offer examples showing students how you might guess the meaning of a word based on the prefix.

4. Guide students through the process of using prefixes to unlock the meaning of words they find in reading.

5. Ask students to take a list of words with prefixes and figure their meaning and give them reading samples containing words with prefixes.

As a follow-up to explicit instruction, you may wish to make card sets with prefixes on one set of cards and base words on another set. Working individually or in pairs, students match cards from the two sets to create their own words, consolidating vocabulary learning. They may also then write the words in their vocabulary journals. Similar strategies may be used with suffixes.

FIGURE 6.10

STRATEGIES OLDER
STUDENTS FOUND MOST
USEFUL

Source: Based on
Schmitt (2000).

DETERMINATION	SOCIAL	MEMORY	COGNITIVE	METACOGNITIVE
Strategies for the discovery of a new word's meaning	Strategies for the discovery of a new word's meaning	Strategies for consolidating a word once it has been encountered	Strategies for consolidating a word once it has been encountered	Strategies for consolidating a word once it has been encountered
1) bilingual dictionary 2) analyze any available pictures or gestures 3) monolingual dictionary	1) ask teacher for paraphrase or synonym of new word 2) ask teacher for a sentence including new word	1) say new word aloud when studying 2) connect word to its synonyms and antonyms 3) study the spelling of word	1) written repetition 2) verbal repetition 3) take notes in class	1) continue to study word over time

Word Learning Strategies Identified as Useful by Older Learners

We have emphasized the importance of guiding students toward independent use of word learning strategies. You might be interested in the results of one study that attempted to identify strategies that students themselves found most useful, in this case Japanese students learning English in Japan (Schmitt, 2002). Figure 6.10 summarizes the strategies using the researcher's five categories: determination, social, memory, cognitive, and metacognitive. Determination and social strategies help students understand a word's meaning. Determination strategies are used independently, while social strategies involve asking the teacher for help. Memory, cognitive and metacognitive strategies help students consolidate word meanings. If you work with older students, you might share and discuss these strategies with them. Let them choose strategies to try out and then evaluate their usefulness. If you are especially curious, you might want to get the article and replicate the study yourself.

One often mentioned strategy not cited by the students in the study (Schmitt, 2002), is the keyword method for memorizing new vocabulary. In this multistep mnemonic procedure, students select and memorize associations between a target word (L2) and its translation (meaning) and a similar sounding word in the L1. Some older students may find the technique helpful. However, we suggest that vocabulary learning time is better spent hearing and using new words in meaningful contexts, such as theme studies. One caveat we offer about teaching any strategy is the learning payoff in relation to the time spent teaching it.

Assessing Second Language Learners Vocabulary Progress

You may assess your student's vocabulary learning informally in several ways. First of all, you may observe and jot notes as students work in small groups while reading or working in cooperative groups on content area tasks. In addition, you may collect their personal dictionaries periodically, analyze their entries, and make a note of strengths and needs to discuss in an individual conference. When you ask students to write or present their understandings as part of your content area teaching, you may watch for and note correct use of technical vocabulary you have taught. Another way to assess vocabulary during instructional time is to engage students in discussion of word meanings (Simpson cited in O'Malley & Pierce, 1996). For example, you may assess how well students recognize and infer relationships by asking how a pair of words do or do not relate, for example, how *football* and *soccer* are alike or different. Or you may ask students to take a list of objects, classify them by common attributes, and name the class to which they belong, for example, *duck, zebra*, and *frog* may be classified as animals. If rock is in the list, it has to be set aside as an outlier. Each of these alternative strategies asks students to do something more elaborate with a word which may reveal a deeper level of word knowledge.

In addition to assessing vocabulary as part of instruction, you may also use traditional means such as multiple-choice tests and matching items. The benefit of these traditional assessments is that they are quick and easy, and may be administered to the whole class at one time.

Looking back, most of us can remember an influential teacher in our lives. One such influential teacher was Professor Featherstone, who gave the freshmen literature class about 25 key terms we should know in order to appreciate and discuss English literature. We knew we would be tested on those terms, so we studied them well. By the end of the semester, we were all rather impressed by the level of sophistication we had achieved in our literary discourse! Starting with those key terms, I (Owen) ended up majoring in English literature. Professor Featherstone, by teaching important literary terms, provided us with the words and ideas we needed to understand literature and literary criticism. And knowing that he would be testing us on those terms motivated us to study!

Differentiating Vocabulary Instruction

Differentiating vocabulary instruction requires us to consider each student's word knowledge in relation to grade level curriculum standards, goals, and objectives. Student contributions to K-W-L charts (see Chapter 3) and your other observations during instruction provide first steps in assessment. Short word lists of important content area terms are another way to assess student word knowledge prior to instruction. Word frequency lists can help you determine other words your students may need. Finally, each student's personal dictionary entries offer an ongoing record of individual vocabulary levels and growth. With this information in hand, you will be able to make use of several features of this chapter to differentiate instruction. One feature is the division of strategies into beginning and intermediate categories. Another feature is the chart in Figure 6.11, which suggests grade levels at which each strategy may be used. Finally, you will be able to assess student learning after instruction using the various techniques suggested.

In Chapter 3, we offered a scaffold for planning differentiated instruction that calls your attention to who, what, how and how well. We use that scaffold now to describe differentiated vocabulary instruction related to a theme study on **travel** and **distance** in a fifth-grade class. The lesson is based on a fifth-grade science standard that requires all students to demonstrate knowledge and understanding of the planets in our solar system, their size, distance from the earth, temperature, and the composition of their atmospheres.

Who: Fifth-grade students who are beginning, advanced beginning, and intermediate English language learners. They represent a variety of primary language backgrounds. They have all enjoyed looking at the night sky and are familiar with the words *moon*, *stars*, and *sun*.

What: The opening lesson focuses on the initial concepts for the theme study and corresponding vocabulary: **solar system, sun, planet**, and **distance**. The next part of the theme study will add: **diameter, temperature, atmosphere, surface, gas**, and **oxygen**

How: Showing a large, colorful picture of the solar system, the teacher points out the sun, the Earth, and the planets, inviting students to offer corresponding words in their primary language for the multilingual wall dictionary. A **K-W-L chart** is created to elicit and develop background knowledge on the topic. Students then work in triads to create an illustrated poster on an assigned planet, using textbooks and other resource materials the teacher has gathered. Each triad will include a **beginning**, an **intermediate**, and an **advanced** English learner. The project involves drawing the planet, labeling it, and writing its distance from the sun. The poster will later become the opening page of a short report on the planets covering subsequent information on the planets, including size, position in the solar system, atmosphere, and other facts.

How well: Beginning English learners will be able to point to the sun and the planets as they are named and state their distance from the sun when asked; **intermediate English learners** will be able to orally describe their planet's location in the solar system and its distance from the sun, using target vocabulary; **advanced English learners** will be able to use facts to explain generalizations about their planet, such as how its distance from the sun affects its temperature. All students will record target vocabulary in their science journals, along with any additional words they wish to include. Next to their words they note the meaning in words, pictures, or translations. Just before students present their posters, the teacher meets briefly with homogenous groups (based on English language proficiency) to provide additional vocabulary reinforcement and assistance, differentiated for beginning, intermediate, and advanced English learners.

Summary

In this chapter we discussed vocabulary acquisition and its relationship to reading comprehension, academic literacy, and general communication in and out of school. With a focus on high-frequency words and content area vocabulary, we explained three major sources of word learning (1) incidental learning of words in context including oral communication, reading, and writing; (2) explicit instruction on specific words; and (3) explicit instruction on strategies to unlock word meaning and help students become independent word learners. Explicit instruction on words and word learning strategies also helps students develop word

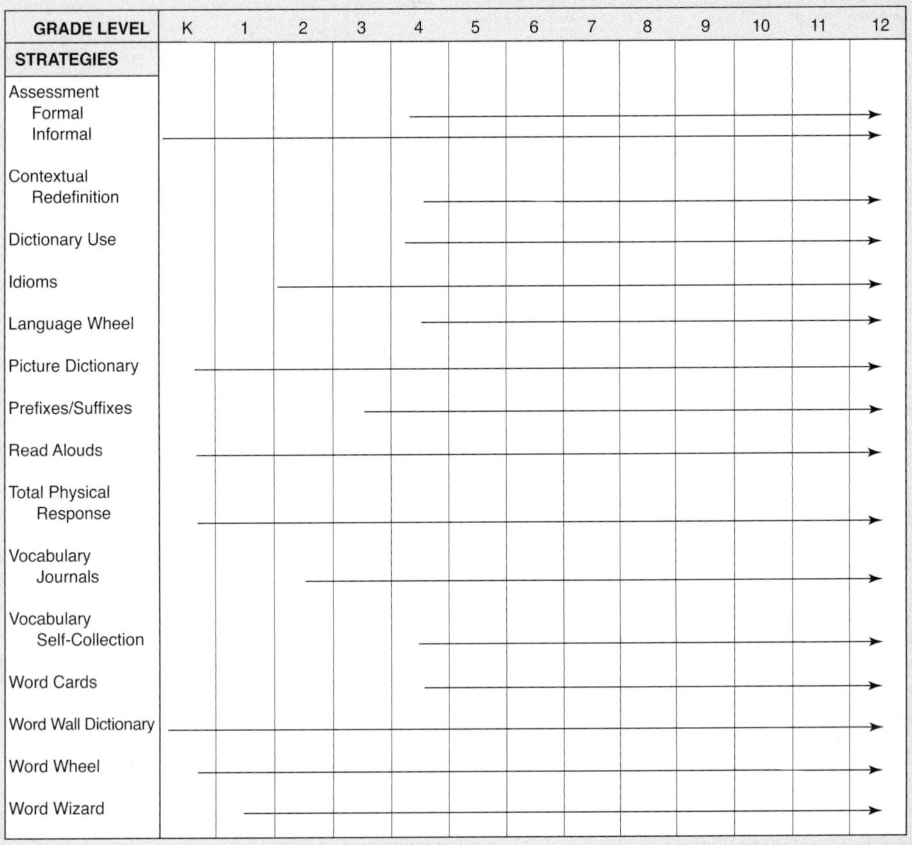

FIGURE 6.11

GRADE LEVELS AT WHICH STRATEGIES MAY BE USED

GRADE LEVEL	K	1	2	3	4	5	6	7	8	9	10	11	12
STRATEGIES													
Assessment — Formal					→————————————————→								
Assessment — Informal	→————————————————————————————————————→												
Contextual Redefinition					→————————————————→								
Dictionary Use					→————————————————→								
Idioms			→————————————————————————→										
Language Wheel					→————————————————→								
Picture Dictionary	→————————————————————————————————————→												
Prefixes/Suffixes				→————————————————————→									
Read Alouds	→————————————————————————————————————→												
Total Physical Response	→————————————————————————————————————→												
Vocabulary Journals			→————————————————————————→										
Vocabulary Self-Collection					→————————————————→								
Word Cards					→————————————————→								
Word Wall Dictionary	→————————————————————————————————————→												
Word Wheel	→————————————————————————————————————→												
Word Wizard		→————————————————————————————————→											

consciousness so that they become more aware of words, word parts and their meanings, new words they come across, and different forms or uses of learned words. Through this awareness and wide reading, students develop fluency in recognizing and understanding words in oral and written communication.

While this chapter has concentrated on teaching specific selected words and on teaching students strategies that will help students learn words independently, later chapters discuss strategies that help students consolidate their learning and elaborate and deepen word meanings and assess the breadth and depth of their knowledge. Strategies that help students elaborate and consolidate words discussed in later chapters include the following: clustering, mapping, semantic feature analysis, and structured overviews.

Figure 6.11 presents the grade levels at which we have seen teachers use the various strategies.

Suggestions for Further Reading

Bear, D. R., Helman, L., Templeton, S., Invernizzi, M., and Johnston, F. (2007). *Words their way with English Learners: Word study for phonics, vocabulary, and spelling instruction.* New Jersey: Pearson/Merrill Prentice Hall.

The title says it all; this is a resource every teacher of English learners should have. Everything you could possibly want to know about word study is here with a great variety of activities and strategies for working successfully with English learners.

Beck, I., McKeown, M., and Kucan, L. (2002). *Bringing words to life: Robust vocabulary instruction.* New York: The Guilford Press.

This book, written by important vocabulary researchers, focuses on native English speaking students. However, it contains many ideas and strategies that can and have been used with second language learners successfully. After a lucid presentation of a rationale for "Robust vocabulary instruction," chapters include topics on choosing vocabulary words, introducing vocabulary, and teaching vocabulary in earlier and later grades.

Folse, K. (2004). *Vocabulary Myths: Applying Second Language Research to Classroom Teaching.*

This book, clearly based on research, may change your mind as it did our's on vocabulary teaching. When you read the various ideas about teaching vocabulary, you may be surprised to discover that the following are myths: "Using word lists to learn second language vocabulary is unproductive;" the use of translations to learn new vocabulary should be discouraged; and guessing words from context is an excellent strategy for learning second language vocabulary. The book discusses research on each topic and suggests appropriate activities and strategies based upon research. An excellent starting place to learn about teaching second language learners and vocabulary.

Krashen, S. (2004). *The Power of Reading: Insights from the Research* (2nd Ed.). Portsmouth, NH: Heinemann.

Krashen's book presents evidence in favor of free voluntary reading (FVR). By free voluntary reading he means reading that is selected by students who are not asked to make book reports or answer questions from a teacher about what they are reading. He states that: "Free voluntary reading is the foundation of language education." He says: (1) "Language is too complex to be learned one rule or word at a time"; (2) "Language users must acquire many words with many nuances of meaning and complex grammatical properties"; (3) "Teaching vocabulary lists is not efficient. The time is better spent reading" (p. 19). Krashen's views on incidental learning are different from Folse's and are important to know.

Nation, I. S. P. (2005). *Learning Vocabulary in Another Language.* Cambridge: Cambridge University Press.

Nation is one of the major scholars and researchers on vocabulary acquisition and teaching. Chapters in this excellent book include: the goals of vocabulary learning, knowing a word, teaching and explaining vocabulary, vocabulary and listening and speaking, vocabulary learning strategies and guessing from context, word study strategies, testing vocabulary knowledge and use, and designing the vocabulary component of a language course. This comprehensive book is a valuable resource for any teacher, but especially for teachers of older students.

Nation, P. (Ed.). (1994). *New ways in teaching vocabulary.* Alexandria, VA: Teachers of English to Speakers of Other Languages, Inc.

This is a resource book with over one hundred activities for use with various levels of English learners. Each activity contains a description of the level of the activity such as beginning, intermediate, and advanced, a description of the aim/purpose of the activity, the class time the activity will take, the preparation time, and resources. Activities range from meeting vocabulary for the first time, establishing vocabulary that has been previously learned, enriching vocabulary, and developing vocabulary strategies such as guessing words from context, word building, using dictionaries, and giving learners control. The last section deals with developing fluency with known vocabulary.

Schmitt, N. & McCarthy, M. (Eds.). (2005). *Vocabulary: Description, acquisition and pedagogy.* Cambridge: Cambridge University Press.
   This excellent resource book, written by experts, contains sections written by many of the top researchers/educators on second language

vocabulary acquisition. Articles cover a range of topics including: vocabulary size, text coverage, word lists, written and spoken vocabulary, vocabulary acquisition: word structure, collocation, word-class, and meaning, what's in a word that makes it hard or easy, some intralexical factors that affect the learning of words, vocabulary learning strategies, and current trends in teaching second language vocabulary. An excellent, sophisticated discussion of many levels of vocabulary acquisition, learning and teaching.

Activities

1. Try reading specific aspects of both Folse's book and Krashen's book. For example, Krashen states that "Teaching vocabulary lists is not efficient. The time is better spent reading" (p. 19). But Folse states that it is a myth that "using word lists to learn second language vocabulary is unproductive" (p. x). Is there a way you can reconcile the two seemingly contradictory views of vocabulary learning? What do Nation and others have to say about learning from lists? How do these various views compare to this chapter's views on the same subject?

2. Look up the different lists recommended for student vocabulary at the beginning, and academic levels. Discuss with a partner or in a group how you might use a list to evaluate student vocabulary levels and to teach students necessary vocabulary. You may want to use the lists mentioned in this book or you may want to look at other lists on the internet to determine what list(s) would be most useful with your specific students.

3. Describe students in a classroom and explain how you would create lessons for the following lists: the first 1,000 words, the second 1,000 words, or a content area word list. Share your

teaching ideas with other students in your class and determine which activities or approaches your group thinks would work best.

4. At the end of this chapter, we suggest giving students a list of words that will provide a foundation for them in a specific content area. Discuss whether you would use this approach or not. In your discussion, talk about how students might learn these words with another approach that may be more interesting or more effective.

5. We shared a specific memory we had learning words in Professor Featherstone's class. Think of your own vocabulary learning in classrooms and beyond. What was most helpful to you? Where and how did you learn most of your vocabulary? How might this knowledge of your own learning inform your classroom teaching?

6. Do you think some students can learn from word lists and that others will not learn as well? How will you adapt your own teaching strategies to meet the needs of students who learn differently from one another, of students who learn well by memorizing lists, and others who do not?

225

Where the Classroom Comes to Life

Video Homework Exercise

An ESL Vocabulary Lesson (Elementary)

In the video, the teacher demonstrates a vocabulary lesson in which she first pronounces each word, has the children pronounce each word, and then asks students to make vocabulary cards of the words for study. Next, she gives a definition of each word or sometimes she has children act out a word. She also describes each word in ways that will help the children become familiar with them. Finally, they write their own sentences with the words and play the children games with the words to build fluency.

Go to MyEducationLab, select the topic "Vocabulary," and watch the video entitled "An ESL Vocabulary Lesson."

1. Using the model presented in Chapter 6, how might you develop your lesson for the same words differently?

2. Would this lesson be different for older students who are beginners in English language development? For those who are intermediate in English language development? How?

3. Describe activities from the video that you might use with English learners and activities you might not use? Give a rationale for your decision based on information in Chapter 6.

Video Homework Exercise

Vocabulary Instruction (Secondary)

In the video, two high school science teachers demonstrate strategies for teaching vocabulary. They try to connect words such as *muggy* and *parasite* to the students' own lives. Finally, they discuss the strategies they are using and the purpose of the strategies.

Go to MyEducationLab, select the topic "Vocabulary," and watch the video entitled "Vocabulary Instruction."

1. In his lesson, is Mr. Gannon teaching students vocabulary that they already know or is he helping students consolidate the meaning of familiar words? What might be the difference between the two approaches?

2. How does the use of absurd sentences, cartoons, and creative writing help students with vocabulary? What can the teacher learn from this student writing?

3. Why does the teacher try to connect a word like *parasite* to the students' own experience? What is the value of this approach?

4. The students in these classes appear to be native English speakers. Would you do anything differently for beginning English learners if you were teaching the same words? What about for intermediate English learners?

226

English Learners and Process Writing

> The difference between the *almost*-right word and the right word is really a large matter—it's the difference between the lightning bug and the lightning.
>
> —MARK TWAIN

> The very nature of writing indicates it must be learned through actual experience in putting words together to express one's own meaning. One does not learn how to create a sentence by adding or subtracting words and punctuation marks in a sentence someone else has created.
>
> —LOU LA BRANT

In this chapter, we look at how English language learners benefit from the process approach to writing instruction. We address the following questions:

1. What does research tell us about writing in English as a non-native language?
2. What is process writing, and how can it be used with English learners?
3. Which classroom contexts and teaching strategies can best assist second language writers?
4. What does the writing of beginning and intermediate English learners look like, and how can it be assessed?
5. How can we work with errors in student writing?

When we went to school, our teachers taught writing just as their own teachers had before them: They gave us topics to write about and then read our papers with red pens twitching in their hands to find errors. Our favorite teacher would hand out a mimeographed tome containing the 162 errors she would be looking for whenever we wrote. Consequently, writing was a little like crossing a minefield and hoping we wouldn't get red-penned on our way. We always wore out the eraser before the graphite portion of our No. 2 pencils. The assumption was that students' writing just needed correcting to make it better and that good thinking came automatically. Some teachers would roll out the tanklike opaque projector, project our papers on the screen, and discuss only the things that were wrong with the writing. Crossing that minefield with short, fearful steps, we learned to write short, correct sentences that fended off red pens but were often empty of thought. Our teachers would reluctantly take home student papers on Friday nights, put off reading them until Sunday evening, and then anesthetize themselves with a glass of red wine to help them endure the dreary reading.

By the 1960s many teachers saw that this concentration on correctness was not working, and many of them moved to what was called creative writing. In the creative writing approach, teachers avoided correcting student writing for fear of stifling creativity. Some would give two grades for writing, one for content and the other for grammar, spelling, and mechanics. Everyone knew that creative content would pull the higher grade. We were often allowed to select our own topics. For our teachers, this meant that instead of reading dreary papers, they read papers that were novel and interesting. We certainly thought so anyway. But some papers contained so many errors that the wonderful ideas were impossible to discern.

Following this confusion about teaching writing, researchers such as Janet Emig (1971) began to look at what students and professional writers actually did when they wrote. They found out that good writers concentrated on ideas first rather than on correctness. When writers concentrated on correctness while drafting ideas, their writing suffered. Gradually, process writing developed from this research and from teacher practice. The creative writing emphasis of the 1960s evolved into writing in phases. In the prewriting phase, writers engaged in thinking and concentrating on forming their ideas with a particular audience in mind. In the next phase, drafting, writers tried to get their ideas down on paper. In the revising phase, writers tested whether they had accomplished their task and made changes accordingly. If they had accomplished their task, then they would correct it in preparation for publication or for sending it to their intended audience. Thus, process writing allowed writers to manage the writing task by breaking it into manageable parts or phases. Writers could now focus on topics they cared about and on each phase of the process: prewriting, drafting, revising, editing, and publishing. Student papers improved so much that many teachers found themselves sharing favorite student papers with one another.

One such teacher is our friend Paul, who has taught immigrant kindergartners in an innercity school for 20 years. Each year, on the first day of school, he invites the children to write. He shows a few examples of student writing from previous years, including drawings, scribble writing, and invented spelling, written in whichever language the child has chosen. Given the invitation to express themselves freely, his students begin to write. Some scribble, some draw pictures, some copy letters and words from the board, some write their names, and a few write messages. Whatever they write, however, Paul listens to their stories and praises their accomplishments, letting them know they're "on their way and getting better every day."

Paul doesn't expect each student to construct elaborate messages on entering kindergarten, nor does he believe in teaching children each little skill before allowing them to begin writing. Rather, he assumes that the best way for them to learn is to express themselves with pencil and crayon from the start—to learn to write by writing. This view has now grown into the highly researched fields of emergent literacy and process writing.

The process approach to teaching writing has gained prominence among educators from kindergarten to college over the last few decades. In recent years, the process approach has also been successfully applied with second language writers. In this chapter, we describe theory and research supporting the rationale for using process writing with English language learners. We describe ways in which students may collaborate to practice and improve their writing. In addition, we provide general descriptions of beginning and intermediate second language writers and outline various teaching strategies to facilitate their progress. Samples of student writing are interspersed to give you a sense of what students are able to do in writing and to illustrate how their writing reflects both written language knowledge and general second language development. Finally, we conclude with procedures for assessing writing progress.

"Write about dogs!"

Source: © The New Yorker Collection 1976 George Booth from cartoonbank.com. All Rights Reserved.

Research on Second Language Writing

Current research confirms the similarity of writing processes for both first and second language writers. For example, second language writers make use of their budding knowledge of English as they create texts for different audiences and different purposes, just as first language writers do (Ammon, 1985; Edelsky, 1981a, 1981b). As students develop control over the language, their writing gradually begins to approximate conventional written English (Hudelson, 1986). In addition, at the early stages, children writing in a second language often support their efforts with drawings (Hudelson, 1986; Peregoy & Boyle, 1990a), just as their first language counterparts do (Dyson, 1982). It makes sense that the task of English writing should be similar for both first and second language learners. After all, the problems writers face are either specific to the conventions of written English, such as spelling, grammar, and rhetorical choice, or they relate to more general aspects of the writing process, such as choosing a topic, deciding what to say, and tailoring the message to the intended audience—elements that go into writing in any language.

Although the processes of English writing are essentially similar for both first and second language writers, there are some important differences in what the two groups bring to the task. First of all, students new to English are apt to experience some limitations in expressive abilities in terms of vocabulary, syntax, and idiomatic expressions. In other words, second language proficiency plays a role in writing. In addition, English learners may not have had the exposure to written English that comes from reading or being read to. As a result, they may not have a feeling for the way that English conventionally translates into written form. The more they read or are read to in English, however, the easier it will be for them to write (Krashen, 1982).

Some students know how to write in their native language, and this knowledge facilitates the English writing task. For example, they are apt to display a sophisticated understanding of the nature and functions of print and confidence in their ability to produce and comprehend text in their new language (Hudelson,

 Internet Resources

The National Writing Project has over 100 sites (**www.writingproject.org/**). The project consists of teachers and researchers from Kindergarten through University backgrounds who work with students throughout the United States and other countries. The site contains over 100 journals on writing, and all of the complete articles in the journals can be downloaded or read. There are many articles and resources on English learners written by their teachers or researchers. The articles and research studies are by many of the top educators/researchers in the nation. Another excellent site for intermediate and advanced writers who need help with grammar and spelling is the OWL Writing Lab: **http://owl.English. purdue.edu./handouts/esl/.** The site contains interactive lessons and teacher handouts on lessons as varied as subject/verb agreement to appositives. Select a lesson to teach to your students or classmates.

1987). In addition, to the extent that their native language alphabet is similar to the English alphabet, first language letter formation and spelling strategies will transfer partially to English writing (Odlin, 1989). Finally, research demonstrates that students can profitably engage in reading and writing in their second language well before they have gained full control over the phonological, syntactic, and semantic systems of spoken English (Goodman et al., 1979; Hudelson, 1984; Peregoy & Boyle, 1991). In fact, providing students with opportunities to write not only improves their writing but also promotes second language acquisition.

Given the similarity between first and second language writing processes, it is not surprising that effective teaching strategies for first language writers tend, with some modifications, to be effective for second language writers as well. One such strategy is the process approach to writing instruction. In fact, process writing has been enthusiastically embraced by bilingual and ESL teachers, and researchers have pointed out the importance of teaching English learners composing, revising, and editing processes (Krapels, 1990; Silva, 1990). We provide ways for both beginning and intermediate English learners to take part in writing. However, full participation in all phases of the process approach described next requires at least some English language proficiency, either advanced beginner or intermediate, depending on your students' ages and prior academic and literacy experiences in English or their primary language.

What is Process Writing? 231

Process writing is an approach to teaching writing that has been researched in depth over the past several years with both first language learners (Calkins, 1994; Emig, 1981; Graves, 1983) and English language learners (Kroll, 1990). As mentioned previously, in process writing, students experience five interrelated phases: prewriting, drafting, revising, editing, and publishing. During the prewriting phase, students choose a topic and generate ideas, often through brainstorming and oral discussion. Once they have chosen and explained their topic, they begin drafting. As they compose their first draft, they are encouraged to let their ideas flow onto the paper without concern for perfection in form or mechanics. After completing the first draft, students reread their papers and, with feedback from the teacher or their peers, get ready to revise. Revisions are aimed at conveying the writer's ideas as effectively as possible. Finally, the paper is edited for correct punctuation, spelling, and grammar to be presented for publishing. Table 7.1 describes the purpose of each phase of the writing process and provides examples of strategies to use with each.

The process approach thus breaks the writing act into manageable parts and puts oral language, reading, and writing at the service of the student's communication goals. As a result, process writing allows students to concentrate on one task at a time and to experience the value of peer feedback in developing their ideas for effective written expression (Boyle, 1982, 1986). Because their writing is published, students learn to tailor their message for a particular audience and purpose. Moreover, as students share their polished pieces, a great deal of excitement and enthusiasm is generated about writing. Not least important, students evolve into a community of writers who know how to listen to what others have to say and to critique each other's writing in a positive and sensitive manner.

TABLE 7.1 • WRITING PROCESS PHASES AND STRATEGIES

PHASE	PURPOSE	STRATEGIES
Prewriting	Generating and gathering ideas for writing; preparing for writing; identifying purpose and audience for writing; identifying main ideas and supporting details.	Talking and oral activities; brainstorming, clustering, questioning, reading, keeping journals in all content areas.
Drafting	Getting ideas down on paper quickly; getting a first draft that can be evaluated according to purpose and audience for paper.	Fast writing; daily writing; journals of all types; buddy journals, dialogue journals, learning logs.
Revising	Reordering arguments or reviewing scenes in a narrative; reordering supporting information; reviewing or changing sentences.	Show and not tell; shortening sentences; combining sentences; peer response groups; teacher conferences.
Editing	Correcting spelling, grammar, punctuation, mechanics, etc.	Peer editing groups; proofreading; computer programs for spelling, etc.; programmed materials; mini-lessons.
Publishing	Sharing writing with one another, with students, or with parents; showing that writing is valued; creating a classroom library; motivating writing.	Writing may be shared in many formats; papers placed on bulletin boards, papers published with computers, papers shared in school book fairs, etc.

Using the process writing approach, teachers encourage students to write daily and to select a few papers for revising, editing, and publishing. They also respond positively to the message of the student's writing first and later to the form of the writing when it is deemed appropriate to do so. Moreover, they concentrate first on what the student is doing right before addressing errors in the papers. When students are doing something right, we should encourage them to continue. Finally, teachers provide opportunities to write for different audiences for different purposes, and to write in many domains or genres, including stories, letters, biographical pieces, and persuasive essays (Boyle, 1983; Boyle & Buckley, 1983).

To give you a feeling for the process approach, we invite you to try the procedure described next, a writing activity based on a personal memory that works well with any age (Caldwell, 1984). After trying it, you may wish to use it with your own students. As you follow the procedure, notice how the five phases of process writing are included: prewriting, drafting, revising, editing, and publishing.

Experiencing Process Writing: "I Remember"

TEACHER: I want you to think of five things that have happened to you. Write down each of the five things, beginning with the phrase *I remember*. When you have finished, share your ideas with a partner [*gives students time to share*].

TEACHER: Now, write down one name associated with each of the five things you selected [*waits a few minutes*].

TEACHER: Can you name our five senses? [*Students generate the five senses: touch, sight, smell, hearing, and tasting.*]
Write down the most important sense that goes with each of your "I remembers" [*waits a few minutes*].

TEACHER: Now, select the "I remember" you would most like to write about. Share the memory with your group [*waits about 15 minutes*].

TEACHER: Next, write the part of the memory that makes it memorable or important to you; share it with your group.

TEACHER: Now, writing as fast as you can for 10 minutes, see how much of the memory you can get on paper. Don't worry about punctuation or spelling; you can think about that later, if you like what you've written.

TEACHER: [*ten minutes later*] Share your papers with your group and ask them to make suggestions that will make your paper clearer.

Questions for Discussion:

1. In what ways did the exercise help your writing?

2. In what ways do you suppose the process approach might help English language learners with their writing?

Students' Responses to "I Remember"

The "I remember" activity ties well into literature study because published authors often make use of their own personal and family memories as the basis of their fiction. For example, in the foreword to *Mirandy and Brother Wind* (1988), author Patricia McKissack briefly relates the "I remember" family story that inspired the book, which is one elementary students enjoy. Mildred Taylor offers a similar note to her readers in *Roll of Thunder, Hear My Cry* (1976), which middle school students may read, and Richard Rodriguez writes of his childhood recollections in *Hunger of Memory* (1982), a book appropriate for high school students. When students read literature, it is important to discuss the authors and make explicit the connection between professional and student authors. Authors are real people who face the same essential challenges when writing as do the students themselves. By discussing authorship in the context of their own reading and writing experiences, students come to see themselves in a new light and gain a deeper understanding of the relationship between reading and writing.

Using literature in this way, teacher Anne Phillips read her second graders the autobiographical piece *When I Was Young in the Mountains* (Rylant, 1989) to introduce the "I remember" process writing activity. Figure 7.1 shows Peter Aguirre's first draft based on the "I remember" procedure.

Writing such as Peter's does not happen by chance. Peter has heard and read numerous stories, he has been taught to use descriptive words, and he has used the writing process as outlined in the "I remember" activity. After generating his first draft, he listened to advice from his group, which suggested that he needed an introduction to make clearer why he was cutting down a tree in his backyard. In addition, he added information at the end of the story to make the milk and sandwich scene fit. He then worked with his teacher to edit his story for publication. In the final draft, he corrected most of his original errors and, incidentally,

FIGURE 7.1 • FIRST DRAFT OF "THE OLD TREE"

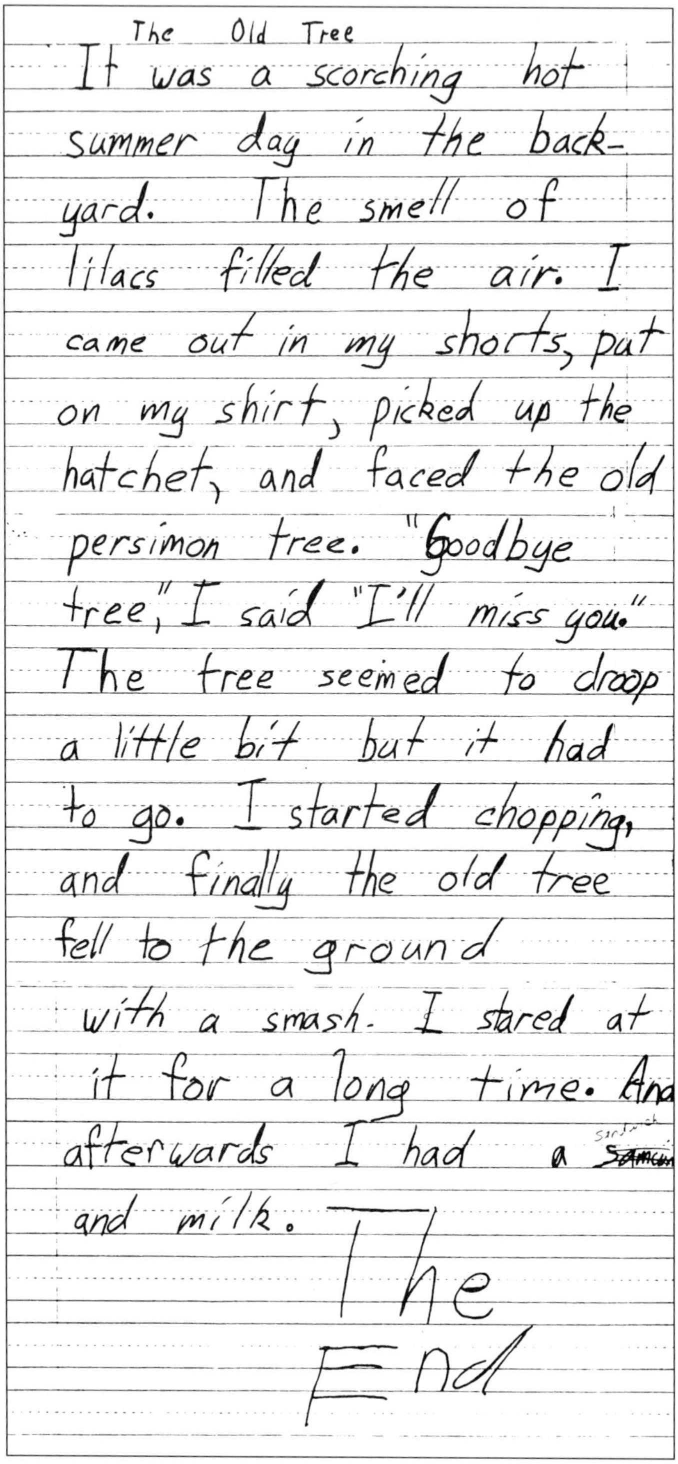

The Old Tree

It was a scorching hot summer day in the back-yard. The smell of lilacs filled the air. I came out in my shorts, put on my shirt, picked up the hatchet, and faced the old persimon tree. "Goodbye tree," I said "I'll miss you." The tree seemed to droop a little bit but it had to go. I started chopping, and finally the old tree fell to the ground with a smash. I stared at it for a long time. And afterwards I had a sandwich and milk.

The End

added a few new ones. Ms. Phillips then asked the students to create a cover for their story and write a dedication, just as their favorite published authors do. For his story, Peter drew a picture of "the old tree" and dedicated it to his pet parrot. Example 7.1 shows Peter's final draft.

Abel, a classmate of Peter's who immigrated from Mexico, produced the piece during the "I remember" activity Example 7.2. He dedicated his story to "Mrs. Grazvawni because she help me with my story."

As English learners write about their memories, we find that they bring a wealth of experience to personal writing topics. One reason personal writing is so useful with English learners is that it provides a bridge between their previous experiences and those of the classroom. In this way, they are validated for what they know, and their teacher and classmates come to understand them better.

Years ago, when Vietnamese students first began to arrive in U.S. classrooms, one well-meaning teacher shared her frustration over a new student in her classroom: "Truc has come along okay with her English, but she never seems to get anything down in writing. She never has anything to say." The resource teacher, however, was able to elicit several pages of writing from Truc during their weekly sessions together. Truc shared the horrors of war, her family's perilous escape by boat, the death of loved ones, and what it felt like to be in a new country with 12 people in a one-bedroom apartment.

Why, we asked, was Truc so reluctant to write in her regular class? In further conversations with her teacher, we found out that writing topics were always assigned. Students almost never chose their own. Truc had difficulty generating ideas under these circumstances. In contrast, she was able to write much more fluently with the resource teacher because she was free to choose her own topic. She may have felt more comfortable in the small-group situation afforded by the resource program. However, there can be no doubt that a great deal of power resides with the freedom to choose one's own topic: power in choice, power in knowing something about the topic, and power in having something to say (Boyle, 1985a).

EXAMPLE 7.1 • FINAL DRAFT OF "THE OLD TREE"

The Old Tree

My favorite memory was when my Dad tought me how to chop down a tree and today was my first test. It was a scorching hot summer day in the back-yard. The smell of lilacs filled the air. I came out in my shorts put on my shirt, picked up the hatchet and faced the old persimon tree. "Goodbye tree," I said "I'll miss you. The tree seemed to droop a little but it had to go. I started chopping, and finally the old tree fell to the ground with a smash. I stared at that tree for the longest time. Then it hit me. I went inside the house. Mom asked what I was sad about. "I miss the tree" I said. "Don't worry" she said I'll fix you some milk and a sandwich.

The End.

EXAMPLE 7.2 • ABEL WRITING HIS "I REMEMBER"

My Favorite Memory

I was in Mexico. It was cold. I was with my uncle. My horse was big and black. I rode slow in the street. I gave grass to him to eat. My uncle jumped in the river; it felt good and cold.

Abel, age 7

235

All students bring rich personal experiences into the classroom. If they are given the opportunities to voice these experiences orally and in writing, you will find that they will often have valid topics to write about and plenty to say.

How Process Writing Helps English Learners

The process approach to writing is especially valuable for English learners because it allows them to write from their own experiences. As they share their writing during writing groups and publishing, their teachers and friends get to know and appreciate them. Thus, personal relationships are enhanced. In addition, second language writers benefit from cooperative assistance among students during both revising (Samway, 1987; Urzúa, 1987) and editing (Peregoy & Boyle, 1990a). As a result, there are numerous opportunities for supporting both clear self-expression and correctness. Cooperative groups not only promote better writing but also provide numerous opportunities for oral discussion within which a great deal of "comprehensible input" is generated, promoting overall language development. Furthermore, the supportive interaction that takes place in effective response groups helps students appreciate and accept each other, another positive factor for second language learning (Cohen, 1986). Finally, by setting editing aside as a separate phase, process writing frees English learners to focus on their ideas first and focus on corrections last. Yet through the editing process they grow in their awareness of English grammar, punctuation, and spelling.

In summary, you can help students with their writing by assisting them with strategies for generating, drafting, revising, editing, and publishing. By introducing students to the writing process, you can show them that they will need to concentrate on various aspects of writing at different times in the process. They must first generate ideas, then form them for different audiences and different purposes, and then revise and edit them to prepare them for publication and sharing. When good literature is combined with opportunities to write often, when strategies are offered to solve problems in writing, and when writing is shared and published, your students will grow both in writing and overall English language development (Boyle, 1985b).

Collaborative Contexts for Process Writing

When you use the process writing approach, writing ceases to be a solitary activity and becomes a highly interactive group endeavor. Of course, individuals ultimately own their own work. However, throughout the phases of the writing process, they have worked with the whole class, in pairs, and in small groups, brainstorming ideas, focusing their topics, considering ways to express themselves, revising their papers, getting ready for publication, and, finally, sharing their polished pieces with the entire class. Thus, the process approach calls for group collaboration and support at every phase: prewriting, writing (drafting), revising, editing, and publishing.

Although cooperative groups are useful during any phase of process writing, group work is particularly crucial during revision and editing. Groups that help the writer during revision are called **peer response groups**, and those concerned with editing are called **peer editing groups** (Beck, McKeown, Omanson, & Pople, 1984; Liu & Hansen, 2002). For both kinds of groups, students need explicit guidelines on what kinds of things to say and how to say them so as to benefit their group members. Thus, students need to learn both the social rules of group work and specific elements of good writing and editing to be effective participants.

Response Groups

After students have chosen a topic and produced a first draft of their papers, they are ready to work in response groups. The purpose of response groups is to give writers a chance to try out their writing on a supportive audience. Response groups usually include three to five people, although other configurations are possible. Each student gets a chance to read his or her paper aloud to the group for feedback, which the writer considers when making revisions to improve the paper (Calkins, 1994; Campbell, 1998; Graves & Hansen, 1983; Healy, 1980). At this point, comments should focus on expression of ideas, not on mechanics, because those will be addressed later during editing. Responding to another's writing is a high-level task, both cognitively and socially, involving careful listening to the author's intent and critical thinking about possible questions and suggestions. Clearly, students need explicit instruction in how to respond effectively and sensitively. Unfortunately, we have seen many groups falter or fail simply because they were not clear about the purpose or function of response groups. How can this be taught? Table 7.2 outlines general proce-

TABLE 7.2 • INITIATING PEER RESPONSE GROUPS

A	By responding to students' content rather than to the form of their writing, you model response to writing.
B	By teaching students specific strategies, such as show and not tell, you give them the vocabulary and means to truly improve their writing in peer response groups.
C	By sharing sample papers with students on the overhead projector, you can model responding to writing and give the students an opportunity to practice response.
D	By sharing papers before and after revision, you can show students the effects of response groups' efforts.
E	By taping or videotaping successful response groups or having successful groups show how they work together, you can assist all children in learning how to be successful response group members.
F	By continually sharing good literature with children, you can help them recognize good writing.

dures for preparing students to work in response groups (see also Berg, 1999). We now describe how teachers can prepare students to be responsive peer group partners.

Before asking students to respond in groups, we suggest that you **model the responding process** by displaying an anonymous first draft paper on an overhead projector and commenting on it yourself (see also Liu & Hansen, 2002). This may be done with the whole class or with a smaller group. First, find one or two things you like about the paper. The golden rule is: "Find something positive to say first." Next, you need to model questions you would ask the writer if there were parts you didn't understand. You might also look for flow of ideas, sequence, organization, and other elements of good writing, such as those listed in Table 7.3. Next, place another paper on the overhead and invite students to

TABLE 7.3 • ELEMENTS OF GOOD WRITING

ELEMENT	DESCRIPTION OF ELEMENT
Lead	The opening of a paper, whether the first line, the first paragraph, or the first several paragraphs, must capture the reader's interest and/or state purpose clearly.
Focus	The writer must choose a single focus for his or her writing, omitting information that does not directly contribute to the point of the piece.
Voice	Voice in a paper is that element that lets you hear and feel the narrator as a real person, even if the narrator is fictitious. Voice should remain consistent throughout a piece.
Show not tell	Good writers learn to create pictures for their readers rather than just make flat statements that tell. Examples also help to show, not just tell.
Ending	A good ending will suit the purpose of the piece to provide closure on the topic but may take the reader by surprise or leave the reader interested in hearing more.

respond to it following the procedure you have just modeled. This procedure gives students a chance to practice responding before they work with one another and boosts their chances of success in collaboration.

Later on, as a variation, you might role-play a good response partner and a poor response partner. Contrasting constructive and sensitive responses with those that are unhelpful or unkind may help beginning responders become effective in their response groups. Students need to see what a good response partner is like and hear the kinds of questions that partners use to assist writers. Once students have practiced as a class with your modeling and guidance, they will be ready to act positively in their groups.

Reading and discussing quality literature also provide students with ideas about how to respond to other's writing. When your students read and share literature, ask them to select writing that is particularly vivid or interesting to them. You might ask them to point out good examples of "showing and not telling," sentence combining, or sentence models (these strategies will be discussed in detail later in this chapter) to try themselves. Ask your students to underline or highlight their favorite parts of a story to share with one another. By sharing good writing by students and professionals alike, you heighten your students' awareness of the author's craft.

Finally, don't forget the power you exert daily as a role model. The way you respond to students' papers will directly influence their ways of responding to others. If you comment in a positive manner, celebrating what they have done well rather than concentrating on mistakes in grammar, punctuation, or spelling, you will find your students doing the same. Your own daily interaction with students is, without a doubt, your most powerful means of modeling response!

In Figure 7.2 we make further suggestions to help students become good responders within the context of an "author's circle," in which writers share their drafts in small groups. Your students now know something about how and what to say in their response groups. As they get ready to move into their groups, you may wish to supply them with a list of questions to help them remember what to say. The sample feedback sheet in Figure 7.3 is one way to guide students until they are confident with their ability to help one another. Another way to guide

FIGURE 7.2

GUIDELINES FOR
AUTHOR'S CIRCLE

Directions to students: You may wish to use the following questions to guide your response to your friends' papers and to help others respond to your writing.

Examples for Authors:
1. Decide what kind of help you would like on your paper and tell your group.
2. Read your paper aloud to your group; you may want your group to have copies of your paper also.
3. Ask your group what they liked best about your paper; ask them to discuss other parts of the paper.
4. Ask your group to respond to the areas you said you wanted help with and discuss their advice, knowing that you will make the decision about whether to change something or not.

Examples for Responders:
1. Listen carefully to authors while they are reading their papers.
2. Respond to the questions the author asks and try to be helpful.
3. Point out sentences, descriptions, or other things you liked about the paper.
4. Point out one thing that might not have been clear to you in the paper.

FIGURE 7.3

SAMPLE FEEDBACK
QUESTIONS

Some questions you may wish to use to assist your students with responding in peer groups:

1. What did you mean when you said _____?
2. Could you describe that scene so we could see it and hear it?
3. What is the most important part of your story? What do you want the reader to think when he or she has finished reading it?
4. What part of the story would you like help with?
5. What part of your story do you especially like?
6. What do you want to do next with this piece?

students' responses is to give them specific tasks each time they meet in their groups, such as looking for "show-and-not-tell" sentences in their writing or for sentences that need combining or shortening. The writing strategies you have taught can become the springboard to successful response groups. Remember, however, that keeping a writing group together is a lot like keeping a good relationship together: It needs constant communication and caring among the group members.

Thus prepared, your students are now ready to work in their response groups. You may assign students to groups or let them choose for themselves. A good way to start is with an author's circle, in which one student reads his or her paper aloud while others listen. The author takes charge of this group and may begin by telling the response group what kind of feedback would be most helpful. When the author is finished, the others respond to the writing, concentrating on making positive comments first, with questions and suggestions later. After one student has been responded to, others may take the role of author, reading their papers and eliciting input from their groups. It is important for students to know that the purpose of response groups is not to count errors or look for mistakes in writing but to provide support to the writer. Because you have carefully explained the procedure, your students will know how to begin. As they all experience the roles of responder and author, their understanding and expertise in responding will grow.

Once the students are settled in their groups, you may move around the room and provide help as needed, but resist the temptation to take over or dominate the interactions. Your students will become more independent if you let them solve their own problems. To reinforce positive group functioning, you may wish to tape-record or videotape the work of a successful group and share it with the class. In addition, you may occasionally review the attributes of a good responder or invite a successful group to share its response to a paper with the entire class. Finally, you may periodically ask students to evaluate strengths and weaknesses in their group work and ask them to suggest ways of improving.

One kind of teacher research project you may wish to carry out is to chart student writing growth in response groups. Two interesting questions to ask might be: Do second language students only learn errors from one another in response groups or do they seem to learn correctness from one another? Would it be better for the teacher to play a more active role in correctness? We do not have definitive answers to questions such as these, but we agree with Hirvela (1999) that when carefully planned, collaboratively oriented tasks enrich and extend English language development, oral and written.

A Sixth-Grade Class Works in Response Groups.

Students in Sam Garcia's sixth-grade class selected their own response groups and responded to one another following the described model. The responders used some of his feedback questions and worked on papers together. Here is an example of one group working with an English learner's paper (Example 7.3). Notice that the responders first concentrate on the content rather than correctness; they also concentrate on what they like about the paper before making suggestions.

When Christa finished reading her paper, the students in her group made suggestions after Christa asked what more she should say.

LISA: I liked the part about the food.

CHRISTA: I should say more about her cooking?

LISA: Yeah—like what's good about the tamales. What else did you eat?

JOE: I like the part about her talking. What accent did she have? You might say that.

LAURA: Maybe you could spell words like she said them, like *Roll of Thunder*.

CHRISTA: That's good, but she talked different.

The group discussed the paper for about 10 minutes, pointing out other improvements, such as naming what animals were on the farm. When they had finished and were ready to work on another paper, Josie volunteered to help Christa with the accent. The session with Christa ended when Martha asked her why she selected that story to tell. Christa replied, "My granma and granpa are gone, and I wanted to remember them; so I wrote this." Christa indicated that her group helped her a lot. She said that she would be able to write a clearer picture of her "granma": "You'll see and hear her now."

Peer Editing Groups

The purpose of peer editing groups is to read over final drafts to make corrections on grammar, punctuation, and spelling. Peer editing groups work well if used at the appropriate time in the writing process, after students are satisfied that their writing says what they want it to say. When students are still revising, it

---

EXAMPLE 7.3 • STUDENT DESCRIBING TRIP TO GRANDMA'S HOUSE

Student's Paper

I went to my grandma's house. She live in the country. We drive for 12 hours. We get on the highway to get ther. She cook so good. We ate tamales and ice cream. She only talk Spanish but she have kind of funny ascent and my sisters and all we love to hear her talk. We love it when she tells about the old days. Like when she talk about other places.

We staying 3 days. Granpa let us help on the farm. I love to visit he's home. I help to cook and help with the animals.

Christa, 11 years old

is inappropriate to concentrate on correctness, like placing frosting on a cake that contains baking soda but no flour, sugar, or eggs. However, once students are satisfied with what their papers say, it is time to edit for correctness.

Correct spelling, grammar, punctuation, and other mechanics are best learned within the context of the students' own writing (Cooper, 1981). We generally address these elements within the context of particular pieces of writing. Students can use computers, if available, to correct their spelling. Allow them to help one another rather than play the major role yourself. You don't need to improve your proofreading skills—they do. Therefore, make them responsible for correctness. One way to begin peer editing groups is to teach a mini-lesson on an element of grammar or punctuation, and then post this element on the chalkboard to focus on during editing. Every so often, teach a new editing element, thus gradually building student knowledge of mechanics. Also useful are editing checklists that students use to help remember elements of grammar, punctuation, or spelling as they edit their own paper or those of their peers. In this way, students apply their mechanical skills directly to their writing, thereby using these skills for purposes of clear communication.

Another possibility is to tutor particular students as "experts" on topics such as capitalization, punctuation, spelling, or subject/verb agreement. Then, when students have editing questions, they go to the "experts" in the class, not to you. This builds self-esteem in your class and also builds independent learners. After all, your main concern in teaching should be to create independent learners, thus making yourself obsolete. Finally, when students select their own topics, when they work in response groups, and when their work becomes important to them, you will find that they are more willing to work in editing groups. Most important, when they know that their work will be published in your class, you will find a renewed enthusiasm for the work that goes into revising and editing.

I can't REvise, I ain't even VISED yet!

Source: Paul Gruwell.

241

Publishing Student Writing

One way to develop a spirit of meaningful collaborative writing is to encourage **publishing projects**. Some teachers like to have classroom newspapers with the students as columnists. Others have students publish newspapers for special holidays. Still others have them write newspaper articles describing calamities, such as tornadoes, earthquakes, or wars. Newspapers are easy to produce and involve students in learning different sections of regular newspapers. They can learn about creating headlines for articles they write; they can learn the difference between editorials and features; and they can learn to write sports, entertainment, and other sections. Publishing projects involve your students in collaborative group work as they organize, write, revise, edit, and publish. Not least important is student enthusiasm. We have seen many resistant students become quite enthusiastic about writing after learning that their work would be published in the classroom newspaper for all to see.

Other publishing activities you may want to try include poetry anthologies, short story collections, and individual publications of student writing. Your English learners will become excited when they know that what they write will be read by others in booklike form. You can create a classroom library by having students publish books that will remain in your room, but you will find that students will value their published books so much that they are often unwilling to let them go. If you explain that their writing will be read by future students, you will get more cooperation. You can also ask students to donate one of their books to the school library or to make copies or second editions of their books.

Another successful publishing activity involves older students sharing their publications with younger children. Third graders, for example, might read their books to a first-grade class. They might also discuss with the first graders how they got their ideas for writing and how they developed the idea into a book. Similarly, high school students can share their writing with younger students. This kind of sharing creates great enthusiasm in the older students, who enjoy a real audience for their writing, and helps younger students see writing as a valuable enterprise practiced by their "elders."

Have you ever noticed that when you take a group picture, the first thing you look at when the developed picture returns is yourself? Why? Did you forget what you looked like? Something similar happens when students publish their writing. They continually return to their own books and reread them. It's not that they don't know the contents of the book but that they find deep satisfaction in reviewing their accomplishments. One way we informally evaluate classrooms we visit is by noticing the number of students who line up to read their books to us. In classrooms in which books are regularly published, students enthusiastically share their writing with others and demand opportunities for more publishing. If you create a publishing center and library, you will find students are motivated to write, revise, and edit their papers.

In summary, we have outlined the process approach to teaching writing, an approach that supports writing success and celebrates English learners' accomplishments through sharing and feedback each step of the way. As students begin to see themselves as authors, they develop pride and ownership in their writing. As the process writing cycle is repeated, as students continually write for real and functional purposes, and as they learn to provide valid feedback to their peers, they grow into more proficient and caring writers. By giving your English learners chances to work on meaningful

Children often choose their own published works to read during quiet reading time.

242

collaborative writing tasks and by having them share their writing through publishing classroom books, you can be assured of their involvement in the revising and editing phases of the writing process. All of these benefits are especially important for English learners because process writing facilitates progress in written expression and promotes second language acquisition as well.

Developmental Phases in Second Language Writing

Second language writers, like their first language counterparts, progress developmentally as they gain control over the writing process. To become truly effective writers, they must coordinate a broad range of complex skills, including clarity of thought and expression, knowledge of different genres to suit different purposes, and the ability to use conventional spelling, grammar, and punctuation. Such coordination depends, among other things, on students' English language proficiency, cognitive development, and writing experience. Because good writing exhibits numerous traits, because these traits vary according to the kind of writing and its purpose, and because individual development of these traits is apt to be uneven, it is not easy to characterize developmental levels. For example, one youngster may write short pieces with correct spelling and punctuation, whereas another writes elaborate, action-packed stories without any punctuation or capitalization. Both are beginners, but neither writer has consistent development in all aspects of good writing. Such variation is to be expected.

243

Despite the complexities in establishing developmental characteristics, developmental descriptions are necessary as a starting point from which to guide your teaching decisions. In this section, we discuss in detail two general developmental phases, beginning and intermediate second language writing. These phases are defined in terms of the matrix shown in Table 7.4 and are analogous to the oral language matrix (student oral language observation matrix [SOLOM]) you saw in Chapter 4. Although we include advanced second language writing characteristics, we restrict subsequent discussion to beginning and intermediate phases, consistent with the rest of the book. For these phases, we offer examples of student writing and suggest strategies you may introduce to help your students progress. Because you know your own students well from daily contact, you will be able to use your intuition and your analytical skills to decide finally which strategies will be most helpful. As a final note, please feel free to use or adapt any of the strategies for any student, according to your own judgment.

In Table 7.4, we describe beginning, intermediate, and advanced second language writing on five trait dimensions: fluency, organization, language use, style, and mechanics. Our concept of an advanced second language writer is defined in terms of an effective first language writer of the same age. In general, if a student's writing tends to be characterized by the trait descriptions listed for beginners, then we suggest that you start with strategies for beginners described in the next section. Similarly, if a student's writing tends to be characterized by the trait descriptions listed for the intermediate phase, we suggest you use the corresponding strategies described for that phase. Bear in mind that your students are apt to vary in phase from one trait to another, and you will need to use your own judgment as to which strategies you will use.

TABLE 7.4 • WRITING TRAITS MATRIX

TRAIT	BEGINNING LEVEL	INTERMEDIATE LEVEL	ADVANCED LEVEL
Fluency	Writes one or two short sentences.	Writes several sentences.	Writes a paragraph or more.
Organization	Lacks logical sequence or so short that organization presents no problem.	Somewhat sequenced.	Follows standard organization for genre.
Grammar	Basic word-order problems. Uses only present tense forms.	Minor grammatical errors, such as -*s* on verbs in third person singular.	Grammar resembles that of native speaker of same age.
Vocabulary	Limited vocabulary. Needs to rely at times on first language or ask for translation.	Knows most words needed to express ideas but lacks vocabulary for finer shades of meaning.	Flexible in word choice; similar to good native writer of same age.
Genre	Does not differentiate form to suit purpose.	Chooses form to suit purpose but limited in choices of expository forms.	Knows several genres; makes appropriate choices. Similar to effective native writers of same age.
Sentence variety	Uses one or two sentence patterns.	Uses several sentence patterns.	Uses a good variety of sentence patterns effectively.

DESCRIPTION OF BEGINNING WRITERS

Beginning second language writers, similar to beginning first language writers, are new to the coordinated efforts that go into creating a good piece of writing in English. They may find writing laborious, producing little at first. If so, organization is not a problem because there is little on paper to organize. If beginners do produce a great deal, logical organization is apt to be lacking. Like their first language counterparts, beginning second language writers may use invented spelling that might include elements from the spelling system of their first language. In addition, during the beginning phase, second language writers may not have a good sense of sentence boundaries or of the conventional word order required in English. Thus, they are apt to make errors in grammar, vocabulary, and usage. In addition, they may exhibit grammatical and other infelicities that may or may not be common to native English beginning writers.

When you evaluate your beginning second language writers, you need to take the time to notice and emphasize what they do well. This may not be natural or easy because errors call our attention like a flashing red fire alarm, whereas well-formed sentences go unnoticed as we focus on their meaning. When a child draws a picture, we don't compare it with Michelangelo's work. Instead, we delight in the accomplishment. Similarly, with beginning writers, we need to find specific elements to praise while pointing out areas to improve. Take for example, the following piece, a beginning-level student's paper referring to the cartoon character Bart Simpson:

> The puppy go to bart. He jump on bart. He look at bart. He see. He go.
>
> Kim, first grade

The child who wrote this paper worked laboriously to produce the final product. As a beginner, Kim uses one type of sentence only. She is able to use the present tense but has not developed the ability to use the past tense. This young beginning writer needs time and practice in both oral and written English. As a first grader, Kim has plenty of growing time, and we suspect that she will improve steadily. Based on this writing sample, we would suggest two immediate strategies. First, additional effort during the prewriting phase of process writing might help her arrive at a more personally meaningful topic. Secondly, oral discussion of her topic combined with drawing would probably result in an elaborated message. Because she is new to English and because she is just a first grader, we would not require her to alter her verb tenses. Such alteration would make little sense to her at this point and would not be likely to transfer to her next piece of writing. In sum, at this point we are aiming at fluency in writing and enjoyment in elaborated self-expression.

Not all beginning writers will be so young as first grader Kim. Quite the contrary. Beginning ESL writers vary in age, interests, prior literacy experience, and second language proficiency. To repeat a point, the beauty of writing is that it accommodates many of the differences related to age, in that the topics are often selected and developed by the students. Thus, age and cultural appropriateness are, to an extent, built in by the students themselves through writing. Older beginning writers may bring a fairly sophisticated concept of the forms and functions of writing to the task, along with a well-developed conceptual system. Example 7.4 shows a writing example of a third-grade beginning English writer, Jorge. In this essay, Jorge attempts to describe the differences between two kinds of birds, mountain dwellers and valley dwellers, based on their portrayal in a cartoonlike picture.

The assignment that led to this essay called for an expository type of writing. As a third grader, Jorge had little experience in writing, especially expository writing in English. He was a fairly fluent Spanish reader and had just begun instruction in reading English. Thus, the cognitive demand of this writing task was rather high. Nonetheless, he was able to convey similarities between the birds' eggs, their heads, and their feet, and differences in food, beak types, and dwelling locations. He used little capitalization or punctuation. His single, extended sentence consists of several clauses conjoined by "and," which is a characteristic of less mature writers. Furthermore, he ends his expository piece

EXAMPLE 7.4 • JORGE DESCRIBES THE DIFFERENCES BETWEEN TWO KINDS OF BIRDS

Tey are the same becaes the bofe of them haves two eggs and there head and there foot and they are not the same becaes they don't eat the same thing and ther beak and one place is the mountain and one is the valley. the end.

Jorge, third grade

with a narrative formula: "the end." These characteristics are indicative of beginning-level writing, though more advanced than Kim's writing. Jorge needs opportunities to write daily for a variety of purposes that he perceives to be real and important. His ability to generate ideas, even within the constraint of a particular assignment, is excellent. With opportunities to create longer pieces of writing on topics that interest him and with the chance to publish and share, it is likely that Jorge will begin writing longer essays. Organization and punctuation are two areas on which he will need to work as he prepares his writing for publication.

STRATEGIES TO ASSIST BEGINNING WRITERS

We have discussed how effective writing requires the coordination of various kinds of skills and knowledge. One way to assist beginning and intermediate writers is to provide them with temporary frameworks that allow them to concentrate on one aspect of the writing process at a time. We refer to such temporary frameworks as **literacy scaffolds**. Just as scaffolding is temporarily provided to help workers construct a building, literacy scaffolds provide temporary frameworks to help students construct or comprehend a written message. In Chapter 3, we defined literacy scaffolds (Boyle & Peregoy, 1990) as instructional strategies that help students read or write whole, meaningful texts at a level somewhat beyond what they could do on their own. In general, literacy scaffolds include predictable elements as a result of repetition of language patterns or routines. Scaffolds are temporary and may be discarded when the student is ready to move beyond them.

Within this definition, the writing process itself is a powerful scaffold in that it breaks a complex process into smaller subprocesses, each of which is aimed at creating meaning. Other types of literacy scaffolds are described subsequently, including dialogue journals, buddy journals, and clustering. Each of these activities provides support for beginning-level writers. We recommend using the activities within the context of collaborative groups in which the students share and respond to one another's writing.

Oral Discussion

Oral discussion prior to writing, which obviously requires some oral English abilities, represents one kind of scaffold to literacy. When students share their ideas orally with the teacher or with their peers, they are facilitated in choosing and focusing their topic. Oral interactions help students organize their ideas and may also provide helpful vocabulary items for English learners. Informal oral language opportunities thus provide a safe arena for children to practice their language production. You don't want your English learners to answer as someone we know did when we asked how she liked school: "I hate school," she said. "I can't read. I can't write. And they won't let me talk." You can avoid that kind of judgment by encouraging your students to talk and share orally throughout the day. We describe several activities next that promote natural use of oral language and pave the way to literacy.

Partner Stories Using Pictures and Wordless Books

One activity that promotes second language development is the use of wordless books. Wordless books tell stories through their pictures and thus offer a unique opportunity for limited English-speaking students to interact with a book. Using wordless books, students orally share their versions of stories in response groups, recognizing that the pictures might yield different interpretations. As a follow-up to wordless books, students may draw their own pictures for a book or a cartoon strip. Students may also try labeling pictures and developing a written story. Wordless books thus offer easy access to literacy events for both younger and older English learners. Whereas elementary students can simply enjoy the illustrations and stories, more advanced wordless books such as *Tuesday* (Wiesner, 1991) can challenge even college students and adults. A few additional wordless books you may want to try are listed here:

Alexander, M. (1970). *Bobo's Dream*. New York: Dial.

*Anno, M. (1978). *Anno's Journey*. New York: Putnam.

Anno, M. (1984). *Anno's Flea Market*. New York: Philomel Books.

Aruego, J. (1971). *Look What I Can Do*. New York: Scribner.

Hutchins, P. (1971). *Changes, Changes*. New York: Macmillan.

Mayer, M. (1967). *A Boy, a Dog, and a Frog*. New York: Dial.

Meyer, R. (1969). *Hide-and-Seek*. New York: Bradbury.

Wezer, P. (1964). *The Good Bird*. New York: Harper & Row.

*Wiesner, D. (1991). *Window*. New York: Clarion.

Concept Books: Creating a Teaching Library

Concept books, excellent for beginning writers, focus on and illustrate one concept or idea. For example, a student, after being introduced to a concept book, might illustrate a color, or the concepts *tall* and *short* or *above* and *below*. Students enjoy making their own concept books. Lisa, for example, made a book illustrating the concepts *little* and *big* by drawing and cutting out pictures to convey the ideas. One page featured a drawing of a little girl with the label *little,* and on the adjacent page was a picture of a big girl with the label *big*. The teacher, Ms. Shirley, kept a collection of concept books that students could use to learn a new concept. Students in her class had favorite concept books and used them as models for their own books. Some of the favorites were large books to illustrate the idea of big, and miniature books to illustrate the concept of small. Other favorite books were pop-up books and peek-a-boo books, in which the students had to guess the concept before they could see the entire picture. Concept books build vocabulary, provide opportunities for productive language use, and create opportunities for successful participation in classroom activities.

————

*Books for older students.

Peek-A-Boo Books for Younger Students and Riddle Books for Older Students

Another effective activity for younger English language learners, peek-a-boo books are excellent for beginning-level writers. Based on Janet and Allan Ahlberg's story *Peek-A-Boo!* (1981), the stories allow young children to become actively involved in a nonthreatening "writing" activity. *Peek-A-Boo!* involves a repeated refrain: "Here's a little baby/ One, two, three/ Stands in his crib/ What does he see?" The page opposite the refrain contains a 3-inch-diameter hole, revealing only part of the picture on the next page. Beneath the hole is the phrase *Peek-a-boo!* When the page is turned, the entire picture is revealed, permitting the child to see whether his or her guess was correct. Children can use the repeated refrain and the peek-a-boo page to create their own first books. They write their own repeated refrain and create a page with the hole and peek-a-boo. On the following page, they can either draw their own pictures for others to guess, or they can cut pictures out of magazines to create their own book. Children then label the picture with a word, phrase, or sentence that describes the hidden picture. One child, Laura, created the following phrase: "Here's little Laura/ One, two, three/ Watching a movie/ What does she see?" Behind the peek-a-boo window, Laura had pasted a picture from her favorite movie and had written the title of the movie, *Home Alone,* below the picture. Peek-a-boo books offer children early access to writing stories because they are visual and because they contain repeated refrains that provide a simple pattern to build on. Children love these easily shared stories that involve them in oral discussions of their writing. For some children, the rhyming and peek-a-boo routine become like a mantra that they will repeat for days at a time. Peek-a-boo stories prepare children for future composing and sharing activities.

Riddle books are an extension of the peek-a-boo books but are adapted for older learners. Using the same format, with riddle books students create a word riddle beneath the cutout opening on the page and ask others to guess what is partially hidden. On the next page, the full picture is revealed and labeled appropriately.

Pattern Poems

Pattern poems are sentence-level scaffolds that make use of repeated phrases, refrains, and sometimes rhymes. The predictable patterns allow beginning writers to become involved immediately in a literacy event. One excellent resource for sentence-level writing scaffolds is Kenneth Koch's *Wishes, Lies, and Dreams: Teaching Children to Write Poetry* (1970). Full of sentence patterns that serve as springboards for writing, the book contains delightful poems written by Koch's high school and elementary multilingual students. Typically, students first write their own poems based on the patterns, sharing them with one another in peer response groups and in classroom publications. Two Spanish-speaking ESL second graders with whom we worked created the following poems using the sentence patterns "I used to be . . . but now I am . . ." and "I am the one who . . ." The repetition of the pattern lends a poetic quality to the full piece of writing.

JUAN: I used to be a baby.
But now I am really big.
I used to be a karate ninja.
But now I am an orange belt.

CHABELA: I am the one who like my teacher.
I am the one who gots new shoes.
I am the one who take care the baby.
I am the one who plays on the swings.

To supplement poetry writing and reading, many teachers also introduce students to predictable literature that contains the same types of patterns and predictable features of Koch's poems. After hearing a story several times, students use pattern books as models for creating, publishing, and sharing books. Typically, they use the given patterns several times before they are ready to experiment with their own patterns and poems. Thus, the pattern offers a scaffold that students abandon naturally when it's no longer needed. Patterns like Koch's and pattern books offer easy and almost instant success to students' first attempts at writing in their second language. One pattern book frequently used with older, less advanced English learners is *Fortunately* (1997) by Remy Charlip. The book follows the fortunes and misfortunes of a boy using the pattern *fortunately* on one page and *unfortunately* on the next page. One high school student used the pattern to create the following story:

Fortunately, I gotta job and I buy me a car
Unfortunately, may car aint running too good
Fortunately, I know this guy and he gonna fix it
Unfortunately, it gonna cost a lot for fix it.
Fortunately, I gotta job.

Arturo, age 15

From Personal Journals to Dialogue Journals to Buddy Journals

You will want to develop fluency in your beginning writers as a first priority. Fluency, the ability to get words down on a page easily, can only come with writing practice and continued English language development. Another word that is integrally related to fluency is **automaticity** (LaBerge & Samuels, 1976). Automaticity is the ability to engage in a complex activity without having to concentrate on each part of it. For example, when you first started learning how to drive a car, you had to concentrate on the steering, on the brakes, on making appropriate signals, and, perhaps, on using a clutch. At first this was difficult, but with practice you began coordinating all of these driving activities at once without having to concentrate on them. Writing and reading work in a similar way. For example, one child might first concentrate on making the letters, working laboriously just to write his or her own name. Only later will he or she go on to writing words and phrases. Other learners aim at getting a lot of "writing" on the page, but it will not as yet conform to conventional script.

Young beginning writers approach the task in different ways, however. You may recall our kindergartner Osvaldo, for example, who filled an entire half page with carefully written but undecipherable words. When asked what his writing was about, he replied that he did not know and returned with great sobriety to his task. We asked him two more times, with the same response, until he explained, "I won't know what I wrote about until I draw my picture." At that point, he created a fine drawing of a boy playing soccer. Writing does indeed involve the coordination of many resources, and the writing process helps students take one step at a time so that they are not overwhelmed by the task.

One of the most popular ways teachers help children develop fluency is through extensive prewriting activities, one of the most powerful being journal writing. By writing in journals daily, students develop fluency and generate ideas on which they might elaborate later. One friend of ours, who has used journals successfully for a long time, told us about a field trip she and her class took to a natural history museum. The students were to take notes in their journals; one fourth grader was overheard saying to another, "Don't look. Don't look. She'll make you write about it!" Unlike these two fourth graders, most students find journal writing nonthreatening and fun. In this section, we discuss ways to use journals for developing ideas, sharing thoughts and feelings, and exploring ideas.

Personal Journals

The first type of journal you may wish to share is a personal journal in which your students get used to writing their private thoughts. When these journals are used, you do not comment on them unless the writer asks you to do so. Students soon learn that the journals are for their own personal and private ideas. We recommend that you ask them to write in their journals three or four times a week at a regular time in the day. Some teachers ask their students to write in their journals at the end of the day, others like them to write after lunchtime or after a reading period. Whatever you decide, set a regular time aside for journals so that your students come to expect and anticipate journal writing. Journals can be constructed by folding pieces of paper in half, stapling at the fold, and decorating the cover.

Dialogue Journals

When students become accustomed to writing in their personal journals, you may want to move toward dialogue journals. First, describe dialogue journals (Kreeft, 1984), explaining to students that they can continue to write about the same topics and ideas as in personal journals except that you will respond to their writing regularly. Make sure you explain that you may not be able to respond to everything they write, but if they have something special to which they want you to respond, they can mark it with a colored marker. In your responses, respond to the content, not the form, of the writing. The purpose of interactive journals is to develop fluency and authentic conversation on paper. Moreover, you are making students' writing functional and purposeful by replying to them and elaborating on what they have said, in the same way that parents scaffold what children say to them in early oral communication. It is only polite to respond to what people say and not correct how they say it. Similarly, in journals, concentrate on positive things you can say. Encourage students to continue writing in their journals but also let them know that some language or topics may be inappropriate for their journals if that is how you feel. If you respond to their journals, make suggestions positively if needed about what they might write about and encourage your students, they will look forward to writing in their journals while eagerly anticipating to your responses. Dialogue journals help develop fluency because they are meaningful, because they are responded to, and because they give writers the freedom to concentrate on what they are saying rather than on how students are saying it. Journals also provide ideas for topics students may write about more extensively later (Peyton & Reed, 1990).

Buddy Journals

A buddy journal is a written conversation between two students (Bromley, 1989, 1995). Buddy journals are a natural extension of personal and dialogue journals. Buddy journals involve students in meaningful, self-selected dialogues about issues that concern them. Moreover, they give them the immediate feedback they require for growth and a real audience and purpose for their writing. After modeling responses in dialogue journals, you can introduce buddy journals to students by explaining that they will be responding to one another instead of to you. Next, assign pairs to work with one another, explaining that they will have an opportunity to work with many other partners throughout the year. You might also provide guidelines for responding to the writing in the journals. Let students see that it is important to be helpful conversational partners in the journals. You might also ask your students to brainstorm potential topics to write about in their journals. Place these topics on the board and suggest that they can write about anything going on in the classroom or anything else they might want to share with one another. Older beginning English learners might share their thoughts concerning a movie or television show they had seen, whereas younger students might write to one another in buddy journals while reading *Harold and the Purple Crayon* (Johnson, 1955), as in the following dialogue:

JOSEPH: I like the crayon magic and how he color thing.
JIMMY: And the pies and things.
JOSEPH: There's a "Harold and Circus" book to read.
JIMMY: Yeah, it has purple coloring.
JOSEPH: Let read it.

Journal writing is a valuable activity for English learners because it involves real and purposeful dialogue and because it is nonthreatening—it will not be corrected or graded. Finally, because journals are structured like an oral conversation and provide a real audience, students see journal writing as a meaningful activity, one worth the extra effort it may require of them. Table 7.5 summarizes several types of journals you may wish to use in your classroom.

Improvisational Sign Language

Using a dictated story or a story students already know, such as "Goldilocks and the Three Bears," "The Parsley Girl," or other folktales, students can create gestures to represent characters and actions in the story. With her second language first graders, Sheila Jordaine asked children to share stories with the whole class before creating their own. Children first dictated a brief story, which Sheila wrote on the blackboard: "Jill had a pet frog. She brought it to school." Next, they determined the symbols for each of the words. Because Jill was a member of the class, all they had to do when her name was read was point to her. They decided that bringing their hands toward them with the palms upward would stand for

TABLE 7.5 • Types of Journals

JOURNAL	PURPOSE	PROCEDURE
Learning log	Develops sense of direction and success in the class; helps teacher evaluate student's progress; helps student articulate what is learned and ask questions for self-assessment.	After certain lessons each day you ask students to keep a daily log of their knowledge or confusions or any elaborations they may wish to make relating to the topics discussed in class. Journal is private or shared with teacher.
Buddy journal	Gets students used to the idea of writing each day; writing becomes a functional and meaningful activity, with almost immediate audience.	Students write and respond to one another about classroom topics and other topics; response is to content and not form of the message; often modeled by teacher in dialogue journal first.
Dialogue journal	Makes writing purposeful in school; gives students audience for their writing and models how to respond to the writing of others.	Journal is used daily or often; teacher responds to content or to something the student has highlighted for the teacher; writing is used as communication.
Project journal	Assists students with preparing for a project in English, science, etc.; students take notes of plants growing in science class in preparation for a report; they take notes of conversations in preparation for story they might write.	Students keep journal with a specific task in mind: plans for writing a story; notes for a social science paper; measurement for a math project.

had, and they made an **A** with their hands, followed by petting their heads for *pet*. For the word *frog*, they got out of their chairs and hopped like frogs. For *she*, they simply pointed back at Jill because *she* refers to Jill. In this way, they naturally learn anaphoric references. When they finished with their symbols, Sheila read the story, pointing to the words, while the children dramatized the story with signs. The next day, the children decided to do a "real" story, "The Parsley Girl," to act out in signs.

The signing activity provides students with several cues for understanding stories. If the story is in a Big Book, the children have the words and pictures in front of them. In addition, the visual dramatization cue for comprehension gives them more information for understanding the stories they are reading. Finally, the activity involves all the students in a meaningful and functional process aimed at comprehension. Children in Sheila's class ask for improvisational signing performances throughout the year, even after they no longer need the extra comprehension support. Older students, even adults, also have a great deal of fun using the technique. For example, older students, who often know many folktales, enjoy creating their own sign language in groups, acting the folktale out and playing a charade-like game that requires other groups to guess the folktale that is being presented in sign language.

Life Murals

Another activity that provides a scaffold for English learners is creating life murals. Using murals, students create drawings depicting significant events, people, and places in their lives and then write about them. For example, one child represented her family by drawing a house with people outside. In another picture she drew the inside of her own bedroom, a trifle messy, to show where she spent most of her time when she was at home. Other drawings depicted a church and school with her friends standing outside in the rain. She also drew a picture of her grandmother, who always read stories to her. When she finished her drawing, she explained these life symbols to her writing partner, and her partner did the same. Finally, she wrote about her life, using the mural to guide her.

Older beginning English learners also use life murals to scaffold their writing. One student in a 10th-grade class compared his life to a soccer game and created a mural showing him sometimes falling, sometimes missing the soccer ball, and sometimes scoring a goal. After creating the mural, he shared it with his group orally in preparation for writing. Then in writing he explained how his life was like a soccer game.

Life murals make writing simpler because they are based on personal experience. Because they are visual, writers can easily get ideas from looking at one another's pictures and hearing their stories. After completing their murals and stories, students read them to their partners. Life murals provide an excellent beginning writing experience, with the drawings scaffolding learners' efforts to compose something more complex than journal entries.

Clustering

Clustering assists writers in developing vocabulary and preparing for writing (Rico & Claggett, 1980). The cluster in Figure 7.4 illustrates different words a student thought of when preparing to write about a personal experience. To create the cluster, Mai simply placed her name and the word *park* in the center of the circle, and then quickly wrote all the other things that came to mind. She thought of different members of her family, of friends, and of a trip she took to an amusement park. When she completed her cluster, Mai shared it with members of her peer response group by telling them about how she got wet on a log ride at the park. In fact, "They all got so wet that they had to buy tee-shirts to change into something dry."

Mai used the cluster as a prewriting strategy to begin thinking about her topic and what she wanted to say. Clusters represent one of the first steps, along with buddy journals, as beginning-level students begin to consider an audience for their writing. The cluster has several advantages: It is easy to create and there are no rules for what can go into a cluster—students decide for themselves; it fills the page and thus assists psychologically in helping the student create a piece of writing; and it is easy to share with others and thus helps the student create a story or experience orally. When English learners are ready to share their writing with their peers, clustering will help them do so. Finally, clustering is used successfully by students when they become older and more advanced; indeed, clustering is used by college and graduate students to improve their writing.

FIGURE 7.4

STUDENT'S CLUSTER
ABOUT TRIP TO
AMUSEMENT PARK

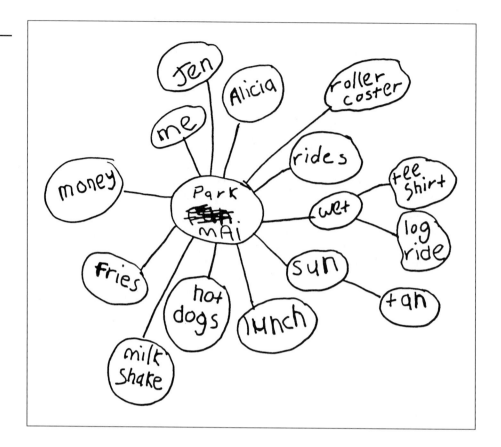

254

Freewriting

Freewriting is a strategy developed by Peter Elbow (1973) in which writers let their words flow freely onto the page without concern for form, coherence, or correctness. In the same way that journals provide opportunities for daily writing, freewriting assists with fluency. Using freewriting, students write quickly to get their ideas down on paper. After freewriting for several minutes, students may select a phrase or sentence they like and write about that for five minutes. They next select their favorite word, phrase, or sentence and write on it for five minutes. This process continues until students have discovered a topic or theme about which they might want to write. The freewriting helps develop writing fluency by allowing writers to concentrate on getting as many words on the page as possible without paying attention to correctness, and it also assists them with narrowing their topic. Through practice with freewriting, writers can be freed from the constraints of having to "get it right." They can instead pay attention to generating and shaping ideas. Along with the use of journals, freewriting assists students with fluency, automaticity, and developing ideas. Thus, it prepares them to move to the intermediate level, where they will pay more attention to refining and editing their ideas.

In summary, beginning-level English language learners can participate successfully in classroom writing events from day one, if you provide support. The scaffolds provided by picture books, concept books, clustering, freewriting, and dialogue journals give students the assistance they need to participate in the classroom. These activities, shared in pairs and collaborative groups, are meaningful activities, not an assortment of abstract skills. Through these activities, English language learners grow from beginning writers to intermediate writers—from writers learning to generate ideas to writers who shape ideas for different audiences and different purposes. They will move on from developing fluency to developing form in their writing and to revising and correcting their work. The strategies in the next section will help them develop into competent intermediate-level writers.

DESCRIPTION OF INTERMEDIATE WRITERS

Whereas your main concern with beginning second language writers will be helping them to generate ideas and develop fluency, your main concern with intermediate writers will be to add form to fluidity in expression. That is, you will want your intermediate writers to begin developing a variety of sentence structures and organizational patterns, from narrative to letter, essay, and more. To do this, you may offer strategies that build on the skills they learned as beginning-level writers, while continuing to share good literature. In addition, you and your students are now in a position to select aspects of spelling, grammar, and punctuation to be focused on during editing.

Intermediate-level writers have developed a general knowledge of simple sentence types and corresponding capitalization and punctuation conventions. However, they need strategies to improve their sentences in quality, style, length, and variety. In addition, as their writing increases in length, they will need to develop organizational strategies, such as paragraphing and logical ordering of ideas. At this point, spelling may be fairly standard, though as yet imperfect, especially if students are using more advanced vocabulary. In addition, some intermediate writers may rely too heavily on one or two sentence patterns as a conservative strategy for avoiding errors. You will want to encourage these writers to try new forms that will improve their writing and strengthen their general knowledge of English. Finally, intermediate writers may still make fairly frequent errors in punctuation, grammar, and usage. In fact, they may make more such errors than beginners because they are producing more writing—a positive sign of writing progress. Recurrent errors may serve as the basis of an individual or group mini-lesson, so that students may correct such errors during editing.

In summary, intermediate writers have developed fluency in their writing. They are able to produce a large number of words on the page, but they still need to work on organization of longer pieces of writing and on sentence variety, grammar, and spelling. The essay shown in Figure 7.5 provides an example of intermediate second language writing, representing the writer's best effort after working in his peer response group.

Juan has worked hard on developing a topic about which he clearly cares very much. Based on the writing traits matrix, his writing exhibits elements of intermediate phase writing. Of particular note, he has organized his essay into a beginning, middle, and end. His teacher gave him special help with this. He writes with considerable fluency but retains errors in his final draft. For example, his writing exhibits minor problems with spelling and verb forms. He misspells *both* as "bouth" and *said* as "sed." However, his inventive spellings are phonetically

255

FIGURE 7.5

JUAN'S STORY: THE FIRST
TIME I SAW HER

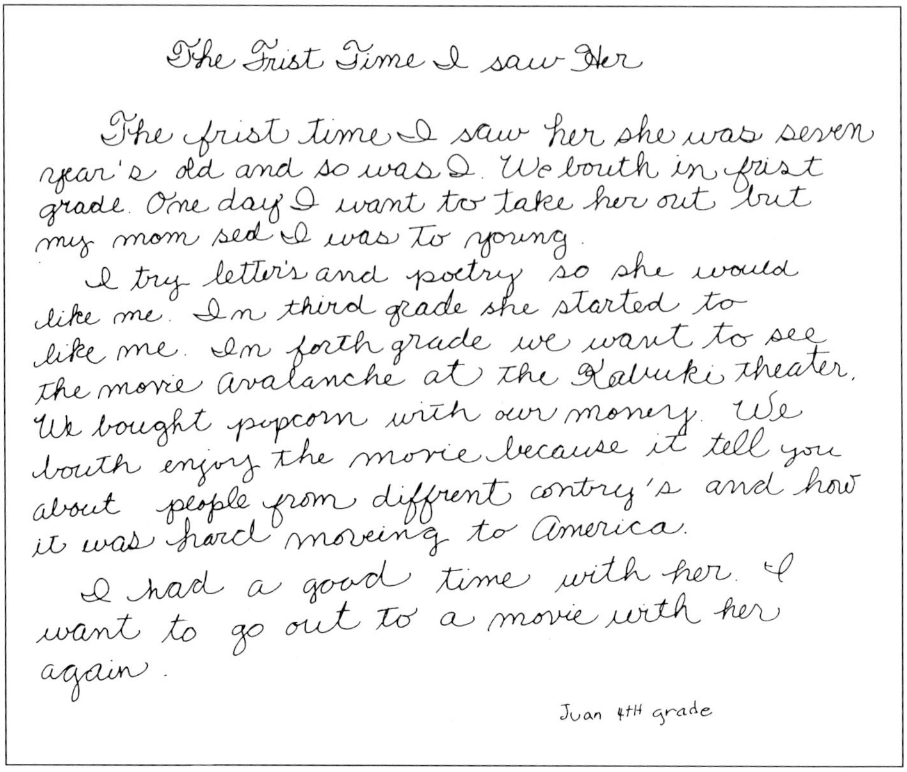

> The Frist Time I saw Her
>
> The frist time I saw her she was seven year's old and so was I. We bouth in frist grade. One day I want to take her out but my mom sed I was to young.
>
> I try letter's and poetry so she would like me. In third grade she started to like me. In forth grade we want to see the movie Avalanche at the Kabuki theater. We bought popcorn with our money. We bouth enjoy the movie because it tell you about people from diffrent contry's and how it was hard moveing to America.
>
> I had a good time with her. I want to go out to a movie with her again.
>
> Juan 4th grade

accurate and thus more logical than conventional English spelling. He consistently uses 's to pluralize "year's," "drink's," and "country's". He also keeps the *e* in moves, for "moveing." His spelling demonstrates substantial sophistication, requiring just a little more refinement to be perfect. Now would be a good time to provide a mini-lesson on plural spellings for Juan. He may keep these spellings in a notebook so that when he edits his own work, he can refer to it if necessary. His overuse of the apostrophe with plurals reflects a previous mini-lesson on the use of the apostrophe to indicate possession. He needs a review of this skill, along with a short explanation of the difference between plurals and possessives.

A different type of error occurs with verb forms. Juan does not yet consistently use the conventional present and past tense verb markers, writing *tell* instead of *tells* or *enjoy* instead of *enjoyed*. These tendencies are probably related to his developing English language knowledge. In our experience, verb agreement of this kind represents grammatical refinement that develops late in second language acquisition. We would not attempt to correct this error if Juan were a beginning English learner. However, because Juan's writing shows substantial fluency in English, he is probably ready for a mini-lesson on the *-ed* ending to indicate past tense. He may list this skill on his editing checklist to remind him to correct this element when editing his work. Juan needs daily opportunities to use the writing process approach. He has a lot to write about and enjoys sharing with his peers during response groups. He needs more opportunities to create finished pieces in which logical organization is needed to convey his message.

Example 7.5 illustrates an intermediate second language writer who is close to moving into the advanced phase. The essay is a piece of expository writing,

---

EXAMPLE 7.5 • ALBERTO'S ESSAY COMPARING OCEAN FISH AND BAY FISH

How the Ocean fish are alike to the Bay fish is that the Bay fish has same eyes like the Ocean fish. And they have same gulls as the Ocean fish. And they have same fins and 3 dots on its tail. And now how they are different is that the Bay fish have claws and the Ocean fish don't even have any teeth. An so the Ocean fish have big tails and the Bay fish have little tails. And the Ocean fish swim on the borrom of the ocean and the Bay fish wim at the top of the Bay. And the Ocean fish eat weed and the Bay fish eat little fish.

Alberto, fifth grade

---

similar to the assignment required of Jorge that we shared with you previously. For the essay, students were asked to compare ocean fish and bay fish based on information they could glean from cartoonlike drawings of the two kinds of fish.

Alberto's essay, a first draft comparing and contrasting ocean and bay fish, exhibits thoughtful and logical sequencing. The topic has been thoroughly covered in a manner that is clear and concise. At the same time, the essay lacks variety in sentence patterns. In general, comparisons call for more complex sentence patterns, which Alberto was not able to produce. Instead, he uses simple statements, beginning new sentences with *And*. To improve this essay, Alberto would benefit from a mini-lesson on sentence variety, which he could then apply in the revision process. In addition, the essay would be improved by an introduction and a conclusion, which Alberto could add rather easily during revision. In the next section, we offer a variety of ideas to help improve the writing of intermediate second language writers working in collaborative groups.

257

Strategies for Intermediate Writers

Successful teachers of writing make sure that students have frequent opportunities to use writing for authentic purposes, often developing topics of students' own choosing and shaping pieces for particular audiences. In addition, teachers provide a variety of opportunities for students to publish their writing in a variety of ways for a variety of purposes. Just as beginning writers work on meaningful writing tasks, so must intermediate writers work on tasks that matter to them. Thus, the strategies we share here are used within the context of meaningful, functional writing assignments. In most cases, your students will have selected the topics they are writing about, and they will share their writing with one another, and with you. Without this meaningfulness, the following strategies will become empty assignments, no better than isolated worksheets. However, when the strategies help students develop and shape their own ideas, they become functional for students.

Show and Not Tell

A sentence that *tells* simply makes a flat generalization (Caplan, 1982; Elbow, 1973). For example, a young writer might write, "The party was fun," or "She has a nice personality," or "The Thanksgiving dinner was delicious." None of these sentences provides any descriptive detail about what the writer wants to convey. Was the party fun because of the food, the games, or the people? We don't know. In contrast, sentences that **show** give specific information for the reader about a party, dinner, or person. D. H. Lawrence once said that in good writing, characters should never merely walk up stairs; they should walk up 15 stairs or 40 stairs. "Show and not tell" is a powerful strategy because students can learn to use it after a brief introduction and a little practice. They can apply it to improve their writing almost immediately. The following passage, from Jean Shepherd (1971), illustrates the "telling" sentence "In the morning, my father could be grumpy":

> He slumped unshaven, staring numbly at the kitchen table, until my mother set the coffee down in front of him. She did not speak. She knew that this was no time for conversation. He lit a Lucky, took a mighty drag, and then sipped gingerly at the scalding black coffee, his eyes glaring malevolently ahead. My old man had begun every day of his life since the age of four with a Lucky and a cup of black coffee. He inhaled each one alternately, grimly, deeply. During this routine, it was sure suicide to goad him. (p. 130)

"Showing" sentences such as Shepherd's make actions specific by illustrating in multisensory detail exactly what happened. After you introduce the concept to writers, ask them to identify showing sentences in literature they are reading. You can also assist them with the strategy by giving them telling sentences to rewrite with partners. The following examples were provided by English language learners in Shirley Vance's class:

TELLING SENTENCE: The band was noisy.
SHOWING SENTENCES: As the band played I felt the drummer was banging on my eardrums and the guitars yelled at me. I thought I would never hear right again.

One of the most powerful reasons to use the show-and-not-tell strategy, in addition to its ease of learning, is that English learners are able to transfer this knowledge to their own writing. They are also able to use it when they are working with peer response groups. They can pick out telling sentences, and they can make suggestions for showing sentences in their own writing and in the writing of others. Giving your students a concrete strategy that immediately improves their writing empowers them and motivates them to learn more.

Sentence Combining

Sentence combining simply teaches students to combine shorter sentences into longer ones while retaining the meaning. Researchers note that as writers mature they begin to write longer, more sophisticated sentences (Loban, 1968; O'Hare, 1973). Practice in sentence combining assists students in producing more mature writing. We suggest that English learners can benefit from sentence combining as well. You may use examples from students' own writing to assist them with sentence combining, or use sentence combining exercises found in books.

The essay on George Washington in Figure 7.6, by a student in a fifth-grade class of language minority students, is typical of what intermediate writers often do when they become comfortable with basic short sentences. A peer response

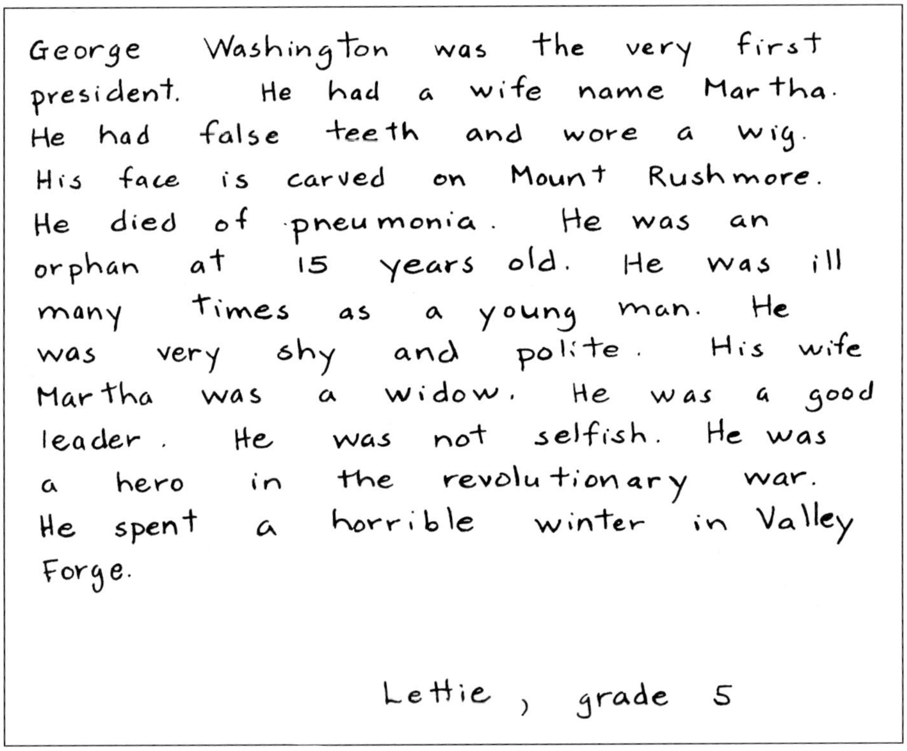

FIGURE 7.6

Essay on George
Washington Before
Sentence Combining

> George Washington was the very first president. He had a wife name Martha. He had false teeth and wore a wig. His face is carved on Mount Rushmore. He died of pneumonia. He was an orphan at 15 years old. He was ill many times as a young man. He was very shy and polite. His wife Martha was a widow. He was a good leader. He was not selfish. He was a hero in the revolutionary war. He spent a horrible winter in Valley Forge.
>
> Lettie, grade 5

259

group suggested combining some of the short sentences into longer, more complex sentences. The essay, of course, needs more work than just sentence combining, and the students who worked on it discovered that they needed to help Lettie organize and delete some of the information in order to complete their task. Example 7.6 presents a revised draft of the essay.

There are, of course, many possible ways to combine the sentences. If you place some examples of sentence combining exercises on a transparency, your students can try the exercises and share results. Through sentence combining, students learn to play with sentence variations and choose the one that best suits their meaning. Moreover, developing writers can apply the strategy to their own writing.

An example of a teacher-made exercise follows:

Example:
1. The boy wanted something.
2. He wanted to buy tickets.
3. The tickets were for a rock group.
4. The rock group was his favorite.

Combination: The boy wanted to buy tickets for his favorite rock group.

EXAMPLE 7.6 • Revised Essay on George Washington

George Washington was the very first president and he had a wife named Martha. He was an orphan when he was young and was ill and very shy and polite. He was a hero in the revolutionary war and spent a horrible winter in Valley Forge. His face is carved on Mount Rushmore.

Sentence Shortening

Sentence shortening, the opposite of sentence combining, assists students with changing wordy sentences into more concise sentences (Peterson, 1981). In the early phases of writing development, some students may write sentences that ramble on and on. You can give students long sentences to revise into shorter sentences that mean the same thing. Arturo Jackson introduces the idea to students in small groups by making a game out of sentence shortening. Using a transparency, he places a wordy sentence on the screen and challenges students to make the sentence shorter while preserving the meaning of the original sentence. Students rewrite the sentence in their groups and then report back the number of words in the reduced version. The object is to write the shortest sentence with no loss of meaning. He also discusses the revised sentences with students so that they can evaluate whether the shortest sentence is actually the best one. A few examples of original student sentences and their revisions follow:

Original Student Sentence:

That man who I know invented something that was entirely new (adapted from Peterson, 1981).

Student Group Revisions:

That man I know invented something.

I know a man who is an inventor.

Original Sentence:

The store over there across the street is owned by three sisters who live in the apartment above the store across the street.

Student Group Revisions:

The sisters live above the store across the street in an apartment.

There is an apartment above the store across the street. Three sisters live above it.

In the latter example, the student groups in the class determined that it was better to break the original sentence into two sentences. They felt that one-sentence versions didn't sound right. Arturo let their decision stand, and they learned that there are no rigid rules for rewriting sentences. They also learned to pay attention to the sound of sentences and to the meaning. They were beginning to develop a sense of style in their writing.

Sentence Models

Sentence modeling, another helpful strategy for intermediate writers, is based on sentences from quality classroom reading materials or from writing produced by students themselves. You can introduce simple sentence models at first, then more complex models. Through the use of sentence models, students develop confidence in their ability to write with power and variety. Sentence models help intermediate-level writers move from a few simple sentence structures to more complex structures, building the confidence that students need to make the transition from beginning to intermediate phases and beyond. The models that follow represent only a few examples of the kinds of sentences you may wish to share. When students are working alone or in peer response groups, they can try the models and immediately develop a more mature writing style. Through these procedures, English learners benefit in both English language development and writing.

A group of fourth graders selected a model based on a favorite sentence in *Charlotte's Web* (White, 1952), consisting of a series of clauses that finish with a major statement (Seigel, 1983). They then developed their own sentences from the model:

> KIM: Leticia reaches in her purse, gets the lipstick, colors her lips, and gets the mirror to see how she look.
>
> NG: Jan runs fast, opens the car door, getting in to go to the rock concert.

All 26 students in the class, with help from their groups, were able to write good examples of the model. Later, in their own writing, the model and variations of it began to appear. The students could show off with the sentence, knowing also that they could punctuate correctly. Finally, they had fun using patterns occasionally introduced by their teacher and began lifting patterns of sentences they liked from their own reading. Using sentence models gave the students confidence to experiment and play with language.

Another more complex sentence model you may want to introduce to intermediate writers is the dependent clause in a pair or in a series. We have found that intermediate writers can follow this model and gain confidence through their success, impressing themselves and others. The model, which is particularly useful as an essay topic sentence or as a concluding sentence in an essay or narrative, contains the following form (Waddell, Esch, & Walker, 1972, p. 30):

If . . . , if . . . , if . . . , then Subject Verb.

Because . . . , because . . . , because . . . , Subject Verb.

When . . . , when . . . , when . . . , Subject Verb.

Student Examples of the Model

Because it is rainy, because it is cold, because I feel lazy, I think I won't go to school today.

When I am home, when I am bored, when I have nobody to play with, I watch television.

If I was rich, if I could buy anything, I would buy my parents a house.

In the last example, the writer did not want to use a series of three, and saw that she could use a series of two if she wanted. Using sentence models, students begin to experiment with the sentences and learn that sentences can be organized in a variety of ways. This gives English learners confidence in their ability to learn new English sentence structures. Using sentence models in their writing not only teaches students to develop variety in their sentences but also shows them how to punctuate.

Mapping

Although show-and-not-tell and sentence models work with form at the sentence level, mapping works with form at story or essay levels. A map is a visual/spatial representation of a composition or story and can assist students with shaping stories or essays they are writing (Boyle & Peregoy, 1991; Buckley & Boyle, 1981). Mapping has been used by students of all ages. The writer Henry Miller used to draw on the walls of his room making maps in preparation for writing his novels.

You can introduce students to mapping by having them work in groups; later they can learn how to map by themselves. Jackie Chi introduces the strategy by giving students a familiar topic and asking them to brainstorm words or phrases for the topic. Here are some words children in a third-grade class brainstormed based on the word *soap*:

hand soap	bar	face	liquid	sink
powder	bathroom	facial	showers	clean
dirty	slippery	kitchen	bath	bubbles
clothes	shiny	colors	hands	dry

After students have generated the words for soap, Jackie asks them to think of words that go together (categories) and to place words under the category names, as in the following example. She reminds them that they can add new words to the list and that some of their words may not fit in any categories.

Type of Soap	Places Used	Used For
liquid	kitchen	showers
powder	bathrooms	baths
bar	machines	hands

After they have placed their words into categories, Jackie asks students to use butcher paper and marking pens to make a map representing their words (Figure 7.7). She provides them with the simple structure in Figure 7.7 to start them out but asks them to be creative in developing maps. For example, they might want to draw pictures to illustrate their words. When each group has finished mapping, she has them share their maps. Later, she might ask students to map their own topics on a piece of paper and share them. They would use the same process Jackie introduced to them: brainstorm, create categories, draw a map. When it is completed, they can use the map to write a story about themselves. Lisa, age 7, developed the map in Figure 7.8 in preparation for a piece about her friends.

The mapping procedure helps students generate ideas and think about how they might organize their ideas before they begin to write. It

FIGURE 7.7 • MAP ON SOAP STUDENTS CREATED WHEN INTRODUCED TO MAPPING

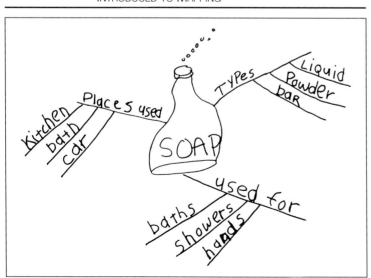

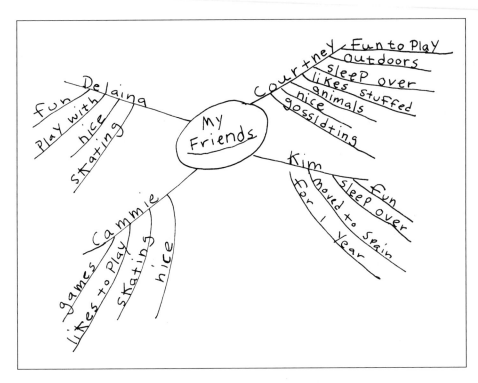

FIGURE 7.8

PREWRITING MAP ABOUT A STUDENT'S FRIENDS

263

helps them think about the content and form their story or essay will take, and allows them to try out different ideas before they commit them to paper. Because mapping is less intimidating than writing a whole story or essay, students gain confidence in their ability to compose. The map in Figure 7.9 and short paper in Example 7.7 are by a student who usually struggled with writing

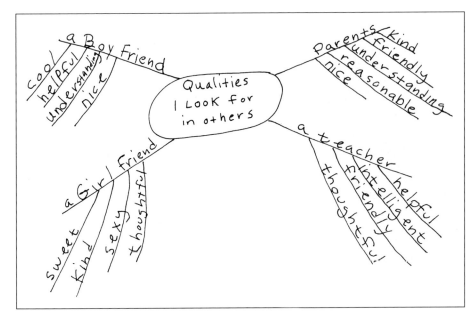

FIGURE 7.9

PREWRITING MAP ON QUALITIES STUDENT ADMIRES

EXAMPLE 7.7 • ESSAY ABOUT QUALITIES STUDENT ADMIRES (BASED ON MAP IN FIGURE 7.9)

This composition is about the way I feel about others. For instance, how I feel about my parents, girl friend, teachers and friend. Sertain kind of people make me sick. I don't like some people that just think that there so perfect, and so fine. I think that you have to look for alot of qualities in a parent. They have to be understanding because if your parents arent understanding you mit as well not call parents. and they must be loveing, thoughtful, and exspecialy helpful, they help you when your sick they help you when your in troble they help you ever day of your life. . . .

Keno, age 12

---

but, with the help of the map and his response group, was able to turn in a paper that far exceeded anything he had written before (Hudson, 1982). We present one of the five paragraphs he wrote.

In summary, intermediate strategies help second language writers organize their thoughts on paper, develop specificity in expression, and use a variety of sentence patterns with conventional punctuation and grammar. Moreover, these strategies help students expand the array of genres they can use, from letters to stories to essays to poetry. As your English learners use the strategies, they will develop confidence and become motivated to work on revision. The strategies also guide students in evaluating the writing of others and making constructive suggestions in their peer response groups. Without specific "how to's," students will falter in response, as we learned in class one day. After peer response groups had not gone well in our third-grade class, we asked Joe to read his paper for class comment. When Joe finished his paper, Sarah raised her hand and commented, "That's a good paper." When we asked her to be more specific, she elaborated, "That's a really good paper." If students are not provided with specific strategies for revision, you might end up as Joe did that day: no farther ahead than if he had worked alone instead of with the

In responding to student writing, teachers model sensitivity and wording that students can use in peer response groups.

group. On the other hand, if you explicitly teach English learners how to revise, you will give them the vocabulary to talk about writing, and you will model response to writing. The strategies we have presented have been proven to be successful with English learners; they have helped improve their writing and promoted their English language proficiency as well.

Assessing English Learners' Writing Progress

The best kind of assessment in any classroom comes from day-to-day informal observations of your students as they write and interact in their writing groups. Such informal assessment gives a much better picture of the student's overall achievement than any single paper, standardized test score, or other one-time performance sample. To accompany your observational insights, we suggest using portfolios and holistic scoring and involving students in evaluating their own writing. In this way, students become aware of their own progress. Remember that the best assessment of student writing is going to be the writing itself, not tests on grammar, spelling, or punctuation, for instance. Finally, when students become evaluators of their own writing and know how and what they need to do to improve it, they will improve.

Portfolio Assessment

Portfolio assessment involves keeping selected pieces of a student's writing in a special folder (Howard, 1990; Murphy & Smith, 1990). You and your student select which pieces should be saved to illustrate the student's writing abilities. Portfolios are useful for several reasons. First, through the use of portfolios you can assess students' growth by viewing all of their writing over the year and thereby assess your own teaching. Second, you can promote self-assessment in your students and motivate them to evaluate their own growth. Third, portfolio assessment motivates students to improve as they see their development throughout the year and helps them to see real growth when they compare what they wrote at the beginning of the year with what they accomplished by the end of the year. In summary, the keeping of writing portfolios assists students in evaluating themselves as writers and assists you in evaluating your own program. Look at the two pieces of writing (Figures 7.10 and 7.11), which are separated by one-and-a-half years, and you can see that you would learn a great deal about Jorge's improvement as a writer.

Now imagine that you are Jorge's teacher and have received the essay in Figure 7.10 along with one he has just written for your class (Figure 7.11); both essays come from the same stimulus, a drawing of two kinds of fish.

Clearly, the two papers might be viewed differently within the context of how far Jorge has advanced if they are found together in a portfolio. If you receive a piece of writing like Jorge's and can compare it with what he was doing last year, you can make certain decisions about what needs to be done next,

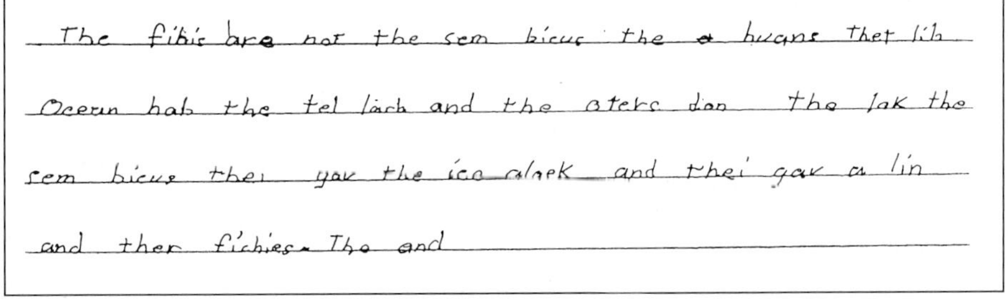
The fibis are not the sem bicus the a buans thet lih
Ocean hab the tel lach and the aters don the lak the
sem bicus thei yav the ico alaek and thei gav a lin
and ther fichies. The and

FIGURE 7.10

JORGE'S FIRST PORTFOLIO SAMPLE: WRITING ABOUT FISH

FIGURE 7.11

JORGE'S WRITING ABOUT
FISH: A LATER SAMPLE

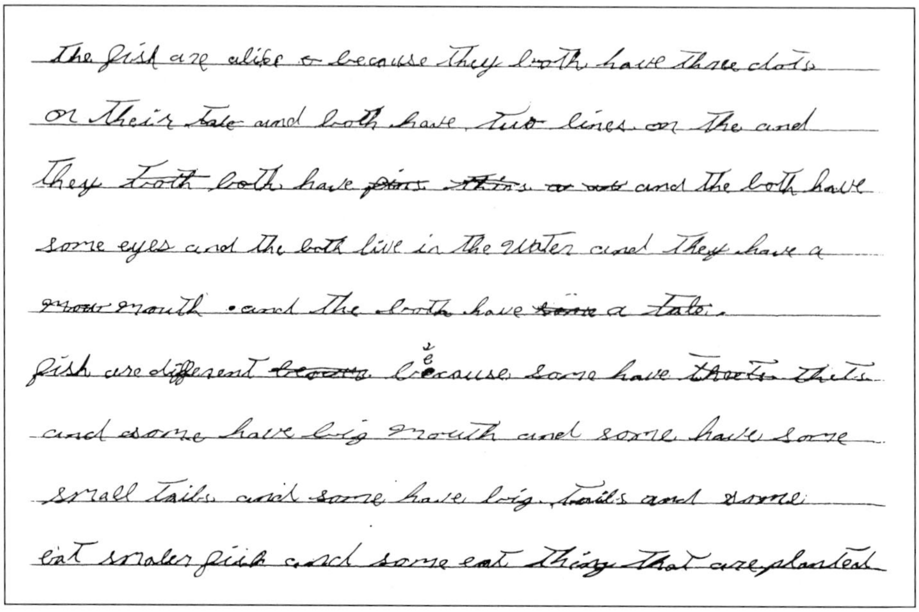

The fish are alike o because they both have three dots
on their tale and both have two lines on the and
They both both have pins mthrn or not and the both have
some eyes and the both live in the water and they have a
mou mouth . and the both have some a tale .
fish are different becaus because some have thoots their
and some have big mouth and some have some
small tails and some have big tails and some
eat smaler fish and some eat things that are planted

about his strengths and weaknesses. You can also ask him to look at the two papers and see his own advancement. Portfolios allow you to contextualize the student's advancement, and better evaluate what is needed and what has been accomplished.

Previously, in Figure 7.5, we shared a piece of writing by Juan ("The First Time I Saw Her") as an example of an intermediate writer. However, Juan's portfolio shows that he didn't write at the intermediate level when he entered the class. Example 7.8 shows his writing in the second month of school, Example 7.9 shows a piece from the fourth month, and Example 7.10 shows the sixth month of school.

EXAMPLE 7.8 • JUAN: SECOND-MONTH SAMPLE FROM PORTFOLIO

To day it was ranning. why? The only men who can tell us is faster dan a speeding bullet. More bigger dan a penut smaller dan my hand. It middy mouse. Yes hes baaaack beeter dan ever. Faster dan ever.

He' parner jast like! But! more dumer dan middy mouse. Its supper Juan. Yes he's back more dumer dan ever. Middy mouse can't belive I he's parnter.

EXAMPLE 7.9 • JUAN: FOURTH-MONTH SAMPLE FROM PORTFOLIO

Dear Eney one

To day I got up. I whast to, I took a shower. I help my brother get dress, and I got dresset too. My mom left me some money. It was five dollars in cash. I went to the story to buy my brother a pice of candey. We got on the bus we came to school and played. Her I am writing this for you.

P.S. See you later!!!

EXAMPLE 7.10 • JUAN: SIXTH-MONTH WRITING FROM PORTFOLIO

The first time I saw her she was seven year's old and so was I.

We bouth in first grade. One day I want to take her out but my mom sed I was to young.

I try letter's and poetry so she would like me. In forth grade we want to see the movie Avalanche at the Kabuki theater. We bought popcorn, and drink's with our money. We both enjoy the movie because it tell you about people from different country's and how it was hard moveing to America.

I had a good time with her. I want to go out to a movie with her again.

Juan, fourth grade

In the three examples, we can see Juan moving from a beginning to an intermediate level. In the first example, Juan uses the pattern from the Mighty Mouse cartoons to create his own pattern in writing. The pattern gives him support while he is still at a beginning level in English. In the second example, Juan writes about more mundane matters in mostly simple sentences. He makes fewer errors in his writing, but he is held back in expression by his limited English. In the third, only four months after the first sample, Juan is beginning to express himself well and in a variety of sentences. His English language ability has grown, and he shows this growth through writing. He also shares matters that are important to him, and he shares them with feeling. In a four-month period, he has moved from copied patterns to familiar sentence models to individual sentence structures. He writes more, he writes better, and he is well launched as a writer. Through portfolio assessment, Juan and his teacher can share his success and determine his next step. These next steps will offer Juan more opportunities to write for different purposes and for different audiences. Moreover, he will be exposed to more sophisticated language in the stories he reads. All of these opportunities will assist him in becoming a better writer. If you ask Juan today what he wants to be, he will say, "A writer."

Students not only share portfolios with their teachers but also refer to them while working with their peers. When students have been working in peer response groups, they become critically perceptive of their own writing and that of their peers. As they look at their writing portfolios, they begin asking the same questions they ask of others in writing groups: What was I trying to say? Did I accomplish what I wanted to? How would I change it?

Some questions you might have students address in their own writing will reveal the strengths and weaknesses of your own program and the perceptions of your student writers. For example, you might ask them to think about one thing they like about a piece of writing. In contrast, you could also ask them to reflect on one thing they did not like about their writing. Students' answers to these questions reveal the depth of their understanding and help you assist them in going beyond such superficial responses to their writing as finding two spelling errors in a paper. Student self-evaluation is at the heart of portfolio assessment, helping you determine what you need to do next, while empowering the students in their own development.

Once students have collected a body of work in their portfolios, you can assist them with procedures for comparing their writing. Ask them to look over their writing and select what they think is the best piece of writing and what is

267

their worst. Then, ask them to respond in writing to questions such as: Why did you select the piece? Why is it good or bad? If you decided to revise the piece, what specifically would you do with it? What have you learned about your writing by evaluating the pieces in your portfolio? What might you do differently when you write next as a result of viewing the writing in your portfolio?

Thinking and writing about the work in their portfolios helps students reflect on their writing and encourages them to share their thinking with others. Most important, perhaps, is the fact that students begin to see that some pieces in their portfolio are incomplete and that others may be worthy of revisions for publication. Moreover, students tend to see writing as the development of ideas rather than the correcting of papers. Portfolio assessment helps students become reflective and self-evaluative writers. When this happens, they can use the revision and editing strategies they have learned to improve their writing and to prepare it for sharing with others.

Holistic Scoring

Holistic scoring refers to the evaluation of a piece of writing as a whole, rather than to evaluation of separate aspects such as spelling, punctuation, grammar, style, or mechanics (Myers, 1980; White, 1985). Holistic scoring is usually used to evaluate a set of papers that have been written on the same topic with the same topic development and writing procedures. In this way, the papers can be compared readily in terms of quality. When teachers assess a paper holistically, they read papers swiftly and rate them on a scale, often from 1 to 6, with 6 as the best and 1 as the worst score. In the evaluation process, reader–evaluators agree on "anchor papers," or essays that typify each rating, 1 to 6. Usually, two readers evaluate each essay to increase the reliability of the score. Generally speaking, scores of 1 and 2 represent our category of beginner; scores of 3 and 4 represent the intermediate category; and scores of 5 and 6 are the advanced writers with the particular group you are evaluating. Holistic assessment has been used to assess a school's or even a whole district's progress in writing, and helps students evaluate their own writing.

Holistic scoring has several advantages over traditional methods of evaluating and grading papers in your classroom. First, you develop the anchor papers along with the students and then specify writing traits that make the papers low or high on the scoring scale. Second, holistic scoring helps students evaluate a paper based on its communication of ideas rather than on correctness alone. Third, holistic scoring provides models for good writing, making the traits of good writing explicit to students. Developing writers can apply these models and knowledge of good writing to their own composing, and they can evaluate their own writing holistically, thinking critically about what it needs to receive the highest evaluation.

Procedures for Using Holistic Scoring in the Classroom

We recommend using the following procedures for holistic assessment with your students, based on Miles Myers's work (Boyle, 1987; Myers, 1980). First, discuss with the students a topic they might want to write on and make sure all students can address the topic with ease. Topics such as "write a description of someone who is important to you," or "write about a favorite object you have," or "write about a person who has influenced you" are good topics because everyone can write about them. After they have selected the topic, give your students a half hour or so to think about the topic, take notes, brainstorm, or perform whatever prewriting strategy they use (Boyle, 1986). Let them know that, on the following day, they will have time to write an essay on the topic. On the next day, give them time to review their prewriting notes and to think about the topic before you ask them to write.

It is a good idea to ask another teacher from another school to have students write on the same topic using the same procedures. Then you can use those unfamiliar papers to discuss assessing and scoring the papers with your students. These papers can be used throughout the year to evaluate papers on other topics. Once you've received the other class's papers, you can go through them and, using a scale of 1 to 6, select papers you feel clearly represent each score on the scale. Simply place the papers on a table and begin ranking them after reading them quickly. After you have done this with all the papers, you will want to select representative papers to become model or anchor papers that the students will use to score their own writing. Be careful that you do not select a high paper that is so perfect that no other student will be able to get a 6. Likewise do not select a low paper that is too low.

Sample Holistic Essays, Rubrics, and Possible Teaching Strategies for Each Level

The six holistic anchor papers here were taken from the essays of two secondary school English language development (ELD) classrooms. They are not meant to represent a holistic scoring done in your classroom but to illustrate the results of two teachers' holistic scoring. The teachers, from different schools in different cities, were able to use their own students' essays and the essays of each other's classes. Once you have ranked papers, you can create a **rubric** that lists the qualities of papers receiving scores of 1 to 6, such as organization, vividness of description, originality of ideas, spelling, grammar, and punctuation. These rubrics you have developed can be used by you and by students to make writing qualities more explicit. The essays in Examples 7.11 through 7.16 represent each holistic score; level one essays received the lowest score in the session, and level six represents the highest score received.

EXAMPLE 7.11 • LEVEL ONE ESSAY

The most important person I have my next door person she always call at me and tell about dog bark in other hose about cats to a lot. she only tell about those things and my mom don't like it or talk to me bout it.

EXAMPLE 7.12 • LEVEL TWO ESSAY

The most important to me is my uncle the way he tell me to go to school and tell me to read my books and do work teacher says. I was to go school and learn things I need to know and get a good work place. My uncle have good work and he is good person. What he told me is right and it help me do pretty good in school. I can think how I learn from my uncle. He my favorite person. What he say is right.

EXAMPLE 7.13 • LEVEL THREE ESSAY

The most important for my life is a man I met in my house. He was friend of papa and he smiled a lot. He tell me about his job and how he fix cars and do this with the engines and mechanical things. He tell he always do work on car when he was 14 like me. And I can learn to do something important like he work on. Alexander always tell he work hard to fix cars and help people drive and enjoy their drives. He would told me work hard, be a good person you will be successful and like life. He was important he told me the right things to do and he was always nice. I will work hard all my life.

EXAMPLE 7.14 • LEVEL FOUR ESSAY

The person who is important is my best friend who taught me to play soccer better. Joseph treat me like a good friend and when he knew I could not play good he showed me how to do it. One thing he showed me was how to practice for along time he say to be a soccer player you had to practice so I practice every day. And I get better to practice and I made the team this year he is on the team too. When I don't play so good he told me that everybody make mistakes and errors a part of the game very good player and even start make mistakes too. And I will make mistakes like stars.

I want to be a star and practice helps meke me better. And Joseph practice with me and he show me how I can be better. We practice kicking the ball and passing the ball and I will be making the first team like Joseph makes it. He is one of the best players and he gives me time to practice and get better like him. Most people don't do that and that why he is important to me and will always be my friend and companion. He tell me the new word it means very good friend.

EXAMPLE 7.15 • LEVEL FIVE ESSAY

I have not known anybody who has been as important to me as Larry. Larry who always wanted to help me. When I first come to this country he was the first person to help me. He told me how I should be in school and how I should raise my hand when I had the answer and to not talk if I don't raise my hand. He told me what shows on television I would like and he was right about that too. Larry was very popular with the other kids and I know I was lucky to have him as a friend. He didn't have to choose me as a friend. Lots of other kids were his friends also. I didn't know many words when I came to this country and he helped me because he could speak Spanish and he could also speak English. That was a great help to me.

Larry did other things that helped me. He introduced me to his friends and he made me part of the teams when we played baseball and he knew I was a good shortstop so I git to play that position sometimes. He showed me how to play other positions too and I got to pitch one time but I wasn't good at that. Because of Larry when I moved to this country it was a lot easier and now we are still friends after four years. Larry taught me how to be with other other people and how to help them and when someone new comes to our class I make sure I help him just like Larry helped me. That's why he is a very important person.

EXAMPLE 7.16 • LEVEL SIX ESSAY

Except for my parents Bob James is the most important person in my life. He is important to me for several reasons and I will relate a few of them. First of all, he has always treated me well even when I have not always treated him well. He accepts my mistakes, lets me know how I have offended him, and communicates with me so I will understand his feelings. Once I got so mad at him for ignoring me at school that I decided I wouldn't be his friend anymore; I decided I would not talk to him when I saw him. But he would not let me ignore him; he called me on the phone and asked me what was wrong and I told him that he ignored me in fornt of his friends. Right away he said that he didn't mean to and that he considered me a good friend. He also thanked me for being honest with him and we become good friends again.

Bob also would make good suggestions about what we should do, go to the movies go to the mall and other things. He always had good ideas and he knew how to have fun no matter what. We didn't just drive around in his car; once we visited all the churches in our town and we met ministers and priests and got to go inside the churches. The churches were interesting but what surprised us was how nice the people were. In every church they showed us around and seemed interested in us. They didn't treat us just like two kids who shouldn't be there. I guess Bob will be the best friend I will ever have and that he will always introduce me to interest and curious things.

Based on these essays, Figure 7.12 illustrates rubrics for each level of writing and possible strategies that might be used with beginning-level, intermediate-level, and advanced intermediate-level writers. The rubrics discuss characteristics of essays, including fluency, organization, mechanical errors, sentence structure, grammar, and communication. The strategies are meant as possible suggestions for the students, not as recommendations for individual students. Your knowledge of students will determine appropriate strategies.

FIGURE 7.12 • RUBRICS BASED ON WRITING IN MIDDLE SCHOOL ELD CLASSROOMS

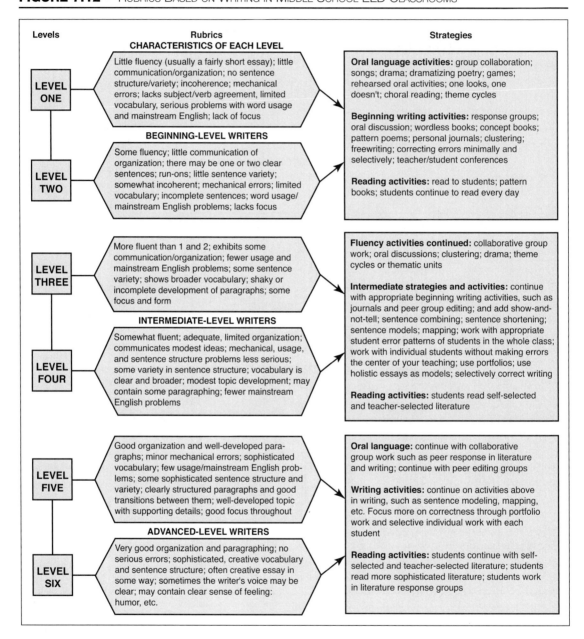

Working With Errors in Student Writing

The goal of writing instruction is to promote student competence in writing effectively and correctly across a variety of genres: letters, stories, poems, essays, and reports. To help students achieve that goal requires explicit instruction, not only on generating and expressing ideas, but also on numerous details, such as text structures, sentence styles, grammar, punctuation, and spelling. When teachers ask how to deal with errors in student writing, they are usually concerned with these mechanical details. We suggest that teachers take time each day to provide explicit instruction on mechanical details, taking into consideration English language proficiency (Echevarria, Vogt, & Short, 2008) and writing development needs that are common (1) to the whole class and (2) to individuals and small groups. These details might include, for example, subject/verb agreement, spelling words related to a theme topic, and perhaps a new sentence style or text structure. Once taught, these items may then be incorporated into peer editing and self-editing checklists.

When choosing writing elements to focus on, you can assess specific needs of individuals and groups by evaluating the writing they produce in class. As students write daily, sometimes taking a piece through all five writing phases including publication, error patterns in their drafts provide information on specific instructional needs. After you have conducted mini-lessons addressing particular error patterns, these items are then incorporated into individualized or group editing checklists.

Balancing Goals: Fluency, Form, and Correctness

Three important goals in writing development are illustrated in Figure 7.13: fluency, form, and correctness. **Fluency**, which is closely related to a student's general English proficiency, is the ability to generate ideas with ease while writing them down on paper. **Form** refers to sentence styles, paragraphing, and text structures; whereas **correctness** concerns the proper use of grammar, punctuation, and spelling. A good piece of writing displays its author's competence at all three levels. Because few students are writing experts, an instructional program that leaves out any one of these aspects lacks balance. Virtually all students need explicit assistance in all three. In the past, instruction often focused only on correctness, leaving students to find their own way into fluency and form. With the advent of the process approach, fluency sometimes took over completely, leaving minimal time for instruction on form and correctness.

The purpose of the model is to remind us to keep fluency, form, and correctness in mind for all students, while focusing attention on one aspect at a time. For example, students who have difficulty getting just a few words on the page need to focus on developing their writing fluency. Nevertheless, it is generally appropriate to assist them with correct use of capitals at the beginning of sentences and periods at the end. Once they are able to write fluently, the focus changes to form, to such matters as paragraphing, sentence models, and creating smooth transitions between paragraphs. The writer also will deal with correctness within the longer piece of writing. Finally, in preparing to share a piece of writing for publication or sharing, writers focus on correctness. Thus, the fluency, form, and correctness model reminds us to focus on one specific aspect of writing at a time but not to the exclusion of others. In sum, all students will work

FIGURE 7.13 • FLUENCY, FORM, AND CORRECTNESS MODEL

on fluency, form, and correctness, but the specific details and relative focus will differ according to (1) the student's individual needs as an English learner and as a developing writer and (2) the phase the student is working on developing the particular piece, that is, prewriting, drafting, revising, editing, or publishing.

Balancing Instruction: Scaffolds, Models, and Direct Instruction

The process approach incorporates an instructional model calling for scaffolds, models, and direction instruction (Cazden, 1983) as shown in Figure 7.14. Process writing provides a variety of **scaffolds** to assist students with all aspects of writing, including correctness. For example, as explained in Chapter 3, the writing routine itself provides a scaffold: Students know that they are going to edit their work for grammar, spelling, and punctuation after they are satisfied with the content. In addition, teacher and peer feedback will help them locate errors in their writing.

Models are provided in several ways. For example, the teacher may model a particular sentence pattern, including correct spelling, grammar, and punctuation. When teachers respond to student's journal entries, they model correctness as well. In addition, when teachers guide the class in editing a paper on the overhead projector, they model both the process and corrections involved.

Direct instruction is essential for helping students revise and edit effectively and correctly. We might teach a lesson to the entire class, a small group, or an individual student based on assessed needs (Ferris, 1995, 2002). One possibility is to use programmed materials or games for students to use on their own or with others. As an alternative, we might suggest a computer program on spelling or some other aspect of writing. Most word processing programs contain spelling and grammar checking capabilities. Although these programs aren't perfect, they can assist students by pointing out potential grammar, spelling, and usage problems and suggesting possible solutions. Students make the final choice as to how to use the suggestions. Another possibility is to keep student workbooks on hand in class to provide specific help as needed. For example, if a student continues to have trouble with a particular sentence type, we may refer the student to the topic and page in the workbook for additional help. Figure 7.15 illustrates one kind of handout you could give to your students.

As students learn writing conventions, they can become effective participants in responding to their peers' writing. Liu and Hansen (2002) make excellent suggestions for assisting students with grammar during peer response and editing:

FIGURE 7.14

MODEL FOR WORKING WITH CORRECTNESS

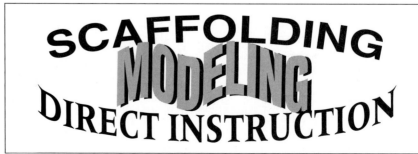

ERROR MADE ON PAPER	DATE STUDENT WROTE PAPER & NUMBER OF ERRORS IN CATEGORY						
	1/7	1/14	1/21	1/28	2/5	2/11	REFER TO PAGE IN WORKBOOK
SUBJECT/VERB AGREEMENT	3	4	2	1	1	0	PAGES 21–22, ESPECIALLY 22
CAPITALIZATION	3	3	2	2	1	1	PAGES 78–86, EXERCISE ON 81
SPELLING	6	7	4	4	3	2	PAGES 123–145; SEE 5 RULES
RUN-ON SENTENCE							PAGES 243–286
VERB FORM							PAGES 92–98; SEE ALSO 21-22
PREPOSITIONS							PAGES 100–111
WORD ORDER							PAGES 300–312
PRONOUN REFERENCE							PAGES 10–14
USE OF ARTICLES							PAGES 410–434
PARAGRAPHING							PAGES 288–296 AND 180–186
OTHER ERRORS							Teacher points out pages for individual student problems

FIGURE 7.15

HANDOUT STUDENT USES FOR CORRECTING PAPERS BASED ON TEACHER RESPONSE

1. The teacher should focus on only a few types of grammatical/stylistic issues per peer response activity to make grammar more manageable and effective.

2. The teacher should provide grammar reviews on what students have already been taught in class to reinforce instruction.

3. Based on learners' error patterns, the teacher should offer a mini-lesson on a particular pattern and then have the students focus on that pattern in responding to each other's papers.

4. During and after peer response activities, students should keep a journal that lists their own errors and ways to correct them, creating a personal self-editing or error log (Ferris, 2002). Students use these personal logs as they revise and edit their own papers in the future. They thus monitor their own error patterns and become self-sufficient in editing.

In summary, we recommend correcting in a careful, focused manner to obtain the best results from our students. Here are some final guidelines for working with beginning- and intermediate-level writers.

Beginning-Level Writers:

1. Work with fluency first.

2. When a student has enough fluency (is able to write a short paragraph with relative ease) correct minimally.

3. Correct relatively "simple" things like beginning a sentence with capital letters or ending a sentence with a period. You as the teacher can make the decisions regarding what is appropriate for individual students.

4. As students gain confidence in their writing, begin to work on other aspects of their writing, such as spelling, punctuation, and grammar.

5. You won't want to correct too many problems in the writing and cause the writer to retreat from learning new sentence structures.

Intermediate-Level Writers:

1. They have developed fluency and are ready for more specific error correction.

2. Using their own writing, respond to the most egregious errors first.

3. Assist them with subject-verb agreement and others aspects of their writing that get in the way of meaning.

4. Have them use handbooks and computers to check on their own writing errors after you have corrected them.

5. As stated previously, you are the best expert in your classroom regarding student errors and advancement.

Finally, and above all, when it comes to working with errors in student writing, we must know our students well enough to make crucial decisions as to how many details the student can handle at one time, whether they respond better to blunt or delicate suggestions, and how much supervision they need in implementing corrections. We don't want to overwhelm them but maybe just "whelm" them a bit. With all these considerations, it becomes clear that correcting student errors is more an art than a science, one that calls for capitalizing on "teachable moments," while at the same time systematically addressing the detailed conventions of good writing. By keeping in mind fluency, form, and correctness, by implementing effective teacher and peer response, and by providing scaffolding, modeling, and direct instruction, we create optimum opportunities for students to learn to write effectively.

Differentiating Instruction for Writing Development

To match writing instruction to student needs, you first need to consider each one's English language proficiency and general literacy abilities. That is, to engage students in writing, a productive act, it is important to know how comfortable they are processing written text and how well they express themselves verbally. In addition, knowledge of students' home languages, cultures, and prior schooling may provide important information about students' prior experience with writing. For example, if a student is able to write in the home language, you can validate the student's knowledge and build on it. On the other hand, if your student has no prior experience with writing in any language, you will need to start at a more basic level, perhaps even using drawing and labeling as a starting point. (See Chapter 5 for additional ideas to adapt to older learners who are new to writing.) One great beauty of writing is that although all students engage in the same general task, such as producing a memoir, they themselves differentiate based on what they are able to produce. Your challenge is to decide how to move them to the next level of development.

For your convenience, in this chapter and throughout the book, we have set up several features to help you differentiate instruction. Because differentiated instruction is always based on assessed student needs, we have provided several tools to help you assess and evaluate English learners' writing, including Table 7.3, Elements of Good Writing, and Table 7.4, Writing Traits Matrix. In addition, we have provided many examples of student writing to illustrate appropriate responses to scaffold student growth in writing. Furthermore, we offered a detailed example of holistic scoring of student essays from two middle school English Language Development classrooms. Figure 7.12 summarizes six writing levels found among those essays and various teaching strategies appropriate to each. Even if you choose not to conduct a holistic scoring in your class, you can still use or adapt the levels and strategies to help you plan. We would also like to refer you to the Scale of Writing Development, Figure 5.15 in Chapter 5. Starting at the early emergent levels and moving all the way up to sophisticated aspects of process writing, Figure 5.15 helps you see what the next level of development might be for each student. In addition to writing assessment procedures, we have divided our strategy descriptions into those most appropriate for beginning and intermediate writers. Finally, at the end of this chapter we indicate the grade levels for which the strategies may be used (Figure 7.16). All these features utilized in concert will help you differentiate instruction and assessment.

You may recall our scaffolding framework for differentiating instruction calling your attention to **who, what, how**, and **how well**. We use that framework now to illustrate a differentiated lesson, an extension for the oral language lesson provided in Chapter 4 around the theme of travel.

WHO: Students in grades 2–4 identified as **Beginning** to **Early Advanced** in English language proficiency. The students are from a variety of primary language backgrounds and cultures; most have had experiences using public transportation and personal vehicles both in their home cultures and in the United States.

WHAT: Students will work in cooperative groups to compile a book on modes of transportation, drawing information and ideas from the previous part of the theme study (see Chapter 4), including their oral language poetry performances, prior reading, and other classroom resources. Students will identify and describe various modes of transportation used around the world.

HOW: Beginning and early-intermediate groups will be grouped heterogeneously with advanced intermediate and early advanced English learners. In this manner, students will be engaged with at least one peer at or above their level of English proficiency. Students in the beginning and early-intermediate group will be expected to write simple sentences with illustrations, whereas the intermediate and early advanced students will write paragraphs with illustrations. All will begin their writing by creating a simple cluster to identify their vehicle, adjectives to describe it, and the places where it is used.

HOW WELL: A developmental writing rubric will be used that assesses a student's ability to use appropriate vocabulary and grammar for descriptive writing. Students can further be assessed individually by asking them to describe in a short narrative their favorite and least favorite vehicle and why. This sample essay can then be assessed using a holistic rubric for descriptive writing.

Summary

We have presented research indicating that second language writers are similar to first language writers in the ways they develop. They use their background knowledge to develop ideas and use the writing process in ways similar to those of first language learners. Process writing, consisting of prewriting, drafting, revising, editing, and publishing, makes writing easier for second language writers because it breaks the writing task into manageable phases. Students, instead of having to coordinate their budding ideas with grammar, spelling, and sentence styles, can concentrate on one area at a time. Once they have gathered and organized their ideas, they can focus on correcting their writing.

In presenting the writing process, we offered examples of writing from beginning and intermediate second-language writers to show what these students are able to do in writing, and to illustrate how their writing reflects both written language knowledge and general second language development. We also showed the strategies that successful teachers often use with English learners who are beginning or intermediate writers. Further, we suggested that you allow your students to work in collaborative and cooperative peer response groups in which they use language to share, discuss, and solve their writing problems. Finally, we advocated that you encourage your students to express themselves in writing, viewing their first attempts as small miracles. With this encouragement, your students will gain confidence in their abilities to learn and will continue to try.

In Figure 7.16 we have listed the grade levels at which we have seen teachers successfully using writing strategies. As your students gain confidence and proficiency in their writing, you may find that they can work easily with strategies

FIGURE 7.16

GRADE LEVELS AT WHICH STRATEGIES MAY BE USED

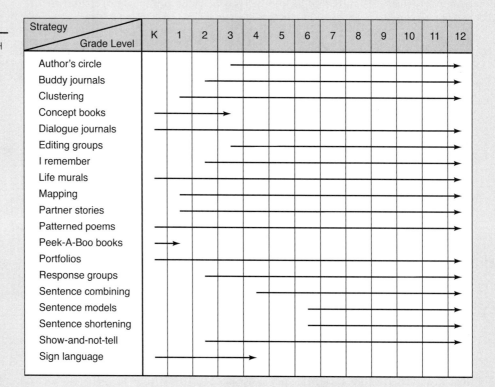

Strategy \ Grade Level	K	1	2	3	4	5	6	7	8	9	10	11	12
Author's circle				→————————————————————————→									
Buddy journals			→——————————————————————————————→										
Clustering		→—————————————————————————————————→											
Concept books	→————————→												
Dialogue journals	→——————————————————————————————————————→												
Editing groups			→——————————————————————————————→									
I remember			→——————————————————————————————→									
Life murals		→—————————————————————————————————→											
Mapping		→—————————————————————————————————→											
Partner stories		→—————————————————————————————————→											
Patterned poems		→—————————————————————————————————→											
Peek-A-Boo books	→——→												
Portfolios		→—————————————————————————————————→											
Response groups			→——————————————————————————————→									
Sentence combining					→————————————————————————→							
Sentence models						→——————————————————————→						
Sentence shortening					→————————————————————————→							
Show-and-not-tell			→——————————————————————————————→									
Sign language		→————————→											

designated in our figure to be beyond their grade level. We suggest you use the chart as a general guideline and adjust according to your judgment. With this in mind you can achieve the highest success with your students.

Small successes lead to larger successes, and all success, when you and the students recognize it, leads to further success. Thus, assess and evaluate student writing not in terms of comparing it to an essay by an accomplished expert but in terms of current accomplishments and next levels of development. In other words, use portfolios to keep in touch with what students know now and what they need to learn next. Moreover, view the assistance you can give them in terms of their development and how you can help them advance to the next level. Successful writing teachers build English learners' confidence, encourage them to continue to write, and point out what they have done well.

Suggestions for Further Reading

Berg, E. C. (1999). Preparing ESL students for peer response. *TESOL Journal*, 8(2), 20–25.

This excellent article presents 11 guidelines for preparing students for peer response addressing (1) the role of peer response, (2) demonstrating and personalizing peer response experiences, (3) conducting a whole-class activity with the class modeling revision, (4) familiarizing students with a peer response sheet, (5) providing revision guidelines, and (6) highlighting good revision strategies. This research-based article will be helpful for new teachers and those who are experienced with peer response groups.

Ferris, D. R. (2002). *Treatment of error in second language student writing*. Ann Arbor: University of Michigan Press.

Every ESL writing teacher should have this book; It presents theory, practice, and advice in a much needed area, that of working with L2 writing errors. Chapters include "Why Is Error Treatment Necessary for L2 Writers?" "Perspectives on Error Correction," "Preparing L2 Writing Teachers to Treat Student Error," "Responding to Student Errors," and "Beyond Error Correction: Teaching Grammar and Self-Editing Strategies to L2 Student Writers," and it has useful and practical appendixes. We wish this book had been available when we first started teaching writing to L2 students. Although the book is primarily concerned with university student writing, the ideas are directly applicable to the secondary level and adaptable to elementary-level student writing.

Ferris, D. R. (2003). *Response to student writing: Implications for second language students*. Mahwah, NJ: Lawrence Erlbaum Associates.

Most of the research here is based on university students, but ideas can easily be adapted to younger students. The book consists of two major sections: research and practice. The practice section in particular is especially useful for teachers of younger students.

Gottlieb, M. (1995). Nurturing student learning through portfolios. *TESOL Journal*, 5(1), 12–14.

This short article on portfolios contains everything you would need to begin portfolio assessment. The article also gives four "rubric modifications" to consider for use for students receiving language education support services. A discussion of documenting achievement and evaluating portfolios is both brief and exacting.

Kinsella, K. (1996). Designing group work that supports and enhances diverse classroom work styles. *TESOL Journal*, 6(1), 24–30.

This article should assist any teacher who wants to use group work in a classroom with diverse learners. Kinsella first describes the characteristics of what she calls analytical and relational learning styles, followed by an instructor self-assessment form for group work design and implementation. The article also contains a classroom work-style survey, which you could give to your students before you embark on collaborative group work. The survey will help you understand student thoughts about group work and individual study, and will assist you with differentiating instruction. All are discussed in detail.

Liu, J., & Hansen, J. G. (2002). *Peer response in second language writing classrooms*. Ann Arbor: University of Michigan Press.

A theoretically sound approach that is helpful for practicing teachers. The chapters cover topics such as: effects of peer response, contexts of peer response, grouping students in peer response, and instructing students in peer response. For teachers who want to establish peer response groups in their classrooms, this book prepares you for the pros and cons, and assists with setting up groups and maintaining them.

Activities

1. Collect one student's writing over a period of several weeks. Collect from journals, notes, letters, stories, or any other type of writing the student may do during the period of collection. At the end of the collection period, compare the student's writing as it developed over time. You might categorize such things as: the topics the student wrote about; the genre of writing; the conditions under which the student did his or her best writing; and the kinds of advancements the student made in developing and organizing ideas, in grammar and spelling, or in any other aspect of writing that interests you. Report your findings to your classmates.

2. Observe classrooms where teachers approach the teaching of writing differently and evaluate the writing that takes place in those classrooms. For example, compare a classroom that uses peer response groups and encourages students to select their own personal topics with a class in which the teacher selects topics and spends a great deal of time correcting papers and returning them to students. What are some differences you find in the writing of the students in the two classes? Do students in different classroom circumstances write differently? Are they motivated differently? What recommendations would you make to your classmates based on your observations?

3. Observe English learners working in peer response groups and take notes on the kinds of questions they ask one another and on the kinds of responses that seem to lead to improved writing. Make a list of questions and responses that seem to be most useful to young writers to share with your class. If you identify a group that appears to work especially well, ask that group to role-play their peer response group in front of the rest of the class.

4. Observe how different teachers prepare students to work with the writing process. How is the writing process introduced? How are topics selected? How are students prepared to function in peer response groups? Does the teacher prepare students explicitly for working in successful peer response groups? For instance, does the teacher remind students to be respectful of others' writing and to make comments concerning what they like about the writing to provide a positive context for any revisions they may ask about? Finally, what is the importance of publishing student writing in the classroom, and what are the varieties of ways teachers value and ask students to share their writing?

5. Collect writing from different grade levels and English language development levels so that you can compare and contrast how students' writing develops over time. For example, how does spelling develop from the first to the third grade? Do students naturally move from invented spelling to more standard spelling without a great deal of instruction, or do they need instruction in spelling to learn how to spell? When is it appropriate to intervene with the students' natural process to help them become better writers? Do students, as they develop in reading and writing, change sentence length and maturity naturally over time or must these be explicitly taught for student writing to grow? Look at the writing you have collected from different grade levels and see what other categories you might evaluate.

PEARSON
myeducationlab
Where the Classroom Comes to Life

Video Homework Exercise
Literature and the Reading Process

In the video, the teacher goes over a paragraph with students and asks them to discuss key ideas from the paragraph. She then asks students to write about what they have learned. She also discusses how she selects articles for her students.

Go to MyEducationLab, select the topic "Teaching with Literature," and watch the video entitled "Literature and the Reading Process."

1. How do you plan to use articles in your own class? What are some of the values of using such fiction and nonfiction?

2. Why does the teacher select articles that may tie in to other content area classes in her reading class?

3. How might previewing and discussing specific paragraphs in readings assist English learners at different levels of language and reading proficiency?

8

Reading and Literature Instruction for English Learners

> " My poems are hymns of praise to the glory of life. "
>
> —Dame Edith Sitwell

In this chapter, we discuss the reading process, compare first and second language reading, and provide suggestions for promoting second language reading through a variety of contexts and strategies emphasizing the use of multicultural literature. The following questions are discussed:

1. What does research tell us about students reading in a second language?
2. Which classroom contexts and teaching strategies can best assist English learners in reading and enjoying literature?
3. What are the characteristics of beginning and intermediate-level second language readers?
4. How may second language reading be assessed?

When Susan Jacobs was absent with the flu for a few days, her students complained about the substitute. "She didn't know any of the rules," one child said. "She made me clean up the sinks, and it was Juan's turn," said Julia. Others complained loudly, "She didn't know anything!!!" Susan asked the students what they thought should be done about the situation. The children told her not to be absent. Knowing she couldn't guarantee that, she asked her students for suggestions to improve things if she should be absent again.

Glad to have been asked, the students eagerly suggested that the substitute needed guidelines about how the classroom functioned, and because they knew the rules, they could write a substitute handbook. One group decided to take charge of the guidelines for cleaning the room. Another group said they would make a list of some of the general rules of behavior. "We have to talk 'bout mailboxes on our desks and that it's OK to pass notes except when something's going on. But no airmail letters!!!" said Tina.

Thus charged, the children spent two weeks developing and refining the handbook, complete with classroom charts, to make it easier for the substitute to know procedures, rules, and student roles. Each group wrote one part of the handbook, revised it, and gave it to other groups for further clarification and revision. Finally, an editorial team edited the handbook and published it using a computer. They told Susan that all she had to do the next time she was ill was tell the substitute to read the handbook.

Because this happened early in the year, the students learned the classroom rules at a deeper level. Susan also allowed them to negotiate new rules that they thought would make the classroom work better. These new rules, added to the handbook, were to be followed by everyone, including Susan. Through the activity, children received validation for their own views on classroom management, learned the system more clearly, and became involved in a meaningful literacy event. Susan decided she would negotiate rules and create a substitute handbook with classes in the future.

You may wonder why we start a chapter on reading with an example of what seems to be a writing activity. We start this way because, although writing and reading are the focus of Chapters 7 and 8, we view them as integrally related

283

 INTERNET RESOURCES

The literacy connections site's (**www. literacy connections.com/SecondLanguage.html**) aim is to "promote literacy and a love of reading." In the site you'll find resources for dictionaries, references, and word books; for nonfiction bilingual and Spanish books; for poetry, rhyme, and songs; and "inexpensive" reproducible Spanish and bilingual books. The Schools of California Online Resources for Educators (SCORE) Project site (**www.sdcoe. k12.ca.us/score/cyberguide.html**) contains detailed lesson plans for K-12 classrooms. There

are specific lesson plans and links to sites that expand lessons. Each "cyberguide" delivers a unit of instruction centered on a core work of literature.

Another excellent site, The Children's Literature Guide: Internet Resources Related to Books for Children and Young Adults (**www.acs. ucalgary.ca/~dkbrown/**) contains lessons and links on literature. The links contain such categories as "Authors on the Web," "Stories on the Web," "Readers' Theater," "Recommended Books," and "Resources for Teachers."

processes. When the students wrote their drafts for the handbook and considered the appropriateness for a substitute, for example, they became readers. When they shared revisions with one another, they became readers. When they worked with other groups and with the editorial team, they became readers. Though we concentrate on reading in this chapter, the emphasis will always be on reading and writing as interrelated processes working together to serve the larger purposes of communication and learning (Heath & Mangiola, 1991).

What Does Research Tell Us About Reading in a Second Language?

Over the past decade, researchers have looked at how people process print when reading in English as a second language (Carrell, Devine, & Eskey, 1988; Goodman & Goodman, 1978; Grabe, 1991; Hudelson, 1981). They consistently find that the process is essentially the same whether reading English as the first or second language. In other words, both first and second language readers look at the page and the print and use their knowledge of sound/symbol relationships, word order, grammar, and meaning to predict and confirm meaning. The linguistic systems involved in reading are commonly referred to as **graphophonics** (sound/symbol correspondences), **syntax** (word order), and **semantics** (meaning). In the process, readers use their background knowledge about the text's topic and structure along with their linguistic knowledge and reading strategies to arrive at an interpretation and to achieve their purpose for reading. If their interpretation does not make sense, they may go back and read again (see Peregoy & Boyle, 2000).

To see for yourself how you use graphic, syntactic, and semantic cues, try reading the passage in Figure 8.1. We made the task more difficult by deleting several words and leaving a blank in their place. Think of the blank spaces as words you don't recognize. In some cases, we provided an initial letter or two as graphophonic cues. Were you able to fill in all the blanks? What kinds of clues did you use to help you create a meaningful whole? Even though this passage was not titled, the first lines provided an important clue: "Once upon a time" signals the fairy tale genre. As you read on, you needed to predict words for each blank that fit grammatically and made sense. To do so, you used your internalized knowledge of the syntax and semantics of English. Your implicit linguistic knowledge allowed you to make two essential judgments: Does it sound right, and does

FIGURE 8.1

PASSAGE WITH SOME WORDS MISSING

Once upon a time, long ago and far away, there lived a gentle queen. It was the deepest and darkest 1. _____ winters, and every day the gentle queen would spend 2. h _____ afternoons sitting with her needlework at the only window in the 3. _____. The castle window itself was framed in blackest ebony, 4. _____ anyone passing below could gaze upon the beautiful queen, 5. _____ as a picture, as she quietly worked at her 6. _____. One day, as she sat sewing, she pricked her finger 7. _____ her needle, and three rich, red drops of blood 8. _____ upon the glistening snow below. At the sight of the red blood upon the 9. _____ snow, the gentle queen whispered: "Oh, how I wish 10._____a baby daughter with hair as black as ebony, 11. _____as red as blood and skin as white as snow." And so it came 12. _____ pass that the queen gave birth to such a 13. _____, whom she called Snow White.

Answers 1. of; 2. -er; 3. sunlight; 4. and; 5. pretty; 6. embroidery; 7. with; 8. fell; 9. white; 10. for; 11. lips; 12. to; 13. child it make sense? In this way, you gradually created a tentative envisionment of the story. A slightly different approach would have been to skim over the passage first to get a general idea of what it was about and then fill in the blanks. If you took this approach, you probably noticed that the story was *Snow White*. This information would have facilitated the task because it would have activated your background knowledge about this familiar tale. You would still make use of your knowledge of the graphophonics, syntax, and semantics of English to predict and confirm specific words to put in the blanks.

Second Language Readers

A reader who speaks English as a second language uses essentially the same process that you did to read the passage. Yet the task is apt to be more difficult. Why? As you have probably predicted by now, the resources that first and second language readers bring to bear are different. The two most important differences are **second language proficiency** and **background knowledge** pertinent to the text being read. Take another look at the *Snow White* passage and consider it from the point of view of a student learning English. Limitations in language proficiency will generally make it more difficult for a second language student to fill in the blanks. For example, you probably had no difficulty filling in *the* or *her* before *afternoons* in the second sentence. However, predicting words such as *a*, *the*, *in*, and *on* is often difficult for students who are still learning English. Formulaic expressions such as "Once upon a time" and "pretty as a picture" may

be unfamiliar and thus difficult to interpret fully. Thus, limitations in second language proficiency affect second language reading comprehension, causing it to be slower and more arduous. When English learners read texts that are fairly easy for them, their reading provides comprehensible input that promotes English language acquisition (Elley & Mangubhai, 1983; Krashen, 1993). With your assistance, they will be able to advance to more difficult texts.

English Learners and Background Knowledge

Although second language proficiency affects reading comprehension, another powerful factor in the equation is the

Providing students with the opportunity to read in their primary language helps boost success in second language reading.

reader's prior knowledge of the topic of a passage or text. In the *Snow White* example, you probably knew the story. This knowledge made it easier for you to fill in the blanks. Fairy tales also follow a particular narrative structure, beginning with the formulaic opening "Once upon a time," moving through a predictable plot sequence, and ending with "They lived happily ever after." Thus, your experience with fairy tales provides you with background knowledge not only about the content of particular stories but about common narrative forms and plot sequences. This background knowledge facilitates comprehension of written stories by helping you predict where the story is leading. To the extent that second language readers are less familiar with the topic and structure of a particular text, their comprehension task will be more or less difficult (Carrell & Eisterhold, 1988). By providing reading material on content familiar to your students and by building background before reading a text, you can offset reading comprehension difficulties stemming from limited second language proficiency.

English learners may experience reading difficulties related to limited second language proficiency and background knowledge that does not match the topic of a particular text. However, English learners who know how to read in their first language bring sophisticated literacy knowledge to the task of second language reading. They know that print is part of a systematic code that represents language and thereby carries meaning. If the student's home language uses a writing system similar to the English alphabet, the transfer from the home language to English reading is fairly straightforward (Odlin, 1989). Students still need instruction and practice in English reading, but they have a substantial head start over students who are preliterate or who must learn the Roman alphabet used for writing English.

Reading Processes of Proficient Readers

Learning to read involves gradually developing the ability to recognize words almost instantly. Good readers become so automatic in word recognition that they concentrate on meaning and are rarely aware that they are attending to almost every letter they see (Adams & Bruck, 1995). Try reading the following passage, observing your own process as you go along, to see if you can identify elements of the reading process we have been discussing (Buswell, 1922).

> The boys' arrows were nearly gone so they sat down on the grass and stopped hunting. Over at the edge of the wood they saw Henry making a bow to a small girl who was coming down the road. She had tears in her dress and also tears in her eyes. She gave Henry a note which he brought over to the group of young hunters. Read to the boys, it caued great excitement. After a minute but rapid examination of their weapons, they ran down to the valley. Does were standing at the edge of the lake making an excellent target. (p. 22)

How aware were you that you were scanning the letters and words as you read? Research on eye movement suggests that good readers attend to almost every word on a page almost without realizing it; moreover, they also attend to almost every letter (Rayner & Pollatsek, 1989; Zola, 1984). You probably perceived the words in this passage quickly and somewhat unconsciously, except for certain tricky words that created problems in meaning. You may also have noticed that the word *caused* was misspelled as "caued"; we misspelled it intentionally to illustrate that when a letter is missing, your reading fluency can be slowed because the information in almost every letter is important to you as a good reader (Bertera & Rayner, 1979).

Because this is a passage that plays tricks with a reader's normal expectations of a text, you probably had problems with certain words or phrases. You probably misread *bow*. We suggest that you did this because your experience with print has told you to use your background knowledge to predict what will come next. Because the text uses words such as *hunting* and *arrows*, your hunting schema or background knowledge has been activated, leading you to choose *bow* (rhyming with *so*) instead of *bow* (rhyming with *cow*). We also predict that you mispronounced the word *tear*. Your knowledge of syntax told you that the word should be pronounced *tear*, as in *teardrop*. English meaning is based largely on syntax, or word order, leading to the difference in meaning, for example, between a *Venetian blind* and a *blind Venetian*. In some languages, such as Latin or Turkish, word order is not as important. When you came to the phrase *Read to the boys* you had a 50 percent chance of getting it right but may have pronounced it *read* (as in *reed*) instead of *read* (as in *red*). We also suspect you may have mispronounced the word *minute* in *After a minute but* because you are more familiar with the common phrase *after a minute* (as in 60 seconds). Finally, we guess that you hesitated but pronounced *Does* properly even though you've repeatedly seen the word at the beginning of a sentence pronounced as does (rhyming with was). No doubt you got this one right because you started adapting to the trickiness of the text and read more slowly and carefully.

The miscues or deviations from the print you made with the text further illustrate the need for readers to use linguistic and background knowledge while interacting with print to make the best prediction possible about what they are reading. This aspect of background knowledge is particularly important when thinking of second language reading because of the different background knowledge that second language readers may bring to a text.

Elements of Reading Comprehension and Metacognition: A Cartoon Example

287

Let's look at a cartoon to further illustrate some features of reading comprehension. Because cartoons are largely pictorial, they provide a fresh way to examine the role of background knowledge, inferences, and metacognition (i.e., reflecting on your understanding) in the comprehension process. Because cartoons include captions and word balloons, they also require reading. Look at this "Far Side" cartoon and answer the following questions so that we can engage in a dialogue about our comprehension processes.

Comprehension Questions:

1. Who are the figures in the forefront of the cartoon?
2. Where are these figures? How do you know?
3. What do the written words tell us about the event the figures are attending?
4. What kind of movie are they going to watch: adventure, comedy, drama, horror, or mystery?
5. Is this cartoon funny to you? Why or why not?

You probably answered most, if not all, of the questions with relative ease. Let's look at what enabled you to do so. First of all, your experience with cartoons would alert you to the idea that there must be humor here. To get the humor, you have to look more closely. For example, you would have to notice that the figures represent flying insects of some kind, that they are sitting in a movie theater, and that the title of the film has just appeared on the screen. You might have also inferred that the event is a horror movie. How were you able to do this?

THE FAR SIDE® BY GARY LARSON

© 1980 FarWorks, Inc. All Rights Reserved/Dist. by Creators Syndicate

RETURN OF THE KILLER WINDSHIELD

The Far Side® by Gary Larson © 1980 FarWorks, Inc. All Rights Reserved. The Far Side® and the Larson® signature are registered trademarks of FarWorks, Inc. Used with permission.

288

Essentially, you made use of your background knowledge to make inferences based on the picture and word cues in the cartoon. To get the humor, you have to make another inference, drawing a parallel between what constitutes a horror movie for people versus what might constitute a horror movie for flying insects. Once you understand the cartoon, you may or may not find it funny. Your response to the cartoon is ultimately personal, similar to your response to a poem or a piece of literature. These processes are similar to those you use to comprehend written texts as we explain next.

Background Knowledge and Inferences

A major element in reading comprehension is **background knowledge** about the genre and subject (see Anderson, 1999). In this case the genre is a cartoon. Your prior experience with cartoons lets you know that you have to interpret the pictures and words to find humor. If you are familiar with Larson cartoons, which have become almost a genre of their own, you may expect rather quirky humor. As you look at the cartoon, you need to engage your background knowledge to recognize the characters and setting: bugs in a movie theater. If you ever watched *Mystery Science Theater 3000* on television, the scene of bugs in a theater might be immediately familiar. If you are an entomologist, you might be inclined to respond to these bugs affectionately as a kind of "extended family." The curtain, screen, and seats helped you identify a theater setting. If you are a theater major, you might have identified the proscenium. As you engage your prior knowledge to interpret the pictures in the cartoon, you need to activate two main schema: flying insects and movie theaters.

Decoding and Vocabulary

Understanding the cartoon is not complete, however, until you decode and comprehend the words on the movie screen. For example, if *windshield* were an unfamiliar word, you might **decode** it by breaking it into parts and sounding it out. Comprehending the word is of course necessary also. We have to know what a windshield is, and the cartoon does not provide clues in this regard, thus the importance of **vocabulary knowledge**. We remember seeing something like "Entschuldigensiebitte" ("excuse me please") on a large sign in Germany. Although we often used this phrase in conversation, we didn't recognize it in print until we had broken it apart and sounded it out. We were surprised to find such a familiar phrase in such an unfamiliar print form.

Recognizing and understanding the words is still not sufficient, however, for understanding the cartoon. Background knowledge is required once again to notice that the words are the film title. This title follows a familiar formula for horror movie titles, but it is only familiar if you have had the experience of watching or have heard of such movies. You have to make an **inference** to conclude that the bugs are watching a horror movie. You make the inference by piecing together clues in the cartoon—the theater setting and the words on the screen—and then applying your prior knowledge of titles, especially horror movie titles. You do the same thing when you make inferences in reading: You use the literal information provided in the text combined with your background knowledge to interpret and draw conclusions about the meaning. Reflecting once again on the various kinds of background you bring, imagine the challenges you would face understanding the cartoon if you had recently arrived, for example, from a village in the Andes, from a large city in China, or from a small town in Russia. Can you see how your knowledge stems from your own particular social and cultural experiences? As you can imagine, humor often does not translate easily across cultures.

Metacognition: "Thinking about Thinking"

If we don't get the humor in a cartoon, we might have to rethink our comprehension process, using metacognitive strategies to repair our lack of understanding (Urquhart & Weir, 1998). **Metacognition** is the process of analyzing our own comprehension processes, or "thinking about thinking." We use metacognition to recognize and repair understanding when something we read does not make sense. Some metacognitive strategies include looking at the cartoon again more closely to see if we missed anything in the picture or in the words. Perhaps there was a caption that we overlooked or some other visual feature. Other metacognitive strategies include questioning ourselves while reading, asking for example, "Where are the bugs?" or "What is the cartoonist trying to say to us?" Explicit instruction on metacognitive strategies is valuable for students when taught in the context of reading literature and content area texts (Grabe & Stoller, 1997).

Text Structure

Another important aspect in reading is text structure (Meyer, Brandt, & Bluth, 1980). The cartoon structure, for example, tells us to look at the pictures, word balloons, and perhaps a caption to get the full meaning. In a similar way, if students recognize the compare/contrast structure of an essay, then they will expect to find objects compared and contrasted. For example, if two schools are discussed in an essay, they will expect the author to discuss how the schools are the same and how they might be different. In other words, the structure helps us make predictions about what will come next, what to expect.

In summary, we have presented three examples (a fairy tale, a passage, and a cartoon) to illustrate elements of reading comprehension. We have emphasized how several kinds of knowledge work together in the process: language knowledge, background knowledge, text structure, decoding, and vocabulary. We have also illustrated the role of cognitive processes such as inferencing and metacognitive strategies such as rereading if needed for full understanding. Explicit teaching of cognitive and metacognitive strategies as students read literature and content texts will increase their academic learning. For English learners, it is especially important to consider their language proficiency and prior experiences relevant to any text they read so that you can prepare them to be successful as they read. Throughout this chapter and also in Chapters 9, 10, and 11, we will illustrate how to help students use and increase their abilities in the elements of comprehension as they read various kinds of texts such as stories, novels, news articles, encyclopedia entries, and textbook selections.

The learning contexts and strategies we suggest for second language readers in this chapter are those in which students are hearing, reading, sharing, and responding to high-quality literature. Just as collaborative work and sharing play an important role in second language writing development, so also do they play a crucial role in second language reading development. These learning contexts will include the whole class listening to and reading fine literature, small groups of students responding to stories they read, pairs of students reading to each other, and individual students reading on their own. Just as process writing helps create a community of writers, shared reading experiences will further develop your students into a community of readers and writers.

We think of the ideal reader as an independent reader—one who responds to literature individually and shares responses with others, listens to other viewpoints and adjusts interpretations, and uses information in a literary text to support interpretations but remains open to the interpretations of others. An ideal environment for literature response gives students opportunities to work in collaborative groups. To provide such an environment, we offer several types of response groups that you may wish to try in your classroom.

Working in Literature Response Groups

Literature response groups, or literature circles, are analogous to writing response groups. The main difference is that in literature response groups students discuss the work of published authors, whereas in writing response groups they discuss the work of their peers. Literature response groups consist of three to six students who have read a piece of literature and are ready to discuss it together. Just as we recommend that you model how to work in writing response groups, we recommend that you model response to literature before asking students to respond in groups. However you decide to work with your own students, you can be assured that English learners, especially those at the intermediate level of English language development, can be active participants in literature response groups (Samway et al., 1991; Urzúa, 1992).

If you have modeled response to writing already, you can easily make the transition to reading response groups because the two are so similar. You may wish to remind students to respond to the content of the literature (i.e., to the problems faced by characters and situations in a narrative). They need to be flexible in their interpretations and tolerant of differing views. For example, they

1. If you did (or didn't) like the book, was there one event, character, or aspect of the book that caused this reaction? What? Why?
2. Do your response group members share a common reaction to the book? What reactions are the same? What are different?
3. If you were faced with the same problems as the main character in the book, would you have responded in a similar manner? Why?
4. How was the main character feeling when we first met him or her? Have you ever felt like the character?
5. How do you feel about the ways the main character behaves with other characters?
6. Did any of the characters remind you of anyone you have known? Yourself?
7. Do you think the author was trying to teach us something? If so, what?
8. Would you change the ending of the book? If so, how?
9. Which character would you like to have met? What would you want to say or do when you met the character?
10. Did your feelings change toward the character(s) as the story progressed? What made your feelings change?
11. If you could step inside the book and be part of the story, where would you enter? Who would you be? What would you do? How would these things change the story?
12. What things would be different in this story if it took place in a different period of time or a different place?

FIGURE 8.2

MODEL GENERIC
RESPONSE SHEET

291

may find that there are several valid ways to interpret what motivates a character to act in a particular way.

At first, some teachers provide groups with response sheets to scaffold their initial response to literature. These sheets provide the students with model questions they may ask of any story. Moreover, the sheets help them begin to develop their own questions. Other teachers ask students to make up their own response sheets based on a story that the children are reading and share that sheet as a part of their own literature activity. One model response sheet developed by teachers is provided in Figure 8.2. It is meant to guide students' response and to prepare them for more independent interpretations of the literature they read.

The response sheet in Figure 8.2 includes the following directions:

This response sheet is recommended for self-paced reading scheduled by students working in literature response groups. Expectations for your responses have been set by your class and teacher. Be ready to accept and respect the opinions of others in your group. You may expect the same from them with regard to your views. Your job is to help one another understand the story you are reading and to share your own views of the story. Remember, there is no one single interpretation of any story you are reading; in fact, there will usually be many different views of stories. You may begin your discussion with the questions listed on this sheet but feel free to develop your own questions as your discussion proceeds.

Steps That Prepare Students to Work in Response Groups

Some of the steps teachers take in preparing students to work efficiently in response groups are as follows:

1. They read good literature to students daily and ask for individual responses informally.
2. They share with students their own responses to characters' dilemmas.
3. They help students connect the characters and situations to decisions and circumstances in their own lives.

4. They encourage different views of the literature, including views that differ from their own.

5. They share their enjoyment of stories and literary language.

6. They emphasize personal response to literature over theoretical literary analysis.

7. They teach students vocabulary to talk about literature.

8. They may provide students with a model response sheet to assist them at first.

After your students have discussed a story in their response groups, you may invite them to extend their interpretations through dramatization, readers' theater, illustration, or some other recreation, such as those in the list that follows. For example, Mary Donal sets up literature centers with materials for carrying out literature extension activities, including art materials for illustration, props for dramatization, pencils and colored markers for writing, and idea cards for further responses to particular stories. Her students sign up for the centers at the beginning of the day. She wants all of her students eventually to try a variety of response extensions, including readers' theater, rewriting stories, and dramatization, instead of illustrating the story every time. By providing centers, she guides her students while giving them choices.

When students begin to respond independently to literature, they can choose from the following list. Additionally, they may respond to the literature in their response journals, perhaps using the same questions they used in group work to focus their reading. By providing students with tools to respond to literature, we motivate them to read on their own.

Ways to Extend Response to Literature

readers' theater	improvisational signing
illustrations	response groups
response sheets	journals
storytelling	creating Big Books
story maps	developing time lines
puppet shows	rebus books
Egyptian hieroglyphs	board games
animated films	collages
making dioramas	mobiles
creating songs	posters
murals	mock court trials
book jackets	dressing up as characters
creating radio scripts	creating videos

How Response to Literature Assists English Learners

Literature response, whether involving the whole class, small groups, pairs, or individuals, offers English learners the opportunity to enjoy good literature. The groups are informal, and there are many chances for students to help each other negotiate the meaning of stories. As story discussion becomes routine, English learners will become familiar with ways of talking about literature, as will their first language counterparts.

The oral discussions thus provide opportunities for comprehensible input (Krashen & Terrell, 1983) and negotiation of story meaning through social interaction (Samway & McKeon, 1999). In many ways, first and second language learners are on an equal footing in that they may all be new to the ways of responding to literature promoted in literature response groups.

Being able to read literature well enough to discuss it in groups, however, requires the development of both reading ability and knowledge of how to talk about it in terms of character, plot development, and so forth. You may wish to research intermediate and advanced students' capabilities in terms of response groups and the strategies that may assist them in working together.

The Many Benefits of Independent Reading

Giving your students class time for reading is a powerful way to promote language and literacy development. In fact, results of the National Assessment of Education Progress (NAEP) indicate that a key feature of schools with high

293

Source: © The New Yorker Collection 1987 Warren Miller from cartoonbank.com. All Rights Reserved.

reading scores is allocation of time for students to read independently (NAEP, 2003). Independent reading can build vocabulary, background knowledge, and interest in reading while improving reading comprehension and overall English language development. Therefore, one of the most beneficial things we can do for our students is to create a comfortable, supportive environment that encourages daily reading. In-class, voluntary reading approaches have been around for decades. We will describe three kinds here, uninterrupted sustained silent reading (USSR), extensive reading, and narrow reading. In addition, we will show how to help students choose books at their independent reading level, an important aspect of all three approaches.

Uninterrupted sustained silent reading (see McCracken, 1971; McCracken & McCracken, 1972) has many different names, such as drop everything and read (DEAR) and our time to enjoy reading (OTTER), and is similar to what some educators call extensive reading (Day & Bamford, 1998; Krashen, 1993). USSR and extensive reading encourage students to read a large number of mostly self-selected books they can read on their own. In USSR, students are generally not required to make book reports or engage in any other follow-up activities. With extensive reading, on the other hand, postreading activities may form an integral part of the program. Follow-up activities might include role-playing the story, designing a poster to advertise the book, copying interesting words and useful expressions in a journal, or sharing views with fellow students (Renandya & Jacobs, 2002). In *The Power of Reading* (2004), Krashen discusses the value of free, voluntary reading (FVR). In practice, teachers don't always make fine distinctions between the different approaches for independent reading: Sometimes they have follow-up activities, sometimes they don't; sometimes they question students, sometimes they don't.

Research, practice, and teacher experience have shown that extensive reading is key to any reading program (Day & Bamford, 1998; Krashen, 1993). Advantages include building vocabulary, background knowledge, and interest in reading in addition to improving comprehension. Krashen has written about the "incidental learning" that comes from a wide variety of reading, and we like to think of the incidental erudition that comes from all reading we do: Even from reading mysteries, we can learn about medicine, law, government, and our environment.

To provide an extensive reading program, you need to have large amounts of culturally appropriate materials, in a variety of genres, at various difficulty levels. In Figure 8.3 we offer guidelines for developing a classroom library so that students can select materials for themselves and you can guide students to books they will enjoy.

Another approach we see as an adjunct to extensive reading is narrow reading (Krashen, 1981b). With narrow reading, students read many texts on the same topic (Schmitt & Carter, 2000). Thus, they are given a chance to read materials that will build their vocabulary and background knowledge, making subsequent reading easier. In summary, through extensive and intensive reading of largely self-selected materials, second language readers can develop their vocabulary, background knowledge, comprehension, and love of books. To assist you with selecting books, Figure 8.4 lists seven guidelines for evaluating appropriate multicultural literature for your classroom.

Next, we discuss other resources for (1) estimating students' reading levels

IDEAS FOR STUDENT SELF-SELECTION AND TEACHER SELECTION OF READING MATERIALS		
GUIDELINES	**COMMENTS**	**RESOURCES**
Have materials in your students' first language and English available in your classroom that address familiar and new topics.	Almost all readers begin by wanting to read about themselves and topics with some familiarity.	www.carolhurst.com/index.html: From this site, you can get information on books in Spanish, Vietnamese, and other languages.
Give students a chance to select their own reading materials.	Any **appropriate** reading is acceptable: magazines, comics, newspapers, etc.	Some appropriate materials may be: *The Week*, Scholastic, classic comics, *TV Guide*.
Help students select reading appropriate for their own reading levels and maturity.	Have graded books available for students at different grade levels.	Leveled readers in English and Spanish available at: Pearson Scott Foresman, reading a-z.
Take students to the library regularly.	If the school library isn't adequate, take students to the city library.	Many libraries have experts on reading for younger and older students.
Look for appropriate books that have won awards and were written for students like yours.	These books are most likely to attract your students to reading.	Caldecott Medal; Newberry Medal; CLA Book of the Year; www.calgary.ca/~dkbrown/.
Read journals that regularly list and discuss books and stories for students.	You can't personally read all the books you may want to recommend; reputable journals can help you select appropriate books.	*The Reading Teacher; Journal of Adolescent and Adult Literacy;* these journal all have regular review sections of many useful books.
Read and know books that are appropriate for your students.	In just a few hours you can read large numbers of elementary books. In several more hours, you can read longer chapter books.	It's surprising how many books you can know within just a few years of teaching. Students can also become a resource.

FIGURE 8.3

GUIDELINES FOR SELECTING APPROPRIATE READING MATERIALS

295

to better guide their choices for independent reading; (2) selecting graded books of a variety of difficulty levels, genres, and topics of interest for your classroom library; and (3) using electronic books (e-books) to enhance your students' reading experiences.

EVALUATION OF MULTICULTURAL LITERATURE	
THINGS TO WATCH FOR	**COMMENTS**
Distortions or omissions of history	Various perspectives should be presented.
Stereotyping	No inaccurate views of groups.
Loaded words	Books should not contain derogatory words such as primitive, backward, savage.
Dialogue	Characters use speech that respectfully and accurately portrays the culture and oral traditions of the community.
Gender roles, elders, and family	Roles are presented accurately within the culture.
Effect on student's self-image	Information in story would not embarrass or offend a student or member of the culture.
High literary quality	Well-written books of cultural significance.

FIGURE 8.4

SUGGESTIONS FOR SELECTING QUALITY MULTICULTURAL LITERATURE

Independent, Instructional, and Frustration Levels of Reading

One way to estimate student reading levels is through informal reading inventories (IRI), which are published reading assessment guides discussed in detail in Chapter 11. Using passages of increasing levels of difficulty, IRIs indicate whether a student can read a particular passage independently, with assistance, or not at all because it's much too difficult. Generally, you want students to choose books at their independent reading level for USSR, extensive reading, and narrow reading. Your students should be able to read graded material with 98 percent word recognition and with 95 percent comprehension to take full advantage of their independent reading. The instructional level for students is 95 percent word recognition and 70 percent comprehension, meaning that this level is appropriate when students have assistance, as in guided reading. If students are below 90 percent word recognition and 70 percent comprehension, the material is probably too difficult for them even with your assistance. Thus, for sustained silent reading you will want your students to be roughly at the independent level, bearing in mind that interest, enthusiasm, and prior knowledge of a topic may facilitate reading at a greater difficulty level than predicted by an IRI.

Five-Finger Exercise

An informal way your students select materials at an independent reading level is one Melinda Thurber calls the five-finger exercise. Melinda teaches her third graders to count the words they don't know on the first page or so of a book holding up a finger for each unknown word. If they reach five fingers, they know the book is probably too difficult for them to read independently. The technique is based on the assumption that the book has about 100 words per page. You may use the same general guideline for students at other grade levels, adjusting the number of unknown words as you see fit.

Graded Books

Graded books and articles consist of specially prepared text controlled for reading level but with content that an older student would find appropriate. For example, you may have a student who is 16 years old but is only able to read at the fourth-grade level. You can select a book or article at the fourth-grade reading level with high interest and mature subject matter appropriate for a 16-year-old student.

Electronic Books

Electronic books (e-books) are an excellent resource for English language learners because there are thousands of books available free, and they can be read on personal digital assistants (PDAs) and other electronic book readers. PDAs are becoming more affordable every day and can be purchased for as little as $38 at the time of this printing. Two available programs are particularly valuable for students: Mobipocket and Palm e-reader. With both of these programs, you merely touch or scan an unknown word with a stylus to get the word's definition and pronunciation. We always travel with our PDAs and other electronic readers, which can literally hold more than 1,000 books with a memory card. Finally, many textbooks are currently available as e-books and probably many more will be available in the future, including this edition of our book. We believe that e-books represent the future; even now, most books, fiction and nonfiction, can be bought for cheaper prices and are immediately available for download from your own computer. Because using the dictionary is so easy and consumes so little time, e-books can facilitate vocabulary and comprehension in a real way.

In the next sections, we discuss strategies for helping students move ahead in reading ability while developing a sense of literary elements.

Beginning Readers: Characteristics and Strategies

In general, beginning-level second language readers, like their first language counterparts, are just beginning to pull meaning from reading short texts. They may still be somewhat unfamiliar with the English alphabet and its unusual, if not unruly, spelling patterns. Chances are they recognize a number of sight words but they need more reading practice to develop a larger sight word vocabulary. Most beginners can read simple texts, such as predictable books, through word recognition strategies, language knowledge, and memorization. However, they may have difficulty processing information beyond sentence-level texts. Regardless of their age, beginners need more experience with written language. If they have never read before in any language, they need frequent reminders of the many ways we use reading and writing for practical purposes and enjoyment. If they are literate in their first language, they probably have some idea of what reading and writing are for, but their literacy concepts should be broadened. In summary, beginners need to be immersed in reading and writing for readily perceived purposes. They need practice to solidify sound/symbol correspondences in English and to remind them that English reads from left to right, top to bottom. Finally, they need enough practice to move them toward being able to read simple texts independently. In this section, we describe a number of teaching strategies that have proven useful for beginning readers.

Language-Experience Approach

The language-experience approach is one of the most frequently recommended approaches for beginning second language readers (Dixon & Nessel, 1983; Tinajero & Calderon, 1988). The beauty of this approach is that the student provides the text, through dictation, that serves as the basis for reading instruction. As a result, language-experience reading is tailored to the learner's own interests, background knowledge, and language proficiency. It builds on the linguistic, social, and cultural strengths and interests the student brings to school. Not least important, this approach works well for those older preliterate students who need age-appropriate texts dealing with topics that interest them.

The core of the language-experience approach builds on stories dictated by individual students, small groups, or the whole class. As a rule, the stories are written down verbatim, after which students read them back. Students are usually able to read their own stories with minimal decoding skills because they already know the meaning. Through this approach, students learn to see reading and writing as purposeful communication about their own interests and

FIGURE 8.5

LAN HUONG'S "SWIMMY" STORY

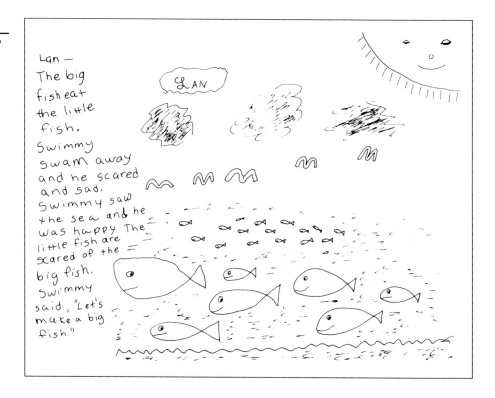

concerns. Moreover, they observe the process by which their own meanings, expressed orally, are put into print form. Important learning about the English writing system is thus conveyed indirectly, preparing students to write. Finally, when they read their own stories back, students are able to experience the success of independent reading. Lan Huong used the book *Swimmy* (Lionni, 1963) to relate her own version, and then read the story to her friends; she created a watercolor for the illustrated page of a book she planned to "write" using the language-experience approach (Figure 8.5).

Although dictation itself provides a useful literacy event for beginners, the language-experience approach (cf. Stauffer, 1970; Tierney, Readence, & Dishner, 1990) provides systematic follow-up to solidify learning. For example, students may underline words in the story that are most meaningful to them, write them on a word card, and place them in their word bank in alphabetical order. In addition, students may cut their stories into sentence strips and rearrange them again to form a coherent piece. The language-experience approach thus bears resemblance to Ashton-Warner's key word approach (Ashton-Warner, 1963) and to Freire's generative theme approach (Freire, 1970; Freire & Macedo, 1987). All three approaches base early literacy instruction on the immediate concerns of students. Thus, as an introduction to reading, the students' own stories become the core of instruction in composition, comprehension, word recognition skills, and general conventions of English print.

One first-grade teacher, Lydia Tanaka, sees language experience as an important part of her literature-based reading program. She reads daily to her students from Big Books and little books, she helps her students make their own Big Books based on predictable story patterns, and she responds to them weekly in their interactive journals. She also uses language-experience stories. The following example shows how.

After an earthquake, Lydia decided to let the children talk about the tremor and share their feelings. She started by asking them to share in groups and brainstorm their ideas for a dictated story. She told them that they were going to create a newspaper about the earthquake and that the front page story would be written by the entire class. When children finished brainstorming and talking in their groups, they began sharing with Lydia, who wrote their statements on the board.

CHABELA: I hear a sound first. Then it shook.

JOSE: Pictures in my house move and dishes too.

LISA: My dad looked at us. He said we better move. We got under tables.

KELLY: We turned on television.

JOE: We watched the world series and it happen.

SAMMY: Glasses broke.

Students continued in this manner until they had related the most important things about the earthquake. At this point Lydia read the group story to the students, pointing to each word as she read it. Next, the students read with her as she pointed to the words. Afterward, she framed individual words and asked the students to read them. Then she asked them to illustrate their story for the newspaper, working in pairs. The class selected one picture to be used for the front page, and the other pictures were presented with short captions on other pages. When the groups had finished their pictures, Lydia asked them to copy the group story.

The next day, students read their story to one another and underlined words in the story they were sure they knew. These words were then copied on separate index cards to be filed alphabetically for each child. Periodically, the child's knowledge of the word bank was checked to make sure the student hadn't forgotten words learned previously.

Lydia's class used the original story and others to create their own newspaper about the earthquake. They then used a computer so that they could publish the paper. Later, the English learners read individual articles to one another and took the newspaper home to read articles to their parents and friends. The initial group sharing of a critical event allowed children to express their fears about the earthquake, helped them become involved in an initial literacy experience, showed them that the words they speak can be written, and gave them a newspaper with words they knew and could share with others.

Lydia doesn't always have events as dramatic as an earthquake (although a year later children wanted to talk about a war), but she uses whatever her students are interested in at the time to develop language-experience stories. She is also quick to point out that these are not the only stories students hear in her class. She reads aloud daily from quality literature, they write in journals, and they hear and act out many stories from the first day of school.

The following text was dictated by Yukka, one of Lydia's first graders. First she drew a picture, then started to write her story. After having some difficulty writing the story, Yukka asked a student teacher to write down what she wanted to say. We include Yukka's writing attempt along with the story she dictated.

YUKKA'S WRITING: I like horse becuss they hav lovely fer.

YUKKA'S DICTATION: They run fast. If I could have horse, he be brown. I ride him in park. I ride him to school and I leave him on the bus.

As Yukka gains experience, her writing will be coordinated enough to keep up with her vivid imagination. Meanwhile, dictation empowers her by providing an adult scribe to get her ideas down on paper. Knowing this, Lydia will encourage Yukka to continue her own writing while taking her dictated stories from time to time. Language-experience stories provide but one important part of Lydia's scheme for assisting children to become literate in their second language. She feels that students must do much more than just read their own stories; therefore, she provides a print-rich environment, full of literature to be heard and read throughout the day. This environment, supplemented with language-experience stories, will enhance the growth of students like Yukka throughout the year. By using English learners' experiences and language, Lydia scaffolds their learning to read and share experiences.

Providing Quality Literature for Beginners

For beginning readers, you will need to create a classroom designed to assist them in making decisions about selecting and responding to quality literature. This does not mean that you won't ever choose a book for students. In fact, you may first want to select a book your entire class reads to model response to literature. Overall, your goal will be to assist students with making choices about what they read, about what they do with what they select, and with their own responses to literature. You will want them to share their reading with one another and to accept different responses to the same literature. However, you'll give beginning-level readers a little more early direction to assure success with their first encounters with a text or story. We have selected several literature-based strategies, sequenced from simpler to more complex, that work well for beginning level readers. These strategies all fit the criteria for literacy scaffolds discussed previously, by working with meaningful and functional communication found in whole texts, by making use of repetitive language and discourse patterns, and by supporting students' comprehension beyond what they could do alone. All of these strategies are meant to provide temporary support to beginning-level students who will drop the scaffolds when they no longer need them.

Pattern Books

Pattern books contain stories that make use of repeated phrases, refrains, and sometimes rhymes. In addition, pattern books frequently contain pictures that may facilitate story comprehension (Heald-Taylor, 1987). The predictable patterns allow beginning second language readers to become involved immediately in a literacy event in their second language. Moreover, the use of pattern books meets the criteria for literacy scaffolds by modeling reading, by challenging students' current level of linguistic competence, and by assisting comprehension through the repetition of a simple sentence pattern.

One popular pattern book is Bill Martin's *Brown Bear, Brown Bear, What Do You See?* (Martin, 1967). The story, amply illustrated with colorful pictures, repeats a simple pattern children use to begin reading. In one first-grade class, for example, Rosario Canetti read *Brown Bear* to a group of nine children with varying English proficiencies. Having arrived recently from Mexico, four of the children were just beginning to learn English as a second language. After hearing the book read once through, the children responded to the second reading as follows:

ROSARIO READS: Brown Bear, Brown Bear, what do you see?
                  [*Rosario turns the page and children see a picture of a red bird.*]
CHILDREN REPLY: Red bird!
ROSARIO READS: I see a red bird looking at me!
                  Red bird, Red bird, what do you see?
                  [*Rosario turns the page and children see a picture of a yellow duck.*]
CHILDREN REPLY: Yellow duck!
ROSARIO READS: I see a yellow duck looking at me.
                  Yellow duck, Yellow duck, what do you see?
                  [*Rosario turns the page and children see a picture of a blue horse.*]
CHILDREN REPLY: Blue horse lookin' at me.

The story continued in this way as other colorful characters were introduced: a green frog, a white dog, a black sheep, a goldfish, and finally pictures of children and a teacher. As a group, the children began to elaborate their responses to include the full pattern: "I see a _____ looking at me." A few children, however, just mouthed the words, participating in the story in a way that was comfortable for them with the support of the group.

After reading several pattern stories to the group, Rosario gives her students opportunities to read the books to each other during self-selection activity time. She also invites them to create their own Big Book versions of the story, or to tell each other the story using flannel board pieces or their own drawings.

One group of Chinese first graders in Audrey Fong's class created their own Big Book after hearing the pattern story *Meanies* (Cowley, 1990). In the story, the question repeated is: "What is it that Meanies do?" This question is followed by an answer repeated three times: "Meanies drink their bath water [in normal voice]. Meanies drink their bath water [louder]. Meanies drink their bath water [shouting in disgust]." And the final phrase: "That's what Meanies do." Using the pattern, the children created their own book: "What is it that Goodies do?" A part of the story is shown here without the illustrations the children drew:

What do Goodies drink?
Goodies drink 7-up.
Goodies drink 7-up.
Goodies drink 7-up.
That's what Goodies drink.

In the book, Meanies eat old bubble gum. The children in Audrey Fong's kindergarten class created their own phrase:

What do Goodies eat?
Goodies eat cake and ice cream.

After becoming familiar with the story and language patterns in books like *Meanies*, children create their own illustrated books following the pattern. Pattern books' most important function is to offer immediate access to meaningful and enjoyable literacy experiences in the student's second language. That may explain why we've seen small second language children carry predictable books around with them all day like security blankets. A partial list of pattern books that have proven successful with older and younger English language learners includes the following:

Allard, H. (1979). *Bumps in the Night*. Garden City, NY: Doubleday.

*Barrett, J. (1970). *Animals Should Definitely Not Wear Clothing*. New York: Atheneum.

Brown, M. (1947). *Goodnight Moon*. New York: Harper & Row.

Carle, E. (1977). *The Grouchy Ladybug*. New York: Crowell.

*Charlip, R. (1971). *Fortunately*. New York: Four Winds Press.

de Paola, T. (1978). *Pancakes for Breakfast*. Orlando: Harcourt Brace Jovanovich.

Flack, M. (1932). *Ask Mr. Bear*. New York: Macmillan.

Galdone, P. (1975). *The Gingerbread Boy*. Boston: Houghton Mifflin.

Hoban, R. (1972). *Count and See*. New York: Macmillan.

Hutchins, P. (1968). *Rosie's Walk*. New York: Macmillan.

Keats, E. J. (1971). *Over in the Meadow*. New York: Scholastic.

Kent, J. (1971). *The Fat Cat*. New York: Scholastic.

Martin, B. (1967). *Brown Bear, Brown Bear, What Do You See?* New York: Holt, Rinehart & Winston.

Mayer, M. (1968). *If I Had . . . .* New York: Dial.

Polushkin, M. (1978). *Mother, Mother, I Want Another*. New York: Crown.

Sendak, M. (1962). *Chicken Soup with Rice*. New York: Scholastic.

*Tolstoy, A. (1968). *The Great Big Enormous Turnip*. New York: Watts.

Illustrating Stories and Poems

Illustrating stories or poems they have read provides another way to develop English learners' response to literature. Students can make a published book of a short story, folktale, or poem, and create pictures that illustrate the literature. Judy Bridges uses this activity because all of the students, even those who speak little or no English, become involved in the illustrations. The activity immediately integrates both older and younger English learners into the collective activities of classroom response groups. The illustrations also assist the students in expressing and defining their own individual responses to the literature and prepare them for verbally sharing in response groups. When students develop illustrations together, they help one another with a basic understanding by illustrating key events. Because they are shared easily, the illustrations provide a communication channel beyond words for assisting comprehension and response to stories.

———

*Books older learners might like.

Shared Reading With Big Books

Big Books, oversized books used to present literature to groups of students in an intimate and joyful way, simulate the kind of lap reading that may take place in the children's homes (Holdaway, 1979). If children have been read to in this way, they move readily from lap reading to large-group shared reading with Big Books. If they haven't been read to often at home, the large-book experience provides an interesting, nonthreatening introduction to reading. Because the books are oversized, all the students can share them in a more personal way than a smaller book would allow. As a result, all of the children become group participants in this delightful and engaging literacy event. Moreover, we've seen teachers use carefully selected Big Books successfully with older students.

Big Books may present predictable stories in patterns that students memorize easily after two or three readings. Then they can "read" the books themselves or to each other, demonstrating a good deal of literacy knowledge. Finally, you can use oversized books to share stories and discussions with students; to point out certain words in the stories that might be difficult to decode; to help them become familiar with reading from left to right, top to bottom; and to assist them with recognizing oral and written versions of the same word.

To use shared reading with Big Books, you will need to develop a small collection of oversized books. Many are available commercially. You and your students may also create your own Big Book versions of your favorite stories using large tagboard for each page and securing the page with ring clasps. Either way, select stories that are predictable at first because these are well loved by all students and easy to understand and remember. When you introduce the story, be sure to read the title and the names of the author and illustrator. When your students create exact remakes of a story, they will include the author's name, too, but the students will be named as the illustrators. If they write new episodes based on a particular pattern, they will be credited with authorship. In this way, reading and writing are integrated, and important learning takes place.

When Thalia Jones introduces *Animals Should Definitely Not Wear Clothing,* (Barrett, 1970), a book appropriate for older and younger students, she starts by asking students to imagine what different animals would look like if they wore clothes. Sometimes, she starts by letting the students draw a picture of an animal wearing clothes to support their thinking and discussion and to help involve students who barely speak English. If necessary, she shows a picture or two of animals wearing clothes to help them start drawing. After this introduction to the topic and title, she reads the story using a pointer to underscore the words from left to right. She reads each word clearly and naturally and gives students time to look at the pictures of each outrageously bedecked animal. She leaves time for laughter, too, especially after their favorite picture, the one of the hen whose newly laid egg is caught in her trousers! When the story is over, Thalia allows students to read small-book versions of the story in pairs. At times, small groups listen to a tape of the story as each child follows along in the book. Finally, she invites students to make their own individual or group books based on the story. Students then make their own oversized books using pictures of animals wearing clothes, labeling each picture with a sentence that models the pattern in the original Big Book and often competing with one another to see who can create the most absurd illustration. As the weeks go by, Thalia occasionally rereads the Big Book and the students' own patterned books. All of the books are kept on hand in the classroom library to choose during free reading.

Big Books, full of rhythm, rhyme, and interesting sequences, motivate students to see reading as fun and interesting. If you are careful to select books with predictable patterns and imaginative language, your students will call for the stories again and again. Their initial engagements with print will be joyful and fun, motivating them to want to read more.

Guided Reading

Guided reading is a strategy in which the teacher works with a small group of students and guides them along as they read stories or other material (Fountas & Pinell, 1996). The teacher selects stories or engages the students in choosing stories that are just a bit more difficult than what they could read unassisted. In other words, the reading material is at the students' instructional reading level. Leveled books and other reading materials of graduated difficulty are readily available for this purpose. For guided reading, students are grouped at similar reading levels, although they may vary in the specific kinds of help needed to become better at decoding and comprehending text. The teacher provides specific, individualized help when students come to a stumbling block while reading aloud, thus differentiating reading instruction. The teacher scaffolds each student through trouble spots, modeling and offering explicit instruction to help them apply the decoding and comprehension strategies needed. Guided reading thus provides ongoing assessment opportunities with immediate, focused instructional assistance. You will want to take a close look at the miscue analysis and running record procedures in the assessment section of this chapter because these will help you decide how to address students' trouble spots during guided reading and document their progress over time. In addition, we offer additional details on guided reading and assessment in Chapter 11.

Directed Listening-Thinking Activity (DL-TA)

The directed listening-thinking activity (DL-TA) provides a scaffold by modeling how experienced readers make predictions as they read. Using DL-TA, you ask questions throughout a story, guiding students to make predictions and to monitor these predictions as subsequent text is provided (Boyle & Peregoy, 1990; Stauffer, 1975). Usually you ask more questions at the beginning of the activity, encouraging students to generate their own questions as the story proceeds. Eventually, students incorporate the DL-TA questioning procedure as a natural part of their independent reading.

Lisa Joiner uses DL-TA with her English learners early in the year as a part of the regular classroom time used for listening to stories; thus, the activity becomes a listening activity at first for her students. She likes to introduce the concept by using Crockett Johnson's magical crayon story *Harold's Circus* (1959). In the story, a little boy, Harold, encounters problems that he is able to solve by drawing something with his purple crayon. For example, he falls into deep water and draws a sailboat so that he can float away safely. Lisa makes overhead transparencies of the pages in the book to share it with the whole class. Before reading the book, she asks children to fold a large piece of paper in quarters and hands each child a purple crayon. Then she asks them to think about what they might draw with the crayon if it were magic and could make anything they drew become real. After the children share their ideas, she introduces the book:

LISA: The story I'm going to read to you today is about a little boy named Harold, who has a magic purple crayon. Harold gets into little troubles at the circus and sometimes has to get out of trouble by drawing something with his magic crayon. What kinds of things do you think might happen to Harold at the circus?

NG: Tiger eat him.

JUAN: A elephant steps on him.

TERRI: A snake swallow him.

The discussion goes on until most of the students have shared their own ideas. The children have fun seeing who can think of the worst thing and say, "Aaaah!!! Ugghh!!!" after each new comment. At this point Lisa quiets the children and introduces the DL-TA strategy.

LISA: I'm going to ask you to draw what you think Harold will draw to get out of trouble. So listen carefully and, when I ask you to, draw a picture of what you think Harold will draw next. [*She reads the text on her overhead pointing at the words as she says them.*]

LISA: One moonlit evening, mainly to prove to himself he could do it, Harold went for a walk on a tightrope. [*The picture shows Harold drawing a tightrope.*] It is easy to fall off a tightrope and Harold fell. By a stroke of luck, a comfortable-looking curve appeared beneath him. [*The picture shows Harold drawing a curve.*]

LISA: [*Speaking to the children.*] I want you to draw what you think that curve was. Remember this is about a circus. Draw your guess on the upper left-hand corner of your folded paper.

The children draw their pictures and share them with partners before Lisa reads on and shows them the picture of what Harold drew—an elephant. Most of the children drew other things, so they laugh when they see that the curve Harold started to draw became the trunk of an elephant. Lisa continues to read the story, and the children get better at guessing and drawing pictures as they catch on to how the story works.

Through DL-TA activities like this, Lisa's children become actively involved in understanding a story that is shown to them on the overhead. They learn how to make predictions when reading, finding out that, as they do so, they get better at understanding what they read. They also see that reading stories like this can be fun, and they frequently ask Lisa to read stories like it again. At first they are only interested in "Harold" stories, but later they ask for other stories too. This activity is sheltered in that pictures accompany the story, and the children themselves respond by drawing. In this way, they are involved through pictorial means in the higher-level processes of story comprehension. They also learn to use drawings on a folded piece of paper to make their own stories and to have others guess what might be on the next page. The stories become little mysteries that they share.

During the DL-TA, Lisa avoids making judgments about students' predictions, so students learn that it is acceptable to make predictions that may be inaccurate. In addition, they learn that, by making predictions, even incorrect ones, they are more likely to get involved in the action and understand the story. Moreover, they learn that good readers may make inaccurate predictions but that they improve as the story progresses. Finally, the children have fun making predictions with stories, as active, rather than passive, involvement engages them in story comprehension and in predicting and monitoring for their understanding while reading. DL-TA has the added advantage of being a strategy that can be used with younger and older students and with beginning and intermediate English learners. Moreover, it can be used with both narrative and expository texts, using the same basic procedures illustrated in Lisa's lesson.

Readers' Theater

Many teachers like to use readers' theater in their classrooms to assist students in responding to literature. Readers' theater is an excellent activity for beginning second language readers and intermediate readers (Busching, 1981; Sloyer, 1982). Beginning readers read and dramatize a script from a story they have read. Intermediate readers, as we describe later, create their own scripts to read and dramatize. For beginning English learners, select stories that have several characters so that more students can participate. In addition, the stories should be somewhat brief and have a simple structure with a clear beginning, middle, and end. Many folktales are excellent for introducing readers' theater because they meet all of these requirements. For example, a story such as *Cinderella* has clear examples of character roles and requires several different parts. In addition, it has a clear beginning, middle, and end, with the slipper fitting only Cinderella's foot. A side benefit of "Cinderella," and other fairy tales or folktales, is that variations exist among different cultures. This allows students to act out and understand different Cinderella stories. Some teachers like to use story maps or Venn diagrams (described in Chapter 10) to assist students in determining the variations in different versions of a folktale.

Once an appropriate story has been selected, you may make performance suggestions to improve diction, dramatization, and expression. Because students have had a chance to rehearse and because they read from a script, they are able to read well during the performance. A good starter story for readers' theater is *Why Mosquitoes Buzz in People's Ears* (Aardema, 1975). The rhythm and rhyme of this delightful cumulative African tale are compelling, and the moral speaks to us all. Your students might want to create masks for the various animal parts in the story before they perform the script.

Partial Readers' Theater Script for *Why Mosquitoes Buzz in People's Ears*

NARRATOR: One morning a mosquito saw an iguana at a waterhole.
MOSQUITO: Iguana, you will never believe what I saw yesterday.
IGUANA: Try me.
MOSQUITO: I saw a farmer digging yams that are almost as big as I am.

Once students have been introduced to the idea of readers' theater, they can act out other scripts of favorite folktales or other stories. Let them select from the many stories that they have heard in your class or from a book or movie they know.

One third-grade class, after consulting with their teacher on their script, performed the story of *The Three Little Pigs* in front of the class. Later, the teacher told them that there was a book that presented the wolf's side of the story, *The True Story of the Three Little Pigs by A. Wolf* (Scieszka, 1989), and that maybe

Someone	Wants	But	So

FIGURE 8.6

STORY MAP SKELETON

they would like to read that script. When they read the story, they were excited and presented it to the class.

When students do readers' theater, they have to analyze and comprehend the story at a deep level to present it again to the class, and they have to share their understanding with others. They also have to determine the tone of voice for the various characters and orchestrate their reading performance into a coherent dramatic production. In short, they have to respond to the story, accept various interpretations from their peers, and offer an effective presentation to the class. Readers' theater gives power over story interpretation to students. Later, as these beginning-level students become intermediate-level students, they will write their own scripts from favorite stories.

Story Mapping

Story mapping is an example of a scaffold because it helps students use story grammar or the basic structure of a story for comprehending and composing stories. For example, many stories have a basic skeletal structure consisting of a major character or two, a goal the character wishes to achieve, an obstacle that makes it difficult to achieve the goal, and a resolution of the conflict between the goal and the obstacle. In the words of novelist John Gardner, "In nearly all good fiction, the basic—all but inescapable—plot form is this: A central character wants something, goes after it despite opposition (perhaps including his own doubts), and so arrives at a win, lose or draw" (Gardner, 1983). The simple story map in Figure 8.6, which is based on this skeletal structure, provides a four-part sequence for students to fill in (Boyle & Peregoy, 1990; Schmidt, n.d.).

Using the story map, one group of five second-grade English language development (ELD) learners produced several story maps after their teacher read "The Three Little Pigs" to them. The children's responses are reproduced in Figure 8.7. Because this was the children's first experience with story mapping, the teacher involved the whole group in creating the maps together. In the process, the children first chose the Big Bad Wolf as the character to map, producing "The Big Bad Wolf wanted to eat the pigs, but they boiled him in hot water, so the pigs lived happily ever after."

Someone	Wants	But	So
the wolf	wants to eat the pigs	but they boil the wolf in water	so the pigs live happily ever after
the pigs	want strong houses to be safe from the wolf	but the wolf blows all but one house down	so the pigs boil him in water and live happily ever after

FIGURE 8.7

SECOND-GRADE ENGLISH LEARNERS' MAP OF *THE THREE LITTLE PIGS*

Another version produced by the group resulted in "The three little pigs wanted to build strong houses to be safe from the wolf, but the wolf blew the houses down, so they boiled the wolf in hot water." Through the process of mapping the story, the children were able to focus on the different perspectives of the wolf and the three little pigs. By the time they created the second map, they had arrived at the type of analysis for which the story map aims.

Students may use the simple story map to focus their attention on important parts of a story. When they use story mapping, it soon becomes evident to students that stories have several characters whose goals often conflict, leading to interest and intrigue as the plot develops. Even a story as simple as *The Three Little Pigs* can be mapped in a variety of ways following the story map model. By sharing and discussing their maps, children deepen their story comprehension and gain awareness of how stories are structured, which assists them with subsequent reading and writing. Once introduced, story maps help English learners not only to understand and to remember key elements of a story but also to create an outline for writing their own stories.

Finally, the story maps provide a starting point for students to share their individual responses to the values and events they perceive in their transactions with the text (Rosenblatt, 1978, 1983, 1984). Through these transactions, English language learners can discuss various views and experiences presented in a story. Ultimately, these responses lie at the heart of literature study, and the maps provide a scaffolding for student explorations and transactions with stories. A different kind of story map was used by Lianna for the story *Bedtime for Frances* (Hoban, 1960) and is shown in Figure 8.8.

FIGURE 8.8

Lianna's Map Based on *Bedtime for Frances*

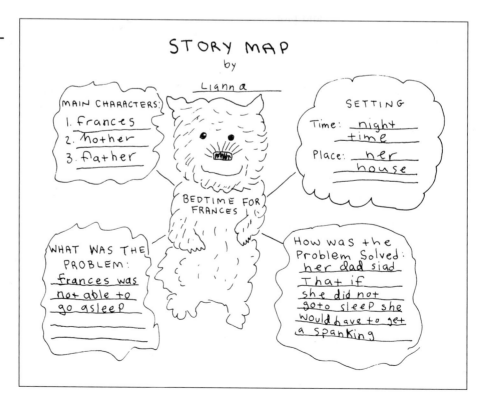

Intermediate Readers: Characteristics and Strategies

Intermediate second language readers will come to you with a rather large sight vocabulary and the ability to comprehend various kinds of texts, such as stories, letters, and some news and magazine articles. Generally, they are apt to speak English well enough to negotiate meanings orally with their peers during literature response groups. They have a fair amount of automaticity in their reading so that they also are able to read with a degree of fluency. They read extended texts but have some difficulty dealing with texts that contain new vocabulary. They will generally need less assistance than beginning-level students and less contextualization of lessons with visuals and other scaffolds. Nevertheless, you will want to provide them with the strategies used with beginning readers in addition to the new ones presented in this section.

Cognitive Mapping

Similar to a story map or a life map, a **cognitive map** is a graphic drawing summarizing a text. Intermediate-level readers can use maps to assist them with comprehending and remembering what they have read, and they can use mapping as a prewriting strategy to generate a plan for their compositions (Boyle & Buckley, 1983; Boyle & Peregoy, 1991; Buckley & Boyle, 1981; Hanf, 1971; Ruddell & Boyle, 1989).

Whereas story maps assist students by scaffolding comprehension and memory of a simple story, such as a folktale, cognitive maps assist them with comprehension and memory of more complex stories containing many characters, settings, and plots. To introduce cognitive mapping for narrative texts, we suggest you follow procedures similar to those you used to introduce mapping as a prewriting strategy. Another good way is to draw a map on the chalkboard or use a mobilelike map, such as the one in Figure 8.9 showing the characters, setting, and plot. Once students have a clear understanding of the categories, you can ask them to generate information from a story they have read to be placed on the map, or you may choose a story with which all the students are familiar to introduce mapping for the first time.

After practicing group mapping, students can begin to create individual maps to summarize information from their reading. The map shown in Figure 8.10 was developed by a fifth grader on the folktale "Beauty and the Beast." Many teachers use maps as a part of their individual reading programs. Because maps help students organize and remember stories, they prepare them to share in their literature response groups.

FIGURE 8.9 • MOBILE MAP ILLUSTRATING STORY PARTS

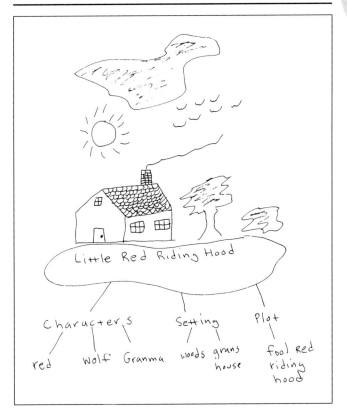

FIGURE 8.10

MAP STUDENT CREATED
AFTER READING "BEAUTY
AND THE BEAST"

310

You will notice that the map in Figure 8.10 differs from the prototype used to introduce the concept to students. That is because students quickly move away from the prototype after they have a clear understanding of what the process is about. They make maps with concentric circles, triangles, ladders, and different artistic shapes to illustrate concepts in their stories. Because mapping is easily learned and easily shared, and because it is visual and spatial, second language teachers and their students find it a particularly useful strategy (Northcutt & Watson, 1986).

Directed Reading-Thinking Activity (DR-TA)

Directed Reading-Thinking Activity (DR-TA) is carried out in the same manner as the DL-TA (Stauffer, 1975). The only difference is that students read the text themselves silently after having made predictions during oral discussion. The activity is actually directed by the teacher, who invites predictions and confirmations on one portion of text at a time and then tells students how many paragraphs to read to find out whether their predictions are correct. This activity provides support at the beginning of a story to help readers get into the text. It also provides students with a model of active questioning during reading. Soon readers carry out the prediction process without teacher participation.

Leticia Palomino models DR-TA using the overhead projector and an index card to cover parts of a story. Uncovering the first paragraph, she asks students to read and predict what they think will happen next. She starts with simple stories, such as "The Magician's Apprentice," and teaches students to ask questions beginning with *who*, *what*, *when*, *where*, *why*, and *how*. *Who* are the characters in the story? *What* happens in the story? *What* are the problems faced by the characters? *When* does the story take place? *Where* does it take place? *Why* did the boy want to be a magician? *How* will the problems be resolved? *What* will happen next? The following is a partial script of Ms. Palomino's students working with "The Magician's Apprentice." First read the part of the story that we have transcribed (Boyle, 1990) and then note the approach she uses to introduce the DR-TA strategy to her students.

The Magician's Apprentice

Once upon a time there was a boy named Julio who wanted to be a magician. He read about magicians and watched magicians on television and bought magic tricks. When he became a magician, there was one trick he wanted to perform. He wanted to make a tiger disappear. One day a circus came to the boy's town. The great Magica the magician was with the circus. Magica was especially known for one trick. She could make a tiger disappear right in front of the audience.

The boy could not wait to go to the circus. That night he had a dream. He dreamed that the magician would teach him the tiger trick. The next day he was very nervous about going to the circus.

Ms. Palomino began by reading the title and asking the students what they thought would happen in the story.

STUDENTS: Magic tricks! Juggling! Balls in air! Disappearing things! Rabbits get lost!

TEACHER: Do you know what an apprentice is? [*The students stared at one another and waited for the teacher.*] That's what they call somebody who helps a person who is very good at what they do. Somebody who has experience. Like a good plumber might have a helper or a carpenter has a helper. Helpers are people who are learning to do something, and they are called an apprentice. So what do you think a story about a magician's apprentice will be about?

STUDENTS: 'Bout man helps magicians? About people helping magicians.

TEACHER: I'm going to read parts of the story and ask you questions. When I do, you guess about what you think will happen next in the story. OK? [*She begins reading after the students nod their understanding. She uncovers only the sections of the story she is reading.*]

TEACHER: Once upon a time there was a boy named Julio who wanted to be a magician.
Class, what do you think will happen to Julio in this story?

STUDENTS: Helps a magician. Rabbits disappear.

TEACHER: He read about magicians and watched magicians on the television and bought magician tricks. When he became a magician, he thought, there was one trick he wanted to perform.
What trick do you think Julio will do?

STUDENTS: Elephant disappear! Ball floats. Card tricks.

311

TEACHER: He wanted to make a tiger disappear. One day a circus came to the boy's town.
What do you think Julio will do when the circus comes to town?

STUDENTS: He'll go to the circus. He'll ride on a elephant. He'll see motorcycle riders. A magician.
Other students seem to agree with the magician idea.

TEACHER: The great Magica the magician was with the circus. Magica was especially known for one trick.
What trick do you think Magica was known for?

STUDENTS: Tricks. Tigers disappear. Tigers disappear!

TEACHER: She could make a tiger disappear right in front of the audience. [*Students laugh.*] The boy could not wait to go to the circus. That night he had a dream.
What did Julio dream, class?

STUDENTS: About the circus. About the magician. About tiger tricks.

TEACHER: He dreamed that the magician would teach him the tiger trick. The next day he was very nervous about going to the circus.

Ms. Palomino continued to read the story, and the students' guesses became more enthusiastic and more accurate. Notice that she did not correct students if they predicted incorrectly. In fact, she encouraged all guesses and made a point of showing them that it really is not as important to guess correctly as it is to make plausible predictions and to check them against the text as new information appears. In this way, students gain experience in predicting and monitoring their comprehension as more mature readers do. After some practice with the DR-TA strategy, Ms. Palomino reminds the students to make predictions in their independent and group reading activities. She starts their independent reading with stories that are amenable to making predictions and monitoring comprehension and then moves them to more difficult texts, in which it may be a little more difficult to make predictions but even more important to do so. In her 20 years of teaching lower and upper grades, Ms. Palomino has used DR-TA with short stories, children's stories, and history texts using the same basic procedures.

Literature Response Journals

Literature response journals are personal notebooks in which students write informal comments about the stories they are reading, including their feelings and reactions to characters, setting, plot, and other aspects of the story; they are an outgrowth of learning logs and other journals (Atwell, 1984). You may wish to let students decide how often they will write in their journals, or you might set a schedule for them. The choice really depends on the purpose. For example, if several students are getting ready for a literature response group, you might suggest that students comment at the end of each chapter and finish the book by a certain date. On the other hand, if the response journal is based on voluntary, free reading, you may wish to leave the choice entirely up to the student. As a middle road, you might want to give students some general guidelines, such as suggesting that they respond once a week or after reading complete chapters.

To help students get started in their response journals, it is useful to provide sample questions they can consider while they are reading, such as: What do you like about the book or characters in the story? How do you feel about some of the decisions characters make in the book? Would you make different decisions? What do you think the main characters should do at a particular point in the story?

In other words, the questions you suggest to students should invite their personal reactions and responses to the experience of the story rather than aiming at literary analysis. That can come later. The purpose of the journal is to encourage dynamic, experiential, and authentic involvement with literature. The following example shows a few brief responses by Sammy, a third-grade intermediate-level reader, to a story he selected to read individually. Following Sammy's response is a high school student's response to *Romeo and Juliet* after seeing an excerpt of a film and reading and discussing the play in his group.

> The story about "The Japanese Fairy Tale" about a very ugly man of long long ago. He ugly becuss he give his pretty to the princess. He loveing her very much to do that. I wouldn't do that I don think so.
>
> Sammy

> The plays about two gans or families that wants to fight all the time. The boy and girl love each one and they don't want the family to fight at all. I dont think they will live very happy.
>
> Joseph

You or your other students may respond to the journals. Either way, be sure to respond to the intent, not the grammatical form. You might ask an occasional question about the literature or a character in the story or what might happen next. Or you might share a similar response to a piece of literature you have read. Whatever your comment, encourage the students in their search for meaning in the literature. To manage your own responding time, you might ask students to highlight sections to which they want you to respond. In this way, literature response journals may become interactive. Some questions you can give students to assist them with responding to the stories they are reading include the following. These questions may be used for journals, response groups, or independent reading.

1. What would you tell characters in the story to do if you could talk to them?
2. What was the most exciting or interesting part of the story for you?
3. Why do you think the author wrote the story?
4. If you wrote this story, what parts would you change?
5. Would you recommend the story to others? Why?
6. What way would you like to respond to the story? Mural, map, summary, etc.?

Developing Scripts for Readers' Theater

When English learners attain the intermediate level, they are ready to go beyond the readers' theater activities that asked them to read, interpret, and act out scripts provided for them. At this point, they can begin to develop and write scripts of their own, based on the stories they are reading. Developing their own scripts requires them to pick out the most important events in a story according to their own interpretations. In addition, they must identify the most important characters in a story and the conflicts and problems they face. Finally, students must interpret the resolution of these problems and think about the tone of characters' voices: Are they happy, sad, or indifferent? After these choices are made, students determine the dialogue that they will use for their script. You may want

Literature response logs help students focus on their own personal reactions to characters, plot, setting, and other aspects of a particular piece of literature.

314

to have them create maps of the stories before they develop their scripts; the maps will help them make decisions about major events and the dialogue that goes with them. To create scripts, students must know a great deal about story structure. Thus, readers' theater at the intermediate level requires substantial sophistication.

Students must be sophisticated in their understanding of character motivation and conflict, and they must be able to show this sophistication in the scripts they write. They must have sophistication concerning the conflicts characters face and interpret these conflicts for their script. Finally, they need to understand the resolution of the story, its meaning and ramifications for various characters, and they must portray this in their script. Developing a readers' theater script provides students with a purposeful and meaningful activity for interpreting stories and involves them in activities that will enhance their comprehension of stories. Because they must negotiate meaning when developing scripts and because they act out the dramatic script, second language intermediate readers benefit from readers' theater, an activity that integrates oral and written language with a dramatic flair.

Adapting Stories into Plays and Scripts for Film and Videotape

Another way you can involve students in meaningful and motivational reading and writing activities is to have them adapt stories into scripts for making animated films or for interpreting stories from television. Animated films require students to develop a story first and then create a storyboard for the film. Storyboards are cartoon strips created by animators to portray the sequence of events both visually and with dialogue. Once they have developed the story, they create a storyboard for the film. Once students have developed the storyboard, they are ready to create cutout or clay characters to be moved on backgrounds for the animated effect. They then make the film, adding dialogue and music to the finished piece of animation. Just as readers' theater requires students to interpret stories at a sophisticated level and provides different channels for assisting students with negotiating meaning and developing scripts, so also the animated storyboard and film provide built-in sheltering to communication.

Using Computers and CD-ROMs to Enhance Learning

If you have computers available for your students, there are programs coming out every day that can assist your English language learners. Some animated programs tell colorfully illustrated stories in both English and another language. In addition, some programs highlight words as they say them. Thus, your students gain access to stories through visual and verbal information. Other programs allow your students to develop and animate their own stories and help students to work together in collaborative groups to develop stories that can be played back by anyone in the class. Many computer stores sell CD-ROMS that contain samples of the stories so that you can preview them in your home. You can also purchase sample programs inexpensively or read reviews in magazines such as *MacWorld*, which offers "free" CD-ROMs containing parts of programs and games you can preview. We recommend that you try these programs before purchasing any at your school. You may also ask students to preview programs to help you develop your own school library for different grade and developmental levels.

315

Assessing Second Language Readers' Progress

Assessing second language reading progress is an ongoing process requiring a variety of information sources. Daily observations while students read in class provide one important source. The advantage of in-class observations is that they focus on students' reading in natural, routine situations involving authentic literacy tasks. These informal assessments will tell you much more than a myriad of standardized tests. Nothing takes the place of a perceptive and observant teacher who knows students and watches for their progress throughout the year. To augment your observations, you may wish to use individual assessment procedures from time to time to document student progress or to understand better a student experiencing reading problems. We describe several individual assessment procedures you can use, including miscue analysis and running records. In Chapter 11, we offer in-depth discussion of individual reading inventories, an analytic procedure for assessing student reading strengths and instructional needs. Here we focus on day-to-day classroom observations and interactions with students as they negotiate meaning through print. A teacher who recognizes and responds to the teachable moment easily takes the place of all the standardized tests and reading labs in the entire school district.

Assessing With Materials Students Bring to Class

One excellent and valid way to assess students' reading abilities is to ask them to bring something to the class to read. This casual approach to assessment is non-intimidating and affords you an opportunity to see what students select. Moreover, from this approach you might discover whether students have anything to read at home or whether they read at all outside of the school environment.

When using this approach, make sure the students understand that they can bring anything they want to school: a TV guide, a record label, a comic book, a magazine, or anything else. When they have brought in their selection, ask them to read it aloud. As they do so, evaluate their performance with their self-selected materials in comparison with materials you've heard them read in class. If the students do quite well with self-selected materials and poorly with school materials, you can begin to select materials more appropriate to their interests and level of reading efficiency. If they do poorly with self-selected materials, you will have a better idea of their proficiency and of how you can assist them with becoming better readers. Be careful not to make judgments too quickly when assessing students, however. Assess them with various materials from school and from home, and assess them informally each day to gain as much knowledge as possible before you draw conclusions about their reading abilities.

Informal Assessment

Informal assessment procedures may be used with individual students to evaluate their reading. They differ from most standardized tests in that they are individually administered to evaluate performance on specific reading tasks. If administered periodically during the year, they establish a profile of progress. We feel strongly that the informal assessment procedures presented here and in Chapter 11 are the ones that will help you to determine how your students are doing. As already noted, we suggest that the best informal procedure for assessing students' reading and writing is to watch English learners as they approach various reading, writing, and oral language tasks and accomplish authentic reading activities throughout the day. The informal procedures presented in the following sections, therefore, represent strategies for assessment to augment your daily informal assessment in the classroom.

Miscue Analysis

Miscue analysis is a reading assessment tool that focuses on the reader's **miscues**, or variations from print made during oral reading (Goodman, 1973; Goodman & Burke, 1972). Rather than carrying the onus of a terrible mistake, miscues provide a valuable source of information about how the reader is processing print. Some kinds of miscues actually indicate good comprehension. By analyzing a reader's miscues or deviations from text, it is possible to evaluate strengths and weaknesses and thereby determine what kind of instructional assistance might be appropriate. By studying the kinds of deviations a reader tends to make, you can infer which reading strategies children use and which ones should be taught to help them improve. Because miscue analysis is based on oral reading, teachers need to separate oral pronunciation style or errors from reading errors. Although the miscue analysis reveals the process of comprehending, a measure of overall comprehension of the text is also needed. This is accomplished by asking the reader for a summary, an oral retelling, of what was read.

Miscue Procedure*

1. Select a student whose reading you wish to assess. Then choose a reading selection somewhat more difficult than what the reader usually deals with easily in class. The selection should be about 500 words in length and should be a meaningfully complete piece. Use your own judgment if you think the selection should be shorter.

2. Gather and prepare materials for tape recording the oral reading:

   (a) a copy of the reading selection for the student (original or copy)

   (b) a tape recorder and blank tape

   (c) a copy of the selection for you to write on (triple spaced)

   (d) notes on the selection that you will use to probe the student's spontaneous retelling of the piece (i.e., what you think are important parts to remember in terms of characters, plot, theme, setting)

3. Find a quiet place to record the session. Start by telling the students that you are going to tape record their oral reading to help you learn more about how students in their class read.

4. Turn the machine on "record" and ask the student to read the passage out loud all the way through. Tell the student: "Here is something I want you to read for me out loud. I can't help you read it, though, so if you come to a word you don't know, try to figure it out and then read on. When you have finished reading, I will ask you to tell me all you can remember about what you have read." After the reading is finished, ask the student to tell you all he or she can remember. Then follow up with questions as needed to see if the student can retell all the parts you consider important.

5. At the end, let the reader listen to his or her voice just for fun.

6. Later, listen to the tape to analyze the miscues.

The coding system in Figure 8.11 defines and illustrates how to mark miscues students may make while being informally assessed.

An example of one reader's oral reading and miscues is shown in Figure 8.12. Juanita was asked to read a passage and the questions following it. The passage (Karlsen, Madden, & Gardner, 1976) is marked according to the information in Figure 8.11.

After reading and answering the questions, Juanita retold the story. What can we learn from her reading and retelling? How can the miscue analysis combined with comprehension questions assist you in determining a reading program for Juanita? Let's analyze Juanita's performance and make some decisions for assisting her.

Interpreting Miscues

Juanita had trouble pronouncing the name Barbara, but this didn't impede understanding. She knew she was reading a girl's name. She pronounces *lived* in a

---

*Based on Y. M. Goodman and C. L. Burke, *Reading Miscue Inventory Manual: Procedure for Diagnosis and Evaluation* (New York: Macmillan, 1972).

FIGURE 8.11

MARKING MISCUES

1. **Insertion:** The child inserts a word not in the text; place a caret where the insertion is made and write the inserted word above it.

   also
   Example: The cat was ᵛin the kitchen.

2. **Omission:** The child leaves a word out; circle the word the child omits.

   Example: Many people find it ⟨difficult⟩ to concentrate.

3. **Substitution:** Child replaces one word with another; place the child's substitution over the replaced word.

   dog
   Example: The doll was in the little girl's room.

4. **Word Supplied by Tester:** Child can't get word and tester supplies it; put supplied word in parentheses.

   (school)
   Example: Joe ran to school.

5. **Word Missed then Corrected by Reader:** Child says word wrong then immediately corrects it; place missed word above word and place a check by it.

   rat ✓
   Example: The cat is sleeping.

nonstandard way, but this mispronunciation was not a problem because she understood the meaning. Again, the miscue is not one that stands in the way of meaning. The same is true of her pronunciation of *loved*; when she was asked what that meant, she answered: "It mean she like baseball." For Juanita baseball and softball are the same thing. Juanita also pronounces the Spanish word *chocolate (cho-coh-lah-tay)* for *chocolate*; clearly she is understanding the passage. When we get to the last sentence, however, we find that she has trouble with words that do impede comprehension. She says *grace* for *grass* and *lunched* for *laughed*. In the retelling, it becomes clear that at that point she is confused. Nevertheless, even the miscue of *lunched* for *laughed* indicates a degree of comprehension up to this point. She matches the word *laughed* with a word, *lunched*, that matches *laughed* syntactically and is contextually appropriate given the previous information concerning lunch.

Based on this analysis, we can see that Juanita has many strengths as a reader. First, she reads for meaning and tries to make sense of the passage. Second, she is able to pronounce most of the words according to her oral language equivalents. She misses a few words in the text, but, with further reading, will probably learn these with teacher guidance. Through the miscue analysis, we are able to gain a

FIGURE 8.12

MISCUE ANALYSIS PASSAGE

Bar-bar-Barbára lee-ved   lov-éd
Barbara lived in a big city. She loved to play softball in the park on Saturday morning. Every
                                        cho-coh-lah-tay
Saturday for lunch, she'd buy a hot dog and chocolate milk. One day, Barbara asked her father
                                        grace   *lunched*
how chocolate milk was made. "The cows eat chocolate grass," her father said. Barbara laughed
              Reet
and said, "Right!"

great deal of information about Juanita, information that will help us determine whether she needs special assistance, whether she is reading for meaning or just for pronunciation, and whether we need to intervene in her progress as a reader.

In contrast to Juanita, who reads for meaning, you might find a student who pronounces every word perfectly but does not comprehend the passage well—a student who seems to be "barking at print." Miscue analysis is a powerful tool for you to use with students to identify strategies and patterns in their reading behavior as a basis for developing an appropriate program for reading.

Now let's take a look at a younger reader with more difficulties, Candy. Candy's teacher, Chris Belmont, told us that Candy was not understanding what she was reading and was having difficulty pronouncing words correctly. He asked us to evaluate her reading and to develop a plan for helping her become a more proficient reader. She had transferred from a nearby school district to his fifth-grade English language development class after being in the United States for three years. She had attended first grade and part of second grade in Guanajuato, Mexico, before coming to the United States. In the process of immigration, Candy missed out on several months of her second-grade year. Consequently, on arrival in this country, she was placed in a second-grade class, one in which English was the primary language of instruction. By the fifth grade, when we met her, her oral English was fluent, she got along well with the other students, and she was eager to become a good reader. In fact, she could read second- and third-grade-level books in English quite easily, and she enjoyed reading poems in the reading textbook series selected by the district, though she had done little writing yet.

Two aspects of Candy's language and literacy profile suggested that English reading instruction was an appropriate choice for her at this point in her schooling. First of all, her English proficiency was at the intermediate level, phase III, based on her teacher's student oral language observation matrix (SOLOM). Second, her English reading abilities were already established, though not yet commensurate with her grade level. In other words, she was able to read simple, connected discourse in English but had trouble with longer, more complex pieces. For beginning English learners who are not yet literate in any language, we usually recommend literacy instruction in the primary language if possible. For Candy, we did not consider primary language literacy instruction to be necessary at this point. Nevertheless, we wondered if her present reading difficulties might have been avoided if she had enjoyed the benefit of full primary language literacy instruction previously in her schooling.

With this background information in hand, we met with Candy, a charming, enthusiastic young girl, who was eager to hear what we would say about her reading. She told us that she had learned a lot from Mr. Belmont, and she wanted to become the best reader in the class. She told us that she had trouble with long words. Clearly, Candy was an articulate, thoughtful, and reflective student with strong expressive abilities in English. We began by asking Candy to read a second-grade passage. She read the passage with several miscues but was able to summarize what she read quite well. Next, we skipped to a more difficult text based on a traditional Mexican story about our Lady of Guadalupe. We taped Candy's reading of the text but chose not to mark her errors on the spot because we did not want her to feel self-conscious. When she completed the text, we asked her to retell the story, but she insisted that she did not remember any of it. However, when we asked her questions about the passage, she was able to remember the main characters and essential parts of the plot. However, her understanding of the passage was

FIGURE 8.13 • CANDY'S MISCUES ON THE GUADALUPE PASSAGE

Long ago in Mexico, there lived an Indian farmer named Juan *[John]*

Diego. Juan Diego went to Mass every Sunday at the Spanish mission. *[misión]*

Then one day, something happened that would change the entire *[en the]* *[cage]*

history of Mexico. *[story]*

On December 9, 1531, Juan Diego rose at dawn to go to church. *[down]*

He put on his best white pants and shirt, covered himself with his *[wit]*

blanket, and began the long walk to the mission. He followed the rocky *[and]* *[misión]*

dirt road over the dry desert hills. When Juan Diego got to the hill *[dree]*

named Tepeyac, he heard a beautiful song coming from the sky. On the *[on]* *[skee]*

hilltop, Juan Diego saw a large white cloud with gold light shining from *[shine]*

it. Juan Diego stopped and looked. Suddenly a lovely voice spoke: *[sop]* *[apok]*

"Juan Diego! Juan Diego!"

Before him stood a beautiful lady dressed in a blue satin robe that *[sashen]*

was covered with a thousand glimmering stars. Her skin was smooth *[tousan]*

and brown, and her long black hair was crowned with a shimmering *[aroun]*

halo.

sketchy. She told us she had not heard this story before, but she had seen a picture of Our Lady of Guadalupe on the calendar at home. Thus prior story knowledge did not assist her in her reading. We thanked her for coming and told her we would be back to see her the following week.

We then proceeded to evaluate her oral reading (Figure 8.13). Overall, we saw that Candy usually used her intermediate-level English language knowledge and reading skill to make sense of the text. She knows that the story is in English, so she reads John instead of Juan in the first line but corrects to Juan the second time the name appears. She also uses the Spanish cognate *misión* for *mission*. Neither miscue creates any comprehension problem. When examining miscues, it is most helpful to look for **persistent miscue patterns**. If a student makes the same kind of miscue repeatedly, the pattern often provides a direction for instruction. One pattern we see in Candy's oral reading is that she omits almost all *-ed* endings of words. She also has problems with **digraphs**, in which two letters stand for one sound, such as *th-* in *thousand* or *sh-* in *shining*. She seems to have difficulty with words beginning with a **blend**, in which two letters stand for two blended sounds, such as *bl-* in *blanket*, *sp-* in *spoke*, and *st-* in *stopped*. She even has trouble with *from*, which should be in her sight word vocabulary by now. When she comes to words with initial blends, she seems to lose the flow of meaning.

After identifying these miscue patterns, we needed to determine whether these types of miscues were preventing Candy from understanding the text. In other words, do these miscues make a difference in meaning? The unpronounced *-ed* ending does not appear to impede comprehension and reflects her present oral pronunciation. The same is true for her digraph errors, such as *tousand* for *thousand*, and *dey* for *they*. We therefore did not choose to address these miscue patterns in our suggested instructional plan. On the other hand, her consistent trouble with initial blends in words, such as *blanket*, *stopped*, and *spoke*, suggests some instruction on this element might help. Comprehension is an issue, indicated both by her difficulty in retelling the story and by the teacher's comments. Thus, we also wanted to build a strong focus on meaning, both within sentences and throughout the story. We explained our analysis to the teacher, reminding him that English learner pronunciation differences per se should not be considered a reading problem with either beginning or intermediate learners. Only miscues that impede meaning should be cause for concern. We then shared the following instructional recommendations:

1. Candy needs wide self-selected reading of materials at her current reading level and just a bit beyond.

Candy should read many trade books at about a third-grade level and some that are a little more difficult. We suggested three ways to promote successful comprehension and enjoyment of these stories: buddy reading, keeping a literature log with story map, and opportunities to talk about books informally with her peers and her teacher. Buddy reading motivates students to keep reading and provides assistance from the reading partner. By keeping a literature log and story map, Candy will have two scaffolds for understanding and remembering the story so that she will be confident in sharing it with others. The teacher may wish to create a set of important questions about plot and characters to guide the comprehension of some of these books to be addressed in the literature log.

2. Candy needs to be reminded to monitor her own reading. Does the text make sense? If not, she should reread the text to see if another way of reading will make sense.

3. Specific skill instruction is recommended on blends, one of the miscue patterns that seemed to make a difference in Candy's comprehension.

4. Because Candy had a similar problem with the words *dry* and *sky*, it should simply be pointed out to her that these words rhyme and are pronounced with a long *i* sound.

With these recommendations in mind, we decided to begin our next session with Candy by asking her about the words that gave her problems, and found that it was easy for her to take the Guadalupe passage and tell us. We began our subsequent sessions by inviting Candy to bring favorite books to read to us. We also arranged with the teacher to begin a buddy reading program for her in class. She read short books and favorite parts of longer books. As she read to us, we emphasized that what she read should make sense to her. If it didn't, then she should reread to see if reading some words differently made better sense. We then told her we would give her some strategies to help her read words accurately so that they would make sense. We began with work on blends, based on our hypothesis that these were creating problems for her. We gave her a series of cards containing blends, such as *bl*, *fl*, and *cl*, and asked her to pair them up with other parts of words. Figure 8.14 illustrates the game.

First, we made sure that Candy knew how to sound out the blends, and then we gave her a few examples of how the game worked. We did this by moving a blend such as *bl* next to the rest of a word such as ue, and then we pronounced the word we made, *blue*. Next we asked Candy to play the game, and we pronounced the words with her until she felt comfortable pronouncing the words on her own. Candy's performance

FIGURE 8.14 • BLENDING GAME

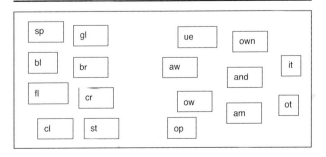

supported our belief that she knew the meanings of these words and was a fast learner. We next moved from blends to digraph games and finally mixed the blend and digraph games together. Even though her digraph miscues did not indicate a need for instruction, we wanted to make sure she distinguished digraphs and blends, which she did easily. She found the games fun and was happy to see how easy it was for her to learn something that helped her become a better reader. Next, we offered her a selection of books to read that used many of the blends she had practiced. Finally, we asked her to read the Guadalupe passage again, first reminding her that many of the blends and digraphs would be found in the passage. In reading the passage over again, she got 90 percent of the blends right and was able to give us a brief, but correct, summary of the passage.

We worked with Candy for three weeks and saw immediate improvement. However, continued growth in reading comprehension would require the teacher to implement our recommendations in the coming months, specifically by providing wide reading with opportunities to summarize and talk about her reading. Nonetheless, by asking Candy to slow down and make sure she saw all of the words, by teaching her about blends and digraphs, and by providing her with opportunities to read with a buddy, keep a literature log, and talk about stories with others, we were able to start Candy toward success. With practice and continued evaluation of Candy's reading, we are certain she will become a proficient reader.

As a fifth grader, Candy will need to read expository material for information efficiently. This kind of reading must be addressed by the teacher for all his students, and we provide strategies for such reading instruction in Chapters 9 and 10. We wanted to base Candy's reading improvement program on stories at this point because she enjoys them immensely and can practice reading longer pieces in this favorite genre of hers.

Not every reader is as easy to work with as Candy. Many do not learn as readily as she did, many take much more evaluation, and many do not have Candy's cheerful attitude and motivation. But generally in our 25 years of working with English learners who are having problems, we follow a similar pattern. We spend time asking the students about their reading and try to find out what we can about their reading background and instruction. Then we give them passages to read, summarize, and answer questions about to probe their level of comprehension. We next look at the miscues they have made to see if they interfere with their comprehension; if they do, we try to set up a program to assist them. Most of the time we try to work with student strengths to assist them. Candy's love of stories and her ability to learn quickly from explicit instruction were major strengths. Finally, if students are progressing well, we continue with the program we've designed. But more frequently, we try many different things before we are able to find the key to each student's learning. We always have resource books on reading that assist us in determining other strategies we might try if a child is not succeeding. (See additional readings at the end of this chapter.)

Informal Reading Inventories (IRIs)

An informal reading inventory consists of graded passages with comprehension questions. When you use passages from the inventory or if you use graded passages you have devised, you tape students as they read the passages aloud and then ask the students to answer the comprehension questions. The comprehension questions, usually both factual and interpretive questions, give you a good sense of what the student does with texts of varying difficulty. Some teachers also like to ask students to summarize the information to help them get a fuller picture of the student's reading abilities. When they do this, they prepare an outline of the major points in the text they expect students to retell.

When the student has completed the passages, you can listen to the tape and evaluate how the student has performed. You can make the comprehension check or summary check and then do a miscue analysis of the student's performance. In this way, if the student is having some comprehension problems, you can see if there are patterns of miscues that might explain the comprehension difficulty. You can also look for general patterns of miscues to see what the student's strategies for reading are. Usually you'll want to begin with a passage that is relatively easy for your student and then have the student read increasingly difficult passages. But only have students read two or three short passages at a time or they may tire. In this way, you can get data on the relative reading level of your students and on what assistance they may need—for example, in determining main ideas—to move up to the next level of reading. You can then develop a plan for your students to help them with becoming more competent readers. Informal reading inventories take some time, but they are well worth it for the data you will get on your students' reading capabilities. We provide further discussion of informal reading inventories in Chapter 11.

Running Records

A running record is a shorthand transcription of a child's oral reading of a text, taken "on the spot," while the child is reading. Running records allow a teacher to evaluate student progress on a day-to-day basis without using copies of the text the student is reading. Instead, the teacher stands behind the reader and marks words the student gets right with checks and takes notes similar to miscue notes to code a reader's deviations from the text.

According to Clay (1979, 1989), teachers use running records to guide instructional decisions about the following:

1. the evaluation of text difficulty
2. the grouping of students
3. the acceleration of a student
4. monitoring progress of readers
5. allowing different readers to move through different books at different speeds and yet keeping track of (and records of) individual progress
6. observing particular difficulties in particular students

Procedures for Running Records

Clay (1989) suggests that you can begin using running records effectively after about two hours of training. You will get better at it with practice and begin noticing more and more about students' reading behaviors. Clay also suggests that it's better to use regular graded books from the program you use; if this isn't possible, you can use graded sets of paragraphs that are available in informal reading inventories discussed in Chapter 11. Teachers normally use passages

FIGURE 8.15 • SOME GUIDELINES USED FOR RECORDING RUNNING RECORDS

1. Check each word that is read correctly. In the example below there are five checks because all words were read correctly.

   Joe went to the store. ✓ ✓ ✓ ✓ ✓

2. When a student gives an incorrect response, place the original text under it.

   Student: sale
   Text: store

3. If a student tries to read a word several times, record all the attempts.

   Student: stare | st- | story
   Text: store

4. If a student makes an error and then **successfully corrects** it, write **SC**.

   Student: stare | st- | story | ("store") **SC**
   Text: store

5. When the student gives no response to a word, use a dash to record it. If a student inserts a word, the word is recorded over a dash. If a student can't proceed unless you give a word use a **T** to record that you **told** the word to the student.

   a. doesn't give response: Student: –
   b. inserts a word: Student: star
   c. student told word: Student: T

Source: Based on M. Clay, *The Early Detection of Reading Difficulties* (Auckland, New Zealand: Heinemann, 1979).

of about 100 to 200 words at different graded levels to see how students work with varying texts. Often teachers use running records with students' self-selected books. Based on Clay's work (1989), we present some of the conventions of running records in Figures 8.15 and 8.16.

Starting with the brief list of running record conventions, many teachers adapt ways that are more efficient for them. In fact, Marie Clay encourages teachers to adapt running records to their own needs and wishes. But with running records, we do not have the text to mark so we have to write quickly to keep notes. Nevertheless, with practice, teachers become comfortable using the procedure.

Strengths of Running Records

The biggest advantage running records have over other methods of evaluating students is that they give you the ability to evaluate your students' reading competencies during classroom instruction. With training and practice you can become used to the conventions of running records (or create your own conventions) to check your students' abilities regularly and without a great deal of time and effort. In addition, we recommend books such as Johns and Lenski's *Improving Reading* (1994) or other books that will give you a good idea of what to do with students who are having difficulties with word recognition, main idea recognition, or the like. Another excellent book you shouldn't be without is Ekwall's *Locating and Correcting Reading Difficulties* (1993). We have worked with reading difficulties among students at every grade level and would not be without these wonderful resource books. With them you will have expert advice at your fingertips that will assist you with assessing and helping your students.

Student Self-Assessment

Throughout our book we have emphasized placing students in charge of their own learning. For example, they are responsible for their own writing and work in writing response groups to shape their narratives. Similarly, they take charge of their reading literature in literature response groups. Moreover, we shall see in Chapter 9 how students set purposes and monitor their comprehension. This kind of self-assessment has often been a missing element in the past. Now, however, there are many writers and researchers who build student self-assessment into their programs (Heath & Mangiola, 1991; Yochum & Miller, 1990).

You may be surprised at how much information students, even young children, can give you about their own reading abilities. They are often able to tell you the kinds of words that give them difficulty or the kinds of reading they find frustrating. We believe in asking them regularly about their interactions with any text they are reading. There are several advantages to this approach. First, students often know more than you or any test will reveal about their reading; you only need to ask them. Second, asking students can save you the time of using any elaborate methods to discover their reading abilities. Finally, and perhaps most important, asking students about their own reading processes helps them become more aware of what they are doing and what strategies or procedures work for them under what circumstances. For example, they may discover that they can read narrative texts rather quickly but that they need to slow down with more complex expository text. They learn that speed of reading and choice of reading strategies must be adjusted according to the demands of the tasks. This metacognitive aspect of reading may be the best gift you can give them in their development as readers. We strongly recommend asking students first; by doing so, you place them in charge of their own advancement without abrogating your own responsibilities.

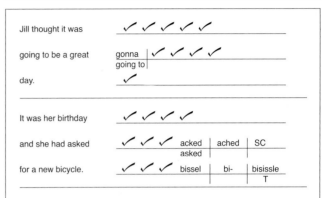

FIGURE 8.16 • A SAMPLE RUNNING RECORD

In the example above, Jody got all of the first line correct. In the second line she changed *going to* to *gonna*, which would be appropriate for her dialect. In the fourth line she got everything correct, but in the next she tried *asked* twice before she got it right and self-corrected (SC). Finally, she was unable to get *bicycle* and had to be told by the teacher (T).

325

Differentiating Reading and Literature Instruction

To match reading and literature instruction to student needs, it's necessary to consider each one's English reading and language development in relation to lesson standards, objectives, and performance expectations. In addition, knowledge of students' home languages, cultures, and interests will help you key into prior knowledge in relation to the literature. By considering these student traits, you will be able to choose appropriate literature selections and set up varied groupings for instruction. Your informal observations will help, as will more focused observations of a student's oral reading in which you take note of **miscues** and **overall comprehension**, as discussed previously in this chapter. Guided reading offers a particularly potent form of differentiated reading instruction because it incorporates ongoing assessment with on-the-spot opportunities for your scaffolding and direct instruction while students read for meaning. Chapter 11 offers additional details on guided reading and how it works hand-in-glove with ongoing assessment.

In addition to guided reading, differentiated instruction for reading and literature may take many other forms, such as shared reading with the whole class, buddy reading, and cooperative group work on a task (e.g., creating story maps or scripts). For each format, you need to consider whether to use homogeneous or heterogeneous grouping and how to plan for all students' active participation, keeping in mind their various strengths and limitations. It is especially important to plan for older learners who may be just beginning to read English. For example, suppose you have identified a novice English learner in your sixth-grade class as a beginning reader, with most of your students well on their way in English language and reading development. If you are introducing a story to the whole class using shared or choral reading, you need to supplement your usual instruction with pictures, gestures, and other cues to meaning for those newer to English. This type of preparation is important for all students, and **essential** for novice English learners and beginning readers, because it paves the way for understanding and responding to literature.

For your convenience, in this chapter and throughout the book, we have set up several features to help you differentiate instruction. First of all, because ongoing assessment is the cornerstone of differentiated instruction, we have described reading assessment tools to use before instruction for planning purposes, during instruction to refine instruction, and after instruction to evaluate student learning. To help you plan for varied student needs, we have grouped recommended teaching strategies into two broad categories of reading development: beginning and intermediate. Then at the end of the chapter, we summarize the grade levels at which each strategy may be used (Figure 8.17). We provide the chart to highlight that some strategies often associated with younger students can also be appropriate for older learners, provided you use age-appropriate reading selections. These features taken together will help you choose teaching strategies matched to individual needs.

You may recall our planning framework for differentiated instruction from Chapter 3 that asks you to consider the questions: **who**, **what**, **how**, and **how well**. We use that framework now to illustrate a literature/reading lesson that forms part of the theme study on **travel** introduced in Chapter 4.

WHO: Students in grades 2 to 4 identified as **beginning** to **early advanced** in English language proficiency. Many students in the class are intermediate readers in English; several are emergent and beginning readers. They represent a variety of primary language backgrounds and cultures; most have had experiences using public transportation and personal vehicles both in their home cultures and in the United States.

WHAT: For this lesson, we have selected a picture book, *The Trip* (Jack Keats, 1978).

HOW: We begin with a **picture walk** through the book with the whole class. By showing the pictures, we preview the main ideas, vocabulary, and concepts essential to the story. We use a DL-TA as we read the first two pages, just to get students started on the book. We keep a close eye on beginning English learners to provide additional sheltering for comprehension as needed. Students now finish reading the story quietly in pairs, **buddy reading**.

Following the buddy reading, students will work with their partner to complete either a **story map** or **cognitive map** of the text that was just read. We see in Figure 8.17 at the end of this chapter that story mapping and cognitive mapping are both appropriate at this grade level. Thus, we have provided a beginning strategy, story mapping, and an intermediate strategy, cognitive mapping. The story map is intended to accommodate beginning readers because it breaks the story down into basic parts students can easily identify. The cognitive map is intended to accommodate more advanced students because it offers more space for interpretation of story lines and characters. Students are given the choice of which map they will create, a task they will carry out with their original buddy.

HOW WELL: Observation checklists are used to document how well students have performed to standards for reading comprehension based on (1) story discussion as they work in pairs, and (2) their completed maps. If we decide we need more information, we may have students retell the story from their maps, assessing for main ideas, sequencing, and details. As a follow-up, we will have students read another story of similar difficulty during guided reading. In this way, students have the chance to apply their learning, and we have the chance to further evaluate each one's reading, providing individual assistance as needed.

Summary

In Chapter 8, we began with a description of the reading process of English language learners, emphasizing the interplay of linguistic knowledge, background knowledge, and reading strategies. We then provided a rationale for literature instruction, followed by specific contexts and strategies for implementing literature study with beginning and intermediate second language readers, using appropriate literature and other reading materials. We emphasize students' selecting their own books and responding to these books in literature response groups. We also suggested a variety of legitimate responses to literature that go beyond the usual discussion of stories: activities that allow second language learners to draw pictures that depict major themes and scenes in stories they are reading or that give them opportunities to dramatize stories in readers' theater or puppet shows. We emphasized variety in responding to the needs of all learners regardless of their language proficiency.

Finally, we described assessment procedures for second language reading development. Through using informal observations, miscue analysis, and running records you can become an expert "kid watcher," assisting children in making regular advancements in language and literacy (Goodman, 1978). In addition, by assisting students with self-assessment, you help them take charge of their own learning and assist you with instructional decisions. In the next chapters, we further our discussion of reading assessment with a thorough discussion of portfolios.

Our belief is that English learners need frequent opportunities to read self-selected literature. You can assist them best by constantly sharing good literature with them and by sheltering the literature and activities involving the whole class. One of the most powerful ways to help students of different cultural backgrounds is to give them choices in their reading and responding to literature. They will choose experientially and culturally appropriate materials for themselves with your help, and they will let you know what they like and what they have difficulty with if you create a secure classroom in which all students are involved in

327

decision making, in choosing to be silent when they wish to, and in taking control of their own learning while trusting your guidance.

Finally, excellent literature is the core of all excellent reading programs. Literature is a human and humane experience because through good books, students may explore their own natures, become aware of potentialities for thought and feeling within themselves, acquire clearer perspectives, develop aims and a sense of direction, and compare their values with the values of characters they meet in books. Literature is the only subject in school that is fully and honestly involved in exploring what it means to be human; it is the written record of human experience.

In a sense, when we read, we discover not only the world around us, but ourselves. Through literature, we can extend our experiences, compare our ethical concepts, relieve emotional frustrations, discover beauty and grandeur in language and in ourselves, and nourish our imaginations. The goal of every literature program should be to enhance these experiences for students, to give them the ability to read literature with enjoyment and understanding, and to nurture a need for further reading. Literature is an intensely personal experience, and it is with this experience that the literature study should be mainly concerned.

Figure 8.17 gives grade levels for using various strategies to enhance students' love for literature. You may want to use the chart to think about your English learners' growth and development and to decide what strategy may be useful. But the chart is not meant to be a rigid one; only you can determine a student's needs and wants when it comes to their growth as readers. Indeed, only you with your student can decide what literature or literature strategies will extend their experi-

FIGURE 8.17

GRADE LEVELS AT WHICH STRATEGIES MAY BE USED

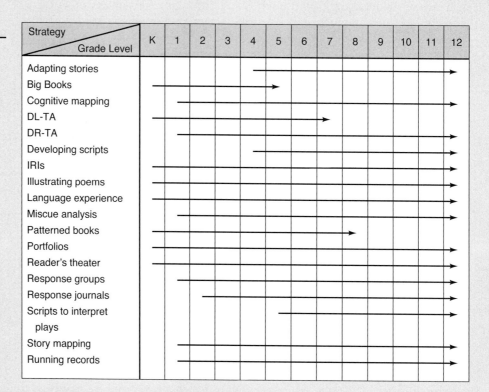

ence and growth. Because literature can be such an intensely personal experience, we all have to pay special attention to our students as they make choices and build their knowledge.

For all students, including English learners, literature not only extends experience and gives chances for comparing values, but also plays an important role in expanding the language of readers. Through literature, students become aware of the delight and magic of words; through poems, short stories, riddles, books, and jokes they can learn about the full range of language use. In our best literature exists the finest use of language. Thus, an excellent reading program for English language learners consists of the best literature. Anything less is a disservice to our students. As Mark Twain once said, "A man who reads poor literature has no advantage over a man who doesn't read at all."

Suggestions for Further Reading

Anderson, N. (1999). *Exploring second language reading: Issues and strategies*. Boston: Heinle & Heinle.

This engaging book begins with a brief, clear introduction to models of the reading process and discusses eight strategies dealing with reading: (1) activate background knowledge, (2) cultivate vocabulary, (3) teach for comprehension, (4) increase reading rate, (5) verify reading strategies, (6) evaluate progress, (7) build motivation, and (8) select appropriate reading materials. The brief book (129 pages), well written and organized, gives valuable, theoretically sound, and practical information in addition to providing a model for teaching.

Birch, B. (2002). *English L2 reading*. Mahwah, NJ: Erlbaum.

Researchers who have developed models of the reading process can be separated into three views: top-down views, bottom-up views, and interactive views (interactive views are a combination of bottom-up and top-down views). This book offers a valuable contribution to the bottom-up view of reading, including chapters on listening skills, processing letters, the English spelling system, phonics, morphophonemic writing, and vocabulary acquisition. This excellent book discusses graphophonic and word-level details of L2 reading, with specific ideas relative to students' particular first language literacy skills.

Custodio, B., & Sutton, M. J. (1998). Literature-based ESL for secondary school students. *TESOL Journal, 7*(5), 19–23.

This article describes how two teachers used literature-based instruction. The article states some advantages to the approach: It promotes literacy development, provides language models, and integrates language skills. The authors go on to explain why content-based instruction (CBI) is effective and suggest how it might be used in a middle school using historical fiction and in high school in a theme-based unit. They note the many advantages of using literature with ESL students and provide a list of multicultural literature that might be used with beginning, intermediate, and advanced students.

Eskey, D. (2002). Reading and the teaching of L2 reading. *TESOL Journal, 11*(1), 5–9.

This article is informative, playful, and insightful. David Eskey pulls from researcher and practitioner information that makes clear the reading process for both first and second language readers. The article contains information, graphics, and humor that teachers will want to use in their own classrooms. The article illustrates Eskey's knowledge and understanding of both first and second language research and practice.

Gee, R. W. (1999). Encouraging ESL students to read. *TESOL Journal, 8*(1), 3–7.

This article, written by a middle school teacher, presents a rationale for extensive reading in

329

classrooms. One statement presents his view: "So, competence in reading, or at least a perception of competence, promotes reading. Conversely, reading promotes competence" (page 3). An excellent article for anyone looking for answers to why more time should be spent reading in our classrooms.

Kamil, M. L., Mosenthal, P., Pearson, P. D., et al. (2000). *Handbook of reading research: Vol. III.* Mahwah, NJ: Erlbaum.

The handbook has been one of the books every reading teacher should have on his or her bookshelf for years. Although most chapters focus on first language reading, there are articles also on second language reading, international issues in reading, and multicultural perspectives on reading policy. The book starts with five articles on reading research around the world: Australia and Aotearoa/New Zealand, United Kingdom, Central and Eastern Europe, Latin America, and the United States. Among the 47 chapters written by experts are 3 valuable ones for EL teachers: "Second Language Reading as a Case Study of Reading Scholarship in the 20th Century" by Elizabeth B. Bernhardt; "Bilingual Children's Reading" by Georgia Earnest Garcia; and a "Multicultural Perspective on Policies for Improving Literacy Achievement: Equity and Excellence" by Kathryn H. Au.

Schmitt, N., & Carter, R. (2000). The lexical advantages of narrow reading for second language learners. *TESOL Journal*, 9(1), 4–9.

This article discusses how narrow reading assists EL students in vocabulary learning. Specifically narrow reading provides "the repetition necessary to establish new words in the learners mind and in supplying the different contexts necessary to elaborate and expand the richness of knowledge about those words" (page 4). With narrow reading, students read about the same topic in a variety of different materials, including newspapers, magazines, and other articles. As students become familiar with a topic, build their background knowledge on the topic, and are confronted with words repeatedly, they build a strong vocabulary.

Tierney, R., & Readence, J. (Eds.). (2000). *Reading strategies and practices: A compendium* (5th ed.). Boston: Allyn and Bacon.

This book contains everything you wanted to know about reading instruction. Although it is not aimed specifically at second language learners, you can adapt most of the strategies for use with your English learners. More than 60 strategies offer ways to assist response to literature and drama, ways to build vocabulary, approaches to cooperative learning, and teaching comprehension. This is the best book of its kind.

Tyner, B., & Green, S. E. (2005). *Small-Group reading instruction: A differentiated teaching model for intermediate readers, grades 3–8.* Newark, DE: International Reading Association.

If you're looking for practical ideas, this excellent book will help you individualize instruction in reading using small groups. Chapters include: Intermediate Reading Instruction and the Small-Group Differentiated Reading Model; Components of and Activities for the Small-Group Differentiated Reading Model; The Evolving Reader Stage; The Maturing Reader Stage; The Advanced Reader Stage; and Assessing Student Performance in the Small-Group Differentiated Reading Model.

Activities

1. Assess a student in reading using a reading miscue inventory or a running record. List the student's specific strengths and weaknesses (e.g., what are the student's decoding skills when reading in context? What is the level of comprehension?). Finally, discuss the kind of program, procedures, or strategies you would suggest for the student. What are the student's strengths that you can build on? For example, if the student is strong in listening comprehension,

you may want to ask him or her to read along with taped stories to help develop automaticity.

2. Observe a class with students working in literature response groups. What are the advantages of creating literature response groups? Are there any disadvantages with which a teacher needs to be concerned? What would you do differently from the classroom you observed to implement literature response groups? Do you think there are times when teacher-directed discussions are more appropriate than literature response groups? When? Why?

3. Develop a readers' theater script for a story in elementary or secondary school, and discuss how you would use readers' theater. Observe how drama is used in the classrooms you visit: What does drama add to students' abilities to respond to literature? How would you use readers' theater differently for older and younger students? For example, would you have older students develop their own scripts? What other dramatic activities would you use with English learners who have limited proficiency versus intermediate proficiency? How can you be assured that all of your students are involved in dramatic activities?

4. Working with a student who is limited in English proficiency, develop a series of language experience lessons. How does the student, within the context of language experience, develop as a reader over time? Does the student seem more or less enthusiastic about reading than a student who has been immersed in literature only? What are some of the shortcomings of a literature-based or language-experience approach to teaching reading? For example, how rich will students' English be if they are only reading from one another's language experience stories? Is it important to introduce patterned stories and other stories to students early on as they are learning to read? Why?

5. Observe several classrooms in which teachers feel that literature is central to students' learning to read. What are the variations in the ways different teachers implement literature programs? What are the views of the teachers, stated or unstated, toward literature study? What role does the teacher play—expert, facilitator, or equal participant in exploring literature? What effect do these different views of literature study have on the students' response to literature? What effect do these views have on students' enthusiasm for reading or independence in reading? Do students choose to read when given free time?

331

Video Homework Exercise

Writing Assessment

In this video the teacher is working with students' narrative writing. She prepares students to meet with her individually for a writing conference. The teacher then meets with one student and provides specific feedback on her paper.

Go to MyEducationLab, select the topic "Writing," and watch the video entitled "Writing Assignment."

1. What connection does this teacher make between reading and writing? How might this help her teach both reading and writing?

2. Do you feel the teacher's work with the girl on her paper was helpful? Would you do things differently? How?

3. How would this assessment process be modified for English learners working on narratives? Consider both beginning and intermediate English learners in your response.

Content Reading and Writing: Prereading and During Reading

In this chapter and Chapter 10, we discuss content area reading and writing, that is, reading and writing in social science, science, mathematics, English, and other subject areas. We address the following questions:

1. What does research tell us about content instruction for English learners?
2. What characteristics of narrative and expository text structure are useful for students to know and why?
3. What kinds of classroom contexts and teaching strategies can assist students to use reading and writing in English as a learning tool?
4. How can teachers prepare students to read and monitor their own comprehension while reading?

The sea is a radiant water galaxy. It's a world of its own in a special way.
Under its foam crested surface, there exists a universe of plant and animal life.
With the tiniest microscopic beings to the most humungus creature that ever
lived, the sea is alive!

Thus opens *Our Friends in the Water* (Kids of Room 14, 1979), a delightfully
written and informative 79-page book on marine mammals: sea otters,
whales, dolphins, seals, sea lions, walrus, manatees, and dugongs. What's different about this book is that it was conceived, written, and illustrated entirely by a
fourth/fifth-grade class. It's a book by kids for kids! The work that went into this
book is remarkable. The reverent wonder expressed in the opening paragraph is
unmistakable. How did it all come about?

As explained by the children, the class expressed curiosity about marine
mammals, and their teacher, Lynda Chittenden (1982), followed their wonder by
facilitating a year-long research project that culminated in this delightful publication. Living near the Pacific coast, the class was able to take a number of field
trips. They visited a seal rookery, spent two days watching gray whales migrate
south, and observed dolphins in training. They also put their imaginations to
work to sense from within what it would be like to live as a marine animal in the
water. One child's conclusion: "Today I learned how important it is to have blub-
ber. Our class went swimming in a 40-degree pool. I did learn that I COULD
swim in that temperature. But, I couldn't even breathe the first time I jumped in.
Gradually I got better. I could swim two laps without flippers. But I still don't see
how a whale could live in 33 degree water, even with layers and layers of blub-
ber" (Steig Johnson's learning log quoted in *Our Friends in the Water,* Kids of
Room 14, 1979, page 16).

Sparked initially by general interest, the class was spurred on by the fascinating information that began to accumulate. The more they found out, the more
they wanted to know. Manatees and dugongs, it seems, were the animals that
gave rise to the mermaid legend and were probably what Christopher Columbus
was referring to in his diary when he mentioned sighting "three mermaids" in the
Caribbean! Thus engaged in the pursuit of knowledge, the class read books,
invited marine mammal experts to visit their class, and wrote in learning logs to
keep track of their growing body of knowledge. Finally, they organized their findings and put them all together in seven coauthored chapters that tell "with facts,
stories, pictures, poems, and dreams the lives of most marine mammals from a
kid's point of view" (Kids of Room 14, 1979, page 9).

We share this extended example with you because it illustrates what we consider the epitome of good learning and teaching. The Kids of Room 14, through
their project, enlighten us as to the possibilities and potentials of students who take
charge of their own learning with the facilitative guidance of an excellent teacher.

Let us take a look at the project in terms of what it might offer English learners. As we do so, we want to illustrate that most of what you or I readily recognize as excellent teaching with first language speakers incorporates strategies that
facilitate optimal learning for English learners as well. The key to success lies
with finding ways for all students to participate and contribute to the learning
enterprise, even if their English language competence is limited.

The marine mammals project, the type of project that could be used at all
grade levels, provided several avenues of learning that we consider highly beneficial to English learners. First, the project emerged from the expressed interests of

the students. Thus, it built on prior knowledge and, more importantly, on the curiosity and concerns of the students themselves. Second, the teacher and the class were able to generate a variety of ideas leading to field trips, providing direct experiences for learning about marine mammals. Third, the teacher herself guided students in processing and keeping track of the information they acquired through oral class discussions, individual written learning logs, and posing questions to further the learning process. Finally, when the class decided to put their findings and illustrations into a book, each chapter was written collaboratively by pairs or small groups of students. Students used process writing with peer response groups to elaborate and refine their writing, keeping in mind the question: "Will other students who have not had the same experiences understand everything we've learned about these most wondrous of animals?" To complement the text, some students made line drawings to illustrate the chapters. Poems and song lyrics were added from student journals and learning logs, giving depth of feeling to the book's overall informational message. In other words, a variety of writing and drawing was published, accommodating individual strengths. Within this type of project, all students can contribute, native and non-native English speakers alike. The theme cycle approach used by this teacher helped the students learn to select and organize the materials they needed to synthesize information for themselves and others and, most importantly, to become independent learners.

In summary, the marine mammals project incorporated six elements that create optimal content learning for English learners:

1. Meaning and Purpose: The topic was meaningful to the students; they selected it and helped shape its development.

2. Prior Knowledge: Learning was built on prior knowledge and direct experience such as field trips.

3. Integration of Opportunities to Use Language and Literacy for Learning Purposes: Oral and written language were used to acquire knowledge and present it to others.

4. Scaffolding for Support: Scaffolds were provided, including group work, process writing, and direct experiences for learning.

5. Collaboration: Students collaborated to build knowledge and organize it for summarizing in a book.

6. Variety: Variety was built in at every step, with oral language, reading, writing, field trips, class discussions, guest speakers, and other avenues of learning provided.

Our Friends in the Water provides a good example of **content-based instruction (CBI)** (Anderson, 1999; Snow, 2001), which integrates language learning opportunities with content instruction. The teacher provides multiple opportunities for extensive reading, student choice, and collaboration in projects (Stoller, 2002). Students are learning language with a great deal of comprehensible input and output (Krashen, 1982; Swain, 1985). Among its advantages, CBI (1) employs English at a comprehensible level, facilitating understanding of subject matter and building language skills simultaneously; (2) often makes use of authentic tasks centered on authentic material, increasing student engagement; and (3) helps students learn appropriate grade-level content, thus providing a bridge to mainstream classes (Custodio & Sutton, 1998). You will find examples of CBI throughout this book.

An important assumption that we make in this book is that all language skills—listening, speaking, reading, and writing—are best developed when students are using those skills to achieve communication goals that are interesting and meaningful to them. This assumption holds true for both first and second language development. When students are involved in projects, such as the marine mammals study, they integrate and practice an astounding number of important social, linguistic, and academic skills related to their own learning: They pose questions; gather data through reading, interviewing, and direct experience; discuss findings with peers; evaluate formats for presenting findings; organize and summarize information for oral, written, and multimedia presentation; and so on. Through the integrated use of these skills, further social, linguistic, and academic development takes place. Our concern with English language learners is to help them participate fully while stretching their language and literacy performance to their next developmental level.

In this chapter, then, we focus on assisting English learners in reading and writing longer, more complex material that becomes increasingly predominant in the upper-elementary grades, middle school, and high school.

By our definition, English learners who are reading and writing longer, more complex pieces in English are intermediate or advanced in English language proficiency. For these students, we offer a wide variety of strategies, scaffolds for support, to assist them as they pursue complex information and ideas relevant to their interests and purposes. The strategies may be used in conjunction with theme cycles or units or with single subject instruction in science, social studies, literature, or any other area of study. As the teacher, you may select from the strategies, as needed, to help an individual student, a small group, or the whole class.

If you have non-English speakers or beginners in your class, they are not likely to be reading and writing long, complex English stories or essays. Nonetheless, it is important to involve them as much as possible in your instruction because their participation will promote both social integration and second language development—top priorities for newcomers. Sheltering your instruction will improve beginners' chances of understanding the general ideas of your instruction and will facilitate language development. However, for older beginners, sheltering alone will not provide full access to the complex information taught in the upper grades. Supplementary instruction in the students' primary language may be needed to preview and review complex concepts you are covering in class. As we present various strategies in this chapter, we will highlight ways to involve beginners in your day-to-day instruction.

This chapter offers strategies you may select before and during reading to promote reading comprehension and strategies that integrate writing into the process of academic learning. First, however, we provide background information on key issues related to helping students read and write longer, more complex pieces as part of their academic learning. In particular, we review the concept of sheltered instruction or specially designed academic instruction in English (SDAIE), describe classroom applications of research on text structure and metacognition, and discuss ways to estimate the difficulty of a text for particular students.

INTERNET RESOURCES

One excellent site for content area instruction and much more is **www. everythingesl.net/**. Here you'll find lesson plans, teaching tips, and many resources. There is also an excellent article on "Challenges for ELLs in Content Area Learning." The article outlines specific challenges ELLs are confronted with in reading, mathematics, science, and social studies. You also might use the Peace Corps site **www.peacecorps.gov/index.cfm** to search for information and lesson plans on culture. After using the site and viewing its resources, create a lesson in which students can select a culture they are interested in and use the Peace Corps site to find information. Students could use K-W-L, or you might create your own format for their completion of the search.

What Does Research Tell Us About Reading and Writing Across the Curriculum for English Learners?

As students move beyond the primary grades, they are expected to read and write about increasingly complex topics in increasingly sophisticated ways. In particular, they must move beyond pattern books and simpler stories to longer literary works and expository prose found in textbooks, magazine articles, encyclopedias, and newspapers. All students, including English learners, can benefit from assistance in dealing with expository texts and complex literature, both in reading and in writing (Singer & Donlan, 1989). In addition, English learners may need assistance related to their English knowledge (O'Malley & Chamot, 1990).

Research is limited on second language students' abilities to read, write, and learn from either expository or narrative texts. Instead, most research and discussion falls under the broader category of sheltered English instruction or SDAIE—instruction designed to be understandable to students with limited English proficiency and also appropriate to the students' ages and academic levels (Northcutt & Watson, 1986; Schifini, 1985). As noted previously, sheltered instruction serves two purposes: (1) subject matter learning, and (2) second language development related to academic work. In other words, sheltered instruction is both comprehensible and cognitively demanding in that content is not "watered down." Without primary language instruction, this goal is not easy to achieve when students arrive in the upper-elementary grades, middle school, or high school. However, for students with an intermediate knowledge of English, sheltered English instruction can be effective.

Sheltered instruction aims to facilitate both language and subject matter learning by building on students' prior knowledge, making use of concrete materials and direct experiences, creating opportunities for students to collaborate on learning tasks, and providing explicit strategies to help students use oral and written language for learning (Chamot & O'Malley, 1986). As you can see, our criteria for teaching English learners include all of these features. To these we add the use of thematically organized instruction to provide a single, meaningful theme to which all reading, writing, and other learning efforts relate. However, sheltered instruction may be successfully implemented in traditional, single subject areas such as mathematics, science, and social studies (Chamot & O'Malley, 1986, 1992; Crandall, 1987; Northcutt & Watson, 1986; Schifini, 1985). In developing instruction, second language acquisition experts typically incorporate learning strategies that have proven successful with first language students, modified to meet the needs of English learners according to their English proficiency and prior experience.

Background Information on Students' Interactions With Texts

Because this chapter focuses on helping students read longer, more complex texts, this section presents background information on some characteristics of longer texts and ways readers interact with them. We present research and theory on (1) aesthetic and efferent stances toward a text, (2) text structure in relation to comprehension and composition, and (3) metacognition. In addition, we discuss how to match students with texts they must use for academic purposes. These are rather complex topics, but they are important because they provide the basis for the reading and writing strategies recommended later.

Aesthetic and Efferent Interactions With Texts

Louise Rosenblatt, in presenting her transactional view of literature response, discusses two attitudes or stances readers may take when reading: efferent and aesthetic (Rosenblatt, 1978, 1984). **Efferent** comes from the Latin word *effere*, meaning "to carry away." When the reader takes an efferent stance toward a text, the central purpose is to carry away information, and this is what we commonly do with expository texts. When we read an article or essay, for example, our major concern is to carry away the information or argument the author is presenting. Rosenblatt defines **aesthetic reading** as aimed at experiencing or feeling a piece of writing. Readers usually set aesthetic purposes when reading literary texts: They are interested in the problems faced by the characters, in the way characters deal with the problems, and in identifying with the characters and situations of a story. Their primary concern is not to carry away information about a particular type of government or about biology, though that may occur.

To illustrate the two purposes, Rosenblatt offers a "pure" example of efferent reading: a mother reading the antidote on a bottle of poison after her child has swallowed from the bottle. The mother's only concern is carrying away the information that will save her child. To illustrate the aesthetic purpose, Rosenblatt suggests we imagine a father reading to his son from *Alice in Wonderland*. When the rabbit says, "I'm late, I'm late, for a very important date," the boy objects, "Rabbits can't tell time and rabbits can't talk." The father replies, "They do in this story!" The boy missed the aesthetic purpose of the story, taking instead an efferent stance, in which the textual information contradicted his knowledge of the real world (Rosenblatt, 1983). These purposes do not mean that a reader cannot gain aesthetic experiences from an essay or that a reader cannot carry away specific information from a story. They simply mean that the primary stance when reading essays and narratives is often different. As John Dewey once said, "Just because a China teacup is beautiful does not mean that it cannot have the pragmatic purpose of carrying tea" (Rosenblatt, 1983).

One of the first things readers must do when approaching a text is to know whether they are to take a largely aesthetic or efferent stance. As the teacher, you can facilitate student success with reading by stating explicitly what you expect students to gain from a text and what you want them to do with what they have read. This holds true for narrative and expository texts, whether the stance is aesthetic or efferent. Theme cycles offer the advantage that students set the purpose themselves and select written materials accordingly, with teacher guidance.

Effects of Text Structure on Comprehension and Memory

An important feature of longer, more complex expository texts is their organization or sequencing of ideas and arguments, often referred to as **text structure**. One familiar expository text structure frequently found in textbooks is the **attributive**, or **enumerative**, pattern, which states a main idea and then lists supporting details. In the attributive structure, words such as *first*, *second*, and *third* typically signal the organization of the list, and words such as *in addition*, *also*, and *moreover* may tie the list together. Three other expository text structures include **compare/contrast**, **problem/solution**, and **cause/effect**. All three of these differ from the basic narrative structure summarized by the someone/ wants/but/so narrative sequence discussed in Chapter 8. These ways of organizing information and ideas are standard conventions that have evolved and become accepted as appropriate for English (Connor & Kaplan, 1987). There are other ways to structure arguments and ideas; in fact, what is considered appropriate text structure in other languages may differ from the patterns to which we are accustomed in English (Chu, Swaffer, & Charney, 2002). Our discussion focuses on English.

Awareness of text structure is important because research indicates that readers use their knowledge of text structure to store, retrieve, and summarize information they have read (Meyer, et al., 1980). In other words, text organization has a profound effect on comprehension and memory (Bartlett, 1978; Meyer, et al., 1980). As students gain familiarity with text structure patterns like compare/ contrast or problem/solution through reading and writing, the patterns form templates that permit predictions of the words and ideas to come, thereby facilitating comprehension. The template also helps students remember the information in the text by providing a conceptual net for keeping the information in mind. Moreover, when students become aware of different text structure patterns, they can use them to structure their writing. Helping students become aware of text structure will help them become more effective in both reading and writing. Study the structures in Figures 9.1 and 9.2 and determine what the structure alone can tell you about the content.

If you have had experience with cooking or baking, you probably identified Figure 9.1 as a recipe structure. You would also be able to guess that the title goes

FIGURE 9.1

Structure Outline 1

```
        _____

  1  _____

  2  _____

 1½  _____

  1  _____

     _____

     _____

     _____

     _____

     _____
```

on the top line of the recipe, that ingredients go after the numbers, and that an explanation of how to do the recipe follows. If you had only the title, such as Chocolate Cake, you could guess even more based on the structure.

The structure in Figure 9.2 represents a business letter. Because you probably identified the structure, you know that the date goes on the upper right side, that the name and address are on the upper left, that the addressee's name follows, that the content is next, and that the person's signature is last. You can also guess that the tone of the letter will be formal.

These two examples illustrate how much information we can derive from structure alone. When we teach students the structure of our textbooks or any of the readings we are using, we assist them with both understanding and remembering what they have read. Similarly, if students recognize a compare/contrast structure, they can begin to look for things that are alike and things that are different about a topic; in other words, knowledge of text structure can help us predict what will come in a text, monitor whether we are getting the information, and help us remember what we have read.

Although there are some pure forms of structure in texts, such as compare/contrast, an enumerative (list) pattern, and cause/effect, many texts use a combination of these forms. Thus, we suggest that you determine and teach explicitly the structure of your own textbooks to your students. We also believe that probably the best strategies for teaching text structures are visual/spatial strategies. For example, you might use a structured overview (see Figures 9.7 and 9.8) for a text organized like a list, a Venn diagram for a compare/contrast structure, or a map for combinations of structures or for less identifiable structures. These visual/spatial strategies are discussed in detail in this chapter and in Chapter 10.

As you familiarize yourself with different text structures, you may call students' attention to the organizational patterns of their texts, thereby helping them read and remember more efficiently. Some research suggests that differ-

FIGURE 9.2

Structure Outline 2

ent cultures structure texts in rather different ways (Connor & Kaplan, 1987; Hinds, 1983a, 1983b). Therefore, explicit explanations regarding the conventions of English text structure may be important for older English learners who have reached substantial literacy development in their home language before immigration. In fact, explicit instruction on text structure is apt to be beneficial for most students, whether native or non-native English speakers.

Cohesive Ties/Signal Words

Another important aspect of text organization is the use of signal words and phrases, called **cohesive ties**, that indicate how arguments and ideas relate within paragraphs and across paragraphs and larger sections of text. Cohesive ties act as signposts to help the reader navigate the text. One way they help is by pointing out the overall structure of a text. For example, words such as *first*, *second*, and *third*, signal to the reader that the author is providing sequenced ideas of similar weight to support a main idea. *Moreover* and *in addition* indicate equal ideas, whereas *nevertheless* and *nonetheless* indicate minimization or negation of previous statements (Halliday, 1975). Table 9.1 categorizes several cohesive ties according to their signpost function: time order, additive, cause/effect, conclusive, and minimization or negation of previous information.

TABLE 9.1 • COHESIVE TIES

TIME/ORDER	ADDITIVE	CAUSE/EFFECT	CONCLUSIVE	CHANGING
soon	in addition	as a result	consequently	nonetheless
when	moreover	because	in summary	despite
finally	also	since	therefore	however

Some cohesive ties can be difficult for English learners to understand and use appropriately because of their abstract quality (Goldman & Murray, 1989, 1992). After all, cohesive ties do not refer to objects, people, actions, or concepts. Instead, they convey relationships between complex ideas expressed in phrases and clauses. To get a feeling for the difficulty they may present, try defining a few for yourself, such as *nevertheless*, *moreover*, and *notwithstanding*. Other cohesive ties are more concrete in meaning, such as *first*, *second*, *third*, and *finally*. One way to help older students comprehend cohesive ties is to provide a bilingual dictionary so that they can find corresponding terms in their native language. This solution is limited, however, because relational words often do not translate directly into other languages. However, dictionary translations provide one way to start. A more useful approach is to show students how to use cohesive ties in their own writing. In this way the student offers the meaning, and you help the student convey that meaning effectively through cohesive ties.

Students can use their knowledge of cohesive ties together with their knowledge of text structure to assist them in comprehending and remembering the information in a text. With these basic structures in mind, students will be ready for strategies such as mapping and Directed Reading-Thinking Activity (DR-TA), which will assist them with learning from texts. Moreover, the same knowledge of text structure assists students with writing expository prose. By learning how authors organize information, students can begin exploring compare/contrast, cause/effect, lists, and other structures in their own writing. Similarly, they can begin to use the same cohesive ties good writers use as signposts to guide their readers.

Headings and Subheadings

Headings and subheadings are another aspect of text structure that students can use to become more proficient readers. For example, students can use headings and subheadings to preview a text to gain a general sense of its content. Students can read headings to assist them in making predictions about the content of a text. Research indicates that middle school and older students often ignore headings entirely. However, students can enhance their comprehension by reading and using headings and subheadings (Bartlett, 1978). Thus, you will want to explain their usefulness to your students.

Teaching Text Structure: One Classroom

In teaching **text structure** for reading and writing, one teacher we know, Leticia Alvarez, places a drawing of a train, such as the one in Figure 9.3, on her bulletin board. Leticia explains that one good structure for an essay is like a train. Each

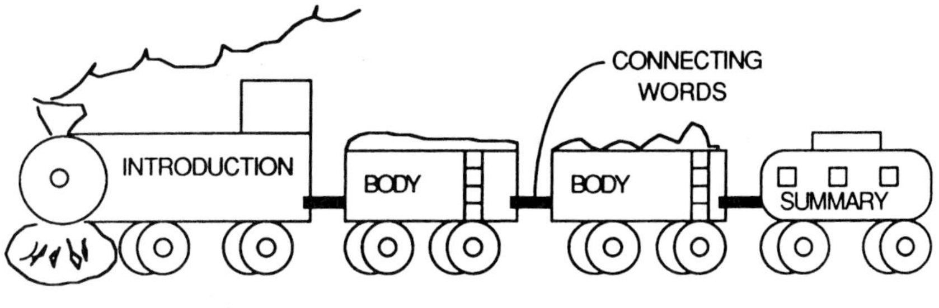

FIGURE 9.3

RELATING ESSAY
ORGANIZATION
TO A TRAIN

Introduction:	In the introduction you should say the main things you want to say in your essay.
Body:	This section gives information that will support the ideas you said in the introduction. Each new paragraph might give different information just as each new train car might be carrying different information, but each new section relates to the main ideas.
Connecting Devices:	You'll want to connect paragraphs to one another to make it easier for the reader to see how each paragraph relates. To do this you might use words such as *moreover*, *in addition*, etc.
Summary or Conclusion:	In the summary you'll want to remind the reader of the major ideas you wanted to present in your essay.

343

section of the train stands for an important part of the essay. For example, the engine of the train knows where it is going, just as the first paragraph of an essay tells the reader where the essay is going. The engine is linked to the car behind it, just as signal words or cohesive ties help link one paragraph to another in an essay. Similarly, each car in the train carries new cargo just as each new paragraph in an essay carries new information. Finally, the caboose in a train looks toward where we've been, just as the final paragraph in an essay tells readers where they have been. We have heard students refer to the train analogy while discussing one another's compositions, and we have heard them talk about the words they will use to link one paragraph to another. In a concrete way, Leticia has taught her students how to develop sophisticated essays. Later, she may teach them other structures to use for both reading and writing.

Literary Structure

As students progress through school, the stories they read will be longer and more complex than the patterned books and short narratives they encountered early on. Thus, a more sophisticated knowledge of literary structure may benefit students in understanding and remembering narratives. In Chapter 8, we shared the some-one/wants/but/so outline as a simple structure young students could use to understand and retell simple stories, but a more detailed way to display narrative content becomes appropriate as students begin to read more complex stories (Boyle & Peregoy, 1991; Buckley & Boyle, 1981; Webster, 1998). The map in Figure 9.4 provides a more sophisticated template for summarizing the literary elements of such stories.

FIGURE 9.4

MORE COMPLEX MAP OF
STORY PARTS

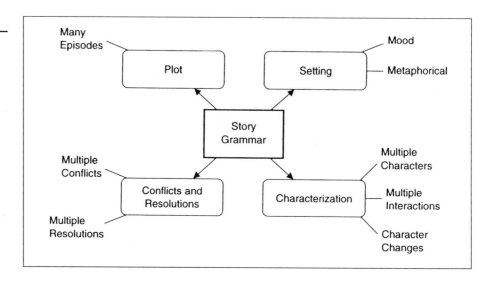

344

Discussion of Story Elements

To add depth to English learners' appreciation of literature, they need to know the basic elements of most stories: the setting, characters, conflict, and dénouement. The **setting** is simply where the action takes place. In more complex narratives, the setting may change often and may even carry symbolic meaning such as good or evil. The **characters** (protagonists) are usually people or animals in the story. In longer narratives characters have time to develop and change, whereas in short stories characters often remain static. Thus, in longer stories we may ask students to look for changes made by characters. The **conflict** or problem usually consists of a situation the character is trying to resolve. In short narratives there is often only one conflict, but in longer narratives, there may be many conflicts and problems to be solved. The solution or **dénouement** consists of the way the situation is resolved.

Metacognition and Learning From Text

Metacognition means thinking about thinking. In research on comprehension and problem solving, metacognition refers to the act of reflecting on one's own thought processes so as to consciously guide the outcome. In reading, metacognition includes the ability to monitor one's own reading processes and the ability to take strategic steps to remedy the situation when one's reading does not make sense. Readers need to be aware of the demands of a reading task to make choices about the strategies they will use (Oxford, 2003). Metacognition is knowing when and how to use strategies to assist in comprehension and composition (Baker & Brown, 1984).

The strategies students need to know in studying texts, described in detail later, involve both retrieval and comprehension of information and remedying problems they may have with understanding texts. Specifically, students need to use strategies to preview texts, to ask questions, to preview headings and subheadings, and to organize information for memory. In addition, students need self-monitoring strategies to help them when they are having problems with achieving their goals in reading. These self-monitoring strategies include setting a purpose for reading, evaluating whether the purpose is being met, and revising goals or remediating their own interactions with texts. For example, students need to recognize that they may have to read a math text more slowly than a narrative text or that they need to recognize when they are not understanding a text. In the last few decades there has been a great deal of concentration on the direct teaching of metacognitive strategies to help students recognize text structures, ask questions of texts, and recall information (Boyle & Peregoy, 1991; Nolte & Singer, 1985; Palincsar & Brown, 1984; Ruddell & Boyle, 1984, 1989).

Matching Students and Texts

In any class, students vary in their ability to read academic material independently. It is axiomatic among educators that variation among students increases with each grade level. Such variation is further accentuated when students vary in English language proficiency. Whether you are collecting materials for theme cycles or teaching a standardized curriculum, it is important to obtain a variety of resources to accommodate varying levels of reading ability and English language proficiency. For example, if your class is studying European exploration of the New World, it is important to supplement any textbook you may use with filmstrips, audiocassettes, and short, simple, illustrated articles on exploration of the New World. In addition, this topic calls for the use of maps, perhaps student made, to post on the bulletin board. The supplementary materials offer a variety of ways for students to access information on the topic. In addition, they build background knowledge that may facilitate students' success in reading more difficult material.

One way to match students with texts, then, is to allow them to select from materials of varying difficulty. You will want to be available to encourage them to try more challenging texts when appropriate. At times, you may want to evaluate directly how your students handle written material from a textbook. **Readability formulas** will give a grade level for an expository text you are using, but because readability formulas are simply based on sentence and word length, they do not give an accurate measure of your students' ability to read a specific text. Similarly, we do not recommend using a **cloze procedure**, in which words are systematically left out of a text and the student tries to replace them; we find that the cloze procedure is extremely frustrating for second language learners and others, and is not predictive, either. We recommend that you try the following procedure, the **group reading inventory (GRI)**, if you want to get valid information about your students' ability to read your specific text.

Evaluating Students' Interaction With Text Using the Group Reading Inventory

The group reading inventory (GRI) (Vacca & Vacca, 1989) allows you to evaluate students' reading based on your text and the kinds of assignments you require. Though intended for group administration, the GRI can also be adapted for individuals. The GRI has the advantage of assessing students on a typical reading of your text and allowing you to get immediate information on their interactions with your text. This information can be used to guide you in adapting your use of the text so that all students can be successful.

FIGURE 9.5

IDENTIFIED CONCEPTS AND
THEIR RELATED SKILLS

CONCEPTS	READING SKILLS
1. The North is industrialized, and the South is agrarian	Compare/contrast the two sides Details of differences
2. Enumeration of differences from wars of the past	Details of differences Vocabulary terms
3. Involvement of different states in the war	Reading a chart and graph Extracting details and major ideas

The first step in developing a group reading inventory is to choose a passage similar in content, length, and complexity to the readings you may require of your class. Next, select the key concepts you would want students to know after reading the passage. Determine the reading skill required to understand each concept. For example, the skill might be understanding vocabulary in context or identification of a main idea and its supporting details. Similarly, the skill might be to understand a cause/effect relationship or a compare/contrast relationship. Or you may want students to understand a graph or chart that illustrates an important concept in the selection you are using. Finally, make up a GRI based on the concepts and skills you have identified. An example of some concepts from a reading on the American Civil War and the derived GRI is presented in Figures 9.5 and 9.6.

The brief example of a GRI in Figures 9.5 and 9.6 is based on the key concepts identified in a chapter. In conjunction with your GRI, you might also ask students to outline the information in the chapter, using the headings and subheadings, or to write a short summary of the pages read. When the students have completed their GRI, you can evaluate their ability to interact with your text. You can determine how much time needs to be spent in discussing vocabulary terms or in modeling ways to determine main ideas using headings and subheadings. The GRI has the added advantage of being a study guide that students can use to develop purpose and monitor their own comprehension of the reading tasks in your class; it provides a scaffold for their reading. We recommend giving GRIs throughout the year as an ongoing informal evaluation procedure.

FIGURE 9.6

SAMPLE GRI BASED ON
THE CIVIL WAR

Directions for Students: Read pages 32–37 in your book and answer the following questions:

Word Meanings: Briefly define or explain the meaning of the following words used in pages 32–37:
(1) emancipation, (2) *writ of habeas corpus*, (3) border states, (4) blockade.

Comprehension—Compare/Contrast Relationships: Read pages 35–36 and answer the following questions:
1. How was the war different from wars of the past?
2. How were the lifestyles of the South and North different?
3. What advantages did the North have over the South in the war?
4. What states were involved on the North and South sides? Compare and contrast why the states *were* involved.

Details: Find the information for the following questions in pages 35–36:
1. Identify three labor-saving devices that helped make the North more wealthy than the South.
2. Give two examples of the Southern view of slavery.

Evaluating Your Own Interaction With One Text

At this point, we would like you to try a brief exercise to evaluate your own efferent reading processes. Read the following passage and answer the questions following the passage without referring to the text (Right to Read Conference, 1972):

> The Echmiadzin is a monastery in the Armenian S.S.R., in 40" 12' N., 44" 19' E., the seat of the Catholicus or primate of the Armenian church. It is situated close to the village of Vagarshapat, in the plain of the Aras, 2,840 ft. above the sea, 12 mi. west of Erivan and 40 mi. north of Mount Ararat. The monastery comprises a complex of buildings, surrounded by brick walls 30 ft. high, which with their loopholes and towers present the appearance of a fortress. Its architectural character has been considerably impaired by additions and alterations in modern Russian style.
>
> On the western side of the quadrangle is the residence of the primate, on the south, the refectory (1730–35), on the east the lodgings for the monks, and on the north the cells. The cathedral is a small but fine cruciform building with a Byzantine cupola at the intersection. Its foundation is ascribed to St. Gregory the Illuminator in 302.
>
> Of special interest is the porch, built of red porphyry and profusely adorned with sculptured designs somewhat of a Gothic character. The interior is decorated with Persian frescoes of flowers, birds, and scrollwork. It is here that the primate confers episcopal consecration by the sacred hand (relic) of St. Gregory; and here every seven years he prepares the holy oil which is to be used throughout the churches of the Armenian communion. Outside the main entrance are the alabaster tombs of the primates, Alexander I (1714), Alexander II (1755), Daniel (1806), and Narses (1857), and a white marble monument erected by the English East India company to mark the resting place of Sir John Macdonald Kinneir, who died at Tabriz in 1830 while on an embassy to the Persian court.

Questions to Be Answered Without Referring to the Text:

1. What direction is Mount Ararat from the monastery?
2. What was the avocation of St. Gregory?
3. What are the five types of architecture mentioned in the passage?

Answers: 1. Southeast; 2. architect; 3. Romanesque, Gothic, Byzantine, modern Russian, Persian.

Did you answer correctly? If not, it may be because you did not know why you were reading the passage. If students don't know why they are reading a passage, they will not monitor their understanding appropriately, and they may remember unimportant details rather than key information. One of the ways teachers prepare students to read texts is by clarifying the purpose, pointing out what students must do with the information. For example, if we had asked you to read the questions before reading the passage, your purpose would have been clearly focused. Once students are prepared for a passage, they are ready to assess their own interactions with the text based on their purpose for reading. Finally, they will be able to organize key information for memory.

In summary, in this section we have discussed current theory and research that informs teaching decisions when students must read and learn from longer, more complex texts, both literary and expository. We described the difference between efferent and aesthetic stances toward a text; elaborated on a variety of narrative and expository text structures; explained how awareness of text structure facilitates effective reading and writing; and defined metacognition in relationship to students' monitoring and evaluating their own reading and writing. In addition, we discussed issues related to matching students and texts to maximize learning. All of these discussions provide the theoretical and practical underpinnings for the reading and writing strategies presented next.

Strategies to Promote Reading Comprehension

Many students read texts passively, waiting for information to present and organize itself for them. Proficient readers, however, know what they are looking for, engage their background knowledge while reading, and monitor achievement based on their purpose (Boyle & Peregoy, 1991; Pearson & Johnson, 1978; Ruddell & Boyle, 1989). In other words, they are thoughtful about reading, using metacognitive processes every step of the way. Figure 9.7 depicts a variety of strategies to help students to become actively self-aware and proficient when reading for academic purposes. The strategies are grouped according to whether they are to be used before students read a text, during reading, or after reading. In the prereading phase, a purpose for reading is established and background knowledge is developed to enhance comprehension; during reading, readers monitor their comprehension based on purpose by asking questions of the text; in the postreading phase, students boost their memory through writing and organizing information. During all three phases, students are encouraged to be metacognitively aware of their reading. In addition, they are taught to use text structure to assist comprehension. Because vocabulary plays a key role in reading comprehension, vocabulary strategies are offered for all three phases.

FIGURE 9.7 • MODEL OF READING/WRITING IN CONTENT AREAS

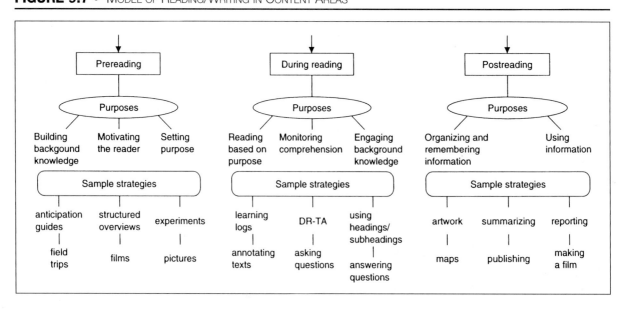

In our previous chapters, we discussed different strategies for beginning and intermediate English learners. For this chapter and the next one we drop this distinction, because the strategies used for both groups are virtually the same. This is not to say that beginning and intermediate English learners will benefit equally from the same instruction. In fact, the strategies generally require intermediate to advanced English proficiency for students to participate fully and learn. However, if you have beginning English learners in your class, you can accommodate them in a variety of ways that will promote both language development and content learning. One way is to provide supplementary texts of varying difficulty along with audiovisual materials. Another way to accommodate beginners is to spend more time on a particular strategy or to combine strategies. Remember to choose strategies that (1) make use of pictures, graphs, dramatization, and other paralinguistic cues to meaning; and (2) incorporate peer support to help beginners glean information from texts. These criteria ensure integration and involvement of newcomers. In addition, you may consider arranging assistance in the primary language from peers, paraprofessionals, and others, including yourself, if you speak the language. Primary language support for beginners has numerous benefits for communication, learning, and social-emotional adjustment.

Prereading Strategies: Developing Motivation, Purpose, and Background Knowledge

The strategies we describe for the prereading phase serve several purposes. First, they motivate student interest and build background knowledge on the topic of the text the students are to read. Students may have little or no knowledge of the text topic, or they may have misconceptions about the topic that can be clarified during the prereading phase. In this way, students are better prepared to read an assigned or self-selected text (Hawkes & Schell, 1987; Herber, 1978). Second, during the prereading phase, students clarify their purpose for reading a particular text. If you have assigned the reading, you'll want to explain to your students why you have selected the material, what you expect them to gain from it, and what they are to do with the information later. In theme cycles, your students have selected their own purpose and already have in mind why they are seeking certain information. The third purpose of prereading strategies is to help students gain a general idea of the text's organization and content by perusing the headings, subheadings, table of contents, and so forth.

Direct and concrete experiences facilitate learning for anyone but are essential for English learners. Thus, if we are trying to teach about whales, the best way would be to visit the ocean when whales are present. If that is not possible, we could show a film about whales or make use of photographs and pictures. All of these are concrete experiences that enhance students' understanding of their reading about whales. The most important thing to give them, however, is a chance to develop their knowledge of a topic before they read about it, through such activities as class discussions, field trips, and films.

Teacher Talk: Making Purposes Clear

Were you ever in a class when the bell rang, and everybody was leaving, and the teacher shouted out, "Read chapter 5 and answer the questions at the back of the book for homework"? Even worse, were you ever simply told to read a chapter without having any idea what the chapter was about, or why you were reading it, or what you needed to know after reading the chapter? We have found that students are often unable to state why they are reading a text or what they are supposed to do with the information later. Lacking clear purpose, they are likely simply to read the words and forget about them.

As the teacher, you can prepare students for reading efficiently by using a few simple, straightforward techniques. One important technique, obvious as it may seem, is to state clearly to your students why you want them to read a particular passage and what they will do with the information later. Sometimes this only requires a few words, whereas at other times it may require a short talk, but we maintain that students should not be given an assignment without knowing its purpose and what they are expected to know when they have finished reading. Without this background, they will end up as you may have with the monastery assignment—not getting the point of the reading or remembering haphazardly. We maintain that no assignment should be made without making explicit what you expect of students after reading the text. One of the easiest ways to accomplish this is simply to tell students your expectations and provide them with the background knowledge they will need to get the information, whether it is efferent or aesthetic in nature.

Field Trips and Films

One of the best things you can do to build background knowledge and vocabulary on a topic is to take your class on a field trip where they will experience directly your topic of study. A visit to a primeval forest, a planetarium, a business or factory, a nursery, or a butcher shop builds students' schema for a topic. In addition to field trips, or in lieu of one, you can create excitement with a good film or videotape or even with simple pictures or transparencies. A good film involves students visually in a topic and contains narration that builds concepts and vocabulary. When English learners have a visual image of a subject that they carry to their reading, they will be better prepared to understand a text and much more motivated to endure a difficult one. In selecting films, it's important that you preview them to assess (1) how easy they will be for your English learners to understand and (2) how well they convey concepts visually that you want your students to acquire. The language complexity and narrational pace of most films are geared to native English speakers. One way to ensure comprehension of the film is to stop it at a crucial place to ask your students questions that clarify or underscore important points.

Simulation Games

Simulations recreate real-life experiences as closely as possible, just as the bridge-building project, mentioned in Chapter 3, involving "companies" in designing, building, and testing bridges, is a simulation of real-life bridge building. When students play the roles of senators and members of Congress, taking a bill from

Individual help is sometimes needed to clarify the purpose and procedures of assignments.

inception through various committees until it finally is voted on, they are recreating the realities of Congress. Simulations thus provide students with direct experience through role-play. As a result, simulations build background knowledge that will help students comprehend texts discussing how bills are passed. Therefore, simulations provide the appropriate background knowledge for students to understand difficult and abstract texts, and they also help motivate students to read.

Simulations may be of particular help to English learners because they provide direct experience for learning, thus engaging nonverbal channels of information. At the same time, the building of background knowledge verbally and nonverbally during simulations develops concepts and corresponding vocabulary in context. Thus, simulations may be especially helpful to students who have difficulty with complex texts. In the past, simulations were often used at the end of a unit of study, but research on second language readers and others indicates the importance of building background knowledge before reading texts on new and unfamiliar topics (Carrell, 1984). Simulations offer a powerful way to do so.

Experiments

Another way to develop background knowledge as a prereading strategy is to involve students in experiments related to a theme or topic. For example, in a science unit on plants, students can experiment with growing plants. They may discover that roots will always grow down, seeking water and the earth, whereas shoots will try to reach the sunlight, even when the plants are placed upside down in a jar. Students can also chart the growth of carrots or potatoes, giving them different kinds of nutrients to test their effect. Students may keep journals, learning logs, or drawings to record growth for reporting later. Such experiments prepare students to read about plant growth, to use the knowledge acquired through their experiments, and to comprehend their texts better. Whether it is an experiment in science, an estimation project for mathematics, or an oral history project for social science, experiments and research build background knowledge for reading, provide motivation, and enhance comprehension.

Developing Vocabulary Before Students Read a Text

All of the preceding strategies for building background knowledge also offer students concrete opportunities to acquire new vocabulary in the context of direct experiences through field trips, simulation games, and experiments. However, it is not possible to provide direct experiences for all vocabulary. Sometimes it is necessary to teach vocabulary separate from direct experience. Whenever possible, it is helpful to illustrate meanings with pictures or diagrams. In addition, it is helpful to teach semantically similar words in a way that shows how they are related, rather than simply presenting a list of words to be memorized. If, for example, you were teaching about the *bow* of a boat, you would teach *fore*, *aft*, *mast*, and other nautical terms at the same time. This gives students a category or cognitive "net" to hold similar words and makes the words easier to remember. As we have stated previously, when information is meaningfully organized, it is easier to remember.

One of the simplest ways to assist students with vocabulary before they read a text is to discuss critical terms before asking students to read. Another is to ask students to brainstorm or cluster around a familiar word to help them expand the word's meaning. For example, if students were going to read about the desert, you might ask them to think of all the words that relate to a desert. One class we observed came up with words such as *hot*, *wind*, *dry*, *sand*, *cactus*, and *scorpions*. The teacher wrote the words in a cluster on the board. The students also discussed each word so that they were prepared to read the text with a better understanding. In this case, the vocabulary activity activated important schema for their reading.

Another way to organize prereading information is to create a map or structured overview of a concept. In this case, the key word is placed in the center of the map, with supporting categories placed on extensions from the center. The map provides a context for understanding the word. For example, a map might have the word *giraffe* in the center. On the extensions might be such categories as "what the giraffes look like" or "food eaten by giraffes." Underneath the extensions would be details describing the category. In this way, students get a more complete view of what the category *giraffe* means before they read about it. In short, you might select keywords or words you anticipate students might have difficulty with before they read the text. You will thus have a better assurance of their successfully engaging the text materials.

Structured Overviews

Structured overviews are visual displays of information, similar to flowcharts and maps, that provide readers with a basic outline of the important points in a book,

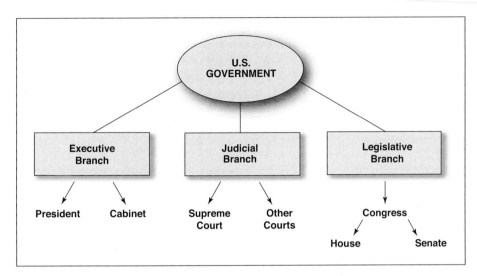

FIGURE 9.8

Structured Overview of U.S. Government

chapter, or passage. Presented on an overhead projector, on tagboard, or on butcher paper prior to reading, structured overviews preview and highlight important information and interrelationships of ideas and corresponding vocabulary (Readence, Bean, & Baldwin, 1981). Similarly, by providing a hierarchy of ideas in a text, structured overviews give readers an idea of the relative importance of ideas and provide categories to assist comprehension and memory of key concepts. The structured overview in Figure 9.8 presents an organized scheme of the different parts of the U.S. government. Look at the overview to see how it might assist a student preparing to read a chapter on the U.S. government and how it might help a reader organize information.

Preview Guides

Preview guides can also help give students an overview of the important ideas in a text because they help them determine how to preview for reading (Vacca & Vacca, 1989). Typically, a preview guide shows students how to read the titles, headings, subheadings, and summaries in a book. By reading these, English learners gain a sense of a text's content and begin to set a purpose for their reading. By reading a summary, for example, your students become aware of what they should know before they begin reading a text. The preview guide in Figure 9.9 teaches students how to preview a chapter and assists them with setting a purpose and monitoring their comprehension.

Directions: Consider the following questions, based on headings and subheadings from Chapter 9, before you read. Try to predict how the chapter will answer each of the questions and check your predictions when you read the chapter.

1. What is meant by prereading and during-reading instruction?
2. How are reading and writing used for learning in content areas?
3. What is the importance of text structure in content reading?
4. What can be done as a prereading exercise to prepare students to read a difficult text?
5. How can teachers assist students during reading?

FIGURE 9.9

Preview Guide for This Chapter

353

FIGURE 9.10

ANTICIPATION GUIDE
FOR *THE GREAT
GILLY HOPKINS*

Directions: Before reading *The Great Gilly Hopkins* answer these questions, which stem from the book's experiences. After reading the book, answer the questions again to see if you still have the same opinions. Answer the questions: strongly agree, agree, agree somewhat, or strongly disagree.

Before Reading	After Reading	
_____	_____	1. Having to move constantly from one foster family to another would make me angry.
_____	_____	2. Most people are not prejudiced toward people who are handicapped or fat or toward African Americans.
_____	_____	3. Prejudice comes from being ignorant.
_____	_____	4. People can overcome their ignorance and prejudice.

Anticipation Guides

You can create **anticipation guides** to prepare students for a story or text. Anticipation guides motivate students and help them predict what will happen in a text (Ausubel, 1968; Holmes & Roser, 1987). A typical guide invites students to state an opinion or predict something about the main ideas or themes in a story or essay before they read it. After reading, students compare the views they held before and after reading.

The guide in Figure 9.10, based on *The Great Gilly Hopkins* (Paterson, 1978), illustrates how an anticipation guide both motivates students to read a passage or book and assists them with setting a purpose and monitoring for purpose during reading. Notice that the guide also provides learners with some background knowledge about the text they are about to read. Though we list anticipation guides under prereading, you can see that they provide support during and after reading as well.

In summary, prereading strategies build background knowledge, create motivation, and help students establish a purpose for their reading. Based on your view of what students need to be successful readers of a complex text, you may choose anticipation guides, preview guides, structured overviews, or less elaborate methods to assist students with comprehension. Finally, when students establish a purpose for reading, they are prepared to monitor their own interaction with a text. Self-monitoring assists students with assessing their own success rather than relying solely on the teacher to evaluate their interactions with a passage.

During Reading Strategies: Monitoring Comprehension

During reading strategies help students monitor their comprehension based on the purpose they have set for reading (Leal, Crays, & Moetz, 1985). They need to ask themselves, "Did I find what I was looking for?" If they have a clearly set purpose, they will be able to determine their success while reading. In addition, they can use the structure of their texts to assist them with finding information based on their purpose. For instance, they can use headings and subheadings to ask questions they think will be answered in a passage. Thus, if they read a heading that says, "The Three Causes of the Civil War," they will know to look for three causes. If they only find two, they will recognize the need to reread. When students know what they are looking for and what they will be doing with the information later, they will be better able to evaluate their own reading. This **metacognitive** aspect is a key to comprehension (Anderson, 2002).

If English learners have not established a purpose for their reading, they will not be able to evaluate whether they have been successful readers. When they check their understanding based on the purpose they have set, then they are monitoring their comprehension. If the purpose for reading is to obtain a football score in the newspaper, they will know they have been successful when they have found the score. If, on the other hand, they are interested in who scored the touchdowns, they will be looking for different information and may scan the print differently. Thus, the purpose established for reading a chapter in your classroom will determine how the student will monitor his or her comprehension during reading.

Most of the during-reading strategies center on **questioning strategies** that you model or that build students' self-questioning abilities. These active comprehension strategies (Nolte & Singer, 1985) model questions for children (Stauffer, 1975), help them ask questions of each other (Palinscar & Brown, 1984), and teach self-questioning strategies after some background knowledge has been provided (Singer, 1978; Yopp, 1987). All of the following strategies attempt to model some form of **self-questioning** to assist readers in monitoring what they are learning as they read (MacDonald, 1986). We present several strategies that assist with purpose setting and self-assessment.

Using Headings and Subheadings

Headings and subheadings not only help students establish specific purpose in reading, but also guide students in monitoring comprehension during reading. Research shows that you can boost your students' comprehension and retention substantially if you simply make sure that they read the headings and subheadings and formulate questions about them (Meyer, et al., 1980). Students sometimes feel they can plow through a text more quickly if they don't bother to read headings. However, they will find that if they read the headings in texts, they will be able to turn the headings into questions and answer the questions when they read the text. For example, if a text heading states, "Three Environmental Dangers of Deforestation," students can create the question "What are the three environmental dangers?" or "What does deforestation mean?" The questions will create their purpose for reading, and they will know that if they only find two dangers in the subsequent paragraphs, then they will have to look for a third danger. By using headings in their reading, students can check whether they have been successful readers. This checking comprehension based on purpose is called **monitoring comprehension**. When you teach students how to turn headings into questions, you help them to monitor their understanding and become independent, successful readers.

Directed Reading-Thinking Activity (DR-TA)

In Chapter 8 we discussed another questioning procedure, DR-TA, in terms of narrative texts (Peregoy & Boyle, 1990a, 1990b; Stauffer, 1975). DR-TA may also be used with expository text. Because expository texts normally contain headings and subheadings, it is sometimes easier to determine when and where to ask key questions. When Lucinda Lim introduces DR-TA with expository text to her students, she uses the following steps. First, she models the procedure with a short

FIGURE 9.11

EDITED DR-TA
TRANSCRIPT

TEACHER: We're going to read an interesting article about the history of soap. What do you think we'll find in the article?

CHILDREN: "About different kinds of soap." "Like bubbles and watery." "Bars of soap."

TEACHER: One of the headings, you'll notice, says, "Cleaning before Soap." How do you think people got clean before soap?

CHILDREN: "They probably jumped in the river." "They didn't get very clean; they smelled." *(laughter)*

TEACHER: Another heading says, "Life without Soap." What do you think our lives would be like without soap?

CHILDREN: "Joey would smell." *(laughter)* "We'd all smell." *(laughter)*

TEACHER: When you read the article, see if your guesses about soap are like article says and make your own guesses using the other headings. what the Remember, if you're guessing you'll have your best chance of understanding what you're reading, even if your guesses are not always right.

reading. Next, she shows students how to create questions using headings and subheadings. She then asks students in groups to make up questions based on headings and answer them in their groups. Finally, she asks her students to report and compare their questions and answers. After some practice in groups, she asks them to use the procedure on their own. She often places beginning-level students in heterogeneous groups or places them with an advanced-level student to assist them with difficult reading. In this way, the advanced student, by clearly articulating the meaning of a text, gains a sophistication about it, whereas the beginning-level student gains access to a difficult text. Figure 9.11 is a brief edited transcript of Lucinda introducing DR-TA to her class with a text about the history of soap.

In this transcript, we can see that Lucinda has prepared her students to read the article on soap. First, she has activated their background knowledge about soap by simply asking some questions. Second, she has shown them how to anticipate and predict what an article might be about by using headings. She has also shown them that it is appropriate to make guesses about something they will read. Finally, she has prepared them to monitor their understanding. Thus, DR-TA combines aspects of prereading activities and questioning procedures to assist students' comprehension.

Vocabulary Strategies During Reading

Students often need strategies to help them comprehend unfamiliar words they may encounter while reading. Two strategies discussed by Tierney and Readence (2000) in their excellent resource book, *Reading Strategies and Practices: A Compendium* are **contextual redefinition** (Cunningham, Cunningham, & Arthur, 1981) and **preview in context**. Both strategies attempt to assist students with comprehending and acquiring vocabulary within the context of their reading. For convenience, we combine features from both strategies to suggest a way to help your students use their background knowledge and the text context to gain a better understanding of their reading. First, you select words you consider important to the understanding of a particular passage. Next, you create several sentences using the words to give your students a chance to predict the meaning of new words in context. You might show students how to use the specific context of the

Deborah and Theresa were happy because Ultima did many of the household _____ they normally did, and they had more time to spend in the attic and cut out an interminable train of paper dolls which they dressed, gave names to, and most miraculously, made talk.

FIGURE 9.12

EXCERPT FROM *BLESS ME, ULTIMA* (ANAYA, 1972)

words to gain knowledge about them. For example, surrounding words can give clues to meaning; headings or subheadings can hint at the meanings of words; or, often, authors paraphrase technical words in common phrases to assure their readers' understanding. When students become aware of the ways authors help them with new vocabulary, they will be more successful in their interactions with texts. Using some form of contextual vocabulary instruction gives students the capability of becoming independent readers who can rely on their own use of strategies to gain meaning from print.

Using Clustering to Develop Vocabulary in Context

One way you can assist English learners with developing their vocabularies through reading is to teach them to guess a word's meaning by the context of its use. One day while we were observing her class, Steffanie Marion used the novel the students were reading to develop vocabulary. First she placed a transparency page of the novel they were reading, *Bless Me, Ultima* (Anaya, 1972), on an overhead projector. She omitted vocabulary words she felt the students might need help with (Figure 9.12). Next, she asked them to guess what word would fit in the first blank space. She placed a circle on the board to represent the unknown word and then surrounded it with students' encircled guesses, as in Figure 9.13. When the students had completed their guesses, she placed the word used in the novel in the center circle in the cluster. Thus, she was able to point out the words in the cluster that were synonyms for the central word. Steffanie's strategy helped the students gain confidence in their guesses and developed their vocabulary further by giving them synonyms for a new and difficult vocabulary word. Steffanie doesn't use the strategy often, she says, but she finds it to be an excellent way to show how to generate the meaning of a new word by using context. In this way she provides students with a strategy that promotes independence in reading.

An example of an excerpt and cluster from a social science passage is shown in Figures 9.14 and 9.15.

Jigsaw Procedure

Jigsaw, introduced in Chapter 3, is another group strategy for assisting comprehension of all students in a class (Johnson, et al., 1986). Using jigsaw, teachers make students responsible for one another's learning, help them with identifying purpose and important concepts in a text, and assist them with reporting information gained. The steps for using jigsaw in a class are the following:

Using the jigsaw procedure, you place the responsibility for purpose setting, questioning, and comprehension monitoring on the shoulders

FIGURE 9.13 • VOCABULARY CLUSTER BASED ON *BLESS ME, ULTIMA*

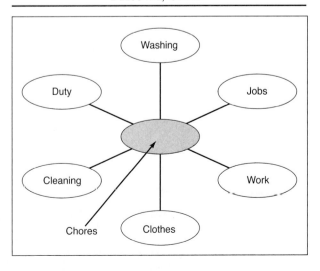

FIGURE 9.14

SOCIAL SCIENCE PASSAGE
ABOUT THE LEWIS AND
CLARK EXPEDITION

After the Louisiana Purchase, President Thomas Jefferson wanted to find out if the Missouri River went all the way through the United States to the Pacific Ocean. If it did, it would provide a possible trade route. To find out he sent Lewis and Clark on an expedition up the Missouri River to, he hoped, the Pacific Ocean. On this _____ Lewis and Clark took 48 men.

Step 1:   Place students in groups of three; each student has a number of 1, 2, or 3.

Step 2:   Students who are 1s become responsible for reading a certain number of pages in a text; likewise for numbers 2 and 3.

Step 3:   Students read the section for which they are responsible.

Step 4:   Groups of 1s, 2s, and 3s get together to form an "expert" group; they share information and decide how to report it back to their main or "base" groups (the groups consisting of the original 1, 2, and 3); 2s and 3s do the same.

Step 5:   1s report information to 2s and 3s in base groups; 2s and 3s do the same.

Step 6:   Some teachers like to have a brief whole-class discussion on the sections that they have read.

of your students. Moreover, all students take responsibility for one another's learning. When students present information to their base group, they present ideas and answer questions about the text for which they are responsible. Similarly, when it is their turn to hear from other members, they will ask questions to clarify their own thinking. The approach, good for all students, is particularly useful for students who might otherwise struggle with content texts because of limited knowledge of English. They will be able to read, question, and understand on their own but will also be able to share their reading and understanding with other students in the "expert" groups. In addition, they will be assisted by other students in their base groups and tutored wherever necessary (Verplaetse, 1998). Because the jigsaw procedure makes each student in a base group responsible for the comprehension of all students in the group, English learners can rely on much more support than they might receive in many content classes. Through the constant negotiating of meaning and continuous use of oral language each day in class, students gain optimal access to comprehensible input for further language and concept development. Jigsaw provides all learners with a maximum amount of support for reading in the content areas. Although this support is provided mainly in the during-reading phase, it is also provided in the postreading phase because students are also asked to organize their information for reporting to their base groups after reading.

FIGURE 9.15 • CLUSTER FOR VOCABULARY WORD: EXPEDITION

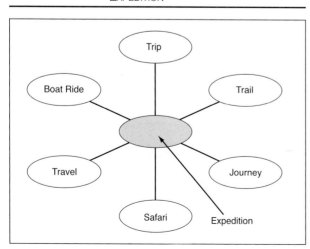

Learning Logs

Journals and learning logs are discussed more fully later, but we want to point out their utility now as an excellent metacognitive learning tool in the during-reading phase (Jaramillo, 1998). Learning logs require students to formulate questions about what they are learning or what might be difficult while they are reading (Calkins, 1994). Using learning logs, students may write specific notes concerning a passage in a text, a formula or experiment, or a period of history. As you review student logs, you can identify concepts that you may need to clarify. In addition, learning logs provide an excellent and natural way to evaluate a student's progress. Most important, learning logs provide students with a way to both assess their own learning and get help from you. One student's learning log shows how a student can create a dialogue of learning with the teacher:

JOSE: I don't understand about photosynthesis. How does the light make air? How do plants help us live and breathe?

TEACHER: This is a very difficult idea. Many students are having some difficulty with it, and I will be going over it tomorrow. We'll be going over it in groups where we'll share questions to help us make the ideas clearer. Then maybe it'll be clearer to everybody.

Differentiating Instruction for Content Area Reading

To differentiate instruction for content area reading, you first need to consider each student's English proficiency and general literacy abilities, especially reading, in relation to your content area standards and curriculum materials. Your previous assessments of oral language (Chapter 4) and reading (Chapter 8) provide a good start. Student writing samples (Chapter 7) also flesh out your appraisal of your students' English language and literacy development. With these general assessments in mind, you may now begin to consider content area standards for your grade level and the textbooks and other materials you will use to help students learn the required curriculum. Your next step is to evaluate your content texts against your students' ability to read and learn from them. One way to do so is to conduct a GRI discussed in this chapter for matching students with texts. It is likely that you will need to find supplemental reading materials that present essential information in brief formats and that include graphic and pictorial cues to support text meaning. Multimedia resources may also help students understand content.

As you review your lesson plans, you need to build in ways for less proficient English learners to understand the material and also for struggling readers to gain from their reading. Sheltering strategies are essential in this regard. At the same time, you need to make sure more advanced students remain interested and challenged. With your content materials on hand, you are now ready to use the prereading and during-reading strategies recommended in this chapter. To give you an overview, we recommend that you take a look at Figure 9.7. This figure summarizes purposes for using particular strategies before and during reading, as presented in this chapter. The figure also shows the postreading strategies that are presented in Chapter 10. At the end of Chapter 10, you will find additional discussion of differentiated instruction for content learning and a detailed differentiated lesson plan.

Summary

The prereading and during-reading phases of reading and writing across the curriculum are crucial. If students don't develop a clear purpose for reading, they will not be efficient content area readers. In addition, they will not be able to monitor their comprehension if they aren't clear about what they should be learning. So the prereading phase of reading and writing across the curriculum prepares students for the during-reading phase. The primary responsibility of students in the during-reading phase is to assess or monitor their comprehension based on their purpose for reading. During-reading strategies also help students keep track of information they may want to present later to others. As a final step, students must consider how they will organize the information so that it will be remembered. Although this chapter has been primarily concerned with helping students comprehend what they are reading, the next chapter, on postreading, focuses on helping students remember what they have understood. Learning requires not only comprehending but remembering.

To assist your students with content learning we have provided several strategies and listed their general grade-level use in Figure 9.16. As the chart shows, most of the strategies are initiated in the fourth or fifth grade and beyond. However, we recommend that you begin introducing purposeful content area reading and writing in earlier grades and also introduce some of the strategies that will scaffold English learners' content reading. With this assistance, your students will be prepared gradually for success in later grades.

FIGURE 9.16

GRADE LEVELS AT WHICH STRATEGIES MAY BE USED

Strategy / Grade Level	K	1	2	3	4	5	6	7	8	9	10	11	12
Anticipation guides						●———————————————→							
Cohesive ties							●—————————————→						
DR-TA	●——————————————————————————————→												
Essay structures							●—————————————→						
Experiments	●——————————————————————————————→												
Field trips	●——————————————————————————————→												
Films	●——————————————————————————————→												
GRI						●———————————————→							
Headings/subheadings						●———————————————→							
Jigsaw procedure						●———————————————→							
Learning logs		●————————————————————————————→											
Preview guides						●———————————————→							
Preview vocabulary	●——————————————————————————————→												
Simulation games						●———————————————→							
Story structure	●——————————————————————————————→												
Structured overviews						●———————————————→							
Teacher talk	●——————————————————————————————→												
Text structure						●———————————————→							

Suggestions for Further Reading

Chapman, C., & King, R. (2003). *Differentiated instuctional strategies for reading in the content areas*. Thousand Oaks, CA: Corwin Press.

This book on differentiated instruction packs a lot of information into 202 pages. We especially like the chapter on "Knowing the Reader," which has sections on reading problems and solutions. For example, the book will give examples of reading behaviors and then suggests briefly what you might try with a student having the problem. Needs word attack skills is followed by four teaching suggestions; over uses phonics is followed by nine suggestions. The book does the same with other areas, such as vocabulary and comprehension. This is an excellent, practical text.

Seda, M. M., Ligouri, O. Z., & Seda, C. M. (1999). Bridging literacy and social science studies: Engaging prior knowledge through children's books. *TESOL Journal, 8*(3), 34–40.

This article provides a clear rationale for using children's literature to enhance the learning of middle school ESL students. It discusses the importance of prior knowledge for students reading in subjects such as history and shows how children's literature can help students build their schema to prepare them to read history texts. The authors give detailed examples of designing and implementing their program and provide examples of what they would do to improve the program. An excellent, thorough article.

Tang, G. M. (1992/1993). Teaching content knowledge and ESOL in multicultural classrooms. *TESOL Journal, 2*(2), 9–12.

This excellent article asks and answers the following three questions: "How can we help students learn new content knowledge written or spoken in English? How can we enable them to demonstrate their content knowledge in English? How can we assist them in using and expressing their background knowledge in English and linking it to new knowledge?" The article then develops a classroom model that includes teacher input and student tasks. Students are asked to construct graphics from a text and to construct texts using the graphics. Sample graphics are used in the article. An excellent article for every middle and secondary teacher.

Vacca, R. T. & Vacca, J. L. (2007). Content area reading: Literacy and learning across the curriculum (9th ed.).

This book, a classic in the area, is in its ninth edition for a reason. Over the years it has provided teachers, including ourselves, important theory and practice in content area reading and learning. Although it isn't specifically written for English learners, there is valuable information on theory and practice for every teacher of ELs.

Wilhelm, K. H. (1999). Collaborative dos and don'ts. *TESOL Journal, 8*(2), 14–19.

This article looks at collaborative learning within the context of project work in classrooms. In particular, the article presents a thorough list and explanation of the dos and don'ts. The list includes several categories: explaining and demonstrating student and teacher roles and responsibilities; modeling the collaboration learning approach; nurturing feedback, reflection, and negotiation; and using well-balanced appropriate grading systems. An excellent article with guiding principles for collaborative work.

361

Activities

1. Visit the classroom of a teacher who has been trained recently in content area reading and writing or of a teacher who has a reputation of being the best teacher in the school and see what they do. How does the teacher prepare English learners and others to read a text? How does the teacher use writing in the class? What would you do differently based on information in this text? What would you do differently based on the success of the teacher you observed?

2. Try creating a GRI on a chapter you might teach. If you are already in the classroom, use the GRI with your class as a study guide and see how it guides your students' learning. Did it prepare them to be more efficient readers? Did it assist them with comprehension? Do you think a GRI will help students become more independent learners eventually or will they simply become dependent on the GRI as a scaffold for their learning? When is it appropriate to take the GRI away and ask students to develop their own questions for their reading?

3. Observe classrooms where teachers try to provide background information in such areas as social science or history for English learners who may have come from a country with a different form of government or who may have a different historical knowledge because of their country of origin. How does the teacher build such students' schema or background knowledge to help them better understand their text? Does this building of schema appear to work for most of the students? If not, what adaptations would you make to the teacher's lesson?

4. As there is a strong relationship between vocabulary knowledge and reading comprehension in content areas, visit content classes and see how teachers approach the teaching of content vocabulary. Do they use worksheets or do they seem to have developed some systematic approach to teaching vocabulary? Do the teachers organize the vocabulary to enhance memory and comprehension or do they simply give students lists or tell them what certain words mean? What kind of vocabulary instruction do you find most useful in the classrooms you observe?

5. If you were preparing a U.S. history lesson for second language learners, how would you develop their background knowledge, vocabulary, and approaches to reading a history text? What strategies discussed in this text or that you have observed in classrooms seem most useful? What scaffolding, SDAIE, or sheltering approaches would you use to enhance the students' learning? How would you teach students to become expert questioners of texts they are reading? How would you develop their confidence as readers?

myeducationlab
Where the Classroom Comes to Life

Video Homework Exercise
Promoting Literacy

The video introduces a form for teaching content area literacy that uses modeling, teaching of strategies, and scaffolding. Next, a middle school teacher discusses the differences between a bar graph and pie graph as part of a discussion about scientific methods. Finally, an elementary teacher helps students think about their reading by visualizing as they read and showing them how to highlight important information for research. She discusses the importance of connecting important information to the students' experiences.

Go to MyEducationLab, select the topic "Content Area Reading and Writing," and watch the video entitled "Promoting Literacy."

1. We have suggested a model similar to the one discussed at the beginning of this video. Our model contains modeling, scaffolding, and direct instruction. Are the two models exactly alike or different? Discuss.

2. A lesson on bar graphs and pie graphs might be an ideal one for English learners because it does not rely solely on verbal explanation. How would you adapt this lesson for English learner students in your class?

3. What value do you think there is in teaching students to visualize information they are reading? Do you think it is a good idea to teach students in primary grades how to highlight information? Why? Why not?

Content Reading and Writing: Postreading Strategies for Organizing and Remembering

"It ain't what you don't know that gets you; it's the things you know that ain't so."

—MARK TWAIN

In this chapter, we discuss ways you can enhance students' comprehension and memory of what they have read in their texts. We discuss such questions as the following:

1. Why should we teach vocabulary in the postreading phase of content reading? What role does this instruction play in assisting students' memory?

2. What is the role of writing in content area reading and writing?

3. Why are collaborative projects particularly valuable for second language content learners?

4. Why do thematic units enhance second language students' learning and memory in content area classrooms?

5. How can we assess English learners in content area learning?

C lare Goldmark's students always develop projects to be presented at the end of specific units in her social science class. Although she provides students with a list of possible projects, she also encourages them to select a topic—within a unit on World War II, for example—that they are particularly interested in. Then she provides students with a model of how they will present the project to their classmates.

She organizes her class so that each group of about five students presents its topic to a cooperative panel of five classmates. The students are to use visuals, including films, maps, collages, or drama they have created, to describe their project, thereby sheltering their presentations. The panel's job is to ask friendly questions about the project so that all the class can learn more about their topic. This project/panel approach requires presenters to prepare, organize, and rehearse their lesson for the panel presentation; thus, they must remember well what they have learned. In addition, because all of the students in the class are involved as both presenters of projects and panelists who must ask questions about the projects, the students are all active participants in the activity. This is especially important because research indicates that students in content classes are often left out in mainstream discussions, etc. (Harklau, 1994; Harper & Platt, 1998). Clare says that the students show a remarkable memory not only for their own project information but for the information provided in other projects as well. These projects require her students to understand, rehearse, remember, and present what they have studied.

364

Postreading Strategies for Students

If students have developed background knowledge for a text, set a purpose for reading, and monitored their comprehension during reading, they must next organize the information so that they can remember what they have read. This is what Clare provides for her students with their project presentations. If content area information is not organized in some way, it will not be adequately remembered (Bruner, 1960; Miller, 1956; Miller, Galanter, & Pribram, 1960). Thus, postreading activities help students organize and remember the information they have gathered in reading. The strategies discussed subsequently, such as semantic feature analysis, mapping, rehearsing, summarizing, and writing, will assist students with remembering important information.

Semantic Feature Analysis for Vocabulary Development After Reading

One method used for reinforcing important concepts and terms after reading is **semantic feature analysis**, which is a graphic method of listing and analyzing the essential traits or features that define members or examples of a particular category or concept. For example, given the category *pets*, one might list *dog*, *cat*, *hamster*, *fish*, and *parakeet* as members. To analyze the essential traits or features of these pets, a list of traits, such as *land*, *water*, *wings*, *fur*, *legs*, and *fins*, must be generated. The final step in the semantic feature analysis is to create a chart and check the features that apply to each member of the category (Figure 10.1).

CATEGORY: PETS					
	Features:				
	land	water	wings	legs	fur
Member: dog cat hamster fish parakeet					

FIGURE 10.1

CHART FOR SEMANTIC FEATURE ANALYSIS OF PETS

After the matrix is set up, students and teacher together check off the traits for each pet. In the process, vocabulary items are reinforced as categories are analyzed and explored. An additional step is to invite students to add other pets to the list for which the feature analysis was carried out. Students may also come up with other traits to analyze, such as whether the animals are carnivores, herbivores, or omnivores.

The semantic feature analysis can be especially helpful in illustrating abstract relationships among complex concepts, as shown in Figure 10.2 on government. After reading and studying about various forms of government, students may work in groups or as a class to list each type of government and establish a list of features, such as freedom to assemble, the right to hold elections, the number of leaders, and so forth. Next, students fill in the chart, analyzing each type of government according to the traits listed in the chart. In this way, students are able to reinforce the meaning of words such as *oligarchy*, *monarchy*, *democracy*, and *dictatorship*, while developing insights concerning similarities and differences among them.

Other visual strategies that help students assimilate special vocabulary are mapping, clustering, and structured overviews. Each of these strategies helps students expand their knowledge of new technical terms and understand them in the

TYPE OF GOVERNMENT	ELECTIONS	FREEDOM	NUMBER OF LEADERS	POWERS	FREE TO ASSEMBLE	FREE SPEECH	OTHER
Monarchy							
Democracy							
Dictatorship							
Oligarchy							

FIGURE 10.2

CHART FOR SEMANTIC FEATURE ANALYSIS OF GOVERNMENT

context of related terms, thus creating a kind of cognitive net for keeping the information in long-term memory. Briefly stated, vocabulary is best taught within a meaningful context, whether you are learning words for a better understanding of government or a better understanding of literary writing. You will want to assist students with special vocabulary terms before they read, with strategies for understanding words during reading and with strategies for consolidating their new vocabulary knowledge after they have completed a text. Because vocabulary knowledge plays a major role in reading comprehension, vocabulary strategies play a central role in our teaching.

Rehearsing to Organize and Remember Information

Rehearsing refers to the reformulation or presentation again of information to oneself or to others. Have you ever studied with someone else? If you have, you rehearsed the information you knew by sharing it with another person. When you repeated what you knew and listened to others present what they knew, you were rehearsing the information. Rehearsing information goes beyond simple memorization and repetition. Having an audience requires you to organize the information so that it is easier to understand. You can also rehearse information culled from a text by talking to yourself or repeating the information aloud. Rehearsing information, whether by repeating orally, paraphrasing in writing, or creating a map, is necessary for memory. Rehearsing requires a deeper level of processing than just reading and assuming that you will remember the information. The Venn diagram and the mapping strategy, presented next, facilitate rehearsal by organizing information visually and spatially to make it easier to access and recall.

Venn Diagrams

A Venn diagram (see Figure 10.3), represented by two interlocking circles, serves to illustrate similarities and differences between two novels, two periods in history, two characters, or any other pair of concepts. Where the circles intersect the two things

FIGURE 10.3

VENN DIAGRAM COMPARING AND CONTRASTING CIVIL WAR SOLDIERS

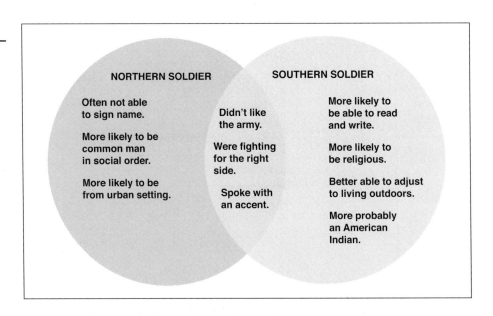

NORTHERN SOLDIER

Often not able to sign name.

More likely to be common man in social order.

More likely to be from urban setting.

Didn't like the army.

Were fighting for the right side.

Spoke with an accent.

SOUTHERN SOLDIER

More likely to be able to read and write.

More likely to be religious.

Better able to adjust to living outdoors.

More probably an American Indian.

being compared and contrasted are similar; where the circles are separate the things being compared and contrasted are different. The Venn diagram in Figure 10.3 illustrates some comparisons and contrasts students made between Northern and Southern soldiers during the Civil War. Venn diagrams can be used to compare and contrast characters in a novel, ideas, or historical situations, and they can become a prewriting diagram students can use when they write a compare/contrast essay of their own.

Mapping

Mapping is a powerful strategy for assisting students with organizing and remembering information. In addition, because maps are both spatial and visual, they assist second language readers with sharing information and their own visual interpretation of the information they have obtained from reading (Boyle, 1982a, 1982b, 1982c; Boyle & Peregoy, 1991; Buckley & Boyle, 1981; Ruddell & Boyle, 1989). A map may simply represent information using headings and subheadings as presented in a text, or it may synthesize the information according to the readers' deeper understanding of a text. Steps for developing a map are the following:

- The student places the title in the center of the map and places headings on extensions from the center.
- The student places the information that he or she found under extension headings.
- When the map is complete, the student checks for important information and reviews the map. If important information is missing, the student places information under appropriate headings.
- The map is studied for a few minutes and is reviewed a few days later for memory. If the student forgets something in the map, he or she checks the text for verification.

The map in Figure 10.4 on soap illustrates how one student developed a map using the headings and supporting details. The student was able to remember the information presented in the chapter "History of Soap" in some detail even a few weeks later.

367

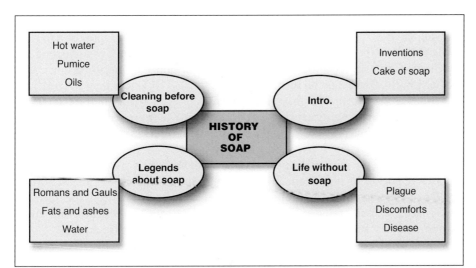

FIGURE 10.4

MAP OF CHAPTER ON SOAP

FIGURE 10.5

GROUP MAP ILLUSTRATING
THE U.S. CONSTITUTION

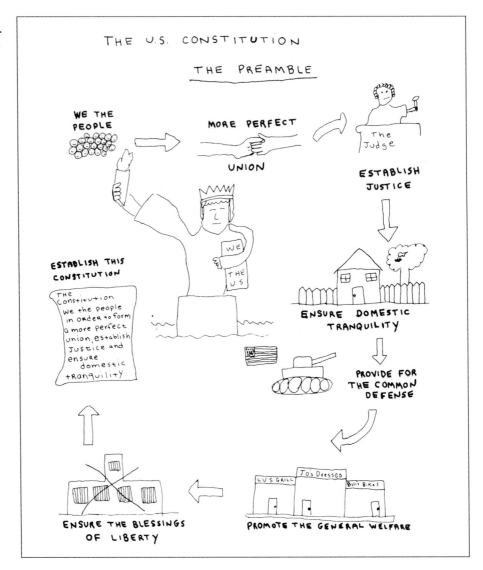

The map in Figure 10.5 was developed by a group of students who had been studying the U.S. Constitution. After reading a chapter and developing a map such as the one on soap, the students attempted to develop a map that went beyond the information, showing relationships among the basic concepts discussed in the text (Boyle, 1982b). Their map on the Constitution (Figure 10.5) was their first attempt to synthesize the information they had derived from the activities in the class unit.

Maps help students organize key concepts in a text and their interrelationships. Mapping thus requires students to reconstruct information and organize it for memory.

In summary, the purpose of postreading strategies is to assist with understanding and retention of important information. Most of the strategies, therefore, involve organizing or restructuring information to make it easier to remember. We have shared several strategies that assist with organizing and restructuring information, such as mapping, Venn diagrams, and semantic feature analysis. These strategies call for a deeper level of processing information because they require students to present information to others in a coherent manner. Next, we discuss writing in content areas.

Writing as a Learning Tool Across the Curriculum

Writing is another powerful strategy that promotes discovery, comprehension, and retention of information (Calkins, 1994). In recent years, teachers have begun to use the writing process and its various phases as an integral part of their content area classrooms. They have found that writing helps students clarify their thoughts and remember what they have learned. Similarly, you will find that you can evaluate and assist your students' learning by reading learning log entries, journals, and notebooks. Recent research has supported the use of writing in content areas by showing that students who write tend to understand more and remember more. We recommend that you ask English learners to write in logs and journals, to write in notebooks, to summarize and comment on their own learning, and to perform hands-on research projects that are reported in correct writing (Reppen, 1994/1995). We believe that journals and learning logs are an excellent way to begin involving students in writing in content areas, and we have found in our own research that even kindergartners can write in journals and evaluate their learning (Peregoy & Boyle, 1990a).

Journals and Learning Logs

We have recommended journals and learning logs for different purposes throughout this book. Table 10.1 illustrates the kinds of journals you can use in various content areas: dialogue/buddy journals, notebooks, learning logs, and response journals (Kreeft, 1984; Rupert & Brueggeman, 1986). In addition, the table notes the general purpose of each type of journal along with an example of its use in different content areas. Although the types of journals are not always mutually exclusive, they give you a feeling for the variety of roles journal writing can play in content areas.

In most cases, you will want to respond to the students' journal entries about once a week. As mentioned in our previous discussion of journals, your comments should concentrate on the content of the journals, not on grammar, punctuation, and spelling. For example, you might clarify a concept over which a student indicates confusion or you might simply give students support for their entries. Journals provide excellent opportunities for students to write daily, to develop fluency, to clarify ideas, and to monitor their own learning and to "become more aware" of their learning strategies (Oxford, 2003). Moreover, writing down information assists memory. You may remember a time when you made a grocery list but found when you entered the store that you had left it behind. Nevertheless, you remembered much of your list because you had written it down; writing had assisted your memory just as writing will assist your students' memory.

Developing Topics and Student Self-Selection of Topics in Content Areas

We generally support the view that students, whenever possible, should select their own writing topics. That is, if your class is studying plants, students

TABLE 10.1 • JOURNAL WRITING IN CONTENT AREAS

JOURNAL TYPE AND PURPOSE	SCIENCE	LANGUAGE ARTS	MATHEMATICS	SOCIAL SCIENCE
Dialogue/ Buddy: to share with another	Explain to teacher or to friend what is happening in class and what is understood	Share with another about a story or poem being read; share other aspects of class	Let teacher or friend know how class or assignments are going	"Discuss" information pertaining to topics in class
Notebook: to take notes to assist memory	Write down information pertaining to an experiment in class	Take down conversations overheard for use in a story to be written	Keep notes about math concepts	Write down key information discussed in class
Learning logs: to discuss and process information from class	Write down notes about what one understands in the class and about what might seem unclear	Write down key concepts from class such as definitions of concepts: setting, theme, characterization	Try to explain math concepts for self or perhaps for another; clarify or try to apply a new concept	Take notes on causes of Civil War or other key ideas; ask self to identify and clarify ideas
Response journals: to respond openly and freely to any topic	Respond to feelings about scientific experimentation or use of animals as subjects or biogenetics	Make any comments on characters or conflicts presented in a story being read	Respond to math in an interesting way, such as ask questions about why people who would never admit to being illiterate will seemingly brag about their math ignorance	Respond to politicians' handling of peace after World War I or about attitudes of pilgrims toward American Indians

INTERNET RESOURCES

Dave's ESL café (**www.eslcafe.com/search/ index.html**) contains over 3,000 links that deal with just about any topic you may be interested in. Topics include literacy, writing, listening, pronunciation, vocabulary, and games. You might evaluate the site on your own or with a student to see how well the site works for teachers and students. In addition, the Wisconsin Literacy Education and Reading Network Source (**http://wilearns.state. wi.us/apps/default.asp**) contains a range of ideas, activities, and strategies. Some areas are: vocabulary, teaching/learning activities, defining comprehension, comprehending different texts, struggling readers, and a large number of literacy links.

should be allowed to select topics that interest them within the context of plants. Additionally, if students are going to do research, they should select and shape their own topics for research. However, we also recognize that you may have important topics for students. When this is so, we recommend that you create **context-enriched topics**, which we define as topics that embed abstract concepts in real-life experiences, allowing students to use their own experiences as part of your assigned topic. The following examples should clarify this process.

Recently, we met a teacher, Joe Allyn, who wanted his students to know something about world economies. Instead of assigning his students to write a paper on the economy of Peru, Mr. Allyn gave them the following situation:

> You are a travel agent, and you intend to take a group of vacationers to a country. To attract enough people for the trip, you will need to prepare a brochure. In the brochure, you will explain the various sights and major cities. You will also need to advise people on how much money they will need and on the clothes they will take, based on the climate and the time of the year. Your travelers will also want to know the kinds of items they might buy and where the best buys are found. Finally, they will need to know how much to expect to pay for hotels, for meals, and what kinds of tips, if any, they should give to waiters. Your brochure should have an attractive cover and should contain any other pieces of information you feel travelers to your country should know. I will supply you with a model of such a brochure.

Joe let students pick a country, work in peer response and revision groups, and share research on the country with one another. He then had a travel day in which each group tried to entice their classmates to "travel" to their country; students used their brochures along with pictures and short films of the country.

The context-enriched topic Joe created has several advantages over traditional, assigned topics. First, the students selected their own country, which allowed some English learners to tell their classmates about their own country and culture. Second, they had an audience for their writing—other travelers and the students in their class. Third, they had a "real" assignment, one that people actually perform in the world. Fourth, the activity involves group collaboration and research. Finally, Joe gave students a model of an appropriate brochure. For English learners, activities might range from doing research on their own home country to drawing pictures for the brochure to adding personal knowledge of travel in another country they may know well. Most traditional writing

371

assignments can be changed into context-enriched assignments by allowing students to use what they already know to create something new.

Noel Anderson also offers context-enriched assignments when she asks her students to select a topic of their own or to use one of her suggested topics after reading a novel. Here is one context-enriched topic she gives to students as a possible writing assignment: "You are Tom Sawyer, and your raft has been carried away in a time warp. Select one of the situations below or create one of your own, and write a letter to Becky about what you experienced and what you think of your experience."

Writing Topic Ideas

1. You find yourself in the school cafeteria where the students are having a food fight.
2. You find yourself on the 50-yard line of the Super Bowl.
3. You find yourself in the middle of a crowd at a rock concert.
4. You find yourself in the middle of a class where the book *Tom Sawyer* is being discussed.
5. Select your own situation.

Noel finds that her students enjoy not only the topics she creates, but also the ones they create for themselves, including some that are modeled after her own and others that are totally original. The opportunity to create their own situation instead of writing an abstract character sketch is particularly useful to English learners because they can start with a familiar situation to use as background for explaining a less familiar character, such as Tom Sawyer, for instance. These questions, furthermore, can be answered individually or in collaborative groups and can model for students questions they might wish to ask.

Photo Essays: Combining Direct Experience, the Visual Mode, and Writing

Photography has great potential for stimulating student interest in school projects, and it forms the basis of the photo essay, a method using visuals to organize thinking before speaking or writing (Sinatra, Beaudry, Stahl-Gemake, & Guastello 1990). In essence, students choose a topic for which they take a set of photographs, or they bring in photos already taken. Then they organize the pictures in a sequence that will support their discussion of the topic. After oral discussion, students write and publish their photo-illustrated essay. We have seen this approach used successfully at both the elementary- and secondary-school levels with students of varying English language proficiency.

In Ms. Guadarrama's third-grade class, for example, children brought in photos of their families, including pictures of themselves. They organized their pictures on construction paper in the order they would tell about them during sharing time. Ms. Guadarrama and her assistant went around the room to listen to the children describe their pictures, helping them reorganize the pictures if necessary for sharing with the class. The students then pasted the pictures onto the paper and orally shared their stories with the entire class. The next day, they used their photo essays to organize the writing of their stories. The written story was

Having rehearsed the information during small-group work, this student is well prepared for her oral presentation on her home country, Haiti.

373

then stapled beneath the photo essay, and the final products were posted around the room for everyone to look at and read. In this activity, the photos not only supported children's writing but also supported reading because students took time to read each other's stories.

In Mia Taylor's sixth-grade class, students were invited to work in pairs to develop a photo essay related to their family, school, or neighborhood. Because Ms. Taylor often used whole-class photo essays as a follow-up after field trips, her students were familiar with the general idea. For the pair projects, Ms. Taylor asked her students to (1) choose a topic and brainstorm how they would develop their ideas through photography, (2) check with her to get approval for their topic and plan, (3) take the pictures, (4) organize their pictures into a storyboard, and (5) write the story, with the final product to be published complete with photo illustrations.

Students' photo essays addressed a variety of topics, including how to make tamales from scratch, a visual inventory of a shopping mall, and a day in the life of a laundromat operator. These photo essays were primarily organized around chronological or spatial sequences. In addition, the photo essay may be set up for classification, as was the case with a pair of students who photographed and analyzed different kinds of businesses in their neighborhood. The procedure also lends itself to thematic organization. Two girls, for example, prepared a photo essay on the problems of being 12 years old. In this case, the girls presented a photo of themselves in the center with the caption, "Problems with Being Twelve." They then presented a wheel of problems, with a photo attached to each spoke depicting problem areas: indecision over hair and makeup, too young to drive, boredom, too much homework, and so forth. The organization of the photographs thus offered a concrete form of semantic mapping.

In summary, the photo essay provides students of all ages and developmental levels with the opportunity to use direct experience and photography around a chosen theme. They are able to manipulate the pictures as a concrete way of organizing their ideas for writing. In the process, they use a great deal of visually supported oral language. Finally, they write the essay and produce an illustrated product for others to read.

Written and Oral Collaborative Research Projects

When entering Fernando Nichol's class, you will sense that he does things a little differently. All four walls of his classroom are covered with books, and this year, 3-by-3–foot airplanes are hanging from the high ceilings. In one corner, a rocking chair with a serape hanging over the back faces a large carpet. Each semester, Mr. Nichol's English learners use the books in his class to do research projects that require reading/writing and oral language use. They use his chair to present their findings to the rest of the class and use the tables around the classroom to work collaboratively on their research topics. Usually, while studying a general topic, such as the Civil War, students select a subtopic such as the role of slaves, to explore more fully and share their findings with their peers. These written research projects involve collaborative reading and writing, and students need to be fairly proficient in English to be totally involved in them. Other teachers use oral history projects to engage students in research and sharing of knowledge.

Oral history projects involve students in selecting a topic of interest, researching the topic by reading and interviewing knowledgeable individuals, and reporting the information orally and in writing. For example, Lee Tzeng

"That's what WE call suppository writing!"

Source: Paul Gruwell.

asks his students to select a topic that relates to what they are studying and to conduct an oral research project. In one case, students decided to do a project on World War II. They had read about the war in their class and had seen several related films. A number of students had relatives who had participated in the war, and they decided to interview their relatives and others in their own neighborhoods who could talk about their war experiences.

To get started on the project, students discussed the types of questions they wanted to ask and the purpose of their project. They determined that their purpose would be to get a personal view of the war and its aftermath. Next, they created questions and discussed how to conduct a good interview. Lee placed them in teams of three, with each member being responsible for one part of the interview: One would be responsible for asking questions, another would tape-record the interview and take notes, and the third person would think of some extra questions that might be asked at the end of the interview.

After completing interviews, students transcribed them. This required them to listen carefully and to work together on mechanics, spelling, and punctuation as they transcribed. After transcribing, they wrote a narrative describing the individual they had interviewed, using Studs Terkel's work as a model (Terkel, 1974). They then refined their written narratives in peer response and editing groups.

Next, each group created a chart with each individual's name and a summary of important elements from the interview. After finishing their charts, they examined them for categories or questions they might suggest. One category that emerged was racial discrimination in the army. One African American man, for instance, shared his experience of all-black troops who were headed by white captains. He said that he and his fellow troopers liked to slow down their work, acting as if they didn't understand the orders if the white captain treated them unfairly or without respect.

As a result of their initial analysis, the students began asking questions about different groups of soldiers. What was the effect of the war on African Americans as opposed to Japanese Americans, for example? What did this mean in terms of job availability for each group? How were Italian Americans and German Americans treated during the war? After students made these generalizations, they created a book about World War II that they disseminated to the people they interviewed and to others in the community. The oral projects represent one ideal type of research because students selected their own topics, decided on important questions, and carried out the topics on their own. In addition, students were involved in oral and written composing, transcribing, revising, and editing a research report on a relevant topic. When the students were ready to publish the results of their research, they could refer to the chart Lee Tzeng provided to assist them with clear interview reporting (see Table 10.2).

The oral interview topic just discussed was used for social science, but we have seen students perform the same kind of oral projects in math, science, and other areas. In mathematics, one class asked business people how math was used in their jobs, and what aspect of math would be most important for students to know. Another class interviewed gardeners and nursery owners to gain information about plants. Wherever we have seen oral projects used, we have seen a great deal of enthusiasm from students and teachers alike. The projects tend to involve students at the deepest levels of oral discussion, critical thinking, reading, and writing. Moreover, they tie learning to real people, real problems, and real life.

375

TABLE 10.2 • ELEMENTS OF GOOD REPORTING

ELEMENT	DESCRIPTION
Opening	At the beginning state what your topic is and how you will develop it; for example, state that you have interviewed World II veterans from different ethnic groups to learn about their different or similar experiences.
Background information	Give readers the background information they will need to know to understand your report. For example, explain the attitudes of North Americans toward different ethnic groups at the time of the war. This might help explain why some troops were segregated from others or treated differently.
Reporting interviews	When reporting the interview of a specific person, give background information on the person that may be important to the reader's understanding of the interviewee. See Studs Terkel (1974) for examples.
Summarizing information	Use your interview charts to find categories of responses that might be similar or different among the interviewees. Remind the readers what your purpose was and state your findings.

In so doing, they tend to override subject matter boundaries, creating integrated knowledge across several traditional disciplines of study.

K-W-L, a Strategy That Fosters Thinking Before, During, and After Reading

Some strategies combine elements of each of the three phases of content reading: before, during, and after. These strategies are particularly helpful in teaching students overall methods for setting purpose, building background knowledge, and monitoring, organizing, and remembering information. K-W-L is such a strategy. **K-W-L** and **K-W-L Plus** provide a scaffolding structure for developing a research question and investigating it. *K*, *W*, and *L* stand for *Know*, *Want to Know*, and *Learn* (Ogle, 1986); the K-W-L Plus strategy simply adds mapping to Ogle's original K-W-L approach (Carr & Ogle, 1987). In the *know* part of the strategy, students can generate, in groups or individually, what they know about a topic; this step taps students' background knowledge and also gives you a chance to see what you may need to clarify in preparing students to read your text. In the *want to know* step, students begin to think of questions concerning the topic; this step helps them generate a purpose for their reading and prepares them to monitor their comprehension. In the *learned* step, students list what they have learned. In the K-W-L Plus extension of the process, students organize what they have learned so they will be able to remember it. The K-W-L strategy helps students become responsible for their learning, assists them with becoming active learners, and provides them with a strategy they may use independently with practice. The worksheet in Figure 10.6 is used with the strategy to guide students through the process.

K (WHAT I KNOW)	W (WANT TO KNOW)	L (LEARNED)

FIGURE 10.6

K-W-L Worksheet

Theme Studies: Providing a Meaningful Learning Context

The theme study "Plants in Our World" described in this section illustrates how English learners can use oral and written language for learning academic material. Special attention is given to assuring a variety of ways students can participate. Ms. Carroll's class of fifth graders has 29 students, including two newcomers and five intermediate English learners. The native languages of the English learners are Spanish, Russian, and Cantonese. Ms. Carroll has no aide, but a resource teacher provides all seven English learners with English language development on a pullout basis.

377

The unit activities take place between 1:30 and 3:15 each afternoon, after sustained silent reading. Students have a 10-minute recess at 2:30. Ms. Carroll provides her students the time from 2:45 to 3:15 to complete any unfinished work. If they are caught up, they may read or choose a game with a friend. Students often use this time to complete projects undertaken during thematic instruction.

Introducing the Topic and Choosing Study Questions

Ms. Carroll has chosen to develop a unit of study on "Plants in Our World," a topic for which she is responsible according to the state science framework. She teaches this topic each year but with some variations, depending on her students' interests and curiosity. In accordance with her own philosophy and the state's guidelines, she makes sure all of her students have opportunities in the processes of scientific inquiry: observing, communicating, comparing events and objects, organizing information, relating concrete and abstract ideas, inferring, and applying knowledge. She is aware that these processes involve critical thinking and that as her English learners engage in these processes they will have opportunities to develop cognitive academic English language skills. The careful and precise ways of thinking, talking, and writing about scientific data are fairly new to all her students, native and non-native English speakers alike.

In addition to making use of the inquiry approach to science, Ms. Carroll is concerned that certain basic information about plants be understood by all her students, as outlined in the state framework. In particular, she wants them to be able to describe the parts of a plant and how each functions to enable plant growth and reproduction. She also wants her students to know the basic needs of plants and to understand and appreciate how plants have adapted to various climate and soil conditions, leading to the remarkable diversity of plant life on earth. Throughout her science and social science curriculum, she weaves the philosophical thread of the interrelatedness among all living things and their environment.

This year for plant study, Ms. Carroll opened the unit by asking students to look around the room to see what was different. Several students pointed out that the room was decorated with potted plants—two ferns, an ivy plant, and a variety of cactus plants. Ms. Carroll then initiated a discussion on plants, inviting the class to name as many kinds of plants as possible. As students volunteered names of plants, she wrote them on a large piece of butcher paper. In this way, Ms. Carroll activated and assessed her students' background knowledge and started a vocabulary list developed in the context of class discussion of the topic.

Next, she asked the class to peruse the list and look for plants that were similar in some way and thus might be grouped together. She then created a map of the students' collective thinking, reproduced in Figure 10.7. Next, she invited the class to work in groups of four to discuss the question: What would our lives be like without plants? Students discussed the question for about 10 minutes and then shared their ideas with the whole class.

378 **FIGURE 10.7**

CLASS BRAINSTORMING ON PLANTS FOR THEME CYCLE

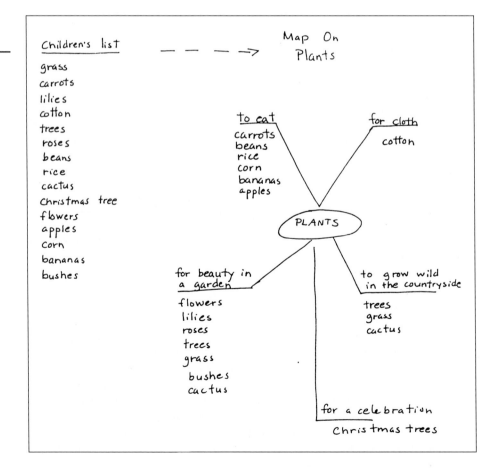

This introduction helped students focus on the general theme, plants. For those few students who were unfamiliar with the word *plant*, the oral discussion with mapping established the concept and its label. As students listed all the specific plants they could think of, the concept was elaborated and additional vocabulary was generated. For all students, the listing and categorizing activated background knowledge about plants to prepare them to discuss the question, What would our lives be like without plants? As students discussed this question, Ms. Carroll was able to get some ideas about what the students already knew about plants. For example, several groups suggested that our food supply would have to come from animals instead of plants. Then someone pointed out that some animals eat only plants, so they could not provide a food source if there were no plants. Another group mentioned the importance of plants for the air, but they didn't know what the effect would be if there were no plants. From this discussion, Ms. Carroll commented that her question had led to more questions than answers! She asked the students to help her list some study questions for the unit on plants. The class settled on the following questions, which were posted on the bulletin board.

1. How are plants used by people?
2. Plants give us so much. Do we give them something?
3. What kinds of plants grow in the rain forests?
4. What would the air be like without plants?

To get started on the first question, students were asked to make note of anything they used that day that came from plants. This was a homework assignment, and they were encouraged to ask family members to help them add to the list, if possible. These lists would be compared the next day in class and posted on the bulletin board. Based on the lists, the class established six categories of things used by humans: food, clothing, medicine, shelter, tools/implements, and aesthetics. Students volunteered for study committees to specialize in finding out more about how plants are used in each category.

Ms. Carroll felt that the second and fourth questions could not be answered without first providing background information on plants, including how they grow and reproduce, what they need to survive, how they make food from sunlight and chlorophyll, and how they give off oxygen and other elements as by-products of photosynthesis. She explained to the class that they would be learning some basic information about plants that they could use to help them answer these questions.

For the question on the rain forests, Ms. Carroll foresaw rich learning possibilities extending beyond just plant life into the delicate balance among all earthly things, living and nonliving. A study of the rain forests would provide her students with a fine opportunity to understand and appreciate how plants adapt to their environment and how they form a part of a larger ecosystem, another topic designated for study in the state framework. She decided to leave the rain forest question for last, preparing her students for its complexities with direct study of plants in class and in the surrounding community. This would also give her some time to gather resources, because this was the first time she had undertaken a study of the rain forests. She explained her thinking to the students and asked them all to be on the lookout for information on rain forests in the form of news articles, television specials, or books they might come across in their research on plants. She established a small classroom corner for these resources and immediately began filling it with books, maps, and other materials that her students could peruse in their free time.

Organizing Instruction

To begin the study of plants, Ms. Carroll established two parallel projects for students to work on: (1) human uses of plants, with six research committees, and (2) plant observation and experimentation to lead to understanding of plant parts, functions, and life needs. Each research committee was to gather information on its topic with the goal of sharing its findings through a poster display, including a short written report, pictures, and objects. Each group was given a section of classroom counter space or a table. The six displays would remain for two or three weeks to give everyone a chance to enjoy and learn from them, creating an impressive tribute to the gifts of the plant world.

For the first week of plant study, Ms. Carroll set up the following schedule:

Week 1:	Introducing the Unit and Getting Started
Monday:	Whole Class: Potting plants
	Ask class what a typical plant needs to grow. List on chart.
	Illustrate with simple drawings, pointing out plant parts and functions.
	Set up experiments with groups of four or five, manipulating variables indicated by students such as water, plant food, sunlight, and soil.
	Each group pots two identical plants and grows them under different conditions. Each day they will observe and record plant size, color, turgor, and other health signs in their science logs.
Tuesday and Wednesday:	Ms. Carroll meets with plant-use study groups to establish goals and plans to help them get started. She meets with three groups each day. While she meets with them, the other groups carry out activities she has set up for them at five science activity centers:

1. Parts of plant and functions: Drawing and labeling for journal
2. Herbs and spices: Classification by plant part; geography of where grown; history of uses and trade
3. George Washington Carver and his research on the many ways to use peanuts
4. Filmstrip on the life cycles of different kinds of plants: conifers, deciduous trees, wild grasses
5. Discussion, listing, and classifying of plants used for food. Group leader needed. List plants used for food. Classify according to plant part. Make a group chart to display the classification.

Thursday:	Groups work on plant-use projects. Groups work at centers. Ms. Carroll is available to assist as needed.
Friday:	Students take a field trip to the nursery to find out what kinds of plants are sold, who buys them, and how they are cared for.

During the first week of the unit, Ms. Carroll has followed a highly structured schedule to build basic background knowledge and get students launched in group study. During the subsequent weeks, students assume greater responsibility for independent work. Ms. Carroll adds several more plant study experiments and reminds students to record results in their science logs. In addition, students work independently on their group projects. At the end of the third week, all six groups set up their poster displays. At this point Ms. Carroll reminds students of the questions they posed at the beginning of the unit. The class, satisfied with the amount of information they have accumulated on how people use plants, know that their rain forest interest will be studied next. However, their second and fourth questions have not yet been answered.

Ms. Carroll explains to the class that they have come up with good questions that require thinking about their current knowledge of plants. She also explains that these questions require using their imaginations to figure out some answers. She suggests that students talk in their groups and write down ideas to address the questions: What do we give plants? and What would the air be like without plants? She reminds her students that questions like these have many possible answers and that the students should use what they know about plants as the basis of their responses. The ideas generated by each group will be posted for each question.

Instructional Modifications for English Learners

Ms. Carroll has not changed the essence of her teaching style to accommodate her English learners. She has always organized instruction around topics and themes. However, in recent years, she has found ways to let students pose questions of their own and choose certain directions of study. These changes in her teaching, motivated by discussions with colleagues and occasional workshops, have aimed at improving instruction for all of her students. In addition, she now scrutinizes her teaching plans with an eye toward maximizing comprehension and participation among her English learners.

For the unit on plants, she used three strategies to this end. First, she introduced the topic with more sheltering than she might have if the students had all been native English speakers. For example, she made sure to have a variety of plants in the classroom on the first day of the unit to make her verbal reference to plants unmistakably clear. She did this specifically for the two non-English-speaking children in the class. She also made sure to illustrate some of the words she wrote on the board. These sheltering techniques, though unnecessary for many of her students, enriched her teaching and added interest for the entire class. The second strategy she used was collaborative grouping. She allowed students to cluster in interest groups around the plant-use categories. However, she balanced the groups in terms of number and social support for students with limited English language knowledge. The two newcomers were placed in the same groups as their assigned buddy. Grouping was not adjusted for the intermediate-level students because they could communicate well enough to be successful in group work. In addition to checking for social support in group membership, Ms. Carroll assigned roles to each student for center activities, which were quite structured and would require students to work independently while she met with the study groups.

Ms. Carroll did not assign roles for the plant-use study groups. However, with her guidance, the groups devised their own division of labor when she met with them during the first week of the unit. In so doing, Ms. Carroll used her third strategy, which was to make sure that within each task there were a variety of ways for students to participate and contribute. By meeting with the study groups one at a time, she was able to make sure that each student had an appropriate way to contribute to both knowledge building and knowledge sharing.

Developing the plant topic into theme studies provided students with several levels of learning. All students were given numerous opportunities to use oral language, reading, and writing for learning. The variety of whole-class and small-group tasks in conjunction with concrete materials and experimentation provided constant opportunities for concept development and language learning. Involvement in the scientific method offered opportunities to use such terms as *hypothesize*, *classify*, *predict*, and *conclude*. Moreover, in using such terms, students were involved in higher-level thinking processes. In addition to the rich learning opportunities through oral language use, the students made use of written language for a variety of functions. For example, all students kept careful observations of plant changes in their science learning logs for the four different experiments they conducted, including drawing and labeling plant parts and functions. They also read the directions and information sheets for carrying out the activities provided at the science centers. They wrote letters requesting pamphlets on the rain forests, and thank-you notes to the nursery following their visit. In addition, they used textbooks, encyclopedias, and magazines to locate information on their plant-use topics.

To summarize the strengths provided by the thematic unit, let's take a look at how Yen, an advanced beginner/early intermediate English learner, participated in the plants unit. But first we will present a little background information about her. Yen arrived three years ago at the age of 7 and was placed in a first-grade class. Now 10 years old, she is in the fourth grade. Yen speaks Cantonese at home because her family is ethnic Chinese from Vietnam. Though fluent in spoken Cantonese, Yen has had little opportunity to learn to write in her native language. However, her written English is fairly good, and she takes great pride in the appearance of her work. Given the choice, Yen likes to illustrate her writing with line drawings. Yen's oral English is adequate for most purposes. She understands Ms. Carroll's instruction and is aided by the sheltering techniques Ms. Carroll uses to make herself understood. At times, Yen herself is hard to understand, however, and she is often asked to repeat herself for clarification.

Ms. Carroll has taken a few special measures with Yen in mind. First of all, she has made Yen the buddy to a new Cantonese-speaking girl, Li Fen, and she has grouped them with two supportive advanced English speakers, Jerome and Linda, for the plant unit activities. Ms. Carroll has noticed that Yen's oral English gets better when she uses it on behalf of her newcomer friend, and, of course, Li Fen benefits from Yen's Cantonese explanations. At the same time, Ms. Carroll has made sure to place them with two advanced English speakers who will be receptive to their communication efforts.

Yen is readily able to do the majority of the activities required for the plant experiments and the science center activities. She draws, labels, records notes in her science log, and negotiates tasks with her group members. For her contribution to the poster display, she researched the topic of herbal remedies in Chinese medicine. She and Li Fen developed this topic together, at Ms. Carroll's suggestion. They began by interviewing family members and looking for information in the encyclopedia. By providing a number of techniques combined with social support, Ms. Carroll has created an environment in which Yen can learn with others in the class. Because Yen has the opportunity to assist another child, she gains in self-esteem and advances in her own content learning.

These boys have worked hard in their cooperative group preparing their oral and visual presentation, "Aquaculture," as part of the class theme study.

Assessment

Assessment of reading and writing for academic learning is similar to assessment in writing and literature. Therefore, we will reiterate some basic, informal ways you can assess students, such as using portfolios, informal observation, and student self-assessment. However, the most important point we want to make here is that all students, and especially non-native English speakers, should be assessed in a great variety of ways: through work in groups and with partners; through participation in projects; through drawings, experiments, and oral talk; and through reading and writing (Huerta-Macias, 1995). If what you want to know is whether a student has learned about plants, you may find that some students can show you with drawings better than with essays, whereas others can perform science experiments meticulously showing a clear understanding of the content. Finally, always try to evaluate students' knowledge through their modalities of strength.

Portfolio Assessment

Whether you use a thematic unit or some other approach, there are many things you can evaluate beyond just whether students understand basic concepts or know the vocabulary of a content area. Using portfolio assessment throughout a unit, for instance, you can ask students to keep their work and evaluate it with you so that they know where they are and what they need to do. In their portfolios, they keep their learning logs or other journals, a record of an experiment they have performed, notes they took from oral interviews, and perhaps tapes or

FIGURE 10.8

POSSIBILITIES FOR INCLU-
SION OF PORTFOLIOS

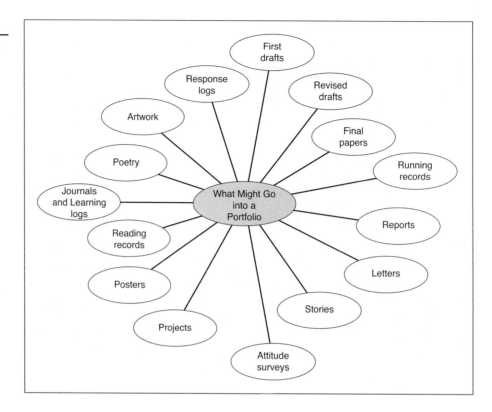

384

pictures they may have collected for a group publication (see Figure 10.8). All of these materials can then be evaluated with the students to determine their level of participation in your class. In addition to the portfolio assessment, your daily observations of students will help you evaluate their work (Gottlieb, 1995).

Selecting Materials for the Portfolio

When selecting materials for the portfolio, students are in charge of their own learning and must self-evaluate; however, you can assist students with becoming more aware of their best work (Smolen, Newman, Wathen, & Lee, 1995). Nevertheless, we have found that students are capable of selecting their best work for inclusion in the portfolio. In addition, you may wish to place all student tests, running records, and other observational materials in the portfolio to show students how far they have progressed throughout the year or semester. Moreover, in an ideal situation the portfolio would follow the student into the next year's classroom to give that teacher insights about the student's progress.

Evaluating Portfolios

You may also wish to set up an evaluation system for the grading of the portfolios. In the holistic scoring section in Chapter 7, we set up model papers with a trait analysis that gives students explicit information concerning excellent and poor papers and what their features are. You can also set up criteria for reading performance, which could consist of how many books students might read throughout certain periods of the year, how many response logs to books should be in the portfolio, and how they might be evaluated. We believe that students should have models of excellent, good, and fair work so that they know what they are working toward. With these models students can evaluate themselves fairly; in fact, we find that when we set up clear criteria for evaluation, students often evaluate themselves more critically than we do. If you need to give a specific grade for work in the portfolio, you may want to set up a point system. Some teachers place a scoring sheet in each portfolio that delineates the number of points for fair, good, or excellent papers. For example, an excellent paper might be worth 10 points, a good paper worth 8 points, and so on. Whatever fits your own teaching situation, we suggest that your system be explicit to your students and communicated to their parents clearly. In this way you can be assured of having the best chance for success. Finally, we think that just as each teacher has to work out a grading and management system that suits them, each teacher has to create a portfolio system designed to work for them.

Figure 10.9 gives an example of Lydia Martinez's portfolio checklist that helps her keep track of her students' progress. Note that every teacher's checklist

FIGURE 10.9

TEACHER'S CHART FOR KEEPING TRACK OF A STUDENT'S READING PROGRESS

Student's Name: ______________	
Reading Behaviors: * reads fluently * recognizes sight words * blends and digraphs * compound words * attends to punctuation	
Comprehension: * identifies main ideas or themes in fiction and nonfiction * makes predictions * monitors comprehension * sets purpose for reading * is able to summarize main ideas or themes in fiction and nonfiction	
Attitudes Concerning Reading: * selects books * reads during free-choice time * reads during silent sustained reading * has favorite books or authors * responds in journals and during literature response time * clearly enjoys reading	
Other Areas Particular to the Student:	

will be different depending on the age of their students, the kinds of readings a teacher expects, the skill level of the students in the class, and the goals of the curriculum. At the end of this chapter we have listed resources we recommend if you wish to gain more knowledge about setting up and evaluating a portfolio assessment program. Finally, we find that classrooms using portfolio systems empower students to take charge of their own learning and self-evaluation and to become more involved with their assignments.

In content instruction you might want to add presentations of both individual and group projects to the other reading and writing assessments in your students' portfolios. You may also add a performance assessment that evaluates how well students present the information they developed in a group project. Whatever you do with portfolio assessment you will want to have your students involved in selecting materials and determining forms of evaluation.

Using Multiple Measures for Assessment

With all students, but particularly with English learners, we recommend that you assess their participation in many different ways. For example, although there are exceptions, the speaking abilities of English learners often surpass their ability to read and write. Therefore, if you assess them only through written exams, you will surely underestimate their capabilities and knowledge of the content you have taught. We have a friend who understands and speaks Italian fairly well and has participated in classes in which the language was used, but if her knowledge of what happened in these classes were assessed in writing only, she would probably fail miserably. If assessed orally or in reading, however, she would perform better. If given a chance to show her abilities with concrete materials, she might receive an "A" for exhibiting her knowledge. Students who may not be able to perform well on a written test may be able to show you through a scientific experiment, for example, that they understood the information at a high level. If you do not assess students in many different ways, you will not find out what they really know.

Differentiating Instruction for Content Area Learning

Content area instruction requires you to teach all students your **grade-level curriculum** in math, science, social studies, and so forth based on your state's corresponding curriculum content standards. In addition, most schools require you to teach from state or district adopted content area texts. Thus, for example, there is a common core of knowledge that all seventh graders are supposed to learn. Given the diversity among English learners, it is no surprise that content area teaching presents big challenges, and differentiating instruction plays a major role in addressing those challenges. Moreover, your content classes may well include both native and non-native English speakers, requiring you to pitch strategies appropriately for a large range of English language development levels. The teaching and assessment strategies in this chapter and previously in Chapter 9 are intended to help you achieve such differentiation.

To best prepare lessons that address grade-level content and learner differences, you'll need to know three areas: (1) the content of instruction; (2) the oral language, reading, and writing abilities of your students; and (3) your students' prior knowledge of content acquired through the primary language or English. The lesson example that follows uses the scaffolding framework for differentiated planning addressing **who**, **what**, **how**, and **how well**, in this case focusing on a fifth-grade science standard:

> Students know that the solar system includes the Earth, moon, sun, eight other planets and their satellites, and smaller objects such as asteroids and comets (*California Science Standards*, Grade 5).

To meet the needs of English learners, we have also identified the following English language development (ELD) standards taken from the *California English Language Development Standards for Grade 5*:

> **Beginning:** Use model to write.
> **Early Intermediate:** Follow a model given by the teacher to independently write at least four sentences.
> **Intermediate:** Read grade-appropriate narrative aloud with expression. Produce independent writing that is understood when read but may include inconsistent use of standard grammatical forms.
> **Early Advanced:** Produce independent writing with standard word order and appropriate grammatical forms. Arrange composition according to simple organizational patterns.

The combination of content and ELD standards provide an outline for selecting lesson content (the same for all students) and matching performance expectations appropriate to different ELD levels. For example, **all** students will be given a model for writing a summary report on one of the nine planets and **all** will be expected to produce writing showing they can understand and use the lesson vocabulary drawn from the fifth-grade science curriculum. In addition, all students will be assessed on **how well** they understand the vocabulary and concepts; **how well** they are able to identify planets; **how well** they know the distance planets are from the sun; and **how well** they know the atmosphere and diameter of the planets. However, the writing students produce (the final product) will be assessed according to their ELD level for writing, as shown previously.

Next, we discuss **how** this differentiated lesson will be accomplished. One way to accomplish the multiple tasks required by your state's standards is to use lesson plans, such as the one given here, that outline how students will read expository text materials on planets and produce a summary report on each planet. As you review this lesson plan, note that the student's native language is allowed as an important aspect of content teaching.

In the opening of this lesson (Part 5, Anticipatory Set), it is helpful to allow students their choice of language in which to express their knowledge of the planets and the solar system. In doing so, you may learn that some students have knowledge of the content, but in Spanish or Vietnamese, for example, and do not have the English language skills to articulate this knowledge. At the same time, you may have native English speakers who do not possess the same content knowledge as a non-native speaker. This situation sets up a process for group organizing that will allow you to pair students who can identify elements of the solar system only in Spanish, for example, with native English speakers who may not have this content knowledge but have the ability to read and write in English. When grouped together, English learners may learn grade-level vocabulary, while sharing some of their own content knowledge. In addition, you immediately validate students' languages and the prior knowledge they bring to your lesson content. The lesson plan here illustrates the step-by-step procedure for developing such a lesson.

SAMPLE DIFFERENTIATED LESSON PLAN FOR CONTENT READING AND WRITING

Theme: Travel/Distance
Grades: 4–7

English Language Proficiency Level: ALL Levels, Beginning to Advanced

Vocabulary/Concepts: *planet, distance, diameter, temperature, atmosphere, surface, gas, and oxygen*

English Language Skills: Reading factual information; Writing simple sentences and expository paragraphs; Orally presenting facts about planets

1. ELD standard
List for each level of proficiency. Select the same content standards for all fluency levels.

Beginning: Use model to write.
Early Intermediate: Follow a model given by the teacher to independently write at least four sentences.
Intermediate: Read grade-appropriate narrative aloud with appropriate pacing, intonation, and expression. Produce independent writing that is understood when read but may include inconsistent use of standard grammatical forms.
Early Advanced: Produce independent writing with standard word order and appropriate grammatical forms. Arrange composition according to simple organizational patterns.

2. Assessment
For different levels of English proficiency; Group accountability; Individual accountability based on ELD standard; Use at end of lesson.

Based on standard(s) for each level; students will collaboratively write or produce a fact sheet on planets, using authentic reading materials at the appropriate reading level. Students will present orally the facts for their planets to the class and place posters with information around the room.

Independently, students will gather information on each planet from posters and write a summary paragraph for each planet in their planet book. Writing should reflect the abilities related to the ELD level of students.

3. Content standard:
Science, Grade 5

Students know that the solar system includes the Earth, moon, sun, eight other planets and their satellites, and smaller objects, such as asteroids and comets.

4. Language objective
Identify the key vocabulary, language structure, or grammar objectives.

Vocabulary development; Content vocabulary for planets and research strategies to locate information. Students will learn paragraph structure for writing factual summaries.

5. Lesson
Anticipatory set

Show the opening five minutes of the movie *Contact* without sound. Ask students to watch and to note everything they see: they can do this in English or their native language. After viewing, do a pair-share and listen as students share what they saw in the video. Following the pair-share, write vocabulary in English as students report to the class what they saw. For students who may have the word in their native language, ask others to translate when possible. As students call out, categorize vocabulary into *galaxy, universe, solar system, earth,* and *home.*

Modeling/instruction

Show a visual chart of the solar system and ask students to identify in small groups what they know about the solar system. Assign a quick write: Write everything you know about the solar system and one thing you want to know. Do a pair-share, having students report "facts" they know and the one thing they want to learn. Write responses on the overhead. Note: Writing can be in English or native language.

5. Lesson (*cont.*) *Modeling/guided practice*	Shared reading of "The Planets" in textbook. Use think-pair-share to have students respond during reading to comprehension questions. Students verify understanding of group project in which they work to gather and report facts on one of the nine planets. Students are all given a copy of a sample fact sheet shown on an overhead; questions to address in their reports are reviewed with the class orally; check that all students understand directions.
Independent practice	Do a shared reading of the Earth facts with the class and model how to highlight important information to answer the questions (e.g., atmosphere, distance from sun). Then as class dictates facts, write the information for the Earth on the Earth fact sheet projected on the overhead. Assign planet groups; have students grouped heterogeneously to read and highlight facts (as modeled). In groups, students will complete fact sheets and do a large illustration of their planet with facts.
6. Lesson evaluation *Assess student learning as described in #2 to determine how well students are progressing toward standards.*	Ongoing assessment during instruction: Check with each group to verify they are reading and highlighting appropriate facts. Check for understanding by asking questions related to each group's reading. Check writing on fact sheets and illustrations for accuracy of vocabulary and writing.
7. Next steps *Reteach or go to next standard.*	If students are having difficulty finding facts, modify the fact sheet by having fewer questions with fewer pages for reading.

Summary

In the upper-elementary grades through high school, students must read and write longer, more complex texts. They must move from short, familiar stories and fables to longer chapter books containing a variety of characters involved in multiple problems, settings, and solutions. Students need strategies that will assist them with these longer narrative texts. Similarly, in curriculum areas, such as history or science, students face texts that are longer, filled with new information, and structured differently from the short narrative texts with which they may be familiar from their previous years of schooling. Therefore, students need special help in negotiating meaning in this new territory. In this chapter, we presented theory, research, and strategies to assist students in their journey.

Reading for academic learning involves reading to understand and remember. We presented strategies in Chapters 9 and 10 pertaining to three phases of the reading process: prereading, during-reading, and postreading. To be successful, students must learn to set a purpose for reading, use their background knowledge, monitor their reading based on their purpose, and organize and remember what is important. Strategies for all of these processes were presented within the context of real classrooms. We also described a variety of ways to use writing for learning across the curriculum, including journals, learning logs, and reports, and for integrating writing into oral and written research projects.

The strategies chart in Figure 10.10 illustrates various grade levels at which we have seen the strategies used successfully. But as with the strategies shown throughout our book, these strategies are to be used at your discretion.

In addition to presenting a great variety of strategies in this chapter, we presented an example of a thematic unit that incorporates many of the strategies. In this way, we illustrated how to select and integrate strategies into the larger learning process in which students are actively engaged in acquiring information and insights to be shared with their peers in written research reports, oral presentations, and creative audiovisual works. In our example, we focused on the use of sheltering techniques, peer support, and oral and written language uses aimed at student learning.

Finally, we described assessment procedures, emphasizing multiple modes of assessment including portfolios, informal observation, and student self-assessment. Multiple modes of assessment help you to gain a complete picture of a student's progress and determine adjustments in your teaching approach. Most important of all, we reiterated that the best way to become an informed teacher is to watch and listen to the students in your classroom.

390

FIGURE 10.10

GRADE LEVELS AT WHICH STRATEGIES MAY BE USED

STRATEGY / GRADE LEVEL	K	1	2	3	4	5	6	7	8	9	10	11	12
Brainstorming	●————————————————————————————→												
Group mapping	●————————————————————————————→												
Journals	●————————————————————————————→												
Learning logs		●——————————————————————————→											
Oral research projects			●————————————————————————→										
Mapping		●——————————————————————————→											
Multiple assessment	●————————————————————————————→												
Photo essays	●————————————————————————————→												
Portfolios	●————————————————————————————→												
Rehearsing				●——————————————————————→									
Semantic feature analysis					●————————————————————→								
Student selected topics	●————————————————————————————→												
Thematic units	●————————————————————————————→												
Theme cycles	●————————————————————————————→												
Written research project			●————————————————————————→										

Suggestions for Further Reading

Armbruster, B. B., & Osborn, J. H. (2002). *Reading instruction and assessment: Understanding the IRA Standards*. Boston: Allyn and Bacon.

The International Reading Association (IRA) is the major international organization for all reading instructors. This book explains the reading instruction standards developed by the IRA. The book presents each reading standard, interprets its meaning, discusses research and other issues, and discusses what the standard means to a teacher. There are seven sections: (1) creating a literate environment; (2) word identification, vocabulary, and spelling; (3) comprehension; (4) study strategies; (5) writing; (6) assessment; and (7) recommendations. This is a useful and readable text.

Chamot, A. U., & O'Malley, J. M. (1992). *The CALLA handbook: Implementing the cognitive academic language learning approach*. Reading, MA: Addison-Wesley.

The authors present their own approach to ELD content-based instruction (CBI). Their model is presented for CBI along with a discussion of the characteristics of learning from different types of content texts. The emphasis throughout is on English language development, and the book contains numerous specific examples of how development can be embedded within content instruction and thematic instruction.

Feyton, C., Macy, M., Ducher, J., Yoshii, M., Park, E., Calandra, B., et al. (2002). *Teaching ESL/EFL with the Internet: Catching the wave*. Upper Saddle River, NJ: Merrill/Prentice Hall.

This book was written for teachers who want to "integrate technology into their teaching." The book contains chapters on listening, oral proficiency, reading skills and comprehension, writing skills, exploring culture, and assessment. Each activity has a teacher's guide, which consists of three steps: schema building, grouping, and post-activity. An excellent book for secondary teachers who have access to computers and the Internet.

Levy, M., & Stockwell, G. (2006). *CALL dimensions: Options and issues in computer-assisted language learning*. Mahwah, NJ: Lawrence Erlbaum Associates.

If you are interested in computer assisted language learning (CALL), this is the book for you. It presents the latest research and practical information on the topic. Chapters include evaluation, computer-mediated communication, research, practice, and emergent and established CALL.

Snow, M. A., & Brinton, D. M. (1997). *The content-based classroom: Perspectives on integrating language and content*. White Plains, NY: Addison-Wesley Longman.

In this excellent edited text, Snow and Brinton have brought together some of the most knowledgeable researchers and educators working with second language learners in content area instruction. Topics include theoretical underpinnings, K-12 instruction, postsecondary instruction, research, practical issues, and connections between content-based instruction and other teaching approaches. An introduction to the best thinking in the field.

391

Activities

1. Observe how different teachers use writing in the content areas. What are the ways students write? What kind of prewriting activities do teachers use to make sure students will succeed in their assignments? Does the teacher respond to the students' writing? Do students respond to one another? Are the content area writing activities authentic and meaningful? For example, do activities involve students in responding to their texts and asking and answering meaningful personal questions about topics?

2. Many students who have been "good" readers in the first few grades, in which mainly short stories are used, begin to have difficulty later with their content texts. Why do you think this is so? What are some possible differences between narrative and expository texts in terms of structure and content? What kinds

of procedures or strategies can a teacher use to assist English learners with content reading? Because students are required to remember a lot of information out of their content texts, how will you help them remember what they have learned?

3. How do teachers use prereading, during-reading, and postreading activities to assist students with content reading? Do all teachers follow a prereading, during-reading, and postreading model? Some elementary teachers use a model they call "into, through, and beyond" instead of prereading, during-reading, and postreading. When you observe them, are they doing something different from the content model presented in this book? Do teachers you have observed assist students with text structure and with using headings and subheadings to create questions and a purpose for reading?

4. Develop a lesson in one content area—English, social science, or mathematics—and discuss how you will use the prereading, during-reading, and postreading model to teach the lesson. For example, what are the best prereading strategies for mathematics instruction or history instruction? What kinds of postreading activities can best assist students in remembering what they learned? Why would you use one strategy over another in a particular content area?

5. Visit a class that uses thematic units to integrate content areas and ask the teacher how a thematic approach might assist students in reading and remembering content materials. Observe for yourself the strengths and weaknesses of a thematic approach to instruction. For example, keep a checklist of your observations consisting of categories such as (1) time students spend reading or working on projects, (2) quality of ideas presented by students, (3) level of involvement in student groups, and (4) learning that appears to take place during the units. Evaluate your checklist and compare it with the quality of work in classrooms where a thematic approach is not used.

---

myeducationlab
Where the Classroom Comes to Life

Video Homework Exercise

Teaching Diverse Learners

In the video a high school teacher in a class whose students come from various language and literacy backgrounds discusses the classroom environment. She then says, "Learning to read is one skill and learning to read in a second language is another skill." She then is shown teaching a lesson on vocabulary focusing on the word *lava*.

Go to MyEducationLab, select the topic "Differentiating Instruction," and watch the video entitled "Teaching Diverse Learners."

1. What are the challenges of working with a class of such diverse students? What would you do to maximize the learning in this class?

2. Do you think the teacher's statement that learning to read in a first language is one skill and that learning to read in a second language is another skill is accurate? Is the statement true for English learners who read in Spanish or Chinese? How might it be true and how might it not be true for students from various cultures and language backgrounds?

3. Evaluate the teacher's lesson on *lava* and discuss how you might modify the same lesson for a class of English learners at various levels of English language development, from beginning through advanced. Give specific examples.

Reading Assessment and Instruction

> " You can observe a lot by watching. "
>
> —YOGI BERRA

In Chapter 3, we discussed the purposes of English learner assessment in terms of (1) identifying and placing students in language education support programs, (2) evaluating the effectiveness of such programs, and (3) assessing student learning and progress. In subsequent chapters we offered various ways to informally assess oral language, emergent literacy, reading, writing, and spelling in English. For each of these areas, we emphasized the importance of directly observing students as they engage in authentic, day-to-day learning tasks so that your assessment ties in directly with your instructional goals and teaching. We noted how important it is to make assessment continuous, ongoing, and multidimensional, that is based on a variety of observations, in a variety of situations, using a variety of instruments. By observing students continuously over time, you gain a solid perspective on their progress. By making assessment multidimensional, you provide the student varied opportunities to demonstrate competence, while giving yourself several information sources from which to construct a more accurate view of the student's abilities. Throughout this book we have also emphasized the benefits of engaging students in assessing their own learning. Students often understand aspects of their own development that would not otherwise come to light. Moreover, by engaging students in assessing themselves, they gain a more sophisticated understanding of their own reading, writing, and learning processes. Finally, we have discussed why it is essential to consider the student's cultural, linguistic, and other special characteristics and needs when collecting and evaluating information to inform instruction.

In this chapter, we return to the topic of assessment with two purposes in mind: (1) to provide an indepth discussion of how to evaluate student reading through an informal reading inventory as one way to assess reading, and (2) to illustrate how to consider information on oral language, reading, and writing to help you form a clearer picture of student abilities and to inform specific instructional choices. In this chapter, we will address the following questions:

1. What are some theoretical views of language proficiency and reading and how do they relate to assessment?
2. What are some of the ways we can informally assess student reading?
3. What is an informal reading inventory (IRI)?
4. How can an informal reading inventory help us systematically evaluate students' reading development?
5. What is the meaning of the three reading levels: independent reading level, instructional reading level, and frustration reading level? How can we use these levels to inform our evaluation and instruction?
6. What are some instructional strategies for addressing students' assessed needs in reading?

Lisa Charles, a student of ours, recently won the award as teacher of the year. We were curious about what she did to achieve this distinction. When we asked her, she was humble, stating only that she worked hard like other teachers in her district. But later in the semester she turned in a paper that illustrated her special dedication to students. In a case study, she described a student, Carlos, who seemed uninterested in reading, and she described what she did to try to change his direction. First of all, she met with Carlos' parents, talked with them about reading to their child, and showed them how they could help Carlos with books she was able to give them. She also paired Carlos with a student who loved reading in a buddy reading situation. Finally, she enlisted the principal of the school to read to Carlos three times a week. Carlos gradually began to look at reading differently and became an enthusiastic beginning reader himself, progressing far enough that he became a buddy reader with another student who needed help at the end of the year.

Lisa identified a problem Carlos was having: valuing reading and perceiving himself as a reader. She then selected several strategies to assist him. Essentially, assessment is about identifying student strengths and needs and finding strategies to help students succeed where they didn't succeed before. You can't always expect the principal of your school to have time to read to one of your students; but you can think about your parents, your community, and your school as resources to assist you and your students. You can also use systematic ways to assess and assist your students in reading development, as we will show you in this chapter.

Theoretical Approach to Literacy Assessment

There can be no aspect of teaching that is more theoretically driven and value laden than assessment. When we assess our students, we must select those aspects of reading, writing, and content learning that we believe are most important for students to know. Decisions about what and how to assess are dependent on both your theoretical perspective and the values you hold. When teachers work together on grade-level, schoolwide or district-level curriculum development, discussions on assessment often become lively and heated. As these discussions yield to consensus, the process itself, difficult as it is, has great potential for clarifying your views and values on literacy and learning, while creating community, cohesion, and common purpose among you and your colleagues. Furthermore, when curriculum and assessment decisions are made schoolwide, students reap great benefits from the articulated consistency in instructional goals and assessment across the grades. Next, we summarize our own views and values concerning language and literacy development as context for the remainder of this chapter on assessment.

Language Proficiency: Listening, Speaking, Reading, and Writing

In Chapter 4, we highlighted interrelationships among the four language processes: listening, speaking, reading, and writing. Because we believe that the strongest communicators are those who are effective users of both the oral and written word, and because we value both oral and written communication, we believe in setting goals for all students in listening, speaking, reading, and writing. In addition to these values and beliefs, we also hold a theoretical view concerning the interrelationships among the four language processes and language proficiency in general. Our theoretical view holds that individuals possess a reservoir of general language knowledge that is brought into play during any act of listening, speaking, reading, or writing. Such knowledge consists of the grammatical conventions, vocabulary, and other linguistic elements of language because these work together to convey and comprehend meaning. In addition to certain general aspects of linguistic knowledge, each language process requires certain elements that are particular to it. Every time a student uses any one of the four language processes, the general language reservoir is exercised, creating a stronger base for subsequent efforts in listening, speaking, reading, and writing.

In addition to developing general aspects of language knowledge, considerable attention is necessary to help students become proficient in the special demands inherent in each of the four language processes, which is why as teachers we, at times, must focus specifically on assessing performance in reading, writing, listening, or speaking in ways that yield useful analyses to inform and guide instruction in each area. When we do so, we zero in on the student's strengths and needs in each area. On the other hand, when we place information on all four language processes in front of us, as in a portfolio, we can see the big picture of a student's language proficiency. Moreover, as we begin to look closely at the various performance samples in the portfolio, we can make comparisons across reading, writing, listening, and speaking that may help us better understand a student's strengths and struggles in oral and written language development. With this understanding, we are in a position to acknowledge and build on the strengths, while providing instruction to meet the student's learning needs. In this chapter, we focus primarily on reading assessment as a result of its importance for all learning and because many non-native English speakers struggle to achieve facility in this important school and life skill. Thereafter, we provide case studies of individual

FIGURE 11.1 • GENERAL MODEL OF ASSESSMENT IN THE CLASSROOM

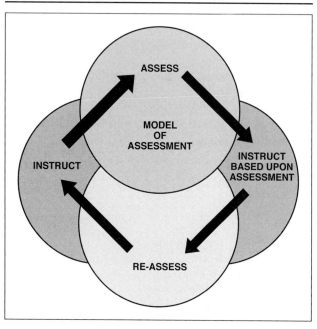

students to illustrate how to glean information from the assessment procedures we recommend. Throughout the chapter, we emphasize ways to use assessment information to guide instruction, as illustrated in Figure 11.1.

Figure 11.1 illustrates our view of assessment as an integral part of the instructional cycle. First, we assess to find a student's strengths and needs, then we instruct the student based on these needs. As we teach, we reassess and adjust our instruction based on how well the student is responding and learning. Finally, we assess the student's progress again. We repeat this cycle until the student is ready to move to more advanced material. Implicit in this approach are several assumptions about how students become better readers and writers. First, students become better at reading and writing by engaging in these processes daily, both independently and with teacher assistance. For example, journal writing and self-selected reading are two ways students apply their literacy abilities at their level of independence, while guided reading and student–teacher writing conferences are two ways to provide teacher assistance. When the teacher is on hand to assist, students work at their next level of development, that is, their zone of proximal development (ZPD), which we discussed in Chapter 3. Thus, our second assumption about how students become better at reading and writing is that they are nudged to read and write texts that are a little difficult for them by virtue of such features as length, content, vocabulary, genre, text structure, and so forth. With teacher assistance, students can work through challenging texts successfully. To work effectively with students in their zones of proximal development, teachers need to have a clear view of general developmental progressions in reading and writing, such as those provided in the scales of reading and writing development at the end of Chapter 5. They also need to be able to analyze specific aspects of reading and writing to determine a student's strengths and needs. For example, we need to know what to do if a student is confusing the letter *d* with the letter *b*, what to do if a student consistently misses the main ideas in passages, and what will help a student remember what they've read or better organize what they have written.

In our view, students' learning needs are addressed through **scaffolding**, **modeling**, and **direct instruction** (Cazden, 1983). Scaffolding, a holistic approach, provides students help with reading or writing a text as a whole, supported by teacher assistance and modeling, as explained in Chapter 3. Scaffolding thus provides practice in coordinating all the complex aspects of comprehending or producing a text. Direct instruction involves explicit teaching of a particular skill or strategy aimed at improving a student's reading or writing and often includes teacher modeling of the skill or strategy as part of the lesson. Direct instruction may address reading and writing processes at any level, from phonics and spelling strategies to higher level critical thinking and composing strategies.

For direct instruction to be effective, however, it is necessary to identify an area of need and teach to it.

We are reminded, for example, of a third grader by the name of Ema. Each time Ema came to a compound word such as *baseball, football, booklist*, or *homework*, she was stymied. When we mentioned this to her teacher, a friend of ours, she told us that Ema would learn compound words on her own. Indeed, many children do intuit such things on their own. However, after several months, we noticed that Ema was still struggling with compound words. With her teacher's permission, we devised a simple mini-lesson showing Ema how compound words are made up of two smaller words put together. We gave her a list of compound words to practice with. After about 10 minutes working on the list, she was able to recognize all the words by breaking them down into their constituent parts. Subsequently, Ema demonstrated her ability to apply the new strategy when reading stories to us. Through a little direct instruction with something she had struggled with for months, Ema was no longer stuck when she came to a compound word. Ema taught us that sometimes it is much more efficient to identify a skill that a student doesn't know and teach it directly. When a student applies that skill during actual reading or writing, what was once an isolated skill becomes a productive literacy strategy (Routman, 1995).

It is not often that a solution as simple as teaching compound words will solve a student's reading problems. More often a systematic, analytic approach to assessment is needed. Moreover, several assessment and instructional strategies may be required over a period of time before substantial progress can be measured. Addressing students' diverse learning needs may mean changing and adjusting our instruction many times. It certainly means that we must have a great many strategies on hand to assist students. All good teachers must be like Shakespeare's Cleopatra, commanding "infinite variety." Figure 11.2 summarizes some of the assessment techniques we have introduced in Chapters 8, 9, and 10. In addition, at the end of this chapter we recommend some valuable resources that will provide you with the variety you'll need to serve your students well. In the next section, we describe some ways to systematically and analytically assess student reading performance. We begin with a discussion of some elements of the reading process in English.

Looking Closely at the Reading Process in English

To assess a student's reading performance using a systematic and analytic approach, you need to have an idea of what proficient reading involves. Here we offer our view of proficient reading, that is, the reading process displayed when a mature reader reads a text closely and carefully, as we hope you are reading this one right now. By delineating various kinds of knowledge that go into the process of reading, we can assess and teach to those areas.

Proficient readers approach a given text, be it a newspaper, a recipe, or a novel, with a **purpose** in mind for reading it. Next comes attention to the print, with visual processing proceeding from left to right, from the top to bottom of the page, given that we are talking about reading in English. Processing the print involves **decoding** the words on the page, producing a mental or verbal equivalent. Fluent readers recognize most words almost instantly, using sound/symbol knowledge, grammar, and meaning cues as they decode. **Comprehension** initially requires processing word sequences as meaningful units at the phrase or sentence

397

FIGURE 11.2 • READING ASSESSMENT OF ENGLISH LANGUAGE LEARNERS

READING LEVEL	INSTRUMENT THAT MIGHT BE USED	WHAT IS TESTED	WHAT MIGHT BE LEARNED
Beginning readers: usually early grades but can be later grades as well.	Running records: As student reads, the teacher checks off words that student reads correctly and codes those student has trouble with.	Student reading fluency and ability to process print: decoding, syntax, use of context, etc.	Whether students have basic ability to recognize words automatically so that they can concentrate on comprehension.
Intermediate readers: students who have learned how to read but may still be having difficulties with processing text.	Miscue analysis: Student reads materials while you are listening or tape recording; words are coded by you and comprehension questions are asked or student recalls information.	Student strategies for processing print, possible difficulties with print, and comprehension of information as given in recall or answering questions.	What student knows or doesn't know based on oral reading. Whether student is "barking at print" or actually comprehending.
Advanced readers: readers who have basic ability to process print automatically and who focus on comprehension.	Comprehension checks: Looking at student's ability to understand both narrative and expository texts, example group reading inventory (GRI).	Student ability to comprehend materials at high levels, including, factual, inferential, and applicative.	Student's sophistication in reading various levels and genres of print.
Appropriate for all readers whether struggling or gifted.	Informal reading inventory (IRI): Using leveled reading passages and comprehension checks, you can establish reading levels of your students.	Student ability to comprehend and process text at independent, instructional, and frustration levels.	How student is able to read and comprehend passages written at various grade levels.
Appropriate for all readers and writers.	Portfolio assessment: Teacher and student together collect in a portfolio various examples of student reading and writing.	How students perceive their literacy ability, general progress.	How student has developed over time. How student perceives work. What might be done next to assist moving the student to the next level of development.

level to begin to construct meaning. Continued comprehension further requires not only understanding the sentences but also relationships among sentences, as text meaning is reconstructed. Decoding, in our view then, provides the reader access to the words on the page; whereas, comprehension requires the reader to process word meanings in the context of the grammatical relationships among the words in a phrase or sentence to arrive at the meaning. It is largely through the relationships of words to each other that English sentences convey meaning. You may have observed how some students read word by word, as if the words in the sentence were nothing more than a random list, sometimes called "barking at print." They have decoded the words without comprehension of the phrase or sentence. To get at the meaning, the reader must attend to the words as meaningful language to understand the ideas in the phrase or the sentence. When teachers ask a beginning reader to "read it again, but this time with expression," they are attempting to focus students on pulling meaning from phrases and sentences, and express that meaning in their oral reading. For example, consider the sentence:

> The frightened fox finally escaped the hunters by diving into its den.

A student who reads this sentence word by word might be able to say each word and even know the meaning of each word. However, only by reading and understanding the words in relation to each other can the reader glean the meaning of the sentence as a whole, making it possible to visualize a fox chased by hunters, running in a panic, and narrowly escaping death. To get that far in comprehension, the reader must understand the meaning of the words in context. For example, the reader must comprehend the word *frightened* as modifying the word *fox*, while understanding *fox* as the subject whose action is conveyed by the verb *escaped*. The fact that the verb is in the past tense is important here, as it lets the reader know that the fox is now safe, because he *did* escape, not that he *is escaping or will escape*. The adverb *finally* modifies the verb *escaped*, implying that the fox has been chased for quite some time. Another grammatical element to understand is the phrase, *by diving into its den*. This phrase elaborates on the verb, telling the reader *how* the fox escaped. Readers understand these grammatical relationships implicitly as a result of knowing the language, not as a result of

 INTERNET RESOURCES

The Reading Assessment Portal for Teachers and Researchers (http://www.iteachilearn.com/index.html) will provide you with articles and many ways to assess your students. The section on literacy testing alone contains miscue analysis, metalinguistic awareness inventory, and an excellent article by Dr. Sheila Valencia on "Understanding Authentic Classroom-Based Literacy Assessment." The Language Testing Student Assessment site (www.ohiou.edu/esl/teacher/testing.html #Testing) contains all the information on testing you could possibly want. The ERIC site on assessment (http://ericae.net/intbod.stm) is so large we've known people who entered it and never returned. It contains 30 pages of links on assessment ranging from alternative assessment to secondary education, early childhood assessment, test reviews, and online tests. You might choose an area such as mathematics and science assessment and evaluate the site's usefulness. Or explore and assess the national results on reading, writing, or mathematics. There are hundreds of links here, most of them annotated.

being able to state the grammatical rules as we have done here. Reading with comprehension thus calls into play the reader's English language knowledge, and is dependent on the reader's ability to understand the specific morphology, syntax, and semantics of the language used in the text.

There is more to reading comprehension than decoding words and comprehending sentences. After all, most passages consist of at least several paragraphs structured in particular ways. Therefore, in addition to knowledge of decoding, syntax, and semantics, the reader's prior knowledge of the passage's content and familiarity with its genre and text structure play a major role in comprehension. Reading along, the reader needs to hold on to his or her ongoing interpretation of the meaning to elaborate, modify, and further build on it, thereby keeping the interpretation going and growing. Reading is thus a complex, cognitive–linguistic process that depends on the reader's ability to engage background knowledge, language knowledge, and memory while processing print. Reading is also a social process in that it involves communicative interaction between the author and the reader. In this view, text comprehension is simultaneously driven by the reader's purpose, prior knowedge, and ongoing interpretation as these interact with the continued decoding and comprehending of the print on the page to achieve communication. Finally, proficient readers monitor their own understanding as they read along to determine whether their interpretation makes sense and to make sure they are achieving their purpose for reading. This view of proficient reading, illustrated with a discussion of how a mature reader might read the following brief passage, provides the theoretical background for our approach to reading assessment.

> One of the most popular pets in today's homes is the cat. Cats were first tamed in Ancient Egypt probably around 3000 B.C. The ancient Egyptians needed cats to keep rats and mice from eating their large stores of grain. The Egyptians grew to admire the cats for their strength, agility, and superb hunting ability. They admired them so much that they not only kept them as pets but also considered them sacred. They even mourned their cats when they died, embalmed them, and took their mummified bodies to a special temple for cats. Today's cats may not be considered sacred, but they are loved by their owners for many of the same traits admired by the ancient Egyptians.

Let us consider how a mature reader might process this brief expository text about cats. In this case, let us assume that the student has chosen to research her favorite animal, cats, for which she will write a short report. The student's purpose for reading the text is to learn new information about cats and choose facts and ideas to include in her report. She brings prior knowledge of cats and their behavior because she has a pet cat at home. However, she is unfamiliar with the ancient Egyptians. She will build on her knowledge of cats as she reads and learns new information about cats in Ancient Egypt. Her prior knowledge, intrinsic interest, and purpose for reading about cats bolster the effort it will take to construct new knowledge from her reading.

Our mature reader begins reading the first sentence, already automatic at reading left to right, top to bottom. As a mature reader, she is able to recognize every word in the first sentence. Decoding is fast and fluent. Notice, however, that to comprehend the subject of the sentence conveyed by a phrase, she must process the **syntax** of the entire phrase, "One of the most popular pets in today's homes." A few of the syntactic relationships that have to be understood include the way that the word *today's* modifies the word *homes* and the way the phrase "one of the most popular" modifies the word *pets*. Important relationships are conveyed by the prepositions *of* and *in* the prepositional phrases, "(one) *of* the most popular pets" and "*in* today's homes." To understand the sentence it is also necessary to know that the verb *is* indicates equivalence between the subject of the sentence, the long phrase we have just discussed, and the complement, "the cat."

In terms of **vocabulary**, some words that may be unfamiliar to our mature reader include *mourned*, *embalmed*, and *mummified*. At the level of word formation, **morphology**, the reader needs to know the meaning of the plural marker *-s* as in *cats* and *homes*, while being able to distinguish it from the possessive marker *'s*, in *today's*. These elements of syntax and morphology can be a bit tedious to think about (and write about). However, the discussion serves to illustrate how knowledge of English syntax and morphology is essential to getting at the meaning of the sentence. That is, understanding the meaning of a sentence requires not only knowing the meaning of the words and their different forms, but also understanding the relationships among the words conveyed by the syntax of the sentence. Thus, reading comprehension at the sentence level depends on the reader's language knowledge.

In addition to our reader's purpose, prior knowledge, decoding ability, and language knowledge, her familiarity with **written language features** helps her read the passage easily. One of the most important written language features is **text structure**. Our passage about cats displays paragraph structure, with an introductory topic sentence, elaborating information, and concluding sentence. Our mature reader knows that she is reading an expository text, one that is written to convey information about cats. Her experiences with this genre of written text create expectations about the kind of content and text structure she will find in this passage. This familiarity assists her in comprehending and remembering the passage.

Finally, our mature reader must put the ideas together that are conveyed in the paragraph as a whole, using **cognitive** and **metacognitive processes**. One cognitive process is inferencing. For example, the reader must infer that the embalming of cats' bodies represents one way in which cats are treated as sacred. That connection is not explicit in the text. Rather, it is an implicit connection that the reader must infer to fully understand the passage. Another cognitive process readers must use is memory. The reader must hold information in memory within and across sentences to build the meaning of the passage. The longer the passage, the more there is to remember and relate. This is where some **metacognitive strategies** are helpful. Our mature reader has a particular purpose in mind for reading: She will be writing a report. Her purpose helps her decide what is important to remember. One of her strategies in achieving her reading purpose is to make notes on ideas she might include in her report.

In summary, our view of the reading process highlights the importance of several components: purpose, prior knowledge, language knowledge, decoding ability, written text knowledge, and cognitive and metacognitive processes. Next we examine these components as they impact non-native English speakers working to become proficient readers in English.

Resources That Non-Native English Speakers Bring to English Reading

Keeping in mind this view of reading, there are three kinds of general information we need to know about our students as non-native English speakers before we even start assessing their reading performance—information that may shed light on their

efforts to read in English, while indicating ways to assist them in becoming better readers. First of all, we need to know something about our students' life experiences, their interests, and their aspirations. With this information, we are better able to make use of their prior knowledge and interests to provide purpose for reading and motivate their desire to read. Second, we need to have a general idea of how well they know English, given the key role of language knowledge in reading. Are they beginners in English? Intermediate? Advanced? With a general sense of a student's **English language proficiency** we will be able to gauge whether language knowledge is making comprehension difficult, and we can guide students toward texts at an appropriate level of linguistic dif-

402

Students who are literate in their primary language bring funds of knowledge about reading and writing that serve them well as they develop English literacy.

ficulty. Third, we need to find out about the student's prior literacy experiences, both in the primary language and in English. Students who are literate in the primary language are generally familiar with various purposes for reading and writing (Peregoy & Boyle, 2000). If they are proficient readers in their primary language, they have exercised the process of constructing meaning from text, a complex process in any language. Thus, they bring substantial **funds of knowledge** (Moll, 1994) specific to written language forms, functions, and processes that they may build on as they learn to read in English. Although much of their **primary language literacy** knowledge is generally helpful as students begin to read in English, there are at least two broad areas English learners need growth in: English language development and understanding the ways that English is portrayed in print; that is, its writing system. Knowing the writing system will permit them to decode the printed words, while knowing English will facilitate text comprehension as we explained in detail previously. Students who read a logographic writing system, such as Chinese, face a different task from those who read an alphabetic writing system, such as the one used for Spanish or French. Nonetheless, all students who are literate in their home language bring funds of literacy knowledge to build on as they learn to read in English.

In addition to the general information about a student's prior knowledge, English language proficiency, and primary language literacy, there are several specific kinds of information to look for in relation to student performance on a particular passage. These specific kinds of information stem directly from the theoretical view of reading described previously and relate to the student's ability to deal with this particular passage. Because we are now discussing a student's ability to read a passage, we are referring to students who are beyond the emergent literacy phase of development discussed in Chapter 5. Thus they are at least beginning readers with at least beginner to advanced-beginner proficiency in

English. In other words, at a minimum, they have sufficient decoding and comprehension abilities to understand a simple passage in English. Among the areas of knowledge we want to learn about are the student's background knowledge about the passage topic itself. If a student doesn't know anything about catalytic converters, for example, he or she might have difficulty with a passage on that topic. Closely related to background knowledge, vocabulary knowledge also plays an important role in comprehension. Perhaps the student knows what a catalytic converter is, but has never heard or seen the term before. Familiarity with **key content vocabulary** can make or break comprehension. Another important knowledge area to assess is the student's **word recognition** and ability to decode with ease and fluency. The more words a student recognizes immediately, the more fluent he or she will be at processing the language of the text and constructing meaning. The better students are at figuring out words they don't recognize on sight, the easier it will be for them to remain focused on the meaning. Thus, sight word knowledge and decoding strategies are important to assess.

In addition to evaluating background knowledge, vocabulary, and decoding, it is also necessary to find out how well the student understands the **syntax** and **semantics** of the text, as they process and relate the ideas across phrases, sentences, and paragraphs. One area that can create difficulty, for example, is understanding the meaning of prepositional phrases, such as "under the tree," or "before returning to the party." Longer and more complex sentences are often difficult to understand because they require readers to comprehend and remember several complicated ideas at once, while mentally juggling the interrelationships among those ideas. Consider, for example, sentences such as the one at the beginning of this paragraph. This sentence connects ideas discussed in the previous paragraph and introduces the direction of the next discussion. Such sentences are more typical of written language than oral, and require facility in English and experience with written text.

Finally, as the student reads, you'll want to find out what strategies, including metacognitive strategies, he or she uses for comprehension of the passage. Does the student make good use of prior knowledge to comprehend? Does the student use text structure to aid comprehension and memory? Does the student slow down or reread complex texts, such as mathematics texts?

As a student reads, then, you are going to look at: background knowledge and vocabulary; word level skills, such as decoding and sight word recognition; language knowledge; and comprehension strategies. With these in mind you can begin evaluating and helping students in their reading progress. Figure 11.3 synthesizes some major categories in reading, some of the things we'll want to know about each category, and examples of techniques we might use to evaluate each area.

Assessing Reading Using an Informal Reading Inventory

Throughout this book we have discussed assessment techniques you can use day to day in your classroom, including checklists, anecdotal observations, miscue analysis, running records, lists of published works, lists and notes on literature students read, writing samples, and teacher-made tests. When items such as these are collected, evaluated, and placed in a portfolio, they provide a rich description of a student's overall language and literacy development. In this section, we share with

FIGURE 11.3

WHAT WE WANT TO
ASSESS WITH READERS

WHAT WE WANT TO LOOK AT	SOME OF THE THINGS WE WANT TO EVALUATE	HOW WE EVALUATE
Background knowledge	What the students know about passages they're reading; whether they engage their background knowledge when they read.	Through questioning and procedures, such as guided reading, DR-TA, and IRIs.
Language knowledge	Language knowledge includes such areas as prepositional phrases, anaphoric references, syntax, etc.	Through miscue analysis and comprehension assessment as students read connected text.
Word recognition	Students' knowledge of sight words, decoding ability, and level of automaticity the student possesses.	Through procedures such as running records, miscue analysis, and informal reading inventories.
Vocabulary	This category is related, of course, to the students' background knowledge. We want to know the extent of the students' vocabulary, including levels of knowledge, such as denotation and connotation.	Students' use of vocabulary in speaking, reading, and writing as seen in daily classroom work, as seen in miscue analysis, and in more formal tests you might give.
Comprehension	Students' ability to comprehend at different levels, including independent, instructional and frustration levels. Students' ability to comprehend at factual, interpretive, and applicative levels	Through students' answering and asking questions at the various levels of comprehension. Through students' recall, learning logs, and other more informal techniques.

you an assessment instrument, the informal reading inventory (IRI), to use when you need indepth information on a student's reading processes, such as a new student or one for whom your day-to-day observations have left you uncertain as to individual strengths and needs. Results of the IRI are another source of information that you may add to the student's portfolio.

IRIs are often used by reading specialists who work with individuals and small groups of students identified as needing special help in reading. Classroom

CALVIN AND HOBBES © Watterson. Reprinted with permission of UNIVERSAL PRESS SYNDICATE. All rights reserved.

teachers who use IRIs with their students benefit in two ways. First, they gain indepth information about each student's reading processes. Second, they benefit from knowing the principles and procedures involved, such as how to systematically collect information about students' reading over time; how to use grade-level materials, such as word lists and grade-level passages, to create benchmarks for students' progress; how to evaluate students' decoding and comprehension strategies; and how to evaluate what students need to progress to the next level of reading development. The IRI process itself can become a mental template that you use when listening to students read during day-to-day classroom activities and instruction. In other words, as you internalize the analytic process, you become a more acute observer and evaluator of student reading performance, even though you are not using the "official" procedure.

Using IRIs to Systematically Assess Students' Status and Progress

An informal reading inventory is a commercially available assessment tool, often published in a spiral-bound notebook format. IRIs include sets of passages of gradually increasing difficulty, usually designated as pre-primer through sixth grade or beyond. By providing a general index of passage difficulty, IRIs offer you a way of determining how a student performs on material at increasing levels of difficulty. Following each passage is a set of comprehension questions for students to answer. The comprehension questions, usually both factual and interpretive questions, give you a good idea of how students make sense of texts of varying difficulty. Some teachers also like to ask students to summarize information to help them get a fuller picture of the student's reading comprehension. When they do this, they prepare an outline of the major points in the text they would expect to be included in a complete retelling. If a student leaves out a major point, you can probe by asking an open-ended question, such as "What happened at the end of the story?" or "What about the dream the boy had?" These questions prompt memory without giving the information in the text. Through probing questions, you can help students display their understanding of a passage while distinguishing lack of recall from lack of comprehension.

When conducting an informal reading inventory, you may tape-record as the student reads each passage aloud, summarizes it, and answers the comprehension questions. It is also possible to have students read the passages silently, and then to assess comprehension. However, oral reading provides you with information on decoding and comprehending that silent reading cannot. Either way, it is best to begin with a passage that you believe is relatively easy for your student because this helps put the student at ease, bolsters confidence, and provides a chance to warm up. Next the student reads passages of gradually increasing difficulty. It's a good idea to have students read only two or three passages at one sitting, depending on their energy and enthusiasm for the task. If the student tires easily, you might want to spread the task out over a few days. The goal is to continue until you arrive at a passage level at which the student has difficulty. In this way you have tapped the ceiling (or plumbed the depths) of their reading proficiency on the IRI passages. In addition, by assessing a student with a challenging passage, you will obtain sufficient oral reading miscues to form the basis of a **miscue analysis** that will assist you in determining the student's reading strategies and potential learning needs.

405

After tape-recording the student to the highest passage level, you listen to the tape to analyze the student's oral reading performance. First, you code the miscues, or oral reading errors, using the system we provided in Chapter 8. Then you assess comprehension by evaluating the student's summary retelling or by checking their answers to the comprehension questions or both, if you have included both in your assessment. In this way, if the student has problems with the comprehension questions or in the retelling, you can look for patterns of miscues in the oral reading that might explain the comprehension difficulty. You can also look for general patterns of miscues to see what the student's strategies for reading are. For example, how does the student figure out an unfamiliar word? Does the student rely on letter/sound cues only or does he or she use a combination of letter/sound cues and context cues? Does the student self-correct? In this way you can get data on your students' relative reading level to help you determine the kind of instruction they may need—for example, in determining main ideas—to move up to the next level of reading development.

Using the results of the IRI, you can then create a strategy development plan for your students to help them become more competent readers. It can be useful to discuss the IRI results with your students in individual conferences, commending them for their strengths, explaining growth areas you would like them to work on, and inviting input from the students themselves. When you do this, you make reading strategies and processes explicit, providing students both the concepts and the words used to talk about strategies good readers use. If you emphasize that your students are in charge of their own learning, and that you will be there to support their efforts, the reading conference will invite mutual commitment between teacher and student toward reading improvement. Informal reading inventories take some time, but they are well worth it for the data you will get on your students' reading capabilities. You can perform an IRI in about 50 minutes with most students and the information will help you every day in your instructional decision making.

Reading Levels Can Be Established Using Informal Reading Inventories

Reading specialists and others often refer to three levels of reading performance on a given passage: the independent reading level, the instructional reading level, and the frustration reading level. Because the terms are used in conjunction with leveled passages—materials that have a designated grade level, such as primer, 10th grade, and so on—you can generalize cautiously as to the difficulty level of materials a student will be able to read independently, which materials will be appropriate for instruction, and which materials will probably be too difficult. When used flexibly and with other assessment information, including your day-to-day observations, IRI results can be quite useful in helping you select both materials and strategies for instruction. In addition, IRI results can help you guide students in selecting materials for independent reading.

Procedures for Determining Independent, Instructional, and Frustration Levels

When you use published IRIs, you will find that they include simple formulas to apply to determine whether a student is reading a particular passage at the independent, instructional, or frustration level. These formulas usually address word recognition and comprehension. For each passage, the IRI will tell you the number or percentage of word recognition errors, or miscues, that indicate independent, instructional, and frustration levels on that passage. In addition, the IRI will tell you the number or percentage of missed comprehension questions that indicate each level. It's important to know that experts disagree slightly on these percentages. Furthermore, it is essential that you combine IRI results with other assessment measures including your own personal judgment to be most accurate in gauging each student's reading abilities. It is especially important for you to use your own judgment when interpreting IRIs with non-native English speakers because all the IRIs that we know of have been designed and tested with native English speakers. Therefore, the calculations used to determine independent, instructional, and frustration levels may well differ for your English learners. The procedure is nonetheless appropriate and useful, as is the general information yielded by the miscue analysis and by the student's ability to deal with leveled passages. Your task will be to decide whether the passage is at the independent, instructional, or frustration level for your student. Next we describe how these levels are usually calculated in the IRIs for native English speakers.

Independent Reading Level

When a student is reading at an independent level, he or she is reading at a level that is relatively easy for him or her, a level at which the student requires little, if any, help from you. In numerical terms, if a student can read the material with roughly 98 percent word-recognition accuracy and with about 90 percent comprehension, they are reading at the independent level. Comprehension is determined according to student performance on the retelling or on the comprehension questions for the passage or on a combination of the two. In an IRI, if students read narrative and expository passages at an independent fourth-grade level, you can have some confidence that they will be able to read other fourth-grade materials with success.

Instructional Reading Level

At the instructional level, students' word recognition is about 95 percent accurate and comprehension is about 70 percent in an IRI or other assessment method using leveled materials. Students are able to read classroom materials at their instructional level when given your assistance. For example, you may do something as simple as developing a topic and building student background knowledge about marine mammals to help them read a passage on that topic. Or you may provide students with a study guide that helps them focus on key ideas in their reading.

Frustration Reading Level

When a student is reading at the frustration level, he or she is having great difficulty with word recognition and comprehension. If students consistently have great difficulty with fourth-grade passages, for example, you will probably want to consider using less difficult texts with them. At the frustration level students are below 90 percent in word recognition and below about 70 percent in comprehension. In other words, this level is simply too difficult for the student, even with help.

Obviously, you don't want to use these percentages rigidly to make decisions about your students. Your students may be highly motivated and willing to work with difficult materials, enabling them to grapple successfully with reading materials you deem to be at their frustration level. Similarly, they may bring a large amount of background knowledge to a passage you would otherwise consider too complex and therefore frustrating for them. These reading levels must be thought of as general guidelines, not as rigid, unchanging levels to be followed doggedly. Nevertheless, using these general guidelines can enhance your knowledge and teaching.

Sample Informal Reading Inventory

Throughout this chapter we will be using materials from one of the best reading inventories we know of, the Qualitative Reading Inventory-II (QRI-II) by Leslie and Caldwell (1995). This reading inventory has several features that we feel are important for all students, but especially for second language learners:

- The QRI-II contains word lists related to each passage provided to help you decide which passage to choose when assessing a student. Research suggests that good readers are able to read from word lists fluently and automatically. In addition, a student's performance on a word list is a quick way to gauge their reading level and start them on an appropriate-grade-level passage for the reading inventory.

- The QRI-II includes "concept questions" to ask before the student reads the passage. These questions assess student familiarity with the topic and under-standing of selected vocabulary or phrases included in the passage. Students are then given the opportunity to make a prediction about what the passage will be about. The concept questions serve two extremely useful purposes. First, they give you important information on what the student knows about the topic; second, they give you an idea of student understanding of some of the words and phrases in the passage. If the student has trouble understanding the passage, you have some information on background and language knowledge specific to the passage that may help you determine the source of difficulty. The concept and prediction questions serve another purpose in that they key the student into the passage topic, activate prior knowledge, and get the student ready to read. The process thus scaffolds student comprehension. For non-native English speakers, in particular, this process is especially helpful both for the information it provides you and for the warm-up it provides the student.

- The QRI-II contains multiple narrative and expository passages at each grade level, from pre-primer to junior high. This feature is useful because students generally have more difficulty with expository passages than with narrative passages. This difficulty may result from the fact that narrative passages tend to be self-contained and relate information that is generally more familiar to readers and because expository passages have different text structures that may play a role in making a passage less familiar and more difficult: for example, expository structures such as problem/solution and compare/contrast among others.

- The QRI-II contains both explicit and implicit questions for checking student comprehension of a passage. Explicit questions are those for which answers are stated explicitly in the text, whereas implicit questions require the reader to infer the answer from information which is not stated explicitly in the text.

- The QRI-II includes retelling as a comprehension measure to complement the information you obtain from student performance on the comprehen-sion questions. A recall checklist is provided to help you determine how much of the passage information the student understood and recalled. We suggest open-ended probing questions to help students recall information they leave out of the retelling.

- The QRI-II miscue scoring counts only errors that interfere with comprehending the meaning of the passage. Thus, repetitions and self-corrections are not counted as errors. Applying this scoring principle to English learners, non-native pronunciations are not counted as reading errors as long as comprehension is demonstrated, given that comprehension is the goal of reading, not pronunciation.

With this information, let's see how one teacher used and adapted an informal reading inventory to gauge her student's general reading abilities and strategies and to determine the student's independent, instructional, and frustration reading levels. Figure 11.4, adapted from Leslie and Caldwell, illustrates categories in a score sheet to help you collect information about your student. The concept questions in Figure 11.4 tap into the student's prior knowledge about the passage which is about to be read. The total number of miscues gives you the accuracy of the student's reading so that you can estimate independent, instructional and frustration levels of reading. In addition, there is a retelling sheet that helps you determine how well the student recalls the passage content after reading. Finally, there are comprehension questions to help you estimate the student's ability to understand the passage that has been read. Let's now look at one student's performance on an IRI.

Case Study of Lou Using an IRI

Lou is a 13-year-old Chinese bilingual eighth grader who speaks Mandarin at home with his parents. Lou's mother speaks no English, whereas his father speaks and reads some English. Both parents are literate in Chinese, and they frequently read newspapers, books, and magazines in Chinese. The family has been in the U.S. public school system for four years. Lou's teacher, Ms. Collins, noticed that Lou was having trouble reading material in her sheltered social studies/English language arts class. In class, Lou works well with his peers, using English effectively in most situations. However, he does not volunteer to participate in whole-class discussions, nor is he eager to make formal presentations to the class. Based on her in-class observations, Ms. Collins rated Lou at a score of 18 on the student oral language observation matrix (SOLOM; see Chapter 4), with vocabulary and pronunciation his lowest areas, rating a 3 each. She rated him as a 4 on comprehension, fluency, and grammar. Based on SOLOM scoring, Lou is rated as upper phase II, limited English proficient. In our terms he is an intermediate English learner.

Ms. Collins decided to assess his reading, beginning with a third-grade-level passage, "A Trip to the Zoo," using her own judgment rather than giving him word lists to decide where to start on the IRI. Figure 11.5 illustrates how Lou read the passage. As we can see, Lou omitted some -*ed* endings that Ms. Collins determined didn't get in the way of his understanding the passage (Lou was able to answer all of the comprehension questions accurately). But he did have trouble with two words: *noticed*, which he pronounced *no-tiched* and he paused at the word *remembered* for a second or two before figuring it out correctly. Ms. Collins determined, therefore, that Lou read the third-grade zoo passage at the independent level. Next, she wanted to see how Lou would read a fourth-grade narrative passage.

FIGURE 11.4

Concept Questions and Partial Scoring Sheet for the QRI-II for Amelia Earhart Passage

Source: Lauren Leslie and Joanne Caldwell, *Qualitative Reading Inventory-2* (Boston: Allyn & Bacon/Pearson Education, 1995). Reprinted by permission of the publisher.

Concept Questions:

1. Who was Amelia Earhart? (3-2-1-0)
2. What are the dangers of flying a small Plane? (3-2-1-0)
3. What is an adventurer? (3-2-1-0)
4. What are women's rights? (3-2-1-0)

Score _____/12 (×100) = _____%

Prediction: _____

Number of Total Miscues
(Total Accuracy): _____

Number of Meaning Change Miscues
(Total Acceptability): _____

Total Accuracy			Total Acceptability
0–6 miscues	_____	Independent _____	0–6 miscues
7–27 miscues	_____	Instructional _____	7–14 miscues
28+ miscues	_____	Frustration _____	15+ miscues
Rate: 263 × 60/ _____ seconds = _____ WPM			

Partial Retelling Sheet for Amelia Earhart Passage

Setting/Background
___ Amelia Earhart was an adventurer
___ during World I
___ she was a nurse
___ who had been hurt

Goal
___ She knew
___ that she must fly

Events
___ Earhart trained
___ to be a pilot

Resolution
___ Her plane disappeared
___ People searched
___ over the ocean
___ for a long time

A Few Sample Comprehension Questions:

1. What was Amelia Earhart's main goal? *Implicit:* to fly; to do challenging things
2. When Amelia Earhart first crossed the Atlantic in a plane, what was her role? *Explicit:* she was a passenger
3. Why do you think her plane was never found? *Implicit:* probably sank in the ocean; ocean was so big; plane was very small

---

Figure 11.6 illustrates Lou's performance on the fourth-grade narrative passage about Amelia Earhart. On the concept questions before reading the passage, Lou indicated that he didn't know anything about Amelia Earhart or what "an adventurer" was; thus, the information in the passage was basically unfamiliar to him. As shown in Figure 11.6, Lou read the passage making only six miscues, which means that he is reading this fourth-grade material at the independent level. Moreover, he correctly answered all of the comprehension questions on the passage and recalled most of the important information in the passage. Therefore, Ms. Collins concludes that Lou probably will be able to read other unfamiliar, narrative material written at a similar level of difficulty, that is, the fourth-grade level. However, his performance

FIGURE 11.5

THIRD-GRADE NARRATIVE
PASSAGE READ BY LOU

Source: Lauren Leslie and
Joanne Caldwell, *Qualitative
Reading Inventory-2* (Boston:
Allyn & Bacon/Pearson Edu-
cation, 1995). Reprinted by
permission of the publisher.

The Trip to the Zoo

The day was bright and sunny. Carlos and Maria jumped [jump] out of bed and
dressed in a hurry. They didn't want to be late for school today. It was a special day
because their classes were going to the zoo. When they got to school, all of the
children were waiting outside to get on the bus. When everyone was there, the
second and third graders got on the bus and rode to the zoo. On the bus, the
children talked [talk] about the zoo animals that they liked best. Joe and Carlos wanted [want] to
see the lion, king of the beasts. Maria and Angela wanted [want] to see the chimps. Maria
thought they acted a lot like people.

When they got to the zoo, their teachers divided the children into four groups.
One teacher, Mr. Lopez, told them if anyone got lost, to go to the ice cream stand.
Everyone would meet there at noon. Maria went with the group to the monkey house
where she spent a long time watching the chimps groom each other. She wrote
down all the ways that the chimps acted like people. Her notes would help her write
a good report of what she liked best at the zoo.

Carlos went with the group to the lion house. He watched the cats pace in
front of the glass. Carlos was watching a lion so carefully that he didn't see his
group leave. Finally, he noticed that it was very quiet in the lion house. He turned
around and didn't see anyone. At first he was worried. Then he remembered what
Mr. Lopez had said. He (traced) his way back to the entrance and found a map. He
followed the map to the ice cream stand, just as everyone was meeting there for
lunch. Joe smiled and said, "We thought that the lion had you for lunch!" (312 words)

on the passage indicates that Lou has some difficulty with multisyllabic words such
as *adventurer*, *frightening*, and *disappeared*. Even though he discussed *adventurer*
with Ms. Collins before reading the passage, he still had difficulty recognizing the
word and understanding it in the context of the passage. This difficulty with decoding and understanding multisyllabic words may cause trouble for him when he reads
other content material containing such words.

Because Lou performed fairly well reading the fourth-grade narrative passage
about Amelia Earhart, Ms. Collins presented him with a more difficult passage to
see how well he might do. She chose a fifth-grade narrative passage about
Margaret Mead. At 357 words, this passage was longer than previous passages.
Furthermore, it contained words that occur infrequently in conversation such as

FIGURE 11.6

LOU'S READING OF
FOURTH-GRADE NARRA-
TIVE PASSAGE

*Source: Scott, Foresman
Social Studies, Grade 4:
Regions of Our Country and
Our World* (Glenview, IL:
Scott, Foresman and Co.,
1983), p. 83. Used with
permission.

Amelia Earhart

Amelia Earhart was an adventurer and a pioneer in the field of flying. She did things no other woman had ever done before.

During World War I, Earhart worked as a nurse. She cared for pilots who had been hurt in the war. Earhart listened to what they said about flying. She watched planes take off and land. She knew that she, too, must fly.

In 1928, Earhart was the first woman to cross the Atlantic in a plane. But someone else flew the plane. Earhart wanted to be more than just a passenger. She wanted to fly a plane across the ocean herself. For four years, Earhart trained to be a pilot. Then, in 1932, she flew alone across the Atlantic to Ireland. The trip took over fourteen hours.

Flying may seem easy today. However, Earhart faced many dangers. Airplanes had just been invented. They were much smaller than our planes today. Mechanical problems happened quite often. There were also no computers to help her. Flying across the ocean was as frightening as sailing across it had been years before. Earhart knew the dangers she faced. However, she said, "I want to do it because I want to do it. Women must try to do things as men have tried. When they fail, their failure must be a challenge to others."

Earhart planned to fly around the world. She flew more than twenty thousand miles. Then, her plane disappeared somewhere over the huge Pacific Ocean. People searched for a long time. Finally, they gave up. Earhart and her plane were never found.

(263 words)

---

anthropology, investigate, ceremonies, and *recount.* Even though the sentences in the passage were fairly short and straightforward, Lou struggled so much with the vocabulary that he was unable to construct meaning from the passage. He made 16 miscues that contributed to loss of meaning, and he was able to answer only half of the comprehension questions. Ms. Collins concluded that fifth-grade material of this type was too difficult for Lou to read; it was at his frustration level.

Given Lou's performance on the Margaret Mead passage, Ms. Collins decided to present him with one more passage, this time moving back to a fourth grade expository passage about Saudi Arabia. Figure 11.7 shows Lou's miscues on the passage. Overall, he made 13 miscues that affected meaning, several involving longer words and compound words. Ms. Collins makes a note of Lou's continuing difficulty with decoding and understanding multisyllabic words, an area she will work on with him subsequently. Ms. Collins was pleased to find that

FIGURE 11.7

LOU'S READING OF
FOURTH-GRADE EXPOSI-
TORY PASSAGE

*Source: Scott, Foresman
Social Studies, Grade 4:
Regions of Our Country and
Our World* (Glenview, IL:
Scott Foresman and Co.,
1983), pp. 244–245. Used
with permission.

Saudi Arabia is a large country. It is about the size of the United States east of the Mississippi River. But it is a country that has not one lake or river!

[Ca-pi-tal] The capital is a city (of) both new and old. There are air-conditioned [aircon] buildings and high-rise [higher] apartments. There are also old buildings made of mud brick. Families often sleep on the roofs at night to escape the heat. They don't worry that it will rain.

Saudi Arabia has very dry, very hot weather. Where do people find water? They dig wells deep into the earth. The capital [ca-pi-tal], a city of many people, is watered [water] by many of these wells.

Outside the capital lies the world's largest sand desert. Strong winds blow the sand. From the air, the sand dunes [du] look like waves of a great (tan) ocean. On the ground, the feel [fill] of sand covers everything. A few islands of palm trees spring up out of the desert. They mean only one thing, water. These islands of life are the oases [oses] of Saudi Arabia which form (around) [come from] the springs or wells. Many people live near the oases in low mud houses. They plant gardens and orchards [orc] and raise camels.

Many groups of people live on the desert itself. They are the Bedouin [Bed/Be] who move from place to place in search of food and water for their animals. The Bedouin [Bedon] depend on camels and goats for milk and meat. They use the animals' [animal/s] hair to make rugs and cloth for tents. The Bedouin [Bedon] know no boundaries [boud]. The open desert has been their home for generations [generat].   (265 words)

Lou was able to answer 4 of the 6 comprehension questions correctly. This performance suggests that expository material at this level of difficulty is about at Lou's instructional level. Ms. Collins decides that Lou has provided her the information she needs to provide appropriate reading material for instruction. She thanks him for his hard work and congratulates him for persisting through reading the various passages.

Summary of Lou's Reading Abilities

Lou's IRI results suggest that he reads fourth-grade narrative passages at an independent level and fourth-grade unfamiliar expository passages at the instructional level. Given that he has been in the United States for only four years and has achieved an intermediate level of English proficiency, this level of reading progress is reasonable, and in fact he should be commended for it. Nonetheless, Lou needs to accelerate his literacy progress to achieve a performance level that will allow him to succeed later on in high school. Examining Lou's performance on the IRI, Ms. Collins noticed several strengths Lou brings to his reading. First,

Lou reads fairly fluently as a result of a good sight vocabulary and he's able to decode simple unfamiliar words, such as *capital* in the Saudi Arabia passage. Second, Lou reads for meaning. He expects the passage to make sense.

Ms. Collins looks for patterns of recurring errors in Lou's reading. When students make errors over and over again, it is more likely that the errors represent an area the student needs help on, provided that the errors are important for reading comprehension. In Lou's reading, one of his recurring error patterns is the omission of the *-ed* endings on past tense verbs. Ms. Collins has to decide whether to work on this with Lou in his reading. To decide, she first examines whether the omission results in lack of comprehension. Does Lou understand that the passage is referring to something that happened in the past? She finds that he does understand, even though he did not pronounce the *-ed* ending. She concludes that this pronunciation error does not affect his reading comprehension. She decides not to concern Lou or herself with this oral pronunciation miscue. Ms. Collins has also noticed, however, that Lou leaves out the *-ed* on some verbs in his writing, which is generally fluent and grammatical. She therefore makes a note that she will work on the *-ed* ending in his writing, where it does make a difference. It will be a detail for Lou to check for when he edits his papers.

A different recurring error pattern that Ms. Collins notices is Lou's difficulty with multisyllabic words, such as *generations* in the Saudi Arabia passage and *anthropology, primitive, investigate,* and *ceremonies* in the Margaret Mead passage. This difficulty interrupts the flow of meaning and impedes Lou's comprehension. Difficulty with these multisyllabic words stems from Lou's lack of familiarity with the words themselves combined with his lack of knowledge about English word formation in the areas of compound words, prefixes, suffixes, and roots. Ms. Collins decides to intensify her work with Lou on vocabulary development and word study related to prefixes, suffixes, and roots as discussed in Chapter 6. Word study of this type will address not only decoding but also word meanings. First, she will ask Lou to keep his own vocabulary self-collection journal (Haggard, 1986) in which Lou keeps a list of new words he comes across in his reading. From this list, Ms. Collins will work with Lou to develop lessons on prefixes, suffixes, and roots to promote his ability to analyze and understand new words. She also plans to provide a computer program that will help him specifically in these areas. In addition, she will set up word games to play with other students who can benefit from similar practice.

Analyzing Lou's reading reminded Ms. Collins of how important it is to prepare all of her students for the reading they will do in class. As a result, she has decided to be more consistent in applying the prereading, during reading, and postreading strategies recommended in Chapters 8, 9, and 10. For her eighth-grade social studies content, it is clear to her that she needs to provide direct experiences, visuals, and graphic organizers to develop both concepts and vocabulary before asking students to read materials on their own. For vocabulary development in reading, Ms. Collins has decided to talk about and model strategies for figuring out new words through word analysis and context, something she had not done much of lately. Finally, Ms. Collins has decided to provide her students with 25 minutes per week of independent, self-selected reading time. During this time, she will conference quietly with individual students, listen to and informally assess their oral reading, discuss strategies to help them read, and find out more about their interests. She may also conference with them on their writing at this time. Such information will further inform her work with her students as individuals and as a group.

All of the IRI testing with Lou took Ms. Collins approximately 55 minutes. With the results of the IRI in mind, she will observe Lou in class during buddy reading, independent reading, and guided reading to discover whether the IRI results are corroborated or not. In addition, she will watch for improvement in the areas for which she has targeted instruction. Later, she may decide to conduct an IRI with Lou again to estimate his progress in reading development.

We chose to use the QRI-II to assess Lou's reading performance for the reasons we stated previously. However, other informal reading inventories may be more useful to you if, for example, (1) you need passages that go beyond the pre-primer to junior high levels found in the QRI-II, (2) you need passages in a language other than English to evaluate reading performance in another language, or (3) you want passages to evaluate both gifted and remedial students. We offer a list of other IRIs that address some of these needs.

A List of Commercial Informal Reading Inventories

Here is a list of some of the commercial reading inventories that you may find useful. We recommend that you go to your school district or county library to find these commercial inventories and evaluate them based on your own classroom needs. Of course, you can also develop your own inventory using classroom or reading program graded materials. You will also find that some reading programs will provide you with informal reading inventories that may be useful.

> Bader, L. A. (2004). *Bader reading and language inventory and reader's passages and graded word lists* (5th ed.). Upper Saddle River, NJ: Prentice Hall.
>
> Flynt, E. S., & Cooter, R. B. (1999). *English–Español reading inventory for the classroom*. Upper Saddle River, NJ: Merrill.
>
> Leslie, L., & Caldwell, J. (2005). *Qualitative Reading Inventory, II* (4th ed.). New York: Allyn & Bacon.
>
> Stieglitz, E. L., & Lanigan, V. (2002). *The Stieglitz informal reading inventory: Assessing reading behaviors from emergent to advanced levels* (3rd ed.). New York: Allyn & Bacon.
>
> Woods, M. L., & Moe, A. J. (2006). *Analytical reading inventory with reader passages* (8th ed.). Upper Saddle River, NJ: Prentice Hall.

Other Procedures for Evaluating and Helping Readers

There are many other ways of evaluating English learners in reading beyond what we have already discussed in previous chapters and in this chapter. Next we list a few other methods that we think may be valuable to you in assessing student literacy. The strategies range from echo reading, which evaluates a student's oral language, syntax, and reading; guided reading, which assists students at the discourse level; to ReQuest procedure, which evaluates and assesses students at the questioning and comprehension level. We begin with Echo Reading.

Linking Assessment and Instruction

Assessment, whether in reading, writing, or any other subject, is only useful if the assessment results inform your instructional decisions. We mentioned previously that your experience assessing students through an informal reading inventory can help you become a better observer of student reading performance during day-to-day classroom activities in which students read aloud. For example, if you pair your students to read aloud quietly to each other during buddy reading, you now have an opportunity to listen in and get an idea of how well the student reads, while making a mental note of areas that might lead to reading improvement, such as providing a mini-lesson later on a particular strategy. Often you will find several students who need similar strategy instruction, leading to the formation of a small group in need of your direct assistance. This kind of group is relatively homogeneous in terms of students' reading development, and represents one kind of flexible grouping designed to meet students' learning needs. It is flexible in that the group is called together for a short time based on a particular, shared learning need. Guided reading, a teaching-learning format described in this section, is a small-group instructional format that calls together several students who read at roughly similar levels.

Echo Reading

Echo reading is a process whereby the teacher reads a sentence and the student repeats or echoes the sentence. Although the procedure has not been researched with second language learners, you may wish to try it with your students. Specifically, echo reading is a method that assists you in discovering the level of syntax a child may possess. Interestingly, if a student is unable to repeat a sentence you have read to them, they will probably be unable to read the sentence. So you can use echo reading to gauge the oral language level of a student and to gain an estimation of what the student may be able to do with reading. This is especially helpful if you have an English learner who is shy, quiet, or reluctant to speak and you are having difficulty finding his or her oral language abilities.

The procedure is fairly simple: First, explain the process to the student; that you are going to read sentences aloud and that their job is to repeat the sentence word for word; second, you'll read the sentence to the student and ask the student to repeat it; finally, as the student echoes the sentence, you'll record what the student has repeated.

We find it easiest to record using the same basic guidelines you would follow if you were doing a miscue analysis:

1. If the student has echoed the word correctly, don't do anything.
2. If the student substitutes or adds a word, write the word above the word or phrase where the substitution takes place.
3. Circle words left out in the student's version.

Follow other procedures discussed in the miscue analysis section to code the student's repetitions and make decisions about the student's English abilities accordingly. As in miscue analysis, if the student substitutes a synonym, such as *table* for *desk*, you'll know that the student is echoing appropriately. On the other hand, if students have to omit many words in a sentence, they indicate that they are having difficulty with the syntax and may have trouble reading similar material. For example, one kind of omission is given below:

ORIGINAL SENTENCE:	The boy went to the store and bought candy.
STUDENT'S ECHO:	Boy went store and candy.

With the echo reading procedure, you can use your own classroom texts to see if students can echo sentences in them. If the student cannot repeat sentences correctly, you may want to carefully select materials the student can read. You could, for example, try pattern books or sentences with the student because they are usually easier to repeat and thus easier to read for second language students and others with less developed English syntax.

Guided Reading

Guided reading is a teaching strategy in which a small group of students is guided by the teacher through reading a text that is at the students' instructional reading level. The text may be narrative, expository, or even poetic, but it must be a text that challenges students a bit. The teacher's role is to guide students toward reading strategies that will enable them to successfully comprehend the text. The strategies on which the teacher chooses to focus will depend on the text itself, along with the strategy knowledge and learning needs of the students in the group. Usually, the guided reading group meets several times a week, if not daily. As a result, the teacher has plenty of time to observe students and gauge their reading abilities informally. During the guided reading session, the goal is to assist students in understanding what was read and responding to it personally and critically. Guided reading can be especially helpful to beginning English learners, but it is also practical and useful for more advanced English learners who are reading complex narrative and expository texts.

Guided reading is a powerful tool because it provides frequent opportunities for students to read challenging material in small groups with the support and guidance of the teacher. In this way, guided reading provides a scaffolding routine, a predictable routine with which students become comfortable and secure. Students know that the reading material will be somewhat difficult, but the teacher will be there to help them with it, and that is how they will become better readers. The teacher's job during guided reading will be to select reading material at gradually increasing levels of difficulty, "upping the ante," as we mentioned in our discussion of scaffolding in Chapter 3. In addition, the teacher must be prepared to observe students, assess informally, and then provide scaffolding, modeling, and direct instruction that address student needs.

Although guided reading may vary from one teacher to another, it usually includes several procedures that are similar to the directed reading-thinking activity (DR-TA) procedure that we presented in Chapter 8. These procedures are as follows:

1. You begin by introducing the story or other text, starting with the title, author, and illustrator, inviting students to make predictions about the text; this helps to create a purpose for reading. With younger children, you may want to go through the pictures in the book, talking about the pictures and inviting predictions as to what the story will be about.

417

2. Based on what they have seen of the story, students engage in a brief discussion about the story based on the title, the illustrations, the topic, and their expectations of what the story will be about.

3. Next, you ask students to read a portion or all of the text; with younger students you may want to read a few pages of the story before asking them to read the rest of the text. The text can be read either aloud or silently depending on your knowledge of the students' capabilities and your purpose.

4. If students read the text aloud in pairs or if you ask them to read aloud quietly to themselves, you can circulate around the group and help individuals solve problems they may have, such as identifying words, understanding punctuation, or understanding a word in a new context. You may have older, more proficient students read larger chunks of the text or story to discuss as a group, providing help and guidance as needed.

5. After reading the story, you will want to facilitate or guide the students to think about what they have read by asking students to share their own responses to the story, to discuss their favorite parts, or to discuss main ideas or themes in a story.

6. You may follow up the last phase of guided reading with a brief, explicit discussion of useful reading strategies for reading and understanding the selection just read. One way is to invite a student to tell how he or she figured out a particular word if you noticed the student applying a good strategy or one you have recently been teaching, such as the use of chunking, or decoding parts of a long word one part at a time. Another way is to provide a brief mini-lesson on an aspect of the text with which several children had difficulty: for example, understanding a simile such as "pretty as a picture." Other mini-lesson topics that might emerge include discussing the text structures, narrative or expository, based on the selection that was read.

7. Finally, following the guided reading lesson you may invite students to respond to a story by creating a puppet show or readers' theater or by responding in their literature response journals.

Figure 11.8, from the excellent book on guided reading by Fountas and Pinnell (1996), illustrates what the teacher and children do before, during, and after guided reading. Although this book focuses on guided reading in the primary grades, guided reading is also a superb tool for upper grades, middle school, and high school. The main differences between younger and older learners relate to the topic, linguistic complexity, and level of sophistication in the reading material used. During small-group instruction using challenging material with teacher guidance, multiple benefits accrue for students of all ages and levels of language and literacy development.

Erlinda Quintanar uses guided reading with her English learners to extend their background knowledge of a story, to expand their understanding of narrative structure, and to enlarge their repertoire of response. Using the American Indian story "Coyote and the Star" from a collection of multicultural folktales she is using in her class, she develops her own approach to guided reading. Here is a synopsis of this appealing story:

> The story explains why coyote howls at the night sky. The reason is that coyote fell in love with a beautiful star which eventually took coyote into the sky. But coyote missed the earth and asked the star to let him go back down to

THE ESSENTIAL ELEMENTS OF GUIDED READING			
	BEFORE THE READING	**DURING THE READING**	**AFTER THE READING**
Teacher	• selects an appropriate text, one that will be supportive but with a few problems to solve • prepares an introduction to the story • briefly introduces the story, keeping in mind the meaning, language, and visual information in the text, and the knowledge, experience, and skills of the reader • leaves some questions to be answered through reading	• "listens in" • observes the reader's behaviors for evidence of strategy use • confirms children's problem-solving attempts and successes • interacts with individuals to assist with problem solving at moment of difficulty (when appropriate) • makes notes about the strategy use of individual readers	• talks about the story with children • invites personal response • returns to the text for one or two teaching opportunities such as finding evidence or discussing problem solving • assesses children's understanding of what they read • sometimes engages the children in extending the story through such activities as drama, writing, art, or more reading
Children	• engage in a conversation about the story • raise questions • build expectations • notice information in the text	• read the whole text or a unified part to themselves (softly or silently) • request help in problem solving when needed	• talk about the story • check predictions and react personally to the story or information • revisit the text at points of problem solving as guided by the teacher • may reread the story to a partner or independently • sometimes engage in activities that involve extending and responding to the text (such as drama or journal writing)

FIGURE 11.8

THE ESSENTIAL ELEMENTS OF GUIDED READING

Source: Irene C. Fountas and Gay Su Pinnell, *Guided Reading: Good First Teaching for All Children* (Portsmouth, NH: Heinemann/Reed Elsevier, 1996).

419

earth; the star took him back to earth. But now coyote misses the star and howls his love for it.

Erlinda introduces and builds background knowledge about the story by reading the title and taking the children on a "picture walk" through the book.

ERLINDA: Class, the title of this story is "Coyote and the Star"; what do you think it'll be about?

SONIA: Coyote and a star in the sky.

CARLOS: How many stars coyote sees.

OTHERS: *(various comments)*

ERLINDA: Those are good ideas.
Let's look at the pictures and see what you think will happen in the story. [*She thumbs through the pictures with the children and stops at certain important pictures, such as the one of coyote embracing the star in the sky, and asks students what's happening in them. Then she reads the first two pages of the story to the children.*] Now I want you to read the rest of the story aloud to a buddy. I'll be right here so if you need any help, just raise your hand and ask me. [*She walks around the table, listens in on their reading, and takes notes on the children's reading strengths and needs.*]

When the children have finished reading the story to one another, she asks them to briefly discuss with their buddy what they thought of the story and what their favorite parts were or who were their favorite characters. Then she asks the group of six students to discuss what they found in their talk with their buddy reader.

JUAN: I thought it was sad how coyote yells.
ERLINDA: Who else felt that way? [*Other children respond in similar ways.*]
LON: I like the part when the star take coyote to the sky.
NGYEN: Me too.

The children continue, with Erlinda's help, answering questions and elaborating on the story and its outcome. After the 10-minute discussion, Erlinda suggests that the children may wish to make a puppet show about the story and the children respond enthusiastically. The children begin gathering materials for the show and work together while Erlinda moves to another group that has been working on stories they are writing themselves. The children will present their puppet show to the rest of the class in two days when they are ready.

We have indicated that there are many variations on the guided reading approach depending on the age and abilities of the students in your class. But the basic outline is similar: (1) the teacher builds some background knowledge before the story is read; (2) the story is read silently or aloud by the students; (3) the students discuss the story with the teacher facilitating the discussion; and (4) sometimes the teacher asks the students to do some kind of follow-up activity with the story, such as writing in their literature response journals or performing the story. With these steps the teacher has guided her students through the story and modeled how one might go about reading any story.

In addition, she uses guided reading to assess the children's progress in reading and understanding stories, making a note of specific kinds of strategy instruction she might provide to improve their reading.

ReQuest Procedure

The purpose of the ReQuest procedure (Manzo, 1968) is to help students learn to develop their own questioning while reading to enable them to be better and more active comprehenders. ReQuest is usually used with students who are advanced enough in English literacy to read short texts. It is a good procedure for small-group instruction but may be used with the whole class. The basic elements of the procedure are relatively simple. You select appropriate material that will involve students in thinking and predicting. Next, you explain the purpose of the procedure to the students. As with most lessons, you'll want to prepare students for reading the text by building necessary background information and discussing difficult and important vocabulary in the text. Next, tell students that they will read a sentence or section of the text and then ask you a question. You will answer the question and then ask them a question about the next section. Your purpose here is to model good questions for the students and to help them with developing their own good questions. When answering the questions, you and the students keep the text closed. After taking students through some of the text, you have them predict what will happen in the rest of the text and then let them read and monitor their predictions. After students have read the text, you might ask them to discuss and recall what they read and what they predicted. You might also have them summarize what they read in their learning logs. Through the ReQuest procedure, you hope to build students' independent reading comprehension and develop confidence in their ability to actively understand and remember what they have read.

Although the procedure relates to older students, it can also be used with students in the primary grades (Legenza, 1974). We saw one second-grade teacher, Lilly Chan, using the method with the book *Fortunately* (Charlip, 1997). First, she told children she was going to play a questioning game with them.

She explained that the rules of the game were simple: She would give an "answer," and their job was to ask a question to go with it. For example, she said, "If I say bat, you might ask, 'What do you hit a baseball with?' or 'What do you hold in your hands when it is your turn to hit in a baseball game?'" After some other examples and clarification, Lilly started the game:

LILLY: The answer is peanut butter. What's the question?
PHAM: What goes good with jam?
JOSE: What sticks to the roof of your mouth?
LEE: What is made out of stomped peanuts?

After naming other topics and developing questions, the children became relatively proficient and enthusiastic about asking questions. So Lilly told the students that she was now going to play the game using a story. They would read the first part of the story, ask a question of her, and she would answer. Then she would ask them a question and they would answer. To introduce the procedure to these young children, she selected a book that was predictable and had pictures that illustrate the action, fortunately and unfortunately. The book has a pattern that repeats something fortunate and something unfortunate that happens. She explained that the word *fortunately* meant something good had happened and *unfortunately* meant something was not good. She also took time to explain that when *un-* was in front of a word it meant "not." She then read the first two lines of the book, asked the students to predict what would happen in subsequent pages, and asked the students to read the following three pages on their own before asking her a question. She would read a line and ask the children a question. Finally, she had the children predict what would happen in the rest of the book and then read it. She finished with a brief discussion of the book.

When you use the ReQuest procedure with either younger or older students, you teach them to anticipate what a story is about, to develop questions that will help them understand the story better, and to predict what will happen next. Moreover, you show them how to be active learners.

Summary

In this chapter on analytic reading assessment and instruction, we began with a theoretical discussion of language proficiency as including both oral and written language: listening, speaking, reading, and writing. We then focused on reading per se. We chose this focus because of the important role of reading in school and beyond. As background for the discussion on reading assessment, we laid out our theoretical view of the reading process of mature readers. We then discussed what non-native English speakers bring to this process, especially in terms of background knowledge, language knowledge, word recognition, vocabulary, and comprehension. Next we presented a detailed description of an informal reading inventory, which we illustrated with the oral reading performance of an eighth-grade English learner. Finally, we showed how small-group instruction for students of similar reading abilities can address students' particular, assessed needs in ways that promote improvement and lead to independence in reading.

Suggestions for Further Reading

August, D. and Shanahan, T. (Eds.) (2006). *Developing literacy in second-language learners: Report of the National Literacy Panel on language-minority children and youth*. Mahwah, New Jersey: Lawrence Erlbaum Associates, Publishers.

This report from the National Literacy Panel offers a comprehensive review of the research on second-language literacy. Every researcher should have this book for future reference. Chapters written by top researchers in second-language literacy and learning provide a close look at the current status of research and suggest areas of future research.

Brantley, D. K. (2007). *Instructional assessment of English language learners in the K-8 classroom*. Boston: Pearson/Allyn & Bacon.

This teacher-friendly text includes a clear theoretical base for assessment, classroom vignettes that bring ideas and strategies alive, and multiple assessment strategies. Each chapter begins with an anticipation guide in which readers check off whether they agree or disagree with a statement. At the end of the chapter, the anticipation guide is repeated with answers to the statements made.

Brown, J. D. (Ed.). (1998). *New ways of classroom assessment*. Alexandria, VA: Teachers of English to Speakers of Other Languages.

This book, part of the New Ways series by TESOL, offers almost a hundred different strategies and approaches to classroom assessment in listening, speaking, reading, and writing. Short articles also include portfolio assessment, self-assessment, group assessment, and much more. If you don't like some of the approaches to assessment in the book, you're sure to find others you do like and will use.

Genesee, F., & Upshur, J. A. (2002). *Classroom-based evaluation in second language education*. Cambridge: Cambridge University Press.

This thorough book on classroom-based evaluation is well written, well organized, and reader friendly. It begins by introducing evaluation, discusses second language evaluation, provides a theoretical framework, and then moves to chapters on topics such as observation, portfolios and conferences, objective-referenced testing, choosing and devising tests, and interpreting tests. Each chapter begins with excellent preview questions and ends with discussion questions you could share with peers in class.

Huerta-Macias, A. (1995). Alternative assessment: Responses to commonly asked questions. *TESOL Journal, 5*(1), 8–12.

In this article, Huerta-Macias fulfills the promise of the title, answering common questions about alternative assessments such as validity, reliability, and objectivity. We recommend the article to anyone who is initiating alternative assessment or anyone who wants to explain it to others.

Hughes, A. (2003). *Testing for language teachers* (2nd ed.). Cambridge: Cambridge University Press.

The brief chapters discuss teaching and testing; kinds, validity, and reliability of tests and testing; stages of test development; and testing writing, oral ability, reading, listening, grammar and vocabulary, and overall ability. The book concludes with chapters on testing young learners and test administration. It is clearly written and organized to make it a user-friendly text for teachers.

Hurley, S. R., & Tinajero, J. V. (Eds.). (2001). *Literacy assessment of second language learners.* Boston: Allyn and Bacon.

This edited text contains articles by key educators and researchers on literacy assessment of second language learners. Articles include topics such as integrated perspectives, assessing acquisition, assessing comprehension and content area learning, and assessing biliteracy development. The articles discuss standardized and informal assessment, and one article assesses work with parents. An interesting collection.

Leslie, L., & Caldwell, J. (2000). *Qualitative Reading Inventory III*, New York: Longman.

We would be remiss if we did not take special note of this excellent informal reading inventory.

It has been praised by researchers and educators as a model for others who are developing inventories. Some of the highlights of this inventory are that it assesses background knowledge for passages being read; the word lists contain words from the actual passages; it provides both expository and narrative passages; and comprehension is assessed through both recall and questioning.

O'Malley, J. M., & Valdez Pierce, L. (1996). *Authentic assessment for English language learners: Practical approaches for teachers.* New York: Addison-Wesley.

This excellent and practical teacher-oriented text helps a teacher construct assessments in oral language, reading, writing, and content areas and helps teachers deliver a curriculum that meets the needs of English learners. Chapters address moving toward and designing authentic assessment, portfolio assessment, oral language assessment, reading assessment, writing assessment, and content area assessment. The last chapter provides examples from the classroom. Each chapter begins with a discussion of the chapter topic, for example, the nature of oral language, the nature of reading, and so on and follows with assessment techniques and ways to use assessment results for instruction.

423

Activities

1. Do a case study of one student. Use a published IRI to discover the student's reading level: independent, instructional, or frustration. Also, discuss the student's strengths and weaknesses and what you would plan to do to assist the student. Be specific about the student's needs and your plan to assist him or her.

2. Assess a student and discover one thing that he or she is unable to do in reading. See if you can teach him or her that one thing. Use books recommended in this chapter to discover a variety of ways you might teach your student one useful strategy for reading that they didn't know before your intervention. Discuss your findings. Did your student learn something? How long did it take him or her to learn? Did learning it make a difference? Did it change him or her as a reader in some way? Did your student become more confident? What did you learn from this process?

3. Have someone administer an IRI with you as the reader. From this you can learn some of the inherent problems in trying to remember information in passages and trying to answer questions. Teachers should be aware that we all will miss questions of recall under the circumstances of reading a passage either aloud or silently. Are students missing questions because they didn't understand a passage or are they missing questions because they can't recall part of a passage? What might a teacher do to gain accurate information using a reading inventory?

4. Administer IRIs to two or three students using different commercial reading inventories. See whether the inventories yield the same or

different results in terms of the students' reading levels: frustration, instructional, and independent. Examine the different inventories to try to explain similar or different results.

5. Work in a group to make up an IRI of your own. Discuss the difficulties you had selecting passages and creating questions for the passages. Reflect on some commercial IRIs. Do

the commercial IRIs have some weaknesses and strengths? What are they?

6. After you have looked over a few IRIs, develop criteria for helping a teacher select an IRI. What major features of an IRI are helpful? What should the passages in the IRI consist of and how would a teacher decide that one IRI is better than another for his or her students?

PEARSON
myeducationlab
Where the Classroom Comes to Life

Video Homework Exercise
Criteria for Evaluation

The video discusses the importance of developing and sharing evaluation criteria for assignments. In parts of the video teachers work with students to develop criteria for making a good poster, and developing criteria for reading and writing assignments are also noted. A key idea is that if students know the criteria, they will know how to achieve at the highest level. Rubrics or scoring guides are discussed briefly; these rubrics are similar to the holistic scoring guides in our text and to reading level guidelines we give.

Go to MyEducationLab, select the topic "Assessment," and watch the video entitled "Criteria for Evaluation."

1. Using the information in the video, how would you develop criteria for a specific assignment? Give an example of the assignment and your approach to developing criteria.

2. How might the development of criteria for evaluation in your classroom assist you as a teacher and assist your students? How would you involve your English learner students in developing evaluation criteria?

3. What is a rubric? Have you ever been in a classroom where a teacher has used a rubric? If so did it help you with the assignment? How will you use a rubric in your own classroom to guide English learners?

424

REFERENCES

Aardema, V. (1975). *Why mosquitoes buzz in people's ears*. New York: Dial.

Aardema, V. (1981). *Bringing the rain to Kapiti plain*. New York: Dial.

Aaronson, E. (1978). *The jigsaw classroom*. Beverly Hills, CA: Sage.

Abedi, J. (2001, Summer). Assessment and accommodations for English Language Learners: Issues and recommendations. *Policy Brief 4*. Los Angeles: National Center for Research on Evaluation, Standards, and Student Testing, University of California.

Abedi, J., Leon, S., & Mirocha, J. (2001). *Impact of students' language background on standardized achievement test results: Analyses of extant data*. Los Angeles: National Center for Research on Evaluation, Standards and Student Testing, University of California.

Ada, A. F. (1988). The Pajaro Valley experience. In J. Cummins (Ed.), *Empowering language minority students* (pp. 223–238). Sacramento, CA: California Association for Bilingual Education.

Ada, A. F., & Zubizarreta, R. (2001). Parent narratives: The cultural bridge between Latino parents and their children. In M. de la Luz Reyes & J. Halcon (Eds.), *The best for our children: Critical perspectives on literacy for Latino students*. New York: Teachers College Press.

Adams, M. J. (1990a). *Beginning to read: Thinking and learning about print*. Cambridge, MA: MIT Press.

Adams, M. J. (1990b). *Beginning to read: Thinking and learning about print: A summary*. Urbana-Champaign, IL: University of Illinois, Center for the Study of Reading.

Adams, M. J., & Bruck, M. (1995). *Resolving the "great debate."* American Educator. Washington, DC: American Federation of Teachers.

Afflerbach, P. (2002). The road to folly and redemption: Perspectives on the legitimacy of high stakes testing. *Reading Research Quarterly, 37*(3), 348–360.

Ahlberg, J., & Ahlberg, A. (1981). *Peek-a-boo!* London: Puffin.

Allen, J. (1999). *Words, words, words*. Portsmouth, NH: Heinemann.

Allen, R. V. (1976). *Language experience in communication*. Boston: Houghton Mifflin.

Altwerger, B., & Flores, B. (1991). The theme cycle: An overview. In K. Goodman, L. B. Bird, & Y. Goodman (Eds.), *The whole language catalogue* (p. 95). Santa Rosa, CA: American School Publishers.

Ammon, P. (1985). Helping children learn to write in ESL: Some observations and hypotheses. In S. W. Freedman (Ed.), *The acquisition of written language: Response and revision* (pp. 65–84). Norwood, NJ: Ablex.

Ananda, S., & Rabinowitz, S. N. (2000). The high stakes of high stakes testing. West Ed Policy Brief. Retrieved August 14, 2003, from www.wested.org/cs/wew/view/rs/181.

Anaya, R. (1972). *Bless Me, Ultima*. New York: Warner Books.

Anderson, N. (1999). *Exploring second language reading: Issues and strategies*. Boston: Heinle & Heinle.

Anderson, N. (2002). The role of metacognition in second language teaching and learning. ERIC Digest. Retrieved August 14, 2003, from www.cal.org/ericcll/digest/0110anderson.html.

Anderson, R. C., Hiebert, E. H., Scott, J. A., & Wilkinson, I. A. G. (1985). *Becoming a nation of readers: The report of the commission on reading*. Washington, DC: National Institute of Education.

Antunez, B. (2002). Reading and English language learners. WFSU Reading Center. WFSU.org. Retrieved May 31, 2003, from http://readingrockets.org/wfsu/article/php?ID=409.

Armbruster, B. B., & Osborn, J. H. (2002). *Reading instruction and assessment: Understanding the IRA Standards*. Boston: Allyn and Bacon.

Asher, J. (2000). *Learning another language through actions: The complete teacher's guidebook* (6th Ed.) Los Gatos, CA: Sky Oaks Productions.

Ashton-Warner, S. (1963). *Teacher*. New York: Simon & Schuster.

Atwell, N. (1984). Writing and reading literature from the inside out. *Language Arts, 61*, 240–252.

Au, K. H., & Jordan, C. (1981). Teaching reading to Hawaiian children: Finding a culturally appropriate solution. In H. Trueba, G. P. Guthrie, & K. H.-P. Au (Eds.), *Culture and the bilingual classroom: Studies in classroom ethnography* (pp. 139–152). Rowley, MA: Newbury House.

Auerbach, E. R. (1991). Toward a social-contextual approach to family literacy. In M. Minami & B. P. Kennedy (Eds.), *Language issues in literacy and bilingual/multicultural education* (pp. 391–408). Reprint Series No. 22. Cambridge, MA: Harvard Educational Review.

August, D., & Shanahan, T. (Eds.). (2006). *Developing literacy in second-language learners: Report of the national literacy panel on language-minority children and youth*. Mahwah, NJ: Lawrence Erlbaum Associates.

Ausubel, D. P. (1968). *Educational psychology: A cognitive view.* New York: Holt, Rinehart & Winston.

Bader, L. A. (2004). *Bader reading and language inventory and readers passages and graded word lists* (5th ed.). Upper Saddle River, NJ: Prentice Hall.

Baker, L., & Brown, A. L. (1984). Metacognition skills and reading. In P. D. Pearson (Ed.), *Handbook of reading research*. White Plains, NY: Longman: 543–558.

Bakhtin, M. (1981). *The dialogic imagination.* Austin, TX: University of Texas Press.

Baldwin, J. (1979/1998). If Black English isn't a language, then tell me, what is? In T. Perry & L. Delpit (Eds.), *The real Ebonics debate: Power, language and the education of African-American children.* Boston: Beacon Press. (Originally published in *The New Yorker,* 1979.)

Barrett, J. (1970). *Animals should definitely not wear clothing.* New York: Simon & Schuster.

Bartlett, B. J. (1978). *Top-level structure as an organizational strategy for recall of classroom text.* Unpublished doctoral dissertation, Arizona State University, Tempe.

Bartolomé, L. (2000). Democratizing bilingualism: The role of critical teacher education. In Z. F. Beyknot (Ed.), *Lifting every voice: Pedagogy and politics of bilingualism* (pp.167–186). Boston: Harvard Education Publishing Group.

Baugh, J. (1999). *Out of the mouths of slaves: African American language and educational malpractice.* Austin, TX: University of Texas Press.

Bauman, R., & Scherzer, J. (1974). *Explorations in the ethnography of speaking.* New York: Cambridge University Press.

Bear, D. R., Helman, L., Templeton, S., Invernizzi, M., & Jounston, F. (2007). *Words their way with English learners: Word study for phonics, vocabulary, and spelling instruction.* Upper Saddle River, NJ: Pearson/Merrill Prentice Hall.

Beck, I., McKeown, M., Omanson, R., & Pople, M. (1984). Improving the comprehensibility of stories: The effects of revisions that improve coherence. *Reading Research Quarterly, 19,* 263–277.

Beck, I., McKeown, M. & Kucan, L. (2002). *Bringing words to life: Robust vocabulary instruction.* New York: The Guilford Press.

Becker, H. (2001). *Teaching ESL K–12: Views from the classroom* with commentary from Else Hamayan. Boston: Heinle & Heinle.

Bemelmans, L. (1939). *Madeline.* New York: Viking.

Berg, E. C. (1999). Preparing ESL students for peer response. *TESOL Journal, 8*(2), 20–25.

Bertera, J., & Rayner, K. (1979). Reading without a fovea. *Science, 206,* 468–469.

Birch, B. (2002). *English L2 reading.* Mahwah, NJ: Erlbaum.

Boggs, S. (1972). The meaning of questions and narratives to Hawaiian children. In C. B. Cazden, V. P. Johns, & D. Hymes (Eds.), *The functions of language in the classroom.* New York: Teachers College Press.

Bolton, F., & Snowball, D. (1993). *Ideas for spelling.* Portsmouth, NH: Heinemann.

Bolton, F., & Snowball, D. (1993b). *Teaching spelling: A practical resource.* Portsmouth, NH: Heinemann.

Bond, G. I., & Dykstra, R. (1967, Summer). The cooperative research program in first-grade reading instruction. *Reading Research Quarterly, 2*(4), 5–142.

Boyle, O. F. (1979). Oral language, reading and writing: An integrated approach. In O. Boyle (Ed.), *Writing lessons that work* (Vol. I, pp. 34–41). Berkeley: University of California/Bay Area Writing Project.

Boyle, O. F. (Ed.). (1982a). *Writing lessons II: Lessons in writing by teachers* (pp. 56–66). Berkeley: University of California/Bay Area Writing Project.

Boyle, O. F. (1982b). Writing: Process vs. product. In O. Boyle (Ed.), *Writing lessons II: Lessons in writing by teachers* (pp. 39–44). Berkeley: University of California/Bay Area Writing Project.

Boyle, O. F. (1982c). Cognitive schemes and reading in the content areas. In H. Singer & T. Bean (Eds.), *Proceedings of the learning from text conference* (pp. 106–114). Riverside, CA: UC Riverside Press.

Boyle, O. F. (1983). Mapping and writing. *Notes Plus.* Urbana, IL: National Council of Teachers of English.

Boyle, O. F. (1985a). Writing research: Present and future. *Quarterly for the Center for the Study of Writing, 4*(1), 3–7.

Boyle, O. F. (1985b). Writing research: Present and future. *The Quarterly of the National Writing Project.* Berkeley: University of California/Bay Area Writing Project.

Boyle, O. F. (1986). Teaching and assessing writing: Recent advances in understanding, evaluating, and improving student performance. *Quarterly of the Center for the Study of Writing, 8*(3), 36–43.

Boyle, O. F. (1987). *Holistic scoring procedures for essays.* New York: Cambridge University Press.

Boyle, O. F. (1990). *The magician's apprentice.* Unpublished manuscript, San Jose State University, San Jose, CA.

Boyle, O. F., & Buckley, M. H. (1983). Mapping and composing. In M. Myers & J. Gray (Eds.), *Theory and practice in the teaching of composition: Processing, distancing, and modeling.* Urbana, IL: National Council of Teachers of English.

Boyle, O. F., & Peregoy, S. F. (1990). Literacy scaffolds: Strategies for first- and second-language readers and writers. *The Reading Teacher, 44*(3), 194–200.

Boyle, O. F., & Peregoy, S. F. (1991). The effects of cognitive mapping on students' learning from college texts. *Journal of College Reading and Learning, XXIII*(2), 14–22.

Bradley, J., & Thalgott, M. (1987). Reducing reading anxiety. *Academic Therapy*, 22(4), 349–358.

Brantley, D. K. (2007). *Instructional assessment of English language learners in the K–8 classroom.* Boston: Pearson/Allyn & Bacon.

Brinton, D. M., Snow, M. A., & Wesche, M. B. (1993). Content-based second language instruction. In J. W. Oller, Jr. (Ed.), *Methods that work: Ideas for literacy and language teachers* (2nd ed., pp. 136–142). Boston: Heinle & Heinle.

Brisk, M. E. (2005). *Bilingual education: From compensatory to quality schooling* (2nd ed.) Mahwah, NJ: Lawrence Erlbaum Associates.

Bromley, K. (1989). Buddy journals make the reading-writing connection. *The Reading Teacher*, 43(2), 122–129.

Bromley, K. (1995). Buddy journals for ESL and native-English-speaking students. *TESOL Journal*, 4(3), 7–11.

Brown, H. D. (2000). *Principles of language learning and teaching* (4th Ed.). White Plains, NY: Pearson Education/Longman.

Brown, H. D. (2007). *Teaching by principles: An interactive approach to language pedagogy* (3rd ed.). White Plains, NY: Addison Wesley Longman, Inc.

Brown, J. D. (Ed.). (1998). *New ways of classroom assessment.* Alexandria, VA: TESOL.

Bruner, J. (1960). *The process of education.* New York: Vintage.

Buckley, M. (1992). Focus on research: We listen a book a day; we speak a book a week: Learning from Walter Loban. *Language Arts*, 69, 622–626.

Buckley, M. H. (1981). *Oral language guidelines.* Unpublished handout from class.

Buckley, M. H., & Boyle, O. F. (1981). *Mapping the writing journey.* Berkeley: University of California/Bay Area Writing Project.

Busching, B. (1981). Reader's theater: An education for language and life. *Language Arts*, 58, 330–338.

Buswell, G. T. (1922). Fundamental reading habits: A study of their development. *Supplementary Educational Monographs*, 21. Chicago: University of Chicago Press.

Cadiero-Kaplan, K. (2004). *The literacy curriculum and bilingual education.* New York: Peter Lang.

Cadiero-Kaplan, K. (2007). Critically examining beliefs, orientations, ideologies, and practices towards literacy instruction: A process of praxis. Unpublished manuscript.

Caldwell, K. (1984, February). *Teaching using the writing process.* Speech presented at the Bay Area Writing Project Workshop, Fairfield, CA.

California State Department of Education (2002). *English-language development standards for California public schools: Kindergarten through grade twelve.* Sacramento, CA: Author.

California State Department of Education, Standards and Assessment Division (2003). *California English Language Development Test: CELDT Communications Assistance Packet for Districts/Schools: Section II: CELDT Overview.* Retrieved on July 7, 2003, from www.cde.ca.gov/statetests/celdt/resources/assistpkts2203.pdf.

Calkins, L. M. (1994). *The art of teaching writing.* Portsmouth, NH: Heinemann.

Campbell, C. (1998). *Teaching second-language writing.* Boston: Heinle & Heinle.

Canale, M., & Swain, M. (1980). Theoretical bases of communicative approaches to second language teaching and testing. *Applied Linguistics*, 1(1), 1–47.

Caplan, R. (1982). Showing-writing: A training program to help students be specific. In G. Camp (Ed.), *Teaching writing: Essays from the Bay Area writing project.* Upper Montclair, NJ: Boynton/Cook.

Carle, E. (1984). *The very busy spider.* New York: Philomel Books.

Carle, E. (1986). *The very hungry caterpillar.* New York: Philomel Books.

Carr, W., & Ogle, D. (1987). K-W-L Plus: A strategy for comprehension and summarization. *Journal of Reading*, 30, 626–631.

Carrell, P. (1984). Schema theory and ESL reading: Classroom implications and applications. *Modern Language Journal*, 68(4), 332–343.

Carrasquillo, A., Kucer, S. B., Abrams, R. (2004). *Beyond the beginnings: Literacy interventions for upper elementary English language learners.* New York: Multilingual Matters Ltd.

Carrell, P., Devine, J., & Eskey, D. (1988). *Interactive approaches to second language reading.* Cambridge: Cambridge University Press.

Carrell, P., & Eisterhold, J. (1988). Schema theory and ESL reading pedagogy. In P. Carrell, J. Devine, & D. Eskey (Eds.), *Interactive approaches to second language reading* (pp. 73–92). Cambridge: Cambridge University Press.

Cazden, C. (1983). Adult assistance to language development: Scaffolds, models and direct instruction. In R. Parker & F. Davis (Eds.), *Developing literacy: Young children's use of language* (pp. 3–18). Newark, DE: International Reading Association.

Cazden, C. (1986). Classroom discourse. In M. C. Wittrock (Ed.), *Handbook of research on teaching* (pp. 432–463). New York: Macmillan.

Celce-Murcia, M. (Ed.). (2001). *Teaching English as a second or foreign language* (3rd ed.). Boston: Heinle & Heinle.

Chall, J. (1983). *Learning to read: The great debate* (Rev. ed.). New York: McGraw-Hill.

Chall, J., & Snow, C. (1982). *Families and literacy: The contributions of out of school experiences to children's acquisition of literacy: A final report to the National Institute of Education.* Cambridge, MA: Harvard Families and Literacy Project.

Chamot, A. U., & O'Malley, J. M. (1986). *A cognitive academic language learning approach: An ESL content-based curriculum.* Rosslyn, VA: National Clearinghouse for Bilingual Education.

Chamot, A. U., & O'Malley, J. M. (1992). *The Calla handbook: Implementing the cognitive academic language learning approach.* Reading, MA: Addison-Wesley.

Chapman, C. & King, R. (2003). *Differentiated instructional strategies for reading in the content areas.* Thousand Oaks, CA: Corwin Press.

Charlip, R. (1997). *Fortunately.* New York: Macmillan.

Cheung, A. and Slavin, R. E. (2005, Summer). Effective reading programs for English Language Learners and other language-minority students. *Bilingual Research Journal, 29*(2) 241–267.

Chi, M. (1988). Invented spelling/writing in Chinese-speaking children: The developmental patterns. From *Dialogues in literacy research*, thirty-seventh yearbook, National Reading Conference.

Chittenden, L. (1982). *Teaching writing to elementary children.* Speech presented at the Bay Area Writing Project Workshop, University of California, Berkeley.

Chomsky, N. (1957). *Syntactic structures.* The Hague: Mouton.

Chomsky, N. (1959). A review of Skinner's *Verbal Behavior. Language, 35,* 26–58.

Christian, D. (1994). *Two-way bilingual education: Students learning through two languages.* (Educational Practice Rep. No. 12). Santa Cruz, CA, and Washington, DC: National Center for Research on Cultural Diversity and Second Language Learning.

Christensen, L. (2000). *Reading, writing, and rising up: Teaching about social justice and the power of the written word.* Milwaukee, WI: Rethinking Schools.

Chu, J., Swaffer, J., & Charney, D. (2002). Cultural representations of rhetorical conventions: The effects on reading recall. *TESOL Quarterly, 36*(4), 511–541.

Cisneros, S. (1994). *The house on Mango Street.* New York: Random House.

Clarke, L. K. (1989). Encouraging invented spelling in first graders' writing: Effects on learning to spell and read. *Research in the Teaching of English, 22,* 281–309.

Clay, M. (1975). *What did I write?* Portsmouth, NH: Heinemann.

Clay, M. (1979). *The early detection of reading difficulties.* Auckland, New Zealand and Portsmouth, NH: Heinemann.

Clay, M. (1982). *Observing young readers: Selected papers.* Exeter, NH: Heinemann.

Clay, M. (1989). Concepts about print: In English and other languages. *The Reading Teacher, 42*(4), 268–277.

Cohen, E. G. (1986). *Designing groupwork: Strategies for the heterogeneous classroom.* New York: Teachers College Press.

Cohen, E. G. (1994). *Designing groupwork: Strategies for the heterogeneous classroom* (2nd ed.). New York: Teachers College Press.

Collier, V. P. (1987). Age and rate of acquisition of second language for academic purposes. *TESOL Quarterly, 21,* 617–641.

Collier, V. P. (1987/1988). *The effect of age on acquisition of a second language for school* (Occasional Papers in Bilingual Education No. 2). Rosslyn, VA: National Clearinghouse for Bilingual Education.

Connor, U., & Kaplan, R. B. (Eds.). (1987). *Writing across languages: Analysis of L2 text.* Reading, MA: Addison-Wesley.

Cooper, C. (1981, June). *Ten elements of a good writing program.* Speech presented at the Bay Area Writing Project Institute, University of California, Berkeley.

Cowley, J. (1990). *Meanies.* New York: The Wright Group/McGraw-Hill.

Crandall, J. (Ed.). (1987). *ESL through content-area instruction: Mathematics, science, social studies.* Englewood Cliffs, NJ: Prentice Hall.

Crandall, J. A., Dale, T. C., Rhodes, N., & Spanos, G. (1985, October). *The language of mathematics: The English barrier.* Paper presented at the Delaware Symposium on Language Studies VII, University of Delaware, Newark.

Crane, F., & Vasquez, J. A. (1994). *Harcourt Brace picture dictionary: Spanish–English.* Orlando, FL: Harcourt Brace & Company.

Crawford, J. (1999). *Bilingual education: History, politics, theory and practice* (4th ed.). Los Angeles: Bilingual Educational Services.

Crystal, D. (1987). *The Cambridge encyclopedia of language.* New York: Cambridge University Press.

Crystal, D. (1997). *The Cambridge encyclopedia of language.* Cambridge: Cambridge University Press.

Cummins, J. (1979). Cognitive-academic language proficiency, linguistic interdependence, optimal age and some other matters. *Working Papers in Bilingualism, 19,* 197–205.

Cummins, J. (1980). The construct of language proficiency in bilingual education. In J. E. Alatis (Ed.), *Georgetown University roundtable on languages and linguistics* (pp. 76–93). Washington, DC: Georgetown University Press.

Cummins, J. (1981). The role of primary language development in promoting educational success for language minority students. In California State Department of

Education (Ed.), *Schooling and language minority students: A theoretical framework* (pp. 3–49). Los Angeles: Evaluation, Dissemination and Assessment Center, California State University.

Cummins, J. (2001). *Negotiating identities: Education for empowerment in a diverse society*. (2nd ed.). Los Angeles, CA: California Association for Bilingual Education.

Cummins, J., Brown, K., & Sayers, D. (2007). *Literacy, technology, and diversity: Teaching for success in changing times*. Boston: Pearson/Allyn & Bacon.

Cunningham, J., Cunningham, P., & Arthur, S. (1981). *Middle and secondary school reading*. White Plains, NY: Longman.

Cunningham, P. (2005). *Phonics they use: Words for reading and writing* (4th ed.). New York: HarperCollins College Publishers.

Custodio, B., & Sutton, M. J. (1998). Literature-based ESL for secondary school students. *TESOL Journal, 7*(5), 19–23.

Dale, T. C., & Cuevas, G. J. (1987). Integrating language and mathematics learning. In J. Crandall (Ed.), *ESL through content-area instruction: Mathematics, science, social studies* (pp. 18–29). Englewood Cliffs, NJ: Prentice Hall.

Darder, A. (1991). *Culture and power in the classroom: A critical foundation for bicultural education*. Westport, CT: Bergin & Garvey.

Day, R., & Bamford, J. (1998). *Extensive reading in the second language classroom*. Cambridge: Cambridge University Press.

De Avila, E., & Duncan, S. (1984). *Finding out and descubrimiento: Teacher's guide*. San Rafael, CA: Linguametrics Group.

Decarrico, J. (2001). Vocabulary learning and teaching. In M. Celce-Murcia. (Ed.) *Teaching English as a second or foreign language*, (3rd ed., pp. 285–299). Boston, MA: Heinle & Heinle.

Delgado-Gaitán, C. (1987). Mexican adult literacy: New directions from immigrants. In S. R. Goldman & K. Trueba (Eds.), *Becoming literate in English as a second language* (pp. 9–32). Norwood, NJ: Ablex.

Díaz, S., Moll, L., & Mehan, H. (1986). Socio-cultural resources in instruction: A context-specific approach. In *Beyond language: Social and cultural factors in schooling language minority children* (pp. 39–42). Los Angeles: California State Department of Education and California State University.

Díaz-Rico, L. T., & Weed, K. Z. (2006). *The crosscultural, language and academic development handbook: A complete K–12 reference guide* (3rd ed.). Boston: Allyn and Bacon.

Dillard, J. L. (1972). *Black English: Its history and usage in the United States*. New York: Random House.

Dishon, D., & O'Leary, P. W. (1984). *A guidebook for cooperative learning: A technique for creating more effective schools*. Holmes Beach, FL: Learning Publications.

Dressler, C., & Kamil, M. (2006). First- and second-language literacy. In D. August & T. Shanahan (Eds.), *Developing literacy in second-language learners: Report of the National Literacy Panel on language-minority children and youth* (pp. 197–241). Mahwah, NJ: Lawrence Erlbaum Associates.

Duke, N. K., & Pearson, P. D. (2002). Effective practices for developing reading comprehension. In S. J. Samuels & A. E. Farstrup (Eds.), *What research has to say about reading instruction*. (3rd ed., pp. 203–242). Newark, DE: International Reading Association.

Dulay, H., & Burt, M. (1974). Errors and strategies in child second language acquisition. *TESOL Quarterly, 8*, 129–138.

Dulay, H., Burt, M., & Krashen, S. (1982). *Language two*. Oxford: Oxford University Press.

Duncan, S. E., & De Avila, E. (1977). *Language assessment scales*. Larkspur, CA: De Avila, Duncan and Associates.

Durkin, D. (1966). *Children who read early*. New York: Teachers College Press.

Dyson, A. (1982). The emergence of visible language: Interrelationships between drawing and early writing. *Visible Language, 16*, 360–381.

Echevarria, J., & Graves, A. (1998). *Sheltered content instruction: Teaching English-language learners with diverse abilities*. Boston: Allyn and Bacon.

Echevarria, J., Vogt, M., & Short, D. J. (2008). *Making content comprehensible for English learners: The SIOP model* (3rd Ed.). Boston: Pearson/Allyn & Bacon.

Edelsky, C. (1981a). *Development of writing in a bilingual program*. Final Report, Grant No. NIE–G–81–0051. Washington, DC: National Institute of Education.

Edelsky, C. (1981b). From "JIMOSALCO" to "7 naranjas se calleron e el arbol-est-triste en lagrymas": Writing development in a bilingual program. In B. Cronnel (Ed.), *The writing needs of linguistically different students* (pp. 63–98). Los Alamitos, CA: Southwest Regional Laboratory.

Eder, D. (1982). Difference in communication styles across ability groups. In L. C. Wilkinson (Ed.), *Communicating in the classroom*. New York: Academic.

Edwards, P. A. (1989). Supporting lower SES mothers' attempts to provide scaffolding for book reading. In J. B. Allen & J. M. Mason (Eds.), *Risk makers, risk takers, risk breakers: Reducing the risks for young literacy learners* (pp. 21–40). Portsmouth, NH: Heinemann.

Ehri, L. (1991). Development of the ability to read words. In R. Barr, M. L. Kamil, P. Mosenthal, & P. D. Pearson (Eds.), *Handbook of reading research: Volume II* (pp. 383–417). New York: Longman.

429

Ehri, L., & Wilce, L. (1985). Movement into reading: Is the first stage of printed word learning visual or phonetic? *Reading Research Quarterly, 20,* 163–169.

Ekwall, E. (1993). *Locating and correcting reading difficulties* (5th ed.). Columbus, OH: Charles E. Merrill.

Elbow, P. (1973). *Writing without teachers.* New York: Oxford University Press.

Elley, W., & Mangubhai, F. (1983). The impact of reading on second language readers. *Reading Research Quarterly, 19,* 53–67.

Ellis, R. (1997). *Second language acquisition.* Oxford: Oxford University Press.

Emig, J. (1971). *The composing processes of twelfth graders.* Champaign, IL: National Council of Teachers of English.

Emig, J. (1981). Non-magical thinking: Presenting writing developmentally in schools. In C. H. Frederickson & J. F. Dominic (Eds.), *Writing: Process, development and communication* (pp. 21–30). Hillsdale, NJ: Erlbaum.

Encarta World English Dictionary. (1999). New York: St. Martin's Press.

Enright, D. S., & McCloskey, M. L. (1988). *Integrating English: Developing English language and literacy in the multilingual classroom.* Reading, MA: Addison-Wesley.

Epstein, J. (1986). Parent involvement: Implications for LEP parents. In *Issues of parent involvement in literacy.* Proceedings of the symposium at Trinity College (pp. 6–16). Washington, DC: Trinity College, Department of Education and Counseling.

Ernst-Slavit, G., & Wenger, K. J. (1998). Using creative drama in the elementary ESL classroom. *TESOL Journal, 7*(4), 30–33.

Escamilla, K., Mahon, E., Riley-Bernal, H., & Rutledge, D. (2003). High-stakes testing, Latinos, and English language learners: Lessons from Colorado. *Bilingual Research Journal, 27*(1), 25–49.

Eskey, D. (2002). Reading and the teaching of L2 reading. *TESOL Journal, 11*(1), 5–9.

Evans, J. (Ed.). (2006). *Ultimate visual dictionary.* New York: DK Publishing.

Facella, M. A., Rampino, K. M. and Shea, E. K. (2005). Effective teaching strategies for English language learners. *Bilingual Research Journal, 29*(1), 209–221.

Faltis, C. J., & Hudelson, S. J. (1998). *Bilingual education in elementary and secondary school communities: Toward understanding and caring.* Boston: Allyn and Bacon.

Ferreiro, E., & Teberosky, A. (1982). *Literacy before schooling* (K. Castro, Trans.). Exeter, NH: Heinemann.

Ferris, D. (1995). Teaching students to self-edit. *TESOL Journal, 4*(4), 18–22.

Ferris, D. R. (2002). *Treatment of error in second language student writing.* Ann Arbor: University of Michigan Press.

Ferris, D. R. (2003). *Response to student writing: Implications for second language students.* Mahwah, NJ: Lawrence Erlbaum Associates, Publishers.

Feyton, C., Macy, M., Ducher, J., Yoshii, M., Park, E., Calandra, B., et al. (Eds.). (2002). *Teaching ESL/EFL with the Internet: Catching the wave.* Upper Saddle River, NJ: Merrill/Prentice Hall.

Fillmore, C. (1968). The case for case. In E. Bach & R. T. Harms (Eds.), *Universals in linguistic theory* (pp. 1–68). New York: Holt, Rinehart & Winston.

Fitzgerald, J. (1995). English-as-a-second-language learners' cognitive reading processes: A review of research in the United States. *Review of Educational Research, 65,* 145–190.

Flores, B., Cousin, P., & Díaz, E. (1991). Transforming deficit myths about learning, language, and culture. *Language Arts, 68,* 370–379.

Flynt, E. S., & Cooter, R. B. (1999). *English-Español reading inventory for the classroom.* New Jersey: Merrill.

Folse, K. (2004). *Vocabulary myths: Applying second language research to classroom teaching.* Ann Arbor: University of Michigan Press.

Fountas, I., & Pinnell, G. (1996). *Guided reading: Good first teaching for all children.* Portsmouth, NH: Heinemann.

Fradd, S., & McGee, P., with Wilen, D. (1994). *Instructional assessment: An integrative approach to evaluating student performance.* Reading, MA: Addison-Wesley.

Freire, P. (1970). *Pedagogy of the oppressed.* New York: Seabury Press.

Freire, P., & Macedo, D. (1987). *Literacy: Reading the word and reading the world.* South Hadley, MA: Bergin & Garvey.

Frith, U. (1985). Beneath the surface of developmental dyslexia. In K. E. Patterson, K. C. Marshall, & M. Coltheart (Eds.), *Surface dyslexia: Neuropsychological and cognitive studies of phonological reading.* Hillsdale, NJ: Erlbaum.

Fromkin, V., Rodman R., & Hyams, N. (2003). *An introduction to language* (7th ed.). Boston: Thomson & Heinle.

Fromkin, V., Rodman, R. & Hyams, N. (2007). *An introduction to language* (8th ed.). Boston: Thomas & Heinle.

Gamez, T. & Steiner, R. (1998). *Simon and Schuster's International Spanish Dictionary (English–Spanish, Spanish–English).* New York: Simon and Schuster.

Garcia, E. (1994). *Understanding and meeting the challenge of student cultural diversity.* Boston: Houghton Mifflin.

Garcia, E. (2001). *Student cultural diversity: Understanding and meeting the challenge* (3rd ed.). Boston: Houghton Mifflin Company.

Garcia, G. (Ed.). (2003). *English learners reaching the highest level of English literacy.* Newark, DE: International Reading Association.

Gardner, H. (1995). Green ideas sleeping furiously. *The New York Review of Books,* (Vol. XLII, No. 5.) New York: Rea S. Headerman.

Gardner, J. (1983). *The art of fiction: Notes on craft for young writers.* New York: Vintage.

Gasparro, M., & Falletta, B. (1994, April). *Creating drama with poetry: Teaching English as a second language through dramatization and improvisation.* Washington, DC: ERIC Clearinghouse on Languages and Linguistics (ED 368 214).

Gee, R. W. (1999). Encouraging ESL students to read. *TESOL Journal, 8*(1), 3–7.

Genesee, F. (1984). *Studies in immersion education.* Sacramento: California State Department of Education.

Genesee, F. (1987). *Learning through two languages: Studies of immersion and bilingual education.* Cambridge, MA: Newbury House.

Genessee, F., Lindholm, K., Saunders W. M., & Christian, D. (Eds.). (2006). *Educating English language learners: A synthesis of research evidence.* New York: Cambridge University Press.

Genesee, F., & Upshur, J. A. (2002). *Classroom-based evaluation in second language education.* Cambridge: Cambridge University Press.

Gentry, J. R. (1980). Early spelling strategies. *Elementary School Journal, 79,* 88–92.

Gersten, R., Baker, S. K., Shanahan, T., Linan-Thompson, S., Collins, P., & Scarcella, R. (2007). *Effective literacy and English language instruction for English learners in the elementary grades: A practical guide* (NCEE 2007–4007). Washington, DC: National Center for Education Evaluation and Regional Assistance, Institute of Education Sciences, U.S. Department of Education. Retrieved July 17, 2007, from http://ies.ed.gov/ncee.

Gesell, A. (1925). *The mental growth of the preschool child.* New York: Macmillan.

Gianelli, M. C. (1990). Thematic units: Creating an environment for learning. *TESOL Journal, 1*(2), 13–15.

Gibbs, J. (1994). *Tribes: A new way of learning together.* Santa Rosa, CA: Center Source Publications.

Goldman, S. R., & Murray, J. (1989). *Knowledge of connectors as cohesive devices in text: A comparative study of native English and ESL speakers* (Technical Report). Santa Barbara, CA: University of California.

Goldman, S. R., & Murray, J. (1992). Knowledge of connectors as cohesion devices in text: A comparative study of native-English and English-as-a-second-language speakers. *Journal of Educational Psychology, 84*(2), 504–519.

Goodenough, W. H. (1981). *Language, culture and society.* New York: Cambridge University Press.

Goodman, K. (1967, May). Reading: A psycholinguistic guessing game. *Journal of the Reading Specialist,* 126–135.

Goodman, K. S. (1973). *Miscue analysis: Application to reading instruction.* Urbana, IL: National Council of Teachers of English.

Goodman, K., & Goodman, Y. (1978). *Reading of American children whose language is a stable rural dialect of English or a language other than English* (Final Report No. C–003–0087). Washington, DC: National Institute of Education.

Goodman, K., Goodman, Y., & Flores, B. (1979). *Reading in a bilingual classroom.* Rosslyn, VA: National Clearinghouse for Bilingual Education.

Goodman, K. S., Goodman, Y. M., & Hood, W. J. (Eds.). (1989). *The whole language evaluation book.* Portsmouth, NH: Heinemann.

Goodman, Y. (1978). Kid watching: An alternative to testing. *Journal of National Elementary Principals, 57*(4), 41–45.

Goodman, Y. M., & Burke, C. L. (1972). *Reading miscue inventory manual: Procedure for diagnosis and evaluation.* New York: Macmillan.

Gottlieb, M. (1995). Nurturing student learning through portfolios. *TESOL Journal, 5*(1), 12–14.

Goulden, R., Nation, P., & Read, J. (1990). 'How large can a receptive vocabulary be?' *Applied Linguistics, 11,* 341–363.

Grabe, W. (1991). Current developments in second language reading research. *TESOL Quarterly, 25*(3), 375–406.

Grabe, W., & Stoller, F. (1997). Content-based instruction: Research foundations. In M. A. Snow & D. M. Brinton (Eds.), *The content-based classroom: Perspectives on integrating language and content* (pp. 5–21). White Plains, NY: Addison Wesley Longman.

Graves, D. (1983). *Writing: Children and teachers at work.* Portsmouth, NH: Heinemann.

Graves, D., & Hansen, J. (1983, February). The author's chair. *Language Arts, 60,* 176–183.

Graves, M. (2004). Teaching prefixes: As good as it gets? In J. F. Baumann & E. J. Kame'enui (eds.), *Vocabulary instruction: Research to practice.* New York: Guilford Press.

Graves, M. (2006). *The vocabulary book: Learning and instruction.* Newark, DE: International Reading Association.

Graves, M., Brunetti, G. J., & Slater, W. H. (1982). The reading vocabulary of primary-grade children of varying geographic and social backgrounds. In J.A. Harris & L.A. Harris (Eds.). *New inquiries in reading research and instruction* (pp. 99–104). Rochester, NY: National Reading Conference.

Graves, M., & Slater, W. (1987). *The development of reading vocabulary in rural disadvantaged students, inner-city disadvantaged students, and middle-class suburban students*. Paper presented at the meeting of the American Educational Research Association, Washington, DC.

Grosjean, F. (1982). *Life with two languages: An introduction to bilingualism*. Cambridge, MA: Harvard University Press.

Gutierrez, K., Asato, J., Pacheco, M., Moll, L. C., Olson, K., Horng, K. L., et al. (2002). "Sounding American": The consequences of new reforms on English language learners. *Reading Research Quarterly, 37*(3) 328–347.

Gutierrez, K., Baquedano-Lopez, & Alvarez, H. (2001). Literacy as hybridity: Moving beyond bilingualism in urban classrooms. In M. de la Luz Reyes & J. Halcon (Eds.), *The best for our children: Critical perspectives on literacy for Latino students* (pp. 122–141). New York: Teachers College Press.

Haggard, M. R. (1986a). The vocabulary self-collection strategy: An active approach to word learning. In E. K. Dishner, T. W. Bean, J. E. Readance, & D. W. Moore (Eds.), *Reading in the content areas: Improving classroom instruction*, (2nd ed., pp. 179–283). Dubuque, IA: Kendall-Hunt.

Haggard, M. R. (1986b). The vocabulary self-collection strategy: Using student interest and world knowledge to enhance vocabulary growth. *Journal on Reading, 29*, 634–642.

Hakuta, K. (1986). *Mirror of language: The debate on bilingualism*. New York: Basic Books.

Hall, J. K., & Eggington, W. G. (Eds.). (2000). *The sociopolitics of English language teaching*. Buffalo, NY: Multilingual Matters.

Halliday, M. A. K. (1975). *Learning how to mean: Exploration in the development of language*. London: Arnold.

Halliday, M. A. K. (1984). *Listening to Nigel: Conversations of a very small child*. Sydney, Australia: Linguistics Department, University of Sydney.

Halliday, M. A. K. (1985). *Spoken and written language*. Oxford: Oxford University Press.

Halliday, M. A. K. (1994). The place of dialogue in children's construction of meaning. In R. Ruddell, M. Ruddell, & H. Singer (Eds.), *Theoretical models and processes of reading* (4th ed., pp. 133–145). Newark, DE: International Reading Association.

Hamayan, E. (1994). Language development of low literacy children. In F. Genesee (Ed.), *Educating second language children: The whole child, the whole curriculum, the whole community* (pp. 278–300). Cambridge: Cambridge University Press.

Hanf, M. B. (1971). Mapping: A technique for translating reading into thinking. *Journal of Reading, 14*, 225–230.

Harklau, L. (1994). ESL versus mainstream classes: Contrasting L2 learning environments. *TESOL Quarterly, 28*(2), 241–272.

Harley, B., Allen, P., Cummins, J., & Swain, M. (Eds.). (1990). *The development of second language proficiency*. Cambridge: Cambridge University Press.

Harper, C., & Platt, E. (1998). Full inclusion for secondary school ESOL students: Some concerns from Florida. *TESOL Journal, 7*(5), 30–36.

HarperCollins. (2006). *Collins cobuild learner's concise English dictionary*. New York: Harper Collins.

Harste, J., Woodward, V., & Burke, C. (1984). *Language stories and literacy lessons*. Portsmouth, NH: Heinemann.

Hawkes, K. S., & Schell, L. M. (1987). Teacher-set prereading purposes and comprehension. *Reading Horizons, 27*, 164–169.

Heald-Taylor, G. (1987). Predictable literature selections and activities for language arts instruction. *The Reading Teacher, 41*, 6–12.

Healy, M. K. (1980). *Using student writing response groups in the classroom*. Berkeley: University of California/Bay Area Writing Project.

Heath, S. B. (1983). *Ways with words: Language, life and work in communities and classrooms*. New York: Cambridge University Press.

Heath, S. B. (1986). Sociocultural contexts of language development. In California State Department of Education (Ed.), *Beyond language: Social and cultural factors in schooling language minority students* (pp. 143–186). Los Angeles: Evaluation, Dissemination and Assessment Center, California State University.

Heath, S. B., & Mangiola, L. (1991). *Children of promise: Literate activity in linguistically and culturally diverse classrooms*. Washington, DC: National Education Association.

Herber, H. L. (1978). *Teaching reading in content areas* (2nd ed.). Englewood Cliffs, NJ: Prentice Hall.

Herrell, A. (2000). *Fifty strategies for teaching English language learners*. Upper Saddle River, NJ: Merrill/Prentice Hall.

Herrell, A. & Jordan, M. L. (2007). *Fifty strategies for teaching English language learners* (3rd ed.). Upper Saddle River, NJ: Merrill/Prentice Hall.

Hinds, J. (1983a). *Contrastive rhetoric: Japanese and English*. Edmonton, Calgary, Canada: Linguistic Research.

Hinds, J. (1983b). Linguistics and written discourse in particular languages: Contrastive studies: English and Japanese. In R. B. Kaplan (Ed.), *Annual review of applied linguistics, III* (pp. 75–84). Rowley, MA: Newbury House.

Hinkel, E. (Ed.). (2005). *Handbook in second language teaching and learning*. Mahwah, N J: Lawrence Erlbaum Associates.

Hirvela, A. (1999). Collaborative writing instruction and communities of readers and writers. *TESOL Journal 8*(2), 7–12.

Hoban, R. (1960). *Bedtime for Frances*. New York: Harper & Row.

Holdaway, D. (1979). *The foundations of literacy*. Portsmouth, NH: Heinemann.

Holmes, B. C., & Roser, N. (1987). Five ways to assist readers' prior knowledge. *The Reading Teacher, 40*, 646–649.

Howard, K. (1990). Making the writing portfolio real. *The Quarterly of the National Writing Project and the Center for the Study of Writing, 12*(2), 4–6.

Hudelson, S. (Ed.). (1981). *Learning to read in different languages*. Washington, DC: Center for Applied Linguistics.

Hudelson, S. (1984). "Kan yu ret an rayt en ingles": Children become literate in English as a second language. *TESOL Quarterly, 18*, 221–238.

Hudelson, S. (1986). ESL children's writing: What we've learned, what we're learning. In P. Rigg & D. S. Enright (Eds.), *Children and ESL: Integrating perspectives* (pp. 23–54). Washington, DC: Teachers of English to Speakers of Other Languages.

Hudelson, S. (1987). The role of native language literacy in the education of language minority children. *Language Arts, 64*, 827–841.

Hudson, W. (1982). Essay writing for reluctant writers. In O. F. Boyle (Ed.), *Writing lessons II: Lessons in writing by teachers* (pp. 14–21). Berkeley: University of California Press.

Huerta-Macias, A. (1995). Alternative assessment: Responses to commonly asked questions. *TESOL Journal, 5*(1), 8–12.

Hughes, A. (2003). *Testing for language teachers* (2nd ed.). Cambridge: Cambridge University Press.

Hurley, S. R., & Tinajero, J. V. (Eds.). (2001). *Literacy assessment of second language learners*. Boston: Allyn and Bacon.

Hyland, K., & Tse, P. (2007). Is there an "Academic Vocabulary"? *TESOL Quarterly, 41*(2), 235–253.

Igoa, C. (1995). *The inner world of the immigrant child*. New York: St. Martin's Press.

Jackson, S. L. (1980). Analysis of procedures and summary statistics of the language data. In B. J. Mace-Matluck (Ed.), *A longitudinal study of the oral language development of Texas bilingual children (Spanish-English): Findings from the first year* (8–14). Austin, TX: Southwest Educational Development Laboratory.

Jaramillo, A. (1998). Professional development from the inside out. *TESOL Journal, 7*(5), 12–18.

Jiménez, R. T., García, G. E., & Pearson, P. D. (1996). The reading strategies of Latina/o students who are successful English readers: Opportunities and obstacles. *Reading Research Quarterly, 31*, 90–112.

Johns, J., & Lenski, S. (1994). *Improving reading: A handbook of strategies* (2nd ed). Dubuque, IA: Kendall-Hunt.

Johnson, C. (1955). *Harold and the purple crayon*. New York: Harper & Row.

Johnson, C. (1959). *Harold's circus*. New York: Harper & Row.

Johnson, D. W., Johnson, R. T., & Holubec, E. J. (1986). *Circles of learning: Cooperation in the classroom*. Edina, MN: Interaction Book.

Johnson, D., with Sulzby, E. (1999). Critical issue: Addressing the literacy needs of emergent and early readers. North Central Regional Educational Laboratory. Retrieved on July 20, 2003, from www.ncrel.org/sdrs/areas/issues/content/cntareas/reading/li100.htm.

Juel, C., Griffith, P., & Gough, P. B. (1986). Acquisition of literacy: A longitudinal study of children in first and second grade. *Journal of Educational Psychology, 78*, 243–255.

Kachru, B. B. (1983). *The other tongue: English across cultures*. Urbana: University of Illinois Press.

Kachru, Y. (2005). Teaching and learning World Englishes. In E. Hinkel (Ed.), *Handbook in second language teaching and learning* (pp. 155–173). Mahwah, NJ: Lawrence Erlbaum Associates.

Kagan, S. (1986). Cooperative learning and sociocultural factors in schooling. In California State Department of Education (Ed.), *Beyond language: Social and cultural factors in schooling language minority students* (pp. 231–298). Los Angeles: Evaluation, Dissemination and Assessment Center, California State University.

Kamil, M. L., Mosenthal, P., Pearson, P. D., & Barr, R. (Eds.). (2000). *Handbook of Reading Research: Volume III*. Mahwah, NJ: Erlbaum.

Karlsen, B., Madden, R., & Gardner, E. (1976). *Stanford diagnostic reading test*. New York: Harcourt Brace Jovanovich.

Katsiavriades, K. (2000). Language families. Retrieved on August 14, 2003, from www.krysstal.com/langfams.html.

Keats, E.J. (1978). *The trip*. New York: Scholastic Books.

Kelly, S. (2004). *Harcourt Brace picture dictionary*. New York: Harcourt Brace.

Kessler, C., & Quinn, M. E. (1984). *Second language acquisition in the context of science experiences*. Paper presented at the meeting of Teachers of English to Speakers of Other Languages, Houston, Texas. (ERIC Document Reproduction Service No. ED 248 713).

Kessler, C., & Quinn, M. E. (1987). ESL and science learning. In J. Crandall (Ed.), *ESL through content-area instruction: Mathematics, science, social studies* (pp. 55–88). Englewood Cliffs, NJ: Prentice Hall.

Kids of Room 14. (1979). *Our friends in the water*. Berkeley: West Coast Print Center.

Kim, H., & Krashen, S. (1997). Why don't language acquirers take advantage of the power of reading? *TESOL Journal, 6*(3), 26–29.

433

Kinsella, K. (1996). Designing group work that supports and enhances diverse classroom work styles. *TESOL Journal*, 6(1), 24–30.

Koch, K. (1970). *Wishes, lies and dreams: Teaching children to write poetry*. New York: Perennial Library.

Koskinen, P., Blum, I., Tennant, N., Parker, E. M., Straub, M. W., & Curry, C. (1995). Have you heard any good books lately? Encouraging shared reading at home with books and audiotapes. In L. M. Morrow (Ed.), *Family literacy: Connections in schools and communities* (12–20). Urbana, IL: International Reading Association.

Krapels, A. R. (1990). An overview of second language writing process research. In B. Kroll (Ed.), *Second language writing: Research insights for the classroom* (pp. 37–56). Cambridge: Cambridge University Press.

Krashen, S. (1981a). Bilingual education and second language acquisition theory. In California State Department of Education (Ed.), *Schooling and language minority students: A theoretical framework*. (26–92) Los Angeles: Evaluation, Dissemination and Assessment Center, California State University.

Krashen, S. (1981b). The case for narrow reading. *TESOL Newsletter*, 15(6), 23.

Krashen, S. (1982). *Principles and practices in second language acquisition*. Oxford: Pergamon Press.

Krashen, S. (1993). *The power of reading*. Englewood, CO: Libraries Unlimited.

Krashen, S. D. (1984). Immersion: Why it works and what it has taught us. *Language in Society, 12*, 61–64.

Krashen, S. (2004). *The power of reading: Insights from the research* (2nd ed.). Portsmouth, NH: Heinemann.

Krashen, S. D., & Terrell, D. (1983). *The natural approach: Language acquisition in the classroom*. Hayward, CA: Alemany Press.

Kreeft, J. (1984). Dialogue writing—Bridge from talk to essay writing. *Language Arts, 61*, 141–150.

Kroll, B. (Ed.). (1990). *Second language writing: Research insights for the classroom*. New York: Cambridge University Press.

LaBerge, D., & Samuels, S. J. (1976). Toward a theory of automatic information processing in reading. In H. Singer & R. B. Ruddell (Eds.), *Theoretical models and processes of reading* (p. 293). Newark, DE: International Reading Association.

Labov, W. (1972). *Language in the inner city: Studies in the Black English vernacular*. Philadelphia: University of Pennsylvania Press.

Lamme, L., & Hysmith, C. (1991). One school's adventure into portfolio assessment, *Language Arts, 68*, 629–640.

Laturnau, J. (2003). Standards-based instruction for English language learners. In G. G. Garcia (Ed.), *English learners reaching the highest level of English*

literacy (pp. 286–305). Newark, DE: International Reading Association.

Leal, L., Crays, N., & Moetz, B. (1985). Training children to use a self-monitoring study strategy in preparation for recall: Maintenance and generalization effects. *Child Development, 56*, 643–653.

Legenza, A. (1974). *Questioning behavior of kindergarten children*. Paper presented at Nineteenth Annual Convention, International Reading Association.

Leslie, L., & Caldwell, J. (1995). *Qualitative Reading Inventory, II*. New York: Longman.

Leslie, L., & Caldwell, J. (2000). *Qualitative Reading Inventory, III*. New York: Longman.

Leslie, L. & Caldwell, J. (2005). *Qualitative reading inventory, IV* (4th ed.). New York: Allyn & Bacon.

Lessow-Hurley, J. (2000). *The foundations of dual language instruction* (2nd ed.). New York: Addison-Wesley Longman.

Lessow-Hurley, J. (2005*). The foundations of dual language instruction* (4th ed.). Boston: Allyn & Bacon.

Levy, M. & Stockwell, G. (2006). *CALL dimensions: Options and issues in computer-assisted language learning*. Mahwah, NJ: Lawrence Erlbaum Associates.

Lightbown, P., & Spada, N. (1993). *How languages are learned*. Oxford: Oxford University Press.

Lightbown, P., & Spada, N. (2006). *How languages are learned* (3rd ed.). Oxford University Press.

Lindholm, K. J. (1990). Bilingual immersion education: Criteria for program development. In A. Padilla, H. Fairchild, & C. Valadez (Eds.), *Bilingual education: Issues and strategies* (pp. 91–105). Newbury Park, CA: Sage.

Lindholm, K. J., & Gavlek, K. (1994). *California DBE projects: Project-wide evaluation report, 1992–1993*. San Jose, CA: Author.

Lindholm-Leary, K. (2001). *Dual language education*. Clevedon, England: Multilingual Matters.

Linquanti, R. (2001). *The redesignation dilemma: Challenges and choices in fostering meaningful accountability for English learners*. The University of California Linguistic Minority Research Institute Policy Report 2001–1. San Francisco: WestEd.

Lionni, L. (1963). *Swimmy*. New York: Random House Children's Books.

Liu, J., & Hansen, J. G. (2002). *Peer response in second language writing classrooms*. Ann Arbor: University of Michigan Press.

Loban, W. (1968). *Stages, velocity, and prediction of language development: Kindergarten through grade twelve*. Urbana, IL: National Council of Teachers of English.

Loban, W. (1982). Personal correspondence.

Long, M., & Porter, P. (1985). Group work, interlanguage talk, and second language acquisition. *TESOL Quarterly, 18*, 207–227.

434

Longman (2003). *Longman children's picture dictionary*. White Plains, NY: Pearson ESL.

Longman (2006). *Longman dictionary of contemporary English* (4th ed.). White Plains, NY: Pearson/Longman.

Lowery, L. (1980). Speech at University of California, Berkeley.

MacDonald, J. (1986). Self-generated questions and reading recall: Does training help? *Contemporary Educational Psychology, 11*, 290–304.

Mace-Matluck, B. J. (1981). General characteristics of the children's language use in three environments. In B. J. Mace-Matluck (Ed.), *A longitudinal study of the oral language development of Texas bilingual children (Spanish-English): Findings from the second year* (23–40). Austin, TX: Southwest Educational Development Laboratory.

Manzo, A. V. (1968). The ReQuest Procedure. *Journal of Reading,12*, 123–126. Urbana, IL: International Reading Association.

Martin, B. (1967). *Brown bear, brown bear, what do you see?* New York: Holt, Rinehart & Winston.

Maslow, A. H. (1968). *Toward a psychology of being*. New York: Van Nostrand Reinhold.

Mason, J., & Au, K. (1990). *Reading instruction for today* (2nd ed.). Glenview, IL: Scott Foresman.

McCauley, J., & McCauley, D. (1992). Using choral reading to promote language learning for ESL students. *The Reading Teacher, 45*(7), 526–533.

McCracken, R. A. (1971). Initiating sustained silent reading. *Journal of Reading, 14*, 521–524.

McCracken, R. A., & McCracken, M. J. (1972). *Reading is only the tiger's tail*. San Rafael, CA: Leswig Press.

McKenna, M., & Robinson, R. (1993). *Teaching through text: A content literacy approach to content area reading*. White Plains, NY: Longman.

McKeown, M., & Beck, I. (2004). Direct and rich vocabulary instruction. In J. F. Baumann & E. J. Kame'enui (Eds.), *Vocabulary instruction: Research to practice* (pp. 13–27). New York: Guilford Press.

McKissack, P. (1988). *Mirandy and brother wind*. New York: Knopf.

McLaughlin, B. (1985). *Second language acquisition in childhood* (Vol. 2). Hillsdale, NJ: Erlbaum.

McLaughlin, B. (1987). *Theories of second language learning*. London: Arnold.

Mehan, H. (1979). *Learning lessons*. Cambridge, MA: Harvard University Press.

Met, M. (n.d.). Content-based instruction: Defining terms, making decisions. Washington, DC., The National Foreign Language Center. Retrieved on January 17, 2007, from www.carla.umn.edu/cobaltt/modules/principles/decisions.html.

Met, M. (1998). Curriculum decision-making in content-based second language teaching. In J. Cenoz & F. Genessee (Eds.), *Beyond bilingualism: Multilingualism and multilingual education* (pp. 35–63). Clevedon, UK.: Multilingual Matters.

Meyer, B. J. F., Brandt, K. M., & Bluth, G. J. (1980). Use of top-level structure in text: Key for reading comprehension of ninth grade students. *Reading Research Quarterly, 16*, 72–103.

Meyer, L. (Ed.). (2000a). *Theory into Practice, 39*(4). Columbus: Ohio State University.

Meyer, L. (2000b). Barriers to meaningful instruction for English learners. *Theory into Practice, 39*(4), 228–236.

Michaels, S. (1979). *A study of sharing time with first grade students: Discourse narratives in the classroom.* Proceedings of the Fifth Annual Meeting of the Berkeley Linguistics Society, Berkeley, CA.

Miller, G. A., Galanter, E., & Pribram, K. (1960). *Plans and the structure of behavior*. New York: Holt, Rinehart & Winston.

Mitchell, R. & Myles, F. (2002). *Second language learning theories*. New York: Oxford University Press.

Mohan, B. (1986). *Language and content*. Reading, MA: Addison-Wesley.

Moll, L. (1994). Literacy research in community and classrooms: A sociocultural approach. In R. R. Ruddell, M. R. Ruddell, & H. Singer (Eds.), *Theoretical models and processes of reading* (4th ed., pp. 179–207). Newark, DE: International Reading Association.

Moraes, M. (1996). *Bilingual education: A dialogue with the Bakhtin Circle*. Albany: State University of New York Press.

Morphet, M. V., & Washburn, C. (1931). When should children begin to read? *Elementary School Journal, 31*, 496–508.

Morrow, L. M. (1983). Home and school correlates of early interest in literature. *Journal of Educational Research, 76*, 24–30.

Morrow, L. M. (1993). *Literacy development in the early years: Helping children read and write* (2nd ed.). Boston: Allyn and Bacon.

Mullen, N., & Olsen, L. (1990). You and I are the same. In J. A. Cabello (Ed.), *California perspectives* (pp. 23–29). San Francisco: California Tomorrow.

Murphy, S., & Smith, M. A. (1990). Talking about portfolios. *The Quarterly of the National Writing Project and the Center for the Study of Writing, 12*(2), 1–3.

Murray, D. (1992). Language in the attic. In D. Murray (Ed.), *Diversity as resource* (pp. 1–17). Alexandria, VA: Teachers of English to Speakers of Other Languages.

Myers, M. (1980). *A procedure for writing assessment and holistic scoring*. Urbana, IL: National Council of Teachers of English.

435

Nagy, W. E., Anderson, R. C., & Herman, P. A. (1987). Learning word meanings from context during normal reading. *American Educational Research Journal*, 24, 237–271.

Nagy, W. E., & Scott, J. A. (2000). Vocabulary processes. In M. L. Kamil, P. B. Mosenthal, P. D. Pearson, & R. Barr (Eds.), *Handbook of reading research: Volume III* (pp. 269–289). Mahwah, NJ: Erlbaum.

Nation, I. S. P. (2001). *Learning vocabulary in another language.* Cambridge: Cambridge University Press.

Nation, I. S. P. (2002). Best practices in vocabulary teaching and learning. In J. Richards, & Renandya (Eds.). *Methodology in language teaching: An anthology of current practice.* Cambridge: Cambridge University Press.

Nation, I. S. P. (2005). Teaching and learning vocabulary. In E. Hinkel (Ed.). *Handbook in second language teaching and learning* (pp. 581–595). Mahwah, NJ: Lawrence Erlbaum Associates.

Nation, I. S. P. (2003). Vocabulary. In D. Nunan (Ed.), *Practical English Language Teaching* (pp. 129–152). New York: The McGraw-Hill Companies, Inc.

Nation, I. S. P. (1990). *Teaching and learning vocabulary.* Boston: Heinle &Heinle.

Nation, P. & Waring, R. (2002). Vocabulary size, text coverage and word lists. In N. Schmitt & M. McCarthy (Eds.), *Vocabulary: Description, acquisition and pedagogy.* Cambridge: Cambridge University Press.

National Assessment for Educational Progress. (2003). Nation's Report Card. Retrieved on http://nces.ed.gov/nationsreportcard/reading/results2003.

National Clearinghouse for English Language Acquisition (2006). FAQ: How many school-aged English language learners (ELLs) are there? Retrieved on June 25, 2007, from www.ncela.gwu/edu/expert/faq/01leps.html.

National Commission on Excellence in Education (1983). *A nation at risk.* Washington, DC: U.S. Government Printing Office.

National Council of Teachers of Mathematics, Inc. (1989). *Curriculum and evaluation standards for school mathematics.* Reston, VA: Author.

Neuman, S. B. & Dickinson, D. K. (Eds.) (2002). *Handbook of early literacy research.* New York: Guilford Press.

Ninio, A. (1980). Picture-book reading in mother-infant dyads belonging to two subgroups in Israel. *Child Development, 51,* 587–590.

Nieto, S., & Bode, P. (2007). *Affirming diversity: The sociopolitical context of multicultural education* (2nd ed.). Boston: Allyn & Bacon.

Ninio, A., & Bruner, J. (1978). The achievement and antecedents of labeling. *Child Language, 5,* 1–15.

No Child Left Behind Act. (Public Law 107–110), 20 U. S. C. Chapter 6301 (2001).

Nolte, R., & Singer, H. (1985). Active comprehension: Teaching a process of reading comprehension and its effects on reading achievement. *The Reading Teacher, 39,* 24–31.

Northcutt, M., & Watson, D. (1986). *Sheltered English teaching handbook.* San Marcos, CA: AM Graphics & Printing.

Norton, B. (1997). Language, identity, and the ownership of English. *TESOL Quarterly 31*(3), 409–429.

Nunan, D. (Ed.). (2003). *Practical English teaching.* New York: McGraw Hill.

Ochs, E., & Schieffelin, G. G. (1984). Language acquisition and socialization: Three developmental stories and their implications. In R. Shweder & R. LeVine (Eds.), *Culture theory: Essays on mind, self, and emotion* (pp. 276–322). Cambridge: Cambridge University Press.

Odlin, T. (1989). *Language transfer: Cross-linguistic influence in language learning.* Cambridge: Cambridge University Press.

Ogle, D. (1986). A teaching model that develops active reading of expository text. *The Reading Teacher, 39,* 564–570.

O'Hare, F. (1973). *Sentence combining: Improving student writing without formal grammar instruction* (Report No. 15). Urbana, IL: National Council of Teachers of English.

Oller, J., Jr. (Ed.) (1993). *Methods that work: Ideas for literacy and language teachers* (2nd ed.). Boston: Heinle & Heinle.

Olsen, L. (1998). *Made in America: Immigrant students in our public schools.* New York: The New Press.

Olsen, L., & Mullen, N. (1990). *Embracing diversity: Teachers' voices from California's classrooms.* San Francisco: California Tomorrow.

O'Malley, J. M., & Chamot, A. U. (1990). *Learning strategies in second language acquisition.* Cambridge: Cambridge University Press.

O'Malley, J. M. & Valdez Pierce, L. (1996). *Authentic assessment for English language learners: Practical approaches for teachers.* New York: Addison-Wesley.

Ovando, C. (2003, Spring). Bilingual education in the United States: Historical development and current issues. *Bilingual Research Journal, 27*(1), 1–24. Retrieved on July 7, 2003, from http://brj.asu.edu.

Ovando, C. J., Collier, V. P., & Combs, M. C. (2003). *Bilingual and ESL classrooms: Teaching in multicultural contexts* (3rd ed.). Boston: McGraw-Hill.

Oxford, R. L. (2003). Language learning strategies in a nutshell: Update and ESL suggestions. In J. C. Richards & W. A. Renandya (Eds.), *Methodology in language teaching: An anthology of current practice* (pp. 124–132). Cambridge, UK: Cambridge University Press.

Palinscar, A., & Brown, A. (1984). Reciprocal teaching of comprehension-fostering and comprehension-monitoring activities. *Cognition and Instruction, 1,* 117–175.

Pappas, C., Kiefer, B., & Levstik, L. (1990). *An integrated language perspective in the elementary school: Theory into action.* White Plains, NY: Longman.

Parker, F. & Riley, K. (2000). *Linguistics for non-linguists: A primer with exercises* (3rd ed.). Boston: Allyn & Bacon.

Paterson, K. (1978). *The great Gilly Hopkins.* New York: Avon/Camelot.

Pearson, P. D., & Johnson, D. (1978). *Teaching reading comprehension.* New York: Macmillan.

Peregoy, S. (1989, Spring). Relationships between second language oral proficiency and reading comprehension of bilingual fifth grade students. *Journal of the National Association for Bilingual Education, 13*(3), 217–234.

Peregoy, S. (1991). Environmental scaffolds and learner responses in a two-way Spanish immersion kindergarten. *Canadian Modern Language Review, 47*(3), 463–476.

Peregoy, S., & Boyle, O. (1990a). Kindergartners write! Emergent literacy of Mexican American children in a two-way Spanish immersion program. *Journal of the Association of Mexican American Educators, 1,* 6–18.

Peregoy, S., & Boyle, O. (1990b). Reading and writing scaffolds: Supporting literacy for second language learners. *Educational Issues of Language Minority Students: The Journal, 6,* 55–67.

Peregoy, S., & Boyle, O. (1991). Second language oral proficiency characteristics of low, intermediate, and high second language readers. *Hispanic Journal of Behavioral Sciences, 13*(1), 35–47.

Peregoy, S., & Boyle, O. (1993). *Reading, writing, and learning in ESL: A resource book for K–8 teachers.* White Plains, NY: Longman.

Peregoy, S., & Boyle, O. (1999). Multiple embedded scaffolds: Supporting English learners' social/affective, linguistic and academic development in kindergarten. *Kindergarten Education: Theory, Research and Practice, 4,* 41–54.

Peregoy, S., & Boyle, O. (2000). English learners reading in English: What we know, what we need to know. In L. Meyer (Ed.), *Theory into Practice, 39*(4), 237–247.

Peregoy, S. F., & Boyle, O. F. (1999b). Multiple embedded scaffolds: Support for English speakers in a two-way Spanish immersion kindergarten. *Bilingual Research Journal, 23*(2 & 3), 135–126.

Perfetti, C., Beck, I., Bell, L., & Hughes, C. (1987). Phonemic knowledge and learning to read are reciprocal: A longitudinal study of first grade children. *Merrill-Palmer Quarterly, 33,* 283–319.

Pertchik, C., Vineis, M. & Jones, J. (1992). *Let's Write & Sing a Song.* New York: Music Plus Publications.

Perry, T., & Delpit, L. (Eds.). (1998). *The real Ebonics debate: Power, language and the education of African-American children.* Boston: Beacon Press.

Peterson, A. (1981, June). *Working with the sentence.* Speech presented at the Bay Area Writing Project Workshop, Fairfield, CA.

Peyton, J., & Reed, L. (1990). *Dialogue journal writing with nonnative English speakers: A handbook for teachers.* Alexandria, VA: TESOL.

Phillipson, R. (1992). *Linguistic imperialism.* Oxford, UK: Oxford University Press.

Philips, S. U. (1983). *The invisible culture: Communication in classroom and community on the Warm Springs Indian Reservation.* White Plains, NY: Longman.

Pica, T. (1994). Monitor theory in classroom perspective. In R. Barasch & C. Vaughn James (Eds.), *Beyond the monitor model: Comments on current theory and practice in second language acquisition.* (pp. 300–317) Boston: Heinle & Heinle.

Pollard, J. (1985). *Building toothpick bridges.* Palo Alto, CA: Dale Seymour.

Purcell-Gates, V. (1995). *Other people's words: The cycle of low literacy.* Cambridge, MA: Harvard University Press.

Rayner, K., & Pollatsek, A. (1989). *The psychology of reading.* Englewood Cliffs, NJ: Prentice Hall.

Readence, J. E., Bean, T. W., & Baldwin, R. S. (1998). *Content area reading: An integrated approach.* (4th ed.) Dubuque, IA: Kendall/Hunt.

Renandya, W. A., & Jacobs, G. M. (2002). Extensive reading: Why aren't we all doing it? In J. Richard & W. Renandya (Eds.), *Methodology in language teaching: An anthology of current practice.* Cambridge: Cambridge University Press.

Reppen, R. (1994/1995). A genre-based approach to content writing instruction. *TESOL Journal, 4*(2), 32–35.

Reyes, M. de la Luz, & Halcon, J. J. (Eds.). (2001). *The best for our children: Critical perspectives on literacy for Latino students.* New York: Teachers College Press.

Reynolds, J., Dale, G., & Moore, J. (1989). *How to plan and implement a two-way Spanish immersion program.* Sacramento, CA: California State Department of Education.

Reys, R., Suydam, M., & Lindquist, M. (1991). *Helping children learn mathematics* (3rd ed.). Englewood Cliffs, NJ: Prentice Hall.

Rhodes, R. L., Ochoa, S. H., & Ortiz, S. O. (2005). *Assessing culturally and linguistically diverse students: A practical guide.* New York/London: Guilford Press.

Richard-Amato, P. (2003). *Making it happen: Interaction in the second language classroom* (3rd ed.). White Plains, NY: Longman.

Richards, J., & Renandya, W. (Eds.). (2002). *Methodology in language teaching: An anthology of current practice.* Cambridge: Cambridge University Press.

437

Rico, G. L., & Claggett, F. (1980). *Balancing the hemispheres: Brain research and the teaching of writing.* Berkeley: University of California/Bay Area Writing Project.

Right to Read Conference (1972). Out-of-print passage used in workshop, Anaheim, CA.

Rodriguez, R. (1982). *Hunger of memory.* New York: Godine.

Romaine, S. (1989). *Bilingualism.* Oxford: Blackwell.

Rosenblatt, L. M. (1978). *The reader, the text, the poem.* Carbondale, IL: Southern Illinois University.

Rosenblatt, L. M. (1983). The reading transaction: What for? In R. P. Parker & F. A. Davis (Eds.), *Developing literacy: Young children's use of language* (pp. 118–135). Newark, DE: International Reading Association.

Rosenblatt, L. M. (1984). *Literature as exploration* (3rd ed.). New York: Modern Language Association.

Routman, R. (1995). *Invitations: Changing as teachers and learners* (2nd ed.). Portsmouth, NH: Heinemann.

Rowe, M. B. (1974). Wait time—Is anybody listening? *Journal of Psycholinguistic Research, 3,* 203–224.

Ruddell, R., & Boyle, O. (1984). *A study of the effects of cognitive mapping on reading comprehension and written protocols.* (Tech. Rep. No. 7). Riverside, CA: Learning from Text Project, University of California.

Ruddell, R., & Boyle, O. (1989). A study of cognitive mapping as a means to improve summarization and comprehension of expository text. *Reading Research and Instruction, 29,* 12–22.

Ruddell, R. B., & Ruddell, M. R. (1995). *Teaching children to read and write: Becoming an influential teacher.* Boston: Allyn and Bacon.

Rupert, P. R., & Brueggeman, M. A. (1986). Reading journals: Making the language connection in college. *Journal of Reading, 30,* 26–33.

Rylant, C. (1989). *When I was young in the mountains.* New York: Bantam Books.

Sampson, M., Allen, R., & Sampson, M. (1990). *Pathways to literacy.* Chicago: Holt, Rinehart, & Winston.

Samway, K. (1987). *The writing processes of non-native English speaking children in the elementary grades.* Unpublished doctoral dissertation, University of Rochester, NY.

Samway, K. D. (2006). *When English language learners write: Connecting research to practice, K–8.* Portsmouth, NH: Heinemann.

Samway, K. D., & McKeon, D. (1999). *Myths and realities: Best practices for language minority students.* Portsmouth, NH: Heinemann.

Samway, K., Whang, G., Cade, C., Gamil, M., Lubandina, M., & Phomachanh, K. (1991). Reading the skeleton, the heart and the brain of a book: Students' perspectives on literature study circles. *The Reading Teacher, 45,* 196–205.

Sartre, J.-P. (1967). *The Words.* New York: Random House.

Saunders, W. M. & O'Brien, G. (2006). Oral language. In F. Genessee, K. Lindholm-Leary, W. M. Saunders, & D. Christian (Eds.). *Educating English language learners: A synthesis of the research evidence.* New York: Cambridge University Press.

Saville-Troike, M. (1978). *A guide to culture in the classroom.* Rosslyn, VA: National Clearinghouse for Bilingual Education.

Schieffelin, B. B., & Eisenberg, A. (1984). Cultural variation in children's conversations. In R. L. Schiefelbusch & J. Pickar (Eds.), *The acquisition of communicative competence* (pp. 377–420). Baltimore, MD: University Park Press.

Schifini, A. (1985). *Sheltered English.* Los Angeles: Los Angeles County Office of Education.

Schmidt, B. (n.d.). *Story mapping.* In unpublished manuscript, California State University, Sacramento.

Schmitt, N. (2000). *Vocabulary in language teaching.* Cambridge, UK: Cambridge University Press.

Schmitt, N., & Carter, R. (2000). The lexical advantages of narrow reading for second language learners. *TESOL Journal, 9*(1), 4–9.

Schmitt, N. & McCarthy, M. (1997). *Vocabulary: Description, acquisition and pedagogy.* London: Cambridge University Press.

Schmitt, N., & McCarthy, M. (Eds.). (2002). *Vocabulary: Description, acquisition, and pedagogy.* Cambridge: Cambridge University Press.

Schofield, P. (1982). Using the English dictionary for comprehension. *TESOL Quarterly, 16*(2), 185–194.

Scovel, T. (1999). "The younger the better" myth and bilingual education. In R. D. Gonzalez, and I. Melis (Eds.). *Language and ideologies: Critical perspectives on the English only movement* (pp. 114–136). Urbana, IL: National Council of Teachers of English.

Scieszka, J. (1989). *The true story of the three little pigs by A. Wolf.* New York: Viking Penguin.

Seda, M. M., Ligouri, O. Z., & Seda, C. M. (1999). Bridging literacy and social studies: Engaging prior knowledge through children's books. *TESOL Journal, 8*(3), 34–40.

Seigel, G. (1983). From speech given at Bay Area Writing Project, Berkeley, CA.

Selinker, L. (1972). Interlanguage. *International Review of Applied Linguistics, 10,* 209–231.

Sheets, R. H., & Hollins, E. R. (1999). *Racial and ethnic identity in school: Aspects of human development.* Mahwah, NJ: Erlbaum.

Shepherd, J. (1971). *Wanda Hicky's night of golden memories and other disasters.* New York: Doubleday.

Shultz, J., Erickson, F., & Florio, S. (1982). "Where's the floor?": Aspects of social relationships in communication at home and at school. In P. Gilmore &

438

A. Glatthorn (Eds.), *Children in and out of school: Ethnography and education* (pp. 88–123). Washington, DC: Center for Applied Linguistics.

Silva, T. (1990). Second language composition instruction: Developments, issues, and directions in ESL. In B. Kroll (Ed.), *Second language writing: Research insights for the classroom* (pp. 11–23). New York: Cambridge University Press.

Silverstein, S. (1974). *Where the sidewalk ends.* New York: Harper & Row.

Sinatra, R., Beaudry, J., Stahl-Gemake, J., & Guastello, E. (1990). Combining visual literacy, text understanding, and writing for culturally diverse students. *Journal of Reading, 8,* 612–617.

Singer, H. (1978). Active comprehension: From answering to asking questions. *The Reading Teacher, 31,* 901–908.

Singer, H., & Donlan, D. (1989). *Reading and learning from text* (3rd ed.). Hillsdale, NJ: Erlbaum.

Skinner, B. F. (1957). *Verbal behavior.* New York: Appleton-Century-Crofts.

Sloyer, S. (1982). *Reader's theater: Story dramatization in the classroom.* Urbana, IL: National Council of Teachers of English.

Smitherman, G. (1986). *Talkin' and testifyin'.* Detroit: Wayne State University Press.

Smitherman, G. (1998a). "Dat teacher be hollin at us"— What is Ebonics? *TESOL Quarterly 32* (1), 139–143.

Smitherman, G. (1998b). Black English/Ebonics: What it be like? In T. Perry & L. Delpit (Eds.), *The real Ebonics debate: Power, language and the education of African-American children.* (pp. 36–46). Boston: Beacon Press.

Smolen, L., Newman, C., Wathen, T., & Lee, D. (1995). Developing student self-assessment strategies. *TESOL Journal, 5*(1), 22–27.

Snow, C. (1977). The development of conversation between mothers and babies. *Journal of Child Language, 4,* 47–56.

Snow, C. (1983). Literacy and language: Relationships during the preschool years. *Harvard Educational Review, 53,* 165–189.

Snow, C. E., Burns, M. S., & Griffin, P. (Eds.). (1998). *Preventing reading difficulties in young children.* Washington, DC: National Academy Press.

Snow, M. A. (2001). Content-based and immersion models for second and foreign language teaching. In M. Celce-Murcia (Ed.), *Teaching English as a second or foreign language* (3rd ed.). Boston: Heinle & Heinle.

Snow, M. A. (2005). A model of academic literacy for integrated language content instruction. In E. Hinkel (Ed.), *Handbook in second language teaching and learning* (pp. 693–712). Mahwah, NJ: Lawrence Erlbaum Associates.

Snow, M. A., & Brinton, D. M. (1997). *The content-based classroom: Perspectives on integrating language and content.* White Plains, NY: Addison-Wesley Longman.

Spolin, V. (1963/1983). *Improvisations for the theater.* Evanston, IL: Northwestern University Press.

Spradley, J. P. (1980). *Participant observation.* New York: Holt, Rinehart & Winston.

Stahl, S. (1992). Saying the "p" word: Nine guidelines for exemplary phonics instruction. *The Reading Teacher, 45,* 618–625.

Stanovich, K. E. (1986). Matthew effects in reading: Some consequences of individual differences in the acquisition of literacy. *Reading Research Quarterly, 21,* 360–406.

Stauffer, R. G. (1970). *The language-experience approach to the teaching of reading.* New York: Harper & Row.

Stauffer, R. G. (1975). *Directing the reading-thinking process.* New York: Harper & Row.

Steinbeck, J. (1958). A teacher I remember. In *Bay Area Reading Association Newsletter.* Oakland, CA.

Stewig, J. (1981). Choral speaking. Who has the time? Why take the time? *Childhood Education, 58*(1), 25–29.

Stieglitz, E. L., & Lanigan, V. (1996). *The Stieglitz informal reading inventory: Assessing reading behaviors from emergent to advanced levels.* (3rd ed.). New York: Allyn & Bacon.

Stieglitz, E.L. & Lanigan, V. (2002). *The Stieglitz informal reading inventory: Assessing reading behaviors from emergent to advanced levels* (3rd ed.). New York: Allyn & Bacon.

Stoller, F. (2002). Content-based instruction: A shell for language teaching or a framework for strategic language and content learning? Retrieved on January 29, 2007, from http:carla.umn.edu/cobaltt/modules/strategies/Stoller2002/READING1/stoller2002.html.

Stoller, F. L. (2002). Project work: A means to promote language and content. In J. C. Richards & W. A. Renandya, *Methodology in language teaching: An anthology of current practice* (pp. 107–120). Cambridge: Cambridge University Press.

Strickland, D. S., & Morrow, L. M. (Eds.). (1989). *Emerging literacy: Young children learn to read and write.* Newark, DE: International Reading Association.

Sulzby, E. (1985). Children's emergent reading of favorite storybooks. *Reading Research Quarterly, 20,* 458–481.

Swain, M. (1985). Communicative competence: Some roles of comprehensible input and comprehensible output in its development. In S. M. Gass and C. G. Madden (Eds.), *Input in second language acquisition* (pp. 235–253). Rowley, MA: Newbury House.

Swain, M., & Lapkin, S. (1989). *Evaluating bilingual education: A Canadian case study.* Clevedon, England: Multilingual Matters.

Swan, M. (1997). The influence of the mother tongue on second language vocabulary acquisition and use. In N. Schmitt & M. McCarthy (Eds.), *Vocabulary: Description, acquisition and pedagogy* (pp. 156–180). Cambridge, UK: Cambridge University Press.

Tang, G. M. (1992/1993). Teaching content knowledge and ESOL in multicultural classrooms. *TESOL Journal, 2*(2), 9–12.

Tatsuki, D. H. (1996). Games with a pronunciation focus. *TESOL Journal, 6*(2) 32–33.

Taylor, D., & Dorsey-Gaines, C. (1988). *Growing up literate: Learning from inner-city families.* Portsmouth, NH: Heinemann.

Taylor, M. D. (1976). *Roll of thunder, hear my cry.* New York: Dial.

Teachers of English to Speakers of Other Languages (1992). *TESOL statement on the education of K–12 language minority students in the United States.* Washington, DC: Author.

Teachers of English to Speakers of Other Languages (TESOL). (2006). *PreK–12 English language proficiency standards.* Alexandria, VA: Author.

Teale, W. H. (1984). Reading to young children: Its significance for literacy development. In H. Goelman, A. A. Oberg, & G. Smith (Eds.), *Awakening to literacy* (pp. 8–20). Portsmouth, NH: Heinemann.

Teale, W. H., & Sulzby, E. (Eds.). (1986). *Emergent literacy: Writing and reading.* Norwood, NJ: Ablex.

Tease, K. (1995). *Literacy rich environments in the preschool and kindergarten classroom: A teacher handbook.* Unpublished master's thesis.

Terkel, S. (1974). *Working.* New York: Pantheon.

Terrell, T. D. (1981). The natural approach in bilingual education. In D. Dolson (Ed.), *Schooling and language minority students: A theoretical framework.* (pp. 61–80) Sacramento, CA: California State Department of Education.

Tharp, R., & Gallimore, R. (1988). *Rousing minds to life: Teaching, learning and schooling in social context.* New York: Cambridge University Press.

Thomas, W. & Collier, V. (1996). Language-minority student achievement program effectiveness. *NABE News, 19*(6), 33–35.

Thomas, W., & Collier, V. (1997, December). *School effectiveness for language minority students.* National Clearinghouse for Bilingual Education (NCBE) Resource Collection Series, No. 9. Retrieved from www.gwu.edu/ncbepubs/resource/effectiveness/index.html.

Thomas, W., & Collier, V. (2002). *A national study of school effectiveness for language minority students' long-term academic achievement.* Santa Cruz, CA: Center for Research on Education, Diversity and Excellence, University of California, Santa Cruz.

Tiedt, P. L., & Tiedt, I. M. (2006). *Multicultural teaching: A handbook of activities, information, and resources* (7th ed.). Boston: Allyn and Bacon.

Tierney, R. J., & Readance, J. E. (2000). *Reading strategies and practices: A compendium* (5th ed.). Boston: Allyn and Bacon.

Tinajero, J. V., & Calderon, M. E. (1988). Language experience approach plus. *Educational Issues of Language Minority Students: The Journal, 2,* 31–45.

Tollefson, J. W. (2000). Policy and ideology in the spread of English. In J. K. Hall & W. G. Eggington (Eds.), *The sociopolitics of English language teaching* (pp. 7–21). Buffalo, NY: Multilingual Matters.

Tomlinson, B. (1986). Using poetry with mixed ability language classes. *English Language Teaching Journal, 40,* 33–41.

Tomlinson, C. A. (1999). *The differentiated classroom: Responding to the needs of all learners.* Alexandria, VA: Association for Supervision and Curriculum Development.

Tompkins, G. (2003). *Literacy for the 21st century* (3rd ed.). Upper Saddle River, NJ: Merrill Prentice Hall.

Topping, K., & Wolfingdale, S. (Eds.). (1985). *Parental involvement in children's reading.* New York: Nichols.

Tragar, B., & Wong, B. K. (1984). The relationship between native and second language reading and second language oral ability. In C. Rivera (Ed.), *Placement procedures in bilingual education: Education and policy issues* (pp. 152–164). Clevedon, England: Multilingual Matters.

Trieman, R. (1985). Onsets and rimes as units of spoken syllables: Evidence from children. *Journal of Experimental Psychology, 39,* 161–181.

Trumbull, E., Rothstein-Fisch, C., & Greenfield, P. (2000). *Bridging cultures in our schools: New approaches that work.* West Ed Knowledge Brief. Retrieved June 17, 2003, from http://web.wested.org/online_pubs/bridging/about_bc.shtml.

Tyner, B. & Green, S. E. (2005). *Small-Group reading instruction: A differentiated teaching model for intermediate readers, grades 3–8.* Newark, DE: International Reading Association.

Ulanoff, S. H. & Pucci, S. L. (1999). Learning words form books: The effects of read aloud on second language vocabulary acquisition. *Bilingual Research Journal, 23,* 4.

Urzúa, C. (1987). "You stopped too soon": Second language children composing and revising. *TESOL Quarterly, 21,* 279–305.

Urquhart, S., & Weir, C. (1998). *Reading in a second language: Process, product and practice.* London: Longman.

Urzúa, C. (1992). Faith in learners through literature studies. *Language Arts, 69,* 492–501.

U.S. Office of Elementary and Secondary Education (2002). The No Child Left Behind Act, Executive Summary. Available at www.ed.gov/offices/OESE/esea/exec-summ.html.

Vacca, R., & Vacca, J. (1989). *Content area reading.* Glenview, IL: Scott, Foresman.

Vacca, R., & Vacca, J. (1993). *Content area reading* (4th ed.). New York: HarperCollins College Publishers.

Vacca, R. T. & Vacca, J. L. (2007). *Content area reading: Literacy and learning across the curriculum* (9th ed.). Boston: Allyn and Bacon.

Valdez Pierce, L. (2003, March/April/May). Accountability and equity: Compatible goals of high-stakes testing? *TESOL Matters 13*(2). Alexandria, VA: Teachers of English to Speakers of Other Languages.

Vásquez, O. (1991). Reading the world in a multicultural setting: A Mexicano perspective. *The Quarterly Newsletter of the Laboratory of Comparative Human Cognition, 13*, 13–15.

Verplaetse, L-S. (1998). How content teachers interact with English language learners. *TESOL Journal, 7*(5), 24–28.

Villaseñor, V. (2004). *Burro genius.* New York: HarperCollins Publishers, Inc.

Vygotsky, L. S. (1962). *Thought and language.* Cambridge, MA: MIT Press.

Waddell, M., Esch, R., & Walker, R. (1972). *The art of styling sentences: 20 patterns to success.* New York: Barron's Educational Series.

Wallat, C. (1984). An overview of communicative competence. In C. Rivera (Ed.), *Communicative competence approaches to language proficiency assessment* (pp. 2–33). London: Multilingual Matters.

Webster, J. P. (1998). Semantic maps. *TESOL Journal, 7*(5), 42–43.

Weinborg, H. (1989). *First things first* [videotape]. Pittsburgh: Public Broadcasting, Inc.

Wells, G. (1986). *The meaning makers: Children learning language and using language to learn.* Portsmouth, NH: Heinemann.

Welty, E. (1983). *One writer's beginnings.* New York: Warner Books.

White, E. B. (1952). *Charlotte's web.* New York: Harper & Row.

White, E. M. (1985). *Teaching and assessing writing: Recent advances in understanding, evaluating, and improving student performance.* San Francisco: Jossey-Bass.

White, T.G., Sowell, J., & Yanagihara, A. (1989). Teaching elementary students to use word-part clues. *The Reading Teacher, 42*, 302–309.

Wiesner, D. (1991). *Window.* New York: Clarion.

Wilhelm, K. H. (1999). Collaborative dos and don'ts. *TESOL Journal, 8*(2), 14–19.

Wink, J. (2004). *Critical pedagogy: Notes from the real world* (3rd ed.). New York: Addison-Wesley Longman.

Wisniewska, I. (1998). Using games to get feedback. *TESOL Journal, 7*(6) 38–39.

Wong Fillmore, L. (1980). Learning a second language: Chinese children in the American classroom. In J. E. Alatis (Ed.), *Current issues in bilingual education: Georgetown University roundtable on languages and linguistics* (pp. 309–325). Washington, DC: Georgetown University Press.

Wong Fillmore, L. (1982). Instructional language as linguistic input: Second-language learning in classrooms. In L. C. Wilkinson (Ed.), *Communicating in the classroom* (pp. 283–296). Madison: University of Wisconsin Press.

Wong Fillmore, L. (1983, February). *Levels of language proficiency: The view from second language acquisition.* TESOL Forum Lecture presented at Teachers of English to Speakers of Other Languages, Austin, TX.

Wong Fillmore, L. (1985). When does teacher talk work as input? In S. Gass & C. Madden (Eds.), *Input in second language acquisition* (pp. 17–50). Rowley, MA: Newbury House.

Wong Fillmore, L. (1991a). Second-language learning in children: A model of language learning in social context. In E. Bialystok (Ed.), *Language processing in bilingual children* (pp. 49–69). Cambridge: Cambridge University Press.

Wong Fillmore, L. (1991b). When learning a second language means losing the first. *Early Childhood Research Quarterly, 6*(3), 323–346.

Wong Fillmore, L., Ammon, P., Ammon, M. S., DeLucchi, K., Jensen, J. A., McLaughlin, B., et al. (1983). *Language learning through bilingual instruction* (Second Year Report No. 400–80–0030). Washington, DC: National Institute of Education.

Woods, M. L. & Moe, A. J. (2006). *Analytical reading inventory with reader passages* (8th ed.). Upper Saddle River, NJ: Prentice Hall.

Wright, W., Betteridge, D., & Buckby, M. (2002). *Games for language learning: New edition.* Cambridge: Cambridge University Press.

Yang, D. (1992). Create a board game. *TESOL Journal, 1*(3), 35.

Yochum, N., & Miller, S. (1990). Classroom reading assessment: Using students' perceptions. *Reading Psychology: An International Quarterly, 11*, 159–165.

Yopp, R. (1987). *Active comprehension: Declarative knowledge for generating questions and procedural knowledge for answering them.* Unpublished doctoral dissertation, University of California, Riverside.

Zola, D. (1984). Redundancy and word perception during reading. *Perception and Psychophysics, 36*, 277–284.

441

AUTHOR INDEX

445

SUBJECT INDEX

Jigsaw, 92, 357–358
Jokes, 133
Journals, 249–251, 369–370
  buddy, 251, 252, 370
  dialogue, 7, 182, 250–251, 252, 370
  literature response, 312–313, 314
  personal, 249
  project, 252
  response, 312–313, 369, 370
  vocabulary, 218

Kamehameha Elementary Education Program (KEEP),
  100–101
Key content vocabulary, 403
Key word approach, 298
Kids Write program, 187
Krashen's five hypotheses, 53–55
K-W-L, 73–74, 221, 222, 376–377
K-W-L Plus, 376

Language
  and identity, 44–46
  and power, 39–44
  role of standard, 44
  social vs. academic, 62–63
Language acquisition device (LAD), 47
Language acquisition theories
  for first language, 46–51
  for second language, 51–57
Language Assessment Scales, 107
Language demands, 85
Language development. *See* Oral language development;
  Written language development
Language domain, 76
Language education support services, 106–107
Language experience approach, 181–182, 297–300
Language family trees, 40
Language functions, 121
Language learning errors, 66–68
Language learning opportunities, 85–86
Language minority/language majority students, 24
Language objectives, 85
Language processes (listening, speaking, reading and
  writing), 117–119, 395–397
Language proficiency, 34–35, 77, 395–397
Language-related lesson modifications, 86
Languages, 41–44
Language subsystems, 35–37
Language Testing Student Assessment website, 399
Language wheels, 216
Learning, cultural influences on, 8–15
Learning logs, 252, 358–359, 369, 370
Lesson plans
  for differentiated learning, 388–389

Internet resources for, 84, 128, 155, 283, 337
  for SDAIE, 86
Let's Write and Sing a Song (Pertchik, Vineis, & Jones),
  147
Letter–sound correspondences, 167
Life murals, 253
Limited English proficient (LEP), 2–3, 107
Listening, speaking, reading, and writing, 117–119,
  395–397
Literacy assessment. *See* Assessment
Literacy backpacks, 175–176
Literacy Connection website, 283
Literacy functions, 161, 162
Literacy scaffolds, 102–104, 246
Literacy traditions, 13–14
Literal language, 37–39
Literary structure, 343–344
Literature development. *See* Reading and literature
  development
Literature response groups, 290–293
Literature response journals, 312–313, 314
Literature response tools, 292
Loban, Walter, 116
Logographic writing systems, 162

Madeline (Bemelmans), 132
"The Magician's Apprentice" (Boyle), 311
Maintenance bilingual education, 24
Mapping
  cognitive, 309–310, 326
  in content area writing, 367–369
  in process writing, 261–264
  story, 307–308, 326
Maslow's hierarchy of human needs, 15
Mathematics, 134–135
Meanies (Cowley), 301
Meaning of a word, 202
Metacognition, 289, 344–345, 354
Metacognitive processes, 401
Metacognitive strategies, 401
Metaphors, 37–38
Mirandy and Brother Wind (McKissack),
  233
Miscue analysis, 316–322, 405
Miscues, 316, 325
Modeling, 237, 396
Models, 260–261, 273
Monitor hypothesis, 54
Monitoring comprehension, 355
Monolingual dictionaries, 212
Morning messages, 179
Morphemes, 35, 54
Morphology, 35, 36, 37, 401
Multicultural literature, 295

PHOTO CREDITS